John Rawls' Theory of Social Justice

AN INTRODUCTION

John Rawls' Theory of Social Justice

AN INTRODUCTION

H. Gene Blocker
Elizabeth H. Smith
Editors

OHIO UNIVERSITY PRESS
ATHENS

Library of Congress Cataloging in Publication Data

Main entry under title:

John Rawls' theory of social justice.

Based on a conference sponsored by the Ohio Program in the Humanities and held at Ohio University in 1976.
Bibliography: p.
Includes index
1. Social justice—Congresses. 2. Rawls, John, 1921- —Congresses. I. Blocker, H. Gene. II. Smith, Elizabeth H., 1939-
HM216.J58 320'.01'1 80-11272
ISBN 0-8214-0445-8
ISBN 0-8214-0593-4 pbk.

Contents

Preface

John Rawls' *A Theory of Justice* has initiated a renaissance in social philosophy unparalleled in this century, stretching across academic boundaries normally separating economists, philosophers, lawyers and social historians. Not since John Dewey has a philosophical theory received so much attention by scholars and even the popular press. Not only are the philosophical journals filled with discussions, analyses and criticisms of Rawls, but the leading periodicals of social commentary, newsmagazines and newspapers have extensively reviewed the book. Just keeping up with the Rawls literature has become a full-time enterprise. It has already become clear that Rawls' work, like that of John Stuart Mill earlier, will have a major impact on social theory and public policy issues for generations to come.

Despite this unprecedented level of interest, however, access to Rawls' thought is difficult. His presentation is rigorously analytical, and the book itself is long and complicated. Moreover, the flood of critical literature on Rawls' book has focused largely on problematic details within the comprehensive scheme of justice Rawls offers and is often highly technical. There is a need, therefore, for a general introduction rendering the fundamentals of Rawls' theory accessible not only to philosophers but to scholars from other fields, students and the general public. Also absent from the current literature is a discussion of the practical consequences of Rawls' theory for issues of public policy. Finally, because of the emphasis on detail in the analysis of Rawls' work, little has been done to place Rawls in a larger historical context of social and political thought. This volume is aimed at filling these gaps in the scholarly literature.

The book is the outgrowth of the bicentennial conference on Rawls, "Justice: Two Hundred Years Later," sponsored by the Ohio Program in the Humanities and held at Ohio University in 1976. The conference highlighted not only the need for a clearly written comprehensive introduction to Rawls, but also the abundance of excellent scholars prepared to work on such a task.

The book is divided into three chapters. The first chapter is designed to introduce the reader to the fundamentals of Rawls' theory of justice, the essential steps in his argument and the key concepts in Rawls' presentation. The second chapter is a series of attempts to draw out the practical applications of Rawls' theory for public policy issues. In many cases the arguments go beyond that actually proposed by Rawls and consider the implications of a Rawlsian conceptual scheme for issues of current public concern. The relevance of philosophy to practical problems of public policy is itself philosophically controversial. Since philosophy is most commonly understood these days to be concerned with conceptual and definitional matters rather than empirical or factual matters, the link between philosophy and social and political affairs is at best indirect and remote. Many social philosophers hold the view, represented in this book by Tom L. Beauchamp, that social philosophy takes place at an ideal level, one step removed from the day to day affairs of political realities and does not therefore have any direct, practical bearing on social policy decisions. Other philosophers, however, disagree. Their view, represented in this volume by John Schaar, is that social philosophy, although admittedly ideal and conceptual, can nonetheless define criteria which can be used with discretion in assessing the justice or injustice of existing social institutions.

This is a subject of legitimate controversy. Our position is that, for better or worse, Rawls is being widely discussed today in terms of the practical applications of his theory, and that philosophers must therefore take a close look at these interpretations of Rawls' theory of justice. The underlying hope of Chapter 2 is that there is a stage of social policy decision-making in which asking higher-order philosophical questions about the criteria or model for an ideally just society is desirable and even necessary. Included in this chapter are discussions of discrimination, civil disobedience, the justification of punishment, the moral basis of allocating resources in a world of scarcity, and the ethical basis on which one nation might be justified in intervening in the domestic policy of another.

In the third and final chapter, Rawls' work is placed in the context of the major philosophical and political traditions. This chapter includes articles about Rawls' relationship to Kant, utilitarianism, Marx and the broad political traditions of the right and the left.

Because of the wide readership intended, this book presupposes very little previous background in social philosophy. Every effort has been made to insure that the language throughout is clear, direct and jargon-free. Since the essays for the book have been selected for their integrated focus within the overall design, it can be read with continuity from cover to cover, and readers with little familiarity with Rawls' work may well choose this approach. But those more familiar with Rawls, as well as those with special interests, whether in economics, political science, or history, may want to pick and choose among the articles those of greatest interest. In the editors' introduction there is a brief description of all sixteen articles which may be of use to the reader in making such a selection.

Inevitably there are some overlapping discussions of the more fundamental points in Rawls' work, but where it was felt that eliminating such material would make the discussion in question more difficult to follow, we have opted for its inclusion, even at the expense of occasional repetitiveness, on the grounds of greater clarity of presentation.

Contributors to this book are a varied and impressive group of scholars. Tom L. Beauchamp is Associate Professor of Philosophy and Senior Research Scholar of the Kennedy Institute of Georgetown University. In addition to numerous articles on causation, biomedical ethics and the philosophy of David Hume, he has edited and coedited seven books, including *Philosophical Problems of Causation*, 1974, *Ethics and Public Policy*, 1975, and *Contemporary Issues in Bioethics*, 1978. He is also coeditor with Norman Bowie of a new book on business ethics, *Ethical Theory and Business.*

Charles R. Beitz teaches political philosophy and international politics in the Political Science Department at Swarthmore. He has written for *Philosophy and Public Affairs* and *Dissent*, and is the author of *Political Theory and International Relations* (Princeton University Press, 1979), where he expands on the theory of international distributive justice presented in his contribution to this collection.

Norman Bowie is Director of the Center for the Study of Values at the University of Delaware. He is the author of numerous books and articles on ethics and political philosophy, including *The Individual and the Political Order* (with Robert Simon), 1977, *Towards a New*

Theory of Distributive Justice, 1971, and two new books on business ethics, *Ethical Theory and Business* (edited with Tom L. Beauchamp) and *Business Ethics*.

Allen Buchanan is Assistant Professor of Philosophy at the University of Minnesota. He has published a number of scholarly papers on Kant, ethics, Rawls and medical ethics and was an active participant in the conference "Justice: Two Hundred Years Later" on Rawls' work which led to publication of this book.

Gail Corrado of Ohio University has had a broad research and teaching background both in philosophy and in the field of economics. She delivered a paper on Rawls and civil disobedience at the conference "Justice: Two Hundred Years Later" at Ohio University in 1976 and another at Ohio Philosophical Association meetings in 1977 which focused on Rawls' use of microeconomic game theory.

Stephen L. Darwall is Associate Professor at the University of North Carolina. He has published a number of articles appearing in *Ethics* and *The Canadian Journal of Philosophy* on reason and morals.

Joseph P. DeMarco is Associate Professor and Chairman of the Philosophy Department at Cleveland State University. Editor of *Philosophy in Context*, he has published widely on topics relating to justice and equal opportunity, including critical work on Rawls. He has recently completed a book on the social political thought of W.E.B. DuBois. His work on the theory of justice is primarily concerned with questions of international distribution and economic development.

Daniel M. Farrell is Associate Professor at the Ohio State University. He has published several articles in philosophical periodicals on political theory generally and on civil disobedience in particular. Recent works include, "Paying the Penalty: Justifiable Civil Disobedience and the Problem of Punishment," which appeared in *Philosophy and Public Affairs*, and "Illegal Actions, Universal Maxims, and The Duty To Obey The Law: The Case For Civil Authority in the *Crito*," which appeared in *Political Theory*.

Leslie Pickering Francis is Adjunct Assistant Professor of Philosophy at the University of Utah. She has published articles on Nozick's theory of the moral significance of rights and existing expectations, especially with regard to property.

Alan Goldman is Associate Professor of Philosophy at the University of Miami, Florida. A recent National Endowment for the Humanities Fellow in Residence at Princeton University and invited participant in the Council for Philosophical Studies Institute on Law and Ethics, Goldman has published widely on issues relating to Rawls and social philosophy. His most recent work is a book published by Princeton University Press called *Justice and Reverse Discrimination.*

Holly Smith Goldman is Assistant Professor of Philosophy at the University of Illinois at Chicago Circle. She is a recent recipient of an American Council of University Women Postgraduate Fellowship and has published a number of articles on ethics and utilitarianism, including "Dated Rightness and Moral Imperfection," in *Philosophical Review* and "Doing the Best One Can," in *Values and Morals.*

David A. Hoekema is Assistant Professor of Philosophy and Tutor in the Paracollege at St. Olaf College in Northfield, Minnesota. A Danforth Fellow from 1972 to 1977 he has written articles and reviews in various areas of applied ethics and philosophy of religion for *Christian Century*, *Christian Scholars' Review*, and *Reformed Journal.* He has appeared in conferences, panels and symposia on Rawls and social philosophy, including conferences at Notre Dame, Ohio University, and University of Minnesota.

Hardy Jones is Associate Professor of Philosophy at the University of Nebraska. In addition to his book, *Kant's Principle of Personality*, 1971, Jones has written a number of articles in various philosophical periodicals, including several recent articles on reverse discrimination.

Louis I. Katzner is Associate Professor of Philosophy at Bowling Green State University. He has written articles on justice, discrimination and equal opportunity, including "Is the Favoring of Women and Blacks in Employment and Educational Opportunities Justified?", which appeared in *Philosophy of Law*, edited by Joel Feinberg and Hyman Gross, 1975. He has also written a book, *Man in Conflict*, 1975, and has taught an experimental philosophy course for sixth graders.

John Schaar is Professor of Politics at the University of California, Santa Cruz. He has written a number of articles in scholarly periodicals on Rawls and equality, and is the author of two books, *Escape from Authority* and *Loyalty in America.*

Mark R. Wicclair is Assistant Professor of Philosophy at West Virginia University. He has written articles in social and political philosophy and aesthetics and during 1977 was a member of a Working Group on Human Rights and Foreign Policy at the Center for Philosophy and Public Policy, University of Maryland.

Many people have given us help and support in the preparation of this book. *Philosophy and Public Affairs* allowed us to reprint "Justice and International Relations" by Charles Beitz which appeared in vol. 4, 1975. Particular thanks are due to J.H. Wellbank of North-eastern University and Pappu S.S. Rama Rao of Miami University for allowing us to use their extensive bibliographies on John Rawls. Professor Wellbank in collaboration with Denis Snook of the University of Oregon is preparing an "Open Rawls Research Bibliography" which will make a continuously updated bibliography on Rawls available. All those involved in the conference on Rawls held at Ohio University in 1976 and funded by The Ohio Program in the Humanities, deserve particular thanks, especially Michael Corrado and Stanley Grean. Special mention must be made of the invaluable assistance given to us by Robert Trevas and Warren Ruchti. Lisa Bibbee, Scott Bodfisch and Sondra Choto were splendid help in preparation of the manuscript, as was Keith Butt who supplied the drawings. We are grateful to the Research Institute of Ohio University for funds to meet certain publication expenses. We also want to thank our contributors, not just for the excellence of their scholarship but for their patience and cooperation.

Editors' Introduction

John Rawls is the most widely read and discussed philosopher of our time. What can account for the remarkable level of interest in the work of an analytic philosopher? The springs of this interest are complex, but it certainly cannot be traced to the popular style of his writing, nor indeed to any concession to popular issues and topics. Rawls' writing has been uncompromisingly rigorous, professional and analytic. A more likely explanation lies in the fact that Rawls' work can be seen as a way of resolving a major political schism of our time, one which separates the libertarian right from the egalitarian left.

Rawls certainly did not set out to reconcile conflicting political ideals; his concern has been with the development of a consistent and sound theory of justice. But the theory he proposed has been suggestive of a way to structure a society which incorporates both individual freedom and a fair distribution of material goods. In this century, western democracies have agonized over how to maintain those individual freedoms as mandated by philosophical justifications of democracy articulated in the 18th century and exemplified by the Bill of Rights, while achieving at the same time some measure of social justice. Is it possible to distribute society's wealth more fairly without encroaching on the rights and liberties of individuals who have acquired, by hard work or circumstance, a greater share of that wealth? The world conscience has been torn between these two essential but apparently irreconcilable goals.

Thus, the political dialogue of our time has been dominated by the leftist demand for equity and social equality and the right's insistence upon conserving institutions and practices which support individual freedom. The demands of the egalitarians have led governments to enact welfare programs, taxation schemes designed to redistribute wealth, programs of affirmative action, and so on, all of which are increasingly under attack for constraining individual liberty (in hiring, in disposing of property, in accumulating wealth, and so on).

Often it seems as though we are attempting to mix oil and water but without the theoretical foundation which might allow us to achieve an emulsion. The popular interest in Rawls' work therefore stems in large measure from the fact that Rawls has in effect constructed a clearly reasoned and fully developed defense of the idea that individual freedom is compatible with a fair distribution of wealth. In Rawls' work many see the hope that a theoretical backing can be provided for the sort of society we have been groping to achieve.

Another source of interest in Rawls' *Theory of Justice* is its attempted reconciliation of historically opposed traditions in social theory. Liberal political thought has long been dominated by two political traditions. The utilitarians and their allies, the legal positivists, have argued for an account of our obligation to the state which is grounded on hard empirical data. Their analysis turns on the distinction between what the law is and what the law ought to be, and insists that both of these are to be examined in terms of the facts. We determine what the laws are by looking to see what the legislature has said and what the executive and judicial officers do. We determine what the law ought to be by calculating which programs produce the most social benefit. Such a theory has considerable appeal for the "tough minded," for it requires that we employ our rational capabilities in the gathering and evaluation of empirical data. In this way decisions about the structure of society are to be guided by quasi-scientific reasoning.

But to followers of the social contract tradition of natural law and natural rights, the utilitarian theory seems set in concrete. The rigid distinction between law as it is and law as it ought to be leads, they object, to a legalism in which an appeal to law and order takes unwarranted precedence over a concern for morality; that is, it leads to an account of legal obligation which confuses might with right. Besides, calculating social benefit is not as easy as it sounds. Even if it were relatively easy to determine which programs and institutions would produce the greatest social benefit, the utilitarian theory is still open to a fundamental objection. It is possible that a program or institution could produce more social benefit than the alternatives, but distribute those benefits inequitably or in some other way violate the rights of some individuals. Hence it is charged that the utilitarian theory is compatible with gross immorality and for that reason cannot provide an adequate backing for a social order.

Philosophers in the social contract tradition emphasize the rights of the individual and attempt to argue that some social arrangements are inherently more reasonable and hence more defensible than others. It is claimed to be reasonable, for example, that all people have the right to life, liberty and property, and equally reasonable for anyone to acquiesce to a government which guarantees these rights. The difficulty has always been that what has seemed reasonable to some has seemed insane to others, especially where hard empirical data of the sort that can be checked and publicly verified is not available to settle the issue. Hence the utilitarians charge that the sort of appeals to "reason" found in the social contract tradition are at best appeals to intuition and unverifiable metaphysical claims about human nature, and that any society founded on such an unsubstantial base will be reduced to anarchy by each person using his own conception of what is right to determine his legal obligation.

The broad appeal Rawls has enjoyed is due in no small measure to his carefully reasoned program for reconciling these competing views. In insisting upon the Kantian foundation of the rights of individuals as against the means-end orientation of the utilitarians, Rawls supports the priority of individual rights and freedoms. Hence the first principle of justice, "The Principle of Equal Basic Liberty," gives priority to the notion of individual freedom. This principle says that each person is to have an equal right to the most extensive total system of equal basic liberties (such as the right to vote, freedom of speech and assembly, freedom of thought, the right to hold property, and so on), compatible with a similar system of liberty for all. But the "Difference Principle" which states that unequal shares of social goods will be allowed only on condition that it benefit the least advantaged seems to incorporate a strong measure of egalitarianism into the theory of justice. The uniqueness of Rawls' approach is that rather than make an appeal to reason he devises a decision-making technique designed to provide a perspective from which a fair, unbiased and unanimous choice of principles to structure can be made. In arguing that some principles of justice provide a reasonable foundation for the structure of society and others do not, Rawls appeals to economic game theory to provide an objective basis analogous to the utilitarian calculus. Hence Rawls' theory seems to provide a way in which to incorporate egalitarian ideals within the social contract tradition and at the same time remedy a crucial defect of that tradition.

Like Kant, Rawls stands then as the man in the middle, a mediator of long-standing disputes. Predictably, his theory has become the target for criticisms from all sides of the spectrum. This indicates the enormous undertaking present in *A Theory of Justice*—a seemingly impossible compromise developed in painstaking detail. Libertarians complain that Rawls has gone too far, giving away too much to better the condition of the have-nots. Egalitarians object that the insistence upon the priority of liberty undermines the effect of the Difference Principle and is compatible with a society of exploitive classes. Rawls also has been charged with inconsistency. *Can* he have it both ways? If constraints are placed on the wealth and power which the most talented members of society can acquire in order to satisfy the Difference Principle, haven't their basic liberties (especially to property) been restricted? But how can inequalities in the distribution of wealth be eradicated without restricting the right to acquire property? And if there are wide disparities in economic well-being, even if they are to the advantage of the worst-off individuals, how can those with less enjoy liberties to the same extent as those with more? What good is it to have a right to stand for office without the means to finance a campaign? The real importance of Rawls' work may well lie in the stimulation it has provided critics to address these basic questions of distributive justice.

Between the covers of this book the reader will find examples of philosophers who criticize Rawls along lines just mentioned, those who are interested primarily in applying the Rawlsian framework to practical issues of public policy making, and those who defend Rawls by trying to answer his critics. Indeed, several articles included in this book indicate the emergence in recent years of at least the main outlines of a Rawlsian response to his critics. Initiated by Rawls himself in an article entitled "A Kantian Conception of Equality," which appeared in Harvard's *Cambridge Review* 1975 and developed and clarified in the articles in this book by Stephen Darwall, Allen Buchanan, and Tom L. Beauchamp, the defense strategy is to strengthen the considerable Kantian orientation of Rawls' approach and to restructure much of the argument which was not originally explicitly Kantian around this Kantian base.

It might be helpful in this introductory section to provide the reader with a brief description of the sixteen articles contributed by scholars of such different persuasions and interests. This will provide the reader with a guide for organizing his reading of these many and varied views of Rawls' theory of justice.

A Description of the Essays in Chapter One

The selections included in Chapter One provide a broad overview of the fundamental features of Rawls' theory.

"A Critical Introduction to Rawls' Theory of Justice" by Allen Buchanan is a general introduction to the fundamental features of Rawls' theory of justice. Buchanan first explains Rawls' two principles of justice and reconstructs three major arguments which Rawls offers to support them. The first argument is that the principles of justice accord with our considered moral judgments. The second argument is contractarian, that the two principles of justice would be chosen by morally neutral or objective persons. The final argument is that the principles of justice accord with a Kantian account of free moral agents as rational, autonomous individuals to be regarded as ends-in-themselves and never as means. Buchanan supports the Kantian defense of the two principles but questions the *maximin principle* which forms the basis of the contractarian argument.

"The Original Position and the Veil of Ignorance" by Louis I. Katzner examines the contractarian basis of Rawls' theory. Katzner explores the relationship between the hypothetical "original position" and the justification of the principles of justice. To eliminate bias and insure that the principles of justice are chosen under fair and impartial conditions, Rawls constructs a hypothetical original position in which the parties who are to choose principles of justice are placed behind a "veil of ignorance." Katzner shows that Rawls is not attempting to deduce the principles of justice from the fair conditions of the original position but rather is arguing that the fact that the principles of justice accord with our considered moral judgments determines the description of the conditions of the original position itself. Hence the notion of reflective equilibrium is the foundation of the the contractarian argument for the principles of justice.

"Rawls, Games and Economic Theory" by Gail Corrado undertakes to make accessible to the non-economist the difficult and technical game theoretical model in which Rawls defends the use of the maximin principle in the contractarian argument, viz., that in the original position, under the veil of ignorance, rational choosers would be more likely to choose Rawls' principles of justice than they would utilitarian or any other principles. Since questions about justice only arise when there are conflicting interests, Rawls employs a mathematical strategy taken from game theory designed to resolve conflicting interests. The problem is deciding which of several game strategies is most appropriate; whether the maximin strategy which best supports Rawls' two principles of justice is indeed the most reasonable. Corrado explains why Rawls has chosen the maximin principle, and why Rawls thinks distributions of economic and social goods made on the basis of the Difference Principle are more consistent with our considered moral judgments than distributions made on any utilitarian rule.

"Equal Basic Liberty for All" by Norman Bowie explains Rawls' account of the notoriously complex and often ambiguous concept of liberty, and explains two crucial distinctions involved in that concept: the distinction between the right to liberty and the worth of liberty. Why liberty is held to be valuable and why everyone should have equal amounts are key issues. Bowie systematically brings together Rawls' scattered remarks on resolving conflicts within a given individual's total system of liberty and resolving conflicts between competing systems of liberty. Bowie emphasizes the role of the constitutional convention in resolving such conflicts within Rawls' hierarchical theory of justice. While Bowie acknowledges difficulties in consistently applying the various levels of Rawls' theory of liberty, he argues that Rawls has provided a fuller account than has been recognized.

"Distributive Justice and the Difference Principle" by Tom L. Beauchamp explains the meaning of the Difference Principle, and discusses some of the problems critics have found with it. Beauchamp discusses Rawls' rejection of a radical egalitarian call for equal distribution in favor of allowing some inequalities in the distribution of social and economic goods, as well as Rawls' contention that talents and other fruits of the natural lottery are morally arbitrary. Critics of the Difference Principle have argued that its application would result in unfairly taking from the talented and industrious to give to the non-meritorious. Beauchamp contends that Rawls is primarily concerned with defining justice in the basic structure of society rather than considering the justice of particular distributions of goods within a basic structure. For this reason Beauchamp questions attempts to apply Rawls' theory to particular public policy concerns.

"Equality of Opportunity and the Just Society" by John Schaar is an attempt to discover the applicability of Rawls' theory to social and political issues. In explaining Rawls' notion of equality, Schaar distinguishes the traditional liberal notion of equality of opportunity from a more far-reaching egalitarianism of results. He defends Rawls' critique of the traditional account of equality as being incomplete, and as failing to take proper account of the moral arbitrariness of natural assets which give some people a head-start over others, and he praises Rawls for developing a more egalitarian account of equality out of the deficiencies of the traditional liberal view. The main problem Schaar finds with Rawls' account is that the theory is so general and abstract it is difficult to see how it can be applied consistently to real social problems. Thus he finds Rawls' work more helpful in diagnosing the ills of society than in affecting a cure. Schaar wonders whether justice really demands that all life styles be regarded as equally valuable or that society not place a greater worth upon the capacities of the better endowed.

A Description of the Essays in Chapter Two

In Chapter Two the essays show how insights gleaned from Rawls' theory of justice might be put to use in addressing political problems of current concern. "Dealing with Injustice in a Reasonably Just Society" by Daniel Farrell raises questions about the justification of civil disobedience within a Rawlsian framework of justice. Farrell argues that Rawls' account of the justification of civil disobedience is unnecessarily restrictive and leads to an account of political authority which places too much emphasis on the obligation to obey the law and too little emphasis on the right (and duty) to resist injustice. According to Rawls, when one is confronted by what one believes is legalized social injustice, one's duty to obey the law usually outweighs one's duty to oppose injustice. Farrell argues that this view is too conservative and criticizes the two primary arguments which support it for depending upon very controversial assumptions. Farrell argues that a less conservative account of legal obligation can be accommodated within a Rawlsian perspective by applying Rawls' methodology to each individual case (that is, by being an act-contractarian) rather than to rules of conduct (that is, by being a rule-contractarian).

"Justice and International Relations" by Charles Beitz explores the applicability of Rawls' framework to international relations. Contract theory has sometimes been thought to be inapplicable to international relations since it is based upon agreement of members within a given society. Beitz argues that the derivation of the two principles of justice depends upon the questionable assumption of national self-sufficiency, and that by interpreting the original position globally it can be shown that justice demands that the have-not nations receive a greater share of the value produced by the world's natural resources. Beitz thinks the natural lottery which endows some states with many resources and others with few resources is as morally irrelevant as the natural lottery which endows some individuals with many talents and others with few. Hence the principles of justice must apply in the first instance to the world as a whole and only secondarily to nation-states. By eliminating the questionable assumption of self-sufficiency, the contractarian model becomes applicable to international relations.

"The Right to Punish and the Right to be Punished" by David A. Hoekema provides an analysis of rights in which the second-order right to punish is traced to the first-order right to protect life, liberty and other goods. Hoekema maintains that systems of punishment whose basic features are determined by deterrence or rehabilitation violate the rights of individuals, and that only a system whose basic features are retributive is able to respect rights. The argument adopts a Rawlsian methodology in placing the issue of punishment in a hypothetical choice situation behind a veil of ignorance and in considering the worst resulting outcome. Rehabilitative or deterrent justifications would produce intolerable outcomes because it would be possible to justify punishment of the innocent or punishment which far outweighs the crime in order to achieve deterrence or rehabilitation. Furthermore, rehabilitation violates the right of the criminal to self-determination. Retributive systems, it is argued, are able to meet these objections.

"A Rawlsian Discussion of Discrimination" by Hardy Jones attempts to extend Rawls' meager discussion of discrimination. While Jones finds problems in applying Rawls' concept of justice directly to the problem of discrimination, he argues that parties to the original position ignorant of their own sex, race, etc. and trying to achieve the safest (i.e. the best worst) outcome would be irrational to select principles which would favor any one sex, race, etc. over the others. The Principle of Equal Basic Liberty also mandates a non-discriminatory society. Jones' most controversial claim concerns reverse discrimination. Jones finds support for reverse discrimination on many levels of Rawls' theory. In societies which have unjustly discriminated in the past, the principle of maximized equal liberty will allow reverse discrimination to insure that the total system of liberty for all is equal over time. Furthermore, if equal opportunity means neutralizing morally irrelevant assets, it is not unjust to give preferential treatment to those with fewer assets. Finally, self-respect does not require that reward correspond to merit if merit is the result of past injustice or the natural lottery.

"Rawls and the Principle of Nonintervention" by Mark Wicclair examines the moral justification of intervention by one nation in the internal affairs of another from a Rawlsian perspective. Since Rawls' principles of justice are derived from a hypothetical agreement among members of a given society, these principles would seem to be limited to members of that society and to have no direct bearing on the relation of states to one another. Utilizing some suggestions offered by Rawls himself, Wicclair argues, however, that Rawls' contractarian approach can be applied in an international context as a means of deciding the question of intervention from a moral point of view. Would the parties in the original position—this time representatives of various nations, rather than individuals—choose a principle of limited intervention or a principle of nonintervention? Wicclair argues that it is more likely that intervention would not be ruled out in cases where the purpose of intervention was to prevent gross violations of human rights.

A Description of the Essays in Chapter Three

In Chapter Three the essays relate Rawls' work to the broader philosophical traditions.

"A Kantian Foundation for Rawlsian Justice" by Stephen L. Darwall argues that features of Rawls' theory reflect and amplify the Kantian requirements of moral autonomy, universalizability, and concern for the moral worth of the individual. He argues, for example, that Kant's own theory implicitly employs the notion of primary goods which Rawls makes explicit, and he suggests ways in which Rawls more consistently employs Kantian principles in social philosophy than Kant himself. Specifically, Darwall examines the Kantian support for Rawls' discussion of the basic structure, the original position, the priority of liberty and the argument against utilitarianism. He also counters major objections to Rawls' use of Kant, arguing that these objections can be met.

"Rawls and Utilitarianism" by Holly Smith Goldman summarizes the main arguments against utilitarianism put forth by Rawls and the responses which can be made from the utilitarian perspective. Goldman points out that only Rawls' distributive principles of justice can be fairly compared with utilitarianism since they are the chief normative component in Rawls' theory. Rawls charges that adoption of utilitarian principles would allow us to sacrifice the interests of the few to increase the happiness of the many. Goldman argues that the differences between utilitarianism and Rawls' theory are less significant than Rawls claims and that none of the arguments intended substantiate Rawls' charge show his theory is superior. Hence Goldman does not find that Rawls' theory of justice is more consistent with our considered judgments about justice than the utilitarian theory. Even from a contractarian perspective Goldman argues that Rawls has failed to show the superiority of his own two principles of justice since either the parties to the original position would choose utilitarianism or would see no significant difference between utilitarian and Rawlsian principles.

"Rawls and Marx" by Joseph P. DeMarco is a consideration of whether Rawls' appeal to our considered judgments as a defense of his principles is any more than an appeal to the unconscious assumptions of western democratic capitalism. Unless it is more than this, the argument is circular and unconvincing. Rawls claims that the support of his two principles is universal, but if Marxist claims about economic determinism of ideas are correct, then the support is far from universal and reflects only the ideas associated with developed capitalistic societies. DeMarco attempts to mediate some of the differences between the Rawlsian and the Marxist perspectives by combining the strengths of each. Rawls' strength is as a short-run thinker who speaks to justice within a static society, while Marx's strength is in his long-run vision of the evolution of society.

"Responses to Rawls from the Political Right" by Alan Goldman examines the wide variety of objections which have been raised by commentators who believe that Rawls' view is too egalitarian. Goldman focuses his discussion primarily on the responses which have come from the libertarian tradition. The key issue concerns the role of merit in a just society. Do people with talent and ability deserve a greater share of social and economic goods or are these characteristics merely the result of the whims of the natural lottery over which no one has any control and hence a morally irrelevant basis for distributing economic and social goods, as Rawls argues? Goldman considers a number of libertarian objections which have been raised at key points in Rawls' argument, such as the description of the original position and the choice of the Difference Principle. The libertarian argues that Rawls' description of the original position begs the question at issue; the libertarian argues that Rawls is willing to sacrifice the interests of the talented and industrious by distributing the fruits of their labor among the less talented and industrious.

"Responses to Rawls from the Left" by Leslie Pickering Francis examines the wide variety of objections which have been raised by commentators who are to the left of Rawls. The paper is a guide to the deep and sustained differences between Rawls and Marxists and focuses on four major areas: Rawls' methodology, his view of rationality, his account of private property and economic life and his portrait of the good community. It is charged that Rawls' methodology is ideological, his view of rationality too close to that of the bourgeois economists and that he underestimates the influence of private property in determining the relationship between individuals and society. A central and that he underestimates the influence of private property in determining the relationship between individuals and society. A central claim made by Rawls' leftist opponents is that a society based upon Rawls' two principles of justice is compatible with a social order founded on deep class divisions which undermine the community and alienate the individual.

CHAPTER 1

Fundamentals of the Rawlsian System of Justice

A Critical Introduction to Rawls' Theory of Justice

Allen Buchanan
UNIVERSITY OF MINNESOTA

THE THEORY

The Importance of A Theory of Justice

Since its publication in 1971, John Rawls' book *A Theory of Justice* has triggered a renaissance in political philosophy in America and the English-speaking world generally.* Even its critics concede that Rawls' work will take its place alongside such classics of the liberal democratic tradition as John Locke's *Second Treatise of Civil Government* and John Stuart Mill's *On Liberty*. In the nine years since its appearance, *A Theory of Justice* has provided a common ground for dialogue between members of disparate academic disciplines which too often suffer from stifling isolationism. Drawn together by a common interest in the issues of social justice which Rawls examines, philosophers, political scientists, economists, sociologists, and law professors are now engaged in an ongoing discussion of exceptional depth and rigor.

Even more importantly, *A Theory of Justice* can provide a sharpened focus for public discussion beyond the limits of the academic community. As persons with a sense of justice, we all have a stake in the problems with which Rawls grapples. Though the various academic

*I am greatly indebted to Rolf Sartorius for his many helpful comments on an earlier draft of this essay.

disciplines each can contribute in their own way to solving the pressing problems of social justice, it is clear that these problems are too important to be left solely to the academic community. What is needed, rather, is a sustained cooperative effort involving the academic community together with the general public. The goal of the present essay is to facilitate such cooperation by providing a critical introduction to Rawls' theory.

Rawls' Aims in A Theory of Justice

Rawls tells us that he has two basic aims in *A Theory of Justice.* One is to articulate a small set of general principles of justice which underlie and account for the various considered moral judgments we make in particular cases. By our 'considered moral judgments' Rawls means the indefinitely large set of moral evaluations we have made and may make about particular actions, laws, policies, institutional practices, etc. Our *considered* moral judgments are those moral evaluations which we make reflectively, rather than in the heat of the moment. They are moral evaluations which we make or would make in circumstances conducive to impartiality and consistency. The judgment that racial discrimination is unjust is an example of one of our most basic, firmly held considered moral judgments concerning justice. An example of a more particular considered moral judgment is the judgment that it would be unjust for a certain employer, Mr. Smith, to refuse to hire a certain job-applicant, Mr. Jones, simply because Mr. Jones is black.

The second of Rawls' two basic aims is to develop a theory which is superior to utilitarianism as a theory of social justice. There are several versions of utilitarianism. Rawls concentrates on two: classical utilitarianism and average utilitarianism. *Classical* utilitarianism may be defined as the view that social institutions are just when and only when they serve to maximize aggregate utility. "Utility" is defined as happiness or satisfaction, or in terms of the individual's preferences as the latter are revealed by his choices. The agregate utility produced by a set of institutional arrangements is calculated by summing up the utility which those arrangements produce for each individual affected by them.

Average utilitarianism, as a theory of social justice, may be defined as the view that social institutions are just when and only when they serve to maximize average utility per capita. "Utility" here, as in classical utilitarianism, is defined as happiness or satisfaction or in terms of preferences revealed through choices. Average utility per capital is calculated by dividing the aggregate utility produced by a given set of institutional arrangements by the number of persons affected by those arrangements. Rawls' second basic aim, then, is to show that the principles of justice he advances are superior to both classical and average utilitarianism.

These two basic aims are closely connected for Rawls. For as we shall see more clearly when we examine Rawls' justification for his principles, he hopes to show that his view is superior to utilitarianism by showing that his principles do a better job of accounting for our considered moral judgments about social justice. In other words, if Rawls can show that it is his principles of justice, rather than utilitarian principles, which underlie our considered moral judgments about social justice, then this will be a point in favor of Rawls' view and against utilitarianism.

The Primary Subject of Justice

Rawls notes that

> Many different kinds of things are said to be just and unjust: not only laws, institutions, and social systems, but also particular actions of many kinds, including decisions, judgments, and imputations. We also call the attitudes and dispositions of persons, and persons themselves, just or unjust (7, all parenthetical references are to John Rawls, *A Theory of Justice* (Cambridge, Mass.: Harvard University Press, 1971)).

Thus there are many different subjects of justice—many different kinds of things to which the terms "just" and "unjust" can be applied. Corresponding to the different subjects of justice, there are different problems of justice. Rawls concentrates on what he takes to be the *primary* subject of justice: what he calls the basic structure of society. By the basic structure of a society Rawls means the entire set of major social, political, legal and economic institutions. As examples of some of the major institutions of our society, Rawls lists the Constitution, private ownership of the means of production, competitive markets, and the monogamous family. The function of the basic structure of society is to distribute the burdens and benefits of social cooperation among the members of society. The benefits of social cooperation include wealth and income, food and shelter, authority and power, rights and liberties. The burdens of social cooperation include various liabilities, duties, and obligations, including for example, the obligation to pay taxes.

The primary subject of justice is the basic structure of society, according to Rawls, because the basic structure exerts such a profound influence on individuals' life prospects:

> The intuitive notion here is that this structure contains various social positions and that men born into different positions have different expectations of life determined, in part, by the political system as well as by economic and social circumstances. In this way the institutions of society favor certain starting places over others. These are especially deep inequalities. Not only are they pervasive, but they affect men's initial chances to life; yet they cannot possibly be justified by an appeal to the notions of merit or desert. It is these inequalities, presumably inevitable in the basic structure of any society, to which the principles of social justice must in the first instance apply. These principles, then, regulate the choice of a political constitution and the main elements of the economic and social system (7).

Rawls' point here can be illustrated by an example. Due to certain discriminatory features of the basic structure of our society, blacks and Chicanos generally have lower life prospects than white males. Their life-prospects are generally lower in the sense that, as a group, their life-time earnings are lower, their educational and social opportunities are inferior, and their access to healthcare is restricted. As another example of how the basic structure apparently influences life prospects, consider the fact that children of uneducated parents—regardless of race or gender—have lower prospects of completing an advanced education.

The Primary Problem of Justice

The primary subject of justice is the basic structure of society because the influences of the basic structure on individuals are present at birth and continue throughout life. The primary problem of justice, then, is to formulate and justify a set of principles which a just basic structure must satisfy. These principles of social justice would specify how the basic structure is to distribute prospects of obtaining what Rawls calls *primary goods.* Primary goods include basic rights and liberties, powers, authority, and opportunities, as well as goods such as income and wealth. Rawls calls all of these benefits *primary* goods in order to emphasize that they are preeminently desirable. According to Rawls, primary goods are

> ...things that every rational man is presumed to want. These goods normally have a use whatever a person's rational plan of life (62).

Primary goods are perhaps best thought of as (a) maximally flexible means for the pursuit of one's goals, as (b) conditions of the effective pursuit of one's goals, or as (c) conditions of the critical and informed formulation of one's plans.[1] Wealth, in the broadest sense, is a maximally flexible means in that it is generally useful for achieving one's goals, regardless of what one's goals are. Freedom from arbitrary arrest is a condition of the effective pursuit of one's goals. Freedom of speech and information are needed if one is to formulate one's goals and one's plans for attaining them in an informed and critical way. A just basic structure will be one which produces a proper distribution of prospects of obtaining primary goods, such as income and health care.

When applied to the facts about the basic structure of our society, principles of justice should do two things. First, they should yield concrete judgments about the justice or injustice of specific institutions and institutional practices. Second, they should guide us in developing policies and laws to correct injustices in the basic structure.

Rawls' Two Principles As a Solution to the Primary Problem of Justice

Rawls proposes and defends the following two principles as a solution to the problem of specifying what would count as a just basic structure.

> First Principle:
>
> Each person is to have an equal right to the most extensive total system of equal basic liberties compatible with a similar system of liberty for all (250).
>
> Second Principle:
>
> Social and economic inequalities are to be arranged so that they are both:
> (a) to the greatest benefit of the least advantaged, and
> (b) attached to offices and positions open to all under conditions of fair equality of opportunity (302-3).

Rawls calls the First Principle the Principle of Greatest Equal Liberty. The Second Principle includes two parts. The first part of the Second Principle is the Difference Principle. It states that social and economic inequalities are to be arranged so that they are to the greatest benefit of those who are least advantaged. The second part of the Second Principle is the Principle of Fair Equality of Opportunity. It states that social and economic inequalities are to be attached to offices and positions which are open to all under conditions of fair equality of opportunity. Before we can hope to assess Rawls' theory, each of these very general principles must be carefully interpreted.

The Principle of Greatest Equal Liberty. The first principle includes two claims. First, each of us is to have an equal right to the same total system of basic liberties. Second, this total system of basic liberties is to be as extensive as possible. The key phrase here is "basic liberties." By basic liberties Rawls means:

(a) freedom to participate in the political process (the right to vote, the right to run for office, etc.)
(b) freedom of speech (including freedom of the press)
(c) freedom of conscience (including religious freedom)
(d) freedom of the person (as defined by the concept of the rule of law)
(e) freedom from arbitrary arrest and seizure, and
(f) the right to hold personal property (61).

The idea of the First Principle, then, is that each person is to have an equal right to the most extensive total system composed of the liberties listed in (a) through (f), compatible with everyone else having an equal right to the same total system.

The Difference Principle. The Difference Principle states that social and economic inequalities are to be arranged so as to be to the greatest benefit of the least advantaged. To understand this principle, two key phrases must be interpreted: "social and economic inequalities" and "least advantaged."

For reasons which will become clearer later on, Rawls' First Principle and the Difference Principle must be viewed as distributing two different subsets of the total set of primary goods. The First Principle distributes one subset of the total set of primary goods: the basic liberties listed above. The Difference Principle distributes another subset: this subset includes the primary goods of wealth, income, power, and authority. Thus the phrase "social and economic inequalities" in the Difference Principle refers to the inequalities in persons' prospects of obtaining the primary goods of wealth, income, power, and authority.[2]

The second key phrase in the Difference Principle is also to be interpreted as referring to this same subset of primary goods. The least advantaged are those who are least advantaged in their prospects of obtaining the primary goods of wealth, income, power, authority, etc. In other words, the phrase "least advantaged" refers to those persons who have the lowest prospects of gaining these goods.

We are now in a better position to understand the Difference Principle. The Difference Principle requires that the basic structure be arranged in such a way that any inequalities in prospects of obtaining the primary goods of wealth, income, power, and authority must work to the greatest benefit of those persons who are the least advantaged with respect to these primary goods.

An example will help illustrate how an institution of the basic structure might produce inequalities which work to the advantage of the least advantaged. Suppose that large-scale capital investment in a certain industry is required to raise employment and to produce new goods and services. Suppose that by raising employment and producing these new goods and services such capital investment will ultimately be of great benefit to the least advantaged members of the society. Suppose in particular, that such capital investment, if it can be achieved, will greatly increase the income prospects of the least advantaged through employing many who are not now employed and by raising the wages of those who are already employed. Suppose, however, that individuals will not be willing to undertake the risks of this large-scale capital investment unless they have the opportunity to reap large profits from the enterprise, should it succeed. In such a case, tax advantages for capital investment and lowered taxes on profits might provide the needed incentives for investment. The Difference Principle would require such tax laws if they were required for maximizing the prospects of the least advantaged. In the case described, the successful investor would enjoy a larger share of the primary goods of wealth and power than other persons in his society. Yet this inequality in prospects of primary goods would be justified, according to the Difference Principle, granted that it is necessary in order to maximize the expectations of the least advantaged. If a different institutional arrangement would do a better job of raising the prospects of the least advantaged, then, according to the Difference Principle, that arrangement would be more just. As a more fundamental example of an inequality in the basic structure which might be viewed as maximizing the prospects of the worst-off, consider the United States Constitution's provisions for special powers for the President. According to the Difference Principle, the inequalities in power which these provisions create are justified only if they maximize the prospects of the worst-off.

Though Rawls first introduces the Difference Principle in the form stated above, he quickly proceeds to restate it using the notion of the *representative worst-off man.* Rawls does not offer a detailed account of how the representative worst off man is to be defined. Instead he sketches two distinct definitions and suggests that "either of [them], or some combination of them, will serve well enough" (98). According to the first definition, we first select a particular social position, such as that of unskilled worker, and then define the worst off group as those persons with the average income for unskilled workers or less. The prospects of the representative worst off man are then defined as "the average taken over this whole class." The other definition Rawls suggests characterizes the worst off group as all persons with less than half the median income, and defines the prospects of the representative worst off man as the average prospects for this class.

This complication in the statement of the Difference Principle is not a minor point for Rawls. It is one instance of Rawls' emphasis on the notion of procedural justice. Rawls distinguishes several varieties of procedural justice, but for our purposes the main point is that procedural justice utilizes institutional arrangements and conceptions, such as that of the representative worst off man, which allow us to apply principles of justice without focusing on actual particular persons. According to Rawls, the great advantage of procedural justice "is that it is no longer necessary in meeting the demands of justice to keep track of the endless variety of circumstances and the changing relative positions of particular persons. One avoids the problem of defining principles to cope with the enormous complexities which would arise if such details were relevant" (87).

The Principle of Fair Equality of Opportunity requires that we go beyond formal equality of opportunity to insure that persons with similar skills, abilities, and motivation enjoy equal opportunities. Again an example may be helpful. Suppose that two individuals A and B both desire to attain a certain position which requires technical training. Suppose further that they are roughly equal in the relevant skills and motivation, but that A's family is extremely poor and cannot finance his training, while B's family is wealthy and willing to pay for B's training. Rawls' Principle of Fair Equality of Opportunity would presumably require institutional arrangements for financial aid to insure that the fact that A was born into a low income class does not deprive him of opportunities available to others with similar skills and motivation.[3]

The Priorities of Justice

Since the Second Principle of Justice contains two distinct principles —the Difference Principle and the Principle of Fair Equality of Opportunity—there are three principles of justice in all.[4] Having advanced these three principles, Rawls offers two priority rules for ordering these three principles. The need for priority rules arises because efforts to satisfy one principle of justice may conflict with efforts to satisfy another. The first priority rule states that the First Principle of Justice, the Principle of Greatest Equal Liberty, is *lexically prior* to the Second Principle as a whole, which includes both the Difference Principle and the Principle of Fair Equality of Opportunity. One principle is *lexically prior* to another principle if and only if we are first to satisfy the requirements of the first principle before going on to satisfy those of the second. So Rawls' first priority rule states that the first priority of social justice is greatest equal liberty. Only after greatest equal liberty is secured are we free to direct our efforts to achieving the requirements laid down by the Difference Principle and the Principle of Fair Equality of Opportunity.

The second priority rule states a priority relation between the two parts of the Second Principle of Justice. According to this rule, the Principle of Fair Equality of Opportunity is lexically prior to the Difference Principle. We are to satisfy the demands of the Principle of Fair Equality of Opportunity before meeting those of the Difference Principle.

The priority on liberty expressed by the first lexical priority rule is one of the most striking features of Rawls' theory. This first lexical priority rule declares that basic liberty may not be restricted for the sake of greater material benefits for all or even for the least advantaged. Where conditions allow for the effective exercise of liberty, liberty may only be restricted for the sake of a greater liberty on balance for everyone.[5] In other words, certain basic liberties may be restricted, but only for the sake of achieving a more extensive total system of liberty for each of us. Freedom of the press, for example, might be somewhat restricted, if this were necessary to secure the right to a fair trial in situations in which unrestricted freedom of the press would lead to biased trials. Trade-offs among basic liberties are allowed, but only if the resulting total system produces greater basic liberty on balance. Tradeoffs of basic liberties for other primary goods such as wealth are not allowed.

Rawls' Justifications for His Principles of Justice

Rawls offers three distinct types of justification for his principles of justice: two based on appeals to considered moral judgments and a third based on what Rawls calls the Kantian interpretation of his theory.

The first type of justification rests on the thesis that if a principle accounts for our considered moral judgments about what is just or unjust, then this is a good reason for accepting that principle. To say that a principle accounts for our considered judgments about the justice or injustice of certain actions or institutions is to say at least this much: granted that principle and granted the relevant facts about the action or institution, it is possible to derive a statement expressing the considered judgments in question. According to the second type of justification, if a principle would be chosen under conditions which, according to our considered moral judgments, are appropriate conditions for choosing principles of justice, then this is a good reason for accepting the principle. If a principle either accounts for our considered moral judgments about what is just or unjust or would be chosen under conditions which, according to our considered moral judgments, are appropriate for choosing principles of justice, let us say that it *matches* our considered moral judgments.

Though both of these first two types of justification appeal to considered judgments, they may be distinguished according to *what* it is that the considered judgments are about. The first of these matching justifications appeals to our considered moral judgments about *what is just or unjust*, and contends that Rawls' *principles* account for these judgments. Let us call this the *principles matching justification.* The second matching justification appeals to our considered judgments, not about what is just or unjust, but rather about what *conditions* are appropriate for the choice of principles of justice. Let us call this second type of justification the *conditions matching argument.*

The conditions matching argument includes three stages. First, a set of conditions for choosing principles of justice must be articulated. Rawls refers to the set of choice conditions he articulates as 'the original position'. Second, it must be shown that the conditions articulated are the appropriate conditions of choice, according to our considered judgments. Third, it must be established that Rawls' principles would be chosen under those conditions.

Rawls describes the conditions matching justification in Chapter 1 of *A Theory of Justice.*

> We shall say that certain principles of justice are justified because they would be agreed to in [the original position]. I have emphasized that this original position is purely hypothetical. It is natural to ask why, if this agreement is never actually entered into, we should take an interest in these principles, moral or otherwise. The answer is that the conditions embodied in the original position are ones that we do in fact accept [as appropriate conditions for the choice of principles of justice] (21).

The following caveat, which Rawls offers immediately after the claim that the conditions constituting the original positions are the ones that we do accept according to our considered judgments, introduces his third type of justification.

> Or if we do not [accept the conditions of the original position], then perhaps we can be persuaded to do so by philosophical reflection (21).

In "The Kantian Interpretation" section of his book, Rawls endorses a certain kind of philosophical justification for the conditions constituting the original position—a justification based on Kant's conception of an autonomous agent, or "noumenal self." For Kant an autonomous agent is one whose will is determined by rational principles rather than by particular desires, and it is the mark of rational principles that they can serve as principles for everyone, not merely for this or that agent, depending upon whether he has some particular desire.

> My suggestion is that we think of the original position as the point of view from which noumenal selves see the world. The parties [who choose from the perspective of the original position] qua noumenal selves have the complete freedom to choose whatever principles they wish; but they also have a desire to express their autonomous nature as rational and equal members of the intelligible realm with precisely this liberty to choose, that is, as beings who can look at the world in this way and express this perspective in their life as members of society...the description of the original position interprets the point of view of noumenal selves, of what it means to be a free and equal rational being. Our nature as such beings is displayed when we act from principles we would choose when this nature is reflected in the conditions determining the choice. Thus men exhibit their freedom, their independence from the contingencies of nature and society, by acting in ways they would acknowledge in the original position. Properly understood, then, the desire to act justly [i.e., to act on those principles that would be chosen from the original position] derives in part from the desire to express most fully what we are or can be, namely free and equal rational beings with a liberty to choose (252).

This passage, like the remainder of "The Kantian Interpretation," is exceedingly condensed and complex, but for our purposes, one central thesis can be extracted from it. This is the thesis that when persons such as you and I accept those principles which would be chosen from the original position, we are expressing our nature as noumenal selves, i.e., we are acting autonomously.[6] There are two main grounds for this thesis, corresponding to two features of the original position. First, since the *veil of ignorance*, which we will discuss shortly, excludes information about particular desires, acceptance of the principles which would be chosen in the original position does not depend upon particular desires which our agent may or may not have. Second, since the *formal constraints* on the choice of principles include the requirement that the principles must be universalizable, the principles chosen will be rational principles in Kant's sense.

In *The Foundations of the Metaphysics of Morals*, Immanuel Kant presents a moral philosophy which identifies autonomy with rationality.[7] Thus, for Kant, the answer to the question 'Why should one act autonomously?' reduces ultimately to the thesis that rationality requires it. If Rawls suceeds in establishing that we act autonomously when we accept those principles which would be chosen from the original position, and if the Kantian identification of autonomy with rationality can be made, the result will be a justification for Rawls' principles which is distinct both from the principles matching justification and from the conditions matching argument.

Granted the critical fire which Rawls' two matching justifications have attracted, the possibility of developing a third, independent type of justification is extremely important. Those who have rejected the matching arguments have done so for one of two reasons. Some have rejected Rawls' assumption that there is considerable consensus among different persons' considered judgments by arguing that either Rawls' principles or his choice conditions fail to match their own considered judgments. Others have argued that even if there is considerable consensus among persons' considered judgments, the mere fact of consensus has no justificatory force. If Rawls' Kantian interpretation can be developed into a plausible Kantian *justification*, then even if these objections to the two types of arguments from considered judgments turn out to be sound, they will not prove fatal to Rawls' theory. Since the Kantian justification will be dealt with in greater detail in another paper in this volume,[8] we can now consider briefly the principles matching and conditions matching justification.

Principles Matching Justification. We have already touched upon the principles matching justification in the second section where it was noted that one of Rawls' basic aims is to provide a theory of justice which is superior to utilitarianism. Rawls believes that one crucial respect in which his theory is superior to utilitarianism (and to other theories he considers) is that it provides a better account of our *most basic* considered judgments about justice. According to Rawls, his principles provide a systematic foundation for these judgments. He also contends that these principles provide a superior guide for extending our considered judgments to new cases which we have not previously encountered.

Rawls argues that his principles of justice are superior to competing principles because, when applied to the relevant facts, they generate our considered moral judgments about what is just or unjust in a straightforward way. The principles he advances are preferable, Rawls concludes, because they provide a *simpler*, more plausible account of our considered judgments about the justice of social institutions.

A crucial instance of Rawls' employment of the principles matching justification is his argument to show that his principles provide a better account of our considered judgments about *liberty* than utilitarian principles do. Rawls suggests that among our most basic considered moral judgments is the belief that a basic structure which discriminates among persons in the distribution of basic liberties is an unjust basic structure. It may be possible, he concedes, to derive this basic considered moral judgment from utilitarian principles and thus to give a utilitarian foundation for the belief in question. However, Rawls argues, in order to derive this basic considered judgment about liberty from utilitarian principles we must make several dubious assumptions, including the assumption that everyone has exactly the same capacity for enjoying the various basic liberties. For unless, as a matter of psychological fact, everyone finds equal satisfaction in the basic liberties, greater utility might be achieved through an unequal rather than an equal distribution of basic liberties. In other words, should it turn out that the empirical assumption of equal capacity for the enjoyment of liberty is false, utilitarianism would require an unequal distribution of basic liberties. The liberty of those who were judged to have a lower capacity for the enjoyment of liberty would be restricted if this produced greater aggregate or average utility. More generally, Rawls objects that, unless it relies on certain problematic assumptions, utilitarianism is likely to allow institutional arrangements which systematically disadvantage some individuals for the sake of maximizing aggregate or average utility.

The Principle of Greatest Equal Liberty, in contrast, provides a straightforward and secure foundation for our considered moral judgment that the basic structure should not discriminate among persons in the distribution of basic liberties. Moreover, Rawls' principles, when taken together, are designed to insure that institutional arrangements will not disadvantage some individuals for the sake of maximizing aggregate or average utility. Thus Rawls concludes that his theory of justice provides the simplest and most plausible account of our most basic considered judgments about social justice: it accounts for our considered judgments while relying on fewer and less problematic empirical assumptions.

Conditions Matching Justification. The most distinctive feature of Rawls' conditions matching justification is his use of the traditional idea that acceptable principles of political organization can be viewed as the outcome of a mutually binding contract among the members of society. The conditions which together comprise the original position are then viewed as conditions under which suitably described parties make a contract with one another.

> ...the principles of justice for the basic structure of society are the principles that free and rational persons concerned to further their own interests would accept in an initial position of equality as defining the fundamental terms of their association. These principles are to regulate all further agreements; they specify the kinds of social cooperation that can be entered into and the forms of government that can be established. This way of regarding the principles of justice I shall call justice as fairness (11).

The idea of a social contract has several advantages. First, it allows us to view the principles of justice as the outcome of a *rational collective choice.* Second, the idea of *contractual obligation* emphasizes that the persons participating in this collective choice are to make a *basic commitment* to the principles they choose, and that compliance with these principles may be rightly enforced. Third, the idea of a contract as a *voluntary agreement* for mutual advantage suggests that the principles of justice should be "such as to draw forth the willing cooperation of everyone" in a society, "including those less well situated" (15).

To utilize the idea of a hypothetical social contract, two things must be done. First, the hypothetical situation in which the agreement is to be made must be carefully described in such a way that it does yield agreement on a determinate set of principles. In other words, the hypothetical choice situation must be described in such a way that, granted the description, it is possible to derive the conclusion that rational persons who found themselves in this situation would choose one set of principles rather than another.

Second, the reasoning from this hypothetical situation must actually be gone through. We must determine exactly which principles of justice would be chosen by rational persons who found themselves in the hypothetical situation described in the first stage. Let us now examine in some detail Rawls' execution of the two stages of the argument, beginning with the first.

Rawls calls his description of the hypothetical choice situation the *original* position to signify that it is the situation of choice from which the principles of justice originate or derive. The original position includes four main elements: (a) the rational motivation of the parties, (b) the veil of ignorance, (c) the formal constraints of the concept of right, and (d) the list of competing principles of justice. To understand the nature of the hypothetical situation of choice as Rawls conceives it, and to see why he thinks it accords with our considered judgments about the conditions which are appropriate for the choice of principles of justice, we must now briefly explicate each of these four elements in turn.

(a) The parties to the contract are conceived of as being motivated to pursue their life plans in a rational way. By a life plan Rawls means a consistent set of basic goals to be pursued over a life time. Each party is conceived of as having a desire to gain as large a share of primary goods as possible, since primary goods are generally useful, whatever one's life plan happens to be. Rawls describes the parties as being mutually disinterested in the sense that each thinks of himself as an independent agent with a worthwhile life plan which he desires to pursue.[9]

(b) The parties in the original position are subject to a set of informational constraints which Rawls refers to collectively as the "veil of ignorance." The idea is that the parties are deprived of certain information. No one knows whether he (or she) is rich or poor, black or white, male or female, skilled or unskilled, weak or strong. The main purpose of depriving the parties of this information is to avoid a biased choice of principles.

> The principles of justice are chosen behind a veil of ignorance. This ensures that no one is advantaged or disadvantaged in the choice of principles by the outcome of natural chance or the contingency of social circumstances. Since all are similarly situated and no one is able to design principles to favor his particular condition, the principles of justice are the result of a fair agreement or bargain. For given the circumstances of the original position, the symmetry of everyone's relations to each other, this initial situation is fair between individuals as moral persons.... The original position is, one might say, the appropriate initial status quo, and thus the fundamental agreements reached in it are fair. This explains the propriety of the name "justice as fairness"; it conveys the idea that the principles of justice are agreed to in an initial situation that is fair (12).

The intuitive idea here is that the choice of principles of justice should not be influenced by factors that are arbitrary from a moral point of view. If, for example, a group of persons in the original position knew that they were rich while others were poor, they might choose principles of justice which produced even greater advantages for the rich while further disadvantaging the poor. Similarly, a person who knew that he was a member of the dominant racial majority might choose principles which would discriminate against certain minorities.

(c) The parties in the original position are also described as limiting their choice to principles which satisfy certain formal constraints. The rationale behind these constraints is that they must be satisfied if the principles of justice which the parties choose are to fulfill their proper role. The proper role of principles of justice, according to Rawls, is to provide a public charter which defines the terms of social cooperation by specifying how the basic structure is to distribute rights, wealth, income, authority, and other primary goods. Rawls suggests that if the principles of justice are to be capable of achieving this goal they must be (i) general, (ii) universal in application, (iii) universalizable, (iv) publicizable, (v) adjudicative, and (vi) final.

They must be *general* if they are to cover all or almost all questions of social justice which may arise. They must be *universal in application* in the sense that their demands must apply to all members of society. The principles of justice must also be *universalizable* in the sense that they must be principles whose universal acceptance we can endorse. If the principles of justice are to guide our actions and policies and to serve as justifying grounds in particular cases, they must be *publicizable* and understandable by everyone. Since questions of justice arise where different individuals come into conflict over the benefits produced by social cooperation, principles of justice must be *adjudicative* in the sense that they must provide a way of *ordering* conflicting claims and thereby settling disputes. Lastly, the principles of justice must be *final:* they must be ultimate principles which provide a *final* court of appeal for disputes about justice (131–35).[10]

(d) Rawls' description of the original position also includes a list of competing principles of justice from which the parties are to choose. The main competitors, according to Rawls, are the two versions of utilitarianism (classical and average) and Rawls' principles of justice.

Setting out the conditions listed in (a) through (d) completes the first stage of Rawls' contractarian argument, the description of the original position or hypothetical situation for the choice of principles of justice. We can now turn to a brief outline of the second stage of the contractarian argument—the attempt to show that granted this description of the original position, the parties would choose Rawls' principles of justice.

By construing the selection of principles of justice as a problem of rational choice, Rawls is able to enlist techniques developed by contemporary decision theorists. Granted the informational constraints imposed by the veil of ignorance, the problem of choosing principles of justice in the original position is what decision theorists call a problem of rational choice under uncertainty.

The idea is that the parties are to choose a set of principles which will then be applied to the basic structure of the society in which they live. Different sets of principles will produce different distributions of prospects for liberty, wealth, authority, and other primary goods. Since the parties do not know their present status in their society, they are not able to predict exactly how the choice of this or that set of principles will affect them personally. The parties are to choose principles which will profoundly influence their life-prospects, but they are to do so in a situation in which the outcome of the alternatives is uncertain.

Decision theorists have proposed various rules for making decisions under uncertainty. Rawls argues that the appropriate decision rule for the parties in the original position to employ is the *maximin rule.* The maximin rule states that one is to choose that alternative which has the best worst outcome. The maximin rule tells one, in effect, to choose the safest alternative.

Rawls' appeal to decision theory in defending the contractarian argument for his principles of justice has two stages. First, Rawls argues that the conditions which make up the original position are conditions which make it rational for the parties in the original position to employ the maximin decision rule. Second, he argues that if the parties employed the maximin decision rule they would choose his principles of justice over the competitors on the list. According to Rawls, the Principle of Greatest Equal Liberty, along with the Principle of Fair Equality of Opportunity and the Difference Principle, insure the best worst outcome of any of the sets of principles on the list.

It is important to understand exactly why Rawls thinks that the worst possible outcome under utilitarianism would be worse than the worst possible outcome under his principles. As we saw earlier, Rawls argues that utilitarianism might require or at least allow severe restrictions of liberty for some if this produced greater overall utility. Thus, the worst outcome under utilitarianism might be slavery or servitude or at least a lesser share of liberty than others have. A person in the original position is to consider the possibility that he might turn out to be a member of the worst off group in society. Rawls' claim is that since utilitarianism may sacrifice the interests of a minority to produce greater aggregate utility, the worst-off under utilitarianism may be very badly off indeed. In contrast, the lexical priority of the Principle of Greatest Equal Liberty eliminates this possible outcome by insuring that no one's basic liberty will be sacrificed for the sake of maximizing overall utility. Further, the Difference Principle requires that inequalities in wealth, income, and authority must work to the greatest benefit of the worst off, subject to the lexical priority of the Principle of Greatest Equal Liberty and the Principle of Fair Equality of Opportunity. Rawls concludes that parties in the original position would adopt a minimal risk strategy, choose his principles, and reject the alternative conceptions, including utilitarianism.

Though it has attracted the most attention, Rawls' maximin decision rule argument does not exhaust his contractarian justification for his principles of justice. He sketches several informal contractarian arguments which do not employ decision theory. Among these are (i) the argument from self-respect, (ii) the argument from the strains of commitment, and (iii) the argument from stability. Granted the limitations of the present essay, we can only sketch these informal arguments very briefly to emphasize their independence from the maximin decision-rule argument.

(i) Rawls stresses that "perhaps the most important primary good is that of self-respect" because

> Without it nothing may seem worth doing or if some things have value for us, we lack the will to strive for them. All desire and activity becomes empty and vain, and we sink into apathy and cynicism. Therefore the parties in the original position would wish to avoid at almost any cost the social conditions that undermine self-respect (440).

He then emphasizes the effects of publicity on self-respect. The public knowledge that the basic structure of society is to be arranged according to his two principles of justice would, Rawls contends, support individuals' self-respect in two ways. First, society's commitment to ensuring everyone greatest equal basic liberty and fair equality of opportunity would be seen as a public expression of unconditional respect for each. Second, Rawls states that the Difference Principle is a principle of *reciprocity* insofar as it insures that the distribution of social goods is to everyone's advantage. The concept of reciprocity or mutual advantage, he observes, is consonant with the assumption that each person's pursuit of the good as he conceives it is to be respected. Thus the common knowledge that the distribution of wealth and income is to be regulated by a principle of mutual benefit also provides social support for the individual's self-respect. Rawls concludes that the parties to the hypothetical contract would recognize that his conception of justice "gives more support to [self-respect] than other principles and [that this] is a strong reason for them to adopt it" (440).

(ii) The strains of commitment argument[11] capitalizes on the fact that it is a condition of the original position that the parties know they are to make a *contract*, a *sincere agreement* not just a unanimous choice.

> The argument from the strains of commitment has an important place in justice as fairness and its concept of contract (agreement) is essential to it...In general, the class of things that can be agreed to is included within, and is smaller than, the class of things that can be rationally chosen. We can decide to take a chance and at the same time fully intend that, should things turn out badly, we shall do what we can to retrieve our situation. But if we make an agreement, we have to accept the outcome; and so to give an undertaking in good faith, we must not only intend to honor it but with reason believe we can do so.[12]

So the parties are actually to make a contract: they are to make a binding agreement, not simply to say that they agree. But if they are to make a binding agreement, then they are to consider whether they will be able to keep it—to comply fully with the principles chosen. And if they are to consider whether they will be able to keep the agreement they must consider whether the facts about human motivation make such compliance possible. Further, it is not even enough to determine that compliance with a certain set of principles is motivationally *possible.* The parties must also determine whether the psychological costs of compliance are excessive. Rawls refers to these psychological costs as "the strains of commitment" and argues that the parties would conclude that the strains of commitment associated with his principles are less serious than those associated with competing principles. Again, the case of utilitarianism provides a central illustration of this contractarian argument. Rawls contends that because it might require that certain individuals' interests be sacrificed for the sake of maximizing overall or average utility, utilitarianism involves greater strains of commitment than his own conception of justice.

(iii) Rawls' third informal contractarian argument, the argument from stability, depends, at least in part, upon the success of the argument from self-respect and the argument from the strains of commitment examined above. He contends that the parties in the original position will choose that conception of justice which, if successfully implemented, will produce a social order which enjoys the greatest stability, other things being equal (138, 177–82). A conception whose implementation will produce excessive strains of commitment, or one which will undermine self-respect, will be unstable. Rawls concludes that since (as he believes he has shown) his conception minimizes strains of commitment and best supports self-respect, it would be chosen in the belief that it is more stable than competing conceptions.

What is perhaps most striking about *A Theory of Justice* is the diversity of particular arguments and types of justification which it contains. Any adequate evaluation of the theory must carefully distinguish and critically evaluate each of the various lines of support which Rawls offers.

Rawls' Model for a Just Basic Structure

Having articulated and argued for his principles of justice, Rawls then provides a brief account of how the basic structure of *our* society could be arranged so as to satisfy those principles. This account does not purport to be a detailed blueprint for the just society, but it is intended to serve two important functions. (1) It helps to specify further the content of Rawls' principles of justice by examining their practical implications. (2) An attempt to apply the principles of justice to the basic structure of our society is necessary if we are to evaluate Rawls' argument from considered moral judgments (see Rawls' Justifications for His Principles of Justice above). For to see whether Rawls' principles provide the best account of our considered moral judgments about justice, we must perform two tasks. First, we must determine what particular judgments about justice Rawls' principles yield when applied to the facts about the basic structure of our society. Second, we must see whether those particular judgments which the principles yield match our considered judgments about what is just or unjust. A fairly concrete plan of how Rawls' principles could be satisfied in our society is crucial for executing the first task and hence also for the second.

In sketching a model for a just basic structure, Rawls concentrates mainly on the institutional arrangements he thinks would satisfy the Difference Principle. The requirements of the Difference Principle in our society could best be met, Rawls believes, through the creation of four branches of government: (a) the allocation branch, (b) the stabilization branch, (c) the transfers branch, and (d) the distribution branch (275–76).

Rawls contends that, granted fair equality of opportunity and greatest equal basic liberty, the Difference Principle would be satisfied by an institutional arrangement exhibiting the following features, corresponding to the four branches of government listed above. (1) There is private ownership of capital and natural resources. A free market system is maintained by the *allocation branch* of government. (2) There is a *stabilization branch* whose function is to "try to bring about reasonably full employment..." (3) The *transfers branch* of government "guarantees a social minimum [i.e., a minimum income for all] either by family allowances and special payments for sickness and unemployment, or more systematically by such devices as a graded income supplement (i.e., a negative income tax)." (4) There is a *distribution branch* whose "task is to preserve an approximate justice in distributive shares by means of taxation and the necessary adjustments in the rights of property." There are two aspects of the distributive branch. "First, it imposes a number of inheritance and gift taxes, and sets restrictions on the rights of bequest." Second, it establishes a scheme of taxation "to raise the revenues that justice requires" (276).

Now what is striking about this model for a just society is that, with the possible exception of the "reasonable" full employment measures mentioned in (2), it purports to satisfy the Difference Principle through purely redistributive measures in the narrowest sense. Rawls assumes, that is, that the Difference Principle can be satisfied simply by redistributing income and wealth through taxing the better off and transferring the proceeds to the worst off. He assumes, then, that the representative worst off man's prospects of wealth, power, authority, etc. can be maximized by boosting the wages earned on the free market with an income supplement. The idea, roughly, is that the market will do part of the job of satisfying the Difference Principle and that taxation and income transfers will do the rest. What is crucial to note here is that Rawls believes that his principles of justice could be satisfied in our society without the abolition of competitive markets and the adoption of socialism. He contends that justice could be attained without a transition to public ownership of the means of production.

CRITICAL DISCUSSION

The Scope of the Discussion

Now that the main features of Rawls' theory are before us, I shall present several basic criticisms.[13] The diversity of these criticisms correspond to the diversity of Rawls' justifications for his principles. I shall argue that (1) the maximin argument is unsound; (2) Rawls' Difference Principle far exceeds the demands of justice and places unacceptable restrictions on freedom; and (3) Rawls' institutional model for a just basic structure is inadequate and misleading. In keeping with the introductory function of this essay, the criticisms I advance are intended more as stimuli for further discussion than as conclusive objections.

The Unsoundness of the Maximin Argument

You will recall that the maximin argument is one of Rawls' arguments to show that the parties in the original position would choose his principles of justice and that the argument consists of two stages.[14] First, it must be shown that the conditions constituting the original position make it appropriate to employ the maximin decision rule—the rule which directs one to choose that option whose worst outcome is better than the worst outcomes of each of the other options. Second, it must be shown that if the parties in the original position employed the maximin rule they would choose Rawls' principles. The first stage is crucial: unless it can be shown that the conditions of the original position make it rational to employ the maximin rule, nothing will be gained by showing that Rawls' principles are the maximin solution to the problem of choice presented in the original position.

Following the decision theorist W. Fellner, Rawls observes that "there appear to be three chief features of situations which give plausibility to" the use of the maximin rule (154). Because of the veil of ignorance (i) there is no basis for probabilistic reasoning in the original position: probabilities of outcomes under the various sets of principles cannot be reasonably estimated since there is no information on which to base such estimates. (ii) Each party in the original position "cares very little, if anything, for what he might gain above the minimum stipend that he can, in fact, be sure of by following the maximin rule" (154). (iii) The worst outcomes of the options other than that option which has the best worst outcome are such that "one can hardly accept" them. Rawls then contends that "the original position manifests these [three] features to the fullest possible degree, carrying them to the limit, so to speak" (153).

Though Rawls does not point this out, condition (i) is in no way peculiar to situations in which employment of the maximin rule is appropriate. Inability to estimate probabilities of outcomes is the key feature which marks that branch of decision theory which deals with decisions under uncertainty.[15] The maximin rule is only one of several decision rules which have been proposed for use in making decisions under uncertainty. Included among these alternative decision rules are a. the minimax regret rule, b. the Bayes rule (i.e., the principle of insufficient reason), c. the Hurwitz α-rule, and d. the maximax rule.[16] Hence to say that the original position does not allow estimates of probabilities of outcomes is not to say anything which indicates that the maximin rule, rather than any of the other rules for decisions under uncertainty, is the rule to employ in the original position. So if the case for the employment of the maximin rule is to be made, it must be made by showing that the original position satisfies conditions in addition to (i).

To make good his claim that condition (ii) is satisfied in the original position Rawls must make a very strong and implausible assumption about the diminishing marginal value of wealth, power, and the other primary goods covered by the Difference Principle. Let us call these primary goods 'nonlibertarian goods' to distinguish them from the goods falling under the Principle of Greatest Equal Liberty. The assumption, call it *a*, is that beyond some minimum, *m* (guaranteed by the Difference Principle), the marginal value of the nonlibertarian goods drops so far and so rapidly that the parties need not even consider possible gains above *m*, once they can be assured of attaining *m*. Now it may be plausible to assume that there is some minimal level of nonlibertarian goods, *m*, such that gains above *m* are of negligible value compared with the disutility of falling below *m*. But from this it does not follow that once they are assured of this minimum the parties will view gains above it as negligible. Further, as we shall see in a moment, even if we grant that there is a minimal level such that anything below it is intolerable, the Difference Principle is not the only principle on the list which guarantees it.

It should be emphasized that assumption *a* is not simply a diminishing marginal value assumption—it is an extremely strong one. There are two reasons why Rawls cannot make it. First, Rawls himself rightly attacks his utilitarian opponents for relying on strong assumptions about diminishing marginal value in their attempts to show that utilitarian principles will not require unacceptable inequalities in wealth or basic liberties. So Rawls' use of a strong diminishing marginal value assumption would undercut one of his main arguments against utilitarianism. Second, assumption *a* seems to be incompatible with Rawls' basic thesis that the possibility of gains above the minimum will serve as incentives for greater achievement in a just basic structure. If the decrease in marginal value of gains above the minimum is as drastic as condition (ii) implies, then there will be no effective incentives. It appears, then, that Rawls has not shown that (ii), the second condition for the appropriateness of the maximin rule, is satisfied in the original position.

Rawls contends that the third condition is satisfied in the original position because all of the "other conceptions of justice may lead to institutions that the parties would find intolerable" (156).

It seems plausible enough to assume that Rawls' main rivals, versions of utilitarianism, may lead to worst outcomes which the parties, as Rawls characterizes them, would find intolerable. The outcomes under utilitarianism, Rawls thinks, might include severe restrictions on some individuals' basic liberties or opportunities. Suppose for a moment that this argument is conclusive, that both versions of utilitarianism are eliminated from the list, and that the parties choose the Principle of Greatest Liberty and the Principle of Fair Equality of Opportunity. Once they have secured equal basic liberty and fair equality of opportunity, it is still an open question as to whether they will choose the Difference Principle or some other principle for the distribution of nonlibertarian goods such as wealth and income. Rawls concedes this when he includes certain "mixed conceptions" on the list of competing conceptions of justice. The several mixed conceptions Rawls mentions are generated by adding various distributive principles to the Principle of Greatest Equal Liberty or to that principle along with the Principle of Fair Equality of Opportunity. He lists the following distributive principles:

1. the principle of average utility; or
2. the principle of average utility, subject to a constraint either:
   (a) that a certain social minimum should be maintained; or
   (b) that the overall distribution not be too wide (124).

It is extremely implausible to maintain, as Rawls must, that condition (iii) is satisfied in the original position on the grounds that both 1 and 2 —and any mixed conception one might device—may lead to *intolerable* outcomes. A mixed conception which not only secures equal liberty and fair equality of opportunity, but also insures an adequate minimum of nonlibertarian goods, does not appear to threaten "intolerable" outcomes any more than the Difference Principle does.

To support the claim that the parties would reject mixed conceptions Rawls suggests two arguments. First, he notes that mixed conceptions which include either an average or a classical utility principle are unattractive because they require interpersonal utility comparisons and because such comparisons involve severe, perhaps insurmountable problems. Second, he says that the notion of a satisfactory minimum of wealth and income is vague and intuitionistic, that reliance on intuitionistic conceptions should be avoided if possible, and that it can be avoided if the Difference Principle is chosen instead (318–20).

The bearing of these two remarks on the question of whether condition (iii) is satisfied in the original position is not clear. Perhaps Rawls' point is that problems of interpersonal utility comparisons and reliance on intuition make mixed conceptions dangerous choices: errors or abuses in their implementation may lead to "intolerable" outcomes for some.

Now it is plausible to claim that, due to the problems of devising interpersonal utility comparisons, implementation of either of the two principles of utility is liable to abuse or error. But a similar objection can be raised against the Difference Principle. Applying the Difference Principle does not require interpersonal utility comparisons. It does require, as it were, *interworld prospect comparisons.* For it requires that we rank all possible arrangements of the basic structure according to the prospect indices of their respective representative worst off positions. How to compare prospect indices across all possible arrangements of the basic structure is not appreciably less difficult than comparing utility functions of actual individuals. If there is a serious possibility of error and abuse in the one case, it is surely present in the other as well. Consequently, Rawls' first argument fails to show the Difference Principle to be superior to all mixed conceptions.

Yet even if the problem of interpersonal utility comparisons is significantly greater than that of comparing prospect indices across all possible arrangements of the basic structure, this is an objection only to those mixed conceptions which include some version of the principle of utility. It is quite irrelevant to the question of whether a mixed conception which includes an adequate minimum principle (without a principle of utility) would be chosen in the original position.

Rawls' second argument against mixed conceptions is somewhat more plausible. It capitalizes on the difficulty of formulating a plausible yet definite adequate minimum principle in the original position. The problem, briefly, is that the veil of ignorance prevents one from knowing the facts needed for determining what an adequate minimum would be in one's own society. Rawls concludes that the parties would not choose an unspecified adequate minimum principle. He fails to consider the plausible suggestion that the adequate minimum could be specified at a later stage of deliberations, when more information is available.[17] Moreover, whatever difficulties might accrue to postponing the specification of an adequate minimum might well be outweighed if the Difference Principle could be shown to be vulnerable to serious objections. I shall consider some of these objections in the next section.

Let us assume, for a moment, what Rawls has not in fact shown. Let us assume that he has shown that all rival conceptions may lead to outcomes the parties would find "intolerable." This would still not suffice to show that the appropriate rule to employ in the original position is the maximin rule, since condition (ii), as I argued above, is not satisfied. It appears, then, that the maximin argument is unsound.

The preceding critique of the maximin argument has important implications for Rawls' three informal (non-decision theoretic) arguments—the argument from the strains of commitment, the argument from self-respect, and the argument from stability. Though I cannot pursue these implications here, I should like to suggest that Rawls has not shown that mixed conceptions which protect basic liberty and opportunity and insure a minimum of wealth and income for all would threaten self-respect, impose unacceptable strains of commitment, or produce instability.

The Difference Principle Exceeds the Demands of Justice and Imposes Excessive Restrictions on Freedom

To determine whether Rawls' Difference Principle exceeds the demands of justice, we must first get clearer about what this principle requires. There is a recurrent ambiguity in Rawls' various formulations of the Difference Principle. Often he states the principle as follows:

> D: The basic structure of society is to be arranged so that social and economic *inequalities* (in wealth, income, and authority) maximize the prospects of the representative worst off man.[18]

This formulation suggests that the Difference Principle imposes a condition on *inequalities* but places no conditions on *equal* distributions. D suggests, that is, that while unequal distributions must maximize the prospects of the representative worst off man, *any* equal distribution is permissible.

There are, however, other passages which suggest the following formulation of the Difference Principle:

> M: The basic structure of society is to be arranged so as to maximize the prospects (of wealth, income, authority) of the representative worst off man.

It is crucial to note that Rawls' arguments for the Difference Principle, including the maximin argument, must be understood as arguments for M, not for D. Consider, again, the maximin argument. If the first stage of the argument were successful, then Rawls would have established that the parties would use the maximin rule. Applied in the original position, the maximin rule requires that the parties choose that principle which maximizes the minimum—that principle which requires the highest minimum share of prospects of obtaining the primary goods. This principle is M, not D. In an article written after the publication of the book,[19] Rawls refers to the Difference Principle as the "maximin criterion." This label also suggests that the proper formulation is M, rather than D, since M, not D, is a criterion which demands that we maximize the minimum.

To see why principle D does not maximize the minimum, it is important to recall that D places *no* conditions on equal distributions. As Rawls himself admits, each person's share under an equal distribution may be lower than the representative worst off man's share under some unequal distribution. Thus principle D, which allows any equal distribution, no matter how small the equal shares may be, does *not* require that the minimum share be maximized. Under an equal distribution the maximum and minimum coincide. Or, to put it more paradoxically, if we define the representative worst off position as that position which is such that no position has lower prospects and if we define the best off position as that which is such that no position has higher prospects, then under an equal distribution the worst off and best off positions are identical.

Principle D, which puts no constraints on equal distributions, does not require that the minimum share be as high as possible. But the maximin rule requires the parties to choose that principle which demands that the minimum share be the highest possible. Therefore, if the parties in the original position employed the maximin rule they would not choose D, but rather M, which does require the minimum to be maximized. Though I shall not argue the point here, I believe that Rawls' other arguments for the Difference Principle are also arguments for M, not D.

We can now begin to see why Rawls' Difference Principle, understood as M, far exceeds the demands of justice. M not only tells us when an equal distribution of wealth, income, and authority is required; it also states the sole condition under which an equal distribution is permissible. According to M, an equal distribution is permissible if and *only if* it is that distribution among those possible to achieve in a given society which maximizes the prospects of the representative worst off man (i.e., which maximizes the minimum share). So in cases in which each person's share under an equal distribution was not as great as the representative worst off man's share under some unequal distribution, M would not only *allow* inequalities, it would *require* that they be instituted. Hence in such cases, even perfect equality would not be enough for distributive justice, according to the Difference Principle!

Surely it is extremely implausible for Rawls to maintain, as he must, that a society which achieves perfect equality in the distribution of wealth, income, and authority is defective from the standpoint of *justice.* It is difficult to see how distributive justice could require *more* than perfect equality. If this conclusion captures the content of one of "our considered judgments" about justice, then the Difference Principle is not plausible as a principle of justice.

An appeal to our considered judgments about justice might, however, support a weaker claim than the one to which Rawls is committed. One might argue that we are required to go beyond equality if equal shares are unacceptably lean. After all, equality is cold comfort where all have nothing or too little.

Such an arrangement of impoverished equality is, no doubt, defective. If means are available for improving everyone's lot (through instituting inequalities in the form of incentives to increase production, say), it may even be *morally* defective. But is the defect a matter of injustice? I am inclined to think not.

Yet even if it were true that justice requires going beyond equality where equal shares are unacceptably lean, this would not rebut my claim that the Difference Principle exceeds the demands of justice. Rawls is committed to the much stronger (and stranger) view that a strictly egalitarian scheme is unjust even when the equal shares are substantial or even bounteous. For according to the Difference Principle, a strictly egalitarian scheme is just only if it is that scheme in which the minimum share is *maximized.*

My objection to the Difference Principle, as a principle of justice, then, is two-fold. First, it is implausible to say that distributive justice requires more than strict equality in wealth, income and authority. Second, even if justice demanded more than equality by requiring inequalities for the sake of raising the minimum where equal shares are lean, it is implausible to say that justice requires *maximizing* the minimum, where equal shares are quite generous. A principle which demands that we continuously raise the minimum *might* be plausible as a principle of supererogation—a principle for the ideally generous society—but it is not a viable candidate for a principle of justice.

I should now like to suggest that the extreme generosity demanded by the Difference Principle would itself be intolerable from the standpoint of individual freedom. In particular, the implementation of the Difference Principle would place several restrictions on the individual's freedom to choose an occupation and on his freedom to engage in what John Stuart Mill called "experiments of living."

Suppose that it is determined that a certain institutional arrangement is that one which maximizes the prospects of the representative worst off man. According to Rawls, the duty of justice requires that we establish this institutional arrangement. Now an institutional arrangement exists only insofar as there are persons actually filling its constitutive roles and positions. It follows that the Difference Principle, when taken together with the principle of the duty of justice, requires that these roles and positions be filled. Rawls apparently assumes that in any given society the use of incentives in the form of larger shares will always be adequate to fill all the needed roles and positions constituting that arrangement which maximizes the prospects of the representative worst off man.

This assumption should give us pause. If the use of incentives fails to elicit individuals' voluntary participation in the needed roles, then the Difference Principle not only allows but indeed requires that individuals be coerced or at least penalized into filling them. There is no freedom of occupational choice under Rawls' Principle of Greatest Equal Liberty to prevent such conscription for the sake of realizing that institutional arrangement which maximizes the prospects of the representative worst off man. To assume that incentives will in fact always eliminate the need for penalties or coercion is gratuitous. To many people the right to pursue—or even to compete for a chance to pursue—the career of their choice is worth more than higher pay or other benefits.

It is not simply that the satisfaction of the Difference Principle may allow or even require that individuals be compelled to fill certain needed social roles in order to establish that institutional order among those possible which maximizes the prospects of the representative worst off man. The Difference Principle also limits freedom by ruling out any and every institution or association—and hence any constitutive role in any such institution or association—whose existence is not compatible with the establishment of that particular institutional arrangement which maximizes the prospects of the representative worst off man. Since the scope of the restriction is so immense, an example will be helpful. Suppose that certain persons in a Rawlsian society wish to engage in what Mill somewhat dramatically called experiments of living. They wish to pool their resources and form a community of a certain sort. Suppose also that the larger society in which they live is one in which there is no poverty in any significant sense—suppose that the worst off enjoy an adequate or even a comfortable share of the primary goods. Suppose also that by using their pooled resources for the purposes on which they have agreed, the individuals in question will not even be doing anything which can be expected to cover the expectations of the worst off in the larger society. Suppose that the experimental community will even contribute some of its resources (through taxes) to improving the lot of the worst off in the larger society.

Even if all of these very strong suppositions hold, the Difference Principle might nonetheless forbid the establishment of such a community. For the Difference Principle would forbid its establishment, on pain of penalty or coercion, if it could be expected to make unavailable certain resources, whether human or material, which were needed for the never-ending task of maximizing the prospects of the representative worst off man. The task is never-ending because the representative worst off man, like the Gospel's poor, will always be with us: there will always be a minimum share.

By requiring too much of the socio-economic arrangements, the Difference Principle would require too much of us. To accept a principle which requires that the minimum be continuously raised, no matter what the cost and no matter how high the minimum already is, would be to view society as a monolithic machine straining after an ever-receding production goal.

In defense of Rawls it might be said that the lexically prior Principle of Greatest Equal Liberty precludes these unacceptable limitations on freedom, or at least can be easily modified to do so. For it might be argued that the basic liberty of "freedom of the person" or "the right to hold (personal) property" would block any attempts to satisfy the Difference Principle through coercion or penalties. Further, it might also be said that the lexical priority of either or both of these basic rights would prevent excessive restrictions on individuals' freedom to form voluntary associations and communities. Or, if these do not do the job, the list of basic liberties can be expanded to protect against potential excesses of the Difference Principle.

There are several difficulties with this reply. First, nothing Rawls says about the two basic liberties in question suggests that they are rich enough to provide effective replies to the libertarian objections considered above. Second, if these basic liberties are stretched to include freedom in the choice of occupation, freedom to associate with others in cooperative ventures, etc., then the problem of determining priorities among basic liberties becomes greatly exacerbated and priorities must be determined if we are to determine which arrangements will produce the greatest equal liberty. Third, if the basic liberties are expanded to include the needed items, then the lexical priority of the Principle of Greatest Equal Liberty threatens to undercut any significant role for the Difference Principle. If, for example, the right to hold personal property is fleshed out as a substantive Lockean property right which includes a person's property in his own labor, then the operation of the Difference Principle will be greatly circumscribed. It is remarkable that Rawls should have included a basic right to property in his lexically prior first principle and an over-arching principle for determining property rights in his second principle, without specifying the content of the former. Until the content of the lexically prior right to personal property is specified, it will be impossible to determine whether libertarian objections to the Difference Principle can be effectively met. Indeed one gets quite different distributive theories depending upon how much or how little one packs into the lexically prior right to property.[20]

The Inadequacy of Rawls' Model for a Just Basic Structure

Rawls' presentation of a model for a just basic structure (see Rawls' Model for a Just Basic Structure above) can be seen as an attempt to rebut objections that the Difference Principle places unacceptable restrictions on individual freedom. The leading idea of the model is that the market will do part of the job of satisfying the Difference Principle and that income transfers through regular, long-standing taxation policies will do the rest. If the Difference Principle could be satisfied through supplementing the distributive mechanism of the market by raking off income from the better off and distributing it to the worst off, the force of the libertarian objections considered in the preceding section would be diminished. For if satisfaction of the Difference Principle were merely a matter of redistributing income through taxation, then there would be no need for coerced labor or other significant restrictions on freedom of occupation. Since well-designed tax laws would provide a stable, predictable framework for legitimate expectations, no one need fear gross or frequent appropriations of his holding or the abolition of institutional roles to which he had aspired. Further, so long as an individual or association meets his or its tax responsibilities there will be no need for government restriction on the development of new life styles, cooperative ventures, or institutions. Finally, taxation and transfer policies would not require the uncontrollable growth of direct economic control which is one of the greatest threats to individual freedom.

Rawls' institutional model for the satisfaction of the Difference Principle can provide an adequate response to the preceding libertarian objections only if Rawls is willing to take either of two drastic and disastrous steps. He must either 1) radically (or rather, conservatively!) transform the Difference Principle by collapsing the range of goods it distributes; or 2) he must stick with the form of the Difference Principle he has argued for all along and make the gratuitous assumption that raising only their *income*-prospects will maximize the representative worst off man's overall index of prospects over the entire range of (nonlibertarian) social primary goods.

Consider the first option, 1. If the Difference Principle were a distributive principle in the narrow sense—if it required only that the *income* prospects of the representative worst off man be maximized—there would be *some* reason to think that its satisfaction would require only taxation and transfer measures, the sorts of measures which are least objectionable from the standpoint of individual freedom. But of course the Difference Principle is not a distributive principle in this narrow sense. What the Difference Principle distributes, it must be remembered, is prospects of a whole set of primary goods, of which income is only one. Among the goods included are not simply wealth and income, but also self-respect, authority, and the prerogatives of power. Further, Rawls himself frequently emphasizes that some of the goods other than wealth or income, such as self-respect, are of special importance and will be given greater weight than others in determining what will maximize the representative worst off man's overall prospects. To attempt to block libertarian objections by paring down the distributive scope of the Difference Principle amounts to abandoning the Difference Principle and replacing it with a much less comprehensive principle. I shall show in a moment that the cost of such surgery would be prohibitive for Rawls.

Consider, then, option 2. Granted that maximizing the prospects of the representative worst off man requires maximizing the weighted sum of prospects of the entire list of these goods—not just maximizing prospects of income or wealth—there is no reason to assume, as this strategy would have us do, that increasing the income prospects of the representative worst off man will maximize his prospects of the whole range of social primary goods. Moreover, Rawls does nothing to support this assumption.

It is important to sort out several versions of the needed assumption about the connection between increases in income-prospects and increases in prospects of other primary goods such as self-respect and authority. Consider first the assumption that in our society at the present time, and for a period extending indefinitely into the future, the overall prospects of the worst off, including especially their prospects of self-respect, can be maximized simply by supplementing their wages through the use of tax revenues. It is not simply that Rawls fails to marshall any empirical evidence to show that this can be done, though this is bad enough. There is the more serious problem that there is a good deal of empirical evidence against the assumption that income and self-respect (and authority) are correlated in this simple fashion even in our society at the present time.[21]
respect is dependent in significant ways upon his belief that his work is meaningful or important, or that it involves the exercise of some of his higher capacities. Though I will not press the point here, I believe that Rawls can be faulted for not having included meaningful work among the primary goods. For surely persons in the original position, realizing as they would that in most societies at most times the nature of a person's work is one of the key factors shaping and limiting his

conception of the good and his values in general, would be concerned to choose a social order which somehow took his interest in this good into account. Rawls does recognize self-respect as a primary good. So to the extent that self-respect is dependent on meaningful work, the comprehensive form of the Difference Principle, which covers self-respect, will require institutional arrangements to provide minimally meaningful work for all. However, it is wishful thinking to suppose that Rawls' simple and rather conservative institutional model for the satisfaction of the Difference Principle will come to grips with the awesome problem of adequately raising the representative worst off man's prospects for self-respect or meaningful work. To assume that these problems can be solved simply by redistributing income through conventional taxation measures is to make the same sort of error for which Marx took the French socialists of his day to task. It is to assume that problems which intimately involve persons' *productive* relations can be solved by purely *distributive* measures in the narrow sense.

If Rawls acknowledges that meaningful work is a primary good, he is faced with a dilemma. Either he must directly take into account meaningful work in determining what maximizes the representative worst off man's over-all prospects, or he must take meaningful work into account indirectly, by taking self-respect into account in determining what maximizes his overall prospects. Regardless of which of these options he takes, there is no reason to believe, and good reason to deny, that mere redistribution of income will adequately solve the problem of meaningful work.

Yet even if Rawls could somehow show that the overall prospects of the representative worst off man can be maximized in our society at the present time by increasing their income, this would not suffice as a reply to the various libertarian objections explored earlier. It would not suffice because, as Rawls himself stresses, an argument for principles for all societies at all times cannot rely on assumptions which apply only to certain societies at certain times. If Rawls is to employ the institutional model he introduces in the second part of his book to meet libertarian objections to the Difference Principle, he must execute the impossible task of showing that the comprehensive distributive requirements the Difference Principle imposes can be satisfied in all or most societies at all or most times through the use of an extremely conservative system of taxation and payments.

Rawls is faced with a dilemma. If he is to invoke the taxation and payment model to block libertarian objections to the Difference Principle, he must either restrict the distributive scope of that principle to prospects of wealth and income, or he must preserve the Difference Principle as a comprehensive distributive principle. If he restricts the distributive scope of the Difference Principle, then he undercuts the supporting role of the theory of primary goods. For the theory of primary goods was employed, it should be recalled, to provide the proper content for a distributive principle. The parties in the original position are described as desiring the whole range of nonlibertarian goods falling under the Difference Principle, not as desiring a severely restricted subset of those goods. Further, to so restrict the list of primary goods would be to weaken the theory of primary goods. Rawls is quite right in maintaining that the contracting parties will be concerned about social primary goods other than wealth and the basic liberties. It appears, then, that Rawls cannot consistently make his institutional model plausible by restricting the distributive scope of the Difference Principle.

Suppose, on the other hand, that Rawls adheres to the full theory of primary goods and to the Difference Principle as a comprehensive principle which distributes prospects covering the whole range of nonlibertarian social primary goods, not just prospects for income or wealth. As we saw earlier, there is no reason to believe that Rawls' taxation and payments model would, in fact, satisfy and continue to satisfy the Difference Principle in our society, much less in all or most societies at all or most times. In fact there is, as I also noted, considerable evidence to the contrary. But if this is so, then again Rawls cannot legitimately invoke the taxation and payment model in reply to the libertarian objections I articulated above. In sum, regardless of which horn of the dilemma Rawls opts for, his model for the satisfaction of the Difference Principle fails to provide an adequate rejoinder to the libertarian's objections. By taking for granted that the Difference Principle could be satisfied by the relatively open and nonrestrictive social structure Rawls presents in the second part of *A Theory of Justice*, we would be overlooking the pervasive and excessive freedom-limiting implications of that principle.

Whether or not these and other criticisms presented in this volume indicate irreparable flaws in Rawls' theory, this much is clear: the systematic study of *A Theory of Justice* affords unique opportunities for grappling with some of the most challenging moral issues of our day. Anyone who works through Rawls' book sympathetically yet critically will emerge from the process with new insights, new questions, and a heightened sensitivity to the problems of justice.

NOTES

1. For a detailed development of this interpretation of Rawls' theory of primary goods, see my paper "Revisability and Rational Choice," *Canadian Journal of Philosophy*, vol. 5, no. 3, December 1975, 395–408.
2. Rawls also sometimes suggests that self-respect should occupy a prominent position in the list of primary goods.
3. I have supplied these examples—they are not taken from the text itself.
4. Rawls adds a "Just Savings Principle" in his final formulation of his principles on p. 302.
5. Though his critics have failed to notice it, Rawls qualifies this commitment to equal liberty with his addition of condition (b) on p. 250.
6. Stephen Darwall has argued that some of Rawls' critics have confused this thesis with the quite different claim that in choosing Rawls' principles the *parties in the original position* are acting autonomously ("A Defense of the Kantian Interpretation," *Ethics*, vol. 86, January 1976, no. 2, 164–70). See, also, Darwall's contribution to this volume.
7. See especially the third part of the *Foundations*.
8. "Rawls and Kant," by Stephen Darwall.
9. Many of Rawls' critics have erroneously assumed that Rawls characterizes the parties in the original position as rational egoists. On p. 127 Rawls distinguishes between (a) one's own conception of the good and (b) a conception of the good which is exclusively a conception of *one's own good* and then characterizes the parties as having (a). This passage shows that it is false to characterize the parties as egoists and rather misleading to characterize them as *self*-interested.
10. Rawls himself does not explicitly distinguish between the requirement that the principles be universal and the requirement that they be universalizable, but he does implicitly invoke both.
11. Rawls' discussion lends itself to two different versions of a strains of commitment argument. According to one version, the parties include strains of commitment in their estimation of outcomes in following the maximin strategy. The other version does not invoke any formal decision principles. My discussion of the maximin argument covers the first version of the argument, so I will concentrate here only on the second.
12. Rawls, "Reply to Alexander and Musgrave," *The Quarterly Journal of Economics*, November 1974, 652.
13. Some of these criticisms, or criticisms similar to them in certain respects, have already been advanced in the vast critical literature on Rawls. My criticism of the maximin argument is very similar to that offered by Rolf Sartorius in *Social Norms and Individual Conduct* (Dickenson, Encino and Belmont, California, 1975), pp. 124–29. Sartorius was extremely helpful in helping me to clarify my criticisms.
14. For another discussion of these issues see "Rawls, Games and Economic Theory" by Gail Corrado in Chapter Three of this volume.

15. ...as distinguished from decisions under risk. For a clear discussion of these decisions rule see W.J. Baumol, *Economic Theory and Operations Analysis*, 2nd edition, (Prentice-Hall, Englewood Cliffs, New Jersey, 1965), chapter 24.
16. And this is true even if the marginal value of the goods does not increase as rapidly (or even decreases) above the adequate minimum level.
17. Rawls himself does acknowledge the need for later stages of deliberation in the task of choosing a political constitution. See pp. 195-200.
18. As I indicated earlier, it may be necessary to add self-respect to this list. Strictly speaking, it appears that the maximin rule would direct the parties to choose that set of principles with the best *worst position*—not the best *representative* worst position. Due to limitations of space, I will disregard this complication.
19. Rawls, "Some Reasons for the Maximin Criterion," *American Economic Review*, May 1974, 141-45.
20. I advance other grounds for the conclusion that Rawls' view suffers from the lack of an adequate theory of property in "Distributive Justice and Legitimate Expectations," *Philosophical Studies*, vol. 28, 1975, 419-25.
21. See, for example, R. Sennett and J. Cobb, *The Hidden Injuries of Class*, (Vintage Press, New York, 1973), especially pp. 4-8, 18, 22, 28-29, 53, and 168.

The Original Position and the Veil of Ignorance[1]

Louis I. Katzner
BOWLING GREEN STATE UNIVERSITY

In *A Theory of Justice*, John Rawls asserts, argues for, and examines the implications of the principles which he believes lie at the heart of a just society. These principles are:

1. The Equal Liberty Principle
   "Each person is to have an equal right to the most extensive basic liberty compatible with a similar liberty for others" (60, all parenthetical citations are to John Rawls, *A Theory of Justice* (Cambridge, Mass.: Harvard University Press, 1971)).
2. The Principle of Democratic Equality
   "Social and economic inequalities are to be arranged so that they are both (a) to the greatest benefit of the least advantaged and (b) attached to offices and positions open to all under conditions of fair equality of opportunity" (83).

Moreover, these two principles are placed in lexical or serial order. "This is an order which requires us to satisfy the first principle in the ordering before we can move on to the second... This means, in effect, that the basic structure of society is to arrange the inequalities of wealth and authority in ways consistent with the equal liberties required by the preceding principle" (43).

Pivotal to this theory of justice is what Rawls calls "the original position" (the most important element of which is the "veil of ignorance"). The centrality of this concept derives from two factors. First,

Rawls argues for his two principles of justice by claiming that they are the principles which would be chosen in the original position. Second, it is the original position which places Rawls' theory of justice in the social contract tradition. In the discussion that follows we shall critically examine this pivotal concept: first looking at the different elements which constitute the original position and then turning to some of the broader issues which surround it.

THE ORIGINAL POSITION

The original position is a specific interpretation of a generic concept —the initial situation. This latter notion refers to the conditions under which agreements concerning the basic rules of society are reached. In other words, the rules agreed to depend upon the way in which the initial situation is described. For example, if it is described as a situation in which one individual is so much stronger than the others that they live in mortal fear of him, then everyone might agree to him being the dictator of all social rules. If, on the other hand, the initial situation is described as one in which everyone knows that some individuals have special talents which are essential to the survival and well-being of the community, there is a good chance that the more talented individuals will be given a privileged position in the structure of the society.

Rawls' basic idea is that the way to arrive at just social rules is to begin with an initial situation which is characterized by fairness. The principles agreed to by rational individuals in such circumstances will be just. He uses the term "original position" to describe this particular interpretation of the initial situation.

The concept of fairness operates at a very abstract level in Rawls' theory. His two principles of justice are rules which govern the basic structure of society; they are not rules to live by in our everyday lives. So, when Rawls speaks of the fair conditions of choice in the initial situation, he is not referring to conditions which apply to the choice of rules which govern our everyday activities. Rather the focus is upon the situation which governs the choice of rules of a more abstract nature.

An illustration will be helpful in conveying what Rawls means by the fair conditions of choice. Imagine a group of youngsters who meet on a playground. One of them has the equipment (perhaps a bat and a ball), and the others are interested in playing a game. The problem that faces them is how to go about establishing the rules of the game. Suppose the youngster with the equipment simply says, "We will play by my rules or not at all." If the other youngsters want to play, and are neither willing nor able to force the owner of the equipment to agree to a different procedure, then they have no choice but to agree to his demand. Although we may question his right to make this demand, there can be no doubt that the situation as described is not a fair situation of choice.

This is because one of the individuals is able to exploit the situation to his own advantage. He can hold out for (i.e. coerce the others into) an agreement which is to his advantage. A fair situation of choice, on the other hand, is one in which either there are no such factors to exploit or, if there are, they cannot be exploited. This shows that unanimous consent in no way ensures that there is a fair situation of choice. Fairness depends upon consent being given under conditions which preclude exploitation by any of the parties involved.

This notion of fairness is introduced into Rawls' version of the initial situation (i.e. the original position) through the veil of ignorance. But the original position involves three other elements as well: the circumstances of justice, the constraints of the concept of right, and the rationality of the parties. Although the veil of ignorance is the crucial concept for understanding Rawls' notion of fairness, each of these elements plays an important role in his overall theory. Thus we shall begin by examining each of them; focusing upon what they involve and the role they play in Rawls' theory of justice.

The Circumstances of Justice

The first element of the original position is what Rawls calls "the circumstances of justice." The central idea is that questions of justice do not arise in all circumstances. Thus if the goal is to derive principles of justice from an initial situation, that initial situation must be defined in such a way as to insure that issues of justice do arise. The definition offered by Rawls involves both objective material conditions and subjective attitudes. He encapsulates the objective material conditions in the notion of "conditions of moderate scarcity" and the subjective ones in the idea of "mutual disinterestedness." Let us look at each of these in turn.

When Rawls refers to moderate scarcity he has several different things in mind. First, when an individual lives entirely by himself, questions of justice do not arise. This is because on Rawls' view, and that of most writers on the subject, principles of justice are concerned with the division of social goods. Obviously such questions only arise if more than one individual makes a claim upon these goods. Hence, when an individual lives entirely by himself questions of justice do not arise.

The term "moderate scarcity" also refers to the material environment in which individuals find themselves. If these conditions are such that resources are plentiful enough for everyone to have as much as he wants or needs, the question of how these resources are to be divided does not rise. The rape of our environment provides an excellent illustration of this point. There was a time when there was more than enough drinkable water for everyone. As industry developed and population increased, however, the pollution of our streams and rivers became a problem. Witness the many companies that now sell bottled water. The distribution of drinkable water has become and is continuing to become a major social problem. And this is a direct result of its increasing scarcity.

On the other hand, this scarcity must not exceed moderate proportions if we are reasonably to expect it to be dealt with through social cooperation. In other words, should drinkable water become so scarce that people are dying of thirst, it is unreasonable to expect that distribution of water would continue to be a subject of social cooperation. What would inevitably happen is that each individual would "take justice into his own hands," and the result would be survival of the fittest. Thus we see that although conditions of scarcity are necessary for issues of justice to arise, they only arise if that scarcity is "moderate." When it becomes too great there is just no way that people will cooperate. Thus one thing that individuals in the original position must be aware of is that the condition of moderate scarcity exists. Otherwise they would have no interest in searching for and agreeing to principles of justice.

In addition to these objective circumstances of justice, there are also what Rawls refers to as the subjective circumstances. As the objective conditions refer to the physical circumstances in which people find themselves, so the subjective circumstances refer to the attitudes individuals have towards these objective circumstances. The basic idea is that each individual has his own conception of the good life, these conceptions often come in conflict with each other, and each individual is solely concerned with promoting his own well-being.

The reason for including these kinds of considerations among the circumstances of justice is that moderate scarcity by itself does not quarantee that the problem of rational choice will arise. In other words, even if things are scarce, if everyone agrees upon the priorities in the distribution of these scarce resources, and acts accordingly, then there is no need to have social rules and regulations governing their distribution. It is only when there is disagreement among the individuals in the society as to how scarce goods should be distributed (or some individuals fail to adhere to the commonly held priorities), that social cooperation requires the development (and enforcement) of rules of distribution. For example, if *everyone* agrees that when resources are scarce they should be distributed on the basis of height (the tallest gets as much as he needs, the next tallest as much as he needs, and so on until the resources are depleted), then disputes over what is just will not arise. It is only when some members of the society do not agree with the principle which elevates the tall, and feel that their claims on the available resources are every bit as legitimate as those of the tall, that conflicts arise and social cooperation is threatened. Thus the attitudes of the subjects are clearly relevant to whether or not issues of justice arise.

It is important to note, however, that Rawls defines the subjective circumstances of justice in more than the minimal way I have just described. It is not merely that individuals put forward conflicting claims to the division of social goods; these individuals are also mutually disinterested (i.e. they take no interest in one another's interests). Indeed it is this mutual disinterestedness that he considers to be the most important of the subjective conditions of justice. But he does not seem to realize that mutual disinterestedness is different from the other subjective circumstances in a very important respect. This is because although questions of justice do not arise unless the other subjective conditions are present, they may well arise even though the individuals involved are not mutually disinterested.

To see this point, let us turn to the example of heightism introduced above. We saw that if everyone agrees that social goods should be distributed according to tallness, there will be no conflicting claims on scarce resources. But notice that there may be conflicting claims on these resources even if the individuals involved are not mutually disinterested. Some individuals in the community may favor the principle of shortism over that of tallism. And this in spite of the fact that some of them are tall. In other words, some of the tall members of the society may place the good of the community above their own interests, and believe that short people contribute more effectively to that good than tall ones do. These individuals are not mutually disinterested (i.e. they do take an interest in the interest of others). Nevertheless conflicting claims to moderately scarce resources may still arise.

None of this is meant to suggest that it is illegitimate for Rawls to include mutual disinterestedness as one of the elements of the original position. It is only to point out that it is both misleading and confusing to include it as one of the subjective circumstances of justice. All of the other circumstances of justice which he mentions, both objective and subjective, are elements which are necessary for questions of justice to arise. The existence of mutual disinterestedness, on the other hand, although it does give rise to questions of justice in conditions of moderate scarcity, is not necessary. We shall see later why Rawls introduces the notion of mutual disinterestedness and how it relates to his theory of justice. For our present purposes it is enough to point out that if it is to be considered a circumstance of justice, it is of a very different order than the others he mentions. And this suggests that for clarity's sake, it would be preferable to introduce the notion of mutual disinterestedness at some other point in the theory.

Not only is moderate scarcity a necessary condition of questions of justice arising, it is also connected to Rawls' two principles of justice in an interesting way. As you recall, Rawls places the two principles in serial ordering with the equal liberty principle taking precedence over the principle of democratic equality. In other words, he insists that it is illegitimate to sacrifice liberty for economic improvement. Yet he qualifies this serial ordering in a significant way. The serial relationship holds only if the minimal level of wealth necessary for the effective exercise of basic liberty has been achieved by the society. As Rawls says: "The supposition is that if the persons in the original position assume that their basic liberties can be effectively exercised, they will not exchange a lesser liberty for an improvement in their economic well-being, at least not once a certain level of wealth has been attained" (542).

Thus we see that there are two minimum levels in Rawls' theory of justice. The first is that defined by moderate scarcity—the level below which issues of justice do not arise. The second is that defined by the serial ordering of the two principles of justice—the level below which, although issues of justice arise, the serial relationship between the two principles does not hold. Obviously Rawls' theory depends in part upon an adequate definition of these two levels. Unfortunately, however, this is an issue that cannot be dealt with here.

The Formal Constraints of the Concept of Right

The second component of the original position is what Rawls calls "the formal constraints of the concept of right." He claims both that these constraints hold for the choice of all moral principles and that they must be assessed by the soundness or reasonableness of the theory of which they are a part: "I do not claim that these conditions follow from the concept of right, much less from the meaning of morality... the merit of any definition depends upon the soundness of the theory that results; by itself, a definition cannot settle any fundamental question" (130).

But there is a tension between these two characterizations of the formal constraints of the concept of right (that they hold for all moral principles but that they must be assessed in terms of the soundness or reasonableness of the theory of which they are a part)—a tension which pervades Rawls' entire discussion of the formal constraints. These two characterizations are not extensionally equivalent. Or more correctly, they can only be made so by insisting that a theory is a moral theory if and only if it is *not* unreasonable. But surely this will not do. The appropriateness of applying the label "moral" to a theory is a function of the kind of theory it is and our understanding of what makes a theory a moral one. Demonstrating that such a theory is unreasonable only shows that it is an unreasonable moral theory, not that it fails to qualify as a moral theory.

Rawls identifies five constraints which the concept of right imposes upon moral theories. They must be general in scope, universal in application, publicly held, ordered and final. Careful examination will reveal that some of these constraints do apply to all moral principles, but not because of the reasonableness of the theory of which they are a part; while others depend upon the reasonableness of the theory of which they are a part, but do not apply to all moral principles.

Generality. The first constraint of the concept of right is that principles must be general: "it must be possible to formulate them without the use of what would be intuitively recognized as proper names, or rigged definite descriptions" (131). The idea is that moral principles should apply to classes or categories rather than to specific individuals. "Everyone should do what Katzner says," is not a moral principle—although it may well follow from the moral principle "everyone should do what is right" and the claim that "Katzner is the only one who knows what is right." It is equally unacceptable to sneak in the equivalent of a proper name by use of a rigged definite description. Thus the principle, "everyone should do what the writer of the paper 'The Original Position and the Veil of Ignorance' for this volume says," is equivalent to the principle "everyone should do what Katzner says." Although the former does not include my name, it involves a description which applies uniquely to me. Thus it is as unacceptable as the principle which includes my name.

Rawls argues for the generality constraint on the basis of the public character of principles of justice. Because these are principles which are chosen by all individuals to apply to the basic structure of society in perpetuity, it would be inappropriate for them to contain proper names or rigged definite descriptions. But surely this does not follow. The principle "everyone should do what Katzner says" (or more correctly, because it holds in perpetuity, "everyone should do what the Katzners say"), could be chosen as the basic principle of our society (although I have sufficient confidence in the intelligence of people to be sure that it would not). What rules this principle out is not the public character of principles of justice, but the constraints imposed by the veil of ignorance (see below).

This conclusion should not be surprising. To the extent that a formal constraint of the concept of right applies to *all* moral principles, it cannot be justified in terms of the public character of such principles. This is simply because not all moral theories are characterized in the public way Rawls describes. On the other hand, such a constraint can be argued for in terms of our understanding of the nature of moral principles. Indeed, this is the way it is normally done. In other words, it is usually argued that in order for a principle to be a *moral* principle, it must be stated in general terms. And this argument applies regardless of whether one views moral principles as having a public or nonpublic character.

Universality. The second constraint of the concept of right, viz, that principles must be universal in application, is usually conceived of in the same way. Indeed, Rawls offers precisely this kind of account when he says of universal principles, "They must hold for everyone in virtue of their being moral persons" (132). For example, if there is a right to life it extends to all moral entities (all beings whose life or death makes a difference), not merely to all men, all women, all Americans, or any other such class. Similarly, if lying is wrong, it is wrong for everyone capable of telling the truth.

So far, so good! But Rawls goes on to offer a second and significantly different account of the universality constraint: "Principles are to be chosen in view of the consequences of everyone's complying with them" (132). In other words, moral principles are to be assessed in terms of the hypothetical consequences of *everyone's* following them rather than the actual consequences of some people following them. Lying is wrong because the consequences of everyone doing it would be undesirable even if, as a matter of fact, so few people will actually lie that the consequences will not be undesirable.

It should be clear that although all moral principles may well conform to the first or weak interpretation of universality, some do not conform to the latter (stronger) interpretation. The weak interpretation simply carries generality to what seems to be its logical conclusion—not only must moral principles be devoid of personal pronouns and rigged definite descriptions, they must hold for all moral agents. The stronger interpretation, on the other hand, by elevating the hypothetical consequences of everyone's doing something over the actual consequences of some people doing it precludes basing morality on what will actually happen. Although one might argue that a theory based upon hypothetical consequences is more reasonable than one based upon actual consequences, this cannot be a formal constraint of the concept of right. For if it is, some of the chief competitors to Rawls' theory of justice are ruled out of the moral domain. In particular, act utilitarianism becomes a nonmoral theory.

Finality. The basic idea of this constraint is that moral principles function as the supreme court of practical reasoning. In other words, when moral obligations conflict with other kinds of considerations, such as those of self-interest or law and custom, it is our moral obligations that hold sway. This is not to say that we should ignore the demands of self-interest, law and custom. It simply means that moral obligations (in the sense Rawls is concerned with) have such considerations built into them—i.e. they are obligations "all things considered." Thus whenever our deliberations result in obligations which conflict with the particular demands of self-interest, law and custom, it is the moral obligations that bind us.

Rawls does not give any argument as to why finality should be a constraint of the concept of right. Yet it does make sense. But this is because of our understanding of what it is for something to be a moral principle, not the reasonableness of the theory of which it is a part. Moral principles are conceived of as the ultimate arbitrators—they are the principles by which we determine our obligations in light of the demands of law, custom, self-interest, etc.

The constraints of the concept of right we have discussed so far—generality, universality (in the weak sense) and finality—are constraints which can plausibly be claimed to apply to the choice of all moral principles. But contra Rawls, this is because of our conceptions of the nature of morality, not the reasonableness of the theory of which they are a part. Basically what these principles rule out of the moral domain are the various forms of egoism (e.g. "everyone should promote *my* interests" is ruled out by the generality constraint). Moreover the question of whether or not egoism is a moral theory—in other words the question of whether or not these really are constraints of the concept of right—is one that is still debated in the literature. Yet the view that Rawls advocates is generally accepted. What is at issue is not the correctness of that view, but rather the kinds of reasons that Rawls gives in support of it. On this score he seems to go astray. The arguments for generality, universality (in the weak sense) and finality as constraints of the concept of right, are not arguments about the reasonableness of the theory of which these constraints are a part. They are arguments about the nature of morality and moral principles.

Interestingly enough, the opposite is the case for the other constraints of the concept of right—publicity, ordering and universality in the strong sense—discussed by Rawls. They should be assessed in terms of the reasonableness of the theory of which they are a part; yet it is illegitimate to insist that they are constraints which apply to the choice of all moral principles.

Publicity. It is this constraint that Rawls believes places his theory of justice in the contractarian camp. The basic idea is to insist upon a public conception of morality. It is not enough that a moral principle satisfy the "What would happen if everyone did that?" test established by the strong sense of universality. We must also consider the effect of a moral principle being publicly acknowledged as one of the fundamental rules of society.

This distinction can be illustrated in the following way. Imagine two different societies. In one, individual conduct is regulated entirely by an intuitive and individual conception of morality. In the other, there is a written constitution and laws are promulgated on the basis of it. In the former, there is no public conception of law. But the operative rules are universal because each individual, in deciding what rules he should follow, asks: What would happen if everyone were to do that? In the latter case, on the other hand, there is a public conception of law. Both the constitution and the laws which are promulgated on the basis of it, are public documents. In this society there are two important but distinct questions that should be asked of a possible law: (1) What would happen if everyone were to follow it? and (2) What will the impact be of including it in our public conception of law?

The reason why it is illegitimate for Rawls to claim that publicity is a constraint for all moral principles should be obvious. Not all moral theories are contractarian. Indeed, the theory which Rawls acknowledges to be the most likely alternative to his, i.e. utilitarianism, is not normally conceived of in contractarian terms. Thus Rawls must either insist that most of the proponents of utilitarianism are not presenting moral theories, or else acknowledge that publicity is not a constraint which applies to all moral principles.

Ordering. The same kind of problem arises with regard to ordering. The idea behind this constraint is that because the purpose of moral principles is to guide our action, a moral theory cannot leave us hanging in this regard. This is not a problem for a theory such as utilitarianism which involves one fundamental principle of morality. It is a problem, however, for those theories which involve more than one such principle. Thus, for example, if one believes that considerations of utility and justice are distinct yet equally important considerations, there is a problem. What is to be done when justice requires one thing and utility another? According to Rawls, these principles must be ordered. The theory must tell us which one takes precedence when the two conflict. And this is a constraint of the concept of right. In other words, any theory which does not do this is not a moral theory.

Surely this is too strong. It requires us to say that all those theories which Rawls labels "intuitionist"—i.e. all theories which rely on the use of intuition to resolve conflicts between principles—are not moral theories. To insist that the reliance on intuition is a defect in any moral theory in which it appears is one thing. But to say that they are not moral theories is something else. It involves much too narrow a conception of what is moral and what is not.

Thus we see that Rawls brings two very different kinds of considerations together under the single heading "the formal constraints of the concept of right." Generality, universality in the weak sense and finality do seem to be constraints which apply to all moral principles. But this must be determined by analysis of what it is for something to be a moral principle, rather than as Rawls maintains by an assessment of a reasonableness of the theory of which it is a part. On the other hand, the appropriateness of publicity, ordering and universality in the strong sense seems to be dependent upon the reasonableness of the theory of which they are a part. Yet they are not constraints which apply to all moral principles.

It should be clear that this discussion in no way refutes Rawls' general characterization of the original position. It merely suggests that there is a need to sharpen some of the specific descriptions of that general characterization. The constraints of publicity, ordering and universality in the strong sense should be treated separately from those of generality, finality and universality in the weak sense. Although it is perfectly appropriate to label the latter "formal constraints of the concept of right," it is misleading to so label the former. To avoid confusion they should be discussed under a different heading.

The Veil of Ignorance

The primary function of the original position in Rawls' theory of justice is to define the fair situation for choosing the principles which govern the basic structure of society. Rawls believes that this can be achieved only by nullifying "the effects of specific contingencies which put men at odds and tempt them to exploit social and natural circumstances to their own advantage" (136). The veil of ignorance is introduced to achieve this end. It requires individuals to select principles solely on the basis of general considerations by denying them knowledge of particulars.

Suppose, for example, that we are trying to decide on the rules for a game of tug-of-war. I weigh nearly 450 pounds with strength to match. You, on the other hand, weigh only 150 pounds. It would be to my advantage to define the game as a one-on-one encounter, you against me. On the other hand, it would be to your advantage to define the game as an encounter based upon weight, so that we each could have as many helpers as we wanted as long as our team's total weight does not exceed 500 pounds. In trying to define the rules of our particular game, we would each hold out for those which are to our advantage. Whatever rules would be agreed to would be the result of a compromise between competing interests. There is no guarantee that rules agreed to in this way (especially given the difference in our respective physical endowments) will be just.

The purpose of the veil of ignorance is to preclude this kind of situation from arising by denying the parties knowledge of the particular facts of the case. In other words, in deciding upon the rules for tug-of-war, neither of us would know our respective physical endowments; although we would know the general principles of human physiology, laws of physics, and whatever other general considerations are relevant. This would prevent us from selecting principles which are tailored to our own particular circumstances and force us to choose rules which would be fair to everyone.

In order to see precisely how Rawls' notion of the veil of ignorance is designed to achieve this end, we must examine that notion in detail. It prevents the tailoring of principles to individual circumstances by concealing knowledge of oneself, one's society, and the relationship between the two. Let us examine each of these in turn.

With regard to oneself, Rawls says that no one knows "his fortune in the distribution of natural assets and abilities, his intelligence and strength, and the like. Nor, again, does anyone know his conception of the good, the particulars of his rational plan of life, or even the special features of his psychology such as his aversion to risk or liability to optimism or pessimism" (137). Each of these elements plays an important role in preventing an individual from insisting upon principles which are designed to promote his particular ends. If one knows the nature of his natural assets and abilities, things which Rawls insists are arbitrary from the moral point of view (see his discussion of the principle of democratic equality), then he would opt for principles which favor individuals with those specific assets and abilities. If, for example, one knows he is very strong, then he would favor principles which are to the advantage of the strong. As we have seen, however, the function of the veil of ignorance is to prevent one from tailoring principles in this way. Hence the veil of ignorance screens out knowledge of one's particular assets and abilities.

For the same reason it conceals knowledge of one's particular conception of the good life. If one had such knowledge, it would be rational for him to favor principles which would lead to the furthering of this conception. For example, if the most important thing in a person's life is listening to a certain kind of music, then he would assess the principles which govern the basic structure of society in terms of how likely they are to make this kind of music readily available. But if one does not know the particular features of his conception of the good life, if all one knows is that he desires what Rawls calls the primary goods (those things such as rights and liberties, powers and opportunities, income and wealth, etc., that all rational persons are presumed to desire whatever else they may want), then one is not able to select principles according to how well they further his conception of the good life.

The last thing about oneself the veil of ignorance hides from view is one's aversion to risk or liability, and one's optimism or pessimism. This limitation is also crucial to Rawls' argument, albeit in a different way. Rawls argues that his two principles of justice would be chosen in the original position because the veil of ignorance makes the maximin rule the appropriate principle of choice. "The maximin rule tells us to rank alternatives by their worst possible outcomes: we are to adopt the alternative the worst outcome of which is superior to the worst outcome of the others" (152–53).

His main argument for the reasonableness of the maximin rule in the original position is that the stakes are very high and that the alternative principles of choice contain risks which would be unacceptable to a rational person. Of course, if a person knew that he liked to take risks, or was extremely optimistic about the way things would turn out, then he might very well opt for one of these principles. But the veil of ignorance prevents us from knowing these things about ourselves. And Rawls concludes that in the absence of any penchant for risk taking or optimism, the rational person would opt for those principles which guard against the worst possible outcome—i.e. his two principles of justice.

The second kind of knowledge that the veil of ignorance conceals is that of the particular circumstances of one's own society. Societies are dynamic entities—they ebb and flow. But Rawls is looking for principles of justice that apply to all societies which have achieved the level of moderate scarcity regardless of their level of economic and cultural development. Should one know the level of development of one's own society, or the generation to which he belongs, it would be possible to opt for principles which favor that level of development or that generation. Again it is precisely this kind of tailoring principles to one's own advantage that Rawls is attempting to prevent. By precluding knowledge of one's particular economic, political and cultural situation he seeks to insure the selection of principles which are fair to all generations at all levels of social development.

Finally, the veil of ignorance also conceals knowledge of one's particular place in society—i.e. one's social-economic position. If this were known, individuals would obviously favor principles which work to the advantage of their class. But the idea of justice as fairness is to select those principles which are fair to everyone, not to a particular individual or class. A fair situation of choice is one in which it is impossible to tailor principles to one's advantage. And this is precisely what the veil of ignorance is designed to do. It rules out knowledge of all particular facts—especially those concerning oneself, one's society and the relationship between the two.

But it does not rule out knowledge of general facts. The parties in the original position have an understanding of the general laws or principles which govern political affairs, economics, social organizations, human psychology, etc. In short, although denied knowledge of all particular facts, they have access to whatever general information affects the choice of principles of justice.

Notice how this account of the veil of ignorance affects the situation of choice in the original position. Rather than having a group of individuals with competing interests coming together to hammer out a compromise agreement which will give each of them part of what they want, the veil of ignorance, by denying all knowledge of particulars, has the effect of totally obscuring individual differences. Unable to evaluate competing principles in terms of how well they further the interests of those who find themselves in their particular circumstances, the parties in the original position are required to choose those principles which will work to their advantage regardless of the circumstances in which they find themselves. But this perspective is the same for all individuals. Denied access to particular facts, all rational individuals will choose the same principles of justice. Thus Rawls believes that in a fair situation of choice (the original position), there would be unanimous consent to his two principles of justice. This presupposes a particular conception of rationality. And it is to this final element of the original position that we now turn.

The Rationality of the Parties

Rawls' account of rationality begins in a very straightforward way. "A rational person is thought to have a coherent set of preferences between the options open to him. He ranks these options according to how well they further his purposes; he follows the plan which will satisfy more of his desires rather than less, and which has the greater chance of being successfully executed" (143). But he adds a rather unusual qualification: "a rational individual does not suffer from envy. He is not ready to accept a loss for himself if only others have less as well. He is not downcast by the knowledge or perception that others have a larger index of primary social goods. Or at least this is true as long as the differences between himself and others do not exceed certain limits, and he does not believe that the existing inequalities are founded on injustice or are the result of letting chance work itself out for no compensating purpose" (143).

Before looking carefully at this special assumption, it is important to point out how this concept of rationality works in tandem with the subjective circumstances of justice (see above) to produce Rawls' full-blown notion of mutual disinterestedness. Rawls' concept of rationality involves evaluating options in terms of how well they further one's own purposes without regard to the fact that others may end up with more than oneself. As you will recall, two of the elements of the subjective circumstances of justice are that each individual has a conception of the good life and that this conception is defined entirely in terms of his own well-being. Thus the purposes in terms of which the rational individual evaluates the options open to him are defined entirely in terms of his own well-being. Moreover, because he does not suffer from envy, he does not view the goodness of his life as being diminished by the mere fact that others may have more.

Clearly the most controversial element in this full-blown notion of mutual disinterestedness is the assumption that a rational individual does not suffer from envy. The basic idea here is that a rational individual will not find the mere fact that others may have a greater share of social goods upsetting. Suppose, for example, that you were asked to choose between the following alternatives: an income of $15,000 per year in a society in which everyone makes that amount, or an income of $20,000 in a society in which some individuals make two or three times that amount. The point of the envy assumption is that a rational individual would not choose the lower income simply to prevent others from making more than he does.

But this is not always the case. Rawls identifies three conditions under which envy is rational: when inequalities exceed certain (unspecified) limits, when they are founded on injustice, and when they are the result of a chance occurrence which serves no compensating social purpose (I assume this is a reference to the natural lottery: the chance distribution of natural abilities and talents.) In other words, Rawls is not claiming that envy is an irrational response when one is being "ripped off" in an unjust system. Under such circumstances it is perfectly appropriate (and rational) to be upset at the fact that others are getting more. But it is not merely that they are getting more that should be the cause of concern to a rational individual. Rather it is that they are getting more *unjustly*.

There is, however, an important ambiguity in these qualifications because Rawls fails to clarify the relationships between them. The latter two seem to be related as genus is to species. In his discussion of the natural lottery, Rawls indicates that one (and only one) of the factors which render inequalities unjust is that they result from chance. But what is the relationship between the requirement that inequalities not exceed certain limits and this genus? Rawls states it as a conjunction. This suggests that envy is irrational only if both of the qualifications are satisfied. In other words, envy is irrational only if inequalities do not exceed certain limits and they are not believed to be founded on injustice. But what if only one of these qualifications is satisfied? What if the inequalities do exceed certain limits even though they are not believed to be founded on injustice? Or they are believed to be founded on injustice even though they do not exceed certain limits? Rawls does not seem to think that the first alternative can arise. He maintains that a society based upon his two principles of justice would not produce excessive inequalities. This of course is an empirical claim and may or may not be correct.

And what should be said of the other case—that in which the inequalities, although not excessive, are believed to be founded on injustice? The answer depends upon what is meant by "excessive." If the inequalities are very small, then envy would seem to be irrational, even if the inequalities were believed to be founded upon injustice. If, on the other hand, the inequalities are large enough to produce significant differences in the life prospects of the individuals involved, then envy would seem to be perfectly rational.

THE BROADER ISSUES

With the particulars of the original position and the veil of ignorance presented and analyzed, it is time to step back and look at some of the broader issues which surround these notions. In particular, we shall examine how they relate to Rawls' methodology (reflective equilibrium) and his contractarianism.

Rawls' Methodology

In order to understand the argument Rawls presents for his two principles of justice, we must examine his methodology. Given his expressed hope that eventually his argument will be strictly deductive (121) and his emphasis upon pure procedural justice (see below), one might well expect him to proceed by sketching his version of the initial situation (i.e. the original position) through an analysis of the notion of fairness, and then deducing his principles of justice from the original position.

But Rawls does not do this. Indeed, at times it seems like he is doing just the opposite. Rather than arguing from the original position to the principles of justice, he seems to be arguing from the principles of justice back to the original position. In other words, he defines the original position in terms of the desired outcome rather than deducing the principles of justice from an independently defined description of the initial situation. "Now the reasons for the veil of ignorance go beyond mere simplicity. We want to define the original position so that we get the desired solution" (141).

The key to understanding what Rawls is doing here is the notion of reflective equilibrium. "In this sense, there are many different contract theories. Justice as fairness is but one of these. But the question of justification is settled, as far as it can be, by showing that there is one interpretation of the initial situation which best expresses the conditions that are widely thought reasonable to impose on the choice of principles yet which, at the same time, leads to a conception that characterizes our considered judgments in reflective equilibrium. This most favored, or standard, interpretation I shall refer to as the original position" (121).

The basic idea of reflective equilibrium is that moral justification is a dynamic process that has two starting points neither of which is unchallengeable. The goal is to hammer out a coherent theory without holding either of the starting points as sacred. In other words, everything is up for grabs. In this particular case, the starting points are (1) the conditions that are widely thought reasonable to impose on the choice of principles and (2) our most confidently held intuitions about justice. The process involves starting at each of these points and working towards the other. We seek to determine which principles of justice would be chosen under what we think are the fair conditions of choice *and* what conditions of choice result in our most confidently held intuitions about justice. Reflective equilibrium is achieved when there is a fit between the conditions of choice and our intuitive conception of justice. Most importantly, in seeking this fit, we work from both ends: modifying our intuitions about justice in light of our conception of the fair conditions of choice *and* modifying our conception of the fair conditions of choice in light of our intuitions about justice.

In other words, Rawls holds a coherence theory of moral justification. Moral claims are *not* justified by showing that they correspond to eternal and unchanging principles. Nor can they be deduced from *a priori* principles. Rather they are justified by showing that they are part of a coherent theory—a theory which unifies our intuitions about justice with the conditions that are widely thought reasonable to impose on the choice of principles by gently pulling and pushing at both ends until a coherent theory is attained.

This methodology is not unique to Rawls. It has a long history in the moral tradition, although Rawls is surely one of its most articulate and perceptive proponents. And because it reflects a middle ground, it opens Rawls up to attack from both flanks. In order to appreciate both the compromising nature of reflective equilibrium, and the kinds of attacks launched against it, let us take a moment to briefly consider the alternatives.

Some moral theorists perceive their enterprise as a process of discovering *the truth.* Be it Plato's theory of forms, which maintains that (the form of) goodness, etc., in some sense exists and is discovered by the truly rational person; or natural law theory which insists that moral laws exist in a way that is analogous to the physical laws of the universe, and are discovered either through divine revelation or the use of reason; or Kant's categorical imperative which he believes can be deduced from the concept of reason, and hence is binding upon all rational beings; there is a belief that moral principles are discovered rather than created. They should guide our lives not because *we* say so, but because *they* say so.

The problems with this conception of morality are manifold. There is the metaphysical problem of making sense out of the notion of existence when it is applied to moral principles. There is the epistemological problem of showing that moral principles can be known—a problem which is exacerbated by the seemingly wide differences of opinion between apparently rational individuals concerning their basic moral beliefs. And there are the logical problems presented by the fact that all purported deductions of such principles are either based upon problematic premises or contain logically questionable steps.

Other moral theorists, convinced by the magnitude of these problems, seek refuge in moral intuitions, feelings or sentiments. Be it one's own, those of the average man, or the ideal spectator, the idea is that moral principles are gleaned from individual feelings or sentiments, rather than "observed" or deduced from *a priori* principles. Thus, the way to find out what is good or just is to consult the feelings or intuitions of the appropriate individual(s). On this view, the purpose of moral philosophy is to tease out of these feelings or intuitions the underlying principles which they contain. In short, moral rules summarize particular judgments. The advantage of identifying the principles which underly these judgments is that when situations arise in which intuition fails to provide guidance—i.e. there are no clear intuitions about what is good or right—we can use the principles as our guide.

The problems with this approach to morality are also manifold. Given that different individuals have divergent feelings about what is good, right, just, etc., how do we know which view is correct? And given that the same individual has different feelings about the same things at different times, how do we know which of these feelings are correct? Or are we to accept the extreme relativist position that they are all correct for the individual who feels them at the time they are felt? Secondly, because our feelings and intuitions about things are at least in part a product of the environment in which we are raised, this view seems to entail that our moral judgments are necessarily culture bound. We make the judgments we do, not because they are correct, but because we have been conditioned to make them. In short, this understanding of the nature of morality conceives of the moral enterprise in a special way. It provides no independent standard by which to assess the feelings or intuitions which are taken as definitive of moral experience.

It is between this Scylla and Charybdis that Rawls seeks to steer his coherence theory. He rejects both the absolutism of the first view and the relativism of the second. He seeks to modify our intuitions about justice in terms of the concept of fairness. At the same time, however, he does not take the concept of fairness as a sacred *a priori*. It too is subject to modification—based upon our intuitions about justice. Thus he presents us with a candle which is literally burning at both ends. And as it burns, reflective equilibrium attempts to forge it into a shape which accommodates both of these pressures on it. This is why, at times, Rawls argues from the concept of fairness to his two principles of justice, while at other times he argues in the opposite direction.

With this account of Rawls' methodology in hand, we are now in a position to understand a rather puzzling aspect of his theory of justice. He claims that the principles chosen in the original position are principles of pure procedural justice. This means that following these principles will necessarily result in a just distribution of social goods because there is no independent criterion by which to assess this distribution (86).

The idea here is clear. The principles of justice are decided upon behind the veil of ignorance. We then go about structuring our society in accordance with these principles, and living in accordance with this structure. But suppose someone does not like the share of social goods that he ends up with. It would defeat the purpose of the veil of ignorance (i.e. to decide what is just in the absence of any information that would enable an individual to tailor the conception of justice to his own particular circumstances) to allow him to claim that the resulting distribution is unjust. Hence the need for principles of pure procedural justice.

The problem is, however, that Rawls does not remain true to this notion of pure procedural justice. He qualifies it in a crucial way, indicating that the distribution resulting from principles of pure procedural justice will be "just whatever it happens to be, *at least so long as it is within a certain range* [emphasis mine]" (85). In other words, the distribution that results from following his principles of justice is not necessarily just.

Making Rawls' theory operational obviously requires a specification of this range. More important for our purposes, however, is why Rawls adds this qualification. It is a crucial qualification because it takes much of the sting out of the notion of pure procedural justice. Following a just procedure no longer quarantees a just result. The distribution of social goods resulting from a just procedure is unjust if it falls outside of an independently established range.

In order to see why Rawls qualifies pure procedural justice in this compromising way, we must examine the relationship between reflective equilibrium and pure procedural justice. The former is the methodology Rawls employs to get his principles of justice—the goal is to establish an equilibrium between our intuitions about *principles* of justice and the conception of fairness from which we attempt to derive these principles. Pure procedural justice, on the other hand, applies to these principles of justice and the distribution of social goods that result from them. The idea is that if the principles are just, the resulting distribution will be just.

Now if it were possible to keep his theory compartmentalized in this way, there would be no need for Rawls to qualify the notion of pure procedural justice. In other words, if reflective equilibrium applied only to the relationship between a fair situation of choice and *principles* of justice, while pure procedural justice applied only to the relationship between the principles of justice and the specific distribution which results from their application, there would be no need to introduce a range of acceptable distributions which function as an independent criterion by which to judge the outcomes produced by the implementation of the principles of justice.

But Rawls does qualify the notion of pure procedural justice, and this suggests an awareness on his part of the impossibility of keeping his theory compartmentalized in this way. Intuitions about principles of justice are intimately connected with one's assessment of the distributions that will result from those principles. Should a resulting distribution fall beyond what we accept as reasonable limits, this would lead us to revise our intuitions about those principles. And it is precisely because of this that Rawls must impose independent limitations upon the range of acceptable distributions.

A second point which must be assessed in light of Rawls' methodology is his expressed hope that his argument will eventually become strictly deductive. One might ask: As long as we are allowed to revise our principles of justice in light of our conception of fairness *and* our conception of fairness in light of our principles of justice, how can we even hope to provide a deductive argument?

The answer involves clarifying what is being deduced from what. Rawls' primary task in *A Theory of Justice* is to argue for, and then trace the consequences of, his two principles of justice. His hope is that the argument for his two principles will eventually become a deductive one. In other words, he hopes eventually to show that the two principles of justice necessarily follow from the original position.

The important point to see is that deductivity is a stronger relationship than reflective equilibrium, but not incompatible with it. Deductivity requires that the two principles of justice can be deduced from the original position. Reflective equilibrium merely requires that the original position and the principles of justice fit together coherently. Two concepts may be coherent even though they are entirely independent (i.e. neither may be deduced from the other). On the other hand, coherent concepts may be related to each other either inductively or deductively.

Thus as long as we understand the nature of a deductive relationship, there is no incompatibility between reflective equilibrium and deductivity. But because the two constitute different requirements, questions immediately arise concerning the relationship between them. Is the desire to achieve a deductive relationship one of the elements to be taken into consideration in the pursuit of reflective equilibrium? The problem arises this way.

Suppose Rawls' two principles of justice and our conception of fairness are in reflective equilibrium, but the former cannot be deduced from the latter. Suppose also that there are two different principles of justice which, although slightly out of tune with our intuitions about justice, can be deduced from the description of the initial situation which embodies our conception of fairness. Does this co stitute a reason to modify our intuitions about justice? In other words, does Rawls build deductivity into his notion of reflective equilibrium so that a less coherent but deductive fit is preferable to a coherent but non-deductive one?

The answer to this question must be "no." This is because Rawls views reflective equilibrium as a dynamic process. This means not only that it is appropriate to modify one's theory on all fronts to achieve a coherent view, but also that today's reflective equilibrium may be tomorrow's reflective *dis*-equilibrium. As our conceptions of fairness or justice change, so too will the theory which reflects an equilibrium between them.

But notice how focusing upon deductivity rather than coherence would constrict this process. What should we do when our views of justice or fairness begin to change, and the deductively established theory of justice no longer reflects our considered opinions in reflective equilibrium? If deductivity is the goal, then we should hold on to our theory of justice until we come up with another one that deductively fits with our new conceptions of justice or fairness; even though that theory of justice is out of phase with our considered opinions. If, on the other hand, reflective equilibrium is the controlling notion, our theory of justice will be more responsive to changes in our thinking about justice and fairness. Destruction of the equilibrium will immediately stimulate the search for a new theory of justice.

It is quite clear that Rawls believes that this kind of responsiveness to our thinking about justice and fairness is one of the important advantages of the reflective equilibrium methodology: "Moral philosophy is Socratic: we may want to change our present considered judgments once their regulative principles are brought to light. And we may want to do this even though these principles are a perfect fit. A knowledge of these principles may suggest further reflections that lead us to revise our judgments" (49).

Thus rather than being an essential ingredient in Rawls' theory, deductivity is merely a hoped for by-product which, even if achieved, may have to be discarded as our conceptions of justice and fairness change.

It is also limited in another important way. Rawls hopes eventually to show that the original position (the instantiation of the concept of fairness) entails his two principles of justice. If he is able to do this, he would surely provide someone who accepts this concept of fairness with a most compelling reason to accept his principles. But he would in no way move a person who does not accept the concept of fairness which underlies the original position.

This is an important point. Rawls believes that one of the strengths of his theory is that its justification relies upon very weak assumptions. The choice in the original position is based upon individual self-interest; hence it is not necessary to assume that the parties will subordinate their interests to those of others, nor even that they will consider the interests of others along with their own. But why should someone, especially a person favored by the natural distribution of talents and abilities, agree to abide by the principles that would be selected in the original position? In other words, even if it can be shown that the two principles of justice necessarily follow from the original position, one might still ask: Why should I accept those principles which can be deduced from the original position? And to the answer, Because the original position is the fair situation or choice, it may be replied: You have not proven that and even if you had, you have not answered the question, Why should I be fair?

Rawls is not really concerned with these problems—indeed he almost totally ignores them. His only attempt to deal with them is in Section 40, where he suggests that the original position should be accepted because it embodies the conditions of free and rational choice. But this issue requires full-blown argumentation rather than mere suggestion. For even if we grant that the two principles of justice follow deductively from the original position, this leaves unanswered the question, Why should I be fair? And without an answer to this question, Rawls' theory stands incomplete in a crucial respect.

Rawls' Contractarianism

Probably the element of Rawls' theory that has received least attention in the literature is his contractarianism. This is indeed unfortunate. For one thing it is clearly the cornerstone of his theory. More importantly, Rawls presents a contract theory only in a special sense of the term; and this has important implications for understanding his theory.

Those who are identified as the major social contract theorists—Hobbes, Locke and Rousseau—view the idea of a contract as a vehicle for answering two important questions: (1) What justifies some individuals having authority over others? and (2) What form (i.e. dictatorship, representative democracy, etc.) should this authority take?

The basic idea of their argument is that living in civil society (i.e. under the authority of rulers) is preferable to living without such authority (the state of nature). And what justifies authority is a contract voluntarily entered into by the members of society.

All of the traditional social contract theorists begin with three assumptions: (1) individual freedom is a good the sacrifice (limitation) of which must be justified; (2) the existence of authority (another good) requires this sacrifice; and (3) the only way this sacrifice can be justified is by having each individual voluntarily consent to the authority. Thus the need for the social contract—the vehicle through which individuals consent to the authority which rules over them.

On this view the state of nature is a hypothetical construct—it is what life *would be like* without the presence of an authority. The social contract stands for the individual consent which justifies the authority. But the consent itself must be real. Without it, the social contract is a nullity and authority is not justified. Moreover, the consent must be individual—i.e. *each individual* must consent to the authority. But the consent itself must be real. Without it, the social contract is a nullity and authority is not justified. Moreover, the con-consent of their parents. Once children reach the age of majority, it is up to them whether to consent or not.

This insistence upon individual consent poses severe problems for social contract theorists. If parents could bind their offspring to the contract in perpetuity, then we would only have to seek an original act of consent which binds all succeeding generations. But since parents cannot bind their offspring in this way, social contract theory requires that each member of each generation consent to the contract.

Explaining how this may be is no mean trick—indeed it is the Achilles' heel of traditional contract theory. The problem is usually confronted by introducing a distinction between express and tacit consent. The former is easy enough. Just as we expressly agree to all sorts of things in our day-to-day living, so we may have the opportunity to consent expressly to living under an authority. This would occur should we have the opportunity to vote for a constitution (although such votes, even when they do occur, do not involve the unanimous consent required by social contract theorists). It more clearly occurs whenever an alien applies for and is granted citizenship in a country.

Obviously, very few of us ever have the opportunity to consent expressly to the authority that rules over us. Hence the need for tacit consent. The basic idea of this notion is that the failure to reject expressly the established authority (perhaps by leaving the country) constitutes a tacit acceptance of it. In other words, accepting the benefits which accrue from living under an authority constitutes tacit consent to that authority.

There are many problems with the notion of tacit consent. But their examination would take us too far afield. The important point for our purposes is the crucial role this notion plays in traditional social contract theories. This is because when one begins with the notion of individual autonomy, authority can only be justified through individual consent. Consequently if a person can show that he never consented to an authority, then he is not bound by it. And because so few people are ever in a position to consent expressly, most of the weight of social contract theory rests on the ability to develop a plausible account of tacit consent.

There are crucial differences between Rawls' notion of the social contract and the traditional one I have just sketched. They result at least in part from the fact that Rawls conceives of his task differently from these traditional theorists. They sought to argue both for the existence of authority and the form it should take. Rawls, on the other hand, is concerned with formulating the principles which should govern the basic structure of society. He is only concerned with the form authority should take derivatively—i.e. as it is implied by his principles of justice. And he is not concerned with justifying authority at all. He simply takes its existence as a given.

This latter point is of major import. Because of it, consent, which lies at the heart of traditional contract theories, is not a factor in Rawls' theory. Thus his version of the social contract turns out to be very different from that of the major figures of the tradition with which he aligns himself. The best way to get at this difference is to distinguish real or actual from hypothetical consent. On the traditional view, the main concern is to show that everyone has actually consented (either expressly or tacitly) to the prevailing authority. If this cannot be shown, that authority is null and void. Thus the claim that someone has not consented to the prevailing authority is a significant problem for those who defend this view.

A hypothetical contract, on the other hand, is one which a person would agree to under certain conditions (in Rawls' case, if one assumed the perspective of the original position). It does not undermine Rawls' theory to show that some or even most individuals have not looked at things from this perspective. Nor would it affect his view to show that some individuals, either because they misunderstand what the original position is, or because they attempt to assume its perspective and fail (i.e. they are unable to totally dismiss knowledge of particulars from their deliberations), opt for other principles. All Rawls claims is that rational individuals who situate themselves behind the veil of ignorance and abide by the constraints of the concept of right would select his principles. If this is so, and if the original position captures our sense of fairness and the two principles of justice our intuitions about justice (problems we have already discussed), then the two principles of justice are justified. And this is true even if no one has ever actually consented to them.

Thus it is obvious that Rawls' notion of the social contract involves something very different from the express consent of his predecessors. But what about tacit consent? Perhaps he is offering us a different account of this troublesome notion. Perhaps he is suggesting that we replace the traditional notion of tacit consent (not leaving a society and thereby accepting its benefits) with a new one (what a rational individual would agree to behind the veil of ignorance while observing the constraints of the concept of right).

There are two problems with this interpretation of Rawls. First, there is no indication that this is the way he conceives of his task. He does not relate his discussion of the original position to the concept of tacit consent. Moreover, there is no reason for him to. Given that he is not concerned with the justification of authority, there is no reason for him to be concerned with the notion of tacit consent.

Secondly, there is a conceptual problem in understanding the notion of tacit consent in the hypothetical way introduced by Rawls. If one tacitly consents to what a rational individual would agree to behind the veil of ignorance, then it is possible to tacitly consent to what one expressly rejects. In other words, assuming that Rawls' two principles are those that would be chosen by rational individuals behind the veil of ignorance, then everyone tacitly consents to them. And this is as true of those who have thought about the matter and expressly rejected those principles as it is of those who have never considered them.

Thus on this interpretation we have an anomalous situation which seems to bend the notion of consent completely out of shape. Because tacit consent no longer depends upon my actions, nor even upon my actual thoughts, but rather upon what I would think under certain circumstances, what I tacitly consent to may turn out to be very different from what I think I am consenting to. In effect, tacit consent now lies outside the hands of those who are doing the consenting. A very strange situation indeed!

Recognizing the differences between an actual and hypothetical contract, and that Rawls' theory is contractarian in the latter sense, is crucial to understanding his argument. Throughout the book he speaks of the "parties" in the original position as if they were real individuals who are actually contracting with each other. For example, "It seems reasonable to suppose that the parties in the original position are equal. That is, all have the same rights in the procedure for choosing principles; each can make proposals, submit reasons for their acceptance, and so on. Obviously the purpose of these conditions is to represent equality between human beings as moral persons, as creatures having a conception of their good and capable of a sense of justice" (19).

Yet at other points he makes it clear that this is mere literary license. "These remarks show that the original position is not to be thought of as a general assembly which includes at one moment everyone who will live at some time;...it is important that the original position be interpreted so that one can at any time adopt its perspective. It must make no difference when one takes up this viewpoint, or who does so: the restrictions must be such that the same principles are always chosen" (139).

Rawls is not interested in showing that it is rational for individuals, in light of the differences that exist between them, to consent (either expressly or tacitly) to his two principles of justice. Rather his point is that if we obscure the differences between people (by imposing the veil of ignorance), his principles would be the rational choice. Thus, one cannot argue against Rawls by showing that there are certain individuals who would not or do not accept his two principles. The argument must be that a rational individual would not choose them under the circumstances he has specified.

This clarification serves to highlight a point we made earlier. The question, Why should I be just? has a rather straightforward answer to traditional social contract theories. You should be just (i.e. follow the rules of your society) because you have consented to them by consenting to the authority that promulgates them. And why should you consent to that authority? Because it is to your advantage to do so. It brings you all of the advantages which result from living under the rule of law. Indeed, the very fact that you have chosen to remain in the society gives silent testimony to these advantages.

But for Rawls, the answer is not so easy. Even if he has shown that it is in the rational person's (i.e., everyone's) interest to adopt his two principles of justice from behind the veil of ignorance, he cannot argue that it is in everyone's interest to agree to abide by those principles which would be chosen from this perspective. It is clearly not to the interest of those who benefited from the workings of the natural lottery. Rawls must argue for their compliance in terms of fairness, not self-interest. He must show that the perspective from which all individuals become one individual is the one that should be adopted in the choosing of the basic principles of society. In other words, even if he has provided us with an acceptable answer to the question, Why should I be just?, his answer immediately gives rise to another question—viz., Why should I be fair? But this is a question that Rawls does not attempt to answer.

NOTES

1. My thanks to Andrew Altman, Jeffrey Perkins, and the editors of this volume for their helpful comments on earlier drafts of this paper.

Rawls, Games and Economic Theory

Gail Corrado
OHIO UNIVERSITY

John Rawls' *A Theory of Justice* is an extended argument for the acceptance of two particular principles of justice. Rawls recommends these principles both because he believes they are consistent with rules that would govern choices made under fair conditions and because the consequences of the principles fit what Rawls feels we mean by "justice." In order to argue that his principles would be chosen under fair conditions, he first describes what he conceives to be a fair situation. Rawls contends that if you are going to choose principles of justice that do not favor any particular man's interest or conception of what is good, i.e., principles that are fair, you must somehow prevent those who are going to choose the principles from allowing their own interests or conceptions of the good to bias the final choice of governing principles. To accomplish this, Rawls proposes a hypothetical vantage point called the original position which guarantees this notion of fairness by lowering a "veil of ignorance" (136, all parenthetical citations are to John Rawls, *A Theory of Justice* (Cambridge, Mass.: Harvard University Press, 1971)). Individuals behind the veil are ignorant of their own interests and personal characteristics. They are not aware of their standing in society, their particular talents, their sex or even their respective notions of the good. They know only "general facts about human society" (137).

Rawls argues that when individuals, whom he calls representative men, actually try to choose principles from the original position they will select his principles over other philosophically popular principles. The principles themselves, however, must stand on their own; we would not be well advised to select a principle of justice simply because we agree that the manner in which it was chosen was fair. Rawls attempts to support the case for his principles by suggesting (I) that they are the most rational choices for a person to make who is constrained to act fairly (the argument from fairness), and (II) the distributive consequences of his principles fit what we mean by justice better than any other of the philosophically popular principles (the argument from intuition).

Both of these arguments are made using the analytic tools of a variety of disciplines. The casual reader may miss the force of some of Rawls' more important arguments because of unfamiliarity with the relatively arcane analytic tools of mathematics and economics. The case for fairness, for example, involves understanding the rudiments of game theory and decision theory. Rawls does not formally deduce his principles from a consideration of the original position. He attempts to show that, given the restrictions on knowledge outlined in the original position and given the procedures of game theory and decision theory, we would be more likely to choose his principles than, say, utilitarian principles. Rawls hopes to show that his principles are consistent with the rational choice procedures of game and decision theories while utilitarian principles are not. When Rawls argues that his principles fit our conception of justice better than competing principles, he uses the techniques of microeconomics. He employs indifference curve analysis to indicate distributions of society's goods and services which we would ordinarily feel is just, without rewarding arbitrarily chosen human characteristics. In other words, Rawls believes his principles distribute goods and services justly without requiring us to make decisions about which human characteristics should be rewarded by being given a greater share of those goods and services.

Game theory and microeconomic analysis, then, play central parts in forming the Rawlsian case for the acceptance of his two principles. The following is an attempt to explain the basic procedures of each, in order to make Rawls' arguments more accessible. We will begin with a discussion of fairness and, therefore, with a sketch of game theory.

GAME THEORY, THE ARGUMENT FROM FAIRNESS AND THE MAXIMIN PRINCIPLE

Game theory is a mathematical attempt to answer certain questions that arise when one is involved with a conflict of interest. In terms of the social problems we are discussing here, a conflict of interest will always exist when there is not enough of the goods and services available to satisfy everyone's desire for them. Rawls believes that the major condition under which a discussion of justice becomes relevant is such a condition of conflict; a concern for whether or not society's goods are distributed justly is only important when the act of distribution itself is important—when it matters how much of the available goods each person gets. Justice, then, involves the notion of a conflict of interest. Game theory provides us with procedures to follow when we are involved in conflict situations. However, before we begin the complicated way in which Rawls uses game theory to make his case for fairness, we must first consider an extremely simple example of a conflict situation: the game of tic-tac-toe.

Suppose I decide to play tic-tac-toe with my son. Game theory would provide a framework whereby I might answer the question, "I have an 'X' in the right hand corner and my son has his 'O' in the left, what should I do now?" The "should" in that sentence, as in all proper uses of that term, suggests a value judgment. In other words, you should do whatever is, by some relevant criterion, appropriate to the situation. For this reason it is conceptually impossible to totally divorce the mathematical analysis known as game theory from the economic and philosophical notion of utility. "What should I do now?" in the case in which I am playing tic-tac-toe with my son depends upon what I want to do. For example, I might want to win in order to demonstrate my skill or I might want to lose to bolster his confidence. "Utility" is the name used to indicate the use a person has for the outcome of a situation. If I won the game of tic-tac-toe and I had wanted to lose it, then the utility for this win would be lower than if I won the game and I had actually wanted to win. In both cases the outcome, or payoff, is the same: I won the game. Game theory provides us with methods for getting as much as we can in a conflict situation, whether what we want more of (what we want to maximize) is measured in terms of pure outcomes or payoffs (in our example winning or losing the game) or in terms of utilities (whether or not I wanted to win or lose). We can, however, suspend any further discussion of just what it is we are maximizing by assuming that there is something we want to get more of in the conflict situation. We will have to also assume that this something can be measured to some extent; the exact description of that extent will be postponed until the discussion of modern utility theory.

Conflict of interest, then, is generally characterized by scarcity, i.e., there is something the protagonists value and there is not enough of that something to satisfy everyone. Game theory is a model which suggests the strategies the protagonists might adopt to get as much of this scarce resource as they can. Rawls uses game theoretical procedures to argue that, given the restrictions on knowledge contained in his original position, we would be more likely to choose his principles than any of the others he considers. If we use "principle" as a synonym for "strategy" and say that the something we want to get more of is the Rawlsian notion of "primary goods" (e.g., liberty, wealth, power, etc.), we have an analogy whereby the tenets of game theory could prove useful in making the case for the Rawlsian principles.

A game can be represented by a diagram called a "tree." Each branch represents an alternative available to a player at that point in the game. A "node" represents a "move." A move is defined as a point in the game at which certain alternatives are available. Imagine that I am playing tic-tac-toe and I have just put my X in the first space and it is now your turn to consider all the remaining spaces to determine where to place your mark. You, as the second player, can consider only the boxes left after I have placed my mark in the first box. I could, however, have put my mark in the second box. If I had, then I would have said, "It is your move" after this action as well, and it still would have been necessary for you to decide where to put your mark. In fact, I could have put my mark in any of the nine spaces of the tic-tac-toe board and then left the next move to you. We will use the word "move" to denote each of the possible different situations the second player has to consider after the first player has moved. The first move, then, in which the first player chooses one of the nine spaces to place his mark (shown on Figure 1B), is represented by the first node on the tree (shown in Figure 1A). Each of the nine spaces in Figure 1B represent alternatives open to him and, as such, are represented by branches on the tree in Figure 1A.

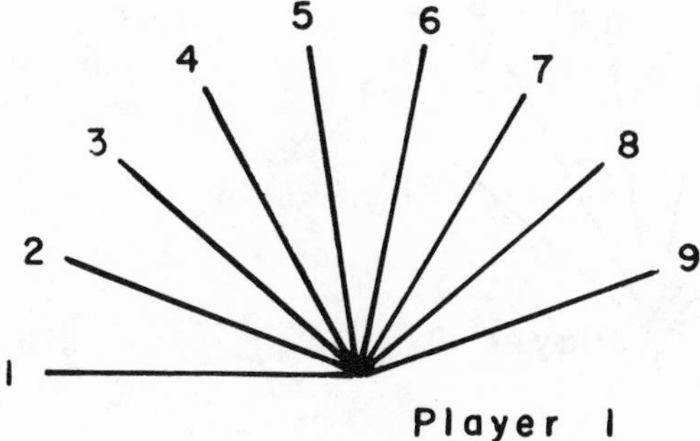

FIGURE 1A

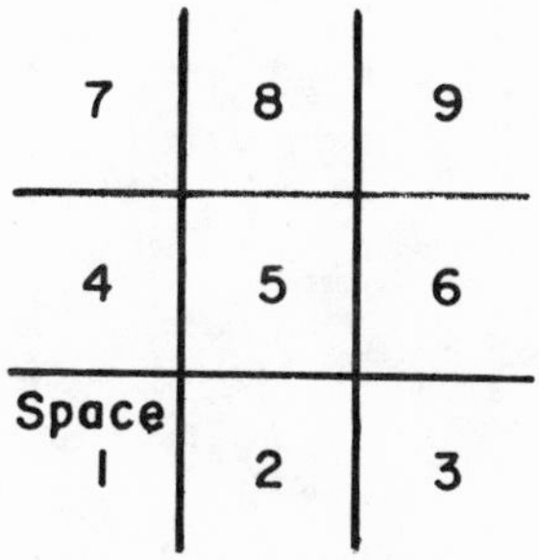

7	8	9
4	5	6
Space 1	2	3

FIGURE 1B

The set of possible alternative situations for the second player is represented by a set of nodes: one on the end of each of the branches denoting possible moves that could have been made by the first player. There will be eight branches on each of these nodes (one less than the original number of spaces available since the first player will already have used one of the spaces). Thus, if player 1 places his mark on space 1 the set of moves player 2 can make (in the remaining spaces 2–9) is represented by a set of nodes at the end of the branch from space 1 as shown in Figure 2.

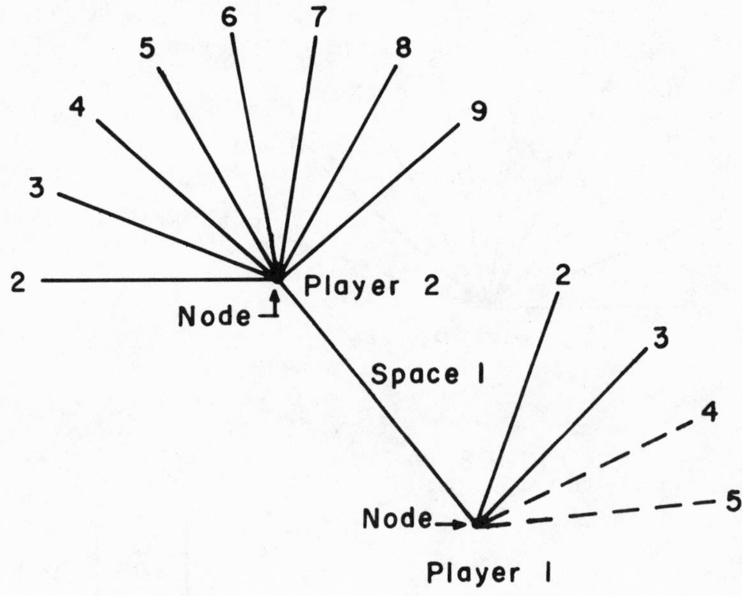

FIGURE 2

There are several basic assumptions used to characterize a game for the purposes of the theory. We will use the eight assumptions used by Luce and Raiffa[1] because they are clear and complete but, more importantly, their exposition is cited in *A Theory of Justice*. These assumptions will help us define the basic requirements of any game. Particular games will differ from each other by how they fulfill these requirements. The first assumption mentioned by Luce and Raiffa is that the game rules must characterize a finite number of branches with the further restriction that we know who moves first.

The second assumption is that each move is labeled so that we can decide which player is eligible to move. The third assumption is made in order to include a game where a "move" is made by a random device, like the spinning of a wheel or the shuffling of cards. This assumption states that there should be a probability associated with each of the outcomes of the random device, e.g., there should be a probability associated with each number on the wheel. This particular assumption is problematic if we do not have knowledge of the relevant probabilities, as we do not in the original position because of the veil of ignorance.

Frequently we are involved in a game where we do not know, for one reason or another, the actual choice of the player preceding us. A good many card games are of this variety, "Twenty-one" or "Black Jack" being the most simple. In the case of "Black Jack", we have to make a decision to take another card or to hold at some number, even if we don't know what our opponent has done (in fact the "game" aspect of this procedure lies in our being ignorant of our opponent's decisions). We can construct a hypothetical game to illustrate both the case in which we know the opponent's move and the case in which we do not. Suppose the second player has moves on two or more branches but is ignorant of the particular branch which his opponent's choice has forced on him. For example, suppose you are playing a game in which the first player has five possible alternatives. If he chooses alternative a, b or c you know exactly what he has done. However, if he chooses d or e the rules of the game prevent you from knowing which choice was made. Under the rules described so far, the game being played would be diagrammed by the tree in Figure 3 in which uncertainty is represented by U.

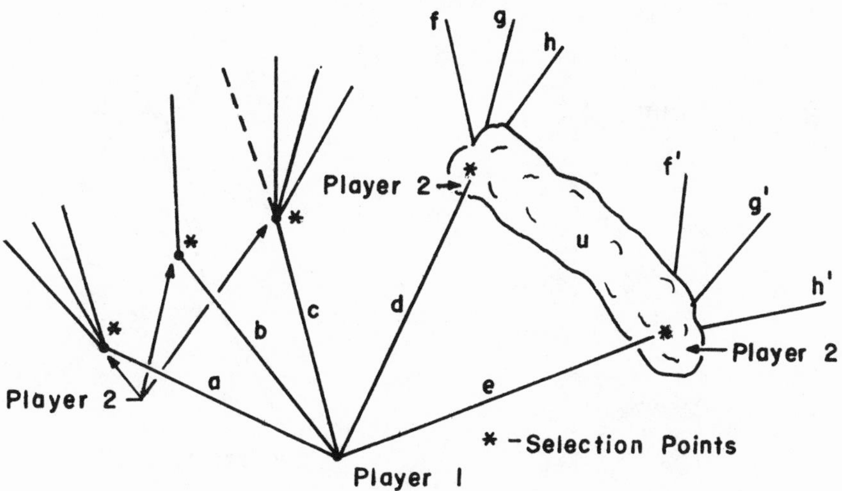

FIGURE 3

If the first player chose either d or e and I want to choose, say, the left alternative, I will then choose one of the pair f-f'. I will not be able to distinguish f from f' because I don't know the choice of the player before; I will not know whether the first player chose d or e. It is as if you were driven, blindfolded, to a fork in the road and then, after the blindfold was removed, you were asked to choose the branch on which to travel. Where you end up obviously depends upon the road you were actually taking while blindfolded. Unfortunately, your only choice is of forks in the road—you know very little about the road you have actually travelled. The set of possible alternatives in this form is called an "information set." The information set in

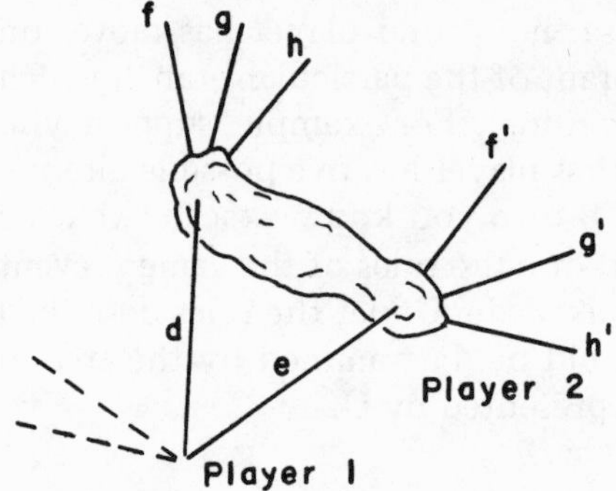

FIGURE 4A

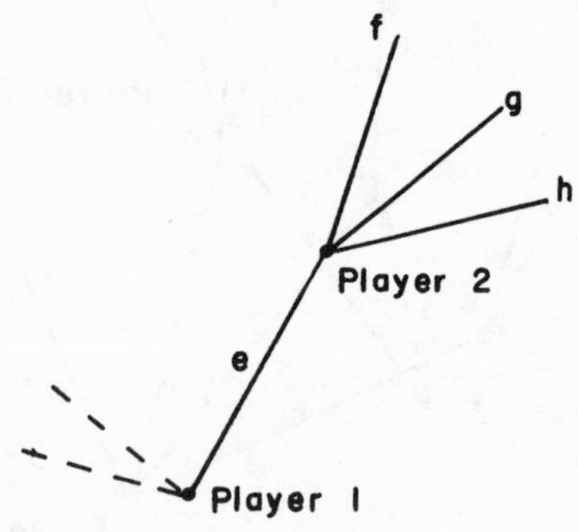

FIGURE 4B

Figure 4A has two moves for player 1. When a player faces an information set such as the one for player 1 in Figure 4B, that has only one move, he is said to be "fully informed." When all moves are of this type the game is said to have "perfect information." To take account of games that lack "perfect information," the fourth assumption[2] states that the rules of such games must define the location and ambiguity of a player's moves. In our example, there would be ambiguity in the first set of moves to be played by the second player (in Figures 3 and 4A) only in the case that the first player chose alternative d or e. The fifth assumption further defines these games by stating that they must have rules which clearly identify the pairs of alternatives which can be chosen; in this case the pairs to be chosen by the second player would be f-f', g-g', and h-h'.

The sixth assumption asserts that the "terminal node," or last set of alternatives any player has, must have an "outcome" or "payoff" associated with it. This assumption requires game rules to relate one outcome from a set of outcomes to each terminal point on a tree. Consider the following example from tic-tac-toe.

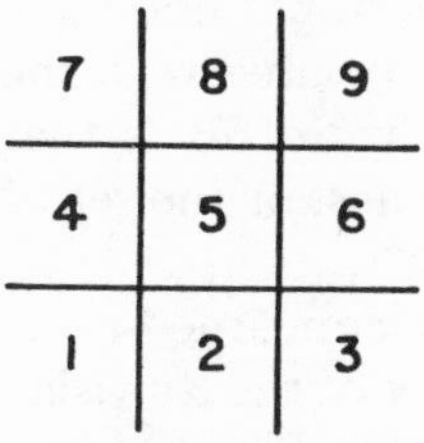

7	8	9
4	5	6
1	2	3

Space Numbers

FIGURE 5A

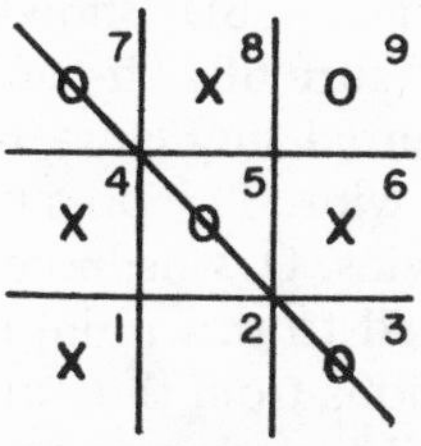

Terminal Point
(alternative moves made by player 1, who makes "X" and player 2, who makes "Y" and space numbers)

FIGURE 5B

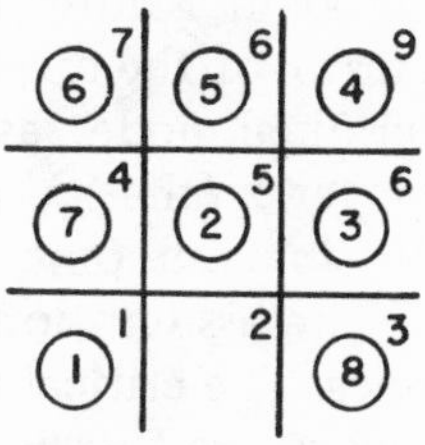

Order of Moves

FIGURE 5C

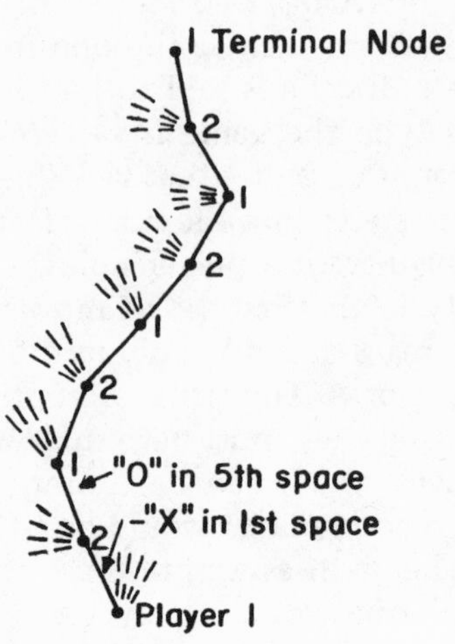

FIGURE 5 D

The spaces are numbered as noted in Figure 5A making the terminal node look as drawn in Figure 5D. The order of the moves has been noted in Figure 5C; the figure (5D) showing the terminal node is a mirror of the diagram in Figure 5B. The outcome associated with the terminal node, as represented in Figure 5D and Figure 5B is that player 2 (the 'O' marker) wins. The possible outcomes, or the set of possible outcomes is: [X wins, O wins, no one wins].

The assumptions outlined to this point have only concerned game rules. The critical assumptions from the point of view of the Rawlsian theory are those which tell the players how to behave. The last two assumptions discussed by Luce and Raiffa[3] limit the behavior of the players. In particular, the seventh assumption says that each of the players must have a distinct "use" for each of the outcomes or payoffs mentioned in the sixth assumption. The theory calls this payoff-to-use correspondence a "utility" function. The eighth and last assumption requires that each player be aware of a move-by-move analysis of the game.

Game rules, then, by assumptions one to six are characterized by the type of information that must be available for and specified to the players. The last two assumptions require that the players must have some particular use for the various outcomes of their moves within the game and that they must know the consequences of the information given in the rules. Particular games will follow these general requirements; they will, however, fulfill them in a variety of ways. Individual games differ from each other by the number of players, number of moves, who moves first, number of alternatives in each move and type of outcome.

One of the most popular game forms for analysis is the constant sum game or a sub-set of it, the zero-sum, two-person, game. These games have one move. The move consists of a set of alternatives actually chosen, given all contingencies, to reach the terminal note of a game tree. The whole tree represented by Figure 5D could be a move of a one-move game if we considered it to be a strategy choice of Player One. That is, if Player One believed that Player Two would respond to his moves in the manner represented on the tree, then Player One might want to choose the alternatives noted for him in that tree, assuming, of course, that Player One had a positive use for the outcome of that tree. The set of alternatives chosen by a player under these circumstances is called a "strategy." A strategy is, in other words, a set of moves a player would make given certain beliefs about the other player's moves. The game as it is now being defined is a game which consists of one actual move. Games described by strategy choices are called games in "normal" form. Games described by a move-by-move discussion of alternative choices are called games in extensive form. A two-person, zero-sum game is a game in normal form where each player chooses a strategy without benefit of knowing what choices the other actually made. The other part of the zero-sum, two-person game to be described is the peculiar way each of the possible outcomes is associated with a terminal point. Zero-sum games, as was noted, are a sub-set of a class of games called constant-sum games. In constant-sum games the outcomes are assigned numbers so that, if there are two people, the sum of winnings and losings always remains constant. If the constant sum in question were 40, then if player A won 30, player B would only win 10. Zero-sum games are constant-sum games where the constant sum is zero, i.e., one person's winnings are exactly the other person's losings. If I win 3, you lose 3. Given the eight assumptions listed above, what can we say about the choice of strategies for A and B? Assuming, for the sake of illustration, that there is a best choice of strategies for A and B, how will A and B choose them? Remembering that both A and B are trying to maximize their respective payoffs, given the choice open to each, we might begin by considering the following matrix:

A↓ \ B→	Z	Y	W
r	4	19	17
q	8	21	2
s	12	3	20
m	22	25	1

FIGURE 6

A's possible strategies, listed vertically, are r, q, s and m. B's strategies are, listed horizontally, z, y and w. The outcomes or payoffs listed in the remaining boxes are the outcomes of A's and B's decisions for A; that is, they represent what A gets as a result of each pair of choices.

If the game is zero-sum, we need only represent the payoff to one player in our matrix—the other will receive the exact opposite (if A wins 4, B loses 4). We have represented A's payoffs in the matrix above. If player A chooses strategy r when player B has chosen strategy y, then player A wins 19. Now, player A, being a rationally self-interested person, is going to try to maximize his possible gains. Assuming this is so, he will inspect his array of payoffs to find which of his four strategies will cause him to do best. Strategy m looks good—he could win 25 or even 22, but he might, at worst, win only 1. Inspecting the rest of his strategies, A might note that strategy r offers him the highest minimum win. If he chooses r he can win 19 or 17 but at worst he will win 4, whereas at worst with strategy g he will only win 2 and at worst with s he will win 3. A might then choose strategy r which offers him the highest minimum winning. This strategy is called a maximin strategy. In analogous reasoning, player B will now inspect his strategy choices z, y and w to see which gives him the possibility of losing the least. The strategy which has the lowest highest number will minimize his possible losses. For example, if A's payoff were 25 this would cause B to lose 25 whereas if A's payoff were only 15, B would only lose 15. The strategy of choosing the lowest-highest, of minimizing the opponent's possible gains, is called minimaxing. If A maximins and B minimaxes, A will choose strategy r and B will choose strategy w. The outcome of this game will then be a payoff of 17 to A. This outcome has the pleasant result of being the best each could have done, since if your opponent maximins then the best thing you can do is minimax. Games which have definite solutions are called games with saddle points.[4]

Rationally self-interested Rawlsian protagonists, however, are neither well-informed nor are they in the essential opposition which characterizes the two-person, zero-sum games described above. The Rawlsian individual's strategies are alternative distribution principles. Rawlsian players are not, strictly speaking, antagonists. How, then, can Rawls use this model to provide evidence for the proposition that his principles are the best selection among currently available alternatives from the point of view of the original position? We need to clearly describe the elements of conflict and we need to define just what a strategy choice will do for a payoff in terms of primary goods.

The first thing to note is that we can play the Rawlsian game as if one party to the conflict were "nature" or "reality." Since every individual is ignorant of his/her peculiar life goals and every individual needs primary goods no matter what these life goals might be, we can list a particular society's payoffs in terms of primary goods; this could make payoffs "inter-personally comparable."[5] We can play the game as if only one person were involved in trying to choose the best distributive principle against only one other player which we have called "nature" or "reality." Reality's strategies are really states of affairs that would occur should our Rawlsian player choose some particular strategy (distribution principle). For example, let player A choose a distribution principle that states that all valuable goods and services in a society should be distributed evenly among the members of the class judged "best" by a society. Suppose that reality chooses a society in which people with big noses are judged to be best. Now, if it so happens that you don't have a big nose, you would get nothing as a payoff.

A more complicated example can be drawn if we suppose there were only three possible choices of principles corresponding to three possible strategies. Let us call these principles A, B and C respectively. Now let us further assume that there are only three possible situations that could occur. These are reality's strategies 1, 2 and 3. In each situation, that is, for each pairing of strategy with states of affairs, we get a particular set of distributions:

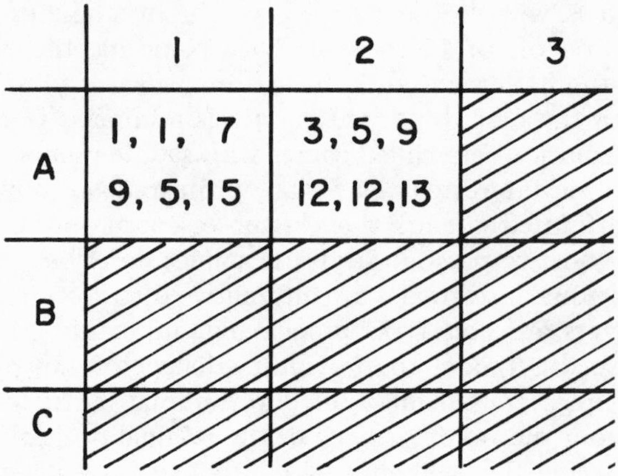

	1	2	3
A	1, 1, 7 9, 5, 15	3, 5, 9 12, 12, 13	
B			
C			

FIGURE 7

Assuming that there are only six representative individuals in each society, the choice A, given reality's choice 1, might lead to the distribution listed in the matrix under A-1. The lowest individual would receive one unit of primary goods, and the second lowest would receive one, etc. Unfortunately, the game still doesn't look very much like the simple constant-sum or zero-sum, two-person game described before. So at this juncture we must make some assumptions which will either force our game model into the two-person, zero-sum variety, or will give us some other criterion for choosing strategies.

The critical difference between the two-person game and the Rawlsian model is that in simple two-person games we are assumed either to have perfect knowledge of the alternatives or, where the choice is left to chance, we are at least assumed to have a knowledge of the probabilities of the various alternatives. The Rawlsian predicament, on the other hand, involves a more severe knowledge constraint. The original position was conceived to guarantee fairness by limiting knowledge which might bias an individual's choice of governing principles. The problem, then, is not strictly analogous to the game theoretical procedures already discussed, situations involving risk. We would be playing a game involving risk if we could reasonably suppose that we would have a 60–30 chance of becoming a powerful figure in a society given a particular choice of governing principles. The Rawlsian paradigm prohibits us from making that sort of inference on the grounds of fairness; we would have to know too much about ourselves to arrive at any statement of probabilities. Rawls has us making choices where there are severe knowledge constraints and serious risk if we make the wrong choices. We are, therefore, going to have to employ a criterion used to guide strategy choices when we have the kind of ignorance suggested by the Rawlsian choice paradigm; we must use a criterion for decisions made under uncertainty. Uncertainty here is used to denote a situation where one does not even have certain knowledge of the probabilities attached to the alternatives available to us. Such is clearly the case for the Rawlsian protagonists.

Decision-making under uncertainty, unfortunately, cannot use many of the rules for decision-making under risk. We must distinguish more carefully between two types of conflict situations; there are games or conflicts under risk in which there is some way to arrive at the probability of an outcome occurring and games or conflicts under uncertainty for which there is no such information. Consider the game tree illustrated in Figure 3. If we are playing a game under risk, and if we have an information set that consists of two or more moves, we will have probabilistic information even if the previous move was made by a random device. We can also say that our player will be able to choose a strategy on the basis of the "expected value" of each alternative open to him.[6] Under uncertainty, however, we are not given any probabilistic information.[7] Stretching the notion of a "tree" diagramming just a bit, we can draw a model of a game under complete uncertainty as follows in Figure 8.

There are many ways to treat situations of complete uncertainty. Each of the possible treatments involves a characterization of the degree of uncertainty under which we are operating. The issue is which decision making rule should determine our strategy in selecting principles of justice. We will follow Baumol's treatment of this problem[8] not only because it is clear and concise, but because it is cited in *A Theory of Justice* as an accessible account of decision procedures.

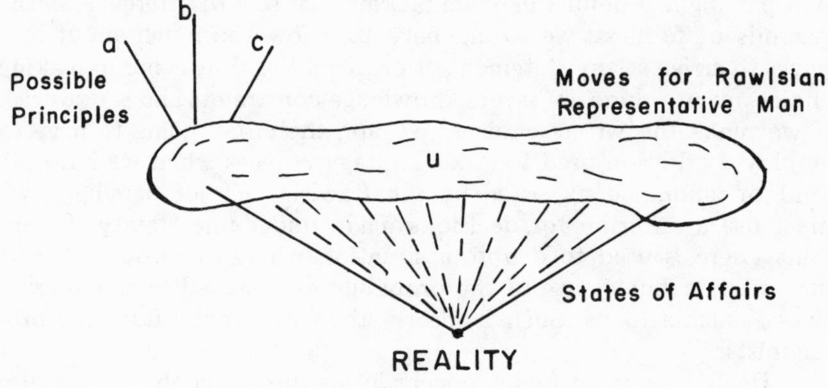

FIGURE 8

The following, then, is an explanation of five major decision rules and Baumol's reasoning concerning the limitations on each. Again, the rationale for doing this is not that Baumol's treatment is indisputable, but that Rawls appears to agree with it and his analysis of what is implied by the original position follows from his acceptance of Baumol's interpretation. We will, therefore, consider the five rules for choosing strategies under uncertainty: maximin, maximax, the Hurwicz α criterion, the Bayes criterion and the minimax regret rule, and the considerations which led Rawls to adopt the maximin rule as the decision making rule to be used in the original position.

The maximin treatment is exactly analogous to the one discussed when we were examining simple two-person, constant-sum games. If you have no idea of the probability of the outcomes and you might really find yourself in a pickle if you choose the wrong alternative, you might use the maximin route to minimize your losses and choose that strategy which offers you the highest minimum payoff. The maximax rule is, in a sense, the opposite of the maximin rule. The man who chooses the maximax rule must be interested only in gain, the sort of person who believes that if he can't have it all he doesn't care what he gets. The maximax man will choose that strategy which offers him the highest possible payoff without regard to his possible losses. The Hurwicz α criterion is a rule which tries to mitigate the possible follies involved in using either of the two rules discussed above. It suggests that to make a reasonable decision we should look at both extremes; in particular, we should choose that strategy which offers us the highest expected average of the lowest and highest payoff under a particular strategy, given a subjective weighting of those extremes. Suppose we have two strategies, A and B, which under different realities give us the following payoffs: (A) 15, 18, 19, 27; (B) 1, 9, 35, 92. Suppose one individual believes that it is very important not to receive a small amount, perhaps because he has fixed expenses so he cannot afford to receive an amount lower than the total of these expenses. Suppose, further, that this individual also believes that receiving a great deal over the total of his expenses is not so important. Let us also imagine another individual who does not mind receiving small amounts, but who feels that obtaining large amounts is worth almost anything. If we told both individuals to rank the highest and lowest payoffs in both A and B on a preference scale of one to ten (where one is low), we might have the following situation:

Payoffs of Strategy A	15	18	19	27
Individual I's Ranking	4	5	6	9
Individual 2's Ranking	3	3	4	5

Payoffs of Strategy B	1	9	35	92
Individual I's Ranking	1	2	2	3
Individual 2's Ranking	2	3	4	9

FIGURE 9

If we call the first individual "the worrier" and the second "the adventurer" we might describe the weighted average of each as follows:

The worrier:	A: $\dfrac{(15 \times 4) + (27 \times 9)}{2}$	151.5
	B: $\dfrac{(1 \times 1) + (92 \times 3)}{2}$	138.5
The adventurer:	A: $\dfrac{(15 \times 3) + (27 \times 5)}{2}$	90
	B: $\dfrac{(1 \times 2) + (92 \times 9)}{2}$	415

FIGURE 10

Following the Hurwicz α criterion rule, the worrier would choose strategy A whereas the adventurer would choose B.

The Bayes rule is a much more sophisticated treatment of decision making under uncertainty. This rule suggests that even if we do not know the requisite probabilities we may make either of two educated guesses. If we have some expert, a habitual observer of the environment within which we are trying to make our uncertain decisions, he or she might provide some educated guesses about the probabilities attached to the various outcomes or payoffs. We could then use expected value calculations to determine the choice of strategy. A calculation of expected value works much the same way as the weighted average discussed in the foregoing treatment of the Hurwicz α criterion. In expected value calculations, we multiply all payoffs times some weighting. In the Hurwicz discussion, the weighting was given by a subjective preference scale from one to ten. More often, however, an outcome is weighted by the probability that it will occur. One can evaluate strategies by comparing their expected averages. We can determine the expected average of a strategy by multiplying each outcome by its weight, adding the results all together and dividing by the number of outcomes. The preferred strategy is the one with the highest expected average. If we do not have expert advice, the other method of determining probabilities is to admit we are ignorant of the actual probabilities and treat all outcomes as if they were equally probable.

The Savage minimax-regret criterion is an analogue of the minimax rule discussed previously. The weakness of the maximin rule is that it fails to take account of any of the alternatives other than the lowest. The Savage minimax-regret treatment draws a new matrix from the one used with a minimax treatment; this new matrix is designed to take account of intermediate values. We can calculate the degree of regret we would have if we choose one strategy over another.

I↓ \ II→	1	2	3
A	4	7	3
B	9	4	12

FIGURE 11A

I↓ \ II→	1	2	3
A	5	0	9
B	0	3	0

(MINIMAX REGRET)

FIGURE 11B

The intuitive idea is that what is really relevant for decision making is how big a mistake we might make if we choose the wrong alternative. Suppose the matrix in Figure 11A shows the payoffs for players I and II under alternate strategies (e.g., A or B; 1 or 2 or 3). A matrix illustrating the minimax-regret rule could then be drawn as shown in Figure 11B. If player I chose strategy A with a payoff of 4 and player II chose strategy 1 and player I could have chosen strategy B with a payoff of 9, he or she will have a "regret" of 5. If he chose strategy B he would have nothing to regret, and so on.

Each of the decision procedures we have discussed have certain weaknesses and strengths, depending upon what we believe to be the exact degree of uncertainty facing us. In what follows we will relate Baumol's discussion[9] of these strengths and weaknesses since it is crucial to an understanding of Rawls' case for his principles from the point of view of fairness.

The minimax regret theorem does take into account intermediate payoffs, but the minimax-regret matrix only makes sense if regret, in the technical sense described above, is an accurate measure of our regret colloquially understood. In other words, the choice of strategies will depend not only on what we might gain if we choose a particular strategy, but how much we value what we could have gained. However, the minimax-regret matrix will only enable us to make decisions on that basis if the numbers in the matrix reflect regret colloquially understood. If a loss of 30 and a loss of 39 are all the same to us, then the numbers in the table will not be an accurate reflection of regret colloquially understood since the numbers reflect a difference which is not perceived. This is exactly what the Rawlsian paradigm prohibits and, therefore, is why this particular rule cannot be used by Rawls in selecting principles of justice. Individual utility values cannot be used as payoffs because not every individual has the same use value for each payoff. Since the numbers in the minimax matrix cannot reflect the actual utilities of the individuals doing the choosing because the veil of ignorance prevents knowing who the individuals are or what they value, the regret values cannot be reflections of the regret of those individuals.

The Bayes theorem requires that we assign probabilities on the basis of equiprobability in the absence of some expert advice. Rawls' veil of ignorance rules out the use of experts, but as Baumol suggests, an assignment of equiprobability to each outcome would be foolhardy since that assignment can only be made if we know the number of alternatives facing us.

> Suppose our player is considering whether to sell ice cream (strategy A) or hot dogs (strategy B) at a baseball game. We may divide nature's strategies into three possibilities; sunshine, C; cloudiness, D; rain or other forms of precipitation, E. In the complete absence of meteorological information we might consider C, D and E to be equally probable and assign them each the probability 1/3. Alternatively, we might have decided that the major contingencies to consider are rain and non-rain. Because we possess no relevant information it can be argued just as persuasively as before that these two contingencies are equally likely and each should be assigned the probability 1/2. We see, then, by the simple act of reclassification the *a priori* probability assigned to the rain's contingency (nature's strategy E) has been raised from 1/3 to 1/2. In other words, unless we have some advance information on the number of categories into which the alternatives should be classified, the Bayes equiprobability-of-the-unknown approach can leave the relevant probability figure completely ambiguous.[10]

Now, returning to the model of decision-making under complete uncertainty in Figure 8, we see that the information set precludes our knowing the choice reality might make and our choice is in no way dependent upon the number of alternatives reality has at its disposal. We are trying to choose a principle which will govern the distribution of society's goods and services. We need to know the ranges of amounts of these goods and services given to each representative man, but the decision is not dependent upon knowing the number of ways this can be done. That information is neither necessary nor available to the Rawlsian man. Therefore the Bayes theorem is not a reasonable strategy to follow in the original position.

The remaining principles, the Hurwicz, maximax and minimax rules have some very peculiar properties. Again, which rule we will choose depends upon the assumptions we make concerning our choice paradigm. Given the fact that we are concerned with actual levels of primary goods distributed over representative men by our hypothetical distribution principle, the Hurwicz criterion seems singularly useless. Whereas a particular distribution might have a weighted average of highest and lowest payoffs of, say, 30, we might find that no one actually received that amount. If we assume that there are five representative men, we could have the following distribution: 2, 3, 3, 5. If we give a weighting of 10 to the highest and 5 to the lowest, we would have a weighted average of 30 although no one would receive such an amount. Hence we can reject the Hurwicz criterion strategy. In eliminating the maximax criterion Rawls makes an additional assumption about the choosers in the original position. Rawls stipulates that they care little for what they get over a certain point. If this is assumed, it makes no sense to disregard, or weigh lightly, the lowest payoffs, since these are going to be relatively more important than high payoffs which have diminishing value. Only the maximin rule remains a plausible rule for choosing principles of justice under conditions of uncertainty. The maximin mandates selection of principles of justice which maximize the lowest payoff. The difference principle, by definition, does exactly that.

The argument for the acceptance of the difference principle, however, rests both on the fact that it is consistent with the maximin rule and that its most prominent rival, utilitarianism, is not. The utilitarian criterion for arriving at a just distribution requires us to maximize either the sum (classical utilitarianism) or the average (average utilitarianism) of individual utilities computed over all individuals. We can at once note that the Rawlsian paradigm and veil of ignorance prohibits considering payoffs in terms of individual utilities.[11] We need not hypothesize that the individuals involved have the same utilities for any particular level of primary goods.

Having shown that the difference principle is consistent with the most reasonable choice of rules under uncertainty, given our particular choice paradigm, and having also mentioned the outline of an argument against utilitarianism from this point of view, we are now in a position to turn to the second part of this discussion and examine whether the difference principle accords with our intuitive notions of justice.

UTILITY THEORY AND THE ARGUMENT FROM INTUITION

In choosing a principle of justice we must have some notion, if not a systematic one, of what justice is. Rawls has been concerned with devising a consistent interpretation of justice conceived as fairness. The aim is to find a principle which will distribute a society's primary goods in a just manner, i.e., fairly. The fairest distribution at first glance would seem to be an equal distribution. Any theorist, therefore, who wishes to propose a principle of distribution which does not result in an equal allocation of primary goods must offer some argument concerning why they are making such a deviation. Deviations from equality have to be rationalized in terms consistent with whatever other convictions we have about just distributions. That is, we might decide that a just distribution is an equal distribution tempered by need, or *desert* or by incentive motivation for the common good.

The use of the maximin rule and the resulting choice of the difference principle sets up some fairly strict requirements concerning exactly how the notion of justice may be tempered. In order to understand how the maximin rule does this, we must understand the rudiments of modern utility theory. In particular we must understand that the use of the maximin rule makes the Rawlsian protagonist a conservative who cannot gamble on a principle of justice which might get him a high payoff of primary goods because he is an extreme risk avoider. It is important to note that this conservatism is a result of the constraints of the original position requiring the use of the maximin rule. Rawls never requires that the representative man be a risk avoider; he has not made conservatism an independent assumption. Conservatism occurs as the result of the choice of rational men constrained to be fair.

The modern theory of utility was thought to provide a theoretical framework which would permit economists to make prescriptions for society based on a consideration of the preferences of the individuals within that society. If we are to make prescriptions concerning the optimum distribution of goods to the members of a society, we cannot base our prescriptions on some notion of the intrinsic worth of the goods in question. Even if we could somehow establish a measure of the intrinsic worth of all the goods to be distributed, we might find that some individuals within our society have different preferences; they might not like a particular good as much as the intrinsic value rating suggests they should like it. If we have begun by assuming that it is the individual's use for, or preference ranking of, the goods and services to be distributed that will determine what society will deem to be a good distribution, then we cannot force individuals to accept any dictated scale of intrinsic value.

If the task is to determine which distribution of economic goods a society prefers on the basis of the preferences of individuals, it must first be established what the individuals within the society prefer. Once the way each individual ranks the various distributions is determined, we must combine the individual preferences to determine the way society as a whole ranks the distributions. These seemingly simple tasks involve grave problems. Suppose, for example, we suggest that there be some unit, call it "utils," which we will use to measure the use-value, or utility, for a particular individual of a particular good or bundle of goods. For example, an apple might have a value of one util for individual Q. The total utility of individual Q is some function of the utility of the apple and the other commodities Q has to consider. The first problem we encounter concerns the nature of this function.

We might suppose, initially, that we may simply add the separate utility or use-value of each of the individuals' goods to arrive at the total utility for the individual. Suppose there are three goods; F, C and H. Let us also assume that a hypothetical individual Q has the following utilities corresponding to each of the above listed goods:

Good F	5 utils
Good G	7 utils
Good H	15 utils

To say that Q's total utility is the sum of the utilities of goods F, G and H (27 utils) would be to make an assumption about the nature of the goods which is not necessarily true. It would be to assume that the utility of F is not affected by the other goods, G and H. If F were ice cream and G were hot fudge this would clearly be false. If the utility of one good affects the utility of another good, then the total utility derived from some consideration of these goods could be greater than or less than the sum of their individual utilities depending on the nature of the interdependency. If we cannot simply add, what functional relationship can we adopt that does not entail special and unacceptable assumptions?

Even if we solve the problem of how to combine the utilities of the individual commodities which form the bundles in the distributions, we still must decide how precise individual measurement must be before we can arrive at a consistent social measure. Ultimately, the individual will be ranking different distributions of bundles of goods. Do we need to require the individual only to say which distribution he or she liked best, next best, etc., in order? But even the weakest definition of a cardinal ordering requires use of a scale for which the difference between, say, 5 and 10 utils of one good is exactly comparable to a difference between 15 and 20 of another good. While we may have no serious difficulties ranking types of goods, we might find it difficult to order them with precision sufficient to use a cardinal scale. It is asking quite a good deal of a person to be required not only to rank apples against bananas, but also to be precise about it and rank them so that a bundle of 8 apples with a 5 util rating is exactly 1/3 as good as a bundle of 20 bananas with a rating of 15 utils. While such a requirement is not logically impossible, modern utility theory has demonstrated that it is not necessary to have this kind of precision.

Before we return to the problem of how we can combine individual rankings to reflect social choice, and its complications, we will first consider a theory of utility for individuals which attempts to solve the two problems mentioned above. If utility theory is to aid in solving these problems, it must provide an unobjectionable method of comparing particular commodities and it must order bundles of commodities consistently for each individual.

The difficulty with providing a consistent ordering of bundles of commodities for an individual is the inability to specify the relationship between the ranking of each particular commodity and the total utility of the individual. Fortunately, it is possible to develop a consistent individual ordering without being specific about the nature of that functional relationship. Suppose we have a world in which there are only two commodities X and Y. We know that the total utility of an individual, Q, is some function (e.g., addition, multiplication, etc.) of the utilities of commodity X and commodity Y for individual Q, but we do not know the precise nature of the function. By definition, each commodity and each bundle of commodities (e.g., amount 5 of X and amount 7 of Y or amount 7 of X and 5 of Y) has one and only one ranking on Q's utility scale. We can picture different combinations of the two commodities, X and Y, and the rankings of each combination on a surface of space called a utility surface and thereby represent the functional relationship between amounts of X and Y and the utility measure without specifying the nature of the function. In Figure 12 various quantities of commodities X and Y are represented along the X and Y axes.

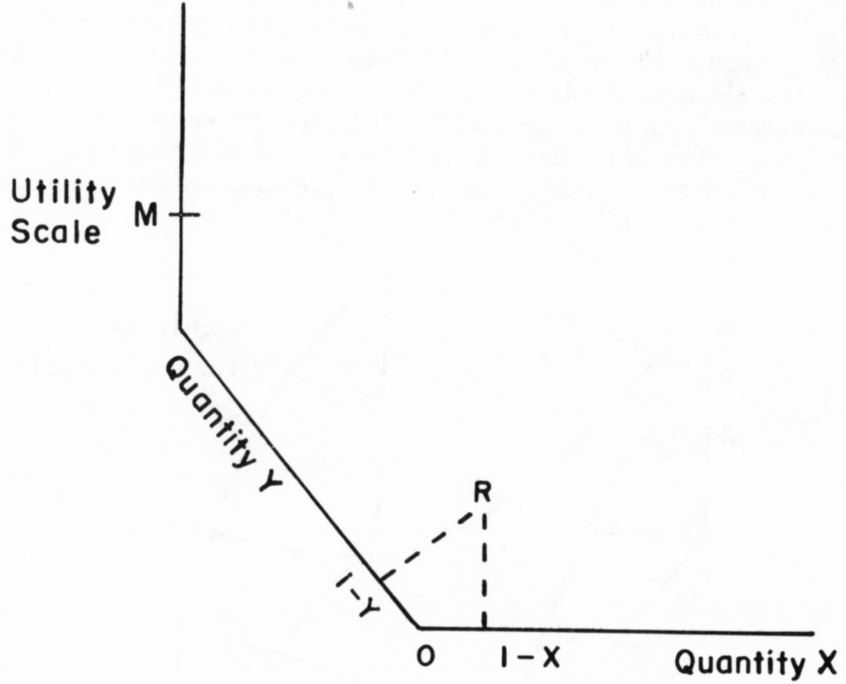

FIGURE 12

Suppose that point 0 represents a zero amount of X and a zero amount of Y. Zero amounts of X and Y have a utility ranking of 0. Point 1-X represents amount of 1 of X and 1-Y represents amount 1 of Y and so on along the X and Y axes. We could draw hypothetical lines at right angles from points 1-Y and 1-X which would intersect at point R which represents the commodity bundle 1-Y and 1-X. Consider point 0, which represents zero amounts of X and Y and a ranking of zero as place of beginning, and suppose we pin there a piece of fabric. If a utility of the bundle 1-X and 1-Y were represented by a vertical measure run up from point R until it reached the height of the ranking (M) given bundle 1-X and 1-Y on the utility scale by individual Q, it would push the fabric up behind point 0. Vertical measures running from the intersection points of other commodity bundles (say 10-X and 10-Y) would have a similar effect. We can generate a three dimensional picture, Figure 13A, on this basis in which we can represent the fabric pinned to point 0 as it is pushed to points S by hypothetical lines drawn from points such as R which represent commodity bundles, the height of the line reflecting the ranking given the bundle by individual Q on the utility scale. The surface stretched from point 0 to points S is the utility surface.[12]

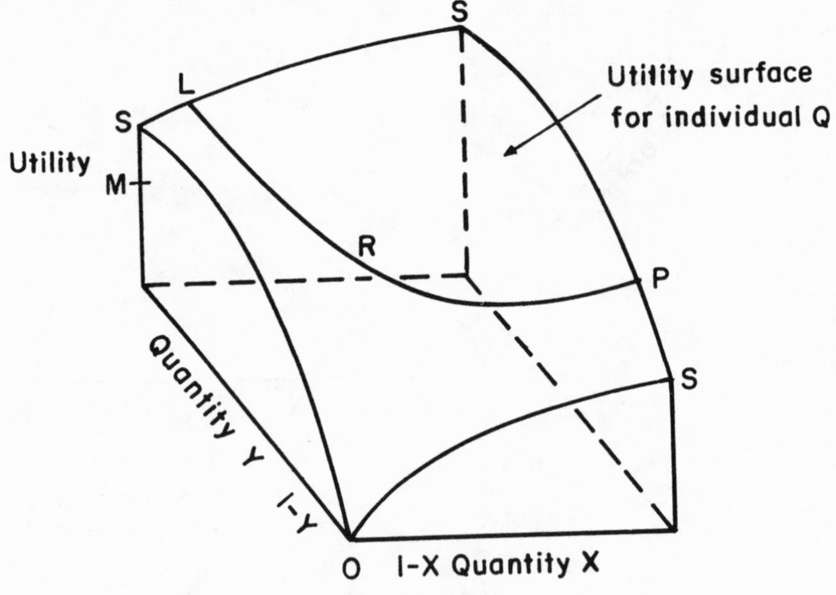

FIGURE 13A

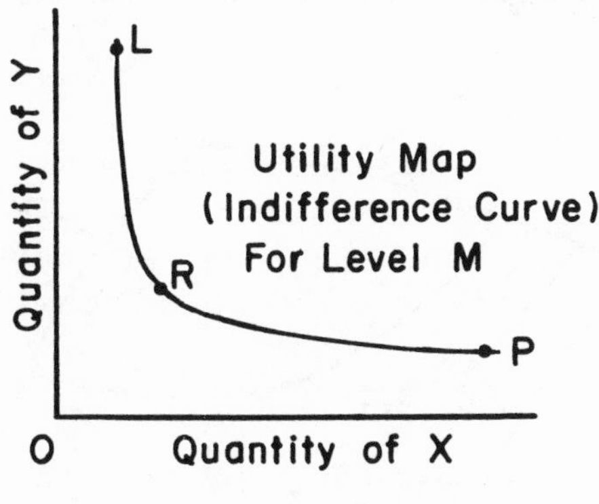

FIGURE 13 B

Any point on the utility surface corresponds to some amount of X and Y being related to some particular utility number. For example, point R relates the commodity bundle consisting of amount 1-Y of X and 1-X of Y with a utility ranking here represented by M. This allows us to relate various amounts of individual commodities to utility without being specific about the way in which they are related. It is, therefore, not necessary to make any additional assumptions about the nature of the functional relationship. Let us call the relationship between commodity bundles and an individual's ranking of them a utility function. One attribute that a utility function should have is the ability to reflect the fact that an individual can give up an amount of one commodity in exchange for an increase in the amount of another commodity and still remain at the same utility level. This particular model takes this into account since if we take a horizontal slice of the utility surface by cutting across the diagram at a particular level of utility, we get a curve (LRP in Figure 13A) which represents the locus of all different combinations of X and Y for which individual Q's utility remains at level M. These horizontal slices are called utility maps or indifference curves. They can be drawn onto X, Y axes as is shown in Figure 13B. We have, then, a way to show that there are different commodity arrangements that leave individual Q at the same level of satisfaction. We have, further, been able to do this without specifying any particular functional relationship as the one that must hold for all individuals, between commodities and total utility. We simply know that for individual Q amount a of X and b of Y (illustrated in Figure 14A) give him greater utility than c of X and d of Y.

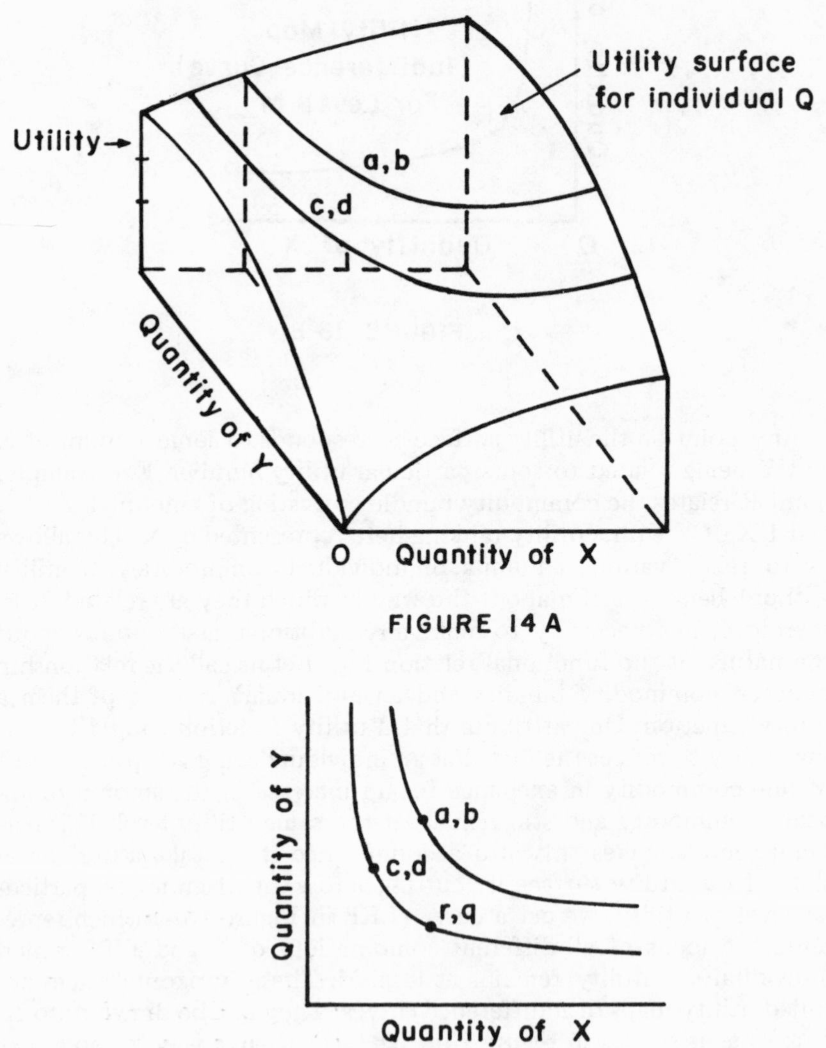

FIGURE 14A

FIGURE 14B

We can also note that bundle c, d and r, q have the same level of utility. The individual is, therefore, indifferent with respect to a choice between the two bundles c, d and r, q. A curve showing the commodity bundles which have the same level of utility is therefore called an indifference curve (14B). It should be obvious now that we need not use a scale that requires cardinal precision. Since all we ultimately require of utility is higher or lower than another level of utility, this can be achieved by use of an ordinal scale.

It would seem, then, that we could arrive at a consistent preference ordering of distributions for society as a whole in an exactly analogous manner. Unfortunately, the transition from individual preference to social preference involves serious problems. Basically we want to be able to analyze preference rankings given to various distributions of goods by society as a whole in terms of preference rankings given by individual members of society. We might suppose that we could say that no matter what the form of the function, each set of individual preference levels corresponds to one and only one social preference or social utility level; further, that by taking horizontal slices of a utility surface, we could arrive at a set of distributions between which society as a whole is indifferent; no one distribution in this set would be socially preferable to another in the same set. Such a slice, theoretically at least, would graphically describe various combinations of rankings of distributions of social goods by particular individuals in the society. The way we combine the individual preferences might well allow the trading of one individual's preferences for another individual's preference as long as society's preference or utility level is unaffected.

Unfortunately, there are problems involved in extending the individual model. Both the degree of precision of individual utility functions and the degree of precision in the social utility measure are problematic. Sen[13] argues that even if we require individuals to order their preferences cardinally, we still need some way of comparing the rankings of one individual with those of another. No matter what degree of precision we require in individual rankings, we must be able to say something like, "Individual A's fifth ranking is equivalent to individual B's third." We need some kind of interpersonal correspondence rules between the utility levels of various individuals. If we try to arrive at a social utility measure (usually called a social welfare function or SWF) without interpersonal comparisons by somehow compiling individual utility functions, giving each equal weight, we will be unable to produce a consistent social preference function. In

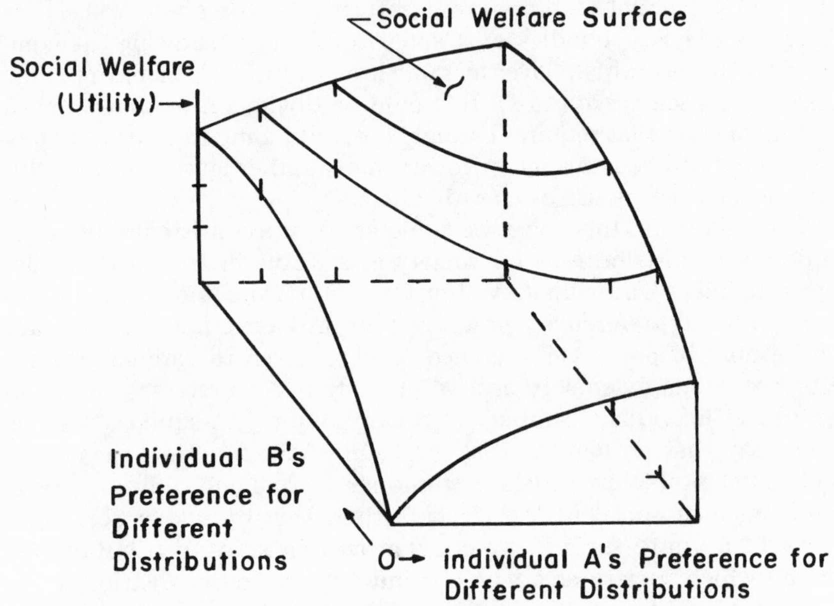

FIGURE 15

fact, Kenneth Arrow[14] demonstrated that even a weak characterization of such a situation involves serious inconsistencies; i.e., the axioms which characterize the situation are inconsistent.

It is a strength of the Rawlsian principle of distribution, the maximin principle, that it provides some way of dealing with this difficulty. The difference principle requires us to locate the least advantaged man and judge the effects of policies by changes in his plight. This forces us, at least initially, to have an interpersonally comparable measure in order to determine who is least well off. However, from then on ordinal rankings will suffice.

We are finally in a position to review Rawls' argument that his principle more nearly fits what we believe to be just, intuitively, than any other philosophically important distribution principle. Rawls' major attack, as it has been throughout *A Theory of Justice*, is on utilitarianism. His argument is that, given the constraints of the original position. the maximin rule is the appropriate strategy to guide our selection of principles of justice. In the discussion of the maximin rule in the section on game theory, it was noted that a player making decisions on the basis of the maximin rule would be a conservative risk avoider and would choose a strategy that would minimize possible losses rather than maximize possible gains. The models of game theory and utility theory are both useful in explaining the strategy of the extreme risk avoider.

Each of the various decision rules for dealing with decision making under uncertainty has its own peculiar shaped indifference curve.[15] To understand why, the notion of an indifference curve has to be altered a bit to accommodate the fact that the player might adopt alternative strategies. The normal indifference curve represents combinations of commodities to which the consumer is indifferent; if one bundle consists of three units of X and four units of Y, the individual who gets the bundle will get them all. In our altered strategy the consumer will receive only one, but not both of the payoffs represented. Consider the payoff matrix illustrated in Figure 16.

Nature → / I ↓	R	Q
A	7	2
B	3	9

FIGURE 16

If individual I plays strategy A then he or she can get either 7 or 2 as a payoff, depending upon the strategy nature selects. Similarly we can draw indifference curves on a set of axes representing the different strategies for nature.

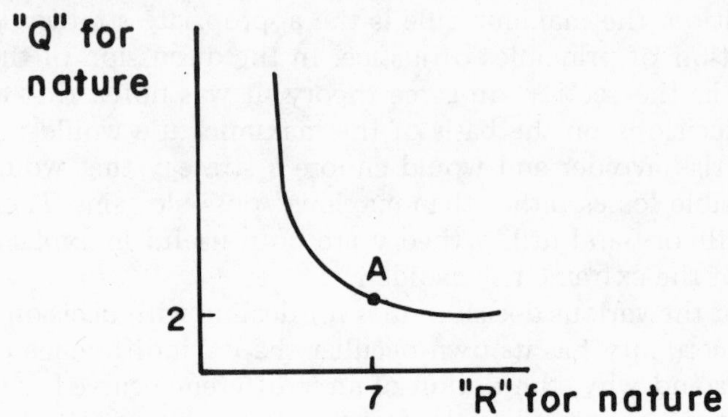

FIGURE 17

A point on this indifference curve represents the payoff pair that would occur should player I choose strategy A. The player might receive 2 or 7; he would receive 7 if nature played strategy R and he would receive 2 if nature played strategy Q, but not both. Baumol[16] argues that an indifference curve for an individual operating on the maximin rule will be shaped like those in Figure 18.

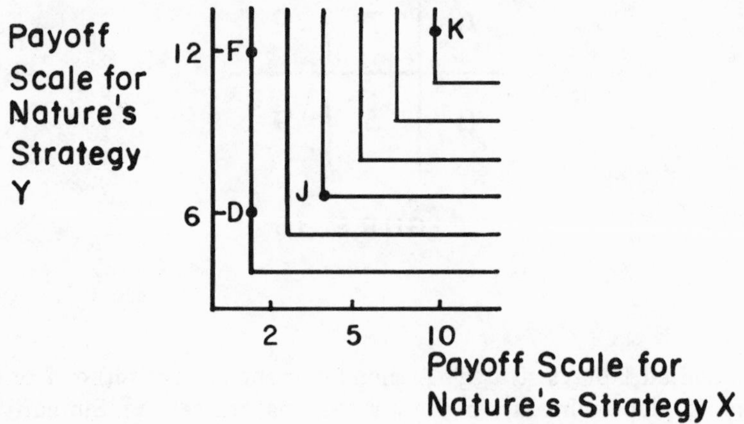

FIGURE 18

Indifference curves of this shape reflect the fact that the player using the maximin rule will always be indifferent to the choice between two strategies unless one strategy raises the lowest payoff he can receive. Pure strategy indifference curves such as we have drawn are curves that connect strategies that, for one reason or another, we cannot decide between. A maximin user will not be able to choose between two strategies unless one of them gives him a higher lowest value; he will not be able to decide between a strategy which offers him a payoff array of 1, 3, 5, 59 and one which offers a 1, 5, 7, 99; but he will be able to choose one which offers 5, 9, 9, 67 over one which offers a 1, 5, 8, 99. Diagrammatically, we see (Figure 18) that player I, a maximin user, is indifferent between two strategies, D and F, which offer him a possible 2, 6 (D) and 2, 12 (F) respectively. We can also note that he would choose strategy J over either D or F. J, which offers a minimum of 5 or 6 depending on nature's choice of strategies, is preferred to D or F which offer minimums of 2. Likewise K is preferable to J (10, 12 is preferable to 5, 6).[17]

It is now possible to make Rawls' argument clear. Let us represent two alternative strategies nature could take on a set of axes and let us draw indifference curves connecting the distributions that we consider equally just. Suppose nature could adopt strategy X which makes individual Q among the best-off in society or adopt strategy Y which would make individual Q among the worst-off in society. These two alternative strategies will be plotted along respective axes so that payoffs for the most-favored-man will be represented on the X axis and payoffs for the least-favored-man will be shown on the Y axis as in Figure 20.

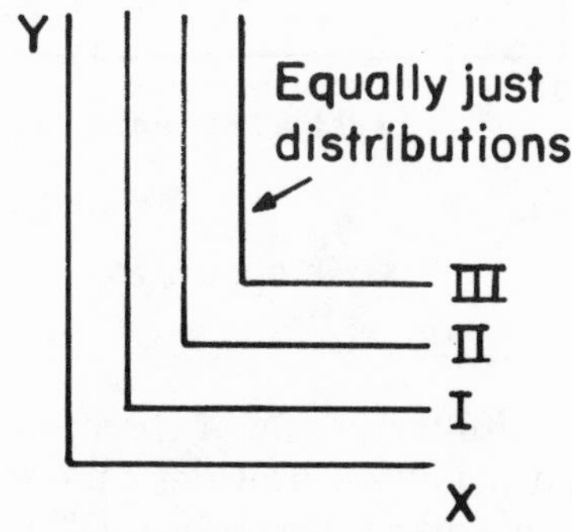

FIGURE 19

Indifference curves can be drawn on the axes whose shape will reflect the rule of choice being used. The square shaped indifference curve in Figure 19 reflects the use of the maximin and shows that all distributions along a given line (e.g., I or II) are equally acceptable to someone using a maximin rule. It can also be shown that a utilitarian strategy of choice would produce negatively sloped indifference curves. As shown in Figure 20, distributions A, B and C are equally attractive using utilitarian reasoning since they all offer a payoff of 101 and since it is only the total payoff package that matters.

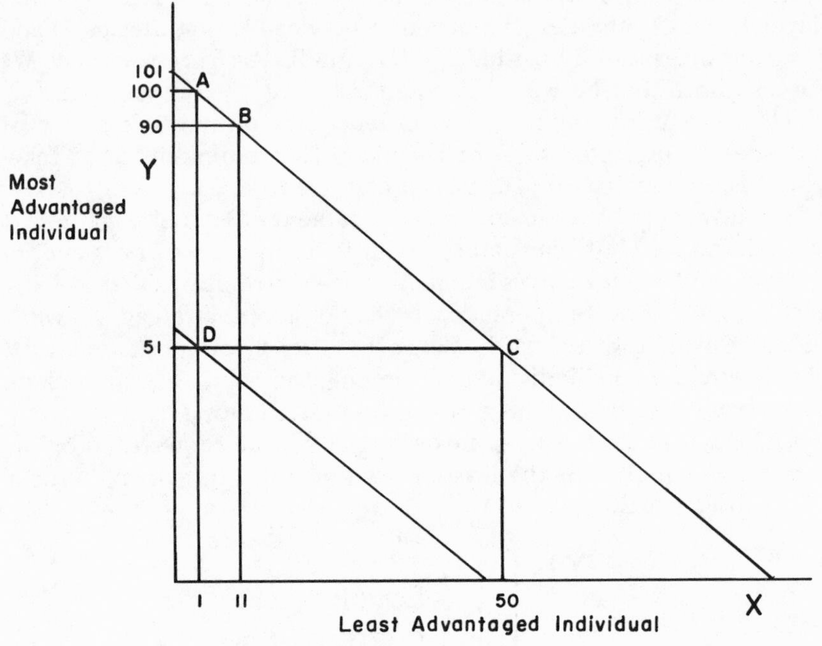

FIGURE 20

The individual using a utilitarian rule of choice does not prefer C over A even though that distribution provides a more nearly equal payoff to the most and least advantaged individual. (Rawls argues this is counterintuitive.) He would prefer, however, A, B or C to D which has a total payoff of only 51.

Suppose that there is a relationship between an increase in the most-favored man's position and an increase in the least-favored-man's lot. Perhaps the most-favored-man, given an increase in his position, would be induced to produce more and his increased production would benefit the least-favored-man as well. Let us represent this relationship by Figure 21.

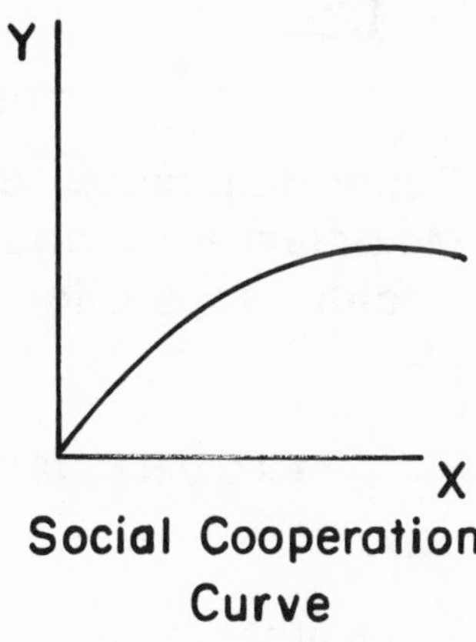

Social Cooperation Curve

FIGURE 21

The curve represented here is a "social cooperation curve." It has a downward sloping portion since, in a world of limited resources, continuing increases to the most-favored-man will not advance the lot of the least advantaged past a given point. If we superimpose the social cooperation curve on a graphic representation of the indifference curves of a maximin user, as shown in Figure 22, we get an indication of the most just distribution such a society can hope to reach; namely, the distribution described by the highest indifference curve reached by the social cooperation curve. Notice that the indifference curve which touches the cooperation curve at its highest point is the one for all those distributions which increase the payoff package for the least well-off members of society more than any others.

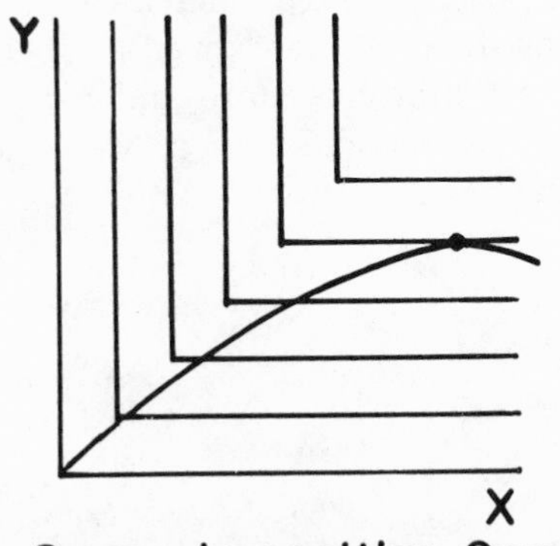

Super-imposition Graph
Maximum Rule and
Social Cooperation Curve

FIGURE 22

Rawls justifies selection of the maximin strategy of choice in the original position by arguing that use of the utilitarian or any other rule of strategy would result in an indifference curve which, when superimposed on the social cooperation curve, would not accord as well with our intuitive idea of justice as does the indifference curve of the maximin principle. Any shape of indifference curve other than that of the maximin rule would make the point at which the social cooperation curve touches the indifference curve a point which could be improved upon. That is, if in Figure 23 we superimpose the utilitarian strategy upon the social cooperation rule, we find that the highest valued indifference curve is touched by the social cooperation curve far from the latter curve's highest point. In fact the least well-off would have to accept considerably less than they would get at a much lower valued indifference curve. In Figure 23 we can see that the highest payoff for best-off people (on the X axis) is indicated by the highest indifference curve intersected by the social cooperation curve (curve A). But indifference curve A yields the worst-off individuals (on axis Y) a smaller return than indifference curve B which intersects the social cooperation curve at a higher point on the Y axis.

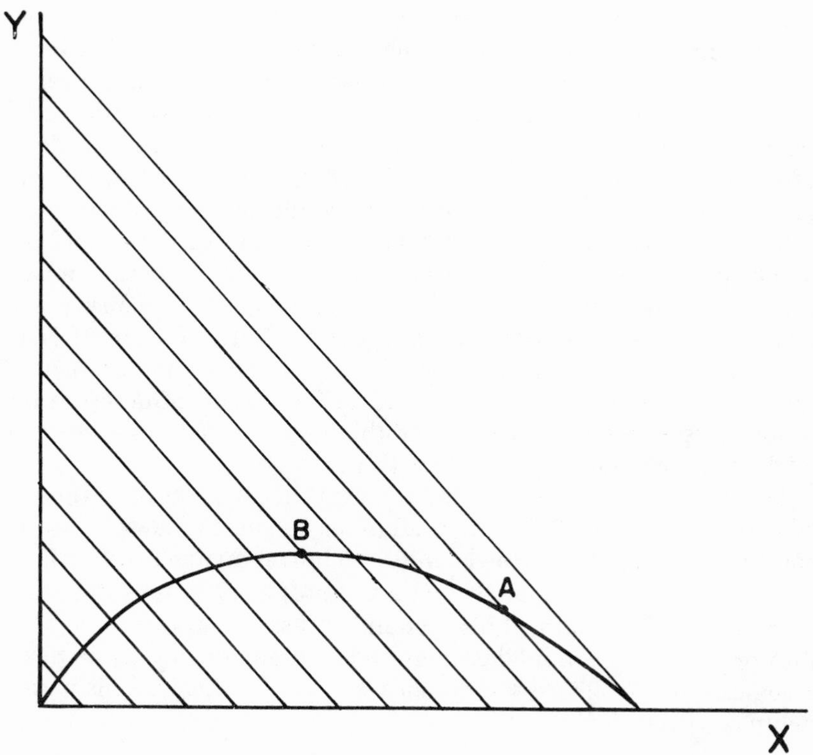

FIGURE 23

Rawls does not deny that this result could be defended, but he argues that in order to justify giving the least well-off individuals less than the maximum available to them through social cooperation, we must make additional assumptions. It might be contended, for example, that the most favored man should get more because he deserves it, but this is an additional assumption and requires us to define "desert." The simplest hypothesis, the one that requires us to make the fewest problematic assumptions, is preferable, and use of the maximin strategy not only accords with our intuition that a distribution in which one individual gets 51 and another 50 is preferable to a distribution in which one individual gets 100 and another 1, but does so with a minimum of problematic assumptions.

What Rawls hoped to show was that his choice of a distribution principle, namely the difference principle, would be the choice of rational men constrained to act fairly. We have shown that, given the Rawlsian interpretation of a fair situation of choice and given the features of the various rules for making choices in a situation of uncertainty, the maximin rule does appear to be the most plausible rule of choice to adopt. If we select principles of justice using the maximin strategy, the difference principle would be selected since it accords better with the maximin rule than do any of the various utilitarian principles of distributive justice. Further, Rawls hoped to show that the difference principle has distributive consequences which are consistent with our considered intuitive notion of justice as fairness. We are not led, under this view, to adopt any problematic assumptions about our worth or define the notion of desert, a definition which would take us beyond the bounds of fairness *per se*, and might not always be compatible with it.

While the foregoing discussion of game theory and utility theory is not complete, it is sufficient to allow us to sketch Rawls' reasoning and provide a guide to Rawls' more technical arguments. Rawls' use of economic theory in analyzing a philosophical issue is one of the sources of the strength of his account of justice and it is to be hoped that making the economic background of his arguments more readily accessible will facilitate the detailed and critical analysis his work so richly deserves.[18]

NOTES

1. R. Duncan Luce and Howard Raiffa, *Games and Decisions* (New York: John Wiley & Sons, 1957), p. 44.
2. *Ibid.*
3. *Ibid.*, pp. 48, 49.
4. A saddle point is the name given to the solution of games which are designed to have solutions. The solution is so named because of the graphic representation of those solutions.
5. While the meaning of this term will be discussed more carefully in the section on utility theory, it generally means that the payoff one person receives can be accurately compared to the payoff of other individuals.
6. See the discussion of the Hurwicz criterion below. The term "expected value" is an expression which names a mathematical procedure which allows us to couple any probabilistic information we have with the payoff information we have.

7. In order to be certain about probability assignments we must know both the full description of the universe we are considering and the portion of the universe taken up by the event to which we are trying to attach a probability. We have no such information.
8. William J. Baumol, *Economic Theory and Operations Analysis* (New Jersey: Prentice-Hall, 1972); for another discussion of the derivation of the maximin principle see "A Critical Introduction to Rawls' Theory of Justice" by Allen Buchanan in Chapter I of this book.
9. *Ibid.*, pp. 574–92.
10. *Ibid.*, p. 578.
11. The following is a discussion of the conclusion noted above that it is not necessary to conclude that the individuals in our society have the same utility function for primary goods. Suppose we have the following situation:

Primary good levels	1	2	3	4	5	6	7
Individual A's utility for each level	7	15	21	39	45	67	89
Individual B's utility for each level	9	32	34	45	79	83	95

The primary good level need only be a monotonic transformation of the individual's utilities. The interpersonal comparability is included in the above in that we are assuming that we can in fact make a monotonic transformation, i.e., we are assuming that everyone wants more rather than less of these goods. This monotonic transformation might leave a good deal of information out concerning an individual's use for any particular level of primary goods. In fact the Rawlsian paradigm seems to require us not to use such information since such information would mean that we know a good deal about the particular talents, life goals and notions of the good of our representative individuals.
12. While the diagram represented here is a general representation of a utility surface described in many standard economic texts, the particular curve drawn here follows the one used in C.E. Ferguson and J.P. Gould, *Microeconomic Theory*, fourth edition (Illinois: Richard D. Irwin, 1975).
13. Amartya K. Sen, *Collective Choice and Social Welfare* (San Francisco: Holden-Day, Inc., 1970.
14. Kenneth Arrow, *Social Choice and Individual Values* (New York: Wiley, 1951).
15. Baumol, *Economic Theory.*
16. *Ibid.*
17. Baumol goes on to describe the indifference curves characteristic of other decision rules under uncertainty. The Bayes criterion, for example, has sloped indifference curves since these individuals are willing to trade a lower lowest for higher highest.
18. I would like to thank Dr. I. Ghazalah for his helpful comments and general patience. I would also like to express my appreciation to Mr. Keith Butt for his transformation of unrecognizable scrawls into attractive graphs and drawings.

Equal Basic Liberty for All

Norman Bowie
CENTER FOR THE STUDY OF VALUES
UNIVERSITY OF DELAWARE

America is the country which insures equal liberty for all. This claim is a tenet of the American creed. The commitment to equal liberty also functions as an ideal against which American institutions can be evaluated. But the phrase "equal liberty for all" needs interpretation and evaluation before it can serve either as a factual claim about America or as a poignant reminder of how American institutions "come up short." John Rawls' *A Theory of Justice* places the Principle of Equal Liberty for All at the apex of his system. The Principle of Equal Liberty has priority over the other principles of justice—at least in developed countries like the U.S. In the first section of this essay I examine some of the key concepts in Rawls' theory of liberty. Rawls' list of basic liberties is compared to the liberties enumerated in The Bill of Rights in the U.S. Constitution. In defining liberty itself, I show how Rawls tries to avoid adopting one of the ideological definitions of liberty—that the only true freedom is freedom from coercion by others or that the only true freedom is freedom to develop one's own essential nature. Rawls' strategy is to draw a distinction between the equal right to liberty and the equal worth of liberty. Rawls is a proponent of the former, but not of the latter. In the second section I explain the sense in which Rawls considers the right to equal liberty to have priority over the right to an equal distribution of economic resources.

Perhaps the most important section of the paper is the third section. As stated, The Principle of Equal Liberty expresses a rights claim that each individual's total system of basic liberties be equal to every other's. But what does Rawls mean by that cumbersome phrase, "that system of basic liberties," and how could such a rights claim, once understood, be implemented? In the third section I attempt to structure Rawls' disorganized remarks on this topic so that these questions might be at least partially answered. In so doing, I discuss Rawls' notion of the Constitutional Convention as the device for implementation, and I analyze a hierarchical set of principles which Rawls uses to both guide and constrain the Constitutional Convention in its work. During the course of the argument, Rawls' remarks on the justice of majority rule are discussed.

In the final two sections of the paper, I consider some of the justification Rawls offers on behalf of his theory, and I assess the adequacy of some of the criticisms leveled against him. With respect to the adequacy of his Principle of Equal Liberty for All, I think his errors tend to be errors in clarity and style rather than errors in substantive analysis. It is the task of this paper to provide some of the needed clarity and organization. After all, the adequacy of The Principle of Equal Liberty for All is of great interest to Americans. Rawls' account deserves nothing less than our earnest study.

DEFINITIONS

Rawls' commitment to equal liberty seems clear. His first principle of justice is

> Each person is to have an equal right to the most extensive total system of equal basic liberties compatible with a similar system of liberty for all. (302, all parenthetical citations are to John Rawls *A Theory of Justice*, (Cambridge, Mass.: Harvard University Press, 1971)).

But what are these basic liberties which compose the system and to which we have a right?

The basic liberties of citizens are, roughly speaking, political liberty (the right to vote and to be eligible for public office) together with freedom of speech and assembly; liberty of conscience and freedom of thought, freedom of the person along with the right to hold (personal) property; and freedom from arbitrary arrest and seizure as defined by the concept of the rule of law (61).

The student of the Constitution will be interested in comparing Rawls' list of basic liberties with the liberties protected by the Bill of Rights. Article I protects our freedom of religion, speech, the press, assembly, and our freedom to petition the redress of grievances. So long as political liberty is fairly broadly construed, Rawls' list includes the Article I liberties. Article IV which protects citizens from unreasonable seizures and searches is included by Rawls. Articles IV–VIII specify the conditions for arrest and trial and these liberties may be captured by Rawls' blanket term "freedom from arbitrary arrest." Rawls also includes items not specifically mentioned in the Bill of Rights—the political right to vote and to be eligible for public office. However, later amendments to the Constitution in conjunction with Congressional mandate have extended voting rights and the right to hold public office to all citizens.

Throughout the book, Rawls places considerable emphasis on freedom of the person. "Freedom of the person" is a fairly general term, however, and it is difficult to be sure what specific freedoms it includes. Rawls indicates that it includes the right to hold personal property. The Constitution does not put it quite the way Rawls does, but the Fifth Amendment does specify that no one shall be deprived of his property without due process of law and that "private property shall not be taken for public use without just compensation." The right to hold private property has been a central tenet in the American ethic and nearly an absolute right for those of libertarian persuasion. The Bill of Rights provides two other instances of freedom of the person—the right to bear arms (Article III) and the right to be free from quartering soldiers in your home—at least in time of peace (Article IV).

Later in this essay we will discuss just what liberties should and should not be included in the list of basic liberties. However, as a starting point, we can see that Rawls' list has many features in common with the list enumerated in the Bill of Rights.

It should be noted that in specifying his list, Rawls tries to avoid becoming embroiled in the debate as to whether or not there is a legitimate distinction between negative and positive liberty and whether or not the state should protect positive liberty. In other words, Rawls tries to avoid one of the emotionally charged debates between contemporary American conservatives and liberals. The traditional distinction runs like this: Negative liberty is freedom from the constraints imposed on a person by others; for example freedom from bodily harm, imprisonment, or the seizure of personal property. Positive liberty is much more inclusive since one has positive liberty when one is free from the impediments of oneself as well as free from the coercive force of others. Examples of positive freedom include freedom from neurosis, ignorance, poverty, and fear. One has negative freedom to see *Star Wars* if no one prevents it; one has positive freedom only if one has the price of admission as well. Provision for positive freedom by the state requires much more state power and control than provision for negative freedom alone. For that reason, conservatives think that the state should only attempt to secure negative liberty. Both parties to the dispute claim that they are concerned with real freedom, while the view of freedom held by their opponent is either narrow and truncated or dangerously broad. Rawls hopes to avoid the debate about what constitutes *real* freedom by following Gerald C. MacCallum's view that freedom is a triadic relation. By a triadic relation, MacCallum means that in discussing freedom one should ask first who is free, second what he or she is free from, and third what he or she is free to do or become. Rawls adopts the MacCallum framework.

> The general description of liberty, then, has the following form: this or that person (or persons) is free (or not free) from this or that constraint (or set of constraints) to do (or not to do) so and so (202).

What are the implications of this triadic account of freedom in ideological debates? The basic implication is that the two ideological accounts of freedom are oversimplified. Whenever legislators debate whether or not to increase taxes to pay for welfare programs, neither side can claim that it is the sole champion of freedom. Proponents of the welfare system can claim that they support the freedom *of the welfare recipients to additional income* so that *the constraints of poverty* might be removed. Opponents champion the freedom *of the taxpayers from government* to *spend their money* as they see fit. The triadic notion of freedom emphasizes *both* absence of constraints and the ability to achieve what one desires.

Since both the conservative emphasis (freedom from) and the so-called liberal emphasis (freedom to) are incorporated into the triadic definition, Rawls must amplify his definition of freedom if he is to avoid the conservative–liberal ideological dispute. After all, most policy disputes can be characterized as conflicts among claims to liberty. The loser in one of the policy disputes will then likely claim that his or her equal right to liberty has been violated. Rawls deals with this problem by drawing a distinction between the equal *right to* liberty and the *equal worth* of liberty. With respect to an equal right to liberty, liberty is the same for all. However, the worth of liberty (the means one has to achieve one's liberty) need not be equal. In other words, people can be hampered in the attainment of their goals or in the fulfillment of their desires by poverty and yet be equal to the wealthy with respect to liberty.

> Thus liberty and the worth of liberty are distinguished as follows: liberty is represented by the complete system of the liberties of equal citizenship, while the worth of liberty to persons and groups is proportional to their capacity to advance their ends within the framework the system defines. Freedom as equal liberty is the same for all; the question of compensating for a lesser than equal liberty does not arise. But the worth of liberty is not the same for everyone. Some have greater authority and wealth, and therefore greater means to achieve their aims. The lesser worth of liberty is, however, compensated for, since the capacity of the less fortunate members of society to achieve their aims would be even less were they not to accept the existing inequalities whenever the difference principle is satisfied (204).[1]

It might seem that critics on the left could argue that Rawls is satisfied with the equal freedom of the sick man and the poor man to sleep under the bridge. In other words, Rawls has sacrificed the liberty *to* condition for the liberty *from* condition. Rawls' response is that the second principle of justice limits inequalities in the *worth* of liberty to acceptable levels. The worth of liberty is subject to what Rawls calls the difference principle. The difference principle requires that all inequalities in the worth of liberty must work out to the advantage of the least well off. Rawls may think he avoids the liberal-conservative dispute by appealing to the triadic notion of freedom. However, Rawls really has a proposed answer to the dispute which uses his distinction between liberty and the worth of the liberty and the difference principle.

THE PRIORITY OF LIBERTY

One of the more controversial aspects of Rawls' theory of justice is that he gives The Principle of Equal Liberty for All priority over the second principle—The Maximin Principle or Principle of Democratic Equality as it is sometimes called. This principle states that "social and economic inequalities are to be arranged so that they are both

(a) to the greatest benefit of the least advantaged and (b) attached to offices and positions open to all under conditions of fair equality of opportunity" (43). This principle is a principle for the distribution of economic goods and for the positions of influence within society. What Rawls is claiming is that the equal right to liberty is morally more fundamental than the principle for dealing with inequalities in the distribution of economic goods and positions of influence. Rawls has a technical term for this priority relation; he refers to it as a lexical ordering. In a lexical ordering, the liberty principle must be completely satisfied before the second principle of justice (The Maximum Principle) is to be applied.

> This (a lexical ordering) is an order which requires us to satisfy the first principle in the ordering before we can move on to the second, the second before we consider the third, and so on. A principle does not come into play until those previous to it are either fully met or do not apply. (43, Parenthetical remark added by author.)

If the lexical ordering were followed completely, Rawls would not allow society to sacrifice any liberty in order to promote greater equality in the distribution of economic goods and services. Such an extreme conclusion seems to be in conflict with our basic notions as to what is morally appropriate. First, it is at least arguable that in economically deprived societies, some restrictions on liberty are necessary so that living standards can be raised. The general thrust of the argument is that the political and constitutional liberties characteristic of a society like our own would cut down on the efficiency through which a centralized government or an industrial elite could manipulate institutional structures to promote economic growth. In defense of temporarily suspending liberties for economic reasons, a number of political theorists argue that both the justification for political and constitutional liberties and the worth of those liberties increase as living standards rise.

Moreover, if the priority rule were strictly followed, one of Rawls' basic liberties, the liberty to hold personal property, would cause special problems. There is considerable debate concerning the extent of Rawls' commitment to a full blown capitalist theory of private property. It does seem clear that Rawls thinks either the public or private ownership of the means of production and distribution could be compatible with his two principles of justice. But there is another issue with respect to the holding of private personal property which is not at all clear. On traditional libertarian accounts, any nonvoluntary taxation for the sole purpose of redistributing wealth is an infringement on the personal property rights of the taxed individual. Rawls has no developed theory of these rights. If the libertarian account were followed, obviously the possibility for redistributing resources to promote egalitarian goals would be extremely limited. This limitation would exist in any society but its impact would be especially severe in poorer countries where basic needs are at stake. It is clear that Rawls cannot hold to a strict lexical ordering of the two principles and he doesn't.

Rawls hedges the priority ruling by recognizing that it can go into effect only when certain minimum standards of living have been achieved.

> ...the idea underlying this ordering is that if the parties assume that their basic liberties can be effectively exercised, they will not exchange a lesser liberty for an improvement in economic well-being. It is only when social conditions do not allow the effective establishment of these rights that one can concede their limitation, and these restrictions can be granted only to the extent that they are necessary to prepare the way for a free society. The denial of equal liberty can be defended only if it is necessary to raise the level of civilization so that in due course these freedoms can be enjoyed....(151, 152).
>
> The supposition is that if the persons in the original position assume that their basic liberties can be effectively exercised, they will not exchange a lesser liberty for an improvement in their economic well-being, at least not once a certain level of wealth has been attained. It is only when social conditions do not allow the effective establishment of these rights that one can acknowledge their restriction. The denial of equal liberty can be accepted only if it is necessary to enhance the quality of civilization so that in due course the equal freedoms can be enjoyed by all. The lexical ordering of the two principles is the long-run tendency of the general conception of justice consistently pursued under reasonably favorable conditions (542).

These concessions in the application of the priority rule are necessary if Rawls' theory is to remain plausible. Of course, one fundamental question remains to be answered. When has a society reached the sufficient standard of wealth? Nonetheless, Rawls' theory is significant in arguing that in a society like our own, justice will recognize that liberty is more valuable than increased economic well-being. Our political and constitutional liberties are more important than two cars in every garage. Rawls' point is one well worth making since in affluent societies like our own it does seem correct although frequently it is in danger of being forgotten.

CREATING THE SET OF BASIC LIBERTIES

Rawls' theory is fairly distinctive in arguing that the equal liberty principle is a commitment to a *system* of equal basic liberties. Let us look specifically at Rawls' statement of the principle.

> Each person is to have an equal right to the most extensive total system of equal basic liberties compatible with a similar system of liberty for all (302).

The commitment is a commitment to a total system. By putting the principle this way, Rawls has created horrendous problems of interpretation and application. The most obvious difficulty is that such a principle seems excessively general and totally ignores the weighing and balancing of the various liberties which must occur in order for an individual to have the most extensive total *system* of basic liberties. Equally obvious is the necessity for having a theory which limits each individual's liberty package so that all the individual liberty systems are compatible one with another. What Rawls needs is a theory which provides for the necessary legitimate restrictions on individual liberty in order that equal liberty for all can be a reality. After all, a just society is not a society where everyone can do as he or she pleases. Rather it is a society where everyone's right to do as he or she pleases is equal to everyone else's.

Rawls tackles this theoretical issue when he considers how the principle of equal liberty for all is to be actualized in the institutions of society. Rawls' means for achieving this is the constitutional convention. It is the job of the constitutional convention to apply the liberty principle to society's institutions, particularly in the writing of a constitution.

> Then I suppose that after the parties have adopted the principles of justice in the original position, they move to a constitutional convention. Here they are to decide upon the justice of political forms and choose a constitution:... they are to design a system for the constitutional powers of government and the basic rights of citizens....To do this the liberties of equal citizenship must be incorporated into and protected by the constitution....The first principle of equal liberty is the primary standard for the constitutional convention. Its main requirements are that the fundamental liberties of the person and liberty of conscience and freedom of thought be protected and that the political process as a whole be a just procedure (196, 197, 199).

One of the first problems that the constitutional convention must face is how to resolve conflicts among liberties. The slogan, "Your freedom to swing your fist ends in front of my nose," will not do.

How are the individual liberty packages adjusted so that everyone's is the equal of everyone else's?

> First of all, it is important to recognize that the basic liberties must be assessed as a whole, as one system...Clearly when the liberties are left unrestricted they collide with one another...Thus the delegates to a constitutional convention, or the members of the legislature, must decide how the various liberties are to be specified so as to yield the best total system of equal liberty. They have to balance one liberty against another. The best arrangement of the several liberties depends upon the totality of limitations to which they are subject, upon how they hang together in the whole scheme by which they are defined (203).

The role of the constitutional convention is very important in Rawls' theory since it is this device which determines the institutions and rules for balancing liberties. Indeed, the constitutional convention writes all the rules for society's implementation of the principle of equal liberty and it provides the regulations for the necessary restrictions on liberty. Since Rawls has developed a theory of imperfect procedural justice, one might think that whatever the constitutional convention decides is *ipso facto* just. This is not the case, however. The constitutional convention is bound by the principle of equal liberty for all. In this respect there is some analogy between Rawls' constitutional convention and the United States Supreme Court. Just as the Supreme Court is the final interpreter of the Constitution while at the same time being bound by the Constitution, so Rawls' constitutional convention interprets the liberty principle while at the same time being bound by it.

Moreover, Rawls does not leave the constitutional convention without some guidance. Unfortunately, the reader of *A Theory of Justice* isn't aware of this guidance until the discussion is well advanced. This guidance is provided by what Rawls calls *The Priority Rule.* Rawls' priority rule reads as follows:

> The principles of justice are to be ranked in lexical order and therefore liberty can be restricted only for the sake of liberty. There are two cases: (a) a less extensive liberty must strengthen the total system of liberty shared by all, and (b) a less than equal liberty must be acceptable to those citizens with the lesser liberty (250).

The first point in the priority rule is very important since it limits any balancing or restrictions to those required by liberty itself. Liberty cannot be sacrificed for or balanced against economic gain.

Rawls' approach can be illustrated by discussing freedom of speech. Unless there are rules governing freedom of speech, discussion and inquiry become impossible (203). The point that Rawls is making is that no individual liberty can be completely unrestricted and still be held equally by all members of society. If freedom of speech is to be equally available to all, there must be rules governing debate and inquiry. Such rules are legitimate restrictions on freedom of speech since they are designed to enhance liberty rather than to achieve economic or social gain, and they enhance liberty to the benefit of all.

In the interest of public order, the priority rule allows other restrictions on freedom of speech. Rawls agrees with Justice Oliver Wendell Holmes that no one has the right to yell "fire" in a crowded theatre. What Rawls must do is find a legitimate place for such restrictions within his theory without adopting the philosophy of utilitarianism. Utilitarianism argues that social institutions should be organized so as to promote the greatest good for the greatest number. With respect to free speech a utilitarian would argue that the rules governing free speech should be those which contribute to the greatest public good. Critics of utilitarianism, however, see a great danger in the utilitarian analysis for adopting rules. The interests of a minority could too easily be sacrificed for the happiness of the majority. For example, some critics argue that utilitarianism would sanction rules which stifle the the expression of unpopular opinions. As one of the chief critics of utilitarianism, Rawls must find a way to avoid sacrificing the interests of an individual on the altar of the public good. Rawls' task is not an easy one. Liberty clearly must be limited, yet it cannot be limited simply because it enhances the interests of the majority. Rawls has at least two strategies. First, liberty can be restricted only when the *liberty* of the majority is threatened. It cannot be restricted simply because the majority would be happy or would approve such restrictions. Secondly, the restrictions would have to be acceptable from the perspective of the original position. They would have to be acceptable to rationally self-interested persons behind the veil of ignorance. Rawls' remarks on liberty of conscience apply here.

> Liberty of conscience is limited, everyone agrees, by the common interest in public order and security....it now seems evident that, in limiting liberty by reference to the common interest in public order and security, the government acts on a principle that would be chosen in the original position. For in this position each recognizes that the disruption of these conditions is a danger for the liberty of all. This follows once the maintenance of public order is

> understood as a necessary condition for everyone's achieving his ends whatever they are.... Furthermore, liberty of conscience is to be limited only when there is a reasonable expectation that not doing so will damage the public order which the government should maintain. This expectation must be based on evidence and ways of reasoning acceptable to all (212, 213).

So far the restraints on freedom of speech can all be justified by the first part of the priority rule, namely, that liberty can only be restricted for the sake of liberty.

Let us now turn to the second part of the priority rule. Inequalities in liberty are justified if they work out to the advantage of the person who is least well off with respect to liberty. What Rawls does is apply the difference principle which is an essential feature of the second principle of justice to the principle of equal liberty itself. It should be noted that Rawls is speaking specifically about political liberty, but I believe his remarks can be generalized to cover the structure of the basic liberties themselves.

> An inequality in the basic structure must always be justified to those in the disadvantaged position. This holds whatever the primary social good and especially for liberty. Therefore, the priority rule requires us to show that the inequality of right would be accepted by the less favored in return for the greater protection of their other liberties that results from this restriction (231).

Suppose the total liberty packages of one group in society were less than all the other members of society: How could such a situation be just? It would be just only if the worse off accepted their disadvantaged position for the reason that any attempt to improve their position would make them even worse off.

The priority rule is not the only constraint placed on the constitutional convention. Given that basic liberties have to be restricted and balanced institutionally, it is important that all citizens have equal liberty to participate in these institutions. For these reasons, Rawls provides a special analysis of what he calls political liberties. He develops a special liberty principle to govern any restrictions which the constitutional convention must place on political liberty. The liberty principle Rawls calls upon is the principle of equal participation. This principle "requires that all citizens are to have an equal right to take part in, and to determine the outcome of, the constitutional process that establishes the laws with which they are to comply" (221).

Rawls then spends considerable time in spelling out the meaning, the extent, and the worth of the principle of participation. With respect to meaning, Rawls is committed to what in common parlance is called one man-one vote. "Starting with the question of meaning, the precept of one elector-one vote implies, when strictly adhered to, that each vote has approximately the same weight in determining the outcome of elections" (223). With respect to extent, Rawls is committed to the principle of majority rule. With respect to worth, Rawls argues that the worth of this particular liberty should be kept fair. The careful reader will note that this involves a shift in Rawls' position. With respect to equal basic liberties, Rawls is *not* committed to preserving approximate equal worth. With respect to the principle of equal participation, however, Rawls argues for moving more in that direction. Rawls' actual language contradicts his earlier position:

> Compensating steps must, then, be taken to preserve the fair value for all of the equal political liberties....For example, in a society allowing private ownership of the means of production, property and wealth must be kept widely distributed and government monies provided on a regular basis to encourage free public discussion (225).
>
> Historically, one of the main defects of constitutional government has been the failure to insure the fair value of political liberty (226). Public resources have not been devoted to maintaining the institutions required for the fair value of political liberty (226).

This long chain of quotations seems to lead us to the following hierarchy concerning The Principle of Equal Liberty for All. At the apex of the hierarchy is The Principle of Equal Liberty which serves as one of the two basic principles of *A Theory of Justice.* This abstract principle must be applied, and conflicts among the basic liberties must be resolved. Now it is the job of the constitutional convention and the resulting constitution to achieve these goals. However, the constitutional convention is not logically prior to The Equal Liberty Principle. Even though the convention applies the principle and resolves conflicts among the basic liberties, it is still bound by the principle. With respect to political liberty, this binding constraint is provided by the principle of equal participation—a principle which Rawls must believe is either derivable from or simply synonymous with The Principle of Equal Liberty itself. The principle of equal participation may serve as a restatement of The Principle of Equal Liberty for All just as the second formulation of Kant's categorical imperative served as restatement of the first formulation.

However, constraints and limitations on the principle of equal participation are in order. By considering Rawls' discussion of these constraints, the priority rule can be further explained. The reader may recall that Rawls believes that the principle of equal participation has its proper extent when decisions are made on the basis of majority rule. However, certain limitations on the principle of majority rule are necessary. These limitations create inequalities in the extent of liberty. How can such inequalities be justified?

At this point, Rawls is coming to grips with one of the key problems in political theory. To what extent is a democracy based upon majority rule a just form of government? If majority rule never infringed on other liberties, majority rule would be just since it embodies the equality of extent of the equal participation principle. However, Rawls is acutely aware of the fact that in the world of practical affairs, the principle of majority rule does infringe upon other liberties and Rawls believes these liberties should be protected. To illustrate this point, consider The Bill of Rights. It protects many of what Rawls calls basic liberties, e.g., freedom of speech, freedom of assembly, and freedom from arbitrary arrest and seizure. Now the point of The Bill of Rights is to protect these basic liberties from being eroded by majority rule. Congress cannot legitimately pass a law abrogating an individual's or group's right to peaceably assemble. It was the judgment of the Founding Fathers that some individual liberties are so fundamental that they are placed beyond the ordinary process of democratic decision making; Rawls concurs in that judgment.

Rawls discusses various ways for limiting the principle of majority rule. Some of the restrictive devices present in our own Constitution which Rawls thinks are justified include a bicameral legislature, separation of powers mixed with checks and balances, and a bill of rights with judicial review. Rawls also believes that it is possible to justify, in theory at least, an element not found in our form of government—specifically John Stuart Mill's device of plural voting which gives extra votes to those with greater intelligence and education.

Rawls is consistent in his defense. He accepts the position that majority rule is sometimes hostile to our basic liberties. Any restraints on majority rule must be introduced only on the basis of protecting these more basic liberties. The restraints can never be introduced on the basis of economic or social benefits. Devices like a bill of rights with judicial review, a bicameral legislature, and other arrangements which protect separation of powers are justified because they strengthen the total system of liberty shared by all.

Perhaps the following quotation from Rawls might serve as a fitting summary of his views.

> ...we should narrow or widen its extent [principle of participation] up to the point where the danger to liberty from the marginal loss in control over those holding political power just balances the security of liberty gained by the

greater use of constitutional devices. The decision is not an all or nothing affair (230).

As our discussion has developed, it is clear that Rawls' theory of liberty is extremely complex. At the apex of the system we have the principle of equal liberty for all. When Rawls speaks of two persons being equal with respect to liberty, he means that their systems of basic liberties are equal. What does the total system of equal basic liberties consist of? The simple, and most obvious answer is that the system consists of only the basic liberties and that one basic liberty is as important as any other. In other words, all basic liberties are on a par.

Unfortunately, this view is not the one adopted by Rawls. It seems that some of the limitations Rawls places on the principle of equal participation are not to be placed on the other basic liberties.

> In many historical situations a lesser political liberty may have been justified ....These constraints do not justify the loss of liberty of conscience and the rights defining the integrity of the person. The case for certain political liberties and the rights of fair equality of opportunity is less compelling. As I noted before (§ 11), it may be reasonable to forgo part of these freedoms when the long-run benefits are great enough to transform a less fortunate society into one where the equal liberties can be fully enjoyed (247).

From this one can reasonably conclude that political liberties as embodied in the principle of equal participation are not on a par with such basic civil liberties as freedom of speech or freedom of conscience. Indeed Rawls says,

> ...it [priority of liberty] allows...that some liberties, say those covered by the principle of participation are less essential in that their main role is to protect the remaining freedoms (230).

We are now in position for a final summary of Rawls' hierarchical view of liberty. If the supreme Principle of Equal Liberty for All is to be more than an empty slogan, the institutions of society must embody it. Not only must they embody it, but at least some institutions must provide a means for ending the conflicts among individual liberty systems, and for introducing the restrictions on freedom which are necessary if the most extensive liberty for all is to result. This task falls to the constitutional convention which takes as its operating principle the priority rule. Since a constitutional convention is required and continued political institutions are necessary, the protection of equal political liberties, embodied in the principle of equal participation, must be ensured. However, additional restrictions justified by the priority rule will be placed on the political liberties. The Principle of Equal Liberty puts a number of constraints on what the constitutional convention can do with respect to either settling conflicts among liberties or in restricting liberty. Everything must be done in the name of liberty itself. More specific instructions to the constitutional convention are provided by the priority rule. Beyond this point, however, imperfect procedural justice takes over. Once the constraints provided by the priority rule and the principle of equal participation are in place, whatever the constitutional convention and the political institutions which are established decide with respect to implementing The Principle of Equal Liberty for All is just. Of course, these results will not be perfect, but it is the best we can do. There may be further constraints on the constitutional convention, but in the absence of further specifications, my remarks seem within the spirit of Rawls' views on imperfect procedural justice.

JUSTIFICATION

Any sound philosophical principle must be adequately justified. Justification of The Principle of Equal Liberty for All is no small matter since there are at least three components that require justification. Rawls must justify his commitment to the value of liberty, his commitment to the priority of liberty, and his commitment to the equal distribution of liberty.

Why should liberty be valued at all? Rawls' answer here is that liberty is a primary good. Primary goods are goods that all rational beings are presumed to want because these goods are the prerequisites for the fulfillment of any life plan whatsoever. Since Rawls seems on strong grounds here, let us turn to a more controversial area, the priority of liberty.

As we noted, the priority of liberty is not absolute. In very impoverished societies the ordering does not hold. However, even when this concession to extreme poverty is taken into account, Rawls' commitment to the supreme value of liberty is very strong. For example, Rawls says,

> Moreover, the initial agreement on the principle of equal liberty is final. An individual recognizing religious and moral obligations regards them as binding absolutely in the sense that he cannot qualify his fulfillment of them for the

> sake of greater means for promoting his other interests. Greater economic and social benefits are not a sufficient reason for accepting less than an equal liberty (207).

But why not?

A possible answer occurs late in the book when Rawls discusses the priority of liberty. In making his defense he appeals to the central place that the primary good of self-respect has in his system. The high value we place on liberty is a result of the high value placed on the primary good of self-respect.

Rawls indicates that self-respect has two aspects. "...it includes a person's sense of his own value, his secure conviction that his conception of his good, his plan of life is worth carrying out. And second, self-respect implies a confidence in one's ability, so far as it is within one's power, to fulfill one's intention" (440).

I do not believe it is stretching the intent of Rawls to argue that he could justify his commitment to liberty as follows. Liberty is a necessary condition, a prerequisite if you will, for the primary good of self respect. Without liberty, one could not have a sense of one's own value or the confidence in one's ability to fulfill one's intentions. Self-respect may be at the top of the ladder of primary goods but liberty is clearly a necessary rung in achieving self-respect. I cannot cite passages in the text where Rawls explicitly holds this view, but I believe the argument presented here is consistent with the tenor of his remarks and does provide some rationale for his very heavy commitment to the priority of liberty.

Finally, we consider Rawls' arguments on behalf of the equal distribution of liberty. Rawls' strategy is to use the device of the original condition constrained by the principle of ignorance as the chief means for justifying the equal distribution of liberty. Rawls selects one of the basic liberties, the liberty of conscience, and then shows that in the original condition the parties to the contract would adopt the principle of equal distribution. Having made the case for this particular liberty, he contends that his argument can be generalized to cover all the basic liberties.

Rawls argues as follows: In the original condition, we are, of course, ignorant as to what our moral and religious convictions are and as to whether or not our convictions will be those of the majority or those of the minority. Given this, Rawls argues that only the principle of equal liberty of conscience makes sense. One does not want to take the chance that one will be in the minority and have his or her religious views suppressed. Would one gamble that his convictions would be in the majority? Rawls answers with an emphatic no. He says,

> ...to gamble in this way would show that one did not take one's religious or moral convictions seriously, or highly value the liberty to examine one's beliefs (207).

Similarly individuals would not consent to the principle of utility because this would subject one's conscience to the calculus of social interests. The influence of earlier political theorists on Rawls is quite clear. Liberty is so fundamental that we don't play games with it. We don't gamble with it and we don't submit it to the process of bargaining in the pursuit of the common good.

Another argument on behalf of the equal distribution of liberty rests on the contribution an equal distribution makes to a stable well-ordered society. For purposes of this argument we must assume Rawls is correct when he argues that justice requires that The Principle of Equal Liberty has priority over The Maximin Distribution Principle. In a society where that priority ordering prevails, it is The Equal Liberty Principle which acts as a stabilizing support for society.

> The basis for self-esteem in a just society is not then one's income share but the publicly affirmed distribution of fundamental rights and liberties. And this distribution being equal, everyone has a similar and secure status when they meet to conduct the common affairs of the wider society (544).
>
> When it is the position of equal citizenship that answers to the need for status, the precedence of the equal liberties becomes all the more necessary. Having chosen a conception of justice that seeks to eliminate the significance of relative economic and social advantages as supports for men's self-confidence, it is essential that the priority of liberty be firmly maintained (545).

Moreover, Rawls argues that it is *irrational* to try to distribute material goods equally. Rawls can make this strong claim on the basis that one would always prefer $100 for himself and $125 for another if the alternative were $90 for both himself and the other. Whether or not Rawls is right on this strong claim, if the priority argument is accepted, the equal distribution of liberty would be supportive of the stability of society.

There is no one specific section of *A Theory of Justice* devoted to matters of justification since the justification for particular principles or concepts is not independent. The entire book illustrates Rawls' reflective equilibrium method of justification. Rawls explains justification through reflective equilibrium as follows: he argues that ethical principles (including the ethical principles of political philosophy) must not contradict the basic moral intuitions of men and women. However, moral philosophy cannot rest on intuitionism. Individual decisions must be made on the basis of an appropriate theory. We then test the results of the theory to see how it squares with the basic intuitions. This constant interaction between theory and basic intuitions should yield a point of reflective equilibrium where both are in harmony. Hence a total justification of The Principle of Equal Liberty for All would require that we see how well all its parts cohere both with our basic intuitions about liberty and with the theory of justice as a whole. Obviously, much more could be said on behalf of Rawls' justification of The Principle of Equal Liberty for All. However, such a discussion would inevitably involve a discussion of the whole book. Perhaps these brief isolated remarks will convey some of Rawls' rationale for The Principle of Equal Liberty for All.

CRITICAL ASSESSMENT

Like so many of the other topics considered in *A Theory of Justice*, Rawls' discussion of liberty is a complex, sophisticated masterpiece of philosophical analysis. Moreover, his discussion on the context of the total theory provides a philosophical justification for many of the institutional structures within the United States designed to promote equal liberty for all. His discussion also humbles us by making us realize that our society has not achieved equal liberty for all.

Given the magnitude of his task and achievement, a critic of Rawls is analogous to a drama critic taking shots at Shakespeare. Nonetheless, although Rawls' discussion of liberty is first-rate, it is clearly not the last word. The critical comments that follow rest on two underlying themes: (1) that Rawls' discussion of liberty is seriously incomplete and (2) that Rawls' discussion of liberty is sufficiently disorganized so that confusion and perhaps even inconsistency inevitably result. For the convenience of the reader, my critical remarks will follow the structural outline of my explanatory comments in the first four sections of this paper.

The first problem focuses on the list of basic liberties. There seems to be no theoretical basis for inclusion and exclusion. For example, Rawls has not included the freedom to select one's own life style among the basic liberties. There is no reference concerning the freedom to use drugs or to select one's own sexual partner! On what basis are these exclusions made? As another critic has succinctly indicated, "Which liberties are basic and why?"[2]

There are also some problems resulting from Rawls' distinction between liberty and the worth of liberty. By insisting that liberty must be equal but the worth of liberty may be very unequal, Rawls sounds like a Harvard Milton Friedman. This impression is corrected when at a later point in the book one realizes that any inequalities in the worth of liberty are subject to the difference principle. However, confusion does set in when Rawls argues that inequalities in the worth of the liberty of equal participation are to be compensated for.[3] In these discussions, The Difference Principle is not mentioned at all. It seems that if Rawls' account is to be both persuasive and consistent, Rawls must say that all inequalities in the worth of liberty are subject to The Difference Principle and, once having said that, all references to compensation should be dropped.

Another problem is presented once Rawls hedges the lexical ordering of the two principles of justice. To salvage plausibility, Rawls must hedge; he cannot say liberty has lexical priority. But now the theory has considerable indeterminacy. What is needed are some guidelines which will tell us when the lexical ordering should be given up. The necessity for guidelines will be even more evident once it is realized that tradeoffs between economic betterment and liberty are desired not only in so-called underdeveloped countries but even in the most affluent countries. Economic betterment is more highly valued than Rawls thinks. Even the most casual observer of the United States cannot help but be impressed by the apparent dominance of pocketbook issues over issues of liberty. It seems that the long-run tendency of society to develop to the point where the lexical ordering will prevail is very long indeed. Of course, Rawls can appropriately argue that current societal values do not reflect the value decisions that would be made by persons operating in the original condition under a veil of ignorance. Even so, Rawls has not shown how persons in the original condition would define such vague phrases as "due course" and "a certain level of wealth." Until this is done we cannot be certain that a hedged lexical ordering would be acceptable from the perspective of the original condition.

The most serious problems, however, focus on Rawls' attempt to apply The Principle of Equal Liberty for All. Many commentators focus on the excessive vagueness and generality of the principle itself. Joel Feinberg says,

> Rawls' discussion of liberty is thorough and sophisticated but it seems to this reviewer to suffer from a somewhat vacuous formalism. First of all, the formulation of the principle itself suggests that a large number of different systems of rules...could in principle satisfy it.[4]

Feinberg then goes on to argue that Rawls does not pay sufficient attention to the fact that the basic liberties conflict with each other. He thinks that Rawls' statement that liberties can only be restricted on the basis of liberty is not very helpful in resolving conflicts among liberties. Feinberg's view is echoed by Schaefer. "How can the liberties to do different things be measured, added, and weighed against one another, in the absence of any standard except liberty itself?"[5]

Now I do think Rawls has done more in providing content to The Principle of Equal Liberty for All than his critics realize. The constitutional convention is designed to resolve the ambiguities and conflicts which his critics focus on. However, Rawls' discussion of the constitutional convention as a device for settling these issues is especially tortured and disorganized. The important priority rule is not introduced until the end of the discussion. Moreover, the wording of the priority rule makes it apply best to the principle of equal participation. Notice the specific reference to "extent"—a word which is only precisely defined in the discussion of equal participation. However, the political liberties embodied in the principle of equal participation are of a lower order than civil liberties. How does the priority rule apply to civil liberties?

Moreover, the critics are right in arguing that Rawls does not indicate how the constitutional convention is to deal with conflicts among basic civil liberties. That clearly is one of the jobs of the constitutional convention (196-97, 199). But rather than discuss conflicts among the basic liberties, Rawls discusses restraints on liberty required by the maintenance of the public order and constraints on the principle of equal participation. What all this has to do with conflicts among basic liberties is not clear.

This apparent confusion and inconsistency may have a common source. I think that many of the problems Rawls has with his discussion of equal liberty for all parallel other difficulties in *A Theory of Justice.* Over the course of the time Rawls spent in writing the book, his views on several of the key concepts matured and his discussion became more sophisticated and complex. The reader will discover, for example, that Rawls' account of rationality at the end of *A Theory of Justice* differs markedly from the very simple economic view of reason as the most efficient means to a given end which Rawls featured in the first part of the book. Rawls did not go back and "correct" his earlier view. The interpretation of The Principle of Equal Liberty for All led Rawls into a number of discussions including general restraints on liberty such as the laws governing debates and restraints on particular features of societal institutions designed to enhance and protect liberty. Early in the text the basic liberties were civil liberties (Bill of Rights). However, to implement these civil liberties, political institutions were required and as a result a whole new category of liberties was created, political liberties. The political liberties were to be equal, but at the same time they were to be subject to constraints. This required a special principle, the principle of equal participation. But restraints on the principle of equal participation required another principle—the so-called priority rule. At this point, Rawls saw that the priority rule could be used to cover the entire discussion. However, Rawls simply incorporated the development of his thought into the book without rewriting the discussion so that the hierarchy of the liberty principle would be clear and the logic of his discussion would be obvious. In writing the first part of this paper, I have tried to impose as much order as I could, while at the same time being faithful to the text. However, the remaining gaps leave Rawls open to the criticisms enumerated above.

It seems to me that later in the book Rawls places less reliance on imperfect procedural justice. The early portions of the book were more compatible with libertarian philosophy. However, once he focused on the problems of insuring that everyone's system of basic liberties was equal and that all inequalities worked to the advantage of the least well-off, then the number of principles grew and the relations among the principles became both more complex and more indeterminate. Perhaps the only way to settle some of the ambiguities and indeterminicies discussed here is to place more reliance on majority rule.[6]

The final item for discussion is Rawls' account of justification. This item causes particular difficulty since the justification for particular principles or concepts is not independent. Rawls begins with certain intuitions about liberty and its value. He then builds a theory for achieving liberty in a just society and finally he tests the results of his theory against the basic intuitions with which he began. As a result, some points of his theory changed—the lexical ordering, for example. Also at some points his intuitions became less clear—that all primary goods were on a par, for example. I also believe that Rawls began with the view that a liberal democratic state is fundamentally the most just state. As a result of his theorizing about justice, he suggested moral constraints which must be placed on a liberal democratic state if justice were to be achieved. *A Theory of Justice* would have been both shorter and clearer if it had contained the final results of Rawls' attempt to achieve a reflective equilibrium on these matters. It also would have been far less rich and revealing. It is the task of commentators, like those in this volume, to tie up loose ends and to make some of the items which are implicit, explicit. For the true flavor of this philosophical masterpiece, the reader is urged to also sample the real thing.

NOTES

1. Critics who make this point include H.L.A. Hart, "Rawls on Liberty and Its Priority," *University of Chicago Law Review* 40 (1973): 534-55 and Robert F. Ladenson, "Rawls' Principle of Equal Liberty" (unpublished paper).
2. David Lewis Schaefer, "A Critique of Rawls' Contract Doctrine," *The Review of Metaphysics* Vol. XXVIII (1974) 97.
3. See p. *12*
4. Joel Feinberg, "Justice, Fairness, and Rationality," *Yale Law Review*, 81 (1972) 1022.
5. Schaefer, *op. cit.*, p. 98.
6. See the discussion in Norman E. Bowie and Robert L. Simon, *The Individual and the political Order*, (Englewood Cliffs, N.Y.: Prentice Hall, 1977).

*Distributive Justice and the Difference Principle**

Tom L. Beauchamp
GEORGETOWN UNIVERSITY
AND KENNEDY INSTITUTE

The terms "justice" and "distributive justice" are used in widely differing ways in contemporary moral philosophy. It would be quite wrong to interpret Rawls' conception of justice through certain commonly accepted understandings of these terms.[1] Accordingly, I begin with a brief analysis of these terms in order to show how Rawls' views differ from those of other writers, both regarding the *implication* of these terms and, more especially, regarding the role of a *theory* of justice. I here briefly treat the difference principle as a distributional principle in Rawls' philosophy. Later both this principle and the notion of "least advantaged persons" are treated in detail.

In an essay largely devoted to Rawls' theory, Hugo Bedau correctly comments that the question "What is a theory of social justice about?" is seldom addressed.[2] As both Bedau and Robert Nozick have recognized, failure to appreciate the objective of principles of justice in Rawls' theory can lead to basic misunderstandings. I concentrate throughout on this question, with special emphasis on what Rawls refers to as "the basic structure of society." He insists that the basic structure is the primary subject of a theory of justice, and this focus

*I am indebted to Arnold Davidson for many suggestions regarding the structure and content of this paper. I am also indebted to Norman Daniels, Norman Bowie, and Louis Katzner for numerous helpful criticisms and positive suggestions.

of his theory most prominently distinguishes his views from other accounts of justice.[3] On the whole I defend Rawls against his critics; my argument is not intended as a critical appraisal of his views. This critical silence should not be construed as a tacit acknowledgment that Rawls is correct on all, or even most substantive issues in the philosophy of justice. On the other hand, I do hold that Rawls has presented a more complex and powerful theory than his critics seem generally to have appreciated.

THE CONCEPT OF JUSTICE AND THE DIFFERENCE PRINCIPLE

Notoriously, Rawls argues that the notion of justice is most closely linked to that of fairness. While there undeniably are close connections between these terms, perhaps the single word most closely linked to the general meaning of "justice" in recent moral philosophy is "desert." According to many writings on justice, one has acted justly towards a person when that person has been given what he is due or owed, and therefore has been given what he deserves or can legitimately claim.[4] If a person deserves to be awarded a law degree, for example, justice has been done when that person receives the degree. What persons deserve or can legitimately claim is said to be based on certain morally relevant properties they possess, such as being productive or being in need. It is said to be wrong, as a matter of justice, to burden or to reward someone if the person does *not* possess the relevant property.

The more restricted expression "distributive justice" refers in this tradition to the proper distribution or allocation of social benefits and burdens. Paying taxes and serving on juries are distributed burdens, while welfare checks and research grants are distributed benefits. This literature on distributive justice has tended to focus on considerations of fair *economic* distribution, especially unjust distributions in the form of inequalities of income between different classes of persons and unfair tax burdens on certain classes. In his development of the difference principle, Rawls too is concerned with economic inequalities and distributions, but he does not conceive desert and allocation as the primary subject of a theory of justice in the way most recent theories have. Let us now see why.

In the current literature on justice, several adjectives are commonly used to modify "justice." Writers tend to speak indiscriminately of social justice, distributive justice, and individual justice, as if the meaning of such terms were unambiguous. It seems to be assumed that distributive justice and social justice are synonymous expressions; and Rawls himself seems at times to treat them synonymously [cf. 87; all parenthetical citations are to John Rawls, *A Theory of Justice* (Cambridge, Mass.: 1971).] But, unlike Rawls, other writers tend to conclude that the basic problem of justice is the allocation of social benefits and burdens according to one or more allocational principles of justice. These principles function to divide given collections of benefits and burdens to known individuals, when there is such a collection to be divided. They are to be parcelled out according to needs, contributions, etc. This conception of distributive justice conforms well with what Rawls calls *allocative* justice (88). This accounting is not an accurate characterization of his own approach, which he describes as a conception of *social* justice. It is critical that allocative and social justice be distinguished as different types of theories of distributive justice.

Allocative Justice

Theories of allocative justice are based on so-called material principles of justice—"material" because they give content to a principle above and beyond the formal principle of justice (equals must be treated equally). Each material principle of justice identifies a relevant property on the basis of which burdens and benefits should be distributed. What makes each principle a plausible candidate is the plausible relevance of the property it isolates. The following is a fairly standard list of the major candidates for the position of valid principles of distributive justice in the allocative sense (though different and longer lists have been proposed[5]): to each person an equal share; to each person according to individual need; to each person according to individual effort; to each person according to societal contribution; and to each person according to merit. There is no obvious barrier to acceptance of more than one of these principles, and some theories of justice accept all five as valid. Most societies use several of them, applying different principles of distribution in different contexts. In the United States, for example, unemployment and welfare payments are distributed on the basis of need (and to some extent on the basis of previous length of employment); jobs and promotions are in many sectors awarded (distributed) on the basis of demonstrated achievement and merit; the higher incomes of wealthy professionals are allowed (distributed) on the grounds of superior effort or merit or social contribution (or perhaps all three); and, at least theoretically, the opportunity for elementary and secondary education is distributed equally to all citizens.

In contemporary writings on justice it is said that *theories* of distributive justice are developed by systematically elaborating one or more of the material principles of distributive justice, perhaps in conjunction with other moral principles: *Egalitarian* theories emphasize equal access to or equal distribution of goods and services; *Socialist* theories emphasize need; *Libertarian* theories emphasize contribution and merit in a free market arrangement; and *Utilitarian* theories emphasize a mixed use of such criteria so that public and private utility are maximized. Of course some socialist theories emphasize production (as does Rawls), while deemphasizing allocation, and libertarians are largely concerned with entitlements deriving from just acquisition and free exchange. Setting pure forms of the latter theories aside, the acceptability of an allocative theory of justice is generally thought to be determined by the acceptability of its moral argument to the conclusion that some one or more selected material principles ought to be given priority (or perhaps even exclusive consideration) over the others.

Social Justice

Although Rawls says that his principles "define the appropriate distribution of the benefits and burdens of social cooperation" (4), the allocative conception is not his primary subject: "The conception of the two principles does not interpret the primary problem of distributive justice as one of allocative justice" (88). Though commentators such as Robert Paul Wolff seem to overlook the point[6], Rawls is not so much concerned with the actual burdens and benefits to be distributed to identifiable individuals with known values and preferences as he is with the cooperative institutional arrangements that produce the benefits and create the burdens that are to be distributed. His principles of justice do not, for example, mention properties possessed by individuals on the basis of which that person's share of social resources is determined. Nor do the principles determine how wealth or other primary goods are to be distributed directly to individuals. Rawls is thus not concerned with principles of allocation in the traditional way (through material principles), for his concern with allocation derives exclusively from the implications the basic structure has for allocation.

Because Rawls sees society as a cooperative venture for mutual advantage, where individuals' entitlements are determinable only within the cooperative scheme, he is interested in the justice of productive social institutions. The benefits deriving from individual contributions he sees as a common product on which everyone has an equal claim. Without productive institutions there could be nothing to distribute, and the social structure defining their cooperative arrangement plainly can itself be either just or unjust. Rawls' problem, especially in the sections on the difference principle, is that of formulating principles of justice that will govern the social structure, since this structure will "regulate the distribution of social and economic advantages" (61). He argues, moreover, that "a distribution *cannot* be judged in isolation from the system of which it is the outcome" (88). Let us call this form of justice, so typically Rawlsian, *social* justice. This usage follows Rawls' own description of his "topic" as "that of social justice" (7), his principles as "principles of social justice" (4), and his "conception" as one of "social justice" (9).

We can sum up the discussion thus far as follows: The generic term "distributive justice" includes both allocative justice and social justice. Whereas most writers on distributive justice have concentrated on allocative principles, an allocative theory of justice is emphatically not Rawls' enterprise, even though there are allocative implications of his theory of social justice as embedded in the basic structure of society.

The Difference Principle As a Principle of Justice

Rawls' *principles* of justice are rooted in the intuitive conviction that all social primary goods, including liberty, income, and opportunity, should be distributed equally, except when an *unequal* distribution of these goods would work to everyone's advantage. The so-called difference principle governs permissible inequality of distribution. The difference principle says that social and economic inequalities are to be permitted only if they are arranged to the greatest benefit of the least advantaged members of society (302f). This principle expresses Rawls' conviction that the justice of the basic structure is to be gauged by its tendency to counteract the inequalities caused purely by luck of birth (family and class origins), natural endowment, and historical circumstance (accidents over the course of a lifetime). This conviction helps explain why Rawls refers to his conception of justice as egalitarian (100). He means that his theory requires society to reduce certain inequalities by pooling advantageous resources for the benefit of everyone, and in particular the least advantaged. He even points out that "the first problem of justice" is to delineate principles of justice that can regulate inequalities and can be used to rearrange the long-lasting effects of social, natural, and historical contingencies. The difference principle rests on the view that because inequalities of birth, historical circumstance, and natural endowment are undeserved, society should reduce inequalities by selecting its naturally disadvantaged members and redressing their unequal situation. "The idea," says Rawls, "is to redress the bias of contingencies in the direction of equality" (100f).

His intention, however, is to formulate the difference principle neither as a principle of redress nor as a principle of equal outcome where all players in the game participate and wind up on equal terms. The point, rather, is to establish *processes* for the distribution of social resources so that the reasonable long-term expectations of the least advantaged are improved. Rawls' problem is thus to find a principle (II.a) to govern the distribution of certain primary goods, especially of wealth and income. His other principles of equal basic liberty (I) and fair equality of opportunity (II.b) act as constraints on the difference principle (though the liberty principle is more than a mere constraint because of Rawls' lexical ordering of principles).

After several tentative formulations of the difference principle (II.a) in *A Theory of Justice*, Rawls states the difference principle in its final formulation as follows: "Social and economic inequalities are to be arranged so that they are...to the greatest benefit of the least advantaged, consistent with the just savings principle..." (302). We shall later examine this principle in detail.

THE BASIC STRUCTURE AS THE PRIMARY SUBJECT OF JUSTICE

First, however, we must ask what "the basic structure of society" is, if it is not some set of allocative rules or precepts. Rawls writes as follows in *A Theory of Justice* (7):

> For us the primary subject of justice is the basic structure of society, or more exactly, the way in which the major social institutions distribute fundamental

> rights and duties and determine the division of advantages from social cooperation. By major institutions I understand the political constitution and the principal economic and social arrangements. Thus the legal protection of freedom of thought and liberty of conscience, competitive markets, private property in the means of production, and the monogamous family are examples of major social institutions. Taken together as one scheme, the major institutions define men's rights and duties and influence their life prospects....

Despite Rawls' repeated emphasis on institutions, he is definite in *A Theory of Justice* that "the basic structure is a public system of rules" (84), a description that most plausibly means that certain sets of rules governing the basic institutions describe and individuate the basic structure. Or perhaps institutions just are public systems of rules (55). In his later article, "The Basic Structure as Subject," Rawls attempts to explicate more carefully what he means by the "basic structure." There he argues that the basic structure is the "all-inclusive social system that determines background justice."[7] But what is meant by an "all-inclusive system" and "background justice"?

The All-inclusive System and Background Justice

The basic structure in the sense of an all-inclusive system includes the set of rules governing legal institutions such as the supreme court, the set of rules establishing permissible marital and familial relationships (e.g., rules requiring monogamous families), rules establishing permissible property relationships, and rules establishing permissible social and economic inequalities. Rawls sees these structural components comprising the all-inclusive social system as central to a theory of justice for two reasons: First, he argues that the rules have pervasive influence over what he refers to as natural, social, and historical contingencies. His view is that abilities, talents, expectations, beliefs, opportunities, etc. are all heavily influenced by the form a given society takes. The form of society determines not only the actual desires, wants, and aspirations of persons, but also their future desires, wants, etc.—including the kind of persons they will become as well as the kind of persons they are. If one alters the form, then one expects different kinds of persons and different social outcomes.

Second, there is a primary social need for procedural rules that regulate the social system over time in order to avoid injustice. What at one time was a free and fair agreement reached by responsible moral agents may over a period of time become so influenced by subsequent agreements and new developments that it is no longer possible for parties under the new conditions to enter into free and fair agreements. A structure does not remain just over time simply because it was at an earlier time free and fair. For this reason Rawls emphasizes that periodic regulation and correction of the basic structure consistent with general social order is essential if we are to protect against injustice. The role of the principles of justice that he develops is to make it possible to regulate and correct the system by the use of (ideal) standards external to the (nonideal) system itself.

> We recognize this principle when we say that the distribution resulting from voluntary market transactions will not in general be fair unless the antecedent distribution of income and wealth and the structure of the market is fair. Thus we seem forced to start with an account of a just basic structure. It's as if the most important agreement is that which establishes the principles to govern this structure.[8]

A theory of justice and its principles, as we shall see, govern the basic structure but are not part of the basic structure.

Although Rawls speaks of public rules as the components of the basic structure, he is not engaged in the trivial enterprise of calling our attention to the social importance of public rules. He is arguing that political constitutions and other rules can become accepted as parts of the basic structure and nonetheless lead to unjust outcomes. Unfortunately, as Bedau has noted, Rawls is never very clear as to the criteria determining whether institutions or rules are *basic* or whether these criteria are relative to other social arrangements. Certainly one might doubt whether the monogamous family is basic, or at least one would want to know why it rather than such institutions as children's games or religious institutions is basic. Rawls does describe an entire institutional arrangement, including a market economy and branches of government, that he believes necessary to insure background justice. However, only if the procedures and agreements in a given institutional framework are controlled and regulated by principles external to the basic structure itself—viz. the principles of justice—can problems of injustice be avoided. "These principles," Rawls argues, "must embody an ideal form for the basic structure in the light of which ongoing institutional processes are to be constrained and the accumulated results of individual transactions continually modified."[9]

The Ideal Form

The notion of an "ideal form" plays a more significant role in Rawls' writings than his commentators have generally noticed.[10] In *A Theory of Justice* he argues (1) that an ideal is fundamental because it determines how nonideal schemes are to be established and (2) that the institutions required by the principles of justice "define an ideal structure" (8f, 241, 261). This "perfectly just basic structure" constitutes a standard such that "institutions are to be judged in the light of this conception and held to be unjust to the extent that they depart from it without specific reason" (245f). In "The Basic Structure as Subject," Rawls argues that an ideal is required in order to protect against injustices that might result if the system were allowed to operate through pure procedural justice alone. The following is one of the most important passages in Rawls' philosophy:

> [The two] principles specify an ideal form for the basic structure in the light of which pure procedural processes are to be constrained and corrected....We need such an ideal to guide the corrections necessary to preserve background justice. As we have seen, even if everyone acts fairly as defined by rules that it is both reasonable and practicable to impose on individuals, the upshot of many separate transactions will undermine background justice. This is obvious once we view society, as we must, as involving cooperation over generations. Thus even in a well-ordered society, adjustments in the basic structure are always necessary. What we have, in effect, is an institutional division of labor between the basic structure and rules applying directly to particular transactions. Individuals and associations are left free to advance their ends more effectively within the framework of the basic structure secure in the knowledge that elsewhere in the social system the necessary corrections to preserve background justice are being made.
>
> The essential point, then, is that the need for a structural ideal to specify constraints and to guide corrections does not depend upon injustice. Even with strict compliance with all reasonable and practical rules, such adjustments are continually required. The fact that actual political and social life is often pervaded by much injustice merely underlines this necessity. A procedural theory that contains no structural principles for a just social order would be of no use in our world, where the political goal is to eliminate injustice and steer change towards a fair basic structure....There is no rational basis for preventing or eliminating injustice if such an ideal form for background institutions is rejected.[11]

Rawls thus holds that no pure procedural theory of justice (such as Nozick's) could be *sufficient* as an account of justice even if a society were, at some point in time, just according to all procedural rules. While he holds both that pure procedural justice may be relied upon for important social distributions, and that the most pressing and difficult problems of social justice (such as those of civil disobedience and criminal justice) must be investigated by nonideal theory, he insists that the ideal theory is a necessary feature of a theory of justice, not a mere Platonic observation about the importance of general standards.[12] Ideal theory is also more basic than nonideal theory because its principles are to be used in the structuring of nonideal theories.

Why the Basic Structure Is the Primary Subject

The basic structure is the primary subject in Rawls' theory for the same two reasons previously encountered in discussing the importance of the all-inclusive system for a theory of background justice. First, Rawls emphasizes the pervasive causal efficacy of the all-inclusive system in affecting persons' initial chances and starting places in society. "The basic structure is primary," he writes, "because its effects are so profound and present from the start" (71). Second, Rawls takes the basic structure to be primary because of its fundamental place in the regulation and adjustment of social outcomes.[13] Both of these reasons derive from Rawls' larger view that it will do little good to tinker with distributional outcomes through material principles if the background conditions creating the problem (and thus creating a need for redistribution) are unjust. No amount of adjustment through such allocative principles will eliminate the problem if it resides deep in the basic structure.

Rawls' favored example against both allocative-principle and distributive-process theories is that of voluntary market transactions, which he believes cannot be just unless antecedent economic distributions as well as the structure of the market are both fair. Suppose the structure of the system of markets is not fair because only those born wealthy are able to engage in investments, while investments alone permit a high standard of living and those not born into wealth are systematically excluded from possibilities of investment. This situation of advantage and disadvantage could be adjusted by redistributing wealth in accordance with a principle of need. Wealth theoretically could be distributed so as to equalize individual income. Yet the social system would remain unjust because the background conditions generating the problem have not been adjusted. To the extent that these background conditions are themselves the cause of unjust outcomes requiring compensatory actions, they are unjust, no matter which compensatory measures are introduced.

If one accepts Rawls' views about the pervasive influence of the basic structure, one will almost certainly agree that the basic structure should be the primary, though perhaps not the exclusive concern of a theory of justice. Other *derivative* principles may, of course, be a secondary concern of a theory of justice. This topic leads to a consideration of what Rawls refers to as "precepts" of justice.

The Secondary Status of Material Principles (Precepts)

Subsequent to the publication of *A Theory of Justice*, Rawls summarized his intent in that work: "I held that the first test of a conception of justice is whether its principles provide reasonable guidelines for the classical questions of social justice in [the case of the basic structure of society]."[14] Rawls believes that theories of justice commonly address classical questions too obliquely because they operate with secondary principles, or mere precepts, of justice—i.e., material principles of distribution. He argues that these conceptions of justice operate "at the wrong level of generality" and tend to overlook the basic structure (308). If his claim is correct, he has located something of major philosophical importance, for the bald accusation he makes is that other philosophers have superficially presupposed basic institutions as a *mere background* against which moral judgments are to be reached, while failing to theorize regarding the justice of this background itself. In any event, to understand why Rawls regards his principles as alone properly applicable to the basic structure is to understand not only how his theory differs from others but also why he regards his as superior.

§ 47 of *A Theory of Justice* is devoted exclusively to "The Precepts of Justice." The following line of argument is present in this brief section: If a basic structure of society satisfies the two principles of justice, distributive results in the social system will be just (or at least not unjust), no matter what those distributive results are. This reliance on what he calls pure procedural justice captures "the suitably general point of view" attempted in *A Theory of Justice* (304). However, Rawls acknowledges that there are many "intuitive ideas" of justice rooted in "common sense precepts of justice"—the material principles preferred by common sense.

Rawls' strategy in dealing with this problem relies on Mill's perceptive treatment of the subject in *Utilitarianism* (Ch. V). Mill argued that common sense precepts or principles such as "to each according to effort" or "to each according to need" lead to conflicts among principles and to contrary moral injunctions. The principles themselves also assign no relative weight to their own demands when they conflict with other principles. Consequently, they are of no help when a judgment of relative merit or overridingness must be made. These precepts obviously fall short of providing a theory of justice because they result in an unhelpful pluralism where a higher principle is needed to arbitrate their conflicts.

Rawls and Mill are thus agreed that common sense precepts are subordinate or derivative principles that cannot be elevated to the status of the supreme principle(s). Accordingly, Rawls must face the issue of the role such principles are to play in his system, if any, including how his system can assign appropriate weights and derivative status to any acceptable principles. Rawls again handles this issue through the example of a competitive market economy operating within the framework of a just basic structure. He argues that in this setting it is easy to see

> how the various precepts of justice arise. They simply identify features of jobs that are significant on either the demand or the supply side of the market, or both. A firm's demand for workers is determined by the...net value of the contribution of a unit of labor....Experience and training, natural ability and special know-how, tend to earn a premium. Firms are willing to pay more to those with these characteristics because their productivity is greater. This fact explains and gives weight to the precept to each according to his contribution....Similarly jobs which involve uncertain or unstable employment, or which are performed under hazardous and unpleasantly strenuous conditions, tend to receive more pay....From this circumstance arise such precepts as to each according to his effort, or the risks he bears, and so on.... Given the aims of productive units and of those seeking work, certain characteristics are singled out as relevant (305f).

Rawls thus regards common sense precepts as the natural outgrowths of pervasive social contexts. He also offers an explanation for cross-cultural variations in the presence and weight of the common sense precepts of justice. If the basic structure of one society acknowledges a principle of fair equality of opportunity or employs the difference principle (Parts II.a and II.b of Rawls' second principle), while the basic structure of a second society does not, then it is predictable that the second society will weight the material principle "to each according to his contribution" (especially when contribution relies on training and education) more heavily than would the first society. The first would tend to weight education, training, and natural endowment less heavily, while the second would weight the reduction of inequalities less heavily.

The conclusion Rawls reaches is the following: "None of these precepts can be plausibly raised to a first principle....Common sense precepts are at the wrong level of generality. In order to find suitable first principles one must step behind them" (307f). Rawls sees, of course, that these principles offer a plausible claim to generality in certain contexts. Distribution according to contribution, for example, seems to be a general principle of fairness; and Rawls admits that his own theory of primary goods is an extension of a principle of need for a special purpose. But he finds these and all material principles deficient in their usual formulations because they fail to appreciate the deep and prevalent importance of the basic structure. He is again appealing to the idea that it is both more important and more difficult to control distribution through the basic structure than through the distribution of shares of the available material means. Contribution, for example, can occur only if there is an opportunity to contribute. Whether the opportunity is present depends on what business firms and buyers want. These underlying market forces must themselves be fair and appropriately regulated before it can be decided whether one's contribution is duly rewarded and appreciated, overly rewarded and overly appreciated, etc.

While Rawls acknowledges that his principles generally *accord* with common sense moral judgments, including its precepts, he also allows that his two principles function to provide "a relatively concrete principle for questions that common sense finds unfamiliar and leaves undecided" (319). Sometimes he places a stronger interpretation on the revisionary quality of his principles: "Most likely we shall have to loosen ourselves from our ordinary perspective and take a more comprehensive viewpoint."[15]

Libertarianism and the Basic Structure

We have just seen why Rawls rejects theories built on common sense precepts. But what of those theories that employ no precepts or material principles whatsoever—or perhaps employ only principles of acquisition, transfer, and rectification, to use Nozick's language? We earlier noted how Rawls conceives it to be necessary to use principles of justice to correct institutional processes, including "the accumulated results of individual transactions." This contention forms the substantive basis for his objection to all libertarian theories of justice—the most prominent form of no-distributive-principle theories. These theories, so wedded to an unmonitored free market arrangement, are referred to by Rawls as systems of natural liberty. Basically, such theories guarantee equal liberties but without any attempt to compensate for advantages resulting from natural and social contingencies (72).

Nozick's libertarianism is perhaps the most viable theory of natural liberty in contemporary philosophy. He argues, specifically against Rawls, that a theory of justice should be structured to protect individual rights against state interference and should not promote the "patterning" of society through distributive arrangements that in effect *redistribute* economic benefits and burdens. As Nozick sees it, any economic arrangements that are freely chosen by autonomous agents are just; for such agents have an entitlement, without interference, so long as they do not violate another agent's rights, to economic benefits that they acquire by their own productive efforts, as well as a right to their subsequent voluntary economic transactions (and in some cases to "rectification" from third parties in order to correct a prior unjust acquisition or transfer). One's rightful holdings are thus exclusively a matter of how they were received. This theory is one of pure procedural justice in the extreme.[16]

Although Rawls' reasons for rejecting libertarian theories, including Nozick's, are implicit in *A Theory of Justice*, they emerge more clearly in his later writings:

> We have a right to our natural abilities and a right to whatever we become entitled to by taking part in a fair social process. The problem is to characterize this process....[17]
>
> [Voluntary market conditions are] not, in general, fair unless the antecedent distribution of income and wealth as well as the structure of the system of markets is fair. The existing wealth must have been properly acquired ....The two principles of justice regulate how entitlements are acquired... within the basic structure.[18]

Rawls' primary reason for rejecting libertarianism is the same as his reason for rejecting theories built on precepts: without a higher governing principle to monitor the basic structure, injustices will emerge from the contingencies of social, historical, and natural circumstance. Rawls' theory here most closely approximates traditional accounts of distributive justice based on the notion of desert. Because neither those who suffer from social inequalities nor those advantaged by these inequalities deserve their situation, fairness demands compensation through a reduction of inequalities. It is this reduction of unequal advantage that Rawls' larger system of basic equal liberties and fair opportunities, together with the difference principle, is intended to allow.

In *Anarchy, State, and Utopia* Nozick argues against Rawls' views as follows:

> If things fell from heaven like manna, and no one had any special entitlement to any portion of it, and no manna would fall unless all agreed to a particular distribution, and somehow the quantity varied depending on the distribution, then it is plausible to claim that persons placed so that they couldn't make threats, or hold out for specially large shares, would agree to the difference principle of distribution. But is *this* the appropriate model for thinking about how the things people produce are to be distributed?[19]

The problem with Nozick's argument is its neglect of the role of the basic structure in Rawls' work. One of the curious features of Nozick's book is his failure to consider how the justice of acquisitions, holdings, transfers, and rectification are to be monitored by social institutions. Problems of regulation and basic institutional structures are simply ignored. At the same time, Nozick is accusing Rawls of neglecting the underlying reason for someone's having an entitlement to something, including the very significant reason that the person *produced* it. Rawls stands accused of incorrectly thinking of social goods as, like manna, given independent of a background history of individual effort.

This, however, is precisely the mistake Rawls does not make, for his theory of the basic structure is intended to provide an account of such a background history. Nozick is perfectly correct to insist that historical considerations such as individual productivity and effort are relevant to the determination of just social outcomes. Rawls would never deny it. However, he would insist both that such historical considerations are not the only considerations and that they are irrelevant considerations if the basic structure regulating the outcome is itself unjust. For this reason Rawls insists that pure procedural theories such as Nozick's are valid only if they function within the framework of a theory of a just basic structure.

Consider an example. Nozick argues that if testators legitimately own their property and wish to give it to other persons, they should have a right to do so. Rawls would agree with this claim if the larger framework within which inheritance functions is itself just. However, if some individuals possess vastly more wealth than others, without deserving it because it arrived purely as a gift, then this inheritance outcome may produce unjust situations of inequality where the least advantaged in the cooperative scheme deserve compensation. Thus, historical contingencies generally have weight but not decisive weight in all circumstances; and in some cases they may have no weight at all.

As we saw previously, notions such as productivity, contribution, and entitlement only gain their meaning from underlying social forces, such as market mechanisms. These mechanisms must be appropriately regulated *before* it can be decided whether a person's "contribution" or "entitlement" is duly or unduly appreciated. Only a theory of how justice can be embedded in the basic structure provides an answer, and this objective guides Rawls' entire theory. If he succeeds in showing that the basic structure determines just outcomes, then Nozick has neither an argument against Rawls nor an understanding of the primary objective of Rawls' work.

Moreover, Rawls' theory significantly incorporates the notion of pure procedural justice. Any distribution of wealth and income resulting from the basic structure is just if the basic structure itself is just (85, 87f). No other independent precepts or principles do or can determine whether any particular distribution of social and economic goods is just or unjust. Nozick distinguishes between *process* theories such as his own and *end-state* theories controlled by distributive principles, of which Rawls' is presumably an instance. Yet this distinction misconstrues Rawls' point. He is arguing for a regulated process, while Nozick is arguing for an unregulated process. Rawls has no end-state vision for society. His approach to pure procedural justice again reiterates the importance of both background justice in the basic structure and his rejection of those common sense precepts that determine individual allocations.

However, it is easy to misunderstand Rawls' perspective on the relationship between his principles, background justice, and pure procedural justice. David Miller, for example, seems to me to misrepresent Rawls' views in the following argument:

> [Rawls' second principle] prescribes a certain outcome, [involving] an arrangement of inequalities which maximizes the benefit of the least advantaged, and...a distribution of offices according to ability and skill. Had Rawls wished to make his account of justice pure procedural, he should have omitted the two principles altogether and prescribed only the institutional framework; for instance, if one maintained that whatever distribution resulted from the workings of a free market economy was fair, this would be a pure procedural interpretation of justice. But in Rawls case the institutions are set up to *satisfy* the two principles.[20]

Miller interprets pure procedural justice in this argument so that only a theory as radically individualistic as Nozick's could qualify. Rawls, however, has a quite different understanding in characterizing his theory as pure procedural. A system counts as justifiably pure procedural even if its basic institutions are, as Miller puts it, "set up to *satisfy* the two principles." Rawls understands the expression "pure procedural justice" to apply to any purely procedural mechanism *within* an established and patterned basic structure. However, and very importantly, until such an established structure exists—whether Rawls' or a utilitarian one or whatever—there could be *no procedures.* Even a pure free market system establishes basic procedural rules in the basic structure that specify permissible outcomes.

Thus Miller and Nozick similarly misinterpret Rawls. Nozick incorrectly claims that Rawls' principles pattern outcomes and that his own theory does not; and Miller inappropriately models pure procedures exclusively on the free market interpretation of the basic structure argued for by Nozick.

THE DIFFERENCE PRINCIPLE

Because parties in the original position are said by Rawls to be free and *equal*, one might suppose that the overriding principle of justice should be strictly equal distribution. No perfectly free and equal person, after all, would expect either more or less than an equal share of primary social goods (150). Rawls even notes that "the obvious starting point is to suppose that...social primary goods...should be equal: everyone should have an equal share."[21] Yet he argues that equal distribution cannot be justified as the sole primary principle. If there were inequalities rendering everyone better off, by comparison to initial equality, these inequalities would be desirable—so long as they were consistent with equal liberty and fair opportunity. More particularly, if these inequalities enhance the position of the representative least advantaged person, as measured by a higher index of primary goods, then it would be self-defeating for the least advantaged or anyone else to seek to prohibit the inequalities. Rawls thus rejects radical egalitarianism in favor of a difference principle.

The Justification of the Difference Principle

I shall now consider the moral justification Rawls offers for the difference principle. This justification is based on the moral reasons he believes would compel free, rational, and equal persons to agree to the difference principle. The difference principle is presumably a rational principle that hypothetically situated persons would choose in order to mitigate the disadvantages they would otherwise suffer if they were to wind up among the least advantaged. Notoriously, Rawls proceeds to justify all his principles—equal liberty, equality of opportunity, and the difference principle—by a procedure of choice in the original position. In particular, Rawls uses the rational strategy of minimizing risks by applying the *maximin rule* for choice under conditions of uncertainty. Because a decision-maker under the veil of ignorance cannot employ a rule based on probability outcomes or highest expected utility, it seems reasonable to choose an action that would promote the highest minimum outcome. The maximin rule justifies a choice of principles that advantage the lowest social strata in society and thus protect against risk at that social level.

Rawls' argument for the derivation of the maximin criterion is complex and controversial. Many have openly expressed doubts that this strategy could lend any support to Rawls' two principles,[22] while others argue that a maximax rule is at least as appropriate as a general solution to the problem of *choice.*[23] I shall concentrate, however, on what I take to be Rawls' main *moral* argument for the difference principle and not on his justification based on the maximin rule (Sec. 26). I begin by considering the following popular interpretation of Rawls, which I believe to be fundamentally misguided:

> [Individuals in the original position] do not choose the principles they do because they believe them to be just. They are concerned with their share of the primary social goods...and seek to look after their own interests. The principles chosen are principles of justice *because* they would be chosen by such persons under the (fair) conditions of the original position.[24]

This interpretation implies that whatever *would* be chosen by rational and free agents under conditions of the original position are justified by this choice procedure as the principles of justice. Thus, if the agents of choice were to choose principles entailing high risk ventures, these would be the principles of justice. Rawls rules this possibility out in his discussions of the veil of ignorance. To be sure, he often uses the language of those principles to which free and equal persons *would agree* (13), but the emphasis is to be placed on *free and equal* in such statements, not on some quasi-prediction regarding that to which they *would* agree. It is no part of Rawls' theory that if free, equal, and rational individuals could convene and choose a set of governing principles—based on whatever reasons each finds to be determinative (each being equal and autonomous)—then those principles are justified *because* they have been contractually agreed to.

This interpretation misconstrues Rawls' theory as based almost exclusively on contract and pure procedural justice. Rawls' view, rather, is that there are (morally prior) good reasons that justify a contractual agreement to the principles of justice. Rawls would consider his principles just whether or not they would actually be agreed to by persons swept behind a nonhypothetical veil of ignorance. Accordingly, I interpret Rawls' views on the original position and the difference principle as follows: The moral reasons that would incline free and equal persons to the choice of the difference principle are defined into, or at least presupposed in the notion of the original position. For example, the moral arbitrariness of contingencies is presupposed in the idea of the veil of ignorance, and the need for fairness is presupposed in the symmetrical position of the parties in the original position. Thus, the choice of the difference principle in the original position is justified not because it is *chosen* by or *would be chosen* by rational agents of choice but rather because it is chosen under conditions which themselves incorporate the moral reasons governing free and equal persons. (A modified interpretation, suggested to me by Louis Katzner, is that Rawls' view *presupposes* the Kantian moral justification identified above, even though Rawls does not actually *structure* his argument in terms of this moral justification. I am unsure on this point.)

That Rawls relies on a moral justification deeper than that of a hypothetical contract follows from our previous discussion of his views on social cooperation. He sees basic institutions as reciprocal arrangements for mutual advantage. The worth of any person's ambitions and talents is contingent upon the scheme of cooperation, and the social benefit derived from one's contribution is thus a collective asset to which all in the reciprocal arrangement can validly lay claim. In any such society, free and equal persons would be justified in rejecting radical egalitarianism and accepting the difference principle in order to advantage everyone. In his summary statements of the moral justification of the difference principle, Rawls appeals to equality as the starting point, not a contract:

> ...we are regarding citizens as free and equal moral persons....Because we start from equal shares, those who benefit least have, so to speak, a veto; and thus we arrive at the difference principle. Taking equality as the basis of comparison those who have gained more must do so on terms that are justifiable to those who have gained the least....
>
> The conception of equality contained in the principles of justice I have described [is] Kantian....Particularly important among the features of the original position...[is] the veil of ignorance....If the two principles would

> be adopted in the original position with its limits on information, the conception of equality they contain would be Kantian in the sense that by acting from this conception the members of a well-ordered society would express their negative freedom. They would have succeeded in regulating the basic structure and its profound consequences on their persons and mutual relationships by principles the grounds for which are suitably independent from chance and contingency.[25]

I would not know how to understand an argument from Kantian premises using principles that are "suitably independent from chance and contingency" except as a moral argument cut free from actions which hypothetical individuals might take behind a veil of ignorance but tied to Kant's view that the categorical imperative would be accepted by all rational beings because it is an explication of the notion of pure reason. Rawls' argument seems clearly aimed at reaching a conclusion regarding what individuals ought to do from the moral point of view—a point of view Rawls chooses to present through the model of the original position.

Perhaps, as Thomas Nagel has argued,[26] Rawls' attempt fails, because the principles he selects presuppose a conception of the good that renders his principles morally *nonneutral* and that is never in fact *justified* by Rawls. I think this criticism implausible, for—as Rawls argues in his article "Fairness to Goodness"—the original position is not morally neutral because the issue is one of fairness rather than neutrality.[27] But whether Rawls succeeds or fails is not the present point. I wish only to note that Rawls sees his principles as ones that rational agents *ought* to choose because of their rightness and not merely as ones such agents *would* choose. Or, to speak more correctly, in the original position what they would choose simply is what they ought to choose.

A related temptation in interpreting Rawls is also to be avoided. Consider Wolff's account. He supposes that Rawls commits himself to the view that the fairness of the two principles of justice "*consists in*" their being "the outcome of a purely procedurally just bargaining game."[28] Wolff then has no trouble in showing that Rawls' Kantian views about rational agents in the original position undermine his pure procedural account: "Rawls has, by the transformations of this theory, undermined the logic of its justification."[29] But this charge can be sustained only if one incorrectly presumes that for Rawls the fairness of the principles consists in their being the product of a purely procedurally just bargaining game. If I am correct that Rawls derives the fairness of the principles from Kantian grounds and not from pure procedural grounds, then Wolff's charge fails.

The Moral Irrelevance of Natural Assets

It might be supposed from the discussion thus far that Rawls regards natural assets as undeserved in the sense that persons do not deserve to have the assets. Rawls says, in fact, that "No one deserves his greater natural capacity...." But Rawls' view in fact reduces to the weaker claim that no one has a right by virtue of the natural lottery and an initial position in society to a system of social cooperation in which his contingently derived talents benefit him at the expense of those who are worse off (102, 104). He contends that the distribution of natural and social contingencies is arbitrary from the moral point of view and thus provides no *moral* grounds for arrangement of the basic structure:

> The natural distribution is neither just nor unjust; nor is it unjust that persons are born into society at some particular position. These are simply natural facts. *What is just and unjust is the way that institutions deal with these facts* (102, italics added).

If such contingencies were made the basis for distributing primary goods, the arbitrariness found in nature would be unjustifiably imported into the basic structure—unjustifiably because there are no supporting moral grounds. Thus, it becomes an open question how the basic structure ought to be arranged so as to thwart morally arbitrary distributions. The difference principle provides Rawls' resolution of the problem, for it is "a fair way of meeting the arbitrariness of fortune" (102).

The Nature of "The Least Advantaged"

The difference principle requires that inequalities be arranged to the greatest benefit of the least advantaged. But who are the least advantaged members of society? Does Rawls mean a single class of economically deprived individuals? Does he intend to include the physically disabled or such mentally disabled persons as the retarded? What Rawls characterizes as "the representative least-advantaged person" must be singled out and carefully described or the difference principle will be impossible to apply for purposes of social policy.

We may begin with two observations. First, any definition of the least advantaged offered by Rawls is not intended as a definition of the *single* least advantaged or worst off individual. Rawls does not select the single worst off individual with respect to come criterion *C* and then argue that the class of the least advantaged includes those similarly situated to the representative individual. Instead, Rawls looks to the range of disadvantaged members in a given society, as judged by natural and social contingencies, and then fixes a threshold below which all persons in that society may be designated as worst off. His idea is thus to arrive at a *representative position.* Second, the benefits to the least advantaged required by the difference principle are always in terms of primary goods. These are goods that all rational persons agree are desirable, however much they may disagree about the desirability of other (nonprimary) goods. Precisely which, if any, primary social goods beyond income and wealth are to be included under the difference principle is unclear. But in Rawls' account, opportunities and powers, income and wealth, rights and liberties, and self-respect are all listed as primary goods (92). Generally speaking, the difference principle maximizes the representative least-advantaged person's expectations of the relevant primary goods, however relevance is established. These goods are objective because needed by everyone, and thus they do not merely measure individual levels of preference or satisfaction. Moreover, Rawls argues that "the measure of benefit to the least advantaged is specified in terms of an index of social primary goods."[30] Because the same index of goods can be objectively used to determine everyone's social status, primary goods can serve as the common standard for interpersonal comparisons in matters of social justice. These comparisons are to be made in terms of expectations of primary social goods, where the term "expectations" is to be understood as the index of these goods that a representative person in a particular position can look forward to (92).

Frank Michelman accepts the following restrictive interpretation of Rawls' views on primary goods, the least advantaged, and the difference principle:

> [I assume] that the prospects of the least advantaged...are to be defined in terms only of the primary social goods of income and wealth (rights and liberties evidently being taken care of by the liberty principle).[31]

This assumption simplifies Rawls' views and makes them more readily applicable to social problems. However, for reasons to be explained below, it is far from clear that Rawls intends the class of the least advantaged to be determined solely through measurements of *economic* disadvantage.

These two observations about representative positions and primary goods lead to a third consideration. Because the difference principle requires maximization of the expectations of primary goods for the *class* of the least advantaged, it does not require that every single individual's expectations be maximized. Because consideration of *representative* positions is uppermost in Rawls' mind, he says the difference principle requires aggregation over the expectations of the worst off. The principle is thus referred to by Rawls as a "limited aggregative principle" (98).

Two Early Formulations of a Definition

Having argued for a theory of primary goods, Rawls considers two possible ways to define the least advantaged in *A Theory of Justice*. He first suggests that a particular social position might be selected—e.g., the position of an unskilled worker. The least advantaged could then be described as the class of persons with the average or lower-than-average income and wealth of this social position (98). Second, he suggests a definition in terms of relative income and wealth, without reference to social position: the least advantaged group would be composed of the class of individuals with less than half of the median income or wealth (98). However, both of these formulations of the class of the least advantaged fail to surmount what is known as the index problem. Both make reference only to the primary goods of income and wealth. It is no doubt for this reason that Michelman makes his assumption about the limited range of primary goods. Yet the difference principle seems suited to govern the distribution of powers and opportunities as well, and it is obviously possible that the class of those with the lowest index of income and wealth will not correspond to the class with the lowest index of powers. Even if these classes generally are coextensive, they are theoretically distinct, and there are many historical examples—invariably in unjust societies—where they have not been coextensive. But if primary goods other than income and wealth must be included, the least advantaged could be determined only if nonhomogeneous indexes of primary goods could be compared and synthesized. Notoriously such comparisons and syntheses are questionable and fail to provide the objective bases of interpersonal comparison sought by Rawls.

In an attempt to circumvent the index problem altogether, Rawls assumes that the goods of income and wealth are "sufficiently correlated" with power, authority, opportunity, etc. that "those with greater political authority, say, or those higher in institutional forms, are in general better off in other respects" (97). Rawls then proceeds, without argument, to the conclusion that this assumption is "safe enough" for his purposes and that the only important matter is "how to define the least fortunate group" (98). This failure to confront the index problem is dangerous, however, because a *definition* of the least fortunate group cannot be provided without relying on this assumption. Some commentators have explicitly questioned the assumption of a correlation, which they regard as an ad hoc stipulation that simply evades the index problem. There is considerable merit in this objection. It is therefore understandable why Rawls might explore a new definition of the least advantaged in his later work.

The Third Formulation of a Definition

Rawls suggests a different definition of the least advantaged in "A Kantian Conception of Equality." Though he qualifies his formulation as "rough," he is definite in stating that

> The least advantaged are defined very roughly, as the overlap between those who are least favored by each of the three main kinds of contingencies. Thus this group includes persons whose family and class origins are more disadvantaged than others, whose endowments have permitted them to fare less well, and whose fortune and luck have been relatively less favorable, all...with the relevant measures based on social primary goods.[32]

Rawls' view here seems to be that the least advantaged are to be defined as the class of persons that overlaps the three classes of those disadvantaged by social, natural, and historical contingencies. That is, one is a member of the class of the least advantaged if and only if one is a member of each of these other three classes. The least advantaged person, then, is the representative person who overlaps each type of contingency.

Does this third formulation successfully resolve the index problem? It might be thought that it does because there is no need to compare such incomparable primary goods as wealth, power, and opportunity. *Comparisons* are not needed because any individual in the lowest strata of all relevant primary goods is obviously a member of the least advantaged, and Rawls' shaky correlation assumption may be simply jettisoned. He thus seems in his later work on his way to the resolution of a problem that plagues *A Theory of Justice*. But, as he says, it is a *rough* formulation—very rough—and potentially this new criterion may pick out a class of least advantaged persons that does not correspond to our intuitive convictions.

There are similar unclarities that we might hope to see reduced. For example, there is a potential problem of either circularity or regress in Rawls' procedure that again subjects it to potential criticism as an ad hoc maneuver. He has defined *the* least advantaged in terms of *three types* of least advantaged. But what are the criteria for being least advantaged in each of these classes? Moreover, it is worth noting that all starting places in society are dependent upon the basic structure of a specific social system. The lowest class of natural and social contingencies cannot be understood in abstraction from a particular social scheme. Thus, a single social system must be relied upon as the background against which the least advantaged are to be determined, and any fixing of the least advantaged is inherently relative to this social system. If the model system changes, so will the class of the least advantaged; or perhaps it is the definition that must be adjusted. The point is that without further clarification it seems a clear implication of Rawls' views that different social schemes will pick out different representative persons as among the least advantaged.* Finally, as Scanlon has pointed out, "Rawls does not discuss his reasons for allowing averaging within a social position when he has rejected it in the more general case."[33] Without further clarification, it looks as if Rawls' allegedly nonutilitarian views could lapse into utilitarianism in at least *some* societies (though this is, of course, not the point of Scanlon's comments). It is to be hoped that in upcoming years Rawls will devote considerable attention to these problems of clarifying the nature of the least advantaged.

Conclusion

In conclusion it is worth considering what Rawls does *not* attempt in his writings on justice. Rawls' emphasis on the basic structure leads him to develop a theory of justice at a "suitable level of generality" (131, 304, 308). As we have seen, this level is that of ideal theory and in no way encompasses elements of nonideal theory. Rawls' theory, then, is not intended to have any immediate application to everyday problems of government and social regulation. Any such "application" is exclusively indirect, as mediated by the basic structure.

The level of generality sought by Rawls is important, because some expositors have interpreted his theory as having a more direct application to social problems than I believe he intends. As noted previously, his principles of justice are not intended to apply directly to any

*I am indebted to Arnold Davidson for the idea that led to this point.

particular distribution of goods, services, opportunities, burdens, etc. Moreover, his principles provide no criteria for the evaluation of any institution's distribution independent of the justice of the institution itself (88). Rawls' analogy to the game of gambling is useful: A gamble is fair whatever its outcome, so long as the rules of the gamble are themselves fair. The rules of a fair gamble, however, are unequipped to judge the fairness of individual gambles—when, e.g., a poor man loses $100 and a rich man wins $100. So it is with Rawls' principles: they can serve to judge what constitutes fair rules of procedure, but once these rules are established the principles are not equipped to judge the fairness of individual outcomes—as when, e.g., the rich turn out to receive more funds in a national health insurance scheme than the poor.

I thus have some reservations regarding even so excellent an interpretation of Rawls as Michelman's. He assumes that the principles have at least a fairly direct application to social problems. Specifically, he argues that the ideal theory has implications for "substantive welfare rights, even though the focus...on the basic structure may pose difficulties for [a] welfare-rights search. This focus means that the theory's principles of justice are selected for their capacity to serve as rather abstract, broad-gauged constraints against which to test more specific and circumstantially contingent proposals at the constitutional and legislative levels."[34] This interpretation seems to me both correct and at the same time potentially misleading. Certainly he is right about the constitutional level, for constitutional rights are components in the basic structure. It is also reasonable to argue that Rawls' principles provide "broad-gauged constraints" against various possible legislative outcomes. It would be incorrect, however, to conclude that Rawls has a *theory* about welfare rights or that his views entail a particular outcome of welfare rights for basic structures. Many different basic structures will be compatible with his broad principles, perhaps even a society without any welfare rights whatsoever. Rawls' "theory of welfare rights," then, is like his theory of representative least advantaged persons. Neither the least advantaged nor particular systems of welfare rights can be ascertained from the viewpoint of the original position, for that position is too veiled in ignorance. Too many facts about a particular society must be known in each case. Moreover, Rawls seems to recognize that there will always be an indeterminacy regarding how to apply the difference principle and that very different applications of this application may turn out to be equally just (201). However, he argues that

> This indeterminacy in the theory of justice is not in itself a defect. It is what we should expect. Justice as fairness will provide a worthwhile theory if it defines the range of justice more in accordance with our considered judgments than do existing theories, and if it singles out with greater sharpness the grave wrongs a society should avoid (201).

For similar reasons, I am led to disagree even more extensively with Ronald Green's careful and probing arguments regarding the ostensible implications of Rawls' views for health care:

> [Contract theory's] focus is not on case to case allocations but on the basic structure of society. As far as this basic structure is concerned, the idea of equal access will suffice. To a large degree we can assume that the problem of differing subjective needs can be handled by professional judgments within the health care system....
>
> Rational agents in the original position are not primarily interested in [utilitarian] aggregates...but would instead employ cautious maximin reasoning to secure the highest minimal level of health care services.[35]

I do not see that Rawls' egalitarian conception of justice has any a priori implications for the health care system. Alternative contemporary proposals for (1) equal access to health care, (2) rights to health care, (3) no federal or state funding of health care, and (4) utilitarian cost/benefit approaches all seem to me to have versions consistent with Rawls' views (contingent upon the nature of particular societies). Moreover, Green's interpretation seems all the more implausible because an account of equal access to health care entails that the health care system is an institution in the basic structure, like the constitution, that ought to be regulated by rules of justice. Yet there is no reason to make this assumption. Access to health care could be handled purely on a voluntary free market basis, where neither allocations for, nor regulation of the institution is required by principles of justice. At most, as Michelman puts it, a legislature would have to bear in mind certain broad *constraints*. Now, *if* Rawls had included health among his social primary goods, then *perhaps* interpretations such as Green's might be more acceptable. But health is not included, and there is reason to think that its inclusion would force alterations in the principles themselves. [For Rawls, health is a natural primary good rather than a social primary good (62).] It is to be hoped that in the future Rawls' expositors will resist claims to have discovered proper applications of his work. The ideal theory is not well suited for this form of interpretation, tempting though it may be to seek to uncover the practical commitments of Rawls' work.

Rawls of course believes that his ideal theory has broad implications for nonideal theory, as we have seen. At the same time, he acknowledges that the immediate and dilemmatic problems of justice confronted in nonideal theory (in the form, e.g., of problems in criminal law) are not resolvable by ideal theory. A reworking of the basic structure always has implications for the way in which concrete decisions must be reached, but only in remote and unusual cases would adjustments in the basic structure be needed in order to carry out the concrete social and political decisions that are the staple sources of just and unjust outcomes in the modern state. It is no part of Rawls' theory to decide whether these decisions are to be reached by utilitarian or nonutilitarian reasoning, left to collective action or individual action, etc.

Rawls seems to me quite correct to have distanced his theory to an appropriate level of generality. Philosophers have long had too grand an enterprise in mind in developing theories of justice. They seem often to have thought that a cosmic theory of justice, public policy, and rights can be applied with consistency and rigor to the solution of many immediate social problems. But policies governing practical matters of great complexity cannot simply be deduced from highly abstract principles, whether of law or of moral philosophy. There also is no single consistent set of rights or material principles of justice that always and predictably applies when problems of social justice arise. There are many such principles, in the form of social rules, and they sometimes apply and sometimes do not apply when urgent questions of social justice emerge. Accordingly, those who would import an abstract theory of justice or a single principle of justice into the arena of public policy, with hopes of thereby resolving such issues, commit as serious an error as those who would totally exclude considerations of justice in favor of the politics of public policy. We are much in Rawls' debt for not making grand claims about the concrete reaches of his theory, while nonetheless showing us how a philosophical account of justice can be both broadly relevant and worthy of careful study for its own sake.

NOTES

1. Such accounts of justice in contemporary philosophy are found, for example, in Joel Feinberg, *Social Philosophy* (Englewood Cliffs, N.J.: Prentice-

Hall, Inc., 1973), Chapter 7, and Nicholas Rescher, *Distributive Justice* (New York: The Bobbs-Merrill Co., Inc., 1966).

2. Hugo Adam Bedau, "Social Justice and Social Institutions," *Midwest Studies in Philosophy*, III (1978), 159-75.
3. Unfortunately, the basic structure is perhaps more ignored by commentators than any major topic in Rawls' book. For example, in the only two full length expository works on Rawls—by Brian Barry and Robert Paul Wolff—there is scarcely a reference to the basic structure, let alone a serious attempt at interpretation and analysis.
4. In addition to Feinberg and Rescher, cf. Norman Bowie, *Towards a New Theory of Distributive Justice* (Amherst, Mass.: University of Massachusetts Press, 1971) and James Rachels, "What People Deserve," in *Justice and Economic Distribution*, ed. John Arthur and William H. Shaw (Englewood Cliffs, N.J.: Prentice-Hall, 1978).
5. For example, see Rescher, *Distributive Justice*.
6. Robert Paul Wolff, *Understanding Rawls: A Reconstruction and Critique of A Theory of Justice* (Princeton: Princeton University Press, 1977), pp. 200f.
7. John Rawls, "The Basic Structure as Subject," *American Philosophical Quarterly*, 14 (1977), 159-65, especially Section IV.
8. John Rawls, "A Kantian Conception of Equality," *Cambridge Review* (1975), p. 95.
9. Rawls, "The Basic Structure," Sec. I.
10. However, cf. Joel Feinberg "Rawls and Intuitionism," in *Reading Rawls: Critical Studies of A Theory of Justice*, ed. Norman Daniels (New York: Basic Books, 1976), pp. 116ff; and Frank Michelman, "Constitutional Welfare Rights and *A Theory of Justice*" also in Daniels, ed., *Reading Rawls*, pp. 329f.
11. Rawls, "The Basic Structure," Sec. VIII.
12. *Ibid.*
13. *Ibid.*, Secs. II-III and "A Kantian Conception" p. 95.
14. *Ibid.*, Sec. I.
15. Rawls, "A Kantian Conception," p. 95.
16. Robert Nozick, *Anarchy, State, and Utopia* (New York: Basic Books, 1974), Chapter 7.
17. Rawls, "A Kantian Conception," p. 98.
18. Rawls, "The Basic Structure," Secs. II, VI.
19. Nozick, *Anarchy*, p. 198.
20. David Miller, *Social Justice* (Oxford: Clarendon Press, 1976), p. 45.
21. Rawls, "A Kantian Conception," p. 97.
22. Miller, *Social Justice*, p. 42.
23. Rolf Sartorius, *Individual Conduct and Social Norms* (Belmont, Calif.: Wadsworth Publishing Co., 1975), p. 125.
24. John Arthur and William H. Shaw, "Introduction," *Justice and Economic Distribution*, p. 16, italics added; cf. Ronald Dworkin, "The Original Position," in *Reading Rawls*, pp. 17, 21.

25. Rawls, "A Kantian Conception," pp. 97-99.
26. Thomas Nagel, "Rawls on Justice," in *Reading Rawls*, p. 9.
27. Rawls, "Fairness to Goodness," *Philosophical Review* (October, 1975), pp. 536-54.
28. Wolff, *Understanding Rawls*, p. 178.
29. *Ibid.*, p. 179.
30. Rawls, "A Kantian Conception," p. 96.
31. Michelman, "Constitutional Welfare Rights," p. 323.
32. Rawls, "A Kantian Conception," p. 96.
33. T.M. Scanlon, "Rawls' Theory of Justice" in *Reading Rawls*, p. 194.
34. Michelman, "Constitutional Welfare Rights," pp. 321f.
35. Ronald M. Green, "Health Care and Justice in Contract Theory Perspective," in *Ethics and Health Policy* (Cambridge, Mass.: Ballinger Publishing Co., 1976), pp. 117f.

Equality of Opportunity and the Just Society

John H. Schaar
UNIVERSITY OF CALIFORNIA, SANTA CRUZ

"All social values...are to be distributed equally unless an unequal distribution...is to everyone's advantage. Injustice, then, is simply inequalities that are not to the benefit of all" (62, all parenthetical references are to John Rawls, *A Theory of Justice* [Cambridge, Mass.: Harvard University Press, 1971]). With that thesis, powerfully argued, John Rawls calls us forward to a vision of the future which captures the deepest yearnings and highest aspirations of the democratic ideal. "Justice is the first virtue of social institutions, as truth is of systems of thought" (3). With that assertion, Rawls recalls us to the very origins of political philosophy, reminding errant political theorists and citizens alike that justice *is* their first concern. Not power, or the GNP, or efficiency, or the endless pursuit of private interest but *justice* is the proper subject of political thought and action as it is the defining characteristic of the good state.

The reminder and the call come to a people as short of memory as they are of vision. We are sleepwalkers approaching a precipice, and our judgments of our prospects are clouded by fear, by cynicism, and by the habit of living well with the knowledge that at least two governments, swollen and stupid with power, can virtually destroy civilization in an hour. The end may be near. There may not be enough time or energy left for the peoples to call up their powers of social invention and devise the means of rescue. Nor do I think for a minute that a book alone can do much to wake us up. Perhaps the most it can do is to remind us of what we have already lost. Still, it is certain that if we do not look upon ourselves as creatures worth saving we shall go down.

John Rawls' book does honor and address us as such creatures, and reminds us that we honor ourselves most when we strive to build social arrangements that encourage self-respect, intelligence, and reciprocity. Only to the extent that a society is just does it provide such encouragement, and the just society is profoundly equalitarian in its basic arrangements. So Rawls argues, and as the argument joins hands with Aristotle in its assertion of the primacy of justice, so does it join hands with Marx and Rousseau in its assertion of the primacy of equality within justice.

The social welfare, or corporate capitalist and state socialist regimes of our day have exhausted their moral resources. We see all around us persons haunted by intimations of the end of the human experiment, whether in war, or in the despoilation of the earth, or in the wasteland of bureaucratic and technological regimentation. The emancipation of the race from political, economic, and social servitude has been the common aim of revolutionaries from 1776 to the present. While accomplishing much, all these vast efforts have lost momentum. We have no widely held conceptions of feasible future alternatives where democracy and human dignity might prevail. The forces of the Left, which once offered hope, nearly all have fallen victim to the theory that the big state and the hierarchical party are the proper instruments for building the good society. Their efforts and achievements, while no doubt more noble than anything offered by the Right, are badly flawed monuments to that bad theory. On the Right, work, thrift, enterprise, and profit are defended as moral values by only a few fanatics. Rather, corporate capitalism is said to be an effective method for raising the GNP and assuring a high level of consumption. No honest writer even pretends that the huge states of the West are in any significant sense democracies. At best, those regimes are praised as reasonably good guarantors of private liberties and reasonably satisfactory reconcilers of conflicting group interests. We hardly even pretend any longer that the whole system is admirable, worthy in its own right of loyalty and devotion. Probably the only real focal value offered us by our societies today is the satisfaction of private desires, largely through consumption. Beyond that, the system is pointless, unable to make a defense for itself, not admired much even by those who live in the rooms at the top.

I paint this familiar picture [once again] to set the context for what follows. John Rawls' book appeared at a time when serious ideas were in short supply, and it has provided the raw materials for a still-booming academic industry. Most of this commentary has been narrow and technical, precisionist and professional. While *A Theory of Justice* perhaps invites responses of that sort, being itself in parts quite technical and professional, the main source of that impulse is found in the Alexandrian tone of social theory in the universities today. We are masters of method, heirs of the Baconian conviction that great and difficult ends can be reached by standard and common means. I think that, in the end, one has not responded adequately to *A Theory of Justice* until one has appreciated the vision of the good society which is at its center. That vision is profoundly equalitarian: As Rawls puts it, in his characteristically moderate and modest tone, the two basic principles arrived at in the original position "express an equalitarian conception of justice" (100). I shall try to have a conversation with Rawls on the subject of equality—its place in the theory of justice; its place in the institutions and policies of the just society.

The subject is of the greatest practical importance. It is plain that the underlying question of all major domestic political debates in the advanced societies with social welfare regimes is the question of equality. What is the desirable degree of inequality? Which inequalities are acceptable and which are not? By what criteria shall we weigh claims to varying shares of the primary social goods? These are the most profound, most underlying questions of political life in the social welfare states, and increasingly it is recognized that we have no coherent answers to them. In the prescence of that (growing) incoherency, policy wobbles and public opinion grows querulous. You will search the literature long to find a serious thinker who supports and respects the present methods and policies of distribution as just and efficient.

Present methods and policies of distribution also are unsupported by any large body of political opinion. Modern economies with welfare structures continue to deal out, with fine and seemingly inevitable impartiality, a consistent portion of want and waste to some, and abundance and uneasy privilege to others. The social welfare regimes themselves, while huge and entrenched, seem increasingly fragile. Buffeted by organized groups pressing for incompatible relative shares, legislatures everywhere are numbed in stasis and confusion, unable to contribute a genuinely intelligent and independent voice to the formation of major policies. Everywhere there is a huge increase of centralized power, located in unstable political executives and unwieldy bureaucracies. The fear grows that the whole system could collapse, due to its own complexity on the one side, and to the excessive expectations and demands of various groups and interests on the other. The welfare state has aroused in many the expectation that government ought to be doing something for them, and as this expectation spreads to more groups in the population, so too spreads the mentality either of parasitical dependence on government handouts or of cynical rooting in the government trough. Policies are made by coalitions of self-interested minorities, with little attention to anything that can be called the public good. Furthermore, increasing numbers of people experience and accept the system as being this way, and in that acceptance, of course, reveal their own self-contempt while expressing contempt for others.

To put this in more neutral language, we might call on the standard distinction between genuinely public or collective goods, goods which must be available to all if they are to be available to any (national defense, or public parks, say, are the usual examples), and particular goods which can be made available to some and denied to others. The social welfare states are increasingly in the business of providing private goods, and the well-being of a great many groups depends on active and extensive government support. These supports are usually made in the form of income transfers and subsidies of many kinds, and it is these, not the provision of public goods, which excite the most passionate interest and provoke the most intense feelings of envy, resentment, and greed. Besides, there is also the issue of who will pay (privately, often indirectly) for public goods: a steel producer forced to install expensive equipment to reduce air pollution passes the charges on to consumers. Our methods of making decisions lead to increasing tension among all sorts of groups, and to pervasive dissatisfaction with a government which tries to do more and more for more and more groups. Even as governmental efforts and agencies expand, gratitude for those efforts and respect for those agencies decline.

Behind these manifest confusions lies a deeper confusion about the meaning of justice and the just society. That, in turn, translates into the question of what inequalities are acceptable and justifiable, and what ones are not. The present stalemate and confusion cannot last, for the system is inherently dynamic (the chief indicator of this is inflation which leads to demoralization, increasing hostility among groups, and the erosion of moral limits). Seen in this perspective, then, John Rawls' book, although it is in the nature of an academic treatise in political philosophy, addresses the most important practical political questions of our time. At stake in the question of justice is the question of democracy itself.[1]

EQUALITY OF OPPORTUNITY

In *A Theory of Justice* John Rawls proposes a basic shift in our operative definition of equality. He wants to revise our present understanding of equality of opportunity to a new meaning which he calls fair equality of opportunity modified by the difference principle and the principle of redress. The former, he says, suffers from a number of serious defects which the latter avoids. The remainder of my discussion centers on this topic. The best place to begin is with Rawls' criticism of the idea of equality of opportunity.

That notion is one of the brightest stars in the liberal firmament and one of the chief aims of liberal reform. Let every individual be assured an equal opportunity with every other individual to gain the goods and achieve the benefits which society affords. No one must enter the contest under socially-imposed handicaps. It is society's duty to see that all have an equal position at the starting gate. Then the race goes to the swiftest, the prize to the most deserving. That way we not only achieve justice among groups but also assure social progress. Each can rise as far as his talents and ambition will take him, so none can justifiably look with envy at those above. Equal opportunity releases energy, assures progress and innovation, and treats everyone with equal justice.

The principle of equality of opportunity sharpens to a cutting edge the primary liberal tenet that the individual is the basic unit of society and that all social arrangements are to be judged by reference to how they aid or hinder the fulfillment of individuals' needs, purposes, and abilities. Thus, the equal opportunity principle was one of the most effective weapons in the assault against the institutions of fixed hierarchy, rigid classes, and ascribed status. All places were to be equally open to all contenders under conditions of fair competition. Birth, patronage, tradition had no claims. Individual merit and ambition alone were to be the criteria for the allocation of places, and the race was to be open to all on equal terms. The implementation of equal opportunity meant nothing less than "a complete social revolution: a change in the social base of status and power, and a new mode of access to place and privilege in the society."[2]

Modern bourgeois society is based on this principle and is inconceivable without it. Equality of opportunity is taken as a rule of justice, and deviations from it bear the taint of illegitimacy and unfairness. Group after group has employed the principle in its struggle to overcome one or another kind of handicap and disadvantage. In its formulation as "careers open to talent" the equal opportunity principle is in theory, if not always in practice, at the very heart of the meritocratic society. That society awards the places of honor and high reward to trained or educated technical ability. Hence, equal opportunity requires equal access to the institutions which provide that training, and to the jobs which follow from it. If individuals or groups have been handicapped by prior social disadvantages, then it is a public duty to take affirmative action to overcome those disadvantages. By a logical extension, then, equal opportunity has grown to include a great variety of measures designed, as former President Johnson put it, to remove the "shackles" previously imposed by social attitudes and conditions on some of the contestants, such as blacks, various ethnic minorities, women, and others who have been weighted down by the burdens of poverty and prejudice.

Up until a few years ago, this understanding of equality as equality of opportunity reigned virtually unchallenged. It is still by far and away the dominant conception of equality in the public mind and the dominant conception employed in the making of public policy. Today, however, in some quarters the principle has come under attack. Far from being a remedy for inequality, and thus a move toward justice, the principle is held to be the fountain of new kinds of inequality, and thus a move toward injustice. Some writers are arguing that equality of opportunity should be replaced by equality of expectations, or even equality of results. John Rawls agrees with much of this criticism, and proposes that the liberal principle of equal opportunity must, as a requirement of justice, be replaced by a new understanding of "fair equality of opportunity." Let us look at his critique.

THE EQUAL RIGHT TO BECOME UNEQUAL

It is not my purpose to discuss the logic by which Rawls derives the principles of justice from the "original position." Rather, I shall cut into *A Theory of Justice* two or three levels above its foundation in order to move quickly toward the topic of equal opportunity. However, for the sake of easy reference, let me set down once again the familiar two principles (302–303): First Principle:

> Each person is to have an equal right to the most extensive total system of equal basic liberties compatible with a similar system of liberty for all.

Second Principle:

> Social and economic inequalities are to be arranged so that they are both:
> (a) to the greatest benefit of the least advantaged, consistent with the just savings principle, and;
> (b) attached to offices and positions open to all under conditions of fair equality of opportunity.

The first of these principles applies mainly to the equal liberties of citizenship—freedom of speech, association, the vote, and so forth. It will not much concern us here, although it should be noted that claims for equality increasingly take the form of expanding the concept and logic of equal citizenship into the areas of economic and social rights and benefits.[3] In a very important way, the notion of equality that is based on the equal status of citizens pervades Rawls' discussion of all other aspects of equality.

The second principle concerns the distribution of what Rawls usefully calls the primary social goods: rights and liberties, opportunities and powers, income and wealth, and a sense of self-worth (92). This is the principle which will concern us most. It proposes that persons in the original position would agree that justice requires an equal distribution of the social primary goods in all cases except where it can be shown that an unequal distribution is to the greatest advantage of the least advantaged group in the society. Rawls is here adopting an idea which was at the heart of primitive Christianity and which was powerfully reaffirmed by Marx: if you want to know whether a society is just, you must examine that society from the point of view of its lowliest members. The eyes of the poor and lowly—the least advantaged, as Rawls calls them—are the eyes that matter when it comes to looking at justice.

Armed with this principle, and standing at this vantage point, Rawls examines two other ways of distributing the primary social goods. The first is the "system of natural liberty" (72). It requires formal equality of opportunity so that all have "the same legal rights of access to all advantaged social positions" (72). Thus, all careers are, in principle, thrown open to talent. But no effort is made to preserve an equality or even similarity of social conditions among the competitors.

Hence, distributive shares are improperly influenced by both natural (e.g., native or genetic strengths and weaknesses) and social (e.g., poverty) factors that are utterly arbitrary from a moral point of view. It is radically defective as a principle of just distribution.

The liberal interpretation recognizes this and improves upon it by trying to "mitigate the influence of social contingencies and natural fortune on distributive shares" (73). This view insists on fair equality of opportunity which means, for example, that such factors as social class should not unduly affect either the conditions of entry or the outcomes of the contest for distributive shares. Society must take affirmative measures to assure that "those who are at the same level of talent and ability, and have the same willingness to use them, should have the same prospects of success regardless of their initial place in the social system..." (73).

The liberal interpretation of equal opportunity is a great improvement over the system of a merely formal right to compete for positions. It insists that careers must genuinely and substantively, and not just formally and legally, be open to talents. Still, it too is defective as an interpretation of equality and as a principle for distributing the primary social goods. At this point in the argument, Rawls finds two major defects in the liberal interpretation. First, although this interpretation tries to reduce the effect of social contingencies, it still "permits the distribution of wealth and income to be determined by the natural distribution of abilities and talents" (73–74). Such an outcome is of course arbitrary from a moral point of view. "There is no more reason to permit the distribution of income and wealth to be settled by the distribution of natural assets than by historical and social fortune" (74). Secondly, the principle of fair opportunity can be implemented only imperfectly, at least so long as the family exists. It is simply impossible in practice to secure similar chances of achievement for those similarly endowed, because the extent to which natural powers and faculties develop is affected by an enormous number and variety of social conditions. Some of these factors are unknown to us, others could be equalized only at enormous cost, and still others could never be equalized at all.[4]

DEMOCRATIC EQUALITY

If we are genuinely to treat all people equally as moral persons and not allow shares in the benefits of social life to be determined by the natural lottery or social fortune, then we need a different interpretation of equality. That needed interpretation is reached "by combining the principle of fair equality of opportunity with the difference principle" (75).

The difference principle asserts that inequalities are justifiable only if they are to the advantage of the worst-off representative man or group. We are to agree to consider the unequal distribution of talents and abilities among a population as a general social resource which can be arranged to work to the advantage of all, rather than as a source of strength for some and weakness for others. No one is to benefit from the contingencies of nature or social position "except in ways that redound to the well-being of others" (100). In the conception of justice as fairness, people in effect agree to share one another's fate. Reciprocity and mutual benefit must prevail over considerations of social efficiency and technocratic values (106–107).

It is important to appreciate here that Rawls is distinguishing between two senses of "desert" which are often confused. On the one side, we say a person "deserves" superior social rewards if he has done what the social system requires or expects of persons. On the other side, we sometimes think that persons with greater natural talents, say, deserve those talents or at least deserve the great advantages that come from exercising them. But this is surely wrong. From a moral point of view no one deserves his place in the distribution of native abilities any more than he deserves the place in society into which he was born. Hence, the more advantaged have no basis for claiming benefits unless those benefits contribute to the welfare of others, and especially to the welfare of those advantaged by nature or social position.

Finally, the democratic interpretation of equality (fair equality of opportunity modified by the difference principle) is completed by adding still one more dimension, the principle of redress. Just as undeserved advantages must be minimized, so must undeserved disadvantages be compensated for. "Thus...in order to treat all persons equally, to provide genuine equality of opportunity, society must give more attention to those with fewer native assets and to those born into the less favorable social positions. The idea is to redress the bias of contingencies in the direction of equality" (100–101).

Now, Rawls does not forward the principle of redress as the sole criterion of justice. It must be weighed in the balance along with others. Still, some examples will show that he goes quite far along the road of redress—certainly farther than anything met in present social policy. He suggests, for example, that greater resources might be spent on the early education of the less intelligent rather than the more intelligent (101). Or, as another example, he proposes that the social minimum (the level of primary social goods below which no one must fall) should be set at the point which maximizes the expectations of the least advantaged group over the long term (285). Obviously, such suggestions travel farther along the equalitarian road than anything contemplated in such established compensatory efforts as "headstart" or skill development or curriculum enrichment programs. It is not excessive to say that by the time Rawls is done, the last are put first; and this is said to be required by the democratic understanding of equality, and by the conception of justice as fairness. Persons must receive not according to their abilities but according to their needs.

A Theory of Justice is the most comprehensive and sophisticated effort in recent social theory to formulate what can properly be called a democratic and even socialist ethic. Rawls is far more consistent and coherent on this subject than Marx—let alone Engels—ever was. He sets nothing like the restrictions on substantive social and economic equality that the early liberals (e.g., Locke) did. Indeed, he goes far beyond even such great democratic thinkers as Jefferson for whom equality under the law of nature implied nothing about equality of condition in society. Indeed, Jefferson comes close to being a "meritocrat," as can be seen in his plan for education, for example, or in his view that the "natural aristocracy" was the most precious asset of mankind, and that the best society was that which brought the natural aristocracy to the fore. In some of his writings, (e.g., *Agrarian Justice*) Tom Paine went as far toward equality as Rawls, but in others he pulled back (e.g., his defense of chartered corporations and unequal incomes in *Dissertations on Government; The Affairs of the Bank; and Paper Money*).

Edward Bellamy (*Equality*) went farther toward "equal shares" than Rawls has, but he encumbered his case with such a heavy scheme for the regimentation of labor and the hierarchical, anti-democratic organization of government that few readers have found it palatable. Among recent writers, only George Bernard Shaw, so far as I know, made an argument for equal shares of the social product anywhere near as far-reaching as the one made by Rawls.[5] Shaw defined socialism as complete equality of income, and proceeded to make a lively, even brilliant, defense of socialism so defined. Unlike Rawls, however,

Shaw's case for equality is largely a case against the absurdities and irrationalities of the wage system as a method for measuring and rewarding individual contributions to the social good. Shaw offers little in the way of philosophical and moral argument for equality.

It should be apparent that in making these comparative assessments of "how equalitarian" Rawls is, I am leaving out of the comparison primitive societies, equalitarian utopian literature (such as More's *Utopia*), and the many—usually short-lived—efforts to establish equalitarian communities. This leaves out a lot, but the exclusion is justified because Rawls himself does not draw on these literatures and experiences. There is no doubt, for example, that the earliest communities of primitive Christians were radically equalitarian. Thus: "And all that believed were together, and had all things common; and sold their possessions and goods, and parted them to all men, as every man had need" (*Acts* 2:44–45). Again: "And the multitude of them that believed were of one heart and of one soul; neither said any of them that ought of the things which he possessed were his own, but they had all things common....Neither was there any among them that lacked: for as many as were possessors of lands or houses sold them, and brought the prices of the things that were sold, and laid them at the apostles' feet: and distribution was made unto every man according to his need" (*Acts* 4:32–35).

Rawls does not consider such materials for perfectly understandable reasons. He is a man of reason, not of faith, a philosopher, not a true believer. Justice may be the first virtue of society, but the theory of justice is only part of the whole theory of the good society. Besides, such experiences and ideas as those described in *Acts*, or those propounded in say, Babeuf's *Conspiracy of Equals*, were entirely and even fiercely "perfectionist" in nature, while Rawls' logic, as we shall see, precludes perfectionism.

Justice as fairness sets the claim for equality above all other claims save that of liberty; and, as we have seen "equal liberty," while formally prior to the difference principle, in the end requires for its implementation a far greater measure of social and economic equality than is presently the case. Rawls does not discuss liberty and equality within the familiar liberal framework which promptly sets them against each other as clashing and nearly incompatible principles. He sees the two as mutually enabling, and he stands as far as possible from the view which sees the moral life as, to use Weber's expression, the battlefield of "warring gods." Moreover, he is utterly unwilling to see equality as just one among many values, none of which has priority over the others.[6]

For Rawls, then, equality comes first. Goods are to be distributed equally unless it can be shown that an unequal distribution is to the advantage of the least advantaged. Furthermore, redress for the disadvantaged has a prior claim on the social conscience and on social policy over any considerations of efficiency or progress. That too is entailed in justice as fairness.

THE AMBIGUITIES OF EQUALITY

No ethical principle is without its ambiguities and uncertainties. No single principle can provide a guide in all cases of judgment and decision, for the complexity and heterogeneity of real situations and events inevitably outstrip the simplicity of abstract principles. And it is doubtful, regardless of the quality of the logic employed, whether all persons will ever agree on a definition of the good society, or even of the primary feature(s) of the good society.[7] Hence, it is no surprise that a number of difficulties can be found in Rawls' democratic interpretation of equality and equal opportunity. I shall discuss a few which I think troublesome, but readers must of course decide for themselves whether they think them so.

To begin, there are some complexities implicit in the principle of redress. On the whole, it is not too far off the mark to say that for Rawls the just society is the society of equals. In pursuit of this society, he proposes that persons or groups disadvantaged by the "natural lottery" or by their social position are to be compensated for these undeserved disadvantages. In general, the claims of the less fortunate take priority over all other claims. Thus, as mentioned earlier, Rawls suggests that "greater resources might be spent on the education of the less rather than the more intelligent..." (101).

Apart from the question of return on investment—trying to make silk purses out of sows' ears—this surely raises questions of justice. Perhaps the least fortunate should come first, but in putting them first Rawls comes pretty close to penalizing or handicapping the more fortunate. If the greater social resources go to the least naturally endowed and least socially favored persons, that in effect puts a handicap on the better endowed and more favored. One might agree with Rawls (104) that the better endowed cannot claim that they deserve social arrangements that do not contribute to the welfare of others. But by the same token, how can the less fortunate claim that *they do* deserve such arrangements? Or, to put the question differently, by what arguments would one persuade the better endowed that they should be penalized for the sake of the lesser endowed? At a certain point, and I expect that point would be reached quite quickly, such persons would find it hard to see such a society as "a collective venture for mutual advantage" as Rawls puts it. Denied the resources needed to develop their high potentialities, seeing those resources diverted to persons of lower potential, such persons would probably find other and harsher words than "mutual advantage" and "cooperative venture" to describe their society.

It is difficult to find the right words here. One feels some shame in questioning that the least fortunate should have priority on the social conscience and in the making of social policy. And today very few wish to return to the cruelties and stupidities of a social Darwinist rationale for ignoring the needs of the poor and the poorly endowed as necessary for progress and the improvement of the race.

Still, it is not easy to see that justice requires the full reversal (the last shall be first) that Rawls says it does. We do sometimes feel it right to "handicap" the most favored, but rarely do we make such arguments in the name of justice. Rather, we bring other considerations to bear. For example, race horces are handicapped according to their track records, but that is done not in the name of justice, but in order to make the race interesting to bettors. Or, a party of backpackers might agree that the strongest members should carry the heaviest loads, not in order to serve justice, but because all the members want to reach the same destination at about the same time. Furthermore, a hiking party has nothing like the complexity of a social order, with its multiplicity of persons, groups, interests, needs, and values. Under actual social conditions it is enormously difficult to explain, justify, and implement the kind of handicapping or redress which Rawls proposes.

Add to these considerations the fact that those who occupy the least favored social positions might occupy them out of choice—or, if not out of choice strictly speaking, out of a combination of personal and social factors so complex that no one really knows how to sort out and untangle them. In the United States today, for example, public education through high school is fairly easily available to all, and yet one-fifth of the students drop out before graduation. I do not think it has been shown that those persons quit mainly out of economic necessity. The reasons are many and heterogeneous, but in the end, the person chooses to drop out. How do the difference principle and the principle of redress apply here? Society may have strong obligations to compensate those who are kept down or held back for faults not their own, but if persons do not avail themselves of socially provided opportunities, then does society have still further and continuing obligations to compensate them for the losses that accumulate over life as a consequence of the early failure to take advantage of offered opportunities?

Suppose we were still to answer "yes"; that regardless of the reasons or factors that put persons among the least fortunate, those persons' needs and claims still take first priority in the distribution of social resources. Now comes an additional problem. Very often, we simply do not know how to help such persons. We do not know what resources provided in what ways would be genuinely helpful. The "problems" of some groups and individuals can seem intractable. Our wisdom is limited; our knowledge uncertain; our means and methods coarse and haphazard. Enormous expenditures can produce very small results, despite the best will and intention in the world.[8] Much experience seems to indicate that probably the only method that genuinely restores the unrestoreable, provides opportunities and liberties to the derelict and destructive, is the "method" of political and social revolution. *A Theory of Justice* moves entirely within what might be called an administrative and technical framework, and never comes close to talking about social revolution.[9]

I make this point because much experience with the efforts of the welfare-oriented regimes shows that it matters. Despite considerable effort, those regimes have been able to do rather little to stop the dynamic which continues to produce and reproduce very unfortunate disadvantaged groups. We have begun to read about families in their second and third generation of dependence on public subsidy. The War on Poverty ended in a decisive victory for poverty. Helping the unfortunate has produced a huge, unwieldy, and expensive bureaucratic establishment, but nobody is very satisfied with the substantive results. Furthermore, in the United States at least, most welfare efforts are aimed only at establishing a social minimum, a level below which no one can fall, and that is a much simpler task than the one set by Rawls' difference principle complemented by the principle of redress. When even this much simpler task has produced administrative, political, and moral problems that are far from solution, we must expect the task proposed by Rawls to strain to the breaking point our resources of social judgment, knowledge, and skill.

So, then, the difference principle appears simple and practical enough until it comes to the point of application, where, I think, it shows less utility as a guide to policy than one would wish. There are social conditions under which the difference principle is easily applied. We might imagine a band of Eskimo, say, who are facing starvation. They decide that the hunters among them should get the largest share of the band's food supplies because if the hunters grow too weak to hunt the whole group will perish. Under such conditions, it is not hard to understand and to apply the principle that goods should be distributed equally unless it can be shown that an unequal distribution is to the advantage of the least advantaged groups. There, something very like what Rawls calls "chain-connectedness" (80 ff.) really does obtain. But that is rarely the case (and even more rarely can it be *seen* to be the case) in large and highly complex societies. In such societies, it is not easy to say what would be required in the way of a showing, a proof, that an unequal distribution is to the advantage of the least advantaged. What would qualify as an argument? Rawls rejects efficiency and progress as criteria, just as he rejects the argument put forward by Keynes that the disproportionate share of wealth and income appropriated by the new rich of nineteenth-century capitalist society was justified because this unequal distribution "made possible the rapid build-up of capital and the more or less steady improvement in the general standard of living of everyone" (299).[10]

It might be possible in fairly simple cases, then, to persuade the members of disadvantaged groups that an unequal distribution is in their interest, whether right now, or at some future time. For example, it might be possible to persuade the disadvantaged that all the expensive resources society devotes to the training of highly skilled surgeons, as well as the rewards of income and status which society lavishes upon such persons, are in the interest of themselves as well, for anyone might at some time urgently require the services of a skilled surgeon. But there won't be many cases so clear cut. Society devotes large resources and lavishes great rewards on many kinds of persons and activities where the question of "advantage to the least advantaged" admits of no answer at all, let alone a clear and simple answer. What about lawyers, or musicians, or psychoanalysists, or professors of classics, or dancers? Try to apply the difference principle to decide whether elementary school teachers or university professors should have the higher salary. And yet, of course, such questions are the very stuff of social policy. I am not sure that the difference principle offers much guidance in dealing with them.

This leads to another question which, given the division of labor of the present collection of essays, properly belongs mainly to other writers but which I must at least mention. Certainly one of the basic propositions—even the keystone—of *A Theory of Justice* is the thesis of the priority of the right over the good (31 ff.). Closely connected with this is the argument that while some view of the good or of goodness is necessary in defending justice as fairness against other conceptions, something less than a full theory of the good will suffice. As Rawls puts it, what is needed is "the thin theory of the good" (See Secs. 15, 29, and 60, and esp. 395–97, 433–34). The basic idea of the thin theory of the good is that "rational individuals...desire certain things as prerequisites for carrying out their plans of life. Other things equal, they prefer a wider to a narrower liberty and opportunity, and a greater rather than a smaller share of wealth and income" (396). These four things, of course, are what Rawls calls the social primary goods which, according to the difference principle, are to be distributed equally unless it can be shown that an unequal distribution is to the advantage of the least advantaged group in the society.

Now, this is clear enough until one adds to the list of primary goods the one which Rawls calls "perhaps the most important," namely, self-respect (440). We respect ourselves when we have a secure conviction that our plan of life is worthwhile and when we are confident of our ability to carry out our intentions. Rawls has already argued that persons in the original position would not adopt the principle of perfectionism: no single plan of life or conception of the best life would be accepted. Hence, "for the purposes of justice [we] avoid any assessment of the relative value of one another's way of life" (442; see whole of Sec. 50). "Democracy in judging each other's aims is the foundation of self-respect in a well-ordered society" (442).

Rawls says that the social bases of self-respect are sufficiently assured if "for each person there is some association...to which he belongs and within which the activities that are rational for him are publicly affirmed by others" (441). In a different vocabulary, we gain our sense of self-esteem largely from our standing in our reference groups.

Now this is certainly correct. But it raises questions for the theory of justice as fairness which, I think, Rawls treats too lightly. Can one even imagine a society whose members are truly neutral ("avoid any assessment of the relative value") among all ways of life and all associations formed around the many particular ways or plans of life? In a very real sense, a society *is* a collectivity whose members agree that some ways of life, some values and activities and characters, are better than others and more to be preferred. Indeed, the decisive feature of real and healthy politics is collective decision-making about the best collective life. No social order is as indifferent toward the variety of plans of life as Rawls suggests, nor as tolerant as he argues the theory of justice requires them to be. Even the most devoted pluralist draws the line somewhere. And I am pretty sure, as an empirical matter, that no actual society regards all associations and activities as equally valuable so long as they "fulfill the Aristotelian Principle (and are compatible with the principle of justice)" (442). Perhaps we are not all "perfectionists" and perhaps most societies are not perfectionist either in the full sense of the term; but each of us has a streak of perfectionism in him, and every society has a tendency that way. Society may be, as Rawls puts it, a "social union of social unions" (520 ff.), but society is also a (whole) social union in which some (partial) social unions are preferred to others.[11]

These considerations matter a great deal when it comes to the question of the distribution of the social product or of the social primary goods. Let us for a moment imagine ourselves as active citizens and policy-makers, considering society from a legislative point of view. Many individuals and groups with different aims and memberships will press their claims for one or another kind of subsidy. Many social needs and possibilities will come to our attention and we shall have to decide which ones we shall encourage and which not. We need criteria to help us decide where and how to allocate the scarce resources at our disposal.

Now, is it likely that we would choose the difference principle as our criterion, and treat all claimants equally unless we could be convinced that an unequal distribution is to the advantage of the least advantaged? As soon as one puts the question this way, one sees the impossibility, even the ludicrousness, of the answer which, as I understand him, Rawls would give. We might employ a variety of criteria, some no doubt more respectable than others, but I doubt whether the difference principle would—or even could—be important among them. We must decide what we want our society to look like, which means that we must decide to encourage some activities, groups, and ways of life and to discourage others. Or, to put this in another vocabulary, we must establish priorities among the many possible needs and purposes which call for assistance. The difference principle, I think, is of virtually no help in doing this. It is, indeed, difficult even to imagine how it has any bearing on the problem. Probably one or another, more-or-less coherent version of perfectionism is needed.

The legislator, or the citizen, who treated all groups and ways of life equally unless to treat them unequally would be to the advantage of the least advantaged would be regarded, I think, not as a just person but as a fool or a shirker—one who either did not understand the very nature of social choice, or one who evaded the burdens of choosing.

If this is approximately correct, it follows, I think, that justice as fairness fails to achieve one of its most important goals—"to establish an enduring basis of self-respect throughout society" (441). Society (the legislator, the citizen) cannot treat all groups and ways of life as equally deserving of respect. To do so is, I think, flatly impossible. Since self-respect does, as Rawls says, come in important part from social approval of one's way of life, and since societies must approve some ways more than others, some groups and persons must find their plans of life socially disapproved relative to others. And insofar as self-respect derives from social approbation, such disapproved groups and persons will partly lack the social basis of self-respect. Just as the difference principle in particular fails to offer a guide to the allocation of social resources among the various ways of life, so does justice as fairness in general fail to provide the social basis for self-respect for all persons pursuing differing paths of life within the social order.

MERITOCRACY AND EQUALITY

The idea of meritocracy has come in for some hard criticism lately.[12] John Rawls seems to align himself with the main thrust of the criticism. In fact, his very "description" of meritocratic society comes closer to denunciation than any other passage in *A Theory of Justice:*

> This form of social order follows the principle of careers open to talents and uses equality of opportunity as a way of releasing men's energies in the pursuit of economic prosperity and political dominion. There exists a marked disparity between the upper and lower classes in both means of life and the rights and privileges of organizational authority. The culture of the poorer strata is impoverished while that of the governing and technocratic elite is securely based on the services of the national ends of power and wealth. Equality of opportunity means an equal chance to leave the less fortunate behind in the personal quest for influence and social position. (106-107)

That is a remarkable formulation. It appears to confuse some of the worst features of the civilization of the United States with some of the best features of the basic concept of meritocracy. Materialism, competitiveness, a wide gap between upper and lower strata, individualism, the passion for political dominion—these are indeed prominent characteristics of our civilization, but they are certainly not the defining properties of the idea of meritocracy. The basic idea of meritocracy is that those who hold the positions of authority and prestige should have earned them through the exercise of some skill, knowledge, or talent that the society desires and honors. The main idea is simply that the best should lead the rest and that social institutions and processes should be arranged so that the places of authority and prestige will be genuinely open to all who have, or who can develop the virtues, skills, and knowledge required to perform ably in those positions. It confuses thought to identify meritocracy as such with the substantive values and goals of a materialist and power-oriented society.[13]

The question of what ends and aims a society should set itself, and of what values, experiences, and types of human beings it should honor—these are political questions of the greatest importance. But they are not as such questions of justice. Nor do they as such have any bearing on the principle of meritocracy, which is simply that the top positions in the social order should be genuinely open to all who have the appropriate talent, knowledge, or virtue. It certainly makes sense to want those who are competent and worthy of praise to occupy the positions of authority and prestige. The big political job is to decide what is worthy of praise and honor, and then to arrange social institutions so that the best persons do get to the places of authority. This, it seems to me, is hardly a question of justice at all. It is a political question. And furthermore, no elaborate theory is needed to explain or to justify the point. The society which does not know what it means by the best way(s) of life, or which does not care, or which chooses the wrong ways, or which does not know how to honor and reward those who are most competent to hold authority might be just or unjust, or neither. What it would certainly be is foolish, contemptible, or vicious, and likely to endure more by lucky accident than by prudence.

Let me put this point sharply. Justice may indeed be as basic to the good society (may be "the first virtue of social institutions") as Rawls says it is, but equality of distribution may *not* be as basic to justice as he says it is—or, at least, not as basic in the ways he says it is. The question of justice really arises when those in the positions of authority either get there by methods which violate other persons, or when, once on top, they exploit their positions and take advantage of those beneath them. Great disparities of wealth, power, and status between the higher and the lower strata are certainly unjust, and *A Theory of Justice* offers us one cogent explanation of why this is the case. Similarly, when the top positions are not genuinely open to all on the basis of merit, that too is unjust, and here again Rawls' book helps us understand why. In these ways and areas, the difference principle and the principle of redress make genuine contributions to our understanding both of equality and of the just society and offer useful guidance in the formation of social policy. These are valuable contributions and *A Theory of Justice* merits much praise for making them.

But, as I have suggested above, when the principles are extended to some of the other areas where Rawls takes them, they offer as much confusion as clarity, and perhaps endanger things worth holding dear. *A Theory of Justice* does, I think, show some traces of the "levelling" spirit which aristocratic temperaments have always feared in democracy—though I do not mean to suggest that there is even the faintest whiff of envy or resentment anywhere in Rawls' book. I think Rawls is persuasive in his general argument for the priority of the claims of the disadvantaged and unfortunate. But I do not think he has found the right way both to acknowledge that priority *and* to open the widest possible avenues for the best to rise to positions of eminence and authority through work and talent. And surely, keeping those avenues open is not a matter merely, or even mainly, of favoring the private advantage of the best and most talented, but a matter of advancing the public good. There is a kind of bias in the book against differences of status and reward. He develops a powerful argument for the equal respect due to each of us as human beings and as citizens of a state that claims to be a democracy. But, I think, he does not find the way to combine this equal respect for all with the greater praise and rewards which are owed to some.

When we think of "the best" we should not restrict ourselves to what is rewarded in this time and among us. The concept is, practically speaking, a universal. That is, there has probably never been a social order without a ranking system, a table of values, a pattern of awarding honor and prestige. This is as basic and as widespread a concept and practice as equality, and at least as important as equality is in any theory of social justice. We might want and deserve to be treated in some respects as equals, but we also want to honor and reward the best. Furthermore, there is probably no labelling or classifying term used by human beings about human beings that does not carry a connotation of high and low, superior and inferior. In the human realm, every comparison or distinction is invidious. We want to be treated alike, but we also want to stand out and be treated as different.

A Theory of Justice understands wholeheartedly the urge toward equality, but it does not appreciate fully, I think, the passion for distinction and the place that passion occupies both in the lives of individuals and social orders, and in the formulation of patterns of distributive justice.

NOTES

1. John Rawls himself never loses sight of this—one-third of his book concerns quite practical questions—but many of his critics have.
2. Daniel Bell, "On Meritocracy and Equality," *The Public Interest*, No. 29 (Fall, 1972), p. 41.
3. On this extension of the logic of the equal status of citizenship to include social and economic equalities, see T.H. Marshall, *Citizenship and Social Class* (Cambridge, England: 1950), esp. p. 9 ff.
4. More and more criticism of the liberal concept of equal opportunity centers on the argument, accepted by Rawls, that the principle cannot be implemented in practice. See, e.g., my "Equality of Opportunity, and Beyond," in *Nomos*, IX, *Equality*, ed. by J. Roland Pennock and John W. Chapman (New York: Atherton, 1967), pp. 228-249; and Christopher Jencks, et al., *Inequality: A Reassessment of the Effect of Family and Schooling in America* (New York: Basic Books, 1972). The Jencks book is especially important, for it casts into doubt both the efficacy of all efforts to equalize educational opportunity, and the belief that excellent educational background and high achievement in later life are directly and strongly correlated. This, of course, brings into question the very foundations of the meritocratic society.
5. Louis Crompton, ed., *The Road to Equality: Ten Unpublished Lectures and Essays by Bernard Shaw* (Boston: Beacon Press, 1971). See especially the essays "Redistribution of Wealth" and "The Simple Truth About Socialism." Both were apparently written around 1910, but not published during Shaw's lifetime.
6. This is of course where positivist and relativist theories leave the matter. For an example, see Isaiah Berlin, "Equality as an Ideal," in Frederick A. Olafson, ed., *Justice and Social Policy: A Collection of Essays* (Englewood Cliffs, New Jersey: Prentice-Hall, 1961) pp. 128, 150.
7. It is important to note that the proposition that "justice is the first virtue of social institutions...." is more in the nature of an assertion than of a rationally justified claim. Rawls does offer a number of strong considera-

tions for the proposition, but they in no way add up to a "proof." Others have brought forward equally strong considerations in favor of say, stability, or the protection and encouragement of religion, or the development of an esthetic, moral, or military elite as the first virtue of social institutions. Rawls lumps all such efforts together as "perfectionist" theories, and tries to show that men in the original position would not choose them. Other papers in this volume deal with these related problems. I mention them only to show that it is possible to disagree with Rawls at the most fundamental level.

8. Most public programs designed to help the unemployed and unskilled gain employable skills illustrate this very inefficient ratio between cost and benefit.
9. To see what I mean here, examine Rawls' discussion of the institutions required to implement the theory of justice (esp. pp. 195-201). The approach is that of the gadgeteer. For a political understanding of how justice is to be achieved, see, e.g., William Hinton, *Fanshen: A Documentary of Revolution in a Chinese Village* (New York: Random House, 1966).
10. Perhaps Keynes' argument is shoddy when judged by the theoretical requirements of justice as fairness, but there is much to be said for it in a rough-and-ready way. The great economic improvements in the condition of the poorer classes during the nineteenth and twentieth centuries were in fact made possible by the cornucopia of goods produced by the technological revolution and the capitalist spirit of enterprise. These forces, and not any theory of justice, have been the mainsprings of improvement in the conditions of the poor. Similarly, it is easier to mount social welfare programs in times of great economic growth than in times of recession. Compare the enormous expansion of redistributive programs in the United States between 1960-65 and today.
11. Of course, the Aristotelian Principle (for definition, see 426) itself contains or provides a standard of judgment among ways of life. And I am not sure Rawls is right in saying that the application of this Principle "is always relative to the individual..." (441). That is certainly not so in Aristotle himself, who argued that one way of life was superior to all others, that the persons who followed this way were superior to others, and that societies which encouraged and rewarded the superior way were superior to those which did not. This raises questions which are central to Rawls' whole theory but not central to the portion of it which most concerns me. Hence, I pursue those questions no farther.
12. In many ways, the finest criticism still remains that of Michael D. Young's fiction *The Rise of the Meritocracy, 1870-2033: The New Elite of Our Social Revolution* (London: Thames and Hudson, 1958).
13. It also confuses thought to identify completely the actual persons and institutions who hold power and authority in the United States with the meritocratic ideal—presenting the actual situation as though it embodied the ideal. This confusion is often made by anxious academic persons who leap to de-

fend their esteemed institutions and privileged positions against the invasion of imagined hordes of the unqualified marching under such banners as "affirmative action" or "equal opportunity." I once overheard a conversation between the Chairman of the Political Science Department of a major university and a black publicist and politician which went to the heart of the matter. The politician observed that he saw very, very few blacks among the faculty. The Chairman earnestly responded that if only qualified minority persons could be found, his Department would jump to hire them. The politician replied, in effect: "No, no, you don't get my point. I know a lot about this campus, and I know there are plenty of dumb white sons-of-bitches on the faculty. What I *don't* see here are dumb black sons-of-bitches."

CHAPTER 2

Applications of the Rawlsian System of Justice

Dealing with Injustice in a Reasonably Just Society: Some Observations on a Rawls' Theory of Political Duty

Daniel M. Farrell
OHIO STATE UNIVERSITY

INTRODUCTION

In Chapter VI of his book, Rawls argues that the members of a reasonably just democratic society have a *prima facie* moral duty to obey the law in that society. He argues, further, that this particular moral duty should be heavily weighted in such a society, so that when it conflicts, or seems to conflict with other *prima facie* moral rights and duties, it will typically override them (350–55; all parenthetical citations are to John Rawls, *A Theory of Justice* [Cambridge, Mass.: Harvard University Press, 1971]).[1] Let us refer to these claims as I and II. In connection with II, Rawls is especially anxious to show that in a reasonably just society, when one's duty to obey the law conflicts with one's right to resist injustice, the duty to obey the law typically overrides the right to resist injustice. On this view, Rawls says, it will sometimes happen—indeed, it may often happen, he says—that a member of a reasonably just society is morally bound, all things considered, to obey what he believes, and believes correctly, is an unjust law or lawful policy. This is because in such a society a law or lawful policy has to be seriously unjust before one's right to resist injustice will override one's duty to obey the law.

Now these claims constitute the core of Rawls' theory of political duty, and hence they are important in and of themselves. However, they are also of interest for another reason: they are among the few concrete examples Rawls gives us of the principles that constitute his theory of right—his general theory of normative ethics, in other words. This theory, which Rawls calls "rightness as fairness" and which has received surprisingly little critical attention, would have us think of the principles of normative ethics as the outcome of hypothetical deliberations that take place behind a carefully constructed veil of ignorance: deliberations, that is, that take place in what Rawls calls "the original position" (111; 184). "The concept of something's being right," on this view, "is the same as . . . the concept of its being in accordance with the principles that in the original position would be acknowledged to apply to things of its kind" (111); ". . . something is right," in other words, "if and only if it satisfies [these] principles" (184).

In what follows, I want to do two things. First, I want to show how Rawls defends I and II and how his defense of these principles ultimately depends upon certain extremely controversial assumptions that he makes in his general theory of right and wrong. Secondly, I want to assess these assumptions, or some of them at any rate, and thereby Rawls' defense of I and II. For purposes of argument, I shall concentrate primarily on Rawls' defense of II. As we shall see, II suggests a rather rigorously legalistic answer to the question of how one ought to react to what one believes to be injustice in a reasonably just society. What I shall show below is that the assumptions Rawls needs in order to prove II are dubious at best and, more likely, just plain false. Hence, I shall show that for all Rawls tells us, II is insupportable. I shall also suggest, in concluding, that Rawls' approach to ethics is seriously imperiled—in a general way—by some of the assumptions that he makes and that in this respect he is in exactly the same position as certain so-called "rule-utilitarians." I shall not attempt to show that Rawls' approach is clearly and unequivocally mistaken, but I will try to show that it faces some very serious problems, problems that it is not at all clear Rawls can get around.

THE ARGUMENT FOR I

Rawls' argument for II is connected with his argument for I, so let us begin with the latter. This argument is based on a principle that Rawls calls "the natural duty of justice," a principle that would supposedly be agreed to in the original position and that requires us to support and uphold just institutions when they exist and apply to us. Since any principle that would be accepted in the original position is a principle that we are bound to abide by in real life, in Rawls' view, other things being equal, he concludes that in real life we have a *prima facie* moral duty to support and uphold just institutions when they exist and apply to us. Let us concede this for now. If we also assume, with Rawls, that a society that comes reasonably close to satisfying his two principles of justice is a just institution, it follows that the members of such a society are morally bound to support and uphold it. That is, it follows that they have a *prima facie* moral duty to do what is required of them for the maintenance of that society.

Now the argument thus far says nothing about obeying the law. If the parties in the original position went no further in their hypothetical deliberations than these remarks suggest, we could imagine them leaving the original position with the natural duty of justice, and whatever other *prima facie* moral principles they have agreed to, and confronting the question of whether or not to obey the law by asking (in real life) what the principles they have agreed to in the original position have to do with the institutions and practices they encounter in real life. Rawls does not imagine them proceeding in this way, however. Instead, having imagined them agreeing to the natural duty of justice, he goes on to imagine the parties in the original position asking themselves the following question: what is required of us if we are to maintain a reasonably just democratic society?[2] The answer, according to Rawls, is that it is impossible to maintain such a society without general compliance with some institutionalized device (or devices) for resolving social conflict. In fact, Rawls is even more specific. He supposes that it is impossible to maintain such a society without general compliance with the principle of majority rule (353–54). Since this is so, he says, and since the parties in the original position have already agreed to do what is required of them to support and uphold such a society, they will conclude that, all other things being equal, the members of a reasonably just society are morally bound to comply with the principle of majority rule and with the duly enacted laws and policies that it produces.

THE ARGUMENT FOR II

The parties in the original position will recognize, Rawls says, that it is inevitable that sometimes the results of the principle of majority rule will be unacceptable, morally, to some members of society. That is, they will recognize that it is inevitable that sometimes the results of the principle of majority rule will be perceived by some members of society to be unjust. Obviously, the argument thus far does not tell people what to do in such cases. For even if it is sound, the most the argument above proves is that, all other things being equal, a member of a reasonably just society ought to abide by valid results of the principle of majority rule. If one also believes that, all other things being equal, one should resist injustice when one believes that one is confronted by it, one will not be in a position to say what one should do, on balance, in cases where these two principles conflict. What this shows, Rawls says, is that the parties in the original position will have to take a stand about what one should do in real life when the results of the principle of majority rule seem to one to be unjust. In other words, they will have to decide what sort of attitude or policy to adopt with respect to cases where one's right to resist injustice seems to conflict with one's duty to obey the law.

Now when this question arises, Rawls observes, the parties in the original position have already agreed that some sort of commitment to the principle of majority rule is better than none at all. Hence, they cannot reject the use of the principle of majority rule altogether, even though they recognize that it is at best an instance of imperfect procedural justice. What then will they do? They will agree to accept the principle of majority rule with its defects as well as its virtues, Rawls says, at least within certain limits. They will agree to abide by the results of the principle of majority rule as such, in other words, within limits, whether those results are just or not (354–55).[3]

THE TROUBLE WITH THE ARGUMENT FOR II

It should be obvious that the argument above will not do, at least as it stands. For suppose we concede that some sort of agreement to abide by the results of the principle of majority rule is preferable to no agreement at all, and suppose we concede as well that no institutionalized decision-making device can obviate the possibility of unjust results. It follows that the parties in the original position must adopt the policy favored by Rawls only if we *also* assume that they must choose between adopting his policy or adopting no policy at all. But why should we make such an assumption? Offhand, it seems the parties in the original position might well undertake a firm but *limited* commitment to the results of the principle of majority rule. For example, they might adopt a policy like the following: "One is to abide by duly enacted legislation, all other things being equal, provided it does not seem to one that that legislation is unjust or otherwise morally objectionable. In cases of the latter sort, one is morally free to do as one sees fit." Of course, Rawls may believe that adopting a principle of this sort is as good as no agreement at all, since he may believe that such a principle amounts to no more than anarachism. But then he needs to prove this and to prove as well that anarchism of this sort is untenable. Otherwise, why should we suppose that it would be unacceptable to the parties in the original position?

TWO POLICIES CONTRASTED

Suppose we take the point of view of the parties in the original position when they are confronted with the problem raised above. They have already agreed to be bound by the results of the principle of majority rule, other things being equal; they must now decide what policy they should adopt with respect to cases where the results of the principle of majority rule seem to be unjust. What sorts of policies are open to them?

One policy represents the attitude of the "institutionalist" as I shall refer to him. This is the policy that is favored by Rawls. On this view, one must generally abide by the results of the principle of majority rule whether one believes that they are just or not. If the putative injustices are serious enough, and if they are of certain specifiable kinds, one may contemplate resisting them illegally provided one is also willing to subject oneself to certain constraints on how illegal dissent is to be conducted in a reasonably just society. Outside of the special circumstances where illegal resistance is even thinkable in a reasonably just society, however, one is morally bound to accept the results of the political process. In other words, outside of these cases, the results of the political process have an absolute weight *vis-à-vis* one's right to resist injustice.[4]

Another, very different policy represents the attitude of the "individualist" as I shall refer to him. This is the attitude of the man who refuses to commit himself to any strict rule or principle with respect to cases of apparent conflict between the right to resist injustice and the duty to obey the law. When the results of the principle of majority rule seem to be unjust, the individualist says, we simply have to ask ourselves whether, *in the case at hand*, justice will be better served by resistance or by compliance. The fact that a certain course of conduct would be illegal is something we have to take into account when we are faced with a conflict of the relevant sort, on the individualist's view, but it is not a feature of a potential course of conduct that should always or even ordinarily be decisive in determining what we do. We should take each controversial case as it comes and try to resolve such cases only as they arise.

Is the individualist committed to any particular *method* for deciding what to do when he is confronted with what seems to be a conflict between his right to resist injustice and his duty to obey the law? It seems to me that he is not. He might say we simply have to "consult our intuitions" in such cases. In other words, the individualist might be an *intuitionist* about conflict resolution, despite the fact that he is what might be called a "contractualist" about the derivation of the primary moral principles that we are supposing will sometimes be in conflict (principles like I above, that is). However, the individualist certainly does not have to be an intuitionist in this respect. In fact, he could very well be a *contractualist* with respect to the question of how we are to determine, in a particular case, whether our right to resist injustice overrides our duty to obey the law. Having refused to use the method of hypothetical agreement for picking a constitutive, second-order moral principle, or a "priority rule," in other words, as Rawls would have us do, the individualist could nonetheless choose to use this method as a device for deciding what to do in particular cases. Thus, when he is confronted by an actual case of apparent conflict—a conflict between his right to resist injustice, that is, and his duty to obey the law—the individualist might go about deciding what to do by asking himself the following question: "What would rational, self-interested parties in an original position of ignorance and equality say about this particular case? Would they say that in this case one ought to go ahead and disobey the law, or would they say that in this case one ought not to disobey the law?" If he concludes that the parties in the original position would endorse disobedience to the law in a case exactly like the one that confronts him, he will also conclude that he is justified in disobeying the law. If he concludes that they would oppose illegal actions in such a case, on the other hand, he will say that—for that very reason—under the circumstances, illegal actions would be morally wrong.

Of course, if Rawls is right, the parties in the original position cannot consider particular cases, since the thickness of the veil of ignorance prevents this. Hence, if Rawls is right, "individualism" is not really an option for the parties in the original position. But this is just to say that Rawls favors making decisions about priority rules in the original position while the individualist is against this. Instead, the latter favors using the idea of agreements reached in the original position—the idea of hypothetical agreements reached behind a certain veil of ignorance, that is—for resolving particular cases of moral conflict. This disagreement—the disagreement between Rawls and the individualist on this particular point—represents a substantive disagreement in meta-ethics, as we shall see. Hence, it will not do for Rawls to *define* the idea of the original position so that judgments about particular cases cannot be made in it. Rather, he must argue for the policy he favors here, and he must argue against the policy favored by the individualist.

"ACT-" AND "RULE-" CONTRACTARIANISM

What can we say about the difference between the two policies described above—that is, about the difference between the institutionalist's policy for dealing with what he believes to be injustice in a reasonably just society and the individualist's policy for dealing with this problem? Notice first that the difference is not one that has to do, directly at any rate, with *how much illegality* each of them is willing to tolerate in a reasonably just society. It might turn out that Rawls and the individualist would actually agree about what one ought to do, all things considered, in every case in which there appeared to be a conflict between the right to resist injustice and the duty to obey the law. Rather, the difference is one that has to do with how they believe a man should go about *deciding* what to do when he perceives a conflict between his duty to obey the law and his right to resist injustice. Rawls believes there are a number of substantive general principles we ought to use in such cases, principles that can be formulated in advance of any actual conflict and that a rational, self-interested agent would be willing to accept, in an original position of ignorance and equality, as defining the nature and extent of his commitment to the principle of majority rule.[5] The individualist, on the other hand, believes that even when principles of the sort Rawls favors can be formulated, they represent nothing more than what might be called "cautionary rules" or "rules of thumb."[6] In particular, he believes that no principle for resolving moral conflicts is a principle that may not be overridden, in a given case, by an individual's decision that justice will be better served by violating the general principle rather than abiding by it. Of course, the individualist-contractualist has at least one important thing in common with the institutionalist: they both believe that, in some sense, when we want to determine what we (morally) ought to do in a given case, we have to determine whether in doing one thing rather than another we will be doing what people behind a certain veil of ignorance would say we ought to do. The difference between them in this regard is of the first importance, however: the institutionalist believes we ought to formulate certain general principles in the original position and use these principles to decide what to do in particular cases, while the individualist—the individualist-contractualist, that is to say—believes that whatever general principles we use as rules of thumb, we are always free, morally, to apply the method of hypothetical agreement directly to the case at hand.

Now when we think of the disagreement between Rawls and the individualist in this way, we can see that it is analogous, in some respects, to the disagreement between certain so-called act- and rule-utilitarians.[7] The analogy is not perfect, as we shall see, but it does help to illuminate the basis of the disagreement between Rawls and the individualist. To see this, consider the following rather simple-minded way of conceiving the act-rule dispute among utilitarians. The act-utilitarian, we might say, is someone who wants us to think of ourselves as at all times free, at least in principle, to apply the principle of utility directly to particular cases. For practical reasons, of course, the act-utilitarian may well urge the adoption of any number of so-called "strategy principles" or "summary rules" for use on a day-to-day basis. However, we are always free, on his view, to abandon these general rules when in a particular case we can promote more good for more people by doing so.[8] The rule-utilitarian, by contrast, is someone who would have us use the principle of utility to derive a number of fairly general moral principles—principles like Rawls' I and II above, for example—and then use *these principles* to decide particular cases of moral conflict. Once we have derived these general rules, on the rule-utilitarian's view, we are *not* free to deviate from them in particular cases, even when it happens that in a given case deviation will actually promote more overall utility than not.[9]

Consider now what Rawls is asking us to do when he asks us to accept a principle like II above in the original position. In effect, he is asking us to agree to something like the following proposal: "Using a certain method for moral decision-making—namely, the method of hypothetical agreement—let us derive certain general principles or moral rules for resolving moral conflicts, and let us agree to stick to these rules, thus chosen, in actual cases of conflict." Like the rule-utilitarian, in other words, Rawls seems to favor one method for deriving moral rules—namely, the direct use of the method of hypothetical agreement—and another method for resolving particular cases—namely the direct use of the rules and, thereby, only an indirect use of the method of hypothetical agreement. This, of course, is precisely what the individualist refuses to do. Like the act-utilitarian, *he* wants to be free to resolve particular moral conflicts by taking each case as it comes—by asking of a given case "What would the parties in the original position say about this particular case?" Even if he recognizes certain moral rules as providing helpful guidelines or useful rules of thumb, the individualist, like the act-utilitarian, is someone who wants us to think of ourselves as at all times free, at least in principle, to use the very principle that the rule-theorist would have us use for deriving moral rules as a principle for resolving particular cases of moral conflict.

Of course, even if this analogy holds—and I shall pursue it in somewhat more detail below—we may note an apparent disanalogy at once. Thus far, we have been discussing the situation of the parties in the original position when, having accepted a constitutive moral principle directing members of a reasonably just society to obey the law, other things being equal, they confront the question of what to do when this rule or principle seems to conflict with another—for example, with the principle that articulates our *prima facie* right to resist injustice. But then for all we have said so far, both the individualist and the institutionalist seem to be in agreement on "rule-" rather than "act-" contractarianism with respect to the *primary* moral rules they recognize. Their disagreement, thus far, is about the secondary moral principles or priority rules that Rawls favors. This contrasts sharply with the situation that exists between act- and rule-utilitarians. *They* disagree "all the way down the line," so to speak. The act-utilitarian, at least as he is commonly conceived, accepts *neither* what we have called primary principles—constitutive ones at any rate—*nor* what we are calling secondary ones (priority rules). In this regard, then, our individualist, or act-contractarian, seems to be a less thoroughgoing act-theorist than his utilitarian counterpart.

THE LOCUS OF THE DISAGREEMENT BETWEEN ACT- AND RULE-CONTRACTARIANS AND ITS EXTENT

Suppose we ask how Rawls would react to the individualist or act-contractarian position described above. Apart from the final paragraph in the previous section, I have been writing as though the disagreement between Rawls and the individualist is a disagreement that would arise in the original position when the parties there are trying to decide whether to adopt an individualist attitude toward apparently unjust results of the principle of majority rule or whether to adopt an institutionalist attitude toward such results. Thus, for all we have said so far, we might suppose that Rawls' argument with act-contractarianism may most naturally be thought of as an argument that would take place at this point in the original position. This, however, would be a mistake. For given the way Rawls structures his inquiry in *A Theory of Justice*, the question of whether to adopt an act- or a rule-oriented attitude about matters of the sort that interest us here is a question that is not *open* to the parties in the original position. They are there only to choose general, second-order moral principles for resolving first-order moral conflicts, and not to decide particular moral cases. There is no question of their *refraining* from picking II, therefore, or some similar priority rule, and adopting instead an act-oriented policy for dealing with injustice; Rawls has already seen to it that they are there to do the one thing and not the other.

Now in light of this fact about how Rawls is proceeding in *A Theory of Justice*, it should be obvious that at this point a really thoroughgoing analysis of his moral theory would have to raise at once the very big question of why it is that Rawls more or less just *assumes* that the parties in the original position are there to choose general moral principles of the sort he favors—why he constructs his argument so that the parties in the original position *have* to choose priority rules, in other words—and what, if anything, can be said for thus precluding, from the outset, the possibility of what I am calling "act-contractarianism." What's more, as we shall see in a moment, a thorough analysis would have to ask not only why Rawls insists on *priority rules*—or general, *second-order* moral principles—but also why he insists on very general *first-order* moral principles, principles like I above, for example. Why shouldn't we be act-contractarians from the start, the individualist might say, agreeing *neither* to I *nor* to II, nor to any other such principles, resolving instead to try to solve our moral dilemmas in real life by asking, in any given case, what rational, self-interested parties behind a veil of ignorance would say about that particular case?

A thoroughgoing and far-reaching analysis of the sort that is really required here is not one we can undertake in the present paper. For one thing, the issue we would be raising is a very big one indeed—one about which a great deal has been written in connection with the act-rule dispute among utilitarians and one about which a great deal would need to be said before we could even begin to hope for a compelling solution to the analogous problem that we would be raising for contractarians. For another thing, we would perforce be turning our attention away from the issue that actually interests us here: namely, Rawls' rationale for II above. To be sure, if my remarks thus far are right, the argument for II ultimately involves, *inter alia*, the assumption that we ought to be rule- rather than act-contractarians; hence, it may be that we cannot assess the argument for II without assessing that assumption in general terms. Nonetheless, I propose to try to do so. After all, it may be that Rawls' assumption has particularly clear and unpalatable implications in the context of normative political theory, even if it is for the most part fairly plausible and unproblematic in other areas of ethics. Holding aside the very *big* question that is implicit in Rawls' approach here—"Shall we, in general, be act- or rule-contractarians, assuming we are bound to be contractarians?"—let us take up in what follows the much more limited question of just how reasonable it will seem to the parties in the original position—at the point where we left them above—to adopt the rule that Rawls favors for dealing with injustice in a reasonably just society rather than no such rule at all. Obviously, in proceeding in this way we will be distorting things somewhat, since we will be allowing the parties in the original position an option which, as we have seen, they do not in fact *have* at this point in their deliberations. Proceeding in this way clearly has some merit, however, despite the fact that it is not quite the way Rawls would have us proceed. For what we will in effect be doing is providing a test case for Rawls' rule-contractarian approach to ethics generally and to normative political theory in particular. If Rawls is right, the decision *not* to choose a priority rule in the case that interests us should not seem very attractive. For anything that can be said against act-contractarianism generally could presumably be said against act-contractarianism with respect to the issue that concerns us here and hence could be said at this point in the original position to anyone who happens to favor the act-contractarian approach. As we shall see, however, the decision not to choose a priority rule *will* seem like an attractive one, while the choice of the priority rule Rawls favors will not.

A final word about the *extent* of the disagreement between so-called act- and rule-contractarians is necessary, however, before we take up the issue that will occupy us in the remainder of this paper. As we saw in the final paragraph of the previous section, if we imagine the individualist's worries emerging only at the point where Rawls is urging him to accept a priority rule like II, there seems to be an important disanalogy between act- and rule-contractarianism, on the one hand, and act- and rule-utilitarianism, on the other. In the latter case, the act theorist refuses to accept binding, general moral principles at any level whatsoever—whether we are talking about so-called "first-order" or "primary" moral principles like I above or so-called "second-order" principles (that is to say, "priority rules") like II. In the former case, on the other hand (the case of contractarianism, that is), at least for all we have said so far, the act-theorist accepts binding and very general moral principles at the one level (the level of primary rules) but not at the other level (the level of secondary rules). Hence, as we have seen, the act-contractarian thus far seems like a less thorough-going act-theorist than his utilitarian counterpart.

Now from what has been said above, it should be obvious that this disanalogy is in fact only an apparent one. For there is certainly no *a priori* reason for limiting the individualist's act-oriented inclinations to the particular point where we have imagined them emerging above. Thus, if someone in the original position were to insist on an act-oriented attitude right from the start—if someone were to reject the idea of adopting binding, general moral principles at *both* the first or "primary-rule" level *and* the second or "secondary-rule" level, that is—he would seem to have a right to do so, *prima facie* at any rate, and a right to demand at once an argument for *not* doing so. Of course, it may turn out that there are reasons for adopting a rule-oriented attitude at the one level (the first level) and not adopting it at the other (the second level); this remains to be seen.[10] The point to be emphasized here is that since we have no reason to preclude the possibility that someone in the original position will want to adopt an act-oriented attitude right from the start, and every reason to ask exactly where and why it is plausible to suppose an act-oriented theory is and is not appropriate, it seems we would be justified in assuming that there is, at least in theory, an even closer analogy between act- and rule-contractarianism, on the one hand, and act- and rule-utilitarianism, on the other, than the discussion in the previous section suggests. For it seems that, like the act-utilitarian, a really thorough-going act-contractarian would refuse to adopt binding (or constitutive) general moral principles at *both* the level of primary rules like I *and* the level of secondary moral rules like II.

Now despite the fact that we might thus imagine our individualist's act-contractarianism emerging even earlier than we have so far supposed, I shall not attempt to evaluate this more thoroughgoing individualism here. A really complete analysis of the implications of act- and rule-contractarianism would indeed require that we do so, of course, and that we do a lot more besides. As I have already indicated, however, a thoroughgoing analysis of this sort is out of the question here. If my doubts about II are well-founded, and if I can show this, perhaps we will then want to go on to question the viability of I. And if both I and II seem ill-grounded, *because* they are cast as binding or "constitutive" moral principles in Rawls' system rather than as mere "cautionary rules" or rules of thumb, perhaps it will seem plausible to question Rawls' rule-oriented approach generally. Here, however, I want to limit my attention to just the one question: why should we suppose that the parties in the original position would choose a priority-rule like II for dealing with injustice in a reasonably just society rather than no rule at all? What are the relative merits of "institutionalism" and "individualism," in other words, or of the so-called "act-" and "rule-contractarian" approaches to the problem of dealing with injustice in a reasonably just society?

THE ARGUMENT FROM EXPERIENCE AND INJUSTICE

Early in his book, Rawls remarks that ". . . an injustice is tolerable only when it is necessary to prevent an even greater injustice" (4). What he means by this, I take it, is that violations of his own two principles of justice are tolerable, morally, only when tolerating them is necessary to prevent even worse violations of those principles. Since the rule-contractarian policy that Rawls favors for dealing with allegedly unjust results of the principle of majority rule would require us to comply with certain violations of his principles of justice, we may infer that at least part of his rationale for adopting that policy is that accepting and abiding by it is necessary for avoiding some even greater injustice than the injustice involved in enforcing and complying with unjust laws. What injustice does Rawls have in mind here, though, and in what sense is complying with unjust laws necessary to avoid it?

Rawls' answer is connected with the so-called natural duty of justice, I think, and is based on Rawls' perception of what is required for the maintenance of a reasonably just society:

> ...our natural duty to uphold just institutions binds us to comply with unjust laws and policies, or at least not to oppose them by illegal means as long as they do not exceed certain limits of injustice. Being required to support a just constitution, we must go along with one of its essential principles, that of majority rule (354).

A bit later, Rawls continues:

> In choosing a constitution, then, and in adopting some form of majority rule, the parties accept the risks of suffering the defects of one another's knowledge and sense of justice in order to gain the advantages of an effective legislative procedure. *There is no other way to manage a democratic regime* (355; emphasis added).

Now I take it that what Rawls has in mind here is something like the following. Suppose we imagine the parties in the original position deliberating about just what attitude one ought to take (in real life) for dealing with what one sincerely believes to be legislative injustice (assuming, of course, the overall context of a reasonably just society). One *could* take the attitude of the individualist, we may suppose. That is to say, one could resolve (in the original position) to leave it to the individual's private judgment (in real life) to indicate, on a case by case basis, what one ought to do in the relevant cases. If we do this, however, we are courting disaster, Rawls seems to think. For even if we suppose for the sake of argument that maintaining a reasonably just society is consistent with generalized noncompliance with demonstrably unjust results of the principle of majority rule, it is clear that the individualist's method will lead not only to resistance to *un*just laws and policies but also, at least some of the time, to resistance to *just* laws and policies. This is because people do not always agree about questions of legislative justice and injustice as they arise in everyday life, Rawls suggests, and also because, acting on a case by case basis, people will inevitably be susceptible to ignorance, bias, and so on. If we adopt (in the original position) the institutionalist's attitude, on the other hand, we will be safeguarding ourselves—and thereby our society—against precisely these dangers, Rawls would say. To be sure, using the latter policy, we will sometimes have to force ourselves to go along with unjust laws and policies, laws and policies which, using the former method, we would have resisted. But this will be for the best in the end, Rawls would say, in the very specific sense that only in this way do we have even a *chance* of maintaining our society.

What evidence is there for Rawls' implicit empirical claim here—the claim that the maintenance of a reasonably just society requires an attitude toward apparently unjust laws and policies like the institutionalist attitude described above and that the maintenance of such a society is in fact *inconsistent* with an attitude like that of the individualist? Rawls himself suggests no evidence whatsoever. Of course, one knows more or less what he has in mind here—the literature on the act-rule controversy among *utilitarians*, after all, is strewn with cases, imaginary and otherwise, where people, using the *principle of utility* on a case by case basis, create just those unfortunate results that general moral rules are supposed to help them avoid. Nevertheless, as we shall see below, it is not at all clear that the individualist cannot get around most of these difficulties in a fairly straightforward way: namely, by urging the adoption of any number of so-called cautionary principles or rules of thumb. Besides, the attitude or policy that Rawls is asking us to adopt here is really quite a conservative one and one which *could*, as we shall see below, have ill-effects just as serious as those it is intended to avoid. Hence, it is rather surprising that he makes no attempt whatever to defend his second assumption—or at least provide some evidence for it—in the course of his argument for II.

Perhaps we should take a somewhat broader view of Rawls' predicament here, however, before we castigate him any further for not providing any evidence in defense of his implicit empirical claim in the argument above. We have seen that the choice between what we are calling "individualism" and "institutionalism" is really a choice that ought to be made on the basis of good, hard empirical evidence. Rather than harping on the fact that Rawls himself does not provide much in the way of evidence, suppose we simply ask what evidence there is. Interestingly enough, when we press this question, we quickly come to see that there *isn't* much evidence, or so it seems to me, other than the "evidence" each of us thinks he has as a result of his own experience in these matters. This is simply because, to the best of my knowledge, there have not been any compelling studies of just the question that would have to be answered if we were to have the answers that we need.[11]

At this point our situation is this, it seems to me. We are supposing that the parties in the original position have to make a decision which they would be best advised to make—as rational, self-interested individuals—on the basis of the best evidence that is available. Unfortunately, the best evidence that is available is not very good (or so I am supposing). Where, then, does this leave the parties in the original position? It leaves them in the following situation, I believe, a situation that Rawls, at least, need not be upset about. They have to make a policy-decision without a lot of evidence about how the various choices they might make are likely to turn out. In other words, they have to make a decision under conditions of restricted knowledge or relative uncertainty. Offhand, this is certainly not an unfortunate upshot for Rawls, since throughout *A Theory of Justice* he deals with very important policy-decisions by assuming restricted knowledge or relative uncertainty of just this sort. Suppose, therefore, we ask how, proceeding as Rawls would proceed, the parties in the original position would handle the question that interests us, supposing they must handle it under conditions of restricted knowledge or relative uncertainty. Would the act-contractarian's approach to the problem of dealing with injustice in a reasonably just society seem at all attractive to them under these conditions, or would they adopt the rule-contractarian's approach, as Rawls supposes?

THE ARGUMENT FROM UNCERTAINTY

Our problem is to decide whether individualism or institutionalism will seem most reasonable to the parties in the original position, if we assume that they really don't *know* for certain exactly what the results of adopting one or the other policy will be. Offhand, it might seem that the parties in the original position would inevitably choose the institutionalist (or rule-contractarian) attitude under the conditions just described, since even if it is not obvious or *certain* that we will get into trouble if we adopt the individualist's approach, it might appear to be much more *likely* that we will get into trouble using this approach, rather than the institutionalist alternative. After all, if we leave it open to people to resist (illegally) valid results of the principle of majority rule whenever they believe that those results are unjust and that justice is likely to be better served (in the long run) by resistance rather than compliance—in other words, whenever they believe that the parties in the original position would endorse illegal action in the case at hand if they were considering it *as a particular case*—we may expect to see considerably more disobedience to the law—much of it unjustifiable—than under the institutionalist alternative. This is simply because given the sort of moral freedom we are discussing here, people are apt to use it and, inevitably, abuse it. People will often apply the method of hypothetical agreement in biased or ignorant ways, for example, if they are allowed to use it on a case by case basis. If they are required to stick to certain general moral rules, on the other hand, there is that much less room for bias and ignorance to lead to untoward results. To be sure, this argument continues, we are assuming that we do not really know exactly how people will use the added moral freedom that individualism or "act-contractarianism" would give them. However, given that there is a good possibility that they will use it badly, at least some of the time, it might seem better to err on the side of encouraging too little individuality in these matters, for the sake of promoting more stability, than to err by encouraging too much individuality.

Now if there were no way for the individualist to get around the difficulties just raised, and if there were no correlative difficulties involved in the institutionalist alternative, I think we would have to conclude that from the point of view of restricted knowledge, the case for institutionalism is indeed better than the case for individualism. It is not the case, however, that there is no way for the individualist to try to deal with the problems raised above, nor is it true that there are no problems of an equally serious sort with the institutionalist alternative to individualism. Let us begin with the latter point, the question of just what difficulties accrue to the *institutionalist's* approach to the problem of dealing with injustice in a reasonably just society.

We may note, to begin with, that one difficulty with institutionalism is that it is at least *possible* that in real life an institutionalist attitude will have adverse effects on a person's capacity to deal with moral conflicts autonomously. After all, even the institutionalist admits that sometimes the presumption in favor of compliance with the principle of majority rule breaks down; his point is simply that the sorts of circumstances under which this is the case can be anticipated, in more or less general ways, and built into the rules of the game as explicit exceptions to those rules. Since part of the point of the institutionalist's position is to inculcate general rules, however, and to inculcate a willingness to go along with them, we must recognize that it is at least possible that over time people will come to rely more on the rules than on their own assessment of the case at hand, even in cases where the institutionalist himself would concede that the rule does not apply.[12]

There is another difficulty with the institutionalist's view, however, which is even more important than the difficulty just described. To see this, recall that the institutionalist point of view has the following consequence: if, in the original position, I agree to adopt the institutionalist point of view in real life, I am agreeing to obey duly-enacted legislation in real life even in certain cases where I *know* that that legislation is unjust and where I know as well that more good than evil would come from *resisting* that legislation. Thus, suppose I am confronted, in real life, by what is obviously a case of economic injustice (within the context of what is all-in-all a reasonably just society), and suppose it is quite clear—or as clear as such things can ever be, at any rate—that the positive effects of resisting this injustice illegally are likely to be considerably greater than the negative effects (I am supposing that the injustice in question is sanctioned by a valid law and that my only way of resisting it would be to disobey the law). According to Rawls' interpretation of II, I must go along with this legalized injustice and I must go along with it despite the fact that if this case were judged by the parties in the original position *as a particular case*, rather than as a *kind* of case, they would say that I ought *not* to go along with it. This is because when we think of the kind of case this is, Rawls says—a case of alleged *economic* injustice—we must admit that it is the kind of case where reasonable people can—and probably often will—reasonably disagree. Unless we ban illegal resistance to alleged economic injustice altogether, therefore, we will be in the position of having to allow it whenever someone is inclined to believe that his is an especially clear and serious case, Rawls argues. Since many people are likely to feel this way, Rawls implies, *much of the time*, and since only a small proportion of them is actually going to be right, we are better off prohibiting illegal resistance to alleged economic injustice altogether rather than leaving people free to resist it if and when they see fit to do so on act-contractarian grounds.[13]

Now I say that the feature of institutionalism just remarked upon is an unattractive aspect of that view because I assume that—all other things being equal—a view that would have us go along with injustice, in a situation where no harm will come from *not* going along with it and where some *good* might be done by not going along with it, is less attractive than a view that does not have this consequence. Of course, Rawls would no doubt concede that this is an unattractive aspect of his view. His point is simply that this disadvantage of institutionalism is the price we have to pay in order to get around the likely disadvantages of individualism. However, suppose the individualist could suggest a way of ameliorating the disadvantages of his own view—the evident tendency to social instability that seems to be inherent in it—and at the same time avoiding the disadvantages of institutionalism just remarked upon. Even if this would not show conclusively that individualism is preferable to institutionalism, from the point of view of uncertainty that we are assuming, it would certainly put individualism in a better light than Rawls allows. For the burden of proof would then quite clearly be on the shoulders of the institutionalist rather than, as Rawls seems to think, on the shoulders of the individualist.

How might the individualist adjust his view, then, so as to avoid the difficulties suggested earlier? Suppose he did what many act-utilitarians have done in exactly similar circumstances: suppose he adopted a so-called "cautionary rule" in the original position, directing him to be mindful (in real life) of the difficulties just described and, for the reasons just mentioned, to be particularly careful when contemplating illegal resistance to economic injustice.[14] The point of such a rule would be much the same as the point of the institutionalist's general rules: for most cases it would in effect tell the individualist how to act and hence for most cases he would not have to ask himself what the parties in the original position would say about that particular case. Such a rule would differ in at least one very important respect, however, from the institutionalist's rules: unlike the institutionalist, the individualist would always be free, in principle, to act against the advice of his general rule if he believed (on act-contractarian grounds) that this would be advisable in a given case. Thus, while an individualist is free, unlike Rawls' institutionalist, to resist economic injustice illegally in a reasonably just society, he will not be likely to do so very often because, like the institutionalist, he leaves the original position with a general principle that creates a strong presumption against such conduct. Still, he *is* free to do so—that is the essence of his position and also what is to him its single greatest advantage.

Now the institutionalist will no doubt reply to this move by arguing that, these cautionary rules notwithstanding, inasmuch as the individualist retains the right to act against the advice of the cautionary rule when he decides that this is advisable in a given case, his position is in the end just as untenable—because just as likely to produce social instability—as the position of the individualist who does not adopt cautionary rules in the first place. How plausible will this rejoinder be, however? Part of the *point* of adopting cautionary principles in the original position, after all, is to put oneself in "double jeopardy," so to speak. That is to say, once articulated, these principles have the effect of making it doubly wrong to disobey the law in certain cases —cases where one ought *not* to have disobeyed the law, on act-contractarian grounds, and where one ought to have been particularly sensitive to the possibility of going wrong because of the existence of the cautionary rule in question. In such cases, if one makes a moral mistake—through hasty judgment, say, or irresponsible ignorance—not only has one made that mistake, which is already to have done wrong, but one has done so in a situation where one has been warned that such mistakes are particularly apt to be made, which is also wrong. With moral safeguards of this sort—that is to say, with cautionary principles the effect of which is to make it doubly wrong for people to err (morally) because of ignorance or self-interest—it seems to me that the individualist could obviate the major portion of the difficulties which the institutionalist is getting at when he warns us of the dangers of the individualist's act-contractarian approach to moral conflict. For if we assume that the moral agents in question are anxious to avoid moral error, we must also assume that, in light of our cautionary principles, they will do their best to avoid hasty, ignorant and self-interested judgments of the sort that worry the institutionalist.

The institutionalist's reply to all this, of course, will be essentially the same as his initial response to the individualist's proposal. Unless we bind ourselves to general rules, in his view, and unless we bind ourselves quite rigorously, there is always room for ignorance, error or bias to lead us astray in our moral decision-making. And this is true, I think; there *is* always room, if we take the individualist point of view, for ignorance, error, and so on, to lead us astray. However, the individualist *can* take steps to minimize the likelihood of our actually going astray in these ways, as I have just shown, and it is not clear that, given these controls, his position is as untenable as the institutionalist contends. In fact, if one asks how most people in our own society act when they are confronted with apparent conflicts between their right to resist injustice and their duty to obey the law, and if one asks as well what the results of the prevalent policy actually are, I think we must concede that (i) most people—I mean, of course, among those who are concerned to act only in ways they would be willing to *defend*, morally—act as individualists, and (ii) their doing so has over the years proven to be quite consistent with the maintenance of a stable society. In other words, so far as I can see, although most people in our own society do have fairly clear and fairly firm general moral principles about (for the most part) obeying the law, they hold these principles not as binding moral principles of the sort Rawls favors but as cautionary rules of the sort suggested above. And the results of this practice—again, so far as I can see--have not been such as to undermine the stability of our society.

CONCLUDING REMARKS

The argument of the preceding section is, of course, inconclusive. What I have tried to show, however, is not that Rawls is clearly mistaken in adopting the institutionalist or rule-contractarian point of view, but that there are no compelling reasons to think that he is correct in adopting this point of view and a number of good reasons for believing that he may be mistaken. I have also tried to show that Rawls' point of view has its costs—costs which, so far as I can see, Rawls nowhere tries to counterbalance by citing relevant, countervailing gains. Of course, it is possible that everything in the preceding *two* sections is quite beside the point, since there may be general, programmatic reasons for supposing that rule-contractarianism is superior to act-contractarianism. Until we hear more about these reasons, however, I think we have to say that Rawls' case for I and II is unproven.[15]

NOTES

1. I shall assume below that the reader is familiar with Rawls' use of the notion of a *prima facie* duty, which is essentially that of W.D. Ross in *The Right and the Good* (Oxford: The Clarendon Press, 1930), and of the correlative notion of an "on-balance" duty or a duty "all things considered." For Rawls' explication, see *A Theory of Justice*, pp. 340-42.
2. Actually, we must say that *sometimes* Rawls imagines the parties in the original position asking themselves this question; at other times, he writes as though the deliberations that concern us here occur at the hypothetical constitutional convention. See p. 353 ff., for example, where Rawls suggests that the deliberations in question take place at the hypothetical constitutional convention, and p. 383, where he says that we must look at his views on these matters "from the standpoint of the persons in the original position." In what follows, I shall think of the original position as the locus of the deliberations that concern us here. Although the parties in question actually

adopt a constitution and commit themselves to some form of majority rule only at the hypothetical constitutional convention, it is reasonable to suppose that they have discussed the relative strength of their ties to these devices in the original position, where the principles of right for individuals (and also, presumably, their relative weights) have already been chosen. (See especially p. 383, where Rawls says that "having chosen principles for individuals," the parties in the original position "must work out guidelines for assessing the strength of the natural duties and obligations, and, in particular, the strength of the duty to comply with a just constitution and one of its basic procedures, that of the majority rule" [383].)

3. Note that in the passage alluded to here, Rawls writes as though the deliberative parties are at the hypothetical constitutional convention. See footnote 2 above in this regard.
4. It is important to notice that the institutionalist (as exemplified by Rawls) concedes that under certain circumstances a member of a reasonably just society *may* be justified in resisting the results of the principle of majority rule. However, he holds that the circumstances under which this will be the case are more or less well-defined. In particular, he holds that unless the results of the principle of majority rule are quite clearly and very seriously unjust, one is morally bound to go along with them (see footnote 5 below for more detail). One is *not* free, on this view, to take each case as it comes and decide for oneself whether justice is likely to be better served in a given case by resistance or by compliance. Rather, one is bound to obey, for the most part, and to obey whether or not one believes that justice will be best served by obedience in the case at hand.
5. Consider, for example, the theory of civil disobedience that Rawls develops in Chapter VI of his book. While he is willing to allow members of a reasonably just society the right to resist (illegally) serious violations of his first principle of justice, which guarantees maximum equal liberty, and blatant violations of the second part of his second principle of justice, which guarantees fair equality of opportunity, Rawls is not willing to allow them the right to resist less serious (and unsystematic) violations of these principles, nor is he willing to allow them a right to resist *any* violations of the first part of his second principle of justice (the so-called "difference principle"), which sets the standards for economic justice in a reasonably just society (371–73). Disagreements about matters of economic justice are both too common and too complicated, Rawls says, to make it tenable to recognize a right to resist what one believes is economic injustice in such a society. Thus, he supposes that the parties in the original position would agree not just to a *presumption* against illegal resistance aimed at putative violations of the difference principle but to a substantive moral principle that prohibits such resistance altogether.
6. See David Lyons, *Forms and Limits of Utilitarianism* (Oxford: The Clarendon Press, 1965), p. 145.

7. I am indebted in what follows to some of Joel Feinberg's remarks in "Duty and Obligation in the Non-ideal World," *The Journal of Philosophy*, Vol. LXX, No. 9 (May 10, 1973). I have also been helped by some of R.M. Hare's reflections in "Rawls' Theory of Justice—I," *The Philosophical Quarterly*, Vol. 23, No. 91 (April, 1973) and, more importantly, in "Rules of War and Moral Reasoning," *Philosophy and Public Affairs*, Vol. 1, No. 2 (Winter, 1972).
8. J.S. Mill is a good example, I believe (see "Utilitarianism" in *Utilitarianism, Liberty and Representative Government* (New York: E.P. Dutton & Co., Inc., 1951), pp. 28-30), though this way of interpreting Mill has been challenged. (See J.O. Urmson, "The Interpretation of the Moral Philosophy of J.S. Mill," *The Philosophical Quarterly*, Vol. 3 (1953), for an interpretation of Mill as a rule-utilitarian, and Maurice Mandelbaum, "Two Moot Issues in Mill's *Utilitarianism*," in J.B. Schneewind, ed., *Mill: A Collection of Critical Essays* (New York: Doubleday & Co., Inc., 1968) for an act-utilitarian interpretation.)
9. For the best statement of this view, see Rawls' own very well-known essay, "Two Concepts of Rules," *The Philosophical Review*, Vol. 65 (1955).
10. Interestingly, such theories are not uncommon, at least among non-contractarians. Ross' well-known theory is an example—see *The Right and the Good*, pp. 17-19 and 29-32—and Hare's is another (see especially "Rules of War", p. 177).
11. For a report of some research that would be relevant—but only in a very general way—to a study of the questions that concern us here, see Stanley Milgram's book, *Obedience to Authority* (New York: Harper & Row, 1974). Even if his very tentative conclusions are sound, however—and this is itself a very controversial question—Milgram's research is certainly not enough to enable us to answer, even tentatively, the questions that we are raising here.
12. Although, as I argued in the previous section, there is not much evidence one way or the other about these matters, what little evidence there is suggests that the possibility raised here is certainly not just an academic one. For some of that evidence suggests that people are all too ready to stick to general rules, even if it involves inflicting the grossest forms of suffering and injustice on others. See Milgram, *Obedience to Authority*, *passim.*
13. Note that it is not important to my argument that we pick *Rawls'* particular brand of institutionalism, though I have done so for the sake of simplicity. Any version of rule-contractarianism will have binding, general moral principles of the relevant sort, even if it does not have the particular principles Rawls favors. Hence, for certain possible cases, any version will be liable to the difficulties suggested here.
14. As indicated above (see note 6), the designation of these principles as "cautionary principles" is due to Lyons. The use of such principles, however, is at least as old as Mill's "Utilitarianism." See Mill, p. 30, where he speaks of such principles as analogous to the calculations summarized in a nautical almanac.

15. A draft of this paper was read at the Conference on Justice at Ohio University in August, 1976, and I am indebted to a number of the participants for helpful comments, particularly to Gail Corrado and Bernard Williams. I am also indebted to Leslie Francis, Don Hubin, William Lycan, Bernard Rosen, Dan Turner and Linda Wentsler.

Justice and International Relations

Charles R. Beitz
SWARTHMORE COLLEGE

> Current events have brought into sharp focus the realization that . . . there is a close inter-relationship between the prosperity of the developed countries and the growth and development of the developing countries. . . . International cooperation for development is the shared goal and common duty of all countries.[1]

Do citizens of relatively affluent countries have obligations founded on justice to share their wealth with poorer people elsewhere?* Certainly they have some redistributive obligations, founded on humanitarian principles requiring those who are able to help those who, without help, would surely perish. But obligations of justice might be thought to be more demanding than this, to require greater sacrifices on the part of the relatively well-off and perhaps sacrifices of a different kind as well. Obligations of justice, unlike those of humanitarian aid, might also require efforts at large-scale institutional reform. The rhetoric of the United Nations General Assembly's "Declaration on the Establishment of a New International Economic Order" suggests that it is this sort of obligation which requires wealthy countries to substantially increase their contributions to less developed countries

*This paper previously appeared in *Philosophy and Public Affairs*, 4 (1975), 360–89 and is reprinted by permission of Princeton University Press. A revised and extended version appears in the author's book, *Political Theory and International Relations*, published by Princeton University Press (1979).

and to radically restructure the world economic system. Do such obligations exist?

This question does not pose special theoretical problems for the utilitarian, for whom the distinction between obligations of humanitarian aid and obligations of social justice is a second-order distinction. Since utility-maximizing calculations need not respect national boundaries, there is a method of decision available when different kinds of obligations conflict. Contractarian political theories, on the other hand, might be expected to encounter problems in application to questions of global distributive justice. Contractarian principles usually rest on the relations in which people stand in a national community united by common acceptance of a conception of justice. It is not obvious that contractarian principles with such a justification underwrite any redistributive obligations between persons situated in different national societies.

This feature of contractarian principles has motivated several criticisms of Rawls' theory of justice (all parenthetical references are to John Rawls, *A Theory of Justice* [Cambridge, Mass.: Harvard University Press, 1971]). These criticisms hold, roughly, that it is wrong to take the nation-state as the foundation of contractarian principles, that, instead, such principles ought to apply globally.[2] I want to pursue this theme here, in part because it raises interesting problems for Rawls' theory, but also because it illuminates several important features of the question of global justice, a question to which too little attention has been paid by political philosophers. In view of increasingly visible global distributive inequalities, famine, and environmental deterioration, it can hardly be denied that this question poses a main political challenge for the foreseeable future.

My discussion has four parts. I begin by reviewing Rawls' brief remarks on international justice, and show that these make sense only on the empirical assumption that nation-states are self-sufficient. Even if this assumption is correct, I then claim, Rawls' discussion of international justice is importantly incomplete, for it neglects certain problems about natural resources. In part three, I go on to question the empirical foundation of the self-sufficiency assumption, and sketch the consequences for Rawlsian ideal theory of abandoning the assumption. In conclusion, I explore the relation of an ideal theory of international justice to some representative problems of politics in the nonideal world.

This is a large agenda, despite the absence of any extended consideration of the most familiar problems of international ethics, those concerning the morality of war, which I take up only briefly. While these are hardly insignificant questions, it seems to me that preoccupation with them has too often diverted attention from more pressing distributive issues. Inevitably, I must leave some problems undeveloped, and merely suggest some possible solutions for others. The question of global distributive justice is both complicated and new, and I have not been able to formulate my conclusions as a complete theory of global justice. My main concern has been to see what such a theory might involve.

RAWLS' IDEAL THEORY OF INTERNATIONAL JUSTICE

Justice, Rawls says, is the first virtue of social institutions. Its "primary subject" is "the basic structure of society, or more exactly, the way in which the major social institutions distribute fundamental rights and duties and determine the division of advantages from social cooperation" (7). The central problem for a theory of justice is to identify principles by which the basic structure of society can be appraised.

Rawls' two principles characterize "a special case of the problem of justice." They do not characterize "the justice of the law of nations and of relations between states" (7–8) because they rest on morally significant features of an ongoing scheme of social cooperation. If national boundaries are thought to set off discrete schemes of social cooperation, as Rawls assumes (457), then the relations of persons situated in different nation-states cannot be regulated by principles of social justice. As Rawls develops the theory, it is only after principles of social justice and principles for individuals (the "natural duties") are chosen that principles for international relations are considered, and then only in the most perfunctory manner.

Rawls assumes that "the boundaries" of the cooperative schemes to which the two principles apply "are given by the notion of a self-contained national community" (457). This assumption "is not relaxed until the derivation of the principles of justice for the law of nations" (457). In other words, the assumption that national communities are self-contained is relaxed when international justice is considered. What does this mean? If the societies of the world are now to be conceived as open, fully interdependent systems, the world as a whole would fit the description of a scheme of social cooperation and the arguments for the two principles would apply, a fortiori, at the global level. The principles of justice for international politics would be the two principles for domestic society writ large, and their application would have a very radical result, given the tendency to equality of the difference principle. On the other hand, if societies are thought to be *entirely* self-contained—that is, if they are to have no relations of any kind with persons, groups or societies beyond their borders—then why consider international justice at all? Principles of justice are suppose to regulate conduct, but if, ex hypothesi, there is no possibility of international conduct, it is difficult to see why principles of justice for the law of nations should be of any interest whatsoever. Rawls' discussion of justice among nations suggests that neither of these alternatives describes his intention in the passage quoted. Some intermediate assumption isrequired. Apparently, nation-states are now to be conceived as largely self-sufficient, but not entirely self-contained. Probably he imagines a world of nation-states which interact only in marginal ways; perhaps they maintain diplomatic relations, participate in a postal union, maintain limited cultural exchanges, and so on. Certainly the self-sufficiency assumption requires that societies have no significant trade or economic relations.

Why, in such a world, are principles of international justice of interest? Rawls says that the restriction to ideal theory has the consequence that each society's external behavior is controlled by its principles of justice and of individual right, which prevent unjust wars and interference with human rights abroad (379). So it cannot be the need to prohibit unjust wars that prompts his worries about the law of nations. The most plausible motivation for considering principles of justice for the law of nations is suggested by an aside regarding the difficulties of disarmament (336), in which Rawls suggests that state relations are inherently unstable despite each one's commitment to its own principles of justice. Agreement on regulative principles would then be a source of security for each state concerning each other's external behavior, and would represent the minimum conditions of peaceful coexistence.

For the purpose of justifying principles for nations, Rawls reinterprets the original position as a sort of international conference:

> One may extend the interpretation of the original position and think of the parties as representatives of different nations who must choose together the fundamental principles to adjudicate conflicting claims among states. Following out the conception of the initial situation, I assume that these representatives are deprived of various kinds of information. While they know that they represent

> different nations each living under the normal circumstances of human life, they know nothing about the particular circumstances of their own society. . . . Once again the contracting parties, in this case, representatives of states, are allowed only enough knowledge to make a rational choice to protect their interests but not so much that the more fortunate among them can take advantage of their special situation. This original position is fair between nations; it nullifies the contingencies and biases of historical fate (378).

While he does not actually present arguments for any particular principles for nations, he claims that "there would be no surprises, since the principles chosen would, I think, be familiar ones" (378). The examples given are indeed familiar; they include principles of self-determination, nonintervention, the *pacta sunt servanda* rule, a principle of justifiable self-defense, and principles defining *jus ad bellum* and *jus in bello.*[3] These are supposed to be consequences of a basic principle of equality among nations, to which the parties in the reinterpreted original position would agree in order to protect and uphold their interests in successfully operating their respective societies and in securing compliance with the principles for individuals which protect human life (378, 115).

One objection to such reasoning might be that there is no guarantee that all of the world's states are internally just, or if they are, that they are just in the sense specified by the two principles. If some societies are unjust according to the two principles, some familiar and serious problems arise. In a world including South Africa or Chile, for example, one can easily imagine situations in which the principle of nonintervention would prevent other nations from intervening in support of an oppressed minority fighting to establish a more just regime, and this might seem implausible. More generally, one might ask why a principle which defends a state's ability to pursue an immoral end is to count as a moral principle imposing a requirement of justice on other states.

Such an objection, while indicating a serious problem in the real world, would be inappropriate in this context because the law of nations, in Rawls, applies to a world of just states. Nothing in Rawls' theory specifically requires this assumption, but it seems consonant with the restriction to ideal theory and parallels the assumption of "strict compliance" which plays a role in arguments for the two principles in domestic societies. It is important to see, however, that the suggested justification of these traditional rules of international law rests on an ideal assumption not present in most discussions of this subject. It does not self-evidently follow that these rules ought to hold in the nonideal world; at a minimum, an additional condition would be required, limiting the scope of the traditional rules to cases in which their observance would promote the development of just institutions in presently unjust societies while observing the basic protections of human rights expressed by the natural duties and preserving a stable international order in which just societies can exist.

Someone might think that other principles would be acknowledged, for example, regarding population control and regulation of the environment. Or perhaps, as Barry suggests, the parties would agree to form some sort of permanent international organization with consultative, diplomatic, and even collective security functions.[4] However, there is no obvious reason why such agreements would emerge from an international original position, at least so long as the constituent societies are assumed to be largely self-sufficient. Probably the parties, if confronted with these possibilities, would reason that fundamental questions of justice are not raised by them, and such issues of policy as arise from time to time in the real world could be handled with traditional treaty mechanisms underwritten by the rule, already acknowledged, that treaties are to be observed. Other issues that are today subjects of international negotiation—those relating to international regulation of common areas such as the sea and outer space—are of a different sort. They call for a kind of regulation that requires substantive cooperation among peoples in the use of areas not presently within the boundaries of any society. A cooperative scheme must be evolved which would create new wealth to which no national society could have a legitimate claim. These issues would be excluded from consideration on the ground that the parties are assumed not to be concerned with devising such a scheme. As representatives of separate social schemes, their attention is turned inward, not outward. In coming together in an international original position, they are moved by considerations of equality between "independent peoples organized as states" (378). Their main interest is in providing conditions in which just domestic social orders might flourish.

THE PROBLEM OF NATURAL RESOURCE REDISTRIBUTION

Thus far, the ideal theory of international justice bears a striking resemblance to that proposed in the Definitive Articles of Kant's

Perpetual Peace.[5] Accepting for the time being the assumption of national self-sufficiency, Rawls' choice of principles seems unexceptionable. But would this list of principles exhaust those to which the parties would agree? Probably not. At least one kind of consideration, involving natural resources, might give rise to moral conflict among states and thus be a matter of concern in the international original position. The principles given so far do not take account of these considerations.

We can appreciate the moral importance of conflicting resource claims by distinguishing two elements which contribute to the material advancement of societies. One is human cooperative activity itself, which can be thought of as the human component of material advancement. The other is what Sidgwick called "the utilities derived from any portion of the earth's surface," the natural component.[6] While the first is the subject of the domestic principles of justice, the second is morally relevant even in the absence of a functioning scheme of international social cooperation. The parties of the international original position would know that natural resources are distributed unevenly over the earth's surface. Some areas are rich in resources, and societies established in such areas can be expected to exploit their natural riches and to prosper. Other societies do not fare so well, and despite the best efforts of their members, they may attain only a meager level of well-being due to resource scarcities.

The parties would view the distribution of resources much as Rawls says the parties to the domestic original position deliberations view the distribution of natural talents. In that context, he says that natural endowments are "neither just nor unjust; nor is it unjust that men are born into society at any particular position. These are simply natural facts. What is just or unjust is the way that institutions deal with these facts" (102). A caste society, for example, is unjust because it distributes the benefits of social cooperation according to a rule that rests on morally arbitrary factors. Rawls' objection is that those who are less advantaged for reasons beyond their control cannot be asked to suffer the pains of inequality when their sacrifices cannot be shown to advance their position in comparison with an initial position of equality.

Reasoning analogously, the parties to the international original position, viewing the natural distribution of resources as morally arbitrary, would think that they should be subject to redistribution under a resource redistribution principle. This view is subject to the immediate objection that Rawls' treatment of natural talents is troublesome. It seems vulnerable in at least two ways. First, it is not clear what it means to say that the distribution of talents is "arbitrary from a moral point of view" (72). While the distribution of natural talents is arbitrary in the sense that one cannot deserve to be born with the capacity, say, to play like Rubinstein, it does not obviously follow that the possession of such a talent needs any justification. On the contrary, simply having a talent seems to furnish prima facie warrant for making use of it in ways that are, for the possessor, possible and desirable. A person need not justify his possession of talents, despite the fact that he cannot be said to deserve them, because they are already *his*; the prima facie right to use and control talents is fixed by natural fact.

The other point of vulnerability is that natural capacities are parts of the self, in the development of which a person might take a special kind of pride. A person's decision to develop one talent, not to develop another, as well as his choice as to how the talent is to be formed and the uses to which it is to be put, are likely to be important elements of his effort to shape an identity. The complex of developed talents might even be said to constitute the self; their exercise is a principal form of self-expression. Because the development of talents is so closely linked with the shaping of personal identity, it might seem that one's claim to one's talents is protected by considerations of personal liberty. To interfere with the development and use of talents is to interfere with a self. Or so, at least, it might be argued.

While I believe that Rawls' discussion of talents can be defended against objections like these, that is not my concern here. I want to argue only that objections of this sort do not apply to the parallel claim that the distribution of natural resources is similarly arbitrary. Like talents, resource endowments are arbitrary in the sense that they are not deserved. But unlike talents, resources are not naturally attached to persons. Resources are found "out there," available to the first taker. Resources must be appropriated before they can be used, whereas, in the talents case, the "appropriation" is a fait accompli of nature over which persons have no direct control. Thus, while we feel that the possession of talents confers a right to control and benefit from their use, we may feel differently about resources. Appropriation may not always need a justification; if the resources taken are of limited value, or if, as Locke imagined, their appropriation leaves "enough and as good" for everyone else, justification may not present a problem. In a world of scarcity, however, the situation is different. The appropriation of valuable resources by some will leave others comparatively, and perhaps fatally, disadvantaged. Those deprived without justification of scarce resources needed to sustain and enhance their lives might well press claims to equitable shares.

Furthermore, resources do not stand in the same relation to personal identity as do talents. It would be inappropriate to take the sort of pride in the diamond deposits in one's back yard that one takes in the ability to play the *Appassionata.* This is because natural resources come into the development of personality (when they come in at all) in a more casual way than do talents. As I have said, talents, in some sense, are what the self is; they help constitute personality. The resources under one's feet, because they lack this natural connection with the self, seem to be more contingent than necessary elements of the development of personality. Like talents, resources are used in this process; they are worked on, shaped, and benefited from. But they are not there, as parts of the self, to begin with. They must first be appropriated, and prior to their appropriation, no one has any special natural claim on them. Considerations of personal liberty do not protect a right to appropriate and use resources in the same way as they protect the right to develop and use talents as one sees fit. There is no parallel, initial presumption against interference with the use of resources, since no one is initially placed in a naturally privileged relationship with them.

I conclude that the natural distribution of resources is a purer case of something's being "arbitrary from a moral point of view" than the distribution of talents. Not only can one not be said to deserve the resources under one's feet; the other grounds on which one might assert an initial claim to talents are absent in the case of resources, as well.

The fact that national societies are assumed to be self-sufficient does not make the distribution of natural resources any less arbitrary. Citizens of a nation which finds itself on top of a gold mine do not gain a right to the wealth that might be derived from it *simply* because their nation is self-sufficient. But someone might argue that self-sufficiency, nevertheless, removes any possible grounds on which citizens of other nations might press claims to equitable shares. A possible view is that no justification for resource appropriation is necessary in the global state of nature. If, so to speak, social cooperation is the root of all social obligations, as it is on some versions of contract theory, then the view is correct. All rights would be "special rights" applying only when certain conditions of cooperation obtain.[7]

I believe that this is wrong. It seems plausible in most discussions of distributive justice because their subject is the distribution of the benefits of social cooperation. Appropriate distributive principles compensate those who are relatively disadvantaged by the cooperative scheme for their participation in it. Where there is no social cooperation, there are no benefits of cooperation, and hence no problem of compensation for relative disadvantage. (This is why a world of self-sufficient national societies is not subject to something like a global difference principle.) But there is nothing in this reasoning to suggest that our *only* moral ties are to those with whom we share membership in a cooperative scheme. It is possible that other sorts of considerations might come into the justification of moral principles. Rawls himself recognizes this in the case of the natural duties, which are said to "apply to use without regard to our voluntary acts" (114) and, apparently, without regard to our institutional memberships.

In the case of natural resources, the parties to the international original position would know that resources are unevenly distributed with respect to population, that adequate access to resources is a prerequisite for successful operation of (domestic) cooperative schemes, and that resource supplies are scarce. They would view the natural distribution of resources as arbitrary in the sense that no one has a natural prima facie claim to the resources that happen to be under his feet. The appropriation of scarce resources by some requires a justification against the competing claims of others and the needs of future generations. Not knowing the resource endowments of their own societies, the parties would agree on a resource redistribution principle which would give each national society a fair chance to develop just political institutions and an economy capable of satisfying its members' basic needs.

There is no intuitively obvious standard of equity for such matters; perhaps the standard would be population size, or perhaps it would be more complicated, rewarding nations for their efforts in extracting resources and taking account of the differential resource needs of nations with differing economies. The underlying principle is that each person has an equal prima facie claim to a share of the total available resources, but departures from this initial standard could be justified (analogously to the operation of the difference principle) if the resulting inequalities were to the greatest benefit of those least advantaged by the inequality (cf. 151). In any event, the resource redistribution principle would function in international society as the difference principle functions in domestic society. It provides assurance to resource-poor nations that their adverse fate will not prevent them from realizing economic conditions sufficient to support just social institutions and to protect human rights guaranteed by the principles for individuals. In the absence of this assurance, these nations might resort to war as a means of securing the resources necessary to establish domestic justice, and it is not obvious that wars fought for this purpose would be unjust.[8]

Before turning to other issues, I must note two complications of which I cannot give a fully satisfactory account. The international original position parties are prevented by the veil of ignorance from knowing their generation; they would be concerned to minimize the risk that, when the veil is lifted, they might find themselves living in a world where resource supplies have been largely depleted. Thus, part of the resource redistribution principle would set some standard for conservation against this possibility. The difficulties in formulating a standard of conservation are at at least as formidable as those of defining the "just savings rate" in Rawls' discussion of justifiable rates of capital accumulation. I shall not pursue them here, except to point out that some provision for conservation as a matter of justice to future generations would be necessary (cf. 284–293).

The other complication concerns the definition of "natural resources." To what extent is food to be considered a resource? Social factors enter into the production of food in a way that they do not in the extraction of raw resources, so it may be that no plausible resource principle would require redistribution of food. A nation might claim that it deserves its abundant food supplies because of its large investments in agriculture or the high productivity of its farmers. On the other hand, arable land is a precondition of food production and a nation's supply of good land seems to be as morally arbitrary as its supply of, say, oil.[9] A further complication is that arable land, unlike iron ore or oil, cannot be physically redistributed to those nations with insufficient land, while food grown on the land is easily transportable. These dilemmas might be resolved by requiring redistribution of a portion of a country's food production depending on the ratio of its arable land to its total production; but the calculations involved would be complex and probably controversial. In the absence of a broader agreement to regard international society as a unified scheme of social cooperation, formulation of an acceptable food redistribution rule might prove impossible.

In failing to recognize resource problems, Rawls follows other writers who have extended the social contract idea to international relations.[10] Perhaps this is because they have attributed a greater symmetry to the domestic and international contracts than is in fact appropriate. Resource problems do not arise as distinct questions in the domestic case because their distribution and conservation are implicitly covered by the difference principle and the just savings principle. When the scope of social cooperation is coextensive with the territorial boundaries of a society, it is unnecessary to distinguish natural and social contributions to the society's level of well-being. But when justice is considered internationally, we must face the likelihood of moral claims being pressed by members of the various social schemes which are arbitrarily placed with respect to the natural distribution of resources. My suggestion of a resource redistribution principle recognizes the fundamental character of these claims viewed from the perspective of the parties' interests in securing fair conditions for the development of their respective schemes.

THE SELF-SUFFICIENCY ASSUMPTION

Everything that I have said so far is consistent with the assumption that nations are self-sufficient cooperative schemes. However, there are strong empirical reasons for thinking that this assumption is no longer valid. As Kant notes in the concluding pages of *The Metaphysical Elements of Justice*, international economic cooperation creates a new basis for international morality.[11]

The main features of contemporary international interdependence relevant to questions of justice are the result of the progressive removal of restrictions on international trade and investment. Capital surpluses are no longer confined to reinvestment in the societies where they are produced, but instead are reinvested wherever conditions promise the highest yield without unacceptable risks. It is well known, for example, that large American corporations have systematically transferred significant portions of their capitalization to European, Latin American, and East Asian societies where labor costs are lower, markets are better, and profits are higher. A related development is the rise of an international division of labor whereby products are manufactured in areas having cheap, unorganized labor and are marketed in more affluent areas. Because multinational businesses, rather than the producing countries themselves, play the leading role in setting prices and wages, the international division of labor results in a system of world trade in which value created in one society (usually poor) is used to benefit members of other societies (usually rich).[12] It is also important to note that the world economy has evolved its own financial and monetary institutions that set exchange rates, regulate the money supply, influence capital flows, and enforce rules of international economic conduct.

The system of interdependence imposes burdens on poor and economically weak countries that they cannot practically avoid. Industrial economies have become reliant on raw materials that can only be obtained in sufficient quantities from developing countries. In the present structure of world prices, poor countries are often forced by adverse balances of payments to sell resources to more wealthy countries when those resources could be more efficiently used to promote development of the poor countries' domestic economies.[13] Also, private foreign investment imposes on poor countries patterns of political and economic development that may not be optimal from the point of view of the poor countries themselves. Participation in the global economy on the only terms available involves a loss of political autonomy.[14] Third, the global monetary system allows disturbances (e.g., price inflation) in some national economies to be exported to others that may be less able to cope with their potentially disastrous effects.[15]

Economic interdependence, then, involves a pattern of relationships which are largely nonvoluntary from the point of view of the worse-off participants, and which produce benefits for some while imposing burdens on others. These facts, by now part of the conventional wisdom of international relations, describe a world in which national boundaries can no longer be regarded as the outer limits of social cooperation. Note that this conclusion does not require that national societies should have become entirely superfluous or that the global economy should be completely integrated.[16] It is enough, for setting the limits of cooperative schemes, that some societies are able to increase their level of well-being via global trade and investment while others with whom they have economic relations continue to exist at low levels of development.[17]

In view of these empirical considerations, Rawls' passing concern for the law of nations seems to miss the point of international justice altogether. In an interdependent world, confining principles of social justice to national societies has the effect of taxing poor nations so that others may benefit from living in "just" regimes. The two principles, so construed, might justify a wealthy nation's denying aid to needy peoples if the aid could be used domestically to promote a more nearly just regime. If the self-sufficiency assumption were empirically acceptable, such a result might be plausible, if controversial on other grounds.[18] But if participation in economic relations with the needy society has contributed to the wealth of the "nearly just" regime, its domestic "justice" seems to lose moral significance. In such situations, the principles of domestic "justice" will be genuine principles of justice only if they are consistent with principles of justice for the entire global scheme of social cooperation.

How should we formulate global principles? As several others have suggested, Rawls' own two principles, suitably reinterpreted, could themselves be applied globally.[19] The reasoning is as follows: if evidence of global economic and political interdependence shows the existence of a global scheme of social cooperation, we should not view national boundaries as having fundamental moral significance. Since boundaries are not coextensive with the scope of social cooperation, they do not mark the limits of social obligations. Thus, the parties to the original position cannot be assumed to know that they are members of a particular national society, choosing principles of justice primarily for that society. The veil of ignorance must extend to all matters of national citizenship. As Barry points out, a global interpretation of the original position is insensitive to the choice of principles.[20] Assuming that the arguments for the two principles are successful as set out in Rawls' book, there is no reason to think that the content of the principles would change as a result of enlarging the scope of the original position so that the principles would apply to the world as a whole.[21]

Rawls' two principles are a special case of the "general conception" of social justice.[22] The two principles hold when a cooperative scheme has reached a level of material well-being at which everyone's basic needs can be met. The world, conceived as a single cooperative scheme, probably has not yet reached this threshold. Assuming that this is the case, on Rawls' reasoning, we should take the general conception, which does not differentiate the basic liberties from other primary goods, as the relevant standard for assessing global economic institutions. In conditions of underdevelopment or low-average levels of well-being, he argues, rational people might opt for a principle allowing rapid growth at the expense of some personal liberties, provided that the benefits of growth and the sacrifices of liberty are fairly shared and that the bases of self-respect relevant to such background conditions are not undermined (see 152, 298–303). The argument is that the prospects of the least advantaged would be less advanced, all things considered, by observing the lexical priority of liberty than by following the general conception of social justice.[23]

The globalization of the two principles (or of the general conception, if appropriate) has the consequence that principles of justice for national societies can no longer be viewed as ultimate. The basic structure of national societies continues to be governed by the two principles (or by the general conception), but their application is derivative and hence their requirements are not absolute. A possible view is that the global principles and the principles applied to national societies are to be satisfied in lexical order. But this view has the consequence, which one might find implausible, that national policies which maximize the welfare of the least-advantaged group within the society cannot be justified if other policies would be more optimal from the point of view of the lesser advantaged elsewhere. Furthermore, no society could justify the additional costs involved in moving from the general to the special conception (for example, in reduced productivity) until every society had, at least, attained a level of well-being sufficient to sustain the general conception.

These features of the global interpretation of Rawlsian principles suggest that its implications are quite radical—considerably more so even than their application to national societies. While I am not now prepared to argue positively that the best theory of global justice consists simply of Rawls' principles interpreted globally, it seems to me that the most obvious objections to such a theory are not valid. In the remainder of this section, I consider what is perhaps the leading type of objection and suggest some difficulties in giving it theoretically compelling form.

Objections of the type I have in mind hold that considerations of social cooperation at the national level justify distributive claims capable of overriding the requirements of a global difference principle. Typically, members of a wealthy nation might claim that they deserve a larger share than that provided by a global difference principle because of their superior technology, economic organization, and efficiency.

Objections of this general sort might take several forms. First, it might be argued that even in an interdependent world, national society remains the primary locus of one's political identifications. If one is moved to contribute to aggregate social welfare at any level, this level is most likely to be the national level. Therefore, differential rates of national contribution to the global welfare ought to be rewarded proportionally. This is a plausible form of the objection; the problem is that, in this form, it may not be an objection at all. The difference principle itself recognizes the probability that differential rates of reward may be needed as incentives for contribution; it requires only that distributive inequalities which arise in such a system be to the greatest benefit of the world's least-advantaged group. To the extent that incentives of the kind demanded by this version of the objection actually do raise the economic expectations of the least advantaged without harming them in other ways, they would not be inconsistent with the difference principle.

Such objections count against a global difference principle only if they hold that a relatively wealthy nation could claim more than its share under the difference principle. That is, the objection must hold that some distributive inequalities are justified even though they are not to the greatest benefit of the world's least-advantaged group. How could such claims be justified? One justification is on grounds of personal merit, appealing to the intuition that value created by someone's unaided labor is properly his, assuming that the initial distribution was just.[24] This sort of argument yields an extreme form of the objection. It holds that a nation is entitled to its relative wealth because each of its citizens has complied with the relevant rules of justice in acquiring raw materials and transforming them into products of value. These rules might require, respectively, that an equitable resource redistribution principle has been implemented and that no one's rights have been violated (for example, by imperial plunder) in the process of acquisition and production leading to a nation's current economic position. (Note that my arguments for a resource principle are not touched by this sort of objection and would impose some global distributive obligations even if the personal merit view were correct in ruling out broader global principles.)

This interpretation of the objection is strictly analogous to the conception of distributive justice which Rawls calls the "system of natural liberty." He objects to such views that they allow people to compete for available positions on the basis of their talents, making no attempt to compensate for deprivations that some suffer due to natural chance and social contingency. These things, as I have said, are held to be morally arbitrary and hence unacceptable as standards for distribution (cf. 66–72). I shall not rehearse this argument further here. But two things should be noted. First, the argument seems even more plausible from the global point of view since the disparity of possible starting points in world society is so much greater. The balance between "arbitrary" and "personal" contributions to my present well-being seems decisively tipped toward the "arbitrary" ones by the realization that, no matter what my talents, education, life goals, etc., I would have been virtually precluded from attaining my present level of well-being if I had been born in a less developed society. Second, if Rawls' counterargument counts against natural liberty views in the domestic case, then it defeats the objection to a global difference principle as well. A nation cannot base its claim to a larger distributive share than that warranted by the difference principle on factors which are morally arbitrary.

A third, and probably the most plausible, form of this objection holds that a wealthy nation may retain more than its share under a global difference principle, provided that some compensation for the benefits of global social cooperation is paid to less fortunate nations, and that the amount retained by the producing nation is used to promote domestic justice, for example, by increasing the prospects of the nation's own least favored group. The underlying intuition is that citizens owe some sort of special obligation to the less fortunate members of their own society that is capable of overriding their general obligation to improve the prospects of lesser advantaged groups elsewhere. This intuition is distinct from the intuition in the personal desert case, for it does not refer to any putative individual right to the value created by one's labor. Instead, we are concerned here with supposedly conflicting rights and obligations that arise from membership in overlapping schemes of social cooperation, one embedded in the other.

An argument along these lines needs an account of how obligations to the sectional association arise. One might say that the greater degree or extent of social cooperation in national sccieties (compared with that in international society) underwrites stronger intranational principles of justice. To see this objection in its strongest form, imagine a world of two self-sufficient and internally just societies, *A* and *B*. Assume that this world satisfies the appropriate resource redistribution principle. Imagine also that the least-advantaged representative person in society *A* is considerably better off than his counterpart in society *B*. While the members of *A* may owe duties of mutual aid to the members of *B*, it is clear that they do not have parallel duties of justice, because the two societies, being individually self-sufficient, do not share membership in a cooperative scheme. Now suppose that the walls of self-sufficiency are breached very slightly; *A* trades its apples for *B*'s pears. Does this mean that the difference principle suddenly applies to the world which comprises *A* and *B*, requiring *A* to share all of its wealth with *B*, even though almost all of its wealth is attributable to economic interaction within *A*? It seems not; one might say that an international difference principle can only command redistribution of the benefits derived from international social cooperation or economic interaction. It cannot touch the benefits of domestic cooperation.

It may be that some such objection will turn out to produce modifications on a global difference principle. But there are reasons for doubting this. Roughly, it seems that there is a threshold of interdependence above which distributive requirements such as a global difference principle are valid, but below which significantly weaker principles hold. I cannot give a systematic account of this view here, but perhaps some intuitive considerations will demonstrate its force.

Consider another hypothetical case. Suppose that, *within* a society, there are closely-knit local regions with higher levels of internal cooperation than the level of cooperation in society as a whole. Certainly there are many such regions within a society such as the United States. The argument rehearsed above, applied to closely-knit localities within national societies, would seem to give members of the localities special claims on portions of their wealth. This seems implausible, especially since such closely-knit enclaves might well turn out to contain disproportionate numbers of the society's most advantaged classes. Why does this conclusion seem less plausible than that in the apples and pears case? It seems to me that the answer has to do with the fact that the apples and pears case looks like a case of voluntary, free-market bargaining that has only a marginal effect on the welfare of the members of each society, whereas we assume in the intranational case that there is a nonvoluntary society-wide system of economic institutions which defines starting positions and assigns economic rights and duties. It is these institutions—what Rawls calls "the basic structure" (7–11)—that stand in need of justification, because, by defining the terms of cooperation, they have such deep and pervasive effects on the welfare of people to whom they apply regardless of consent.

The apples and pears case, of course, is hardly a faithful model of the contemporary world economy. Suppose that we add to the story to make it resemble the real world more closely. As my review of the current situation above makes clear, we would have to add just those features of the contemporary world economy that find their domestic analogues in the basic structure to which principles of justice apply.

As the web of transactions grows more complex, the resulting structure of economic and political institutions acquires great influence over the welfare of the participants, regardless of the extent to which any particular one makes use of the institutions. These features make the real world situation seem more like the case of subnational, closely-knit regions.

These considerations suggest that the amount of social and economic interaction in a cooperative scheme does not provide a straightforward index of the strength of the distributive principle appropriate to it. The existence of a powerful, nonvoluntary institutional structure, and its pervasive effects on the welfare of the cooperators, seems to provide a better indication of the strength of the appropriate distributive requirements. This sort of consideration would not necessarily support a global difference principle in the apples and pears case; but it does explain why, above a threshold measure of social cooperation, the full force of the difference principle may come into play despite regional variations in the amount of cooperation.[25]

Proponents of this objection to a global difference principle might have one last resort. They might appeal to noneconomic features of national societies to justify the special obligations that citizens owe to the less fortunate members of their own societies. On this basis, they could claim that the difference principle applies to national societies despite regional variations in cooperation but not to international society. Probably the plausibility of this sort of argument will depend on the degree to which it psychologizes the ties that bind the members of social institutions.[26] There are problems, however. First, it needs to be shown that psychological ties such as national loyalty are of sufficient moral importance to balance the international economic ties that underwrite a global difference principle. Second, even if this could be persuasively argued, any account of how institutional obligations arise that is sufficiently psychological to make plausible a general conflict of global and sectional loyalties will probably be too psychological to apply to the large modern state (cf. 477).

Perhaps this line of objection can be made good in some way other than those canvassed here. If this could be done, it would not follow that there are no global distributive obligations but only that some portion of a nation's gross product would be exempt from the requirements of the global standard provided that it were used domestically in appropriate ways. The question would not be whether there are global distributive obligations founded on justice, but rather to what extent considerations relevant to the special features of cooperation within national societies modify the egalitarian tendencies of the global standard.

CONCLUSION: THE RELATION OF THE IDEAL THEORY TO THE NONIDEAL WORLD

We have now reached two main conclusions. First, assuming national self-sufficiency, Rawls' derivation of the principles of justice for the law of nations is correct but incomplete. He importantly neglects resource redistribution, a subject that would surely be on the minds of the parties to the international original position. But second, the self-sufficiency assumption, upon which Rawls' entire consideration of the law of nations rests, is not justified by the facts of contemporary international relations. The state-centered image of the world has lost its normative relevance because of the rise of global economic interdependence. Hence, principles of distributive justice must apply in the first instance to the world as a whole, then derivatively to nation-states. The appropriate global principle is probably something like Rawls' general conception of justice, perhaps modified by some provision for intranational redistribution in relatively wealthy states once a threshold level of international redistributive obligations has been met. Rawls' two principles become more relevant as global distributive inequalities are reduced and a higher average level of well-being is attained. In conclusion, I would like to consider the implications of this ideal theory for international politics and global change in the nonideal world. In what respects does this interpretation of the social contract doctrine shed light on problems of world order change?

We might begin by asking, in general, what relevance social ideals have for politics in the real world. Their most obvious function is to describe a goal toward which efforts at political change should aim. In Rawls' theory, a very important natural duty is the natural duty of justice, which "requires us to support and to comply with just institutions that exist and . . . constrains us to further just arrangements not yet established, at least if this can be done without too much cost to ourselves" (115). By supplying a description of the nature and aims of a just world order, ideal theory "provides . . . the only basis for the systematic grasp of these more pressing problems" (9). Ideal theory, then, supplies a set of criteria for the formulation and criticism of strategies of political action in the nonideal world, at least when the consequences of political action can be predicted with sufficient confidence to establish their relationship to the social ideal. Clearly, this task would not be easy, given the complexities of social change and the uncertainties of prediction in political affairs. There is the additional complication that social change is often wrongly conceived as a progressive approximation of actual institutions to ideal prescriptions in which people's welfare steadily improves. An adequate social theory must avoid the pitfalls of a false incrementalism as well as what economists call the problem of the second best.[27] But a coherent social ideal is a necessary condition of any attempt to conquer these difficulties.

Ideal justice, in other words, comes into nonideal politics by way of the natural duty to secure just institutions where none presently exist. The moral problem posed by distinguishing ideal from nonideal theory is that, in the nonideal world, the natural duty of justice is likely to conflict with other natural duties, while the theory provides no mechanism for resolving such conflicts. For example, it is possible that a political decision which is likely to make institutions more just is equally likely to involve violations of other natural duties, such as the duty of mutual aid or the duty not to harm the innocent. Perhaps reforming some unjust institution will require us to disappoint legitimate expectations formed under the old order. The principles of natural duty in the nonideal world are relatively unsystematic, and we have no way of knowing which should win out in case of conflict. Rawls recognizes the inevitability of irresolvable conflicts in some situations (303), but, as Feinberg has suggested, he underestimates the role that an intuitive balancing of conflicting duties must play in nonideal circumstances.[28] Rawls says that problems of political change in radically unjust situations must rely on a utilitarian calculation of costs and benefits (352–353). If this is true, then political change in conditions of great injustice marks one kind of limit of the contract doctrine, for in these cases the principles of justice collapse into utilitarianism. It seems to me, however, that this conclusion is too broad. At least in some cases of global justice, nonideal theory, while teleological, is not utilitarian. I shall try to show this briefly with respect to questions of food and development aid, the principle of nonintervention, and the obligation to participate in war on behalf of a nation-state.

The duty to secure just institutions where none exist endows certain political claims made in the nonideal world with a moral seriousness which does not derive merely from the obligations that bind people regardless of the existence of cooperative ties. When the contract doctrine is interpreted globally, the claims of the less advantaged in today's nonideal world—claims principally for food aid, development assistance, and world monetary and trade reform—rest on principles of global justice as well as on the weaker duty of mutual aid. Those who are in a position to respond to these claims, despite the absence of effective global political mechanisms, must take acacount of the stronger reasons provided by the principles of justice in weighing their response. Furthermore, by interpreting the principles globally, we remove a major source of justifying reasons for not responding more fully to such claims. These reasons derive from statist concerns, for example, a supposed right to reinvest domestic surpluses in national societies that are already relatively favored from a global point of view. The natural duties still require us to help members of our own society who are in need, and a wealthy nation would be justified on this account in using some of its resources to support domestic welfare programs. What cannot be argued is that a wealthy nation's general right to retain its domestic product always overrides its obligation to advance the welfare of lesser-advantaged groups elsewhere.

An ideal theory of global justice has implications for traditional doctrines of international law as well. Consider, as a representative example, the rule of nonintervention. It is often remarked that this rule, which is prominently displayed in a number of recent authoritative documents of international law, seems inconsistent with the international community's growing rhetorical commitment to the protection of human rights, which is also prominently displayed in many of the same documents.[29] The conflict can be illustrated with reference to South Africa: the doctrine of nonintervention seems to prevent other states from giving aid to local insurgent forces explicitly committed to attaining recognition of basic human rights for the vast bulk of the South African population. Ordinarily, such conflicts are regarded as simple matters of utilitarian balancing, but the global interpretation of social contract theory shows that more can be said. The global interpretation introduced an asymmetry into the justification of the rules of international law. These rules impose different obligations depending on whether their observance in particular cases would contribute to or detract from a movement toward more just institutions.

The nonintervention rule is to be interpreted in this light. When it would demonstrably operate to advance or protect just arrangements, it furnishes a strong reason not to intervene. In the absence of compelling reasons to the contrary, it imposes a duty to comply. This is typically the case when intervention would interfere with a people's right of self-determination, a right which protects the fair exercise of political liberty. Thus, American intervention in Allende's Chile certainly violated a basic requirement of global justice. But sometimes, as in South Africa, observing the nonintervention rule cannot be justified in this way. Rather than resting on considerations of justice, which give strong reasons for compliance, it rests on considerations of natural duty—such as protection of the innocent against harms that might be suffered if large-scale military intervention occurred—and of international stability. These are certainly not negligible reasons for nonintervention, but, from the standpoint of global justice, they are weaker reasons than those provided by global justice itself. Obviously, peaceful resolution of cases such as that of South Africa is to be preferred. But when this goal cannot be attained, or when insurgent forces fighting for human rights request foreign assistance, intervention cannot be opposed as a matter of justice (as it could be on the traditional interpretation of this international rule, preserved in Rawls' own brief discussion), for its effect would be to help secure rights, including the right of self-determination, protected by the global principles. Again, in the absence of compelling reasons to the contrary (of which, certainly, a great number can be imagined), there might be an international duty to intervene in support of insurgent forces. I say that there may be an *international* duty because it seems clear that unilateral intervention can almost always be successfully opposed on grounds of international stability. But a decision by the international community to enforce principles of justice would be less susceptible to this sort of objection. Here I note what has too often been overlooked (except, perhaps, by American multinationals), that intervention in another country's internal affairs can take many nonviolent forms, including economic blockades, nonmilitary aid to insurgent forces, diplomatic pressure, etc. While such forms of intervention obviously carry no guarantee of success, it is fair to say that their potential effectiveness has been widely underestimated.[30]

Finally, what are the implications of global justice for participation in a nation's military forces? From what I have said thus far, it should be clear that the global interpretation supplies reasons for acting or not acting which are capable of overriding the reasons provided by traditional rules of international law. These reasons are also capable of overriding the rule that demands compliance with internally just domestic regimes. One important consequence is that conscientious refusal to participate in a nation's armed forces would have far broader possible justifications than on the account given in Rawls (cf. 377–382), assuming for the moment that, given the great destructiveness of modern weapons and war strategies, participation in national armed forces could ever be justified at all. For instance, in some circumstances, a war of self-defense fought by an affluent nation against a poorer nation pressing legitimate claims under the global principles (for example, for increased food aid) might be unjustifiable, giving rise to a justified refusal to participate in the affluent nation's armed forces.

These three examples show that the contract doctrine, despite limitations noted here, sheds light on the distinctive normative problems of the shift from statist to global images of world order. The extension of economic and cultural relationships beyond national borders has often been thought to undermine the moral legitimacy of the state; the extension of the contract doctrine gives a systematic account of why this is so, and of its consequences for problems of justice in the nonideal world, by emphasizing the role of social cooperation as the foundation of just social arrangements. When, as now, national boundaries do not set off discrete, self-sufficient societies, we may not regard them as morally decisive features of the earth's social geography. For purposes of moral choice, we must, instead, regard the world from the perspective of an original position from which matters of national citizenship are excluded by an extended veil of ignorance.

I do not believe that Rawls' failure to take account of these questions marks a pivotal weakness of his theory; on the contrary, the theory provides a way of determining the consequences of changing empirical circumstances (such as the assumption of national self-sufficiency) for the concept of justice. The global interpretation is the result of recognizing an important empirical change in the structure of world political and social life. In this way the theory allows us to apply generalizations derived from our considered judgments regarding familiar situations to situations which are new and which demand that we form intelligent moral views and act on them when action is possible and appropriate. This is no small achievement for a moral theory. Some might think, however, that our moral intuitions are too weak or unreliable to support such an extension of the theory. I doubt that this is true; rather, it often seems to be a convenient way to beg off from unpleasant moral requirements. But if I am wrong about this—if we cannot expect moral theory to provide a firm guide for action in new situations—one might wonder whether moral theory has any practical point at all.

NOTES

I am grateful to Huntington Terrell, who stimulated my interest in questions of international ethics, for comments and criticisms on an earlier version and to Thomas Scanlon, Richard Falk, and Dennis Thompson, for many helpful discussions of earlier drafts.

1. "Declaration on the Establishment of a New International Economic Order," Resolution No. 3201 (S-VI), 1 May 1974, United Nations General Assembly, *Official Records: Sixth Special Session*, Supp. No. 1 (A/9559) (New York: United Nations General Assembly, 1974), p. 3.
2. Such criticisms have appeared in several places. For example, Brian Barry, *The Liberal Theory of Justice* (Oxford: Clarendon Press, 1973), pp. 128-33; Peter Danielson, "Theories, Intuitions and the Problem of World-Wide Distributive Justice," *Philosophy of the Social Sciences*, 3 (1973), 331-40; Thomas M. Scanlon, Jr., "Rawls' Theory of Justice," *University of Pennsylvania Law Review*, 121, no. 5 (May 1973), 1066-67.
3. These principles form the basis of traditional international law. See the discussion, on which Rawls relies, in J.L. Brierly, *The Law of Nations*, 6th ed, (New York: Oxford University Press, 1963), especially chaps. 3 and 4.
4. Barry, *The Liberal Theory of Justice*, p. 132.
5. Immanuel Kant, *Perpetual Peace*, trans. and ed. Lewis White Beck (Indianapolis: Bobbs-Merrill Co., 1957), pp. 10-23.
6. Henry Sidgwick, *The Elements of Politics* (London: 1891), p. 242; quoted in S.I. Benn and R.S. Peters, *The Principles of Political Thought* (New York: Free Press, 1965), p. 430. Sidgwick's entire discussion of putative national rights to land and resources is relevant here—see *Elements*, pp. 239-44.
7. William N. Nelson construes Rawlsian rights in this way in "Special Rights, General Rights, and Social Justice," *Philosophy and Public Affairs*, 3, no. 4 (Summer 1974), 410-30.
8. On this account, United Nations General Assembly Resolution 1803 (XVII), which purports to establish "permanent sovereignty over natural resources," would be prima facie unjust. However, there are important mitigating factors. This resolution, as the text and the debates make clear, was adopted to defend developing nations against resource exploitation by foreign-owned businesses, and to underwrite a national right of expropriation (with compensa-

tion) of foreign-owned mining and processing facilities in some circumstances. While the "permanent sovereignty" doctrine may be extreme, sovereignty-for-the time-being might not be, if it can be shown (as I think it can) that resource-consuming nations have taken more than their fair share without returning adequate compensation. United Nations General Assembly, *Official Records: Seventeenth Session*, Supp. No. 17 (A/5217) (New York: United Nations General Assembly, 1963), pp. 15-16.

9. This statement needs qualification. After a certain point in economic development, a society could make good much of its apparently nonarable land, e.g. by clearing and draining or irrigating. So we ought not regard the total amount of arable land as fixed in the same sense as the total of other resources like oil. This was pointed out to me by Huntington Terrell.
10. Two classical examples are Pufendorf and Wolff. See Walter Schiffer, *The Legal Community of Mankind* (New York: Columbia University Press, 1954), pp. 49-79.
11. Immanuel Kant, *The Metaphysical Elements of Justice*, John Ladd, ed. (Indianapolis: Bobbs-Merrill, 1965), pp. 125ff.
12. Cf. Richard J. Barnet and Ronald E. Müller, *Global Reach* (New York: Simon and Schuster, 1975), chaps. 2, 6 and passim. See also Stephen Hymer, "The Multinational Corporation and the Law of Uneven Development," in *Economics and World Order*, ed. J.N. Bhagwati (New York: Macmillan, 1972), pp. 113-41.
13. Suzanne Bodenheimer gives an account of the role of foreign investment in exploiting the resources of Latin American countries in "Dependency and Imperialism: The Roots of Latin American Underdevelopment," *Politics and Society* I (1971), 327-57.
14. Peter B. Evans, "National Autonomy and Economic Development," in *Transnational Relations and World Politics*, ed. Robert O. Keohane and Joseph S. Nye (Cambridge, Mass.: Harvard University Press, 1972), pp. 325-42.
15. See Richard N. Cooper, "Economic Interdependence and Foreign Policy in the Seventies," *World Politics*, 24, no. 2 (January 1972), 159-81.
16. This conclusion would hold even if it were true that wealthy nations such as the United States continue to be economically self-sufficient, as Kenneth Waltz has (mistakenly, I think) argued. A nation might be self-sufficient in the sense that its income from trade is marginal compared with total national income, and yet still participate in economic relations with less developed countries which impose great burdens on the latter. (See fn. 17, below.) To refute the claim I make in the text, it would be necessary to show that all, or almost all, nations are self-sufficient in the sense given above. This, plainly, is not the case. Waltz argues his view in "The Myth of National Interdependence," *The International Corporation*, ed. Charles P. Kindleberger (Cambridge, Mass.: MIT Press, 1970), pp. 205-226; he is effectively refuted by Cooper, "Economic Interdependence" and Edward L. Morse, "Trans-

national Economic Processes," in *Transnational Relations and World Politics*, ed. Keohane and Nye, pp. 23-47.

17. The situation is probably worse than this. A more plausible view is that the poor countries' economic relations with the rich have actually worsened economic conditions among the poor. Global trade widens rather than narrows the rich-poor gap, and harms rather than aids the poor countries' efforts at economic development. See André Gunder Frank, "The Development of Underdevelopment," in James D. Cockcroft et al., *Dependence and Underdevelopment* (Garden City, N.Y.: Anchor Books, 1972), pp. 3-18. This raises the question of whether interdependence must actually benefit everyone involved to give rise to questions of justice. I think the answer is clearly negative; countries A and B are involved in social cooperation even if A (a rich country) could get along without B (a poor country), but instead exploits it, while B gets nothing out of its "cooperation" but exacerbated class divisions and Coca-Cola factories. If this is true, then Rawls' characterization of a society as a "cooperative venture for mutual advantage" (4) may be misleading, since everyone need not be advantaged by the cooperative scheme in order for requirements of justice to apply. It would be better to say that such requirements apply to systems of economic and social interaction which are nonvoluntary from the point of view of those least advantaged (or most disadvantaged) by them, and in which some benefit as a result of the relative or absolute sacrifices of others.
18. For example, on utilitarian grounds. See Peter Singer, "Famine, Affluence, and Morality," *Philosophy and Public Affairs*, I, no. 3 (Spring 1972), 229-43.
19. For example, Barry, *The Liberal Theory of Justice*, pp. 128-33; and Scanlon, "Rawls' Theory of Justice," pp. 1066-67.
20. Barry, *The Liberal Theory of Justice*, p. 129.
21. David Richards also argues that the principles apply globally, but he fails to notice the relationship between distributive justice and the morally relevant features of social cooperation on which its requirements rest. It is this relationship, and not the simpler, blanket assertion that the original position parties are ignorant of their nationalities, which explains why Rawlsian principles of social justice should be thought to apply globally. See David A. J. Richards, *A Theory of Reasons for Action* (London: Oxford University Press, 1971), pp. 137-41.
22. The general conception reads as follows: "All social primary goods—liberty and opportunity, income and wealth, and the bases of self-respect—are to be distributed equally unless an unequal distribution of any or all of these goods is to the advantage of the least favored" (303).
23. It must be noted that the question whether the general conception is more appropriate to developing societies turns heavily on empirical considerations. In particular, it needs to be shown that sacrifices of liberty, equally shared, really do promote more rapid advances in average levels of well-being than any other possible development strategy not involving such sacrifices. After

considering the evidence, it might seem that an altogether different conception of justice is more appropriate to such societies than either of Rawls' conceptions. Perhaps, in the end, the general conception will turn out to be the best that can be advanced, but it would be interesting to canvass the alternatives. See Norman Bowie's attempt to do this in *Towards a New Theory of Distributive Justice* (Amherst, Mass.: University of Massachusetts Press, 1971), pp. 114ff.

24. This, roughly, is Robert Nozick's view in *Anarchy, State, and Utopia* (New York: Basic Books, 1974), chap. 7.
25. I do not claim to have resolved the problem which underlies this objection, although I believe that my remarks point in the right direction. It should be noticed, however, that what is at issue here is really a general problem for any theory which addresses itself to institutional structures rather than to particular transactions. One can always ask why institutional requirements should apply in full force to persons who make minimal use of the institutions they find themselves in. This point emerged from discussions I have had with Thomas Scanlon.
26. For a suggestive account of a similar problem, see Michael Walzer, *Obligations: Essays on Disobedience, War, and Citizenship* (Cambridge, Mass.: Harvard University Press, 1970), pp. 3–23.
27. On the problem of the second best, see Brian Barry, *Political Argument* (London: Routledge and Kegan Paul, 1965), pp. 261–62.
28. Joel Feinberg, "Duty and Obligation in the Nonideal World," *Journal of Philosophy*, 70 (10 May 1973), 263–75.
29. For example, the U.N. Charter, articles 2 (4) and 1 (3), and article 1 of the "Declaration of Principles of International Cooperation . . . ," approved by the General Assembly on 24 October 1970. Both are reprinted in *Basic Documents in International Law*, 2nd ed., ed. Ian Brownlie (Oxford: Clarendon Press, 1972), pp. 1–31 and 32–40.
30. See Gene Sharp, *The Politics of Non-violent Action* (Boston: Porter Sargent, 1973).

The Right to Punish and the Right to be Punished

David A. Hoekema
ST. OLAF COLLEGE

John Locke argued in the *Second Treatise* that the laws of nature confer on every individual the right to punish those who violate that law. Punishment may take place, he believed, even in the absence of social institutions or positive law.

> And that all men may be restrained from invading others' rights, and from doing hurt to one another, and the law of nature be observed, which willeth the peace and preservation of all mankind, the execution of the law of nature is, in that state, put into every man's hands, whereby every one has a right to punish the transgressors of that law to such a degree, as may hinder its violation. . . .
>
> And thus, in the state of nature, one man comes by a power over another; but yet no arbitrary or absolute power, to use a criminal, when he has got him into his hands, according to the passionate heats, or boundless extravagancy of his own will; but only to retribute to him, so far as calm reason and conscience dictates, what is proportionate to his transgression, which is so much as may serve for reparation and restraint: for these two are the only reasons why one may lawfully do harm to another, which is that we call punishment.[1]

The doctrine that each person has a right to punish even in a state of nature is likely to strike the modern reader as one of the less plausible aspects of Locke's theory of natural law and natural right. It seems a mistake to speak of punishment apart from social institutions which give rise to it and sanction its application. Perhaps in the context of a family a parent has a right, apart from other social institutions, to punish children. There may be other special relationships which give rise to justified punishment.[2] But surely the right to punish another individual to whom one bears no special relationship is a right which, if it exists at all, is conferred by social institutions. The right to punish must in this respect be like the right to vote, or the right to due process: it is a right which has no application—whose assertion does not even make sense—apart from the social institutions which confer it.

For Locke the legitimacy of punishment in the state is a straightforward consequence of the right of all to punish transgressions of the law of nature. But if we do not accept Locke's claim that there is such a natural right, then the justifiability of punishment must rest on some other basis, if indeed it is justifiable at all.

My intent in this essay is to explore questions concerning the justification of punishment in the context of a theory of rights. Is there a right to punish, and if so, who holds such a right and on what grounds? How may it be legitimately exercised? And how can its exercise be reconciled with the rights of the punished?

Theories of punishment which attempt to answer questions such as these have tended to fall into three categories according to whether they have offered retributive, deterrent, or rehabilitative defenses for the practice of punishment. I shall consider these theories by employing an extension of the contractarian approach whose fruitfulness Rawls has demonstrated in the area of distributive justice.

Rawls has suggested that one way of assessing the justice of social institutions is to ask whether persons would choose to establish such institutions from a hypothetical position of equality and fairness. In what Rawls calls the "original position," everyone is imagined to be ignorant of his or her identity and social position. The intent of this and other ignorance conditions is to prevent anyone from making choices based on personal advantage. In the original position each party must choose a set of principles which will govern the basic structure of society (3–21; all parenthetical references are to John Rawls, *A Theory of Justice* [Cambridge, Mass.: Harvard University Press, 1971]). By approaching questions of justice in this way, Rawls in effect divides such questions into two stages: First, what would be a fair situation from which to choose principles to govern basic institutions? Second, what kind of principles would be chosen from such a situation? In the original position as he describes it, Rawls argues that the parties would choose two basic principles, a principle of equal liberty and a principle requiring that inequalities benefit everyone, even the worst off (60–65; cf. 302–3).

A strategy substantially similar to Rawls' is useful, I believe, in developing a theory of punishment. In this study I will employ an argument which makes reference to a hypothetical contract to defend a particular theory of punishment against the principal alternatives. Rawls makes only a few brief remarks about punishment in his book (see 241, 245–51, 314–15, 575–76), and I shall not comment specifically on these; rather, I shall be using a broadly Rawlsian approach to address a different set of questions than those which were his principal concern.

Before taking up the topic of punishment I shall outline a general theory of the nature and structure of rights, particularly natural rights, which will provide a framework for discussion of the relationship between punishment and rights. I shall then distinguish the three alternative accounts of the justification of punishment and develop the contractarian approach which I want to use to evaluate them. I shall argue that, given a certain institutional background and certain circumstances, one person has a right to punish another; I shall also argue that any institution of punishment whose structure is not at bottom retributive will fail to protect adequately the rights of individuals subject to it.

In what follows I shall be concerned for the most part only with legal punishment, not punishment as exercised in the family or in other institutions apart from a system of law and adjudication. Punishment in the legal sense is the deprivation of certain of the normal rights of an individual by the recognized legal authorities of a state.[3] It is an interesting exercise to extend an account of punishment in the state to the practice of punishment in other contexts—the family, schools, clubs, armies—but I shall not attempt that here.

THE NATURE AND STRUCTURE OF RIGHTS

The concept of a *right* is one of a small number of basic moral concepts; it is one of the conceptual tools we employ in defending and criticizing acts and institutions. Ronald Dworkin has distinguished *goals*, *rights*, and *duties* as the fundamental justifying devices in a political theory and has suggested that any political theory must take one of these as the fundamental moral category. Rawls' theory, he argues, rests on a "deep theory" in which rights are central.[4]

What is a right? What is asserted when it is claimed that a person has a right to have something or do something?

Rights are claimed in a variety of contexts: one may claim a right to speak one's mind, assert a right to receive one's inheritance, deny that another has the right to use one's property without permission.

To assert the right of one person is also to assert duties or responsibilities of others. Rights carry with them correlative duties not to interfere with their exercise. Such duties may be duties of noninterference, as in the right to free exercise of religion, or duties to contribute, as in the right, if there is one, to a certain level of welfare.[5]

Further, rights may be held with respect to all other persons or only with respect to some. In H.L.A. Hart's terminology, some rights are special rights, rights which arise from transactions or special relationships. Among these are the power of attorney, the right to use a person's property which is granted by giving permission for its use, and the right of a parent to make decisions on behalf of children. Other rights are general rights held with respect to all others, rights which impose duties not on a special class of persons but on all others.[6]

The features identified above are standard features of the concept of rights, and the distinctions between the several kinds of right can be captured by a disjunctive definition: to have a right is to have a right to do something which imposes a duty on others not to interfere, or a right not to suffer something which imposes a duty to refrain from a certain action, or a right to have something which imposes a duty to contribute or a duty not to refuse to contribute.[7] But there is another feature of rights whose importance has seldom been noted: a distinctive feature of rights among moral concepts is the peculiar appropriateness of force or coercion in ensuring their recognition.[8] Few would recommend, for example, that the moral duty to show kindness to others be backed by the threat or use of force—the suggestion seems inappropriate or incongruous. But there is no such incongruity in the suggestion that rights should be protected by forceful means if necessary. Rights are frequently asserted as a justification for the use of force.

Let me clarify the place of force with an example: suppose that a person has property rights to a certain piece of land. What is implied by the assertion of this right?

First, the right justifies the person's use of the land. He is at liberty, other things being equal, to use it as he will. Second, those with respect to whom he has this right—presumably all others, or all others in a certain community—have a duty not to interfere with his using his land as he will.

Now suppose that another person indicates that she intends to take the land from its owner or to use it in ways that the owner does not want it used. An additional element is included in the property right of the owner: he is also justified in undertaking to prevent the other person from interfering with his use of the land.

There are many means by which the owner might do this, of course. He might tell the other person, "Please don't do that." Or he might kill her. The former is justified, but likely ineffective, while the latter, though effective, is unjustified. The property right does not license the holder to prevent its infringement by any means whatever.

Compare this situation with one in which rights are not involved. Suppose that Yves has declared that he intends to commit a breach of a duty toward Xavier. Perhaps he intends to insult and humiliate Xavier in the presence of friends. Though his act will displease and possibly harm Xavier, it will not violate Xavier's rights. In such a case it is permissible for Xavier to try to prevent Yves from carrying out his intention in several ways. He may admonish him, try to persuade him, plead with him. But he may not *force* him not to do as he intends; it is not permissible for him to physically restrain or to threaten Yves.

If Yves' intention is to violate Xavier's rights, however, Xavier is justified not only in attempting to persuade but also, if necessary, in forcing him to refrain. If in this case Xavier physically restrains Yves or induces him to refrain from the intended action by a coercive threat, he may defend his action by citing his right that the action not be done to him.[9]

So, if a person has the right to exclusive use of a piece of property, we would condone his use of coercion or force if necessary to protect that right. He may post "Keep Off" signs, thereby attempting to keep trespassers away by admonition; he may put up fences, employing a kind of physical compulsion; or he may post signs or publish notices threatening harm to those who use his land without permission.

I shall refer to the right to prevent violations of one's rights as a *second-order right*. The thesis I propose is that every right includes as one of its elements a second-order right. This thesis is supported, I believe, by our willingness to accept the assertion of the need to protect a right as a defense for use of force or coercion. Explicit recognition of this feature of rights is helpful in establishing the place of rights in moral judgments.

If this account of rights is correct, then when Xavier employs force he may defend his action on the ground that it was necessary to protect his rights. Xavier may thus claim that, according to his assessment of the circumstances, the use of force was necessary. In support of his claim he might cite Yves' threat to violate his rights, or past behavior which suggested that Yves intended to do so and Yves' failure to be moved by admonitions.

The claim that force is necessary may be mistaken. The situation is parallel to the assertion of a first-order right: a right provides a defense for acting in a certain way, but a person's claim that his action is justified as an exercise of a right he holds may be incorrect, and in such a case—even if he has the right he asserts—the right does not justify the action. The same holds for a mistaken assertion of a second-order right. A person who beats up a passerby cannot justify his action by claiming that doing so was necessary to prevent him from stealing his watch, any more than a person can morally defend his roasting a neighbor's child on a spit by invoking the right to practice his Molochian religion.

THE NATURAL RIGHTS

Thus far I have been concerned with the structure and nature of rights. But in order to clarify the implications of rights for a theory of punishment, a more substantive account is necessary. What rights do persons have, and how do these bear on the justification of punishment?

Limitations of space prevent me here from attempting to provide arguments for the existence of various particular rights. I shall simply make the assumption—one which is open to debate but which has a good claim to being one of our most widely shared moral assumptions—that rights are an important ground of the moral judgments we make and that persons have rights. I shall further assume that among the rights of persons are certain rights which a long tradition has identified as natural or human rights: rights which all persons have simply because of their status as persons, not because they have entered into special transactions or relationships or because the rights have been conferred on them by social institutions.[10]

Defenders of natural rights have offered different lists of the specific rights concerned. Locke spoke of the right to life, liberty, and property; the writers of the Declaration of Independence substituted the pursuit of happiness for property. The United Nations *Universal Declaration of Human Rights* asserts the right of all to life, liberty, and security of person, along with a great many other rights, ranging from the right not to be subject to slavery or torture to the right to "rest and leisure, including reasonable limitation of working hours and periodic holidays with pay."[11] Among the rights recognized by nearly all defenders of human rights are the following: the right to life (i.e., the right not to be deprived of one's life involuntarily), the right to freedom of expression and of religion, and the right to freedom of the person (i.e., freedom from arbitrary arrest or imprisonment, from torture, from intentional and preventable injury). Included in each of these rights, I have suggested above, is a second-order right to protect the first-order right with force if necessary.

According to the traditional doctrine, natural rights are absolute and inalienable. If absoluteness is taken to mean that these rights can never be overridden by any other moral considerations, it is unlikely that any rights are absolute. But if absoluteness means that, even when other moral considerations are sufficiently urgent to override the right, the right still exists and its infringement counts as a moral cost, the doctrine of absoluteness seems correct.[12]

The force of these natural rights requires that they be recognized as inalienable. If it is even possible to transfer to another the right to decide whether one will live or die or what religious beliefs and practices one will embrace, such a transfer of right would be morally objectionable.

The second-order rights included in these rights, however, are by no means inalienable. One might well decide that the most effective means of protecting the exercise of one's rights is to transfer to another person or to some institution the right to use force for their protection.[13]

The state may be viewed as a system of social institutions which acquires the second-order rights of individuals to protect their rights. This is the meaning of the doctrine that the state holds a monopoly on the legitimate use of force: in the context of a state, certain institutions have the right to use force when necessary to protect the rights of individuals, and individuals no longer have such a right, or have it subject to legal as well as moral limitations.

The right to punish violators of the law is a right which only certain individuals occupying special places in institutions have. And this right derives from the second-order right of the state to protect rights.

I shall go on shortly to explore the support that can be given for the claim that the state has acquired second-order rights from individuals and to explore the ways in which the exercise of the right to use force may respect or infringe individual rights. But before turning to those topics, I wish to look more closely at the role which rights play in supporting moral judgments.

It is clear, in the first place, that general rights—rights to an activity or a kind of object which is described in general terms—imply rights to engage in specific activities or right to specific objects. Their assertion serves as the major premise of a kind of moral syllogism:

> Horace has a right to free exercise of religion,
> Horace's erecting an altar in his driveway is an exercise of his religion.
> Therefore Horace has a right to erect an altar.

> Hypatia has a right not to be deprived of her property without her consent;
> she owns that ring;
> therefore she has a right not to be deprived of that ring involuntarily
> (and everyone else has an obligation not to take it, etc.)

So much is obvious. From the more abstract statement of a right we may infer as its concrete consequences specific rights, and these support moral judgments, though other considerations may override them.

One may also argue in the other direction, from the more concrete to the more abstract. A more abstract right may provide the best explanation of certain rights which are its consequences. Hart has argued, for example, that the assertion both of special rights and of general rights implies an underlying equal right of all persons to be free.[14] Ronald Dworkin similarly posits as the foundation of Rawls' theory of justice a right of all to equal concern and respect in the design and operation of the institutions to which they are subject.[15]

Without attempting to argue the point in detail here, let me suggest that the natural rights enumerated above may best be understood as supported by a more general and more abstract right, the right of all to make choices and to make their choices reasonably effective in determining their future condition. I shall take this right as fundamental; other natural rights need not be taken as primitive but may be supported as consequences or expressions of the basic right. In order to be able to make and carry through one's choices it is necessary to enjoy freedom of the person from arbitrary interference, for example; and in order to make choices with full knowledge of their significance and of the alternatives available, freedom of expression is necessary. Similar arguments for the other natural rights can be based on the underlying right of all to make and carry out choices. I shall refer to this right as the right to self-determination.

THE JUSTIFICATION OF PUNISHMENT: THREE ACCOUNTS

The difficult cases of moral judgments based on rights are those of conflicting rights, or conflicting claims based on rights. Punishment and the threat of punishment pose one of the more perplexing such cases: how can the second-order right to enforce rights be reconciled with the first-order rights of those to whom force is threatened or applied? The question I now take up is whether an institution of punishment is either permitted or required by the recognition of the rights of individuals. Does the state indeed have a second-order right to employ force to protect individuals' rights? If so, is it possible for the state to exercise this second-order right without violating the rights of individuals?

Were the state to undertake to defend certain rights of individuals by employing arbitrary and capricious arrest and treatment, it would be seriously violating individuals' rights, even if its intent in doing so were the protection of other rights. Zeal to protect property rights cannot justify denial of due process to those suspected of theft. Might there be institutions of coercion and punishment which do not thus violate individual rights?

I shall argue that any system of punishment whose basic features are determined by deterrent or rehabilitative considerations will violate the rights of individuals. A system whose basic features are determined by retributive principles, however, need not.

These three defenses of punishment might be summarized as follows: The *deterrent* theory of punishment holds that punishment is justified by its effect in discouraging the person punished and others from committing future offenses similar to that for which the punishment is inflicted.[16] A purpose closely related to deterrence is the *incapacitation* of the person punished, rendering him incapable, either temporarily or permanently, of repeating his offense.[17] Capital punishment is of course the most effective means of incapacitation; but imprisonment also disables a person temporarily from committing most crimes. According to the deterrent theory, of which I take incapacitation as a particular application, punishment is justified by the socially useful effects of deterrence and incapacitation of known criminals and potential criminals. Its application and severity should therefore be set in such a way as to achieve these ends effectively and economically.

In contrast, the *rehabilitative* or reformative view of punishment sees the purpose of punishment above all in its beneficial effects on the individual. Criminal acts are taken to be symptoms of malfunction or maladjustment of the person who commits them; the treatment of criminals, on this view, should aim at restoring them to psychological health and making their behavior conform to socially acceptable standards. Although I have referred to the rehabilitative view as a theory of punishment, what it proposes is not so much a defense as a substitute for it, since treatment of law-breakers for therapeutic ends lacks some of the characteristic features of punishment. On this view, each criminal should be subjected to that treatment which will most effectively heal him or improve his behavior.[18]

The deterrent theory of punishment is frequently supported by a utilitarian theory of ethics. A justified system of punishment, according to utilitarianism, is one which brings about the greatest benefit to all, and a deterrent and incapacitative system of punishment may be constructed with this end in view. Utilitarian considerations may also be offered in favor of the rehabilitative view, however, stressing the benefit done both to the criminal and to society by his reform.

The deterrent and rehabilitative theories have arisen as reactions against the traditional *retributive* defense of punishment, which holds that the justification of punishment lies in its exacting retribution for the offense committed. Retributivism holds that the person who has committed a crime deserves to be punished accordingly. This account of punishment, unlike the others, is backward-looking: it judges the appropriateness of punishment by the offense that a person has committed, not by the expected effects of his punishment on himself or on society.[19]

The question to which I shall devote the remainder of this discussion is which of these alternative accounts, if any, provides adequate support for a system of punishment and which poses the least serious threat to individual rights.

I would like to approach this question by putting it before parties in a hypothetical choice situation who must choose a set of principles to govern institutions of punishment in ignorance of the particular facts about themselves and their position in society. The motivation for employing this approach, as for Rawls' use of the same device in approaching questions of distributive justice, is that disagreement over features of social institutions which arises not from considerations of justice and fairness but from considerations of personal advantage may be ruled out by imagining that the relevant principles must be chosen under suitable ignorance conditions.

Let us begin, therefore, by constructing a choice situation from which principles to govern institutions of punishment will be chosen. The parties to the choice are ignorant of their position in society, of their natural talents and abilities, and of their particular desires and inclinations. They have full access to general knowledge about psychology, economics, and the nature of social interaction, but they do not know the particular circumstances of their society or its stage of historical development (136-142).

That the question of institutions of punishment is raised at all indicates that the choice situation is different from that which Rawls describes. For Rawls postulates full compliance with the laws and policies of society, describing the "ideal theory" thus generated as a necessary step in the construction of a full theory of the state (8-9, 245-46). Questions of punishment belong for the most part to partial compliance theory; an institution of punishment is necessary under the assumption of full compliance only in order to provide assurance for each that others will also comply with the law (315-16). However, one of the facts about human nature and social interaction which the parties to the hypothetical choice know is that the assumption of full compliance is unquestionably false. Under any imaginable social order, people will disobey laws and policies from time to time for a variety of reasons, particularly when it appears to them that personal advantage may be served by doing so. The parties in our choice situation do not assume full compliance, and they know that if there are laws they will be broken.

But to say that laws will be broken is not to say that a system of punishment is necessary. Punishment is the deliberate deprivation of rights or infliction of hard treatment on individuals by duly constituted authorities, and one option open to the parties in the choice situation is to omit any such institution from the design of their society. They might substitute a system of persuasion and exhortation, or they might decide not to include any institutional way of dealing with violation of the law.

Or they might choose to create an institution of legal punishment; and if they do, they will need to choose how it will be organized and administered. They must decide what principles will determine who will be punished and in what way. The theories of punishment enumerated above are the principal options: the parties might choose to select persons for punishment and set their treatment in order to maximize deterrence and incapacitation, in order to bring about reform, or by retributive criteria.

The choice has to do with a kind of distribution: it is a choice of the way in which a society will distribute a particular set of benefits and burdens among its members. Among these are the costs of imprisonment and other penal sanctions. Also included are the costs of being subject to harm through violation of law and the benefits of being free from such harm, since the structure and operation of the system of punishment will greatly affect the decisions of individuals to commit crimes. The parties in the choice situation will want to maximize the benefits and minimize the harms to which they will be subjected.

In order to account for the motivation of the parties we need a version of Rawls' "thin theory of the good," the theory of what it would be rational to want whatever else one wants (395–99). Rawls provides a list of several categories of primary goods—income and wealth, powers and opportunities, rights and liberties, and self-respect—which he regards as means for the attainment of anyone's particular ends (90–95; 440). We need not call on the full list for our purposes: the "goods" to be distributed by a system of punishment are above all liberties, especially freedom from imprisonment and other sanctions (i.e., freedom of movement, freedom of choice of occupation, and the other liberties of which persons being punished are deprived) and freedom from harm and invasion of rights by others (brought about by the effects of punishment on the behavior of others). There are important difficulties with Rawls' list of primary goods,[20] but the shortened list we need for a theory of punishment is less problematic.

I shall follow Rawls in supposing that each party in the choice situation is interested in securing for himself or herself the greatest quantity he can obtain of primary goods—i.e., in this case, the greatest measure of personal freedom—but is indifferent to the outcome for others. The fact that others end up with significantly more or significantly less freedom than he or she does does not bother our imagined chooser, unless the inequality could be eliminated in a way that would benefit him or her. This is in effect a stipulation not of self-interested motivation—since the parties do not know who they are, or which "self" they are interested in—but of individualism. As Stephen Darwall points out in his contribution to this volume, the very same result would be obtained by supposing each of the parties to be interested solely in some individual other than himself.[21]

Application of a hypothetical contract to questions of punishment raises unique problems about who the parties are that are counted in as choosing parties. In particular, are criminals counted in? Do they also get a choice in determining the existence and nature of institutions of punishment, and is one of the positions which each choosing party might turn out to hold the position of a violator of the law—whether career criminal or one-time offender?

If criminals are excluded and the choices which govern the institution of punishment are those which law-abiding citizens would accept, there is no reason in principle why extremely harsh treatment of criminals might not result. The only bar to this outcome would be benevolence on the part of the choosing parties, for they know that the institutions of punishment they design will not normally inflict sanctions on them. But this is unfair: criminals retain many, though not all, of the rights of other members of society, and their situation surely deserves consideration. Therefore I shall count criminals in as parties to the agreement. Will this lead to complete rejection of punishment? It will not, for, in the first place, general compliance with the law which is brought about by institutions of punishment benefits criminals also. More important, under the conditions of ignorance criminals do not know that they are criminals.

This has a peculiar ring. It would be peculiar indeed if the choice of principles of punishment were thought of as prior to the establishment and operation of society. In that case, whether the parties would turn out to be criminals once the ignorance conditions are lifted would be up to them, depending on their future decisions and actions. But I want to take the hypothetical contract as a means of justification which is not temporally prior to the institutions it deals with. At any time we may appeal to this construction in order to find principles which all the members of society, apart from considerations of personal advantage, would accept. Some of these members are criminals, but the principles we arrive at should be acceptable even to them, once they take the standpoint of justice and consider their situation as only one among the many in society.

Moreover, to say that each person may ensure that he or she is not a criminal simply by diligent effort is an oversimplification. Many influences converge on those who commit crimes, and the pressures of one's situation and the lack of evident alternative means of attaining one's goals may greatly restrict one's choice. From the viewpoint of the original position, each individual must consider the possibility that he will occupy whatever position in his society most disposes toward crime, and in such a position his own determination to obey the law may in the long run be ineffective.[22]

THE INSTITUTION OF PUNISHMENT

Let me summarize the options which are open to the parties in the choice situation by constructing a branching tree. They must choose first whether to include an institution of punishment in their society and subsequently, if they choose to have such an institution, must choose a principle to govern its basic structure:

- (I) No institution of punishment.
  - (A) Laws with systematic persuasion and admonition to encourage compliance
  - (B) Laws with no institutional reinforcement, or no laws
- (II) Institution of punishment
  - (A) Application of punishment determined by deterrence and incapacitation
  - (B) Application of punishment determined by rehabilitative considerations
  - (C) Application of punishment determined by retributive considerations

After having chosen one or the other option at each of these two branchings the parties will then choose, subject to the principles they have chosen to govern the institution of punishment, some of the particular features of the institution: what sanctions will be employed, what safeguards included to prevent misdirected punishment, what range of penalties, and the like. I shall not discuss these features systematically but will mention many of the most important below.

The first choice to be made, as I have presented it, is the choice of whether to include an institution of punishment in society. The parties would choose to include a system of punishment, I believe. They would do so because the harm they are likely to suffer if no such institution exists poses an unacceptable cost.

The parties know that they are individuals who pursue particular goals and who hold rights to engage in certain activities and rights not to be interfered with in certain ways. Since they know all relevant general facts about human behavior, they know that individuals frequently come into conflict and attempt to impose their own goals on others without proper consideration for others' rights. But they also know that a system of laws and punishment designed to protect the freedom of each person and to preserve the rights of all will have the effect of diminishing harmful conflict and infringement of rights.

In certain kinds of organizations the most appropriate decision is to include no system of punishment. In clubs, committees, and even relatively large organizations such as political parties, appeals to the good will of members may be sufficient to ensure general compliance with rules, and the circumstances may offer few opportunities for serious violations of rights. But in the basic structure of a society the situation is different: a shared sense of purpose and general good will are not likely to exist, and the opportunities for violation of rights are limitless.

But have the choosing parties any right to include a system of coercive sanctions in the structure of society? The account offered above of the structure of rights shows that they have. The parties conceive of themselves as the holders of rights such as the rights to freedom of expression and to freedom of the person. Included in their recognition of these rights is a recognition of the right to employ force if necessary to protect these rights. In deciding to include an institution of punishment in the structure of society, the parties are in effect deciding to transfer to a certain institution the second-order right to use forceful means to protect their rights.

Since the option of no punishment is ruled out by these considerations, I shall not further examine the various forms which such a choice might take. There are many nonforceful means of affecting behavior, means whose appropriateness and effectiveness varies with the kind of social unit at issue, ranging from simple advice and suggestion to some sort of official and emphatic denunciation.[23] The possibilities of affecting behavior by nonviolent means deserve more consideration than they have received, both in the context of domestic law enforcement and in dealing with aggression from outside. But I shall leave the matter aside for now, since it seems clear that such means alone will leave individuals open to a very high and unacceptable risk of harm and violation of rights.

So branch (II) on the chart above will be chosen by parties in the choice situation because of the risks which attend the other choice. In a society without an effective institution of punishment to back up laws, a great many people will be subject to frequent and serious infringements of rights. In order to avoid the risk of such an outcome the parties will choose to include a system of punishment in their society and thereby reduce this risk substantially. They may defend their decision to create institutions which employ the use or threat of force by pointing to their second-order right to protect their rights.

The reason for choosing (II) over (I), therefore, has to do with deterrence. The parties choose to include an institution of punishment in order to reduce the incidence of crime and bring general compliance with the law. In contrast, a traditional retributivist such as Kant would call on retributive considerations at this point, insisting that we must include institutions of punishment in society because we have an obligation to impose on criminals the penalties they deserve, whatever the effects of the practice may be. This raises many questions: on what grounds ought we to impose punishment? Whom do we wrong if we fail to do so? Is punishment morally required of a state but not of other organizations?

The retributive argument for the existence of an institution of punishment appears to rest on a view of the state as a moral judge and arbiter, an entity charged with upholding true moral laws. Whether any such laws exist is a matter of dispute; Kant's confidence that they are implicit in the very notion of a self as a rational agent seems inadequately grounded. But even if such laws exist and can be reliably identified, the purpose of upholding morality by punishing moral wrong is not one which the choosing parties would be willing to entrust to governmental institutions. Even if the choosing parties are assumed to have full knowledge of the facts about morality, they will also know that there is a substantial possibility that they may at some point act out of different moral convictions. To allow societal institutions to punish those who act in a way which is wrong by the society's moral standards, that being the sole justification for punishment, is a particularly severe infringement of the individual's right to make fundamental choices for himself. If punishment exists for the sake of bringing about compliance with the law, persons in such circumstances may be punished nevertheless; but their punishment will be justified not simply by their alleged immoral act but by the necessity of an institution of punishment which includes their being punished in order to bring about a tolerable life for all.[24]

In the absence of such a moral view, a retributive reason for the existence of an institution of punishment seems to me to have little foundation. Hegel argued that the criminal wills his own punishment when he commits a crime, so that the infliction of punishment is the fulfillment of his will and not an imposition of others' will on him.[25]

Though there may be important insights into the character of criminal acts in this view,[26] it does not seem to me to offer a satisfactory grounding for the institution of punishment.

Considerations of deterrence, then, provide strong support for the existence of an institution of punishment. Retributive arguments, if I understand them correctly, do not. I do not believe the rehabilitative view adequately supports the existence of such an institution either, but since the choice of (II) over (I) is already required by the deterrent arguments, I shall put the rehabilitative theory aside briefly and return to it below.

The account I have given so far is incomplete, however: for there are other ways of achieving deterrence besides punishment, and deterrence alone cannot choose between them. Although deterrent arguments do indeed provide support for a system of punishment over its absence, they support equally any other method of achieving the same result.

When I spoke above of the alternative of omitting an institution of punishment from society, I mentioned the possibility of systematic persuasion and admonition designed to encourage compliance with law. But there are far more effective ways of bringing about compliance, as contemporary police states have demonstrated. The methods of indoctrination, intimidation, and surveillance employed by such states to prevent commission of crimes by citizens are enormously varied, and vast new opportunities for such supervision and control are opened by electronic technology.

Imagine that a well-organized and humane police state created such effective means of intimidation and surveillance that scarcely anyone ever committed a crime. Perhaps each citizen is fitted with a tiny radio-transmitter collar which relays his location and activities to the precinct station at all times. Anyone who is suspected of engaging in illegal activities is immediately warned to stop by the voice of a police officer (or, if this turns out to be more effective, by the taped voice of his mother) issuing from the receiver portion of his collar. If the person refuses to stop, a team of officers is at his side almost instantly to hold him securely until he satisfies them that he has no intention of committing a crime. An electric shock device might be an optional accessory for emergency use.

The point is that under such a system hardly anyone would ever succeed in committing a crime. The deterrent purpose of punishment is therefore undercut. Other influences besides the deterrent effect of punishment would reduce the incidence of crime to very low levels, thus satisfying the demand which led us above to choose a system of punishment; and the number of successful criminals to be dealt with would be so small that their treatment would have little effect on others' behavior. Perhaps, therefore, out of humaneness the officials of such a state would simply let anyone who succeeded in committing a crime go free, confident that neither he nor anyone else is likely to succeed in doing likewise. (Perhaps they now add the electric shock unit.) Indeed, if they are utilitarians they must do so unless punishment would in fact cause a further reduction in crime sufficient to outweigh the suffering of the punished.

Such a humane police state would achieve the goal of deterrence even more effectively than a system of punishment with procedural protections and extensive personal freedom. Deterrent considerations would therefore suggest that we eliminate punishment in favor of such a system. Perhaps a system as effective as the one I have sketched is not yet possible, but then we have all the more reason to work on developing such technology rather than spend our resources on punishment of criminals.[27]

What is wrong with our kindly totalitarian state, of course, is that it achieves deterrence only by trampling on everyone's rights, such as the right to privacy and to freedom of the person. The reason why we would choose a system of punishment over a police state without punishment is that we want to reduce the incidence of crime only by means which respect the rights of individuals. In the following section I will argue that respect for individuals' rights requires that retributive principles govern the application of punishment. The example of the police state shows that even in the choice of (II) over (I) above, it is not just deterrence but deterrence subject to the constraints of right that we are seeking. These constraints are not retributive, properly speaking; as I explained above I do not believe there are acceptable retributive reasons for creating an institution of punishment. But the constraints show that the choice of an institution of punishment is motivated not merely by the result achieved but by the manner of achieving it. Consequential considerations alone are not sufficient to support this choice; the character of the means employed in bringing about compliance with the law must also be considered.

THE RETRIBUTIVE SYSTEM OF PUNISHMENT

Once having chosen to include an institution of punishment in the basic structure of society, the parties must next select a set of principles which will govern its application. By what standards shall persons be selected to be punished and particular sanctions imposed on them?

Would the parties employ deterrent arguments at this step? I do not believe they would. Considerations of rights and liberty—the interest which the parties have in preserving their integrity as choosing and self-determining agents—will lead them to adopt instead a fundamentally retributive set of principles as the basis for the application of punishment.

In order to see the reasons for this it is necessary to spell out more clearly just what the distinctive features of a retributive system of punishment are. I have argued above that punishment should not be conceived as exacting the moral price of crimes. Are there other features distinctive of a retributive theory of punishment?

First, a retributive theory requires that the justification of punishment be essentially *backward-looking.* Punishment is justified by an individual's violation of the law. It is to a past act of the person that we turn when asked to provide a moral defense for an act of punishment. Both the utilitarian and the rehabilitative accounts of punishment, in contrast, are essentially forward-looking: punishment is justified by its expected effects, either on the individual or on society.

Second, and more specifically, the retributive theory requires as a necessary condition for the justification of punishment that the individual punished *be responsible* for the offense for which he or she is punished. There can be no question of punishing someone who committed an act which was a violation of law without knowing what he was doing, e.g., while insane. Of course, criminal acts may be committed through negligence: failing to take proper care to avoid committing certain offenses may itself be a punishable offense. But responsibility for the act being punished is a necessary condition for punishment which is insisted on by the retributive view.

Finally, the specific way in which past acts are held to determine the appropriateness of punishment is through *proportionality* between the offense and the sanction. The more serious a crime has been committed, the more serious ought to be the penalty imposed for its commission. A retributive view of punishment need not specify a cardinal scale of seriousness of offenses and punishments—it need not attempt to specify how many years' imprisonment is required by an armed robbery. What is essential is that there be an ordinal ranking of seriousness of crimes and severity of penalties and a mapping of offenses onto punishments in order of severity. Judgments of the severity of offenses and of sanctions will make reference to rights: the more serious offenses are those which more seriously infringe the rights of others, and the more severe penalties are those which involve farther-reaching and longer-lasting deprivations of rights.

A retributive theory of punishment, as I understand it, does not propose an exact matching of punishment to offense but requires that the reason for a certain penalty be the seriousness of the offense for which it is imposed. Different societies, and the same societies at different times, are likely to have widely different scales and kinds of punishment. What retributivism demands is that, at a given time in a society, the imposition of a punishment of greater severity on one offender than on another be justified by the greater seriousness of the offense committed. In contrast, deterrent considerations would judge the appropriateness of penalties by their expected effectiveness introducing the incidence of crime, and a rehabilitative view would rest the severity of sanctions entirely on the effects on the individual.

But in addition to requiring this comparative proportionality, even a retributive theory weaker than full-blown moral retributivism can set at least some outer cardinal limits on the severity of punishments. From what has been said so far it would appear that a retributive theory would offer no ground for choosing between a scale of punishments which imposes a ten-dollar fine for murder and lesser fines for everything else and a system which imposes death for overtime parking and ranges up to slow and painful death by torture. Either of these might conceivably be defended on deterrent or rehabilitative grounds: it is possible, if unlikely, that either a very lenient system or a very cruel system is the most effective and economical way of securing deterrence or reform. But neither is acceptable on retributive grounds: although retributive arguments do not require any specific penalty for a particular act, they rule out systems which fall outside of what could sensibly be defended as the appropriate penalty for crime. Thus, to cite two factual examples, neither the sentencing of political activist John Sinclair to ten years' imprisonment for possession of two marijuana cigarettes nor the absolution of former president Nixon from any punishment for abuse of high office can be defended as penalties appropriate to the seriousness of the offense.

The decision which must be made at the second branch of the above scheme is a choice between systems of punishment governed by distinct sets of principles. In choosing one of these systems,[28] while ignorant of their particular place in society, they are choosing to occupy some position or other in respect to institutions of punishment. In making their choice they will consider the cost of ending up in any of the resulting positions and the risk of being in that position.

Rawls argues that the parties to the Original Position as he conceives it would choose a maximin rule and select the set of principles which assures the best worst position (150–161). Even if Rawls is correct that a maximin choice is rational in the conditions he stipulates,[29] the conditions for adopting a maximin rule do not appear to be present in the case of institutions of punishment.[30]

Yet the worst position under a system of punishment is important, and even if a maximin strategy would not be adopted I believe the worst position would function as a criterion in a different way. The system with the best worst position would not necessarily be chosen, but a system with an intolerable worst position would be excluded from consideration. The parties will not be willing to choose a system of punishment with a worst position which they cannot accept the risk of occupying. In particular, since the parties think of themselves as agents with a right to self-determination, they will not be willing to accept a system some of whose positions effectively undermine this fundamental right. A kind of "worst-position veto" will thus be involved in their choice.

But both the deterrent and the rehabilitative systems of punishment have intolerable worst positions, as I shall now argue. The only acceptable choice is a retributive system of punishment.

If the parties extend the reasoning for choice (II) to the level of principles to govern punishment, they will choose to determine who is punished and what punishments are imposed by the expected effects of punishment on the incidence of crime. The reason for imposing a sanction on a particular offender will be that doing so tends to bring about general compliance with the law, and the reason for punishing a person with a certain degree of severity will be that this penalty is most effective in preventing crime. Utilitarianism, which commonly underlies the deterrent view, limits punishment to that degree of harm which will bring about the greatest net benefit to all the individuals affected, but it also forbids any penalty less than this. If sentencing a burglar to ten years' imprisonment rather than one will be measurably more effective in deterring others from committing burglary and thus will increase the general well-being of others, the additional sanction is justified if and only if the benefit to others exceeds the cost to the person punished. If an additional twenty years will lead to benefits that outweigh the cost, thirty years it must be.

An obvious objection arises: does not the deterrent theory require that the innocent be punished when doing so will yield a net benefit and forbid punishment even of persons guilty of serious crimes when their punishment will not have a deterrent effect? Many writers who defend deterrence on utilitarian grounds have attempted to answer this objection.[31] The above account of the consequences of the practice of punishment, several writers point out, is incomplete: the benefits to society include not only freedom from criminal invasion of rights but also general confidence that institutions deal with people fairly and punish only those who have committed crimes. Punishment of the innocent, though it might be an effective deterrent, would pose an unacceptable cost in the fear and anxiety caused ordinary law-abiding citizens.

But these considerations do not show that only the guilty should be punished. Rather, they show that *either* punishment should be restricted to the guilty *or* punishment of the innocent should be carried out in such a way that the innocence of the punished person is a closely guarded secret. The chance that the secret will get out must be counted in as a cost, as must the difficulty of maintaining the secret for those few who are in on it. For these reasons a situation in which punishment of the innocent is required on utilitarian grounds is no doubt unlikely to arise in practice, but we need only imagine a wave of crime which is sufficiently serious and sufficiently difficult of detection to override these costs.

Some utilitarians have accepted this consequence, with or without flinching.[32] But from the viewpoint of the hypothetical choice situation, it represents a risk which is inconsistent with the recognition of the rights of persons, since it allows one person to be subjected to severe deprivation solely for the sake of benefiting others, provided that the others' need is pressing enough. The worst position under a system of utilitarian punishment is the position of an innocent person punished for the sake of general deterrence. Even if this position is very unlikely to be occupied at any given time in a society, the risk of occupying it is one which the choosing parties' commitment to the rights of persons will rule out.

There are other positions under a utilitarian system which are similarly objectionable. Considerations of deterrence would allow and even require exemplary punishment of the guilty—punishment which is unusually harsh for reasons of deterrence. A utilitarian system would punish one person more severely than another, and more severely than retributive standards would allow, when there is reliable evidence that doing so will lead to a sufficient increment in prevention of crime to outweigh the additional suffering imposed on the criminal. But in this case also the individual is being treated in a way inconsistent with recognition of his right to self-determination; he is being treated harshly without regard to his act for the sake of benefits to others. The possibility of such treatment, too, poses an unacceptable risk from the standpoint of the choice situation.

In the case of exemplary punishment of the guilty, the parties to the choice must consider the consequences not only if they always obey the law but also if they violate it: they must consider the risk that they will be criminals. The parties know that there will be persons who violate the law, and they take into account the possibility that they will turn out to be among them, whether through mistake, through powerful environmental influences, or by deliberate choice.

Finally, a utilitarian system of punishment will include procedural safeguards such as the requirement of *mens rea,* which excuses acts done while mentally ill and unaware of one's actions, only if their inclusion brings about on balance a greater sum of benefits. It may be argued, for reasons similar to those cited above concerning punishment of the innocent, that these safeguards are justified on utilitarian and deterrent grounds, since they assure all of us that acts we cannot avoid and are not aware of doing will not render us liable to be punished. But there is a cost attached also: the existence of these protections makes it possible for some to commit crimes deliberately and escape punishment by falsely claiming not to have met the *mens rea* requirement. To adopt a utilitarian system of punishment is to take the risk that, should these protections prove at some point to cost more than they are worth in the benefits they bring about, the safeguards will be abolished. It is unlikely but by no means impossible that conditions might be such, either at present or in the future. But to allow the elimination of these safeguards is to open the possibility of punishment for acts which one did not intentionally commit. The support for procedural safeguards offered by utilitarian arguments is conditional, and I believe this would be a further reason for rejection of this system of punishment by choosing parties who take their freedom to determine their condition by their deliberate acts as of central importance.

The objections to the rehabilitative principle as the basis of punishment, or as a substitute for punishment, are equally conclusive. Such a system will select those individuals for treatment who are judged most in need of therapy or reform and most likely to benefit from it, and it will judge the appropriateness of their treatment by the improvement brought about, measured by a certain standard of mental health or by expected behavior and the likelihood of future crime. On this model, punishment of the innocent is not only permissible but preferable to punishment of the guilty. It may sometimes be necessary to wait until a person commits a crime to identify his need for treatment, but it would be less harmful to society, and probably more effective therapeutically, to identify those who are likely to commit crimes and subject them to treatment before they actually do so.

Although the rehabilitative account of punishment has recently received broad support, it is clearly unacceptable as a justification of punishment.[33] It divorces the treatment of individuals radically from their choices, since liability to punishment or treatment is not dependent on one's past acts. It therefore systematically disregards the individual's right to self-determination, a right which the choosing parties are concerned to protect. Under a rehabilitative system I cannot control my future condition by my acts or even predict my future condition. Whether I will be subject to imprisonment and rehabilitation depends on whether those in authority judge that I need such treatment.

Furthermore, such a system imposes on individuals standards of health or normality which may be in sharp conflict with their own conceptions. Treatment is imposed until the individual is judged either to be sufficiently improved to warrant release or to be so resistant to change that further treatment is ineffectual. But to presume that everyone who violates the law is in need of such treatment is to disregard flagrantly the rights of individuals.

The case against the rehabilitative view of punishment is clearest in the context of conscientious disobedience to an allegedly unjust law. A person who deliberately violates a law, believing the law to be unjust and intending by his violation to draw attention to its injustice, may justly be punished for his offense. Many defenders of civil disobedience have included the suffering of the legal penalty as part of their intention, as a way of demonstrating their seriousness and integrity; and, although there are reasons for avoiding punishment in some such cases, no injustice is done if it is imposed. But punishment defended on rehabilitative grounds—treatment with the intent of correcting the abnormality shown by the act or of preventing the individual from committing similar acts in the future—is clearly unjust and an affront to the integrity of the person.

I do not mean to suggest that there is no place for therapy and rehabilitative programs in a society, even compulsory treatment for some. Without question there are persons who commit crimes because of mental disease or incapacity, and such people ought to be given treatment and, if they pose a danger to others, confined until they are able to take responsibility for their actions. The error of the rehabilitative view is to include *all* violators of the law in this category. To make rehabilitative principles determinative of the application of punishment is to misconceive the purpose and justification of punishment; to justify the existence of punishment on rehabilitative grounds is to mistake one kind of institution for another. There is a need for rehabilitative institutions in society, but their purpose and application are not the same as those of penal institutions.

The parties to the choice situation would reject the rehabilitative principle as a basis for a system of punishment, therefore, because it fails to respect the rights of individuals to freedom and self-determination. The worst position in such a society would be unacceptable. The parties would be unwilling to take the substantial risk of being subjected to compulsory treatment because of acts—or because of an authority's prediction that they would commit acts—which they might choose freely and deliberately. And they would be unwilling to allow a standard of mental health or normal behavior to govern their treatment unless they were genuinely unable, because of severe mental illness or disability, to choose and act responsibly.

The remaining choice on the diagram is that of a fundamentally retributive system of punishment. On retributive principles, persons are selected for punishment according to their past deliberate acts of violation of law, and the severity of punishment is set by proportionality to the seriousness of the offense committed.

The worst positions under the other two systems will not exist in a retributive system. Retributive grounds cannot allow deliberate punishment of the innocent or harsh punishment for exemplary reasons. And punishment will be gauged according to the severity of the offense committed, not according to an imposed standard of normality.

What is the worst position under a retributive system? Perhaps it is that of the criminal. But his treatment is justified by his past acts; though he is made to suffer deprivation of rights, that outcome is not unconnected with his deliberate choices. The victim of crime also suffers violation of his rights. But if laws are well formulated, publicized, and enforced, the incidence of crime will be less than it would otherwise be. To the objection that the victim will still suffer, we may respond that further deterrence is not available without doing injustice.

But the procedures of justice are imperfect, and it is inevitable not only that the guilty will sometimes go undetected and unpunished but also that the innocent will sometimes be mistakenly convicted and punished. This seems to be the worst position: that of a person punished by mistake. Does this position pose an unacceptable risk?

I do not believe it does. First, recall that a retributive defense of punishment requires procedural safeguards such as the *mens rea* requirement, presumption of innocence, and the like. It is never justified, whatever the consequences, to punish a person who is known not to have intentionally committed the act for which he was punished. For this reason cases of mistaken punishment will be fewer than they would otherwise be.

Second, though the risk of being mistakenly punished is an important cost, it is one which can be avoided only by eliminating the institution of punishment altogether. Any system of punishment administered by fallible human beings is bound to impose punishment by mistake in some cases. The alternative is to punish no one, but that alternative poses far greater costs.

Therefore this worst position, though it does pose a significant cost, does not invalidate the retributive system from the standpoint of the choice situation. The parties will take the risk of occupying this position rather than risk either the worse and more likely outcomes of the other systems of punishment or the highly undesirable outcome of having no system of punishment. But they will include provisions to make mistaken punishment unlikely and to provide for its correction, such as stringent procedural safeguards and extensive rights of appeal.

CONCLUSION

Let me return to the questions with which I began. First, is there a right to punish? There is: it is not a natural right, as Locke thought, but a right which is socially conferred. It is held by those entrusted with the power to administer a judicial and penal system. Although it is a socially created right, it derives its legitimacy from the second-order natural right of individuals to protect their rights. In society this second-order right is transferred to and exercised by a certain set of office-holders rather than by individuals.

Second, is there a right to be punished? If there is, it is an odd sort of right.[34] Few claims are based on any such right, except in aberrant cases like that of O'Henry's vagrant who vainly attempts to be thrown back into jail.

But perhaps we do have such a right, in a roundabout way. Given the facts of social circumstances and human motivation—the existing moderate scarcity of goods and of altruism—our right to self-determination gives rise to a right that there exist a fair system of punishment. The absence of a system of punishment violates our rights, and so does a system based on deterrent or rehabilitative considerations. Therefore our right to freedom can be protected only by the existence and consistent operation of a retributive system of punishment. We have a second-order right that others be punished when they violate our rights, since this is a necessary means for the protection of our rights.

But we might reason by a moral syllogism like those cited above to the conclusion that we have a right even to our own punishment:

> I have a right to the operation of a fair system of punishment.
> My being punished is required by the operation of a fair system of punishment.
> Therefore I have a right to be punished.

The conclusion sounds paradoxical, perhaps even nonsensical. But if we assume the universal perspective of justice in assessing the institution of punishment, we must recognize that a fair system of punishment is the most reliable way of protecting the rights of all, not merely of those who are never punished. Failure to punish is a failure to respect the rights of all, including the person punished.[35]

NOTES

1. John Locke, *An Essay Concerning the True Original, Extent and End of Civil Government*, the second of the *Two Treatises of Government*, sections 7-8; in Ernest Barker, ed., *Social Contract* (Oxford University Press, 1947), pp. 6-7.
2. To speak of families, of course, presupposes a certain kind of social structure; perhaps in a true state of nature, whatever that may be, there would be no families and no relations of authority between parent and child. But punishment within the family seems the closest we can come to Locke's natural right to punish.
3. These are among numerous defining features mentioned by Hobbes in *Leviathan*, ch. 28; ed. Michael Oakeshott (Oxford: Basil Blackwell, 1960), pp. 202-209. They are also mentioned by Rawls in "Two Concepts of Rules," *Philosophical Review*, 64 (January 1955), 3-32; reprinted in John Stuart Mill, *Utilitarianism: Text and Critical Essays*, ed. Samuel Gorovitz (Indianapolis: The Bobbs-Merrill Company, Inc., 1971), pp. 175-94, at 179.
4. Ronald Dworkin, "The Original Position," *Chicago Law Review*, 40, no. 3 (Spring, 1973), 500-33; reprinted in Norman Daniels, ed., *Reading Rawls* (New York: Basic Books, Inc., 1976), pp. 16-53, at 38-42. Cf. Stanley I. Benn, "Rights," *Encyclopedia of Philosophy*, 7, 195-99.

5. Benn, in "Rights," asserts that the relation between right and duty is not correlation but identity; cf. Stanley I. Benn and Richard S. Peters, *Social Principles and the Democratic State* (London: George Allen & Unwin, Ltd., 1959), pp. 89, 98, where it is asserted that the relation is a logical entailment. The former claim seems overstrong, since there is at least an explanatory priority to a right over its correlative duty: it makes sense to explain a duty by asserting a right, but explanation does not seem to make sense in the other direction. The relation between rights and duties is explored at greater length in my *Coercion, Rights and Punishment* (doctoral dissertation, Princeton University, in progress), ch. 4.
6. H.L.A. Hart, "Are There Any Natural Rights?" *Philosophical Review*, 64 (1955), 175-91; reprinted in Anthony Quinton, ed., *Political Philosophy* (Oxford: Oxford University Press, 1967), pp. 53-66.
7. More precisely, I would suggest the following compound definition, where X and Y are persons and A is an activity or an object:

   (R1) X has a right_1 to A over against Y just in case X is at liberty with respect to A and for this reason Y has a duty not to interfere with X's doing or having A.

   (R2) X has a right_2 not to suffer A over against Y just in case Y has a duty not to do A to X.

   (R3) X has a right_3 to A over against Y just in case X is at liberty with respect to A and Y has a duty not to refuse to assist X in doing or having A.

   (R4) X has a right_4 to A over against Y just in case X is at liberty with respect to A and Y has a duty to assist X in doing or having A.

   I understand a right to be a right of any of the above kinds, or perhaps a compound of two or more of the four kinds. This account, which is developed at greater length in my *Coercion, Rights, and Punishment*, ch. 6, represents an elaboration of the account of legal rights offered by Wesley Hohfeld in *Fundamental Legal Conceptions* (New Haven: Yale University Press, 1923), ch. 1. Cf. also Benn, "Rights"; Hart, "Natural Rights"; Joel Feinberg, "The Nature and Value of Rights," *Journal of Value Inquiry*, 4, no. 4 (Winter, 1970), 243-57.
8. Hart in "Natural Rights," pp. 55-56, suggests that the concept of rights marks off a particular part of morality, the "morality of law," in which the use of force is appropriate.
9. Not all threats are coercive. A coercive threat is one which threatens the victim with intolerable harm unless he complies with the coercer's demands. I develop this account of coercion at length in the first three chapters of my *Coercion, Rights, and Punishment.*
10. Natural rights doctrines are defended by Aquinas, Hobbes, and Locke; among recent attempts to provide arguments in support of natural rights are Hart, "Natural Rights"; Gregory Vlastos, "Justice and Equality," in *Social Justice*, ed. R.B. Brandt (Englewood Cliffs, N.J.: Prentice-Hall, Inc., 1962), reprinted in part in A.I. Melden, ed., *Human Rights* (Belmont, Cal.: Wadsworth Publishing Co., Inc., 1970), pp. 76-95; and Richard Wasserstrom, "Rights, Hu-

man Rights, and Racial Discrimination," *Journal of Philosophy*, 61, no. 20 (Oct. 29, 1964), reprinted in Melden, *Human Rights*, pp. 96-110.

11. General Assembly of the United Nations, *Universal Declaration of Human Rights* (1948), articles 3, 5, 24; reprinted in Melden, *Human Rights*, pp. 143-49.
12. These matters are discussed at greater length in my *Coercion. Rights and Punishment*, ch. 4; cf. also Benn and Peters, *Social Principles*, p. 96; and J.D. Mabbott, *The State and the Citizen* (London: Arrow, Ltd., 1958), pp. 57-58, cited in Wasserstrom, "Rights," p. 97. Above I follow Wasserstrom for the most part. Vlastos observes that the absoluteness of natural rights is not directly asserted by Locke and questions whether it is reasonably inferred from his view; see "Justice and Equality," p. 81.
13. I omit mention above of a third traditional property of natural rights: their imprescriptibility. Prescription consists in the acquisition of rights, e.g., of title to property, by regular possession or use over a period of time. I relegate this property to a footnote since the denial of the imprescriptibility of the rights I have mentioned is highly implausible. But property rights, included by Locke and others in the list of natural rights, are prescriptible. In most American jurisdictions, for example, the right to use of property and in some cases title to property may be acquired by its regular occupation or use, provided either that its use is necessary as a way of access to property owned by the user or that the owner of the property in question makes no attempt to prevent or discourage its use. See Vlastos, "Justice and Equality," pp. 82-83 and n. 25; "Prescriptive Rights and Easement to Title," *Dictionary of Business Law for Laymen*, in Clarence L. Barnhart, ed., *American College Encyclopedic Dictionary* (Chicago: Spencer Press, 1952), Encyclopedic Supplements, pp. 291-92.
14. Hart, "Natural Rights," pp. 64-66.
15. Ronald Dworkin, "The Original Position," pp. 46-53.
16. Classic defenses of the deterrent view of punishment include Cesare Beccaria, *On Crimes and Punishment* (1764), tr. Henry Paolucci (Indianapolis: The Bobbs-Merrill Company, 1963); and Jeremy Bentham, *An Introduction to the Principles of Morals and of Legislation* (1789) (New York: Hafner Publishing Co., 1948).
17. I know of no sources which take this as the principle justification of punishment. Bentham explicitly includes it in his statement of the goal of deterrence: see ch. XIII, n. 1 (pp. 170-171); ch. XV, para. xviii-xix (pp. 196-197). In Bentham as elsewhere the goal of incapacitation is prominent in discussion of capital punishment.
18. This argument seems to be relatively modern. One version is defended by A.C. Ewing in *The Morality of Punishment* (London: Kegan Paul, Ltd., 1929); he emphasizes the role of punishment in moral education. Rehabilitative arguments have recently been put forward by a great many psychologists and psychiatrists. See, for example, Karl Menninger, *The Crime of Punishment* (New York: Viking Press, 1968); B.F. Skinner, *Science and Human*

Behavior (New York: Macmillan Publishing Co., 1953). Bentham explicitly rejects the rehabilitative argument in ch. XV, para. xxv (pp. 200-201).

19. The classic statement of the retributive theory is in Immanuel Kant, *The Metaphysics of Morals* (1797), tr. H.B. Nisbet, in Hans Reiss, ed., *Kant's Political Writings* (Cambridge: Cambridge University Press, 1971), esp. section 49. Other retributive accounts of punishment are found in G.W.F. Hegel, *Philosophy of Right* (1821), tr. T.M. Knox (Oxford University Press, 1942); Bernard Bosanquet, *The Philosophical Theory of the State* (London: The Macmillan Company, Ltd., 1923).
20. For example: is it always rational to want more rather than less income, wealth, power, and the like? Or is there a certain point at which the desire for still more of such goods becomes irrational? What effects does this have on the derivation of principles for distribution? These questions have been taken up in the critical literature on Rawls; see, for example, Thomas Nagel, "Rawls on Justice," *Philosophical Review*, 82 (1973), 226-29; Adina Schwartz, "Moral Neutrality and Primary Goods," *Ethics*, 83, no. 4 (July, 1973), 294-307. Rawls responds to these criticisms in his article, "Fairness to Goodness," *Philosophical Review*, 84 (1975), 536-54.
21. Stephen Darwall, "A Kantian Interpretation of the Original Position," below, section IV. 3. I shall have to leave aside the significance of this individualistic motivation assumption; I hope to explore elsewhere the consequences for a theory of punishment of altering it in a more collectivist direction.
22. On these issues see T.M. Scanlon, "Freedom of the Will in Political Theory" (unpublished ms.).
23. Does such a system constitute a system of *law*? Or is a directive without force or the threat of force to back it something other than law? I cannot address these interesting issues here; cf. H.L.A. Hart, *The Concept of Law* (Oxford: Clarendon Press, 1961), ch. II; Herbert Fingarette, "Punishment and Suffering," *Proceedings and Addresses of the American Philosophical Association*, 50, no. 6 (Aug. 1977), 499-525.
24. For Rawls the retributive argument is obviously ineligible; it would be ruled out by the exclusion of conceptions of morality from the original position. But for a number of reasons which space forbids me from presenting here I believe this exclusion is poorly motivated.
25. *Philosophy of Right*, sections 99-103.
26. See, for example, the concluding sections of George Sher, "An Unsolved Problem About Punishment," *Social Theory and Practice*, 4, no. 2 (Spring 1977), 149-65.
27. The possibility of such an institution and its consequences in the justification of the institution of punishment were suggested to me by Fred Stoutland, but he is not to be blamed for its fiendish details.
28. Or some other system; I am assuming that the three outlined represent the chief alternatives.
29. Whether a maximin rule is rational even in those circumstances is open to question; see Allen Buchanan's discussion in "A Critical Introduction to Rawls' Theory of Justice," above, section II. 2.

30. For example, it is surely not the case that the person choosing an institution of punishment "cares very little, if anything, for what he might gain above the minimum stipend that he can, in fact, be sure of by following the maximin rule" (154).
31. See, among many discussions of these charges and of the possible replies to them, H.J. McCloskey, "Utilitarian and Retributive Punishment," *Journal of Philosophy*, 64, no. 3 (Feb. 16, 1967), 91-111; J.J.C. Smart, "An Outline of a System of Utilitarian Ethics," esp. section 10, "Utilitarianism and Justice," in Smart and Bernard Williams, *Utilitarianism: For and Against* (Cambridge: Cambridge University Press, 1973); Rawls, "Two Concepts."
32. See J.J.C. Smart, "Utilitarian Ethics," p. 72; for flinching see pp. 70-71.
33. Among discussions of the objections to this view, see Herbert Morris, "Persons and Punishment," *The Monist*, 52, no. 4 (Oct., 1978), 475-501, reprinted in Melden, *Human Rights*, pp. 111-34; C.S. Lewis, "The Humanitarian Theory of Punishment," in *God in the Dock: Essays on Theology and Ethics*, ed. Walter Hooper (Grand Rapids, Mich.: William B. Eerdmans, 1970), pp. 287-95; Jeffrey Murphy, "Criminal Punishment and Psychiatric Fallacies," *Law and Society Review*, 4, no. 1 (Aug., 1969), reprinted in Murphy, ed., *Punishment and Rehabilitation* (Belmont, Cal.: Wadsworth Publishing Co., Inc., 1973), pp. 197-210; Joel Feinberg, "Crime, Clutchability, and Individuated Treatment," *Doing and Deserving* (Princeton: Princeton University Press, 1972), pp. 252-71.
34. Herbert Morris argues in "Persons and Punishment" that there is a right to be punished, but his claim is misleading. What he really argues is that, given a choice between therapy and punishment, we have a right, based on our status as persons, to be punished rather than treated. But this is a bit like asserting that we have a right to be beaten up, given the choice between a beating and death. Morris does not consider whether we have a right to be punished rather than set free, for example.
35. In working out the ideas presented in this paper I have benefited immeasurably from the conversations and comments of friends and colleagues. Among those to whom I am particularly indebted for having read and criticized earlier versions of the material are Thomas M. Scanlon, Jr., Charles R. Beitz, James P. Sterba, Jan Narveson, Edward Langerak, and Frederick Stoutland.

A Rawlsian Discussion of Discrimination

Hardy Jones
UNIVERSITY OF NEBRASKA-LINCOLN

The moral and social problems of discrimination are of immense concern to many persons. As this is written the legal ramifications of direct and reverse discrimination continue to ignite intense, even hostile controversy. Those rejected by schools and jobs protest that discrimination, no matter what its form or what its purpose, should not have been the basis for their exclusion. Others argue that discrimination against the better qualified is sometimes justified. The clashes of interests, claims, rights, attitudes, and beliefs on the matter are serious and pervasive. It would be surprising if John Rawls' *A Theory of Justice* had no significant practical implications for the confrontation of these issues. That already much-discussed work is a book of permanent, classic importance in the history of ethical theory; and it is natural to seek whatever guidance it might provide concerning the problems of discrimination. I shall argue that, though its application to these problems is not always easy to discern, Rawls' theory is applicable nonetheless. I shall try to show how Rawls' principles of justice relate to the discrimination issues of current concern.

It is useful to state at the outset what it seems reasonable to expect of Rawls' theory. Oversimplifying greatly, I summarize here two main themes that serve to structure the interpretation I propose: (1) Rawls' theory will hold that discrimination against persons *because of* their sex, race, color, and religion is wrong and, therefore, unjust. (2) Rawls' theory under certain circumstances allows, and perhaps requires, discrimination for the purpose of rectifying injustice and compensating victims of injustice. The latter is currently far more controversial than the former, and more attention is given to it in subsequent sections. I shall not attempt to argue at length that reverse discrimination is justified, but instead concentrate on whether and why the Rawlsian theory allows or requires it.[1] It is worth noting, however, why we should expect a theory of justice and *A Theory of Justice* to condemn the form of discrimination mentioned in (1).

WHY IS DIRECT, "OLD-FASHIONED" DISCRIMINATION WRONG?

Very early in his book Rawls says, "There are questions which we feel sure must be answered in a certain way. For example, we are confident that religious intolerance and racial discrimination are unjust. We think that we have examined these things with care and have reached what we believe is an impartial judgment not likely to be distorted by an excessive attention to our own interests. These convictions are provisional fixed points which we presume any conception of justice must fit" (19-20, all parenthetical citations are to John Rawls, *A Theory of Justice* (Cambridge, Mass.: Harvard University Press, 1971)). Rawls purports to speak for those of his readers who have met the minimal conditions of reflection and impartiality to which he alludes. It is useful for us to try to say *why* such persons have the conviction that discrimination of this form is wrong. And it is worthwhile to say this in an informal, even pre-theoretical way since any proposed theory of justice must presumably yield results consonant with this conviction.

I shall understand racial, sexual, and religious discrimination to be based on race, sex, and religion. Persons who are discriminated against are so treated because they are of a certain race, sex or religion.[2] One reason for thinking this to be bad is that it involves treating complex human individuals, not as full-fledged persons in their own right but as mere members of groups or totalities.[3] Now of course it is not always offensive to members of racial or other groups to be treated as members of those groups. Indeed, in some roles and in some contexts, persons may strongly desire to be regarded and treated as group-members. It is not surprising, though, that the reason for this preference is linked to the need to combat a long tradition of invidious discrimination and unfair prejudice. Voluntary, self-conscious identification with other oppressed members of oppressed groups provides a source of the solidarity necessary for reform. Here, as in several other facets of this subject, what would be offensive within a just system and without a history of unjust treatment becomes attractive when there is an immense need for rectification. The basic point, though, is that group characterization of a person is often seriously detracting from one's merit, status, or achievement as an individual. One's abilities, interests, aspirations, unique unto oneself, are eclipsed in an unwanted, offensive identification with a certain totality.[4]

A further reason for regarding racial and other forms of discrimination as unfair is that it involves assigning places and distributing goods to persons according to morally irrelevant characteristics. Being a particular color or sex seems irrelevant to a determination as to whether a person should be protected from assault, defended when accused, provided educational opportunity, and afforded career aspirations. Such factors are of the sort that Rawls terms *arbitrary* from the moral point of view (74). Again, of course, such factors can become relevant after a period of injustice during which, when they really were irrelevant, they were treated as relevant. The relevance at the new level is for the purpose of rectifying the injustice and compensating the victimized. It is misleading, however, to state, without significant qualification, that the once irrelevant characteristics become relevant even for this purpose. It is not that *being black* or *being female* become in themselves relevant. Rather, having such characteristics is indicative of a serious likelihood of having suffered from unfair treatment. The decisive characteristic—only contingently associable with being black, being female, or being Jewish—is *being a victim of injustice.* And while it is controversial precisely how we should take account of this feature, it is surely not a morally irrelevant characteristic.[5]

Another morally objectionable feature of direct discrimination is that it deprives and hurts persons because of *immutable characteristics* over which they lack control. Such characteristics have been taken as desiderata for what the Supreme Court will regard as "suspect classifications." It should not be assumed, of course, that discrimination on the basis of features that are not unalterable through the individual's control is justified. After all, one's religion and one's sex are now not immutable, even though most persons are understandably resistant to the changes. The point is suggestive of an important and especially difficult aspect of the problems of discrimination. Persons are discriminated against in our society for a variety of personal characteristics—for being short, fat, malodorous, ugly, and bald. Recently a person—who also happened to be black, female, and legally trained—was denied an apartment for being too intelligent. It is not easy to say just which characteristics are permissible bases for discrimination and which are not. I think it consistent with (what Rawls calls) our considered judgments, however, to say that being rejected because of one's sex, color, or race is *more likely* to be wrong than being rejected for being short or fat. Also, when both forms are wrong, the former is *morally worse* than the latter. Generally at least, persons can more readily control and change their appearances than characteristics such as race and sex. Though it is often distasteful, it is sometimes feasible to avoid the invidious treatment by making the changes. But where the treatment is based on immutable features, the discrimination is likely to be very seriously unfair.

A final factor, especially relevant to judgments in our own society, is that racial and sexual discrimination are bad because such practices have occurred so much and for so long. There is unquestionably a long history of rigid, repetitive actions of discrimination. When it occurs now, its occurrence is not occasional or temporary—it is no aberration. Persons who are victimized have, in large numbers, come to regard it as drearily expectable and linked with a pervasive tradition not easily halted or even eroded. This point also helps to account for why racial and sexual discrimination seems worse than invidious treatment of the fat or the thin, the short or the tall. When all four factors are combined and reflected on as a unit, it is readily understandable, I think, why we regard direct, "old-fashioned" discriminatory treatment as wrong and unjust. It is no surprise that Rawls would select this judgment as a benchmark for the evaluation of ethical theories.

PRELIMINARY DIFFICULTIES FOR THE APPLICATION OF RAWLS' THEORY

The most important task in subsequent sections will be to discuss the implications of Rawls' principles of social justice for the issues of discrimination, especially reverse discrimination for the sake of compensation and rectification. Rawls makes several claims in the first chapter of *A Theory of Justice* which may seem to pose obstacles for interesting applications of this sort. In the hope of dispelling whatever doubts such points may raise, it is well to take note of them now. Rawls' principles are standards for judging the justice of social institutions. They are not, as he stresses in several places, principles for individuals (54). But the problems connected with direct and reverse discrimination are, quite obviously, ones that pose difficulties for individuals as well as for institutions. Does this mean, then, that study of Rawlsian principles of justice can yield nothing of value that is both true to the spirit of Rawls' enterprise and helpful in attaining a better perspective about discrimination?

A related point is that the social institutions that Rawls deems relevant are not small-scale ones but rather the institutions for the basic structure of a society. The principles designed to regulate the distribution of social goods apply to distributions on a large scale. In accord with this constraint, the "individuals" to whom the goods are distributed are not real-life, ordinary, human beings but what Rawls calls "representative individuals." The representative individuals occupy certain representative social positions to which the goods assigned may or may not be equally distributed. The two significant representative social positions of the basic structure are citizenship and economic status. A society is deemed just, from the standpoint of the theory of justice as fairness, provided that representative individuals have distributions of goods required by the principles (63-64, 87).

Another problem is that Rawls says very little about compensating victims of injustice and rectifying past injustices. He is concerned with what he calls "full compliance theory." The arguments for the principles and the modes of their application are worked out on the assumption that they will be followed. In view of this and the other constraints, it may seem that Rawls' theory has little to do with various social procedures for dealing with injustice—for instance, rules for fair trials and just punishment, and techniques of compensation for private wrongs, such as personal injuries. More directly related to our topic, the theory of justice as fairness might seem virtually inapplicable to processes for rectifying unjust conditions of actual human beings—compensating individual persons for their sufferings from patterns of unfair discrimination, unjust prejudice, arbitrary exclusion, and intolerant suppression.

In view of all this, how are we to proceed? A variety of responses are appropriate. First, if the theory of justice *were* so inapplicable, that would indicate a serious weakness, a seemingly unjustifiable lacunae in that theory. A significant proportion of the genuine, practical problems of social justice are problems of rectification in which we should be concerned with real human beings, not merely "representative" ones. Second, despite Rawls' stress on the basic structure, large-scale social positions and representative individuals, it is, or so I shall attempt to show, possible to extend his principles to the doings and sufferings of actual human individuals. And even if some rational reconstruction is required along the way, the theory will only be strengthened if shown to have these ramifications beyond the cautious limits that Rawls sets.

Third, even if the principles of justice are initially restricted to moral evaluations of institutional forms, there will inevitably be implications for how individuals should act. An individual's actions, at the least, must be consonant with the requirements of justice for institutions. And Rawls says explicitly that one principle for individuals demands that persons support and further just institutions (114–5). A minimum requirement would be that persons ought not to frustrate or subvert the development and maintenance of institutions that are just. Fourth, it would seem well within the spirit of Rawls' overall efforts for there to be a similar principle for small-scale institutions such as schools and businesses. The latter are, of course, precisely the sorts of institutions within which many issues of discrimination for purposes of compensation arise.

Fifth, even though Rawls doesn't specify any special set of principles for the rectification of injustice, it is not clear that such principles are necessary. The principles that he does provide serve to show when certain situations in society are unjust; but they may also be used as devices for correcting the injustices. There is reason to think that reverse discrimination can serve as a useful tool for bringing about, or more closely approximating, the conditions required by Rawls' principles. Finally, it is important to note a qualification that Rawls makes on the claims about representative positions. Since this matter is intimately connected with our topic, I quote at length:

> As far as possible, then, justice as fairness appraises the social system from the position of equal citizenship and the various levels of income and wealth. Sometimes, however, other positions may need to be taken into account. If, for example, there are unequal basic rights founded on fixed natural characteristics, these inequalities will single out relevant positions. Since these characteristics cannot be changed, the positions they define count as starting places in the basic structure. Distinctions based on sex are of this type, and so are those depending upon race and culture. Thus if, say, men are favored in the assignment of basic rights, this inequality is justified by the difference principle (in the general interpretation) only if it is to the advantage of women and

> acceptable from their standpoint, and the analogous condition applies to the justification of caste systems, or racial and ethnic inequalities (99).

Without further comment on this or other important passages, I now turn to the fundamental elements of Rawls' theory and to their relation to our issues about discrimination. First, then, some remarks about the contracting parties and their original position.

ON WHAT THE CONTRACTING PARTIES MIGHT THINK ABOUT DISCRIMINATION

As is well known to readers of Rawls and of articles in this volume, the principles of justice are chosen or agreed to by rational persons concerned to advance their own interests. They are situated in an "original position" and are subject to various constraints, such as the "veil of ignorance." I shall not attempt a thorough description of the parties and the contracting situation; but it is useful to consider what illumination these features of the theory might provide as regards discrimination. The decisions of the persons in the original position are rather *general.* The parties are supposed to select general moral/social principles for the governance of their common life, but they are not to do so *from a moral point of view.* If they agree to a principle, that will be a principle of justice since it is chosen in a setting in which persons are fairly situated with regard to one another. Any principle agreed to is selected on terms that are fair, but it is not picked because it is *believed* to be fair. The motivation of each of the parties, with one important qualification, is self-interested.[6]

In another respect, also, their decision-making is general rather than specific. They do not take up for consideration the particular moral problems likely to arise in real societies—problems of taxation, social security, welfare, or discrimination. There is no reason to think that, at the original position stage, the parties would worry about the tangled issues of discrimination, compensatory treatment, and reverse discrimination. Any developed "position" they would have on such matters would, at most, be only implicit in their *general* choices of broad social principles. Whatever arrangements regarding discrimination are allowed and required by the general principles constitute their position.

Even so, the contracting parties are likely to have certain propensities concerning discrimination. The very descriptions of them and their situation makes this seem plausible. The rational individuals have general knowledge about the nature of human society but no personal knowledge about themselves. They do not know who they are in any specific sense. These persons are ignorant of their sex, race, color, economic status, social class, and age. As already noted, they are self-interested and mutually disinterested. More specifically, they do not (intrinsically) want to help or to hurt others, but only desire to maximize their individual stocks of primary social goods. They do not know their own ends and life plans; but they do assume that acquisition of primary goods is a useful means of realizing their goals, whatever (once the veil is lifted) those goals turn out to be (136–150). In view of all this, it is reasonable to suppose that their initial inclinations in the original position would be attitudes against discrimination on the basis of sex, race, class, age, and religion. Having their self-interest in view and being ignorant of what they and their fellows are like with regard to sex, race and other features, they would be irrational to use sexual or racial preference in imagining, debating, and selecting principles to which all must be committed.

This result should come as no surprise. The guiding intuition that religious, racial and other forms of intolerance and discrimination are wrong influences the preliminary descriptions of the contracting parties. Within the limits set by whatever constraints are necessary to avoid a bad kind of circularity, Rawls' methodology requires this. One characterizes the original position persons in such a way that the principles they choose accord with what we antecedently believe to be minimal requisites of justice. The choice situation is designed so that it yields results consonant with our considered moral judgments arrived at, independently of theory, through reflective, impartial consideration (19–20, also 17–22, 46–54). It is reasonable, then, to expect that the general principles chosen will reflect the propensities against direct discrimination mentioned above; for these propensities reflect the description of the parties, which reflects Rawls' guiding methodological intuitions, which reflect our considered moral judgments. Thus far, at least, the Rawlsian enterprise is consonant with the explanations for our views on "old-fashioned" discrimination suggested in the first section.

DISCRIMINATION AND EQUAL LIBERTY

The equal liberty principle requires that each citizen have the largest amount of liberty consistent with a like liberty for everyone. This principle is of fundamental importance for what Rawls terms the "special conception" of justice as fairness. Within this conception there are no justifiable exceptions to the requirement of equal distributions of liberty. There *must* be equal liberty for everyone if a society is to be adjudged just. The difference principle—a principle for regulating and judging inequalities in basic goods—does not apply to the primary good of liberty. Even in cases in which a person (a real person, not a "rational contractor") would prefer and would freely choose lesser liberty—lesser than the maximum and lesser than that possessed by his fellows—in exchange for greater wealth, any such transfer or trade would be unjust. In light of this, may we conclude that Rawls' theory requires absolute equality in the treatment of school and job applicants? Should we conclude that justice as fairness absolutely prohibits discrimination, and thus absolutely prohibits reverse discrimination?

It might be tempting for opponents of compensatory discrimination who find Rawls' theory congenial to argue along these lines. That would, I think, be a mistake. There are several reasons for not drawing the conclusions to which the questions refer. First, the "special conception" does not always hold. The special conception, placing so high a premium on liberty, is to be applied only under certain economic and social conditions. Liberty is required to be equal and to be maximized only when society has reached a certain level of cultural and technical advance. Below an indefinitely specified floor of material wealth and progress, there is no special place for liberty or any other particular primary good. Here the "general conception" becomes applicable. The difference principle, then, under certain conditions applies also to liberty, as well as to income and power; and inequalities in liberty may be countenanced (61–62).

Second, Rawls' arguments for the priority of liberty (even under special conditions) are quite inconclusive. A good case can be made that the occupants of the original position would choose a generalized difference principle over any principle of utility (a principle that requires the maximization of total or average welfare). But the arguments that they would assent to the "priority of liberty," and thus adopt the special conception of the equal liberty principle, are far less persuasive. This issue has been treated extensively by other writers, and I see no need for a detailed discussion here.[7]

Third, Rawls' account of "liberty" is much more narrow than the general statement of the liberty principle initially suggests. The relevant liberties are the political liberties (such as the right to vote and to hold office), freedom of speech and of assembly, liberty of conscience, and freedom of thought (61). Much of what we commonly regard as liberty—for instance, economic freedom—is not covered by Rawls' first principle. Furthermore, our problems of "equal treatment versus discriminatory preference" arise in contexts in which liberty, as so restrictedly conceived, is not the only relevant basic good. People are concerned over whether various forms of discrimination in hiring and admissions are justified not only or even primarily because of fears of threats to the liberty to which persons are entitled. The concern over discrimination is at least as strongly due to believed threats to the wealth, power, status, and esteem that it is thought persons deserve. Attention to these matters, then, requires discussion of Rawls' other principles of justice. That is the subject for the next section.

But what of the "liberties" to which the first principle, within the special conception, *does* apply? Is any form of discrimination ever allowable with regard to these? The best answer to the question, I believe, is a tentative "yes." It *seems* initially that the equal liberty principle would forbid any discrimination with respect to speech or voting. The rights to these things are "equal liberty" rights in the theory. The passages in which Rawls suggests that arrangements could justifiably be otherwise are those in which he writes of the need for the strongest possible "total system" of liberty. He says that some of the liberties (perhaps freedom of speech) can be lessened only if having less strengthens the total system. So lesser liberty in one domain is justifiable only if, with the loss, the net amount of overall freedom is greater (243–251).

Rawls applies this "lessening and compensating" idea to the different liberties and appears to assume that from person to person the total amount of liberty will be the same with regard to each type of freedom. That is, even if there is less freedom of speech, everyone will have an equal right to speak. Similarly, if freedom of speech is decreased so as to produce greater freedom of assembly, everyone will have equal liberty with respect to freedom of assembly. But why should the application of the principle of maximum equal liberty be restricted this way? I shall consider three types of cases in which it seems intuitively reasonable to allow (or even require) more liberal applications. In the first, suppose that all members of a certain group—let it be either blacks or whites—share an unusual but not wholly uncommon property. The only way, let us imagine, for them to have as much total liberty as the other group is for them to have half as much freedom of speech and twice as much freedom of assembly. If we stipulate that the worth of the two kinds of liberty is equal, it would seem to be within the spirit of the concept of "maximum equal liberty" to allow this. This seems especially appropriate if the only alternative way of securing equal total liberty is to reduce everyone's freedom of speech to the level of the first group. So here is a case in which (what may misleadingly be called) discrimination with regard to color appears allowable.

The second case is similar to the first, but with a striking difference. Suppose that members of one color group, say the whites, have tremendous power. They are able to control distributions of liberty. Their oppression, however, is rather quirky. They absolutely refuse to allow the blacks to have an amount of freedom of speech equal to their own. Indeed, they declare that blacks will have no more than half as much of this freedom as they have. But they say that they will, if the blacks choose, allow this "loss" to be compensated. Their plan of compensation is to give the blacks twice as much freedom (as they, the whites, have) with respect to voting. Having no real "choice" in the matter, the blacks accede to this arrangement. Again, given that the only realistic alternative is less total liberty for the blacks, the arrangement indicated is better. It is not ideal; but, as Rawls stresses, there are degrees of injustice. A broadened equal liberty principle, then, would declare this further form of "discrimination" to be not unreasonable.

The amounts and kinds of liberty in the last two cases exist at the same time in the development of a society. The third case is more similar to the real problems that confront us. Suppose that, for a ten-year period, the equal liberty principle is violated. During this time whites have been deprived of one half of the freedom of speech that is due them. Suppose further that at the end of this period the oppressors, here the blacks, recognize the wrongness of the past situation and propose a method of rectification. They suggest that during the next ten years they have one half as much freedom of speech as the whites and that after that time of rectification, everyone have equal amounts of this form of liberty. I see no good reason why we, or Rawls, should think this to be wrong. It is consonant with a broadened version of the maximum equal liberty principle since the aim is to secure, despite gains and losses over a twenty-year period, a total amount of liberty that is equal for everyone. The aim cannot, in any real society, be very easily achieved to perfection; but some effort, of this sort, at rectification seems better than simply allowing the first ten-year losses for the whites to fall wherever they lie. A complication that would ensure even closer approximation to the demands of justice would be, during the second ten-year stretch, to allow certain members of the black group to have an amount of liberty equal to that of certain members of the white group. The persons to be treated equally with regard to one another would be blacks, who (because of age) were not beneficiaries of the original injustice, and whites who (again because of age) were not victims of that original injustice. Here, I think, is a fairly clear case in which reverse discrimination would be just: it is a reasonable mode of compensation for past direct ("old-fashioned") discrimination that was unjust. In principle, then, even the equal liberty principle of the special conception would allow for certain forms of discrimination.

DISCRIMINATION AND EQUAL OPPORTUNITY

Many of the problems of discrimination arise in the context of competition for such primary goods as power and wealth. The difference principle and the principle of equal opportunity are designed to regulate distribution of these goods. Rawls presents these as two aspects of what he calls the "second principle." Its function is to supply the conditions essential for the justification of inequalities. The only inequalities that are fair are those that benefit those who have lesser amounts. Unequal power, for example, is justified provided that those with less power are better off that way than they would be were they to have more (an amount equal to that of all the others). This is the difference principle, and I shall discuss it more fully in the next section. The equal opportunity principle requires that relatively advantaged positions be "open to all."

What is involved in having equal opportunity? Rawls' notion of equal opportunity is not the one often appealed to by opponents of all forms of discrimination, direct or reverse. A conception of this that he explicitly rejects is that of "careers open to talents" which means that positions are "open to those able and willing to strive for them" (66). This is seriously inadequate because it provides only a "formal equality of opportunity" in which "...all have at least the same legal rights of access to all individual social positions" (72). What is bad about this limited conception of equal opportunity is that it allows distributions of goods to be heavily influenced by factors (such as accident, birth, and fortune) that are "arbitrary from a moral point of view" (72). In order to counter the effects of such factors, it is essential to go beyond holding positions "open in a formal sense" and ensure that all "have a fair chance to attain them." The following brief passages provide Rawls' understanding of the concept of "fair equality of opportunity":

> ...those with similar abilities and skills should have similar life chances...those who are at the same level of talent and abilities...should have the same prospects of success...regardless of their social class or income class to which they are born...chances to acquire cultural knowledge and skills should not depend upon one's class position, and so the school system, whether public or private, should be designed to even out class barriers. (73).

Even, however, with full equality of fair opportunity, distributions would still be influenced by arbitrary contingencies that are irrelevant from the standpoint of justice. Even one's motivation and effort are influenced by factors over which one has no control. One reason the difference principle is needed is to neutralize the effects of such factors even further (74).

How does all this relate to discrimination? Does Rawls' conception of equal opportunity forbid, allow, or require discrimination? Not surprisingly, the answer depends on who the discrimination is for, who it is against, what the affected persons' pasts have been like, what their present circumstances are, and why the discrimination is undertaken. It is important to remember that Rawls' conception of equal opportunity involves correction for the invidious effects of the natural lottery—the accidents of birth, parentage, training, encouragement, and luck. In view of this, mere abstention from "old-fashioned" discrimination on the basis of sex, race, and color does not automatically assure equal opportunity. Might such assurance require preferential treatment for members of groups who are victims of injustice (including the "natural" unfairness of the natural lottery)?

Rawls explicitly allows, we have seen, "extra" benefits designed to even out class barriers and thereby to increase the level of competence or actual qualifications of the disadvantaged. A way of doing this is to provide welfare supplements for additional training and education. Such "preferential treatment" is at the stage of *preparation*—preparation for careers and for life success. Those who are not disadvantaged, and thus not selected for special help, might complain of discrimination. The complaints would perhaps be especially bitter if most of those favored in this way were members of a particular racial or color group. But this "discrimination" would not be *on the basis of sex or color* and since no one "merits" whatever natural abilities he possesses through good fortune, it is no injustice to allow disadvantaged persons to improve their abilities even at some cost to those naturally more fortunate.

Today the most strident objections to reverse discrimination occur at a different level—that at which jobs and admissions are actually awarded. Do the corrective mechanisms Rawls proposes as required by fair equality of opportunity apply here? I see no good reason for thinking that they should not. Though *A Theory of Justice* is not explicit on the matter, compensatory treatment in the form of preferential hiring, for example, is surely congenial to the Rawlsian conception of equal opportunity. Even reverse discrimination favoring the somewhat less qualified would seem to be acceptable. May those who are discriminated *against*—for instance, better qualified white males—reasonably complain of injustice when this is done? It is difficult to see what their basis of reasonable complaint would be. They do not "deserve" their places in the natural lottery. Nor do they deserve the better chances that would accrue to them through getting the breaks, having a supportive family, and enjoying fortunate childhood experiences. Nor do they even deserve the fruits of their hard work insofar as this is traceable to inculcated motivation and helpful encouragement. But most especially, they do not deserve the benefits that would flow to them as a result of unfair discrimination against others and of (other) unjust treatment of others.

As I have argued in other writings, doing justice in employment involves far more than careful consideration of actual, present qualifications of job applicants. What is also relevant, and very important, is how qualifications have been acquired and what barriers there have been to attainment of good qualifications. Many good qualifications have been developed by some because of injustice to others even where the better qualified are mere beneficiaries, rather than perpetrators, of injustice. And many with relatively poor qualifications would have done much better had they not had to suffer from injustice. It is appropriate, and even imperative, that such factors be taken into account. Not to do so would victimize the victims even further by allowing the effects of past injustice to continue to affect the present and the future.[8] This justification of reverse discrimination for purposes of rectification applies to *all* who lack equal opportunity because of injustice, not just to blacks and to women. And the fact that we may not be able to bring everyone up to a fair equality of opportunity status does not justify us in doing nothing for anyone. We cannot do everything for all; we can do something for some. As

Rawls appears to acknowledge, the most that we can realistically hope for is to minimize and to decrease injustice to some degree. Programs of reverse discrimination, intelligently administered, are ways of achieving this.

DISCRIMINATION AND THE DIFFERENCE PRINCIPLE

The reflections in the last section lead us to consider more closely Rawls' difference principle. The corrections, for the sake of justice, that require us to go beyond the "careers open to talents" notion of equal opportunity mandate the difference principle. One function of this principle is to assure justice to those for whom even fair equality of opportunity cannot adequately provide. *A Theory of Justice* does not always make this point as perspicuous as is desirable. Given that there are to be unequal positions, those seeking the best ones should be accorded equality of opportunity. But when one sees what genuine equal opportunity involves and why it is important, it becomes clear that the difference principle does what equal opportunity cannot do alone. That principle serves one of the functions also served by fair opportunity; and its employment is, in a way, a mode of providing a more pervasive, and much needed, form of equal opportunity.

The difference principle says that, though primary goods are prima facie to be equally distributed, there is a way for certain inequalities to be just. Any inequality must work to the benefit of everyone, in particular the least advantaged. If the latter are better off with the unequal situation than they would be with equality, there is no injustice. The "benchmark" for social justice, then, is equality. Movements toward equality are justified as long as they do not worsen the situation of the least advantaged; movements away from equality are justified only if they benefit the least advantaged. Rawls says that "...the difference principle gives weight to the considerations singled out by the principle of redress. This is the principle that undeserved inequalities call for redress; and since inequalities of birth and natural endowment are undeserved, these inequalities are to be somehow compensated for. Thus the principle holds that in order to treat all persons equally, to provide genuine equality of opportunity, society must give more attention to those with fewer native assets and to those born into the less favorable social positions" (100). It is worth stressing again that inequalities due to unfair discrimination are also undeserved. A supplement to Rawls' point is that in order to treat all persons equally, society must give more attention to those victimized by injustice and to those thrown, by unfair treatment, into the less favorable social positions.

In view of this, preferential treatment in employment and school admissions would seem to be an acceptable instrument for realizing incremental advances in the direction of equality—that equality, of course, that benefits the lesser advantaged. Indeed, not providing preferential treatment for such persons would only involve prolongation of unjustified inequality and, thus, perpetuation of conditions due to injustice. The point is especially apt in situations in which the better qualifications of certain applicants are due to unjustified inequalities with respect to wealth and power. Even when the qualifications are not wholly due to this factor, the differences in qualifications between, say, the better qualified white male and the somewhat less qualified black female will often be caused by it. In cases of this sort the theory of justice as fairness would seem to require reverse discrimination to correct the imbalances flowing from the differences in wealth and power condemned by the difference principle. Indeed, hiring even the incompetent might be justified by this principle. If doing so would contribute to a shift toward equality without worsening the situation of the disadvantaged, this would be justified. In many professions such as law and medicine, though, hiring the incompetent would presumably benefit (if at all) only some of the disadvantaged to the detriment of others also disadvantaged.[9]

It is important to stress that this use of reverse discrimination to satisfy the demands of the difference principle would not involve, according to Rawls' theory, using some persons as mere means to the greater well-being of others. It does not involve, that is, treating *some* persons unjustly so that others can obtain more of what they deserve. Since the better off are not antecedently entitled to their "extra" goods (some of which have led to better job qualifications), they are not treated unjustly when others are given preferential treatment. Unfortunately, to many it will seem otherwise. Expectations have developed over many years to the effect that if one takes one's natural endowment, becomes a good steward of one's resources, works hard, and does not perpetrate injustice, one will get healthy rewards. Among the most important of these are a satisfying career, a good salary, social prestige, and job security. No good theory will, and no fair-minded person should, flippantly upset such expectations. But *as mere expectations*, they cannot carry the moral weight so often attributed to them. Many such expectations will, unfortunately and through no fault of those who have them, simply not be grounded in the requirements of justice. When this is so, it is necessary to give special attention to those who for so long have had to live with far less felicitous expectations—the expectations of facing continual, pervasive, debilitating injustice. It is these expectations that ought to be upset.

DISCRIMINATION AND RESPECT

The concepts of respect and self-respect are prominent in Rawls' theory of justice. He regards respect as a primary social good—a value more important than money and power. He thinks that parties in the original position will recognize the worth of respect and choose principles accordingly. Thus it is thought that they will rank maximum equal liberty above wealth and adopt the "priority of liberty" according to the special conception (Chapters 7 and 8). Self-respect is deemed essential for a decent life in which one strives to secure one's ends, and equal liberty enhances the self-respect accruing to full citizenship. An aspect of self-respect for individuals in a community is the sense that one's ends are respected by others as worthy of attainment. At the least, the latter involves their refraining from official or political attempts to block one's efforts to achieve one's purposes. In a just society run by a conception of justice as fairness, one is free to attain one's ends so long as they are within the bounds set by the demands of justice. Self-respect and respect are thus enhanced when one gives and receives just treatment (Chapters 7 and 8).

There is often much mention of respect in conversations about discrimination. It is said, for instance, that programs of preferential treatment for the victimized will result in less self-respect both for those greater qualified who are not chosen and for those lesser qualified who are chosen. In each, or so it is claimed, the diminished respect is linked to not being treated strictly according to one's actual merits, abilities, and qualifications. To be rejected when best qualified is not to have one's merits recognized and rewarded. To be accepted when less qualified is only to gain from "being black" or from "being a woman" and, again, not to be recognized for one's abilities. Does this provide a good argument against the practice of reverse discrimination for purposes of rectification?

The opponent of preferential treatment in the last paragraph distorts the issue by over-emphasis on only one, and not clearly the most important, source of self-respect. There is no doubt that one's esteem is often enhanced by having one's true merits, rather than factors perceived as extraneous, recognized and rewarded. But, as I have stressed throughout, higher and lower qualifications often rest against a background and history of gross injustice. That which has benefited some has victimized others. In view of this, some qualifications may not be deserved and may not represent one's true merit as closely as is commonly thought. If so, these qualifications cannot be sure guides as to how persons should *now* be treated in hiring and in admissions.

If all this is correct, why should one have a loss of self-respect if given preference over those whose higher qualifications are due to the sorts of injustices from which one has suffered? The answer, of course, is that one shouldn't. Also, one should not have enhanced feelings of self-respect if rewarded because of qualifications acquired through patterns of injustice to others. Moreover, one shouldn't experience a diminishing of respect if victimized persons with somewhat weaker qualifications are preferentially treated.[10] The better qualified do not have a rational basis for respect if that is linked to actual qualifications alone. Reasonable respect—the sort that is worth having—is more securely tied to justice, to doing justice, and to receiving justice. And justice, as we know, requires the rectification of injustice.

NOTES

1. I have discussed these issues in "On the Justifiability of Reverse Discrimination," in *Reverse Discrimination*, ed. Barry R. Gross, (Buffalo, N.Y.: Prometheus Books, 1977), pp. 348-57; and in "Fairness, Meritocracy and Reverse Discrimination," *Social Theory and Practice*, 4, (1977), 211-26.
2. I have not attempted to enumerate all the possible categories to which the subsequent discussion applies. Other obvious ones, though, are national origin, age, and parentage.
3. This is the key to understanding one form of "totalitarianism." I am indebted to Marcus Singer for this point.
4. A friend of mine, sporting a mustache and long hair while attending a college reunion, was confronted by a former classmate with the remark, "Oh, you became one of *them*!" I have Gary Baran to thank for this story.
5. On these points, see David A.J. Richards, *The Moral Criticism of Law* (Encino: Dickenson, 1977), pp. 162-179.
6. To deal with the problem of justice between generations, Rawls alters the motivational assumption and stipulates that each cares for someone in the next generation. It would seem that this problem could as easily be handled

by making each of the parties ignorant of his or her own generation but knowledgeable that some are members of different generations.

7. For criticism, see Brian Barry, *The Liberal Theory of Justice*, (Oxford: Clarendon Press, 1973), pp. 59-82. And H.L.A. Hart, "Rawls on Liberty and Its Priority," in *Reading Rawls*, ed. Norman Daniels, (New York: Basic Books, 1974), pp. 230-52.
8. See note 1.
9. See note 1 and also Alan H. Goldman, "Justice and Hiring by Competence," *American Philosophical Quarterly*, 14, (1977), 17-28.
10. See note 1.

Rawls and the Principle of Nonintervention

Mark R. Wicclair
WEST VIRGINIA UNIVERSITY

The central focus of Rawls' *A Theory of Justice* (all parenthetical citations are to John Rawls, *A Theory of Justice* (Cambridge, Mass.: Harvard University Press, 1971)) is a contractarian account of his much discussed two principles of justice.* These principles purport to apply to the basic political, economic, and social arrangements within nation-states, not to relations between those states. Accordingly, Rawls admits that the subject of his book is "a special case of the problem of justice" (7). However, in discussing conscientious refusal, he indicates that it is possible

> to relate the just political principles regulating the conduct of states to the contract doctrine and to explain the moral basis of the law of nations from this point of view (377).

Thus Rawls suggests that his contractarian approach can also be utilized to resolve moral issues pertaining to international relations. In this paper I will discuss a contractarian analysis of one such issue of particular current interest, namely, the legitimacy of intervention on behalf of human rights.

*Earlier drafts of parts of this paper were read at a meeting of the New Jersey Regional Philosophical Association and at the Pacific Division meetings of the American Philosophical Association. Helpful comments were provided by Charles Beitz and Nell Senter.

The urgency of this question is underscored by the International Security Assistance and Arms Export Control Act of 1976, which stipulates in part that "a principal goal of the foreign policy of the United States is to promote the increased observance of internationally recognized human rights by all countries."[1] For insofar as a serious commitment to this goal requires interventionary activity, it would seem to be incompatible with the commonly held belief that it is morally wrong for nations[2] to intervene in the affairs of other nations. To be sure, those who have argued against the legitimacy of intervention have rarely, if ever, supported an absolute prohibition against interventionary activity. Two types of qualifications have generally been acknowledged. On the one hand, there are what might be termed *general* exceptions to a comprehensive nonintervention rule, whereby specified types of interventionary activity are thought to be excluded from the rule. On the other hand, there are what might be termed *special* exceptions, whereby it is conceded that extraordinary circumstances can override a presumption against interventionary activity of a specified type. Among the standard general exceptions which have been recognized at one time or another are the following: intervention for the purpose of (legitimate) self-defense; intervention to protect citizens of one state when they are within the territory of another state; intervention in the interests of the balance of power; and intervention in response to illegitimate intervention (intervention to enforce nonintervention).[3] Defenders of a general rule of nonintervention normally have not recognized intervention on behalf of human rights, a sub-class of what is commonly referred to in the literature as "humanitarian intervention," as a general exception to the rule of nonintervention. Moreover, even though they usually allow that certain cases involve such flagrant abuses of human rights (e.g., the treatment of Jews in Nazi Germany) that the presumption against humanitarian intervention is overridden, it is not uncommon for such a statement to be followed by the reminder that these cases are indeed "extraordinary." Thus, insofar as a serious commitment to the goal of promoting human rights in foreign countries requires interventionary activity, it is indeed subject to challenge by those who have argued for a general rule of nonintervention.

It is to be expected, then, that some would object to giving United States foreign policy a strong human rights orientation on the grounds that this would be "interventionistic." Ernest Lefever, for one, has argued that

> Making human rights the chief, or even major, foreign policy determinant carries dangers...International law forbids any state from interfering in the internal political, judicial and economic affairs of another. Fundamentally, the quality of life in a political community should be determined by its own people....[4]

As Lefever rightly indicates, international law prohibits certain forms of interventionary activity. And those who argue that the promotion of human rights should not be a basic aim of United States foreign policy sometimes claim that such a policy would commit the United States to a violation of principles of international law. But for the purposes of this discussion, I will not consider what international law has to say on the subject of intervention.[5] Instead my concern is with the claim that, as a rule and *independent of what international law proscribes or prescribes*, intervention on behalf of human rights is *morally impermissible.*

To be sure, writers on international law sought to justify a general nonintervention rule long before the appearance of *A Theory of Justice.*[6] Christian Wolff and his follower, Emer de Vattel, two eighteenth century natural law theorists who are regarded as having been among the first to write treatises on international law which recognized a nonintervention rule,[7] attempted to derive that rule from the claimed "natural freedom and independence" of states.[8] And quite recently, R.J. Vincent[9] has attempted to defend a general nonintervention rule by invoking a conception of international order among sovereign states. But since it would only be a minor overstatement of the significance of Rawls' theory to say with Robert Nozick that ethical theorists and political philosophers "must either work within Rawls' theory or explain why not",[10] it would seem that Rawls' contractarian approach merits special attention. In particular, the question which I shall consider is this: Does a contractarian analysis support a presumption against intervention on behalf of human rights?

However, before proceeding, a few preliminary remarks about the notion of intervention are in order. The literature on the subject of intervention includes a wide range of definitions of the term.[11] At the one extreme, intervention is interpreted narrowly to mean "coercive interference" involving "the use or threat of force,"[12] and the target of interventionary activity has been identified as "the structure of political authority in the target society."[13] At the other extreme, intervention is construed broadly to include almost any attempt by one nation to influence events in, or the behavior of, another state.[14]

As the following remarks will indicate, neither of these two extremes is acceptable for the purposes of this discussion.

To begin with the broad interpretation of intervention, it would be implausible to construe *any* attempt by one state to produce or prevent changes in other states, or in the behavior of those states, as an instance of interventionary activity. Surely international relations involve continual efforts by states to influence events in, and the behavior of, other states. Since it is advisable to restrict the label "interventionary" to a specified class of such efforts to influence, the broad interpretation of intervention should be rejected. Moreover, if that interpretation were accepted, then the claim that efforts to promote human rights in other countries are generally illegitimate because they are "interventionary," could be dismissed out of hand. For certain efforts to influence affairs in other states (e.g., through negotiation or "quiet diplomacy") are commonly accepted as legitimate.

On the other hand, the following considerations suggest that the stipulation that an act is interventionary only if *force* is used or threatened is also unsuitable for the purposes of this discussion.[15] First, it can be argued that there are strong independent reasons for prohibiting the use or threat of outright force as an instrument of foreign policy. Thus, it is important to consider whether there are substantial moral reasons for supporting a qualified presumption against attempts by one state to produce or prevent changes in another state, even if no use or threat of force is involved. Second, it seems to me that those who object to giving United States foreign policy a strong human rights orientation on the grounds that it would commit the United States to an "interventionistic" foreign policy are not merely invoking the specter of marines or clandestine agents landing or operating on foreign soil. Rather, their objection seems to be of a more general nature, namely, that it is illegitimate for the United States, or any country, to "meddle" in the affairs of another nation.[16] Third, the public debate over whether the United States should seek to promote human rights in foreign countries has not been occasioned by proposals by policy makers to send military units to, or to finance clandestine operations in, foreign countries. Rather, it has focused primarily upon measures such as imposing conditions on bilateral military and economic assistance to, and imposing economic and other sanctions on, governments which have poor human rights records. Thus, for example, the International Security Assistance and Arms Export Control Act of 1976, referred to above, includes the following additional provision:

> It is further the policy of the United States that, except under circumstances specified in this section, no security assistance may be provided to any country the government of which engages in a consistent pattern of gross violations of internationally recognized human rights.

By and large, then, the controversy has concentrated on the legitimacy of efforts by the United States to *compel*[17] foreign governments to improve their human rights records.

The use of United States military and economic assistance programs and its votes within various international lending institutions as "leverage"[18] to compel foreign governments to improve their human rights records has been opposed on the grounds that such efforts to influence affairs in other countries are "interventionistic." Now one obvious way of meeting such criticisms would be to appeal to a definition of "intervention" which would rule them out in advance. But given the controversy surrounding the definition of the term, those who claim that the United States has no business promoting human rights abroad would likely view such a move as nothing less than an arbitrary fiat. Consequently, I think that it is important to consider whether a contractarian justification can be provided for a presumptive rule against intervention on behalf of human rights which includes a presumption against attempts to compel foreign governments to improve their human rights records; and this is what I propose to do in the remainder of this paper.

A contractarian approach involves formulating a hypothetical situation in which agents come together to select principles to regulate their affairs. This hypothetical situation is termed the "original position" by Rawls. On a contractarian account, principles are justified if it can be shown that they would be selected in a suitably described original position. In *A Theory of Justice*, Rawls attempts to derive and justify "the principles of justice for the basic structure of society" (11). These are principles which assign basic rights, liberties, and duties and which specify entitlements and conditions of access to wealth, occupations, etc. Accordingly, the parties to the contract are to be thought of as citizens of the same nation-state who seek "to decide in advance how they are to regulate their claims against one another and what is to be the foundation charter of their society" (11). On a contractarian account, then, to ask whether the political and economic institutions of a particular society are just is to ask whether they are compatible with principles which the members of that society would acknowledge if they were to adopt the perspective of the original position. However, as I indicated above, Rawls suggests that a similar procedure can be utilized to derive and justify principles of justice among nations. That is, principles of international justice are to be thought of as principles which would be selected by the parties to a hypothetical *international* social contract. The question which we shall have to consider, then, is this: Would the parties to a Rawlsian hypothetical international social contract select a rule of nonintervention which includes a presumption against intervention on behalf of human rights?

First, it is necessary to formulate an international original position on an analogue with the domestic contract situation. With this end in view, let us briefly review some of the basic features of the domestic original position. In the domestic case, Rawls utilizes a methodological device which he refers to as the "veil of ignorance" to restrict the knowledge of the contractees in a number of ways. Among the "particular facts" which the veil of ignorance prevents the parties from knowing are the following:

> [N]o one knows his place in society, his class position or social status; nor does he know his fortune in the distribution of natural assets and abilities, his intelligence and strength, and the like. Nor, again, does anyone know his conception of the good, the particulars of his rational plan of life, or even the special features of his psychology such as his aversion to risk or liability to pessimism...[T]he parties do not know the particular circumstances of their own society. That is, they do not know its economic or political situation, or the level of civilization and culture it has been able to achieve (137).

However, the veil of ignorance does *not* exclude knowledge of what Rawls refers to as "general facts about human society." Specifically, he states that the parties to the contract

> understand political affairs and the principles of economic theory; they know the basis of social organization and the laws of human psychology...There are no limitations on general information, that is, on general laws and theories... (137-138).

Another important feature of Rawls' description of the domestic original position is a set of conditions which he refers to as the "circumstances of justice." These, according to Rawls, are "the normal conditions under which human cooperation is both possible and necessary" (126). He distinguishes between two types of conditions: "objective" and "subjective" conditions. Among the former are the following: individuals are "roughly similar in physical and mental powers"; and there exists a condition of "moderate scarcity" such that "[n]atural and other resources are not so abundant that schemes of cooperation become superfluous, nor are conditions so harsh that fruitful ventures must inevitably break down" (127). Among the "subjective" conditions which Rawls mentions are the following: each individual has his own "life plan," i.e., a more or less systematically structured array of goals and values; persons "take no interest in one another's interests"; and individuals have needs and interests which are "in various ways complementary, so that mutually advantageous cooperation among them is possible" (127).

One additional feature of Rawls' description of the original position merits our attention. This is his stipulation that the parties are to assume that the principles selected in the contract situation will be generally observed by the members of a society. As Rawls puts it, his primary concern is with "strict compliance" or "ideal," in contradistinction to "partial compliance," theory: "[S]trict compliance is one of the stipulations of the original position; the principles of justice are chosen on the supposition that they will be generally complied with" (245). That is, the parties to the contract do not have to consider whether conditions in *actual societies* might require and justify certain departures from ideal principles. Nor do they have to consider how to deter, and/or deal with, injustices. In effect, then, strict compliance or ideal theory "works out the principles that characterize a well-ordered society under favorable circumstances" (245). This, according to Rawls, makes it possible to determine "what a perfectly just society would be like" (8).

Let us now turn to the international analogue of the domestic contract situation. In the brief section in which he addresses the issue of justice in international relations, Rawls characterizes the international original position in the following manner: (1) The parties to the agreement are "representatives of different nations" (378). That is, we are to think of them as advancing the interests of the states which they represent (the "national interests" of their respective states)[19] rather than their own individual interests. In effect, then, arguments are to be considered from the perspective of the interests of the various states represented. (2) The contractees are to be thought of as choosing "the fundamental principles to adjudicate conflicting claims among states" (378). (3) Under a modified veil of ignorance, they know that they "represent different nations each living under the normal circumstances of human life"; but knowledge of "the particular circumstances of their own society, its power and strength in comparison with other nations,... [and] their place in their own society" is excluded (378). Thus, no one would possess knowledge concerning the size, power, culture, level of economic development, political institutions and ideology, or particular "national interests" of the state which he represents.

Rawls does not offer an argument to show that the principles of international relations which he mentions, and, in particular, a nonintervention rule, would be chosen by the parties to the international social contract. However, the argument would presumably proceed along the lines of Rawls' argument in the case of his two principles of (domestic) justice. The maximin rule for choice under uncertainty figures prominently in Rawls' argument for the selection of those principles. If an agent is confronted with a choice among various alternatives to which he cannot assign probabilities, the maximin rule instructs him to select the alternative the worst outcome of which is the least unfavorable to him. As a result of the veil of ignorance, the known interests of agents in the original position are restricted to "primary goods," i.e., those goods which any individual would want, irrespective of his particular goals and values. The primary goods which Rawls mentions are rights and liberties, powers and opportunities, income and wealth, and self-respect. Thus, in applying the maximin rule, the parties to the contract assess the various alternatives in terms of their projected indeces of primary goods under the worst outcome of each alternative. Rawls' argument for his two domestic principles rests upon the claim that if they *maximined*, the contractees would prefer those principles to any other competing alternative.[20]

Can a similar argument be used to show that the parties to the international contract would select a general nonintervention rule which includes a presumption against intervention on behalf of human rights? For the moment let us suppose that this question can be answered in the affirmative. Still there would be a problem which merits close scrutiny. In the domestic case, Rawls claims that the constraints on the knowledge of the parties imposed by the veil of ignorance and other elements of the description of the original position are each "natural and plausible" (18). In the domestic original position, agents confront one another "in an initial situation of equality"; and the various constraints incorporated into the description of the original position "express what we are prepared to regard as limits on fair terms of social cooperation" (21). Rawls spells this out further by claiming that the description of the domestic original position insures that whatever principles are selected,

> whenever social institutions satisfy these principles those engaged in them can say to one another that they are cooperating on terms to which they would agree if they were free and equal persons whose relations with respect to one another were fair (13).

If the description of the original position did not satisfy these conditions, one might object that the *moral* significance of the fact that Rawls' two principles of (domestic) justice would be selected in a *hypothetical* contract situation is questionable. Rawls himself takes cognizance of this problem when he states that "It is natural to ask why, if this agreement is never actually entered into, we should take any interest in these principles, moral or otherwise" (21). The statement that the description of the original position insures that the principles which are selected are principles "which free and equal moral persons would assent to under circumstances which are fair" is Rawls' answer to this question. This, of course, assumes that a principle of respect for individuals as free and equal moral persons is a basic moral principle.[21]

However, in the case of the *international* social contract, since the parties are to be thought of as advancing the interests of the states which they represent, and not their own individual interests, it would seem that it cannot be asserted that a consideration of "what we are prepared to regard as limits on fair terms of social cooperation" among free and equal *individuals* informs the description of the appropriate original position. If considerations of "fairness" analogous to those in the domestic case determine the description of the international contract situation, it would seem to be a principle of respect for the autonomy or sovereignty and moral equality of *states*, not individuals. This suggests that Rawls' account of justice in international relations presupposes a principle of state sovereignty, a principle which recognizes and requires respect for the autonomy of states. But this is problematical for two distinct reasons. First, whereas it might be plausible to claim that a principle of respect for persons as free and equal moral agents is a basic moral principle; it is not equally plausible to assert that a principle which expresses respect for the autonomy and moral equality of nation-states is a basic moral principle. In any event, an argument is needed to show why collectivities like nation-states should be recognized as objects of respect on an analogue with persons. Second, Rawls states that "The basic principle of the law of nations is a principle of equality. Independent peoples organized as states have certain fundamental equal rights" (378). But if it is a "principle of the law of nations," the principle of equality (among sovereign states) cannot be assumed for the purposes of justifying the principles of justice among nations without begging the question.

This suggests that the principles of state sovereignty and nonintervention[22] should be thought of as protecting against external interference *domestic arrangements which satisfy Rawls' two principles of justice.* For if this were the case, then insofar as Rawls' two principles embody a principle of respect for persons as free and equal moral agents, the same would hold for the principles of state sovereignty and nonintervention. From a contractarian standpoint, this would mean that we should think of the international contract as the second phase of a two-stage sequence. In the first stage, the parties think of themselves as members of the same nation-state, and they are presented with the task of selecting principles which will apply to the basic political, economic, and social arrangements of particular nation-states. In the second stage, the contractees think of themselves as representatives of nation-states *which satisfy the principles they selected in the first stage*, and they are presented with the task of selecting principles of interstate conduct which will protect the (just) basic institutional arrangements of the nations which they represent. From a Rawlsian perspective, then, a nonintervention rule would have the status of a norm which would apply in the ideal or limiting case of a world of internally just nation-states. This seems to be consistent with Rawls' stipulation that his primary concern is with "ideal" or "strict compliance" theory. Consequently, the international contract is to be thought of as generating principles which would govern a world comprised of well-ordered nation-states "under favorable circumstances."

But this would tell us nothing about the legitimacy of intervention in the event that the domestic arrangements of particular nation-states are unjust. And it is precisely this type of case which is involved when considering intervention on behalf of human rights. However, before moving on to examine how cases of this type might be dealt with from a contractarian perspective, a few remarks about the ideal case are in order. First, in virtue of the manner in which Rawls defines the choice for the parties in each of the phases of the two-stage sequence, they never question whether the world should be divided into separate and more or less politically independent nation-states. But this is a fundamental question, and, hence, one which the parties to the contract should consider. It is clearly of paramount importance to determine, say, whether the contractees would prefer a world divided into more or less politically independent nation-states to a single world-state, or some other alternative. Surely, a comprehensive theory of global justice would have to address this issue. Second, it appears that Rawls must have the contractees assume that each state is more or less self-sufficient and materially independent, thereby disregarding the fact that actual states are economically interdependent; and that he must have them fail to consider the issue of the distribution of natural resources. Otherwise, the contractees would presumably consider questions of distribution analogous to those considered in the domestic case. And it can be argued that if they were to do so, they would agree to apply Rawls' two principles, or his general conception of justice, to the world as a whole, and not simply to particular nation-states.[23] But this would seem to require a fundamental revision of the conventional statist conception of the world order, the conception which underlies commonly acknowledged rules of international relations, including the principle of nonintervention. Thus it would seem that Rawls can provide a contractarian account of those commonly acknowledged norms of interstate relations only if he makes a number of strong and questionable assumptions.

This, however, is not the place to challenge these assumptions or to provide an alternative account of principles of global justice. Rather, my aim is limited to showing that even if the statist model is not directly challenged, a contractarian analysis will not provide a justification of a presumption against intervention on behalf of human rights. To this end, I will assume that in the second phase of the two-stage sequence, the parties to the contract believe that some actual societies are likely to be grossly unjust. This involves a departure from strict compliance theory, but it is required in order to address the question of the legitimacy of intervention on behalf of human rights. Moreover, the veil of ignorance does not exclude knowledge of "general facts"; and it seems plausible to claim that the proposition that some societies are likely to be grossly unjust could be inferred from the sorts of "general laws and theories" which pass through the veil of ignorance. Thus the belief in question would not violate the constraints which Rawls imposes on the knowledge of the contractees.

Let us suppose that the parties to the international contract are presented with the following alternative. They are to choose between a broad rule of nonintervention PN which, among other things, prohibits "humanitarian intervention" in the affairs of unjust states, and a limited intervention rule PI which reads as follows:

> It is legitimate for one nation N1 to temporarily intervene in the affairs of another nation N2 provided: (1) The basic political, economic, and/or social arrangements of N2 are grossly unjust. (2) The government of N2 has consistently failed to take positive steps toward promoting just arrangements, and in the absence of external intervention it is unlikely that any timely and significant improvement will occur. (3) One of N1's goals is the promotion of more just arrangements in N2. (4) There is a reasonable likelihood that N1 can successfully accomplish the goal referred to in (3).

If the parties had to choose between PI and PN, which of the two principles would they prefer?

In order to answer this question, more must first be said about the interests of the parties to the contract. As representatives of states, they are to be thought of as advancing the interests of the states which they represent. But how are we to interpret this rather vague stipulation? At this point it is necessary to bear in mind that we want to insure that the hypothetical choice situation is *morally* significant. That is, the aim is to establish that the principles of interstate conduct agreed to by the contractees have a *moral basis.* Now in view of what was said before about the role of a principle of respect for individuals as free and equal moral persons in Rawls' theory, it would seem that the aim of the contractees should be construed as follows:[24] The fundamental aim of each of the parties at the second phase of the contract is to see to it that the legitimate claims and fundamental rights of individuals within the state he represents are duly recognized and respected.[25] Presumably, the principles which the parties select in the first of the two stages of the contract serve to identify these rights and claims.[26]

Let us now see how an agent in the original position might go about deciding between PN and PI. He might reason as follows: "Although I cannot assess the likelihood that the particular state I represent is unjust, I have good reason to believe that the basic institutions of some actual states are grossly unjust. Thus, I must consider the possibility that I have the misfortune of representing a nation whose basic arrangements are essentially unjust. This would mean that certain legitimate claims and fundamental rights are not respected within the state I represent. Now if I were to select PN, I would run the risk that the basic institutions of the state I represent would remain grossly unjust for an indefinite period of time with no real prospect for improvement. On the other hand, I would not run such a risk if I were to select PI. If the state I represent is essentially just, then PI would be superflous. However, if the state I represent is essentially unjust, then PN would prohibit, and PI would permit, actions which might be required to bring about a significant improvement. Thus I should select PI."[27]

However, it might be objected that this line of reasoning is incomplete since it fails to take certain other important "general facts" into account. Thus, it might be claimed that the contractees should recognize that states tend to act in self-serving ways and, in particular, that foreign policy decisions are shaped primarily by domestic interests rather than by considerations of the interests of foreign nationals. To this it might be added that they should also take into account that as "outsiders," states, or the governments of states, lack the information, insight and understanding which is required to know what is best for persons in other states. Thus, in the words of Benn and Peters, it might be asserted that the parties to the contract should conclude that "the claims of a state's members will generally be better served if they are left to work out their own salvation."[28]

Now although I do not want to minimize the seriousness of these claims, I nevertheless do not believe that they afford conclusive reasons for rejecting a limited intervention rule like PI. To begin with the argument from lack of knowledge, insofar as it presupposes a form of epistemological and/or moral skepticism, it would not be accepted by agents in a Rawlsian original position. But suppose the claim is simply that the government of no other state is as likely to know what is in the best interests of the citizens of a given state than the government of that particular state. Then the contractees would also have to consider that foreign governments might well be no less able and willing to make such determinations than governments who have shown a persistent disregard of the legitimate claims and interests of large segments of their respective societies. In any event, it seems plausible to claim that they should reject the assertion that governments can *never* know what is in the best interests of persons, or the "worst-off," in other states.

With respect to the claim that states do not conduct their foreign policy in an impartial manner, the contractees would reason that this is merely a claim about states' motives, and that PI protects them against interventionary activity which would benefit only the intervening state. But suppose it is argued that the lack of impartiality of states means that they cannot be trusted to strictly observe PI. Then the contractees would also have to consider that this might well mean that if they selected PN, it too would not be observed by states. Hence, they would recognize that they might not risk a worse outcome by selecting PI than they would by selecting PN. Further, they might reason that the threat of external intervention can act as a deterrent to governments who might otherwise violate, or allow to be violated, basic principles of justice, and that this tips the balance in favor of PI. Moreover, to further protect themselves against the possibility that states will intervene in ways which benefit only themselves, the parties to the contract might add a condition to PI specifying that intervention is legitimate only if it is reasonable to assume that it would be approved, say, by the worst-off in the target state. Alternatively, they might consider empowering an international organization like the United Nations to decide when intervention is permissible. However, they would also have to consider that given the nature of international politics, this might have the unwanted effect of seriously reducing the prospect that intervention would ever be approved. In any event, I think it is plausible to conclude that even though the parties might agree that it is *sometimes* the case that "the claims of a state's members will be better served if they are left to work out their own salvation", it does not follow that, all things considered, they would reject a limited intervention rule like PI which permits intervention on behalf of human rights.

I have argued that Rawls' contractarian model does not provide a justification for a presumption against intervention on behalf of human rights. To be sure even if I am correct, there may be other grounds for supporting a nonintervention rule which would include a presumption against this type of intervention. However, this discussion should serve to indicate that the apparently widespread belief that it is morally wrong to intervene in the affairs of nations, even for the purposes of improving the rights situation of foreign nationals, requires closer scrutiny. Since so much is at stake, it would be irresponsible to allow an unexamined assumption to play a critical role in deciding what actions, if any, are permissible for states to take on behalf of the rights of citizens of other states. At the very least, more careful study should be made of the likely effects of various possible interventionary measures in particular instances rather than dismissing in advance any effort to compel foreign governments to improve conditions in their respective societies on the grounds that any such action would be "interventionary." Still, it would be unreasonable to expect that such occasional interventionary actions alone will suffice to promote justice in the world. In certain instances, occasional intervention may force governments to significantly curtail the use of torture and the denial of various civil liberties. But when one considers, say, the plight of the poor in less developed nations, it is doubtful that occasional intervention by richer, industrialized nations would be sufficient or appropriate. For one has to recognize that conditions in less developed nations may be in part attributable to the existing pattern of international political and economic arrangements which fosters a relationship of dependency between poorer, less developed nations and richer, industrialized nations.[29] Thus justice may require a rather systematic restructuring of those arrangements. This indicates a pressing need for a careful analysis of existing arrangements as well as a comprehensive theory of global justice, a topic which merits more careful study by philosophers and political theorists.

NOTES

1. P.L. 94-329, 90 STAT. 748.
2. According to one usage, the term "state" refers to a political association and the term "nation" implies ties of history, character, and culture among individuals. Following Rawls, I will adopt another common usage of the term "nation" and will treat it as extentionally equivalent to the term "state." For a discussion of both usages, see Stanley French and Andres Gutman, "The Principle of National Self-determination" in Virginia Held, Sidney Morgenbesser, and Thomas Nagel, eds., *Philosophy, Morality, and International Affairs* (New York: Oxford University Press, 1974), pp. 138-153.
3. See R.J. Vincent, *Nonintervention and International Order* (Princeton: Princeton University Press, 1974), pp. 283-293.
4. "The Rights Standard," *New York Times*, January 24, 1977, "Op-Ed" Page.
5. The status of human rights violations in international law has been the subject of considerable controversy. Lauterpacht, for example, does not share Lefever's view on this matter. He asserts that "the question of human rights and freedoms...has become an international matter by virtue of the terms of the Charter [of the United Nations]." Hersch Lauterpacht, *International Law and Human Rights* (New York: Frederick A. Praeger, Inc., 1950), p. 180. Article 2, paragraph 7 of the Charter states that "Nothing contained in the present Charter shall authorize the United Nations to intervene in matters which are essentially within the domestic jurisdiction of any state..." (as quoted in Lauterpacht, p. 166). But, according to Lauterpacht, other parts of the Charter impose a legal obligation upon states to respect fundamental rights and freedoms. As a result, he claims, the Charter explicitly re-

moves fundamental rights and freedoms from the ambit of matters essentially within the jurisdiction of individual states. Nevertheless, he holds that only "such measures of protection and implementation as fall short of coercive intervention" are legitimate (p. 180).

6. Rawls refers to "the right of a people to settle its own affairs without the intervention of foreign powers" (p. 378).
7. Vincent, pp. 26–27. See also P.H. Winfield, "The History of Intervention in International Law," *British Yearbook of International Law*, Vol. III, 1922-1923. Vattel allowed two exceptions to the rule of nonintervention: intervention on behalf of the just side in a civil war and intervention in the interests of the balance of power. See E. de Vattel, *The Law of Nations or the Principles of Natural Law*, 1758, trans. by Charles G. Fenwick (Washington: The Carnegie Institution of Washington, 1916), Bk. II, Chap. IV, section 56; Bk. III, Chap. XVIII, section 296; and Bk. III, Chap. III, section 49.
8. Wolff holds that for one nation "[t]o interfere in the government of another, in whatever way indeed that may be done, is opposed to the natural liberty of nations, by virtue of which one nation is altogether independent of the will of other nations in its action." Christian Wolff, *Jus Gentium Methodo Scientifica Pertractatum*, 1764, trans. by Joseph H. Drake (Oxford: At the Clarendon Press, 1934), Chap. II, section 256. Vattel asserts that "[i]t clearly follows from the liberty and independence of Nations that each has the right to govern itself as it thinks proper, and that no one of them has the least right to interfere in the government of another." *The Law of Nations or the Principles of Natural Law*, Bk. II, Chap. IV, section 54.
9. R.J. Vincent, *Nonintervention and International Order* (Princeton: Princeton University Press, 1974).
10. Robert Nozick, *Anarchy, State, and Utopia* (New York: Basic Books, 1974), p. 183.
11. Thomas and Thomas, for example, make the following observation: "Some authorities would include in their definition of intervention almost any act of interference by one state in the affairs of another. For example, it has been said that mere official correspondence carried on by one state with another concerning some action of the other amounts to intervention, while conversely it has also been intimated that a failure of a state to concern itself with the affairs of another might amount to negative intervention. To go to the other extreme, there are jurists who drastically limit and qualify intervention. Some are of the opinion that intervention does not exist unless there is a dictatorial interference by one state in the affairs of another. A dictatorial interference is then defined as one involving the use of force or threat of such use." Ann Van Wynen and A.J. Thomas, *Non-Intervention: The Law and Its Import in the Americas* (Dallas: Southern Methodist University Press, 1956), pp. 67-68.

    Moore claims that the term intervention "is used indiscriminately to refer to a range of practices as diverse as student exchange programs and the dispatch of Soviet tanks to the streets of Budapest." John Norton Moore, *Law and the Indo-China War* (Princeton: Princeton University Press, 1972), p. 84.

Rosenau observes that "Notwithstanding the voluminous literature on intervention, there appears to be no agreement whatsoever on the phenomena designated by the term." James N. Rosenau, "Intervention as a Scientific Concept," *Journal of Conflict Resolution*, Vol. XIII, No. 2, June 1969, p. 161.

12. Vincent, p. 8. This definition derives from Oppenheim. See L. Oppenheim, *International Law*, 8th ed., ed. by H. Lauterpacht (London: Longmans, 1955), Vol. I, *Peace*, p. 305. Winfield states that intervention "occurs where one state interferes by force or threat of force in the affairs of another state." Percy H. Winfield, "Intervention," *Encyclopedia of the Social Sciences*, Vol. 8 (New York: Macmillan, 1932), p. 236. See also J.R. Brierly, *The Law of Nations*, 4th ed. (Oxford: At the Clarendon Press, 1949), p. 284.
13. Rosenau, p. 161.
14. See note 12.
15. Despite the fact that he offers no alternative, Vincent admits that the definition of intervention as "coercive interference" involving "the use or threat of force" has "its shortcomings." For, he concedes, "it can be objected that it is at once too inclusive and too exclusive." Vincent, p. 8.

    Whereas I agree with Vincent that this definition is too narrow, he fails to offer a decisive reason for concluding that it is too broad. It is too inclusive, he claims, "because in any case of interference by a great power in the affairs of a small power, the small power can plausibly claim that the activity was coercive due to the implicit threat of force which a powerful state can hold over a weak state." Vincent, p. 8. Now let us assume that the notion of an "implicit threat of force" is to be understood in the following manner: There is a reasonable likelihood that a relatively powerful state S1 will employ force to get what it wants in the event that a relatively powerless state S2 fails to comply with its "request"/demand. Surely, it would be arbitrary to reject S2's claim that S1's action was interventionary, and, hence, illegitimate, by responding that if S2's claim were accepted, then a large number of interactions between relatively powerful and relatively powerless states would be subject to moral criticism. This claim would clearly be unpersuasive from the point of view of S2 and other less powerful states. But this appears to be the only reason which Vincent suggests for holding that the definition he cites is too inclusive.
16. John Vorster, then Prime Minister of South Africa, apparently thought that he would win the sympathy of some Americans when he made the following statement in the course of an interview: "It is fast reaching the stage where we feel that the United States wants to prescribe to us how we should run our country internally and that is of course unacceptable to us. It is a fool who doesn't listen to advice but nobody can allow outsiders, however well-intentioned, whatever their motives, to meddle in their internal affairs."

New York Times, September 17, 1977. It goes without saying that Vorster's remarks were directed against economic and other sanctions short of outright (military) force.

17. Thomas and Thomas state that intervention involves "actions taken by one state to impose its will upon another against the latter's wishes....The essense of intervention is the attempt to compel." Thomas and Thomas, pp. 68-69 and 72.

    Compulsion need not involve force or the threat of force. Rather, it occurs whenever an attempt to modify behavior contrary to an agent's wishes is carried out by the production of, or a threat to produce, undesirable states of affairs in the event of noncompliance. Thus a state S1 attempts to compel the government of another state S2 if the former seeks to get the latter to act contrary to its wishes by threatening to produce some undesirable state of affairs if S2 refuses to comply. It might be claimed that since military and economic assistance is a "gift" by one nation to another, a threat to terminate such assistance cannot be counted as compulsion. However, this would not seem to apply when the following conditions obtain: (1) there has been a long history of assistance; (2) as a result of this assistance, a relationship of dependency has developed between the recipient and donor nations; and (3) past relations between the two countries lead the recipient nation to expect that assistance will continue.

18. It is commonly assumed that military and economic assistance programs give the United States considerable leverage over foreign governments. Accordingly, one of the aims of withholding or threatening to withhold assistance to governments with poor human rights records is to compel those governments to change their policies. This construal of the purpose of imposing conditions on aid appears to assume that the United States shares no responsibility for human rights violations. Those who believe that the United States has directly or indirectly contributed to rights violations might advocate imposing restrictions on aid to end United States complicity. It would of course be disingenuous to charge those who take this position with advocating "interventionary" policies. Still another aim of terminating aid, or severing all relations with governments with poor human rights records, may be to disassociate the United States from those governments. On this view, the termination of assistance is not necessarily associated with the expectation that it will improve the rights situation of foreign nationals.

19. I cannot address here the question whether the notion of "the national interest" is an intelligible concept.

20. Rawls pays particular attention to the choice between utilitarian principles and his two principles of (domestic) justice. According to Rawls, if they accepted the maximin rule, the agents in the original position would prefer his principles to utilitarian principles. If an agent in the original position were to select utilitarian principles, Rawls argues, he would run the risk of a serious loss of freedom and a need to forego other primary goods for the sake of others. According to Rawls, the parties in the original position could

protect themselves against such grave risks by selecting his two principles. This is not the place to assess Rawls' argument for his two principles of (domestic) justice or for the maximin rule.

21. Ronald Dworkin argues that a "right to equal concern and respect" is the fundamental feature of Rawls' "deep theory." Ronald Dworkin, "The Original Position," *University of Chicago Law Review*, 40, 3 (Spring 1973), 500-533.
22. Vincent construes the relation between the two principles in the following manner: "The rule of nonintervention can be said to derive from and require respect for the principle of state sovereignty. Sovereignty can be a statement expressing the idea that 'there is a final and absolute political authority in the political community' and that '*no final and absolute authority exists elsewhere*'...The principle of nonintervention identifies the right of states to sovereignty as a standard in international society and makes explicit the respect required for it in abstention from intervention." Vincent, p. 14. Rawls claims that "the right of a people to settle its own affairs without the intervention of foreign powers" is a "consequence of" the "basic principle of the law of nations," a principle of equality (among sovereign states). Rawls, p. 378.
23. For a perceptive discussion of this and related issues see Charles R. Beitz, "Justice and International Relations," *Philosophy & Public Affairs*, 4, 4 (Summer 1975), 360-389, reprinted in Chapter Two of this volume.
24. An alternative would be to think of the parties as "representatives of various states" in the relatively weak sense that citizens from each of the various nations of the world are present and that each knows that at least one person from each nation is present. Then, arguments would in effect be considered from the perspective of individuals, and each party to the contract should be thought of as advancing his own interests. Although I cannot pursue this line of inquiry here, I think that arguments for the selection of a limited intervention rule similar to those discussed below would apply in this case as well.
25. Suppose, for example, that the parties are thought of as advancing the interests of the *governments* of the states they represent. Then, even though they might well select a broad nonintervention rule like PN, the moral significance of such a hypothetical choice would remain in doubt.
26. An important question is whether the parties would assign a priority to some rights over others. For suppose, say, that they were to assign "lexical priority" to so-called "political rights." Then they might agree to prohibit intervention for the purpose of eliminating economic injustice when such intervention would likely result in an overall decrease in political liberties. I cannot pursue this issue here. All I wish to show is that the parties would acknowledge the legitimacy of intervention on behalf of *some* rights.
27. Indeed, it might be argued that the parties would prefer a stronger rule to PI, namely a rule which imposes an *obligation* on foreign governments, or on some international body, to intervene in certain specified circumstances.

28. S.I. Benn and R.S. Peters, *Social Principles and the Democratic State* (London: George Allen & Unwin, 1959), pp. 362-363. Both of the claims considered above are advanced by Benn and Peters.
29. For an analysis of this purported relationship of dependency and some of its alleged effects, see André Gunder Frank, "The Development of Underdevelopment," *Monthly Review*, 18, 4 (September 1966), 17-31; Theotonio Dos Santos, "The Structure of Dependence," *American Economic Review*, Vol. LX, No. 2 (May 1970), pp. 231-236; and Suzanne Bodenheimer, "Dependency and Imperialism: The Roots of Latin American Underdevelopment," *Politics and Society* 1 (1971), 327-357.

CHAPTER 3

Rawls in Perspective

Is There a Kantian Foundation for Rawlsian Justice?

Stephen L. Darwall
UNIVERSITY OF NORTH CAROLINA

It is fruitful to view the course of Anglo-American moral and political philosophy of the past three decades as a Kantian response to the earlier ascendancy of the views of David Hume. For just as Hume's philosophy forms the background of the period stretching roughly from the twenties through the forties, Kant's thought looms large in the period beginning more or less in the fifties and continuing to the present.

John Rawls' *A Theory of Justice* is not unusual in its attempt to claim a Kantian pedigree. At least two other recent and influential works in political philosophy, Robert Paul Wolff's *In Defense of Anarchism* and Robert Nozick's *Anarchy, State and Utopia*, self-consciously appeal to Kantian premises to support political philosophies radically different from Rawls' and from each other.

Kant's writings have assumed something like the status of a sacred text, both in forming current trends in moral and political philosophy and in being interpreted and reinterpreted in the light of these trends. There is a legitimate task to be performed by the Kant scholar in trying to separate the "historical" Kant from the contemporary use to which his views have been put. I shall not take this tack, however. In this essay I will be rather less interested in the integrity of Kant's own thought than in the way it illuminates and informs Rawls' ideas. There is almost no doubt that Kant would have found Rawls' theory of justice to be unacceptable. His own writings on the subject were much more conservative in substance. Nevertheless, it may still be the case that Kant's more fundamental concerns, expressed in his work on the foundation of ethics, lend support to Rawls. The Kantian ideals of autonomy and respect for rational nature and his view of the connection between morality and reason, themes which lie at the very center of Kant's moral thought, find expression, Rawls believes, in the conception of justice as fairness. It is this idea that we shall explore. Most certainly Rawls extends Kant's ideas here and makes emendations there. The question to be addressed is whether this is done in a way that respects and extends the fundamental insights of Kant's moral philosophy.

RAWLS' KANTIANISM IN THE CONTEXT OF RECENT MORAL PHILOSOPHY

Before we turn to that task it would be useful to place Rawls and his Kantianism in the context of recent moral and political philosophy. This will help us to understand the role that Kant's thought has played recently and to see what is distinctive about Rawls' Kantianism. To understand Kant's influence in this most recent period, though, we must first grasp the Humean roots of the period just preceding.

In many ways the figure of David Hume dominated Anglo-American philosophy in the first part of the twentieth century. The Humean thesis that all substantive knowledge must derive from sense-experience grounded both the early positivist program to base science on theory-neutral observation and even more widely held skepticism about metaphysics.

In moral philosophy Hume's influence was equally profound. To many, Humean reflections seemed to lead to the emotivist position that moral judgments do not make assertions which might be discovered to be true or false, but rather express the speaker's own feelings or attitudes toward the matter under discussion. Philosophers who were led to this conclusion took their texts from Hume's theses regarding the independence of morality from reason, the impossibility of deductive argument from sense-experience to moral judgment, and the dependence of moral judgment on sentiment.[1]

Emotivism and its close cousins had a narrowing effect on the way in which moral philosophers saw their own task. If there was no fact of the matter to seek after in morals, the philosopher's task seemed to be restricted to "meta-ethics": the philosophical analysis of the nature of moral judgment, moral debate, and the like. Any attempt to articulate an ethical system or to speak to particular moral issues was at best an expressive act and one to which the philosopher could claim no special competence.

Though many of Hume's modern followers thought that his ideas ruled out the possibility of articulating an ethical system which was other than a mere expression of one's own feelings, Hume did not agree. Indeed it is an interesting fact that insofar as concern with ethical system and theory had a place at all in the first half of this century, it was largely characterized by discussion of Hume's own substantive theory, utilitarianism. To be sure, other ethical conceptions were advanced, but rarely in a systematic way and most usually as a reaction to utilitarianism.

Early versions of emotivism seemed to make moral judgment and moral attitude entirely independent of reason. A.J. Ayer and Charles Stevenson held that we may "speak with the vulgar" and *say* that we have reasons for holding a moral view, but when we "think with the learned" we must realize that all this can mean is that our feelings are caused or determined by the beliefs which we give as our reasons. Moral views can be neither reasonable nor unreasonable, nor are there rational methods for arriving at a moral judgment or for attempting to influence the moral views of others. Engaging in moral "argument" is no more or less rational a way to influence the moral views of another than is rewiring his brain.

The view that moral judgment is expressive of feeling and independent of reason, when stated this baldly, provoked a Kantian response. For Kant there is a fundamental distinction between those attitudes which we merely happen to have towards things and our moral attitudes. In order for an attitude to be one of moral approval or disapproval, as opposed to mere favor or disfavor, we must conceive of the attitude as one which is based in reason. This point was seized on as an account of our ordinary moral notions and applied against emotivism. Whatever else they are, moral judgments are essentially conceived to be judgments which are based on reasons and thus something of which, unlike tastes or preferences, one can be persuaded or convinced. Thus, it was urged, emotivism must be false as an account of our moral sensibility.

Furthermore, moral attitudes are, in a way that tastes and preferences need not be, implicitly universal. If one thinks that one's friend ought (morally) to receive a benefit then one must think that any relevantly similar person in relevantly similar circumstances ought to receive such a benefit as well. The relevant features depend on what one's reasons are for thinking one's friend ought to be benefited. Thus the implicit universality of moral judgments follows from their reason-dependence. By contrast, one may want one's friend to be benefited without wanting others to be. R.M. Hare, who refers to this feature of moral judgments as their "universalizability," acknowledges the roots of this idea in Kant's Categorical Imperative: "Act only according to that maxin by which you can at the same time will that it should become a universal law."[2]

Thus, the initial attraction of the Kantian position for moral philosophers of this century was that it provided an alternative conception of morality in terms of which emotivism might be successfully challenged. Moral judgment was based in *some* way, it was thought, on reasoning. And in the nineteen fifties a spate of articles and books were published by philosophers anxious to make this point.[3] Hare's view was that reason only required universalizability, and thus system and coherence in one's overall moral view. Others, for example, Baier and Foot, tied morality to a more material conception of reason involving human good or interest. And still others, for example Toulmin, connected morality to a conventional conception of reason. None of these approaches were particularly Kantian. As against Hare, Kant clearly thought that his meta-ethical views regarding the connection between morality and reason determined substantive moral propositions, not merely the demand for ethical consistency. And he would have rejected an account of reason which was *based on* either interest or convention. To quote Onora Nell, Hare's account gave "formality without fertility,"[4] whereas the opposing views, though clearly capable of generating substantive moral conclusions, did so at the price of not being based on a formal and thus *a priori* conception of rationality.

Thus, to the extent that Kant figured in the critique of emotivism it was because he offered what that theory lacked: a conception of morality based on reason. However, Kant's conception of the connection between morality and reason was not pressed in detail. Nor, interestingly enough, were the substantive moral conclusions which Kant believed to follow from this conception of morality.

More recently, however, moral and political philosophers have argued for substantive moral and political conceptions based on what they claim to be Kantian grounds. The last ten years have seen the publication of Robert Paul Wolff's *In Defense of Anarchism*, Robert Nozick's *Anarchy, State, and Utopia* and John Rawls' *A Theory of Justice.* It is a signal fact that all three of these philosophers invoke Kant's moral philosophy in their argument. Wolff appeals to the Kantian ideal of autonomy to argue for philosophical anarchism.[5] Nozick, though not an anarchist, argues for a minimal "nightwatchman" conception of the justified state on the grounds that any state which makes further requirements of individuals violates rights that they have in virtue of being persons. Such states violate the Kantian requirement that persons are never to be treated "simply as a means, but always at the same time as an end."[6]

What these philosophers share with Rawls is a conception of persons as having a special moral status in virtue of their nature as rational beings. Thus Wolff: "Every man who possesses both free will and reason has an obligation to take responsibility for his actions,"[7] an obligation which makes it unjustifiable to relinquish our autonomy. Nozick answers the question "in virtue of precisely what characteristics of persons are there moral constraints on how they may treat each other or be treated?" by citing rationality, free will, and moral agency which together enable persons to formulate long-term plans of life and to act on the basis of abstract principles or considerations.[8] Finally, Rawls argues that individuals may make claims of justice and have the right not to be treated as a means only in virtue of their moral personality: their having some conception of the good and a capacity for a sense of justice (12, 19, 505f, all parenthetical citations are to John Rawls, *A Theory of Justice* (Cambridge, Mass.: Harvard University Press, 1971)).

In the background of all three of these views is the Kantian thesis that the characteristic of human beings that is the fundamental object of moral concern is their rational nature. This forms the basis for these writers' rejection of utilitarianism. Any ethical theory which judges institutions or actions on the basis of how much pleasure they generate or how many desires they satisfy fails to consider this most important fact about us.

Interestingly enough, the failure of utilitarianism on this diagnosis is due to the same cause as the failure of emotivism: an insufficient attention to our nature as rational beings, and to moral agency as including rationality. For Kant these are two sides of the same coin. Moral questions only (and necessarily) arise for rational beings. Therefore the moral must be grounded in the rational. At the same time, however, our nature as rational beings marks us as objects of special moral concern, both for ourselves and for others. The Kantian critique of utilitarianism is thus of a piece with the Kantian critique of emotivism and of Humean philosophy generally: namely, that it abstracts from the constitutive role of reason.

RAWLS' USE OF KANTIAN MORAL PHILOSOPHY

Now that we have a rough picture of the place of Rawls and his Kantianism in a larger historical framework, we can approach the difficult tasks of understanding and assessing the ways in which he makes use of Kantian moral philosophy. The task of understanding will be difficult because unlike Wolff and Nozick, who appeal to one or another Kantian principle in the course of their arguments, Rawls' debt to Kant is more systematic. Nor will the task of assessment be a simple one. Rawls' claim that his theory is Kantian in important respects has been subject to a veritable barrage of criticism.

What precisely, then, is the nature of Rawls' Kantianism and what role does it play in his theory of justice? References to Kant occur throughout *A Theory of Justice* and are by no means limited to the section which Rawls entitles "The Kantian Interpretation of Justice as Fairness." What ties these disparate references together is an attempt to provide support, at different levels of theorizing, for the proposed principles of justice. The references to Kant are neither merely rhetorical, nor an attempt to aid understanding of Rawls' own views by placing them in the context of the Kantian tradition. They are a significant part of the overall argument for justice as fairness.

Rawls' two main arguments for his principles are well known: first, that the principles best systematize our considered judgments about justice when we consider them in "reflective equilibrium" with those judgments, and second, that the principles would be chosen from a perspective (the original position) which embodies constraints that seem morally compelling. Rawls appeals to Kant's moral philosophy to deepen the appeal of both of these arguments.

Rawls' First Argument ("Reflective Equlibrium")

To buttress the first argument Rawls argues that a basic social structure satisfies the Kantian precept that persons are to be treated always as ends in themselves and never simply as means only if it satisfies his proposed principles of justice. They are the best interpretation of the Kantian requirements applied to the basic framework of society.

Consider the difference principle. It requires that inequalities work to the advantage of the worst-off group, or at least not to their disadvantage. If society is arranged so that some profit at the expense of others, then these latter are treated as mere means. Since the difference principle requires that there be no alternative arrangement of the basic structure which makes the worst-off group better off, it ensures that no one is treated as a means in the way indicated. Thus the difference principle receives direct support from the idea that people are never to be treated as means only (180f).

The problem with this argument is that it is open to the better-off to claim that they are being treated as a means by the worst-off if the worst-off profit at their expense. They might claim this if there were alternative arrangements where the better-off would be even better off. The claim of the better-off can only be denied if we make the assumption that treating people as ends in themselves makes an equal distribution of primary goods morally preferable.[9]

Rawls' Second Argument ("Original Position")

The real heart of what Rawls terms the "Kantian Interpretation," however, is the role that it plays in the second argument for the principles, the argument from the original position. It is useful to distinguish two different levels of theory here: a more basic level which grounds the very idea of an argument to moral principles from a perspective such as the original position, and a level which attempts to ground the specific features of the original position itself.

Basic Level: Moral Principles. At the most basic level Rawls argues from Kantian theses about the nature of morality for the position that moral principles must be principles which an agent *would* will or choose from a perspective that is in some sense inescapable for him and essential to the very idea of morality. This idea, which we might call the autonomist thesis, is deeply embedded in Kant's moral thought. Perhaps the clearest statement of it occurs in the Introduction to the *Rechtslehre:*

> ...a person is subject to no laws other than those that he (either alone or at least jointly with others) gives to himself.[10]

In the *Grundlegung* Kant characterizes this idea as one that "all previous attempts which have ever been undertaken to discover the principle of morality" have failed to capture:

> Man was seen to be bound to laws by his duty, but it was not seen that he is subject only to his own, yet universal, legislation, and that he is only bound to act in accordance with his own will....[11]

It is this fundamental idea of Kant's to which Rawls lays claim as underlying the very idea of an argument to principles of justice from a perspective such as the original position. Such a perspective must be one which there are compelling reasons for any person to adopt and from which the principles of justice would be regarded as a suitable object of choice:

> ....[he] [Kant] begins with the idea that moral principles are the object of rational choice (251).

> Kant's main aim is to deepen and to justify Rosseau's idea that liberty is acting in accordance with a law that we give to ourselves (256).

Another central Kantian thesis which Rawls marshals at the most basic level is the idea which he renders by the slogan that the concept of right is prior to that of the good. For Rawls to say that justice as fairness gives priority to the concept of right is to say that on that theory one "does not take men's propensities and inclinations as given, whatever they are, and then seek the best way to fulfill them" (31). As I understand it, this idea is the same as that which Rawls expresses by saying that justice as fairness is not a teleological ethical conception. Teleological ethical theories are those in which "the good is defined independently from the right, and then the right is defined as that which maximizes the good" (24). These two ideas come to the same thing if one takes what is good, independently of consideration of what is right, to be what satisfies our propensities and inclinations.

It is a commonplace of moral philosophy that Kant is a deontological rather than a teleological theorist. This may seem initially puzzling given the fact that Kant begins his foundational work in ethics, the *Grundlegung*, with a discussion of the claim that the only thing which can be called unqualifiedly *good* is the good will. Appearances are somewhat misleading here, however. The claimed judgments of goodness at the beginning of the *Grundlegung* are made from within the moral point of view. Indeed the very idea of a good will cannot be defined, for Kant, independently of the idea of right action:

> Therefore, the pre-eminent good can consist only in the conception of the law in itself (which can be present only in a rational being) so far as this conception and not the hoped-for effect is the determining ground of the will.[12]

The unqualified moral goodness of the good will consists in its acting on an adequate conception of the moral law. A teleological ethics rests its account of the right on what is held to be good *independently* of moral considerations.[13] It is precisely this idea which Kant found most repugnant.

To see why this is so and to understand the relation between Kant's rejection of teleologism in ethics, the autonomist thesis and the argument from the original position in Rawls, we must appreciate the roots of all these ideas in the Kantian thesis that we are subject to morality in virtue of our rational nature. That Kant considers rationality to be a necessary condition for ascriptions of moral worth we have already seen. Only the behavior of rational agents can be morally evaluable because only they are capable of having a conception of moral requirement and of expressing that conception in what they do. Though the moral assessment of action cannot be made independently of such a conception of the right, it is still the agent as acting or not acting on such a conception which is the fundamental object of moral evaluation. Thus only rational beings may be esteemed as having moral worth in virtue of what they do. But rational nature is not merely necessary to be genuinely subject to moral requirements; for Kant it is also sufficient. Kant's account of what we *ought* to do is to be understood in terms of what we *would* do "if reason completely determined the will."[14] If we will but attend to "our common idea of duty and moral laws" we will see that:

> ...the ground of obligation here must not be sought in the nature of man or in the circumstances in which he is placed, but sought *a priori* soley in the concepts of pure reason....[15]

To be rational is to be faced with moral imperatives just because moral imperatives are those which are based on our rationality. Kant expresses this idea by his famous claim that the imperatives of morality are categorical rather than hypothetical. Unlike hypothetical imperatives which:

> ...present the practical necessity of a possible action as a means to achieving something else which one desires (or which one may possibly desire). The categorical imperative would be one which presented an action as of itself objectively necessary....[16]

This idea of *objective necessity* is itself to be understood in terms of being required by an *objective principle:* one "which would serve all rational beings also subjectively as a practical principle if reason had full power over the faculty of desire."[17]

Kant takes the springs of human action to be of two radically different kinds. As beings with an affective nature we respond agreeably or disagreeably to the world in its many aspects and find ourselves, accordingly, with desires and aversions. But as beings with reason we are capable of being moved directly to action by the thought that there is reason to be. A principle which we adopt because it will enable us to accomplish something we desire is ultimately based in our affectivity. But Kant argues

> ...we cannot know, a priori, of the idea of any object, whatever the nature of this idea, whether it will be associated with pleasure of displeasure or will be merely indifferent.[18]

Therefore, any principle thus based in our affectivity cannot be categorical and thus cannot be a genuine moral requirement.

This, then, is the source of the Kantian idea which Rawls expresses by saying that the concept of right is prior to that of the good. Morality cannot be *based* on the satisfaction of our desires *as such*. Rules or principles which are thus based are hypothetical, not categorical, imperatives.

It is also the source of the autonomist thesis. We are subject to moral requirements because of our rational nature. Furthermore, something is a genuine moral requirement only on the condition that it can be grounded in our rational nature. Thus a particular individual is bound by a moral principle only if that principle can be grounded in his own practical reason. But since for Kant reason is genuinely practical, this entails that the principle may be regarded as a product of the agent's own will.[19]

The root idea is that there is a structure of will which is common to rational beings as such and that moral requirements must be based on this. This idea underlies both the autonomist thesis and the thesis that the conception of the right is prior to that of the good. It is also the fundamental idea behind the argument from the original position. For if there is such a structure of will, we should be able to define a perspective which lays it bare. It is just this that the original position is designed to be. Rawls suggests that "we think of the original position as the point of view from which noumenal selves see the world" (255). It is so conceived as to abstract away idiosyncratic features and to enable us to see what principles we would will *qua* rational beings to govern the basic structure of our mutual relations. Whether it does so successfully is an issue that will occupy us below. In any case, the very idea of an argument from a perspective such as the original position is grounded in the Kantian conception of morality as based in rational nature.

Second Level: Specific Features. The second level of theory at which Kant's moral philosophy is invoked to undergird the argument from the original position is in the specific characterization of that perspective. It is one thing to be convinced on Kantian grounds that there must be some such perspective from which morally binding principles would be the objects of choice. It is quite another to argue that the original position is such a perspective. This is the task which Rawls takes on in the section entitled "The Kantian Interpretation of Justice as Fairness" and to which he has addressed himself in several subsequent papers.

In characterizing the choice from the original position we may distinguish three different sorts of features. The first feature is the characterization of the information available to the parties in making a choice. Here Rawls includes a veil of ignorance with respect to knowledge of particulars, but full knowledge of "the general facts about human society." The parties do have some particular knowledge, however. They know their society to be in the "circumstances of justice": a condition of moderate scarcity which makes human cooperation both necessary and possible. The second feature is the characterization of the parties making the choice. Under this heading is included their motivation and the characterization of their rationality. The third feature is the specification of the range of alternatives. The most general characterization of the alternatives is that they are principles which will be regarded as final and overriding with respect to the moral assessment of the basic structure of society. In addition these principles must meet various requirements: they must be public, applicable to all moral persons, formulable without reference to individuals and able to establish an ordering of conflicting claims.

Essentially, the idea of the Kantian Interpretation is that these various elements of the original position may be argued for on Kantian grounds. We shall proceed by considering each of these elements in turn.

Information: Veil of Ignorance. Rawls' argument for this constraint is based both on the Kantian idea of autonomy and on Kant's thesis that we ought to regard all persons as ends in themselves. These two ideas are related by Kant through his notion of a realm of ends.

Kant understands autonomy as "the property of the will to be a law to itself."[20] As rational beings we are capable of forming a conception of practical laws: principles we would act on if "reason had full power over the faculty of desire."[21] The existence of practical laws, then, depends on the existence of a structure of will which is common to rational agents as such. The veil of ignorance defines a perspective in which one abstracts from one's own idiosyncracies (also those of others, and of one's time and place) and consequently may only consider what one has in common with other rational (human) agents. Furthermore, the principles are chosen to be applicable to all persons. To adopt the original position, then, is to adopt a perspective one has in common with other rational human beings and which bases choice in a structure of will shared with them. On this account Rawls regards the original position as "a procedural interpretation of Kant's conception of autonomy" (256).[22]

The ideal of autonomy is connected in Kant's thought to the requirement that we treat others as ends in themselves through the notion of the *realm of ends.* As an autonomous agent one must regard oneself as the source of moral principles:

> ...every rational being must be able to regard himself as an end in himself with reference to all laws to which he may be subject, whatever they may be, and thus as giving universal laws.[23]

But the rational nature in which one's autonomy consists is equally present in others:

> It also follows that...he must take his maxims from the point of view which regards himself, *and hence every other rational being,* as legislative...In this way, a world of rational beings *(mundus intelligibilis)* is possible as a realm of ends.[24]

To express one's autonomy one must consider what one would will *qua* rational being, and in so doing one takes the perspective of *any* rational being. The veil of ignorance, by forcing an abstraction from any knowledge about oneself in particular, makes one's own perspective the perspective of any person. Thus, Rawls claims the original position is expressive both of the ideal of autonomy and of the requirement that all persons be treated as ends in themselves.

Interestingly enough, Kant himself suggested a method of abstraction such as the veil of ignorance as a way to understand the concept of the realm of ends:

> By "realm" I understand the systematic union of different rational beings through common laws. Because laws determine ends with regard to their universal validity, *if we abstract from the personal difference of rational beings and thus from all content of their private ends*, we can think of a whole of all ends in systematic connection, a whole of rational beings as ends in themselves.[25]

Thus Kant's own exposition of the realm of ends explicitly refers to the kind of abstraction from knowledge of particular ends which is accomplished by the veil of ignorance.

Motivation and Rationality of the Parties. There is a widespread misconception that the parties to the original position are self-interested in the sense that their exclusive motivation is to secure the greatest utility for themselves once the veil is lifted. The parties are behind a veil of ignorance with respect to what their actual preferences are and, it is thought, they have no other preferences in the original position except to maximize the satisfaction their actual (i.e., extra-veil)[26] preferences, *whatever* they turn out to be. On this view the parties to the original position have no interest at all in what their extra-veil interests are.

This is a mistake, and it is important to see why it is, for it imports a much less Kantian conception of the person into the original position than Rawls actually intends.

To begin with we should note that Rawls assumes the parties to accept the "thin theory of the good": namely, that a person's good consists in the successful execution of a rational plan of life (395f). This is already a departure from the idea that the parties are soley interested in satisfying their desires whatever they happen to be. A defining characteristic of a *rational life plan* is that it be that plan of life which one would choose if one were fully and imaginatively aware of all the relevant facts about, and consequences of, pursuing it. Since something might satisfy one's actual preferences but not preferences one would have under such ideal conditions, it is a mistake to think of the parties as exclusively concerned to maximize their extra-veil preference satisfaction.

In addition, in several papers published subsequently to *A Theory of Justice*, Rawls has stressed that, as he conceives it, the parties are assumed to have a fundamental interest in maintaining their status as choosers of their own ends:

> They do not think of themselves as inevitably bound to, or as identical with, the pursuit of any partiuclar complex of fundamental interests that they have at any given time.... Rather, free persons conceive of themselves as beings who can revise and alter their final ends and who give first priority to preserving their liberty in these matters.[27]

This characterization of the person coheres better with a moral theory in which the conception of the right is prior to that of the good. Theories such as utilitarianism which seek to maximize aggregate satisfaction of desire identify people with their actual desires or interests. But this forms too ephemeral a basis on which to ground the fundamental distinctness of persons. For Rawls, however, a person is not to be identified with his or her actual desires or interests. Part of what it is to be a rational person is to be capable of revising one's ends and of controlling and adjusting to some extent even one's desires:

> Persons do not take their wants and desires as determined by happenings beyond their control. We are not, so to speak, assailed by them, as we are perhaps by disease and illness....[28]

Because persons have the capacity to have some control over their desires, the mere fact of desire does not support claims to the means of satisfaction in the way that disease and illness support claims to medicine and treatment. The right is prior to the good in that people may be held *responsible* for revising their aims and preferences if they are required to do so by just institutions.[29]

The emphasis on our capacity as rational beings to choose our pursuits and the identification of the person with this capacity rather than with our actual desires is distinctly Kantian. For Kant, our freedom consists in the capacity to abandon or take on pursuits on seeing it to be required by principles which are grounded in practical reason. As agents this capacity constitutes our very identity and accordingly something we cherish. Indeed, it is our duty to cherish it: "Act so that you treat rational nature, *whether in your own person* or in that of another, always as an end and never as a means only."[30]

The fundamental interest of the parties in flourishing as rational choosers of ends provides the basis for the theory of primary goods and for the priority of liberty. If the parties to the original position were only interested in maximizing the satisfaction of their extra-veil preferences, it would be mysterious for them to opt for principles which measure well-being with a theory of objective good, such as the theory of primary goods, rather than the notion of utility. There is, of course, the problem of interpersonal utility comparisons, but though Rawls is certainly mindful of this problem he does not think that it should be given great weight (91). The real basis for taking primary goods as the index of well-being is the conception of the person as a rational chooser of ends. Primary goods are of value to the parties not just because they will enable them to advance their aims, whatever they happen to be, but also from the standpoint of the parties flourishing as rational choosers of ends. Liberties, opportunities, and wealth assure the scope rationally to criticize pursuits in a meaningful way. Closed opportunities, unprotected liberties, and unavailable resources undermine the rational criticism and choice of ends. A person's actual preference schedule might be maximally satisfied with but a minimal level of these primary goods, but the interest in flourishing as a rational chooser of ends is much less likely to be.

This grounding of the idea of primary goods in the fundamental end of flourishing as a rational chooser of ends must be emphasized. As Rawls has suggested, Kant himself makes implicit use of the idea of primary good.[31] In the next major section I shall argue that Kant's dependence on the idea of primary goods is rather more systematic. And this is precisely because of their basis in an end which all rational beings necessarily have. In the third example of the application of the "universal law" formulation of the Categorical Imperative, Kant argues that a person could not will it to be a universal law that people not develop their talents. His reason is that "...as a rational being, he necessarily wills that all his faculties should be developed, inasmuch as they are given to him for all sorts of possible purposes."[32] That any rational being would necessarily will the development of *all* of his talents seems somewhat excessive (and most likely unrealizable), but the root idea is sound. Talents, in general, are a primary good, and one cannot will, rationally, that they be generally squandered as they are a necessary means for the pursuit of ends in general.

Likewise the fourth example of the application of the Categorical Imperative assumes a notion of what would be in the interest of, or good for, a rational agent conceived of as such. To will that people never help others except when it is in their interest to do so will, given certain plausible contingent assumptions, lead to one's lacking the help one may well need in the pursuit of one's ends. The help of others may, given certain assumptions about the world, be regarded as a primary good. It is likely to be an asset regardless of what one's specific ends are, and it could be an essential need. An agent in ignorance of his specific ends would, on that account, be loathe to will that people never help others, except when it is in their interest to do so, because in doing so "he would have robbed himself...of all hope of the aid he desires."[33] Thus both Kant's third and fourth examples employ the idea of what one would will as a rational chooser of ends, the idea which forms the basis of Rawls' theory of primary goods.

Some writers, though they accept the original position as a perspective for assessing principles of justice, argue that the parties would choose a variant of utilitarianism, most usually average utilitarianism.[34] It is argued that if the parties suppose it to be equiprobable that they are any person in society, then they will maximize their expected utility by picking the principle of average utility.

This argument depends, however, on supposing the parties to be motivated solely by a concern to maximize their extra-veil utility. From this assumption it would follow as a corollary that the parties have no interest at all in what their extra-veil preferences are. We have seen that this is a mistake. As Rawls conceives it, the parties have a fundamental interest in flourishing as rational choosers of ends. This includes a complex of desires and propensities: an openness to argument and criticism, a desire to take responsibility for one's ends and pursuits, a propensity to seek out information and experience which is relevant to the assessment of one's pursuits, and the like. The parties are anything but indifferent to whether they have these preferences and a social environment which will support them.

We can see this clearly with the primary good of self-respect.[35] The connection between self-respect and the satisfaction of one's preferences may be somewhat tenuous. We can imagine people with preferences who are content though they lack self-respect; for example, the happy slave. But if one has a fundamental interest in one's nature as a rational chooser of ends, one will necessarily have an interest in being in a social environment which provides the basis for self-respect.

The rational choice of ends is a self-reflective activity. People can only take responsibility for their ends if they so understand their activity. A social environment which sustains a person as a rational chooser of ends must therefore sustain a person's having that conception of him or herself. By supporting a person's self-respect a society supports a person's recognition of him or herself as a moral person, as a being who takes responsibility for his or her pursuits. In so doing, it makes possible the person's maintenance as a rational chooser of ends. Clearly it is possible for social environments to withhold such support. Slavery is only an extreme example. People may be encouraged not to take responsibility for their pursuits, and thus not to affirm a respect for themselves as moral persons, in a variety of subtle ways. One of the great contributions of both the civil rights and the women's movements have been to emphasize how subtly pervasive and undermining such social influences can be. The parties in the original position are aware of the effects of social environment and

> ...regard themselves as having a highest-order interest in how all their other interests, including even their fundamental ones, are shaped and regulated by social institutions.[36]

Thus their choice of principles is not independent of their beliefs regarding the kind of effects social institutions satisfying those principles would have on their desires, interests, and self-conception. We have seen how this might affect the principles chosen in virtue of the primary good of self-respect. Though space does not permit further exploration here, Rawls also believes it to underlie the priority of liberty.

The Objects of Choice: Conditions on Principles.[37] Most of the features characterizing the range of permissible principles are relatively straightforward. That the principles are to be general and universal, applying to all in virtue of their being moral persons and formulable in a way that does not make reference to individuals, are both stipulations with clear Kantian roots. Worth discussion, however, both because it affects Rawls' argument, and because Rawls invokes Kant on its behalf, is the constraint that the principles are to be chosen as a *public* conception of justice. Insofar as ultimate moral claims are lodged by individuals against the society, they are to be made on the basis provided by the chosen principles.

This is by no means a trivial requirement. It may not necessarily promote the greatest aggregate or average utility for a society to have a principles of utility as its *public* conception of justice. Suppose a public utilitarian conception would undermine people's self-respect which, as a matter of fact, they highly value. This would be a utilitarian reason not to use the principle of utility as a public standard for the criticism of the basic structure of society.

This possibility affects the proposed argument from the original position for the principle of average utility discussed in the preceding section. Even if one is convinced by the argument that it is rational to try to be a member of that society which has the highest average utility, it does not follow that it is rational to select the principle of average utility as a public conception of justice.

Rawls cites passages in Kant's political writings[38] where he speaks of justice as requiring the application of a public standard, but the idea seems implicity in his notion of the realm of ends also. Part of what it is to treat others as ends in themselves is to act in ways which one could justify to them by principles which they could accept.

Another important feature of the choice in the original position, which is not, strictly speaking, a formal constraint on eligible principles, is the idea that the principles are to be chosen as a standard for the final moral assessment of the *basic structure* of society. This is an extremely important idea in Rawls' theory. It is the idea which he expresses by saying that "the basic structure of society is the primary subject of justice.[39] By the *basic structure* Rawls means "the way in which the major social institutions fit together into one system, and how they assign fundamental rights and shape the division of advantages that arises through social cooperation."[40]

The appropriateness of the basic structure as the subject of justice springs from the two sources considered above in the discussion of self-respect. First, the parties to the original position are persons who have a fundamental interest in their status as rational choosers of ends. Second, they are aware of the ways in which the desires, aspirations, and self-conceptions of individuals are shaped by social institutions. Thus they cannot be indifferent to the basic structure of society:

> Everyone recognizes that the form of society affects its members and determines in large part the kind of persons they want to be as well as the kind of persons they are. It also limits people's ambitions and hopes in different ways, for they will with reason view themselves in part according to their place in it and take account of the means and opportunities they can realistically expect.[41]

Whether human beings flourish as rational choosers of ends is not independent of the social institutions within which they find themselves. For this reason individuals concerned not to undermine their rational nature must be concerned about the basic structure of society.

Kant was himself well aware of the ways in which social and economic institutions could undermine the capacity of individuals to make rational choices, but he drew rather different political philosophical consequences from it. Both in the *Rechtslehre* and in his essay "On the Common Saying: This May be True in Theory But It Does Not Apply in Practice," Kant makes very insightful remarks about the relationship between independence of judgment and independence in social and economic relationships. His view is that to be fit to vote (and thus to be active rather than merely passive citizens) individuals must be independent and make decisions of their own accord.[42] But there are many individuals in society who are not in a position to do this:

> an apprentice of a merchant or artisan; a servant (not in the service of the state); a minor *(naturaliter vel civiliter)*, all women; and generally anyone who must depend for his support (subsistence and protection), not on his own industry, but on arrangements by others (with the exception of the state)....[43]

In a passage from the essay on "Theory and Practice" which sounds almost as if it could have been a part of Marx's 1844 *Manuscripts*, Kant makes it clear that the last category includes all wage laborers. Those who sell their labor are dependent on others in a way that those who sell their products to others are not:

> For the latter, in pursuing his trade, exchanges his property with someone else *(opus)*, while the former allows someone else to make use of him.[44]

Since individuals who are in such socially or economically dependent relationships to others are incapable of genuinely independent will, they are not fit to take part in political decision-making. Therefore they should not be allowed to vote. Curiously enough Kant holds that this is not "incompatible with the freedom and equality that men possess as human beings."[45] Indeed he goes so far as to say that

> ...uniform equality of human beings as subjects of a state is, however, perfectly consistent with the utmost inequality of the mass in the degree of its possessions....[46]

Where Kant has gone wrong, Rawls must believe, is in not taking seriously enough the political implications of his own moral philosophy. Kant finds individuals in socially and economically dependent circumstances and then concludes that because they are not independent they are not fit to vote. But why are the existing social and economic conditions themselves not open to moral criticism? Is it not heteronomous in the extreme to allow a fundamental principle of one's political philosophy, the denial of the right to vote, to be fixed by contingencies of social and economic relations? For Rawls the proper projection of Kant's moral philosophy into the political realm is a society governed by principles which would be chosen by persons from a perspective that expresses their character as equal, moral persons. Just because of the sort of social insights that Kant had and their concern to establish and maintain themselves as rational choosers of ends, such individuals would be most careful to avoid the possibility of undermining that independence through their own choice. Accordingly they would choose principles for the assessment of the basic structure of society with an eye towards which ones would be most likely to require a social environment in which they could flourish as rational choosers of ends.

Robert Nozick's interpretation of the Kantian idea that people must be treated as ends in themselves and never simply as means seems subject to a similar criticism. Nozick argues that it is sufficient to show that a person is not using another only as a means if:

> ...the other party stands to gain enough from the exchange so that he is willing to go through with it, even though he objects to one or more of the uses to which you shall put the good.[47]

This interpretation makes the issue of whether individuals are being treated as means dependent upon questions at the level of individual transaction where the socio-economic structure of society is taken as given. As we have seen, Rawls takes the issue of whether individuals are treated as ends rather than means to turn on whether they are treated in accordance with principles which they could will as rational beings. Furthermore, for reasons that we have just considered, some such principles (the principles of justice) take the basic structure of society as subject. Whether people are treated as a means, on this view, cannot be assessed in abstraction from the larger socio-economic structure.

Nozick's interpretation of the Kantian *dictum* is a common one. It arises, however, from an imprecise appreciation for the way in which that dictum is formulated. What the principle actually says is, "Act so that you treat humanity, whether in your own person or in that of another, always as an end and never as a means only."[48] Humanity is an adequate translation for "Menschheit" the word Kant actually uses. Nevertheless, the context makes it clear that what he really has in mind is that aspect of human beings which we would share with any rational being:

> Now, I say, man and, in general, every rational being exists as an end in himself...[49]

Thus a more adequate rendering of the principle would be that we are to treat rational nature, whether in ourselves or in others, as an end in itself. Formulating the principle in this way enables us to see more clearly its connection to the argument from the original position. We treat rational nature in others *and* ourselves as an end in itself when we acknowledge and respect principles which any of us would will from a perspective in which we consider ourselves and our interests as rational choosers.

This, then, is the substance of Rawls' Kantian Interpretation. It is an argument in support of the major elements of the original position from a Kantian perspective. It is an important link, therefore, in the argument to justify the two principles of justice. For if it succeeds, it provides a much stronger basis for the principles of justice than is provided alone by the claim that those principles best systematize our considered judgments about justice. If the principles would be chosen by the parties to the original position, then because of the grounding for that perspective of choice in widely and deeply held Kantian theses about the nature of morality, significant additional support is provided. Of equal importance is the fact that if the Kantian theses regarding the connection between reason and morality can actually be made out, then the theory of justice is embedded in a theory of practical rationality. There is then an answer to the question of what reason there is to be interested in the principles of justice: namely, that the principles would be the object of rational choice from a perspective which is inescapable for rational beings.

This way of putting the matter is actually neutral between Rawls' coherence view of justification and Kant's view that justification must proceed from principles with *a priori* validity. Everywhere a Kantian would speak of something as following from the very nature of morality, Rawls might speak about its support from deeply held beliefs about morality. That proposed principles of justice can be made to cohere in a reflective equilibrium both with particular conceptions of morality and rationality would be an extremely powerful coherentist argument for them.[50] It is a mistake therefore to think that Rawls' Kantian Interpretation is necessarily at odds with his view about justification, however, the Kantian Interpretation provides the hope of grounding the principles on a firmer foundation.

THE NEED FOR A THEORY OF PRIMARY GOODS

We saw above that a notion of goods for rational agents conceived of as such is arguably implicit in Kant's third and fourth examples of the application of the universal law formulation of the Categorical Imperative. In this section I want to argue for a stronger claim: that the universal law formulation of the Categorical Imperative cannot be used to generate a tenable account of right action unless an account of primary goods, of goods for rational agents conceived of as such, is invoked. This is a stronger claim because though Kant utilized a conception of primary goods to derive the duties of virtue (*ends* which are duties) in the *Grundlegung*, he clearly thought that the derivation of duties of justice (duties to perform or forbear specific acts in specific circumstances) in the first and second examples did not depend on any such notion. My aim in this section is to show that a tenable grounding of such latter duties, and thus of an account of right action, in the universal law formulation of the Categorical Imperative depends crucially on an account of goods for rational agents conceived of as such. If this is correct, a theory of primary goods plays an ineliminable role in any tenable Kantian theory of right action.

Consider the universal law formulation. It enjoins us to "Act only according to that maxim by which you can at the same time will that it should become a universal law [law of nature]."[51] This gives us a necessary condition of the moral permissibility of acting on a maxim. It is morally permissible to act on a maxim only if we can will that everyone do so. What precisely is included in a maxim, however? At the very least it will include the intended action together with the conditions on which one's intention to act is dependent.[52] But is this all? Kant sometimes includes the motive out of, or the end for, which the intended act is to be taken. Thus the maxim in the first example includes the motive: "For love of myself, I make it my principle to shorten my life when by a longer duration it threatens more evil than satisfaction."[53] And in the second example, Kant makes it clear that the contemplated end for the sake of which the false promise is to be made is relieving distress.

This is important, because if the reason why one could not will that a maxim be universal law depends essentially on the end or motive one has in acting, then all that can be established is the moral impermissibility of performing a particular act in particular circumstances *for a particular end*, or *out of a particular motive.* Nothing directly follows about whether it would be morally impermissible to act in such circumstances for some other end or out of some other motive. Thus, consider the second example. One reason Kant gives why it is morally impermissible to make a false promise to escape a distressed state is that if everyone were to act on the maxim, that "would make the promise itself and *the end to be accomplished by it* impossible." [54] Not only is this something that Kant relies on, but it seems to have moral force with us. To the extent the argument depends on the end pursued, however, all that is established is the moral impermissibility of making false promises in order to better one's disadvantaged position. It does not follow that it would be wrong to make false promises when one was in distress, if one's end in so acting were something else.

In order for the Categorical Imperative to be able to establish the wrongfulness of performing a particular action in particular circumstances, regardless of motive or end, one would have to establish the impossibility of willing that everyone act on a maxim which does not mention the end or motive, but includes only the intended act and the features of the situation on which the intention to act is conditional. Such a maxim would, in general, have the form: "If in C, do A."

It will be remembered that Kant distinguished between those actions which are such that "their maxim cannot even be thought as a universal law without contradiction" and those that it is "impossible to will that their maxim should be raised to the universality of a law of nature."[55] Let us consider the second sort of case first. How could one show the impossibility of willing that everyone act on a maxim of the form "If in C, do A"? Since there is no mention of the end for the sake of which one is doing A, it is impossible to establish a clash between *that* end and what would be accomplished by everyone's acting on the maxim (as in the false promise case above). Clearly any argument that it would be impossible for one rationally to will that everyone act on a particular maxim will have to appeal to one's ends. Furthermore if the argument is to establish the wrongfulness of *anyone's* doing A in C, it must appeal to ends that anyone would have. Finally, in Kant's argument the fact that everyone's acting on the maxim would lead to the frustration of an end which anyone would have is used to show that it is impossible *rationally to will* that everyone so act; but if so, then it must be the case that the end is one which it would be rational for anyone to have. Thus the derivation of duties from the impossibility of willing that a maxim be universal law depends on an account of ends which it would be rational for agents to have, whatever their other ends, i.e., an account of primary goods. Thus it is that Kant utilizes such an account in the third and fourth examples. For it is precisely these examples which he holds to manifest the impossibility of *willing* that a maxim be universal law.

However, there are also, according to Kant, maxims in which it is impossible even to *conceive* (let alone will) to be universal laws. In such cases we have a direct demonstration of the wrongfulness of doing A in C, and that demonstration does not depend at all on an account of primary goods. Kant regards his first two examples as demonstrations of this sort. Furthermore, he takes the distinction between those cases where we cannot will a maxim to be universal law and those where we cannot even so conceive it to generate another important distinction between duties of virtue and duties of justice. The former are duties to pursue particular ends, and though what they require of us in particular circumstances may sometimes be determinate, more often their requirement is somewhat vague. Duties of justice, however, are tied specifically to the performance or forbearance of specific cacts in specific circumstances. Thus Kant holds that a significant portion of his account of right action does not depend on an account of primary goods in the same way that his account of duties of virtue does.

It seems to me, however, as it has seemed to a number of other writers that the fact that a maxim cannot even be conceived to be a universal law is a moral irrelevancy. There are certainly cases where it is difficult to give coherent sense to the idea of a particular maxim holding as a universal law. For example, Kant argues that we could not even conceive of a world in which the maxim "Whenever I am in distress which may be relieved by making a false promise, I will do so" holds as a universal law. If we grant certain reasonable empirical assumptions about the world, enough people acting on this maxim would lead to such a diminution of moral credit that promising would become impossible. Thus no coherent sense can be given to the idea of the maxim's holding as a universal law. However, this line of reasoning applies equally well in cases where our moral intuitions run exactly contrary. Hegel gives as an example the maxim of helping the poor.[56] Could one conceive the maxim "When I am not neglecting other duties by so doing, I will help the poor" to hold as a universal law? Hegel argues that one cannot, for if enough people act on the maxim there will then be no poor to help. Aiding the poor depends on the existence of the poor in just the same way that false promising depends on the existence of the practice of promising. Surely, however, the impossibility of conceiving the maxim to hold as a universal law does not show that it is morally impermissable to act on the maxim to help the poor. Many similar cases can be imagined: for example, liberating slaves.[57]

Merely demonstrating the impossibility of conceiving a maxim to hold as a universal law is morally irrelevant to whether we ought to act on it. What is important rather, is the nature of what would be threatened by universal compliance with the proposed maxim. Annihilation of promising, of the poor, and of slavery impact rather differently on ends which we may be presumed to have as rational beings. Whatever one's specific ends a social practice for fixing mutual expectations is a valuable asset. The elimination of slavery and of poverty do not threaten rational interests, quite the contrary.

Thus it is difficult to see how the universal law formulation of the Categorical Imperative can be used to ground duties to perform particular actions in particular circumstances without reference to an account of the good for rational agents conceived of as such. This would play the role that the "thin theory of the good" does in Rawls' original position. As with the parties in that position, we may assume that rational agents conceived of as such have a fundamental and overriding interest in flourishing as rational choosers of ends. Kant explicitly says both that all rational beings necessarily conceive of their own rational existence in this way and that the existence of an "objective end" (valid for all rational beings) is both necessary and sufficient to ground genuine categorical imperatives.[58]

THE OBJECTIONS TO RAWLS' KANTIAN INTERPRETATION

Finally we are in a position to consider and assess the various objections which have been leveled at Rawls' claimed Kantian Interpretation. Some writers focusing on the *a priori*, non-contingent character of Kant's notion of categorical imperative and his related idea of autonomy argue that principles chosen from the original position are ineligible as categorical imperatives because that perspective is essentially a *human* perspective. The parties choose in the light of information about themselves as human beings motivated by a desire for primary goods: what one writer has called "universal, trans-historical human wants."[59] A related criticism is that principles chosen in the original position cannot be categorical imperatives because the argument for them depends on *desires* for primary goods. Finally, several writers have argued that any principles chosen in the original position are heteronomous and merely hypothetical imperatives because the parties choose principles based on self-interested considerations. Let us consider these in turn.

The Original Position Is an Essentially Human Perspective

To what degree does the knowledge of the contingencies of human life and a desire for primary goods affect the Kantian grounding for the original position? It is certainly true that in various places Kant makes the strong claim that categorical imperatives must be valid for all rational beings. For example, in a passage frequently quoted by Rawls' critics, Kant says that a categorical imperative "would be one which presented an action as of itself objectively necessary."[60] For Kant, to say that an action is objectively necessary is to say that it is required by an objective principle or practical law.[61] And this latter idea is explicated as a principle "which would serve all rational beings also subjectively as a practical principle if reason had full power over the faculty of desire.[62] Thus, to the extent that the argument from the original position depends on human contingencies it would seem incapable of generating genuine Kantian categorical imperatives in this sense.

The case would be airtight were this all that Kant had to say about categorical imperatives. But as Allen Buchanan has pointed out, Kant's characterization of the hypothetical/categorical distinction is ambiguous.[63] Given the above account of categorical imperatives and Kant's claim that "All imperatives command either hypothetically or categorically,"[64] it would follow that any imperative which was not valid for all rational beings would be merely hypothetical and thus lacking in moral force.[65] But Kant also explicitly characterizes hypothetical imperatives as those which express "...the practical necessity of a possible action as a means to achieving something else one desires (or which one may come to desire)."[66] By contrast, categorical imperatives would be those which do not merely express the practical necessity of action as a means to something desired. An imperative might not be valid for all rational beings as such and still be categorical on this second account.

Kant's own argument for the duty to make the happiness of others our end (the fourth example) makes it a categorical imperative in this second sense though surely not in the first. That argument depends on the contingent assumption that it is likely that there will be situations which will require the help of others in which it will not be to their direct advantage to give help, an assumption remarkably like that of the circumstances of justice.

Kant certainly regarded The Categorical Imperative, which grounds among other specific duties the duty to make the happiness of others our end, as valid for all rational beings. Indeed he says at one point that it is the *only* categorical imperative,[67] a remark which can only be interpreted in this strong way. But that does not rob the moral force of those imperatives which are grounded in it. Adopting a principle because it is seen to be required by the Categorical Imperative makes it categorical in the second sense. Though it may not be a principle valid for all rational beings, neither is it adopted as a means to one's ends. Most importantly, its moral force is assured because adopting it is required by a principle which *is* valid for all rational beings, The Categorical Imperative.[68] It is precisely this status which Rawls claims for principles arrived at in the original position.

It might be complained, however, that if the argument for Rawls' principles depends on the assumption of particular human desires, that must surely put it beyond the pale of any plausible Kantian interpretation. I will deal below with the criticism that principles which depend for their derivation on desires of *any* sort cannot be categorical imperatives. Here I wish to consider the complaint that desires for primary goods are merely "trans-historical human wants" and therefore "merely contingent, particular ends"[69] which are incapable of grounding categorical imperatives.

Let us examine the primary goods to see how closely they are tied, in fact, to the human condition. They include "rights and liberties, opportunities and powers, income and wealth," and the social bases of self-respect (92). Is it not plausible to think that these are goods which would be valued by any rational pursuer of ends? It is difficult to see how they are tied to the pursuit of characteristically human ends and interests in particular. If it is true, as I have argued above, that the primary goods are of value to the parties in virtue of their fundamental interest in flourishing as rational choosers of ends, then it is a mistake to characterize them as "merely contingent ends." This criticism fails to appreciate the role of primary goods in supporting this fundamental interest of any rational agent.

Categorical Imperatives Do Not Depend on Desires

A somewhat more deeply-cutting criticism is the suggestion of Thomas Nagel and Oliver Johnson that any principles chosen in the original position could only be heteronomous and hypothetical simply because they depend on desires for their derivation. Thus Johnson argues that Kant counts as hypothetical any imperatives that "presuppose the desire for some end, whether specific or general."[70]

An imperative might "presuppose" a desire in two very different ways, however. One way, which clearly renders an imperative hypothetical, is if the imperative recommends action or is adopted as a means to something which one desires or might desire. Clearly Rawls' principles of justice are not hypothetical on that account. We are not to adopt them as a means to satisfying our desires.

There is another way in which an imperative might presuppose desires, however. It would do so if the argument grounding the principles were to appeal to a desire in any way at all. In this sense the principles of justice must be said to presuppose desires, but so likewise do the principles which Kant derives in the third and fourth examples. To derive a contradiction in the will in each of these examples Kant must appeal to what one wills as a rational being: the development of one's talents and the resources to pursue one's ends which, given a contingent assumption, includes the good offices of others. Furthermore, if my analysis in Section III is correct, Kant must appeal to such willings systematically. It is true that he would hesitate to use the word which we translate as desire ("Begehren") when referring to such willings, since for him "desire or aversion always involves pleasure or displeasure and the susceptibility to pleasure or displeasure is called feeling."[71] But surely the attribution of a desire for primary goods to the parties involves no such appetite or affection. Rawls means nothing more than that parties have an interest in primary goods born of their fundamental interest in flourishing as rational choosers of ends.

Directly to the point here is Kant's distinction between *subjective* and *objective* ends. The former include those "ends which a rational being arbitarily proposes to himself as consequences of his action" which "are material ends and are without exception relative, for only this relation to a particularly constituted faculty of desire in the subject gives them their worth."[72] Objective ends, by contrast, are ends valid for all rational beings. Just after Kant has made this distinction, he puts forth the view that "every rational being exists as an end in himself."[73] One's existence as a rationally choosing being is not a merely subjective end. Insofar as one wills that, one wills the means indispensable to it: primary goods. Thus the desire for primary goods is not directed at a merely subjective end.

That the arguments to the principles of justice depend on desires, then, does not render the principles ineligible to be categorical imperatives. The desires assumed are constitutive of having an end valid for all rational beings. As Kant's own practice demonstrates this secures, rather than vitiates, the status of the chosen principles as categorical imperatives.

Principles That Depend on Self-interest Cannot Be Autonomous

The final criticism to consider is that the principles chosen from the original position can be neither categorical nor autonomous since the parties are assumed to be self-intereested. In this spirit Robert Paul Wolff argues that

> What Rawls claims is that the "veil of ignorance deprives the persons in the original position of the knowledge that would enable them to choose heteronomous principles" (252), but in fact only guarantees that their principles will be, so to speak, generally heteronomous rather than particularly heteronomous. The choice of principles is motivated by self-interest, rather than by the Idea of the Good.[74]

Oliver Johnson makes the same objection:

> An action originally heteronomous is not rendered autonomous, even though performed under a veil of ignorance, if the nature of its motivation is unchanged.[75]

These writers see the question of whether the principles of justice are autonomous as dependent on the question of whether the parties make an autonomous choice within the original position. Since their choice is self-interested, they do not. Since they do not, the principles they choose cannot be autonomous.

If this line of reasoning were correct it would likewise follow that particular imperatives argued by Kant to be required by the Categorical Imperative cannot be autonomous. Recall the fourth example. We find ourselves rationally incapable of willing that everyone act on the maxim of not helping others when it is not to their advantage to do so since that would conflict with our willing that we have their help when we require it. This latter willing is no less self-interested than the motivation of the parties to the original position. But this does not make the principle of beneficence heteronomous. For if we adopt that principle on account of its being required by the Categorical Imperative, we do not adopt it out of self-interest. Likewise to support the principles of justice because they would be chosen in the original position is not to support them out of self-interest. The *hypothetical* assumption of self-interested motivation comes in to determine what the Categorical Imperative (and its "procedural interpretation," the original position) would require.

The complaint that the parties are assumed to be self-interested is a red herring in any case. Because of the veil of ignorance the original position is not a perspective of self-interest, but rather of an *interest in selves*, or individuals, as such. The assumption of self-interested motivation plays no essential role in this argument. Together with the veil of ignorance it is a convenient device for focusing the concern of the parties on the interests of an individual person, though of no individual in particular. To see this we need only notice that the same principles would be chosen, and the same arguments for them found convincing, were the parties not assumed to be self-interested, but to be completely *other*-interested in the following sense. Suppose the parties to be wholly concerned with the interests of some other person. Because of the veil of ignorance there will be no way to pick out that individual (just as there is no way to pick out oneself). Thus any argument that Rawls gives to persuade the parties that it is in their own interest to choose the two principles will be equally persuasive if the parties are assumed to choose among principles having the interest of some other person exclusively at heart.[76] From the point of view of the original position, *there is no difference* between perfectly egoistic and perfectly individual-other-regarding motivation. What is crucial to the perspective is the idea of a concern for *individual* rational beings, or selves, as such.

It seems that the major objections that have been brought against the Kantian Interpretation can be met. At least this is the case if we interpret Kant's views in the ways I have suggested. It is true that there are places where Kant's enthusiasm for the *a priori* carried him to heights unreachable even by individuals in so ethereal an atmosphere as that of the original position. It is my view, however, that to saddle Kant with such excesses, especially when it is inconsistent with much of what is so profound and so convincing in his moral philosophy, is to do him no favor. It is to consign him to the heap of philosophical curiosities. If I am right this is a mistake and we are indebted to Rawls for showing us a way to make Kant's moral philosophy live for us again.[77]

NOTES

1. Hume's own meta-ethical position is in fact much more complicated than contemporary versions of emotivism. See W.D. Falk, "Hume on Is and Ought," *Canadian Journal of Philosophy*, 6, (1976), 359–78; and "Hume on Practical Reason," Philosophical Studies, 27, (1975), 1–18.
2. Immanuel Kant, *Foundations of the Metaphysics of Morals*, trans. L.W. Beck, (Indianapolis: Bobbs-Merrill Co., Inc., 1959), p. 39. Preussische Akadamie edition, p. 421. Beck's translation as well as many others uses a reference system in which page references to the Preussische Akadamie edition are cited. Further references to this work will cite the Preussische Akadamie numbers which can be found in Beck's translation as well as many others. See R.M. Hare, *Freedom and Reason* (New York: Oxford University Press, 1969), pp. 34f. Hare also emphasizes what he calls the prescriptive character of moral judgments. This has affinities with the Kantian emphasis on what one could *will* to be universal law.
3. Their very titles are suggestive: Stephen Toulmin, *The Place of Reason in Ethics*, (Cambridge: Cambridge University Press, 1950): Kurt Baier, *The Moral Point of View: A Rational Basis for Ethics*, (Ithaca: Cornell University Press, 1958): R.M. Hare, *Freedom and Reason.*
4. Onora Nell, *Acting On Principle* (New York: Columbia University Press, 1975), pp. 14f.

5. Robert Paul Wolff, *In Defense of Anarchism*, (New York: Harper Torchbooks, 1970), pp. 12f.
6. Kant, *Foundations*, Preussische Akadamie, p. 429, quoted in Robert Nozick, *Anarchy, State, and Utopia*, (New York: Basic Books, 1974), p. 32.
7. Wolff, *Defense of Anarchism*, p. 13.
8. Nozick, *Anarchy*, pp. 48f.
9. See also "Response to Rawls from the Political Right," by Alan Goldman in Chapter III of this volume.
10. Immanuel Kant, *The Metaphysical Elements of Justice*, trans. John Ladd, (Indianapolis: Bobbs-Merrill Co., Inc., 1965), p. 24, Preussische Akadamie, p. 223.
11. Kant, *Foundations*, Preussische Akadamie, p. 432.
12. *Ibid.*, p. 401.
13. See William Frankena, Ethics, (Englewood Cliffs, N.J.: Prentice-Hall, 1963), p. 13.
14. Immanuel Kant, *The Critique of Practical Reason*, trans. L.W. Beck, (Indianapolis: Bobbs-Merrill Co., Inc., 1956), p. 18, Preussische Akadamie, p. 20. Compare Kant's characterization of autonomy as "the property of the will to be a law to itself," Preussische Akadamie, p. 447.
15. Kant, *Foundations*, Preussische Akadamie, p. 389.
16. *Ibid.*, p. 414.
17. *Ibid.*
18. Kant, *Practical Reason*, Preussische Akadamie, p. 21.
19. See Kant, *Foundations*, Preussische Akadamie, p. 412: "...will is nothing else than practical reason."
20. *Ibid.*, p. 447.
21. *Ibid.*, p. 400n.
22. As it stands this argument is much too sketchy. Most importantly, it is unclear that what one would will *qua* rational being is to be identified with what principles one would choose *qua* rational being, as principles of justice.
23. Kant, *Foundations*, Preussische Akadamie, p. 438.
24. *Ibid.*, emphasis added.
25. *Ibid.*, p. 433.
26. I use this term as a shorthand to refer to what it is the parties would know about their desires and interests but for the veil of ignorance.
27. John Rawls, "Reply to Alexander and Musgrave," *Quarterly Journal of Economics*, 88, (1974), 641. This same idea is expressed in "Fairness to Goodness," *Philosophical Review*, 84, (1975), 553; and "A Kantian Conception of Equality," *Cambridge Review*, (1975), p. 94. T.M. Scanlon has emphasized this aspect of Rawls' notion of the person in "Rawls' Theory of Justice," in *Reading Rawls*, ed. Norman Daniels, (New York: Basic Books, 1974), p. 178. Allen Buchanan has demonstrated its role in the argument for the priority of liberty and as an underpinning for the theory of primary goods. He also argues for its basis in any adequate conception of practical

rationality: "Revisability and Rational Choice," *Canadian Journal of Philosophy*, 5, (1975), 395-408.

28. Rawls, "A Kantian Conception of Equality," p. 97.
29. Rawls, "Reply to Alexander and Musgrave," pp. 642-643.
30. Kant, *Foundations*, Preussische Akadamie, p. 429, (translating 'Menschheit' as rational nature).
31. Rawls, "A Kantian Conception of Equality," p. 99.
32. Kant, *Foundations*, Preussische Akadamie, p. 423.
33. *Ibid.*
34. See J.C. Harsanyi, *Essays on Ethics, Social Behavior, and Scientific Explanation*, Dordrecht: D. Reidel, 1976), pp. 37-63.
35. Rawls tends to conflate self-esteem and self-respect in *A Theory of Justice* though he distinguishes them in "A Kantian Conception of Equality," p. 97. For some general points about respect and self-respect see my "Two Kinds of Respect," Ethics, 88, (1977), 36-49.
36. Rawls, "Reply to Alexander and Musgrave," p. 641.
37. For a different account of these conditions, see "The Original Position and Veil of Ignorance," by Louis Katzner in Chapter I of this volume.
38. See *Kant's Political Writings*, ed. Hans Reiss, (Chicago: Chicago University Press, 1970), pp. 125-170; and the *Rechtslehre*, Preussische Akadamie, p. 311.
39. John Rawls, "The Basic Structure as Subject," *American Philosophical Quarterly*, 14, (1977), 159.
40. Rawls, "Basic Structure," p. 159.
41. *Ibid.*, p. 160.
42. Kant, *Rechtslehre*, Preussische Akadamie, p. 314.
43. *Ibid.*
44. Kant, "On the Common Saying: This May Be True in Theory but it Does Not Apply in Practice," *Kant's Political Writings*, p. 78.
45. Kant, *Rechtslehre*, Preussische Akadamie, p. 315.
46. Kant, "On the Common Saying," p. 75.
47. Nozick, *Anarchy*, p. 31.
48. Kant, *Foundations*, Preussische Akadamie, p. 429.
49. *Ibid.*, p. 428.
50. See *A Theory of Justice*, p. 41, where Rawls speaks of different kinds of reflective equilibrium.
51. Kant, *Foundations*, Preussische Akadamie, p. 421.
52. This formulation raises deep problems. Dependent how? On any condition which is causally relevant? On any condition which one takes to be a consideration? Neither alternative is unproblematic, but space does not permit an examination of this problem.
53. Kant, *Foundations*, Preussische Akadamie, p. 422.
54. *Ibid.*, emphasis added.
55. *Ibid.*, p. 424.

56. Referred to in Walter Kaufman, *Hegel*, (Garden City, N.Y.: Doubleday & Co., 1965), p. 103.
57. It could be objected that there is really no difficulty in any of these cases in imagining the respective maxim to hold as universal law. This would be true in the sense that we could imagine each of these maxims to be among the stock of everyone's practical principles and that whenever the occasion for acting on them arose, (i.e., whenever the antecedent of the maxim was satisfied) people would act on them. The problem is just that the occasion never arises. For example, one just never is in a position to relieve distress by making the false promise if promising is impossible.

    Onora Nell has presented a way of understanding Kant's "contradiction in thought" which gets around this problem (See Nell, *Acting on Principle*, pp. 59f). She reads Kant as requiring that one be able simultaneously to will *the action*, on the proposed maxim, and to will that everyone act on the maxim. By willing that everyone act on the maxim of false promising one makes impossible the willing of the specific false promise that one intended to make. Thus Kant: "it would make the promise itself... impossible," *Foundations*, Preussische Akadamie, p. 422. Evidently this way of understanding Kant still makes him subject to the objection raised in the text.
58. Kant, *Foundations*, Preussische Akadamie, pp. 428-9.
59. Andrew Levine, "Rawls' Kantianism," *Social Theory and Practice*, 3, (1974), 51. See also Robert Paul Wolff, Understanding Rawls, (Princeton, N.J.: Princeton University Press, 1977), pp. 114-5.
60. Kant, *Foundations*, Preussische Akadamie, p. 414.
61. *Ibid.*, p. 413.
62. *Ibid.*, p. 400n.
63. See Allen Buchanan, "Categorical Imperatives and Moral Principles," *Philosophical Studies*, 31, (1977), 249-60. The analysis of the succeeding few paragraphs owes much to Buchanan's paper. Many of the same points are made independently in R.F. Atkinson, "Categorical Imperatives," *Aristotelian Society* supplementary volume 51, (1977), 1-19. The basic distinction between The Categorical Imperative and particular substantive categorical imperatives is noted in C.D. Broad, *Five Types of Ethical Theory* (Totawa, N.J.: Littlefield, Adams and Co., 1965), pp. 120f; H.J. Paton, *The Categorical Imperative*, (New York: Harper & Row, 1967); and other writers.
64. Kant, *Foundations*, Preussische Akadamie, p. 414.
65. *Ibid.*, p. 419f.
66. *Ibid.*, p. 414.
67. *Ibid.*, p. 421. See also *Ibid.*, p. 436 where the other formulations of the Categorical Imperative are said to be "only so many formulas of the very same law."
68. This is what distinguishes such imperatives from others, for example those of etiquette, which though on the second rendering of the categorical/hypothetical distinction would have to be judged categorical might still lack moral force. See Philippa Foot, "Morality as a System of Hypothetical Imperatives," *Philosophical Review*, 81, (1972), 305-16.

69. Andrew Levine, "Rawls' Kantianism," p. 51.
70. Oliver Johnson, "The Kantian Interpretation," Ethics, 85, (1974), pp. 53-66; Thomas Nagel, "Rawls on Justice," in *Reading Rawls*, ed. Norman Daniels, p. 4n. See also Stephen L. Darwall, "A Defense of the Kantian Interpretation," *Ethics*, 86, (1976), pp. 164-70; and Oliver Johnson, "Autonomy in Kant and Rawls: A Reply," Ethics, 87, (1977), 251-54.
71. Kant, *Elements*, Preussische Akadamie, p. 211.
72. Kant, *Foundations*, Preussische Akadamie, p. 427.
73. *Ibid.*, p. 428.
74. Wolff, *Understanding Rawls*, p. 155.
75. Johnson, "The Kantian Interpretation," p. 62.
76. For this point I am indebted to Terry R. Moore and to Arthur Kuflik.
77. For many conversations on Kant and Rawls over the years, I am very much indebted to Arthur Kuflik and to Allen Buchanan. Kuflik provided the original impetus to both Buchanan and myself to think along Kantian lines in understanding Rawls. Buchanan developed many of the details of the Kantian Interpretation in his dissertation, "Autonomy, Distribution, and the State," (Ph.D. diss., University of North Carolina, 1975).

Rawls and Utilitarianism

Holly Smith Goldman
UNIVERSITY OF ILLINOIS
AT CHICAGO CIRCLE

One of the major polemical concerns of John Rawls' *A Theory of Justice*—perhaps *the* major polemical concern—is to provide a satisfactory alternative to the utilitarian account of social justice (15, 22, 166; all parenthetical citations are to John Rawls' *A Theory of Justice* (Cambridge, Mass.: Harvard University Press, 1971)).

In its most general form, utilitarianism is the theory that objects of moral appraisal, such as actions, social institutions, moral codes, or traits of character, can be evaluated strictly in terms of their impact on general human welfare. If an action (or institution, code, etc.) has better consequences for human welfare than those of its rivals, then it is morally acceptable; otherwise, it must be rejected. Utilitarian thought, which flowered in the writings of the classical utilitarians, Jeremy Bentham, John Stuart Mill, and Henry Sidgwick, has been the dominant conception in Anglo-American moral and social philosophy for roughly the past two centuries.[1]

The appeal of utilitarianism is clearcut. First and most important, it identifies effects on human welfare as *the* criterion to use in assessing social phenomena. It is impossible to deny that human welfare is relevant to such assessments, and it is difficult at least initially to imagine that anything else could possibly be relevant. Second, utilitarianism presents us with a *single rule* which covers all decision-making. This is one of its major advantages over what Rawls terms "intuitionistic theories," theories which present us with a plurality of rules to use in making decisions, but which typically fail to guide us in balancing the importance of these rules when they conflict (51). Thus one such theory tells us both to do good and also to treat people equally, but it does not tell us what to do when, for example, treating people equally would produce less good than treating them unequally.[2] Utilitarianism, which employs only one criterion, can never be faced with such a problem. Finally, utilitarianism promises to provide us with a *precise formula* for making decisions, one which resolves every dilemma by a process of calculating the effect on human welfare which is relatively invulnerable to the whims and biases of all-too-human decision-makers. Here again, intuitionist theories fall short, for their application typically relies on decision-makers' intuitions about the weights to be assigned the various conflicting considerations, intuitions whose moral basis is uncertain, and which are likely to be distorted by personal interest in the case.

For these kinds of reasons, utilitarianism has seemed to many to be the only serious contender in our search for an adequate moral theory. Nevertheless severe criticisms have been brought repeatedly against utilitarianism in its turn. In the resulting stand-off, Rawls' theory appeared in 1971 as a long-awaited alternative which managed to avoid the defects of both utilitarian and previous intuitionistic views. Despite the criticism which Rawls' book has attracted, many critics agree with A.M. MacLeod in holding that one of its prime merits is that it "succeeds brilliantly in displaying the inadequacy of a utilitarian theory of justice."[3] In this article I will attempt to assess the truth of this claim, by summarizing Rawls' main arguments in *A Theory of Justice* against utilitarianism, and then exploring and evaluating the responses which may be made in defense of utilitarianism. Since many of Rawls' arguments involve comparing his principles of justice with utilitarianism, of necessity much of the following discussion will have the same character. I will assume that the reader is familiar with the general structure of Rawls' theory and the argument for it.

EVALUATION OF RAWLS' EXTRA-CONTRACTARIAN ARGUMENTS

The Contrast

Since Rawls' theory of justice and utilitarianism are viewed as *rival* theories, we must first be clear on what the character of the two rivals is. This is problematic on both sides. Rawls' theory is a general theory of social justice which includes not simply principles of justice, but also an elaborate edifice supporting those principles, an edifice which has no counterpart in utilitarianism proper. Utilitarianism, on the other hand, appears in many forms, and we must narrow the focus of inquiry down to the one which is the most clearcut rival to Rawls' system. This is consonant with Rawls' own practice, since his discussion focuses on one version of utilitarianism which he takes as representative of the best utilitarian thinking, even though he states that his theory represents an alternative to utilitarian thought generally (22).

Strictly speaking, utilitarianism is a normative theory: a theory to be used in evaluating human phenomena and deciding among them. This theory may be, and has been, argued for in many different ways. For example, some have argued that utilitarianism provides the best explanation of our common moral beliefs, others have argued that "right" simply *means* "conducive to the greatest good," while others have argued that utilitarianism provides us with a rational decision procedure which is better than any alternative. We may call such arguments "meta-ethical" justifications for a normative theory. The major *normative* components in Rawls' theory are his principles of social justice. Thus it is these which are to be compared with utilitarianism. Other salient aspects of the theory—the argument from reflective equilibrium, the idea of an original position, the derivation of principles of justice from an original position—are to be viewed as primarily meta-ethical devices used in arguing for these principles. Thus these aspects are not necessarily in contention between utilitarianism and Rawls' theory of justice, since potentially they may be, as Rawls himself notes, used to argue for utilitarian principles rather than the ones Rawls proposes (121).

Rawls takes the subject of principles of justice to be what he calls the "basic structure of society," that is, the ways in which the major social institutions distribute fundamental rights and duties, and determine the division of advantages from social cooperation. Major social institutions are such things as the political constitution, and the principal economic and social arrangements (7). On his view, principles used in assessing this basic structure must satisfy what he calls the "formal constraints on right"—conditions such as universality and publicity. Since he concedes that utilitarianism can meet these requirements, we need not investigate them in more detail (130–131; but see discussion in "The Strains of Commitment: Psychological Stability" below).

Rawls proposes two different conceptions of social justice which he calls the "general" and the "special" conceptions of justice. The general conception is the more basic one and is expressed as follows:

> All social primary goods—liberty and opportunity, income and wealth, and the bases of self-respect—are to be distributed equally unless an unequal distribution of any or all of these goods is to the advantage of the least favored. (303)

This conception of justice applies when the social wealth is low enough that the basic liberties cannot be effectively established or exercised for all citizens (152, 542–543). As the level of civilization improves, a special case of this conception comes into play, the famous two principles of justice which comprise Rawls' "special conception." For our purposes, the following will serve as a statement of these principles:

> First: each person is to have an equal right to the most extensive basic liberty compatible with a similar liberty for others (60).
>
> Second: social and economic inequalities are to be arranged so that they are both (a) to the greatest benefit of the least advantaged and (b) attached to offices and positions open to all under conditions of fair equality of opportunity.[4] (83)

As is well-known, the two principles of the special conception are "lexically ordered," so that society concerns itself first with satisfying the first principle, and only then with satisfying the second.

We now have an account of Rawls' two conceptions of justice which form his side of the contrast. Let us turn to the utilitarian side. As noted above, the utilitarian criterion may be applied to many different objects of moral appraisal. In this century it has perhaps been most common to view it as a principle for appraising the individual acts of human agents. This version of utilitarianism contrasts with what Rawls terms the system of natural duties and obligations for individuals (333–335). But what we are interested in here is the version of utilitarianism which applies, as Rawls' principles of justice do, to the basic structure of society. Such a version states that the basic structure is just if and only if its consequences for human welfare are at least as good as those of any alternative structure.[5]

This statement leaves two important questions open. In assessing the consequences of a social system for human welfare, do we consider the *total* human welfare, or the *average* human welfare? Classical utilitarianism concentrated on total welfare, and indeed it makes no difference which is chosen in cases where changes in population size are not an issue. But if total population can be increased in such a way that total welfare increases, even though the average welfare falls, then the classical view advocates increasing the population, whereas the average view does not. Rawls concurs with the utilitarians who have taken the average view on this problem to be more satisfactory, and therefore takes the average view as the rival to which his principles of justice are to be compared (161–164).[6] Although there are problems with the average view, for the sake of argument, I shall do the same.

The second question to be addressed is how the notion of "human welfare" is to be interpreted. In the history of utilitarianism, many accounts have been given, the predominant ones identifying human welfare with happiness, pleasure, or the satisfaction of desire. Rawls addresses himself to a form of utilitarianism which defines the good as the satisfaction of desire, or more accurately the satisfaction of rational desire (25). A desire is satisfied when the state of affairs desired obtains, whether or not the person desiring it is aware that it obtains. The notion of "rational" desire has received many interpretations; for our purposes, we can say that a desire is rational just in case it is based on true beliefs concerning the matter at issue.[7]

One of the greatest contributions of Rawls' book is his development of the theory of the good, but he states that the main idea is that "a person's good is determined by what is for him the most rational long-term plan of life given reasonably favorable circumstances.... To put it briefly, the good is the satisfaction of rational desire" (92–93). Thus the theory of the good is "not in dispute between the contract doctrine and utilitarianism" (92). What is in dispute is the relation between justice and the good. Our concern then is the contrast between Rawls' general and special conceptions of justice on the one hand, and on the other hand, a version of utilitarianism which states that the basic structure of society is just if and only if the average satisfaction of rational desire which it produces is at least as great as that which would be produced by any alternative structure.[8]

The First Extra-Contractarian Argument: Reflective Equilibrium

Let us now turn to the arguments by which Rawls attempts to show that this version of utilitarianism is inferior to his own principles of justice. These arguments can be divided into two categories. Some are designed to show that utilitarianism is inadequate without invoking all of Rawls' contractarian apparatus, that is, the original position, the veil of ignorance, and so forth. I shall call these arguments "extra-contractarian" arguments. Others are designed to show that parties to the original contract would not adopt utilitarianism by preference to Rawls' principles of justice. I shall call these the "contractarian" arguments. In some cases, an argument may fall into both of these categories, or it may not be clear which category it is intended to fit. In such cases I shall classify the argument for expositional convenience. The remainder of this section will be concerned with four major extra-contractarian arguments: (i) the argument that utilitarianism generates prescriptions which violate our considered moral judgments concerning what is just and unjust; (ii) the argument that the reasoning in favor of utilitarianism illegitimately "merges persons"; (iii) the argument that utilitarianism requires us to make interpersonal comparisons of utility, or welfare, which have no scientific basis; and (iv) the argument that utilitarianism prescribes the satisfaction of desires which themselves are the product of possibly unjust institutions. Only the second of these arguments is novel, but for many readers, Rawls has given them a statement which is especially forceful and illuminating.

This section will be devoted to a consideration of the first of these extra-contractarian arguments. Let us note initially that Rawls must regard it as one of the most fundamental available to him, for one of the major justifications (perhaps *the* major justification) he offers for the entire contractarian apparatus he describes is the fact that it generates principles and prescriptions for individual cases which are in "reflective equilibrium" with our considered judgments about what is just and what is not. The final court of appeal is to these judgments, or "intuitions," and a showing that utilitarianism violates them would provide Rawls with what he views as the definitive argument against it. Since the contractarian apparatus is designed precisely to ensure that principles which are in reflective equilibrium are chosen by the parties in the original position, any arguments against utilitarianism derived from that apparatus are logically secondary to the extra-contractarian arguments, and specifically to the first of them (19–21; § 9, § 87).[9]

In arguing that utilitarianism generates prescriptions which violate our considered judgments on justice, Rawls advances two related claims. Both arise from the fact that utilitarianism is fundamentally unconcerned with how welfare, or the satisfaction of desires, is distributed over the population. First, he claims that utilitarianism requires some individuals to suffer lesser life prospects simply so that others may enjoy a greater sum of advantages (4, 14, 26, 177–178, 180). Second, he claims, as a special case of greater concern, that utilitarianism requires that the liberties of some be sacrificed for the sake of greater goods for others (3–4, 26, 176). Thus it has sometimes been held that utilitarianism could justify either slavery or serfdom, or other serious infractions of liberty, for the sake of greater social benefits (156).[10] According to Rawls, our considered judgments of justice reject such social systems: "[according to] our intuitive conviction...[e]ach person possesses an inviolability founded on justice that even the welfare of society as a whole cannot override. For this reason justice denies that the loss of freedom for some is made right by a greater good shared by others. It does not allow that the sacrifices imposed on a few are outweighed by the larger sum of advantages enjoyed by many" (3–4; also 27–28). It may appear that Rawls' theory cannot condone such inequalities, for the first principle of the special conception of justice prohibits liberties from being traded for any gain in other social goods, and part (a) of the second principle, called the "Difference Principle," only allows inequalities in economic goods when they benefit the least well-off, not merely when they maximize the average welfare. Rawls claims in fact that such inequalities must benefit *everyone* (80, 102–104, 178–179).

What response can the defender of utilitarianism make to this argument? The first thing he may do is challenge the premise that our considered moral judgments provide a relevant criterion for assessing the adequacy of a normative theory. Rawls takes it that our considered moral judgments are the "class of facts against which conjectured principles can be checked" (51), because he is attempting to provide a "theory of the moral sentiments...setting out the principles governing...our sense of justice" (51). But the utilitarian (or any other moral theorist) may feel that *he* is trying to establish the true, or correct, principles of justice, not simply characterize or systematize the judgments we currently make. And he may feel that our actual moral sentiments are no test of truth, since they are likely to "derive from discarded religious systems, from warped views of sex and bodily functions, or from customs necessary for the survival of the group in social and economic circumstances which now lie in the distant past."[11] Thus he may choose to ignore the pronouncements of common sense.

Other utilitarians have taken a slightly different attitude towards our reflective moral judgments. On their view, our judgments do not express discarded religious systems or outmoded empirical beliefs. Rather they are based on a moral code whose currency *under our social conditions* tends to promote human welfare. Thus even though our judgments may appear nonutilitarian in character, in fact they typically accord with what the principle of utility would recommend. And it is *this* fact which makes them a valid test of truth. Now, it is frequently argued, with some plausibility, that the principle of utility only allows grave infractions of personal liberty in social conditions which are significantly different from our own.[12] Our code deems such infractions to be unjust. However, there is no reason to suppose that the currency of our code in social conditions significantly different from our own would promote human welfare. Thus it is invalid to apply our code to social circumstances unlike ours. We feel that slavery is always unjust, but our feeling is conditiond by our own circumstances, which may not be replicated elsewhere. Where slavery would promote human welfare, it must be recognized as permissible, even though *we* feel, on the basis of our code, that it is wrong. Once again, inconsistency with reflective moral judgments is rejected as irrelevant.[13]

To resolve the issue of whether or not considered moral judgments form a test for the adequacy of any moral theory would require us to provide a complete account of how moral theories are to be justified, a matter beyond the scope of this paper. We must leave the problem here, therefore, with only the preceding sketch of the arguments which may be made on either side.[14]

Let us turn to the substance of the argument, the claim that the precepts of utilitarianism and those of reflective morality do differ in at least some cases. According to Rawls, we intuitively feel that it is unjust to impose sacrifices on a few in order to gain a larger sum of advantages for others (3–4). He states that utilitarianism violates this precept (178). It is not completely clear how we are to interpret this objection. Rawls may have in mind here the classic complaint against utilitarianism that it is *non-egalitarian*, i.e., that it justifies any distribution of goods as long as it maximizes average utility, however unequal that distribution may be. Thus imagine a society which must choose between two arrangements, in the first of which the worst-off persons receive an annual income of five hundred dollars while the best-off persons receive five million, and in the second of which the worst-off persons receive five thousand while the best-off persons receive fifty thousand. If the first of these arrangements would maximize average utility, then utilitarianism prescribes it even though it involves far greater disparity between economic classes than the second. Many of us would find the first arrangement the less just and so would disagree with utilitarianism's recommendation.

Many utilitarians have felt they have an adequate response to this charge. They concede that it is *logically* possible for a society to confront the choice just described. However, they claim that the facts of human psychology make it *empirically* impossible for the first arrangement to be the one which maximizes average utility. They argue, for example, that human beings have similar utility functions for goods such as income, utility functions which satisfy the conditions of diminishing marginal utility (see Rawls' discussion, 159). Thus a hundred dollars taken away from someone who has five million will produce greater utility when given to someone who only has five hundred. In light of this, utilitarians have argued that under conditions as we know them, utilitarianism would not produce radically unequal distributions of goods or utility.

Rawls is quite prepared to reject arguments against utilitarianism which claim that it generates unacceptable prescriptions for *merely* logically possible conditions. He states that he is not interested in what he calls the "ethics of creation," but only in determining what ethical theories are appropriate for the natural and human world as we know it (159–160). Indeed he defends his own theory against certain objections by pointing out that those objections involve applying his theory to abstract, but empirically unrealistic, possibilities (157–159). Thus he must argue against utilitarianism that it generates unacceptably non-egalitarian results under realistic conditions. But his statements on this score are surprisingly ambivalent. Sometimes he says that utilitarianism may "demand that some should forego advantages for the sake of the greater good of the whole" (177). But at other points he seems to concede the utilitarian response: "...there is no reason in principle why the greater gains of some should not compensate for the lesser losses of others....It simply happens that under most conditions, at least in a reasonably advanced state of civilization, the greatest sum of advantages is not attained in this way" (26). Rawls' ambivalence is understandable here since no one really knows enough about the relevant empirical facts to be sure what utilitarianism implies for our world.

However, we can point out that Rawls himself makes empirical assumptions which would be sufficient to show that utilitarianism probably mandates strongly egalitarian distributions. In arguing that the parties in the original position would employ a maximin strategy in choosing their principle of justice, he assumes that there is a satisfaction threshold beyond which goods such as income have a sharply declining marginal utility, and also that there is a toleration point below which amounts of such goods would be intolerable (see "The Second Feature" and "The Third Feature" below). But if these conditions hold, it is extremely likely that average utility would be maximized by allocating to each person an amount of these goods which falls between these two points. Any amount of goods less than the toleration level would produce such severe disutility that it could only be counterbalanced by huge numbers of persons above that level; while amounts of goods greater than those at the satisfaction point would have to be possessed by huge numbers of people in order to counterbalance any amount below that level experienced by others. Neither of these possible patterns of distribution is likely to be one which realistically would be faced by a society. Since Rawls also assumes that the satiation point could be guaranteed to every member of society under Rawlsian justice, it seems unlikely that the difference between that point and the tolerance level can be too large. Thus utilitarian distribution, while it may not be precisely egalitarian, should not involve too glaring disparities between the rich and the poor—at least on Rawls' own empirical assumptions. Given Rawls' reluctance to criticize theories of justice for their applications in unrealistic conditions, and given the empirical assumptions he makes in arguing for his own theory, he himself is not in a strong position to press the objection that utilitarianism leads to radically non-egalitarian distributions in realistic cases. Neither are we in a position to accurately assess the matter until we have more empirical information and in particular some account of how utility is to be measured, a problem which has long hamstrung utilitarian theory. The egalitarian or non-egalitarian tendencies of utilitarian theory must remain a matter of conjecture only.

Rawls' language in his statements that utilitarianism violates common morality suggests that he may have something slightly different in mind than the objection we have examined so far. As we have seen, he repeatedly asserts that utilitarianism requires "sacrifices" from a few in order to gain a larger sum of advantages for others. Let us consider what might be meant by this. Normally, when a person sacrifices something, he voluntarily gives it up. Clearly, however, Rawls does not envision voluntary sacrifices but rather something like the *imposition*, through institutions like the taxation and welfare systems, of lesser prospects for some than they might have enjoyed, so that others are assured of better prospects than they might have endured.[15] But what are we to use as the standard of reference, the situation these individuals might have enjoyed or endured, relative to which their sacrifice or benefit is measured? One possibility is that we should use as this standard of reference the situation that *would have obtained* if the present social system had not been in force. Thus to ascertain whether or not some members of a utilitarian society are making sacrifices, we must ask what their expectations would have been under the principle of justice which would have prevailed if utilitarianism had not. But this is a useless question: in any concrete situation, it would probably be impossible to know what system would have prevailed instead of utilitarianism. Insofar as we have any grasp on the issue, what seems to be true is that utilitarianism and Rawls' principles are on an equal footing here. That is, in most utilitarian societies, there will be some members who would have done better under the form of justice which would have prevailed if utilitarianism had not. But the parallel statement is true of most Rawlsian societies. By this criterion, utilitarianism fares no worse than Rawls' own principles —and probably no worse than any other plausible theory of justice, either.

However, this standard for measuring sacrifice is probably mistaken. When we believe someone has been sacrificed, we mean, not that he is worse off than he would have been in the situation that would have obtained if the present social system had not been in force, but rather that he is worse off than he would have been had the *correct* system of minimal justice or morality prevailed. Thus, when stolen goods are taken from a thief and restored to their rightful owner, we do not say that the thief's interests have been sacrificed for those of the owner—even though, had the present social system not been in force, the thief would have retained possession. A thief is required by minimal justice or morality to return whatever he has taken, so that his doing so, or being forced to do so, is not seen as an occasion of sacrifice.

By this standard, the question for Rawls is whether or not reflective morality would view the arrangements dictated by utilitarianism as requiring transfers or allocations of goods beyond those required by minimal justice. Quite conceivably this is so. (It should be kept in mind here however that many of the "sacrifices" it is traditionally alleged utilitarianism would require involve only one or two "victims." What may have positive utility when done, perhaps in secret, to one individual is far less likely to have the same utility when institutionalized in the basic structure of society.) However, it appears that reflective morality would also view *Rawls'* principles as calling for sacrifices. In defending his principles on this score, Rawls emphasizes the fact that those in the worst-off position in society are nevertheless in the best position they could hope for, and hence cannot be viewed as making sacrifices. However, this defense is inadequate. First, while it may be true that the worst-off class is better off than the *analogous* worst-off class in any alternative society, it is *not* true that any given individual who is a member of this class is *himself* as well off as he might be under some different organization of society. Typically, for every individual, there will be some alternative society in which he would have done better. Moreover even the worst-off class itself, identified as Rawls suggests—e.g., as "unskilled workers" (98) —might well do better under a different organization. Since we are not yet at the point in Rawls' argument where the veil of ignorance can be introduced as a device to prevent individuals from being concerned with their personal fates, Rawls' focus here on the respective worst-off classes under different social arrangements is premature.

Second, whatever we conclude about the sacrifices suffered by those in the worst-off class, it is certainly not true of those in better-off positions that they are in the best possible position under Rawlsian justice as opposed to some alternative, for his conception of justice only allows them to better their positions when doing so is not to the detriment of those below them. If improved wages for them do not act to stimulate the economy and so indirectly to benefit those lower down, then transfers of income through welfare payments are called for which will directly benefit those on the bottom (§ 43). The question is whether or not reflective morality regards such transfers as *sacrifices* on the part of the better-off, perhaps sacrifices which generosity or benevolence recommends but which justice does not require. There is ample evidence that such transfers are precisely so regarded by many who are presently required to make them: the current American "taxpayers' revolt" is at least partly fueled by this feeling. Of course, it is unknown to what extent such a feeling is "reflective," in Rawls' sense, much less "philosophically reflective" (§ 9). Still, the force of the sentiment should make us suspect that

Rawls' principles, as well as utilitarianism, would be seen as requiring sacrifices. Thus in comparing utilitarianism and Rawls' principles on the issue of sacrifices, we must ask which theory would be found by common opinion to require the *more objectionable* sacrifices. Presumably Rawls believes his theory does better in this regard. But until we know more surely what current moral feeling holds as the minimal standard of morality, and what precise distributions utilitarianism requires, it appears that we had better leave the issue unresolved without attempting to declare either conception of justice the clear winner in this matter.

Let us look at the much narrower claim to which Rawls devotes the greater part of his attention, namely the contention that utilitarianism may require unacceptable sacrifices of *liberty.* In an earlier work, Rawls maintained that "ordinary conception of justice... [holds] that slavery is always wrong."[16] This is probably incorrect, but let us grant for the sake of argument that this is true. It is also undoubtedly true that utilitarianism condones the institution of slavery under some imaginable conditions, perhaps conditions in which slavery is more humane and less exploitative than the forms with which we are familiar.[17] (Note that our condemnation of slavery becomes less and less certain as its form becomes more humane, and as it becomes more likely that utilitarianism would allow it.) Thus utilitarianism and common morality (we shall say for the sake of argument) do conflict. But this fact in itself is not enough to show the superiority of Rawls' principles of justice, for they too permit slavery and serfdom under some circumstances. The illusion that they absolutely prohibit these forms of servitude is encouraged by Rawls' practice of speaking as though we need only compare utilitarianism with his *special* conception of justice, that is, the well-known two principles. These principles do indeed appear to bar slavery because they do not allow liberties to be traded for economic goods.[18] However, the proper comparison is between utilitarianism on the one hand and Rawls' special *and* general conceptions of justice on the other. And the *general* conception of justice, which permits liberties to be traded for other social values, would allow slavery in a case where the slaves were better off overall under slavery than they would be if all social values were distributed equally. Such a case might arise when a harsh natural environment and low degree of capital development make it impossible to sustain everyone unless some submit to a condition of servitude, or when the necessity of repelling powerful external enemies makes it necessary to organize the state on a militaristic basis. Thus Rawls' system of justice—taken in its entirety—violates the common moral stricture against slavery and serfdom just as utilitarianism does.

The question we must pose then is whether or not utilitarianism violates this stricture in some more objectionable fashion than Rawls' principles do, for example by allowing slavery in circumstances where the special conception of justice is in force and would prohibit slavery and serfdom. At this juncture of the debate, several critics have claimed that utilitarianism would bar slavery and serfdom in all the same circumstances that mandate the application of Rawls' special conception of justice, and hence that there is nothing to choose between utilitarianism and the special conception on these grounds.[19] Their argument proceeds as follows. Rawls claims that the special conception of justice would come into force when the advancing level of civilization makes the effective exercise of basic liberties possible, and so gives them such value to each individual citizen that he would be unwilling to accept a lesser liberty in trade for any increase, however great, of other goods such as income and wealth. Under these circumstances it is in the best interests of each to have in force a principle of justice, such as Rawls' special conception, which accords absolute priority to justice.

> Now the basis for the priority of liberty is roughly as follows: as the conditions of civilization improve, the marginal significance for our good of further economic and social advantages diminishes relative to the interests of liberty, which become stronger as the conditions for the exercise of the equal freedoms are more fully realized. Beyond some point it becomes and then remains irrational from the standpoint of the original position to acknowledge a lesser liberty for the sake of greater material means and amenities of office.... To be sure, it is not the case that when the priority of liberty holds, all material wants are satisfied. Rather these desires are not so compelling as to make it rational for the persons in the original position to agree to satisfy them by accepting a less than equal freedom. (542-543).

Thus Rawls makes the empirical assumption that at a certain point in economic development, each individual places such a high relative value on liberty that he finds no increase in his material wealth to be worth the amount of liberty he would have to give up in order to secure that increase. But this is an assumption about individuals' *utility* functions for the various goods: the satisfaction they would derive from economic and social goods is infinitesimal compared to what they would derive from liberty. We may infer that Rawls also assumes that the value of liberty for one individual is not infinitesimal compared to the value of liberty for another. If these assumptions are correct, then utilitarianism would require giving each individual the maximum amount of liberty compatible with no reduction in the amounts of liberty assigned to other citizens. Among the states which accomplish this goal, it would then select the one which maximizes average satisfaction over economic goods. But it would not trade liberties for economic goods.[20] Thus, in the circumstances envisioned, *neither* Rawls' special conception *nor* utilitarianism would allow some to be enslaved that others might enjoy greater economic advantages.

This leaves the possibility that under social circumstances where the special conception would come into play it might maximize average utility for society to reduce one person's (or group's) liberties in order to increase the *liberties* of others. However, in Rawls' more elaborate statement of his special conception, he also allows liberties to be unequal if the inequality is acceptable to the person who bears the lesser liberty (250, 302). Presumably this would occur when the least well-off person, in terms of liberties, sees that even so he is better off in terms of liberties than he would have been had liberties been arranged equally (see 247). Utilitarianism of course will permit this sort of case as well since average welfare would thereby be increased. The question is whether utilitarianism would go *beyond* this, allowing some to have less liberty than they would at the equal-liberty point so that others may have more. In principle of course this is possible. But whether or not it would actually occur depends on empirical facts about the level of economic and social development necessary to bring the special conception of justice into play, the character of people's utility functions at that point for liberty, and other matters which Rawls gives us little guidance on and which it is difficult to judge in the abstract. The moral we should draw here is that (at least if Rawls' own empirical assumptions are true) the contrast between utilitarianism and Rawls' principles of justice with respect to treatment of basic liberties is far less dramatic than much of Rawls' discussion would suggest. Rawls himself admits this in one passage, where he states that "It simply happens that under most conditions, at least in a reasonably favored stage of civilization, the greatest sum of advantages is not attained [by a system in which] violation of the liberty of a few... [is] made right by the greater good shared by many" (26). This "favored stage of civilization" is exactly the same one in which Rawls' own special conception of justice prohibits violations of liberty, and outside of which his general conception does not. Despite the rhetoric which has arisen following publication of his book, Rawls' arguments in themselves do not establish a great disparity between the adequacy of his treatment of liberty and that given to us by utilitarianism, although the door remains open for future investigators to accomplish this task.[21]

The Second Extra-Contractarian Argument: Merging Persons

Rawls' second argument against utilitarianism, from the extra-contractarian standpoint, criticizes it on the grounds that reasoning in favor of the principle of utility fails to take seriously the distinctions among persons. The reasoning in favor of utilitarianism is depicted as taking two different forms.

This reasoning, as it appears in the first form, goes as follows. An individual, in attempting to advance his welfare, must take into account the fact that he has competing desires, not all of which can be satisfied. Most thinkers have held that the rational solution to this problem is for the individual to act so as to maximize his overall satisfaction: to sacrifice the satisfaction of less intense desires in order to satisfy more intense desires, and to sacrifice the satisfaction of a smaller number of desires in order to satisfy a larger number. But, the argument continues, this same principle may be applied to a society as well as to an individual because the society faces the same problem, that of advancing the welfare of the group when the desires of some members conflict with the desires of others. If it is rational for an individual to maximize overall satisfaction, it is rational for society to do so as well, sacrificing the satisfaction of less intense desires in order to satisfy more intense desires and sacrificing a smaller number of desires in order to satisfy a greater number. Thus a utilitarian principle is argued for by extending to society as a whole the decision principle which is rational for an individual (23–24).

The second version of this argument for utilitarianism takes the following form. It is pointed out that we believe a person is likely to make a correct moral judgment when he is impartial, considers all sides of the issue, knows all the relevant facts, and so forth. Our belief is then elevated into a definition of rightness: a social system is said to be right when an ideally rational and impartial spectator would approve of it from a general point of view should he possess all relevant knowledge of the circumstances. From this definition one cannot derive any actual assessments of the rightness or wrongness of particular systems because it is still indeterminate what such an ideal observer would approve of. However, this defect can be remedied by stipulating in addition that the ideal observer is to be *sympathetic*—that is, he completely identifies with, and in fact acquires himself in the same degree of strength, the desires of all the parties involved in a given case. Thus if Jones desperately wants the last eclair and Smith desires it only mildly, the ideal observer wants it desperately for Jones and mildly for Smith. Such an ideal sympathetic observer will incorporate in himself all the interests and desires which are relevant to a particular assessment and so approve of a social system only if the existence of that system would maximize the satisfaction of his (expanded) set of desires. Thus from such a definition of "right" is deduced the principle of utility as the correct criterion for determining social justice (27, 184–188).

Rawls appears to object to these lines of reasoning on three separate grounds. The second form of the argument, according to him, has been put forward by those who believe that the sympathetic impartial observer provides us with the correct interpretation of the notion of "impartiality" which is so crucial in moral judgment. However, he claims, another interpretation of this notion is available, namely that provided by the idea of principles which would be chosen in the original position, for the parties in the original position are ones whose situation and character enable them to judge without bias or prejudice (189–190). This point is not decisive, for the fact that *two* interpretations of some notion are available does not show one of them to be mistaken.

Second, and more relevantly, Rawls seems to believe that the interpretation of impartiality embodied in the second form of reasoning depicted above is incorrect because it mistakes impersonality for impartiality. Evidently Rawls believes that the ideal sympathetic spectator must be understood as an impersonal being, not an impartial one. But this is wrong: the sympathetic spectator may be superpersonal insofar as he incorporates in one system of desires, desires identical to all the desires of those around him, but he possesses a full personality and all other attributes of human character. He is impartial because he gives equal consideration to the desires of everyone concerned. Any serious worry that impersonality may have illegitimately been substituted for impartiality should instead be directed at *Rawls*' account of impartiality, because the parties in the original position possess no recognizable human personality. Rawls denies them any knowledge of their place in society, their social status, their natural abilities and assets, their idiosyncratic psychological features, even their conception of the good (137). Some writers have claimed that even *ignorance* on their part of these matters is not sufficient since we can be moved by desires of whose existence we are unaware; to achieve his aims Rawls must deny that they possess these desires at all.[22] But surely such a creature is an impersonal agent if anyone qualifies for this title. Thus Rawls' second concern here seems to cut more severely against his interpretation of "impartiality" than it does against that proposed in the utilitarian reasoning.

Rawls' third objection is his charge that extending to society the principle of choice appropriate for one individual involves not taking seriously the distinction between persons (27, 187). It is true that utilitarianism does not take the distinction between persons seriously in the sense that it does not protect an individual in principle from having his interests neglected in order to promote the interests of others. Presumably this is what Rawls really objects to. But we need not read into this doctrine any confusion concerning the metaphysical difference between persons, as Rawls' words might suggest. There is no more grounds for discovering a confusion here than there is for discovering one in Rawls' own theory that the distribution of natural talents is to be viewed as a common asset whose benefits are to be shared by all (101-102, 179).

Kenneth Arrow argues in addition that the notion of conflating all desires into one system cannot be faulted. A theory of justice is presumably an ordering of alternative social states and therefore is formally analogous to the individual's ordering of alternative social states. Moreover, there is widespread agreement that justice should reflect individual's satisfactions, so social choice made in accordance with *any* of these theories of justice necessarily involves "a conflation of all desires"—albeit one which is purely formal, and not envisioned as embodied in some individual.[23] Rawls' objection cannot be so much to the conflation as to the principle of choice utilitarianism employs.

Before leaving a consideration of this objection to utilitarianism, we should note briefly that the lines of argument Rawls describes only serve as reasoning in support of the *classical* form of utilitarianism, not the *averaging* view which is his and our selected rival to his theory. Moreover they are ones which only a few advocates of the classical view have actually proposed (see 188n.), and are not found in any contemporary defenders of utilitarianism.

The Third Extra-Contractarian Argument: Interpersonal Comparisons of Utility

Rawls' third objection to utilitarianism, from a standpoint independent of contractarian theory, arises from the fact that utilitarianism requires us to make theoretically difficult interpersonal comparisons of utility while Rawls' principles supposedly do not. If we are to maximize average utility, we must have a cardinal measure of each person's welfare, plus the ability to make sensible comparisons between the welfare level of one person and that of another (90). Some utilitarians have been content to leave these comparisons and measurements to unguided intuition, but as Rawls correctly points out, this is a poor basis for social policy. We do not want large-scale allocative decisions to rest on intuitive judgments which are likely to be distorted by self-interest or irrelevant moral notions. Some objective basis for these judgments is necessary so that widespread agreement to them can be elicited and social discord minimized. At the present time, no satisfactory method for making such objective judgments concerning welfare has been found (90–91, 321–325).

Rawls' theory, on the other hand, measures social expectations in terms of "primary goods," things which are necessary means to the success of one's rational life plan, so that it can be supposed a rational man wants them whatever else he wants. The primary goods identified by Rawls are rights and liberties, opportunities and powers, income and wealth, and, in the context of some issues, a sense of one's own self-worth (92–93). Rawls does not suggest this different index of human welfare reflects a different theory of the good for man; on the contrary, he states that the theory of the good is not in dispute between utilitarianism and the contract doctrine (92). According to both theories, a person's good is determined by his rational long-term plan of life. A person is happy when he is more or less successfully in the way of carrying out his plan. And a person's plan of life is determined by his desires, since the plan is designed to permit the harmonious satisfaction of these desires. Primary goods provide a suitable index of good because they are the necessary means for the accomplishment of this long-term plan, whatever its precise content (92–93).

Rawls' argument that his theory is preferable on this score to utilitarianism rests on the claim that while it is possible for society to arrive at an objective measure of primary goods, it is not possible to measure the satisfaction of desire. Partly because he does not assume this is a *theoretical* impossibility, Rawls does not wish to rest much weight on this objection. Nevertheless he does regard it as a significant difficulty (91, 321).

Of course, for Rawls' theory to compare favorably with utilitarianism, it must in fact be possible to measure the quantity of primary goods in some objective way. Little attention has been paid to this fact, but the availability of such a measure seems questionable. Rawls evidently understands "income and wealth" in terms of monetary sums which are relatively easy to measure. However, in a society such as ours, an important part of one's income (much contested in union contracts) is frequently the "fringe benefits" and "perquisites" which accompany one's salary, such as health insurance, paid vacations, or access to recreational facilities.[24] It may be far more difficult to measure the value of such benefits. Moreover the same income in different societies will have different value. Commodities which are available in exchange for financial considerations in one society will not be so available under different cultural and economic arrangements (for example, human organs for transplant purposes are not typically available through the market in our society, although one can imagine them being so under different circumstances.) And the same income has one value when faced with one price structure in one society and a different value when faced with a different price structure in another society (if you like pears and hate apples, ten dollars is worth less to you in a society where pears cost a dollar apiece while apples are fifty cents than it is in a society where apples cost a dollar and pears are fifth cents apiece).[25] How to measure rights, or liberties, or powers, or opportunities, seems an even more difficult problem.[26]

Rawls discusses whether or not his theory involves a serious "indexing problem," that is, a problem of measuring the value of a quantity of one primary good *as compared to* the value of a quantity of some other primary good. He argues the problem is not serious, for the following reasons. Under the special conception of justice, the first principle concerning liberty and the principle of equal opportunity call for all persons to have the *same* amounts of the *same* liberties and opportunities. Thus we need not consider whether or not, for example, the right to vote is equivalent to the right to propose candidates for office since everyone will have both rights, or neither one. Moreover, these principles are ranked lexicographically relative to the difference principle, so the primary goods covered by them need not be compared with those covered by it. Thus, states Rawls, the only possible problem arises in the application of the difference principle itself. But in effect its application only requires us to identify the least well-off representative person (or position) and maximize his situation by finding the social scheme which will leave him best off. Everyone else will perforce be better off than he is. In deciding which social system makes the worst-off representative person best off, we need only make ordinal judgments about his situation, not cardinal judgments as is required in utilitarianism. Rawls claims that defining the bottom position will not in practice be a problem, since although in principle primary goods could vary relative to each other, which would make it impossible to define the bottom position without some weighting scheme, in fact the primary goods tend to vary together, so that persons in the better positions tend to have more of *every* good. Thus the indexing problem reduces to the problem of deciding when the worst-off person is best-off for the various possible combinations of primary goods which may define his expectations. According to Rawls, this judgment can be made by taking up the standpoint of the representative individual from this group and asking which combinations of primary goods it would be rational for him to prefer. This involves an unavoidable, but limited, reliance on intuitive judgments, but one which is less egregious than that required by utilitarianism (93–95).

This argument has not been well received by Rawls' commentators. For one thing, the alleged insulation of liberties, rights and opportunities from comparisons with other primary goods only occurs under social conditions when the special conception of justice is in force. Under more primitive conditions, when the general conception obtains, rights, liberties and opportunities *may* be traded for the economic goods, and we need some measure of their value relative to each other. Critics have also found it extremely unlikely that the primary goods will vary with each other (so that a representative person who has more power also has more income), as Rawls suggests, under all possible social arrangements. Moreover, the likelihood that persons will have different degrees of desire for the various primary goods throws into question Rawls' solution to the problem of ascertaining which possible society's worst-off position is best. One group may find increased powers and responsibilities a more effective tool in pursuing their life plans than increased income while another group may find the opposite. Any society which assumes a universal scale of relative values in determining what arrangements to make for the worst-off group will not be acting with sufficient sensitivity to human variation. Altogether, Rawls' use of the notion of primary goods to solve the problem of interpersonal comparisons of utility is subject to problems almost as severe as those which vitiate the utilitarian account of justice.[27]

There is a related problem which we should note. As remarked above, Rawls states that the theory of the good is not at issue between contract theory and utilitarianism—at bottom they are both concerned with the satisfaction of rational desire (92-93). However, according to Rawls' theory, "justice as fairness...does not look behind the use which persons make of the rights and opportunities available to them in order to measure, much less to maximize, the satisfactions they achieve...once the whole arrangement is set up and going no questions are asked about the total of satisfaction..." (94). One may ask why this failure to enquire into satisfactions is appropriate. An interpretation that has been proposed is that society should concern itself with the distribution of *opportunities*, not the distribution of happiness. What is unjust is not that some people are less happy than others but rather that some people have fewer chances than others. It is up to the individual to decide how to employ his life-chances.[28] This may indeed be Rawls' guiding idea. However, the language in Section 15 suggests another interpretation, namely that the state is genuinely concerned as a matter of justice with the *satisfactions* obtained by individuals; but because of the practical problems in measuring extent of satisfaction, it attempts to affect satisfactions indirectly through the allocation of primary goods which are means towards desire satisfaction. It assumes that "the members of society are rational persons able to adjust their conceptions of the good to their situation" (94), that is, able to maximize their satisfactions given their allotment of primary goods. However, there is no reason to suppose that quantity of primary goods correlates well with degree of desire satisfaction. Although primary goods are *necessary* means to satisfaction of most desires, there is no assurance that they are *sufficient* for the satisfaction of these desires. To show this, Arrow adduces an example of two individuals whose incomes (and presumably other primary goods) are equal, and who therefore qualify as "equally well-off" under Rawls' theory. Yet one of these individuals may be a hemophiliac who requires four thousand dollars a year of coagulant therapy to achieve a state of security from bleeding at all comparable to that of the other. It is by no means clear that they are equally well off in terms of desire-satisfaction or any other intuitive measurement.[29] In this connection one might also point out that whether or not possession of primary goods assures men of greater success in advancing their ends depends on how society is organized. In our society, if I have a consuming desire to collect Persian rugs, a greater income will assist me in pursuing this interest. But here are other imaginable societies in which Persian rugs are not available on the open market at all, but only (say) passed down through family lines. In such societies, possession of primary goods will be of far less use to me. For these kinds of reasons, we cannot expect any important correlation between primary goods and satisfaction of desires. Of course, any argument that there is an important correlation would require us to measure satisfaction of desires, something which Rawls (and many others) have claimed we cannot do. Thus it appears the employment of primary goods to measure social expectation cannot be justified on the grounds that it gives us an indirect, but practical, way of measuring satisfaction of desires. (If it could be so justified, it would be open to utilitarians to use primary goods as well, so that Rawls' theory would not be superior to theirs in terms of practicality. Rawls himself admits the possibility of so reconstruing utilitarianism (175)). But without this kind of connection, it is unsufficiently clear why primary goods provide a relevant measure of social expectations, particularly in light of Rawls' theory of the good. And as we have seen, even the alleged ease of measuring them is in serious dispute.

The Fourth Extra-Contractarian Argument: The Source and Quality of Desires

The final extra-contractarian argument we shall consider goes as follows. Rawls points out that utilitarianism sets as its goal the maximal satisfaction of people's desires. It makes no judgment about the source of those desires or their content or nature. Thus utilitarianism takes existing desires as given, whatever their characteristics. However, it is well known that political and economic institutions influence the desires of those who live under them—thus it is frequently claimed, for example, that capitalism creates the desire for more material goods. Moreover, some desires may seem morally objectionable in themselves, such as the desire to see members of other races occupy lower social positions, or the abhorrence of certain sexual or religious practices. But utilitarianism must take all these desires as grist for its mill, as legitimate as any others, so that the course for the state which it charts out will always be affected by the particular character of the time at which its reforms are initiated.

According to Rawls, however, *his* theory enables one to define an "Archimedean point" for assessing social systems without contamination by existing institutions, whatever their nature might be. His principles of justice are chosen by the parties in the original position on the grounds that they will best advance their interests as measured in primary goods. But the primary goods are taken to be things which are wanted as parts of rational plans of life which may include the most varied ends. Thus basing a conception of justice on these goods does not tie it to any particular pattern of interests as these might be generated by an historical arrangement of human institutions. Since the two principles of justice are not contingent on existing desires or social conditions, they define the long range aim of society, regardless of what it is like at the time they are implemented. Moreover, the parties in the original position implicitly agree not to press claims on each other which violate whatever principles of justice are chosen. Thus, since they give liberty lexicographical priority, they agree not to give any weight to any subsequent desires that the liberties of some be restricted. Such desires receive no value at all, unlike what happens under a utilitarian principle of justice (30–32, 258–263, 450).

It is not wholly clear what the nature of Rawls' complaint against utilitarianism in these passages is. There seem to be three separate concerns. One is that utilitarianism's placing equal weight on all desires, whatever their content, will lead to institutions which would be considered unjust by reflective judgment (see 450). For example, not enough assurance would be given of individual freedom. This concern is simply a restating of the reflective equilibrium argument considered in "The First Extra-Contractarian Argument" above rather than an independent line of reasoning. As we saw there, the real degree of difference on this subject between Rawls' theory and utilitarianism is open to question. Powerful utilitarian arguments for liberal institutions are well known (see 209ff.).

A second concern seems to be the thought that some desires in themselves are recognized by reflective moral judgment as immoral, and consequently that utilitarianism goes wrong in allowing these desires the same status as other more innocent desires. However, utilitarians have long argued, with a good deal of plausibility, that no desire is evil in itself, but only evil insofar as it involves evil consequences. Thus we might normally think of a sadistic desire that others suffer as an evil desire. But on reflection, there seems nothing wrong with the satisfaction of such a desire simply taken *as satisfaction;* the desire is only objectionable because satisfying it necessarily involves the suffering of others, suffering which they desire not to undergo. One of the cases traditionally urged against utilitarianism is that where the sadistic desires of one group (say, the Roman masses) outweigh the desire not to suffer on the part of others (say, the Christian martyrs). However, this sort of infringement on individual freedoms would be objectionable even if the majority's desires were perfectly innocent in character, for example, the desire to see how human beings react under stress.

Although utilitarians have argued that no desire is evil in and of itself, they have also recognized that some desires tend to have worse effects than others because they are incompatible with the satisfaction of opposing desires. They have urged therefore that society encourage the replacement of these desires by other, more harmonious ones which will lead to a greater overall level of satisfaction within society (262). Thus utilitarianism provides us with consequentialist grounds for criticizing certain desires, and plausible grounds at that.

The third concern Rawls expresses in these passages is the concern that utilitarianism does not take into account the *source* of the desires whose satisfaction it seeks to maximize, and in particular disregards the fact that these desires may be the outgrowth of existing institutions. It is difficult to see precisely what is objectionable about this. Rawls may have in mind the fact that these institutions will in some cases be unjust and so give rise to desires which will lead to further unjust institutions, or which are "immoral" in themselves. If so, this point is not distinct from the first two. Or Rawls may be concerned by the fact that social systems tend to breed in their members artificial desires designed to perpetuate the system. Thus many corporations in capitalist economies spend substantial sums on advertising upholding the values of free enterprise. However, this is only objectionable if the resulting attitudes and desires are irrational, that is, based on false beliefs. Since we are concerned with a form of utilitarianism that maximizes the satisfaction of *rational* desires alone, any irrational desires stemming from this source would not be counted in the calculus. Alternatively, Rawls may believe that principles of justice should define a social ideal which is universal, that is, which *any* society should aspire to, whatever its present social and cultural forms.

In any very strong form, such a thesis seems implausible. In our culture, there is great interest in organized sports, and it is prima facie desirable that an ideally just version of this culture would maintain the economic arrangements which make this possible. It would appear that maintaining such arrangements would not necessarily be part of the idealized version of some culture which has no interest in such activities. But if we weaken the thesis to allow room for such diversity, it becomes unclear how the results would diverge from those obtained by applying utilitarianism.

We must conclude that insofar as this final extra-contractarian argument has weight, it is primarily the weight which accrues to it as a version of the argument that utilitarianism fails to accord with our reflective moral judgments. And as we saw before, no conclusive argument has been proposed which shows that utilitarianism fares worse in this arena than Rawls' own theory.

EVALUATION OF RAWLS' CONTRACTARIAN-DEPENDENT ARGUMENTS

In the last four sections, we considered the most salient arguments against utilitarianism that Rawls offers from a perspective which is independent of his contractarian approach. None of these arguments proved to be compelling, and certainly not as demonstrations that Rawls' theory is clearly superior to utilitarianism in the respects at issue. In the following sections we will consider the major arguments Rawls advances against utilitarianism from within the contractarian standpoint. All take the form of attempting to establish that the parties in the original position would choose Rawls' principles of justice, rather than utilitarianism, to govern the basic structure of their society.

To this sort of argument, the defender of utilitarianism has four different kinds of response. He can claim, first of all, that what principles the parties in the original position would select is an entirely irrelevant test for the correctness of a given principle of justice, and therefore that utilitarianism is in no way shown defective by any argument that it would not be so chosen. This is clearly an important strategy, but I shall not explore it here since evaluating it involves a deeper foray into matters of meta-ethics than is appropriate within the confines of this paper. The utilitarian can claim, secondly, that what principles the parties in the original position would choose is indeed relevant, but that Rawls has failed to describe the correct original position, and that the parties in the correct original position would choose utilitarianism rather than Rawls' principles. Rawls recognizes this line of response when he states that for each traditional conception of justice there is an appropriate original position from which it would be selected, and that one of the objects of his argument is to establish that his original position is the correct one (121, 141). The third response available to the utilitarian is to concede that Rawls' original position is the correct one, but to argue that the parties in it would choose utilitarianism rather than Rawls' principles. The fourth and final possibility is to admit that Rawls' original position is the correct one, but to claim that utilitarianism and Rawls' principles are equivalent for the central range of cases, and therefore that the parties in that original position must be indifferent between them. We shall see each of these strategies adopted in response to one or another of Rawls' arguments.

Rawls' argument that his principles of justice, rather than utilitarianism, would be chosen by the parties in the original position rests on the claim that these parties would adopt a maximin strategy in choosing principles, and that his theory of justice constitutes the maximin solution to their decision problem (152, 175). The maximin strategy of decision-making requires choosing an alternative whose worst possible outcome is better than the worst possible outcome of any other alternative. It is the strategy one would select if one knew one's enemy were to determine which outcome would come about. Rawls argues that his principles of justice are the appropriate ones to select if the parties in the original position are trying to maximin, since these principles, in effect, only condone societies which maximize the position of the least well-off group. Thus if one assumed one would be assigned one's place in society by one's enemy, it would be rational to select Rawls' principles to govern that society, for then one would be assured that one's expectations would be as high as possible for that society (152–153).

Rawls is at pains to point out that the parties in the original position are not to make the false assumption that their enemies will assign them their places, and that in general the maximin strategy is not an adequate guide to decision-making (153). The question, then, is why it is appropriate for the parties in the original position to employ it. Rawls has two answers to this question. One is that there are three features of decision-situations which are generally recognized to call for employment of the maximin rule, and that the situation of the parties in the original position manifests all three of these features to a high degree. The second is that the strains of commitment which accompany any public conception of justice and the necessity for psychological stability offer special reasons for the parties to select his principles of justice. We shall look at these in turn and finally shall examine Rawls' criticism of Harsanyi's attempt to derive utilitarianism from a variant on Rawls' own original position.

The First Feature: No Knowledge of Probabilities

Since the maximin rule takes no account of the likelihoods of the possible outcomes of choice, use of the rule is much more plausible if there is some reason for sharply discounting estimates of the probable consequences of one's choices (154).[30] Rawls argues that there is good reason in the original position to discount such estimates. The parties in the original position not only lack all knowledge about themselves as individuals or their place in society, but they also lack any knowledge of the course of history or how often society has taken one form or another (200). In such circumstances, Rawls claims, estimates of probabilities cannot be objective or based on knowledge of particular facts (172–173). The only ground on which the parties might make probability estimates is appeal to the Principle of Insufficient Reason, a principle which directs the decision-maker, when he cannot assign probabilities on actual evidence, to identify the possibilities in some natural way and then assume that each is equally likely. But Rawls argues that it is inappropriate to make use of this principle in the original position because the decision is of such fundamental importance, and because one would desire to have one's decision appear responsible to one's descendants who would be affected by it (169). Thus the parties have "no basis for determining the probable nature of their society, or their place in it" (155). Without probability estimates, they must make use of a decision-principle which does not take probabilities into account such as the maximin rule.

This argument has perhaps attracted more attention from Rawls' critics than any other. The grounds for their objections are diverse. First we might note that even if it is agreed that the parties must employ some decision-rule which takes no account of probabilities, it doesn't follow that they should employ the maximin rule. The maximin rule is only one member of an entire family of decision-principles which take no account of probabilities, and the fact that *some* member of this family must be used hardly shows that maximin in particular must be.[31]

Second, as some critics have pointed out, there is something slightly bizarre about Rawls' arguing that the knowledge of the parties in the original position is insufficient to allow them to make probability estimates. The argument that they cannot make such estimates relies on the *stipulation* that they possess no knowledge of the course of history or the frequency with which society assumes various forms. But this stipulation seems to have no independent rationale. Unlike the stipulation that they possess no knowledge of themselves as individuals, it is not needed to prevent them from "tailoring principles to their own circumstances" (139). Unlike the stipulation that they have no knowledge of the particular details of their own society, it is not needed to secure proper justice between generations (137). It does not seem necessary to secure unanimous agreement on principles (140). Thus its *only* apparent role is to prevent them from making probability estimates of the various possible outcomes, despite Rawls' statement that all features of the original position are to be "natural and plausible" (18). The same comments apply to the parties' inability to estimate the probability of their turning out to be any given individual in a society. The parties' transformation into members of society is not a natural process. a matter of fact about which they could have ordinary evidence. Rather it is a fictitious event whose nature is wholly governed by Rawls' stipulations. His failure to stipulate what the probabilities are, and to allow the parties to know what these probabilities are, needs explanation, and the explanation seems simply to be the desire to secure their selection of his principles of justice. But if this is the case, then Rawls could have secured the same result more straightforwardly by simply stipulating that the parties in the original position are not to make probability estimates. It would then have been clearer that the only rationale for this feature of the original position is that it enables us to derive principles which Rawls finds to be in accord with our considered moral judgments, and in particular to avoid utilitarianism.[32]

Some critics have argued that the situation may be even worse than this discussion reveals, for they contend that independent considerations show that the parties in the original position *must* assume they have an equal probability of being any person in the society for which they are choosing principles of justice. Thus Harsanyi has suggested that the equiprobability assumption is not to be interpreted as the result of using the Principle of Insufficient Reason, but rather a feature designed into the original position which reflects our normal moral assumption that the interests of each person in society are to be given equal weight—as opposed to giving more weight to the interests of the poor.[33] Somewhat along the same lines, Narveson has argued that it is one of our pre-analytic precepts of fairness that rules are fair only when they do not load the dice in favor of anyone, whether rich or poor, and that this is what the equiprobability assumption amounts to.[34] We can certainly agree that it would be coherent for a theorist to design an original position to include an equiprobability assumption for this reason.

It might be noted, incidentally, that Rawls' specific arguments for rejecting the use of the Principle of Insufficient Reason in the original position are not [both] equally compelling. The first argument, that the decision is so important, has found many adherents.[35] But the second one, that abjuring use of the Principle allows the parties to defend their decision to their descendants who will be affected by it, seems off the mark. First, as Hare has noted, it is not at all clear that the descendants will thank their parents for being so conservative; they might well respond, "Nothing ventured, nothing gained."[36] But more telling is the fact that the descendants themselves are potential parties in the original position; by hypothesis, if the parents adopt a certain principle of justice in that situation, the children will also. And it would hardly seem rational for the children to reproach their parents for choosing a principle affecting them when they would choose the very same principle on their own behalf. Thus possible reproach from one's descendants does not seem to be a factor which the parties in the original position need to worry about.

We have seen in this section that Rawls' argument for the parties adopting the maximin strategy because they lack the knowledge to make probability estimates has no independent grounds, beyond the fact that adopting this strategy leads to a principle of justice which allegedly accords with our reflective moral judgments better than utilitarianism. And we have seen reason to question this latter claim.

The Second Feature: A Guaranteed Minimum

Use of the maximin strategy in the original position is plausible, Rawls argues, because of a second feature of that situation: the fact that the parties in it know their conception of the good is such that they care very little, if anything, for what they might gain above the minimum stipend they can be sure of by following the maximin rule. Since this is so, Rawls claims, there is little reason for them to try to do better, for example by following the rule of maximizing expected utility (154–155).

This argument relies on the assumption that the principles of justice selected by following the maximin strategy, namely Rawls' principles, will ensure a socially acceptable minimum which no one will carè greatly about going beyond. Rawls argues that his principles will guarantee this minimum because they provide a workable theory of justice and are compatible with reasonable demands of efficiency (156). However, as a number of critics have pointed out, this argument is dubious.[37] Whether or not such a minimum is achievable depends on the natural resources available to the society, the health of its members, its relations with other societies, and other matters which are largely unaffected by the principle of justice which governs the society. In this connection it should be remembered that Rawls' *general* conception of justice, in addition to his special conception, represents a maximin solution to the choice in the original position.[38] But the general conception is explicitly designed to apply to situations of extreme poverty and social underdevelopment, situations where establishment of a minimum beyond which no one is much interested in going seems ruled out by definition. Some critics have pointed out that indeed the satiation point for wealth and power is higher for most people than the minimum obtainable by Rawlsian principles in even the richest societies.[39] Barry pursues this point by arguing, persuasively, that if the minimum level achievable by maximin policies in a society falls either below or above the threshold of satiation, there is little reason to think, merely on the basis that such a threshold exists, that the maximin policy is obviously the right solution. For example, if apples are to be distributed among ten people whose Rawlsian threshold level is twelve apples, and we can choose between giving everyone ten apples, or giving nine of them twelve apples and the remaining person nine apples, it is not at all clear that the second division isn't better.[40]

Last, it should be pointed out that if there is such a threshold point, and if it is the same for everyone, as Rawls implicitly assumes, then this means that the marginal utility of primary goods effectively diminishes to zero after this point. If this is true, then in all probability utilitarianism would mandate the same institutions as Rawls' principles of justice, since it would increase average utility to distribute goods so as to raise everyone up to the threshold point, rather than giving fewer to some and more to others. If so, utilitarianism satisfies the second demand as well as Rawls' principles of justice do.[41]

We can see, then, that the "second feature" of the original position involves an implausible assumption about human good whose truth would not support Rawls' conception of justice more strongly than it would utilitarianism.

The Third Feature: Avoidance of Intolerable Outcomes

Rawls cites a third feature of the original position which makes it rational for the parties to employ the maximin strategy: use of other choice rules (for example, the rule of maximizing expected utility) would lead to conceptions of justice (for example, utilitarianism) which would permit intolerable institutions (such as slavery and serfdom) which the parties could hardly accept (156).

There are three problems with this argument. First, the desire to avoid intolerable outcomes does not in itself require the maximin strategy. It requires what Hare calls an "insurance" strategy, one which guarantees avoidance of unacceptable outcomes. If the maximin strategy could ensure acceptable outcomes, then it would qualify as an insurance strategy. However, at best it is only one of several possible insurance strategies because it goes beyond what is required of a policy to qualify as an insurance strategy. In particular, it dictates what social arrangements must be selected even in a rich society where the minimum level obtainable is far above the point of toleration. Thus the "intolerable outcome" argument at most gives us reason to think the maximin strategy satisfies a necessary condition for being adopted, but not a sufficient condition.[42] Second, as the argument in the last section allows us to infer, there is no good reason to think that adopting the maximin strategy will actually avoid intolerable outcomes, especially at the low levels of social advancement which call for Rawls' general conception of justice. Finally, as we have already seen in "The First Extra-Contractarian Argument" above, it is far from clear that utilitarianism at any rate would lead to intolerable institutions under conditions when Rawls' principles would not. If slavery and serfdom are genuinely intolerable, then it appears their disutility is so great that no social system permitting them (except under very severe conditions) would maximize average utility. This means that utilitarianism may provide as good "insurance" against these institutions as Rawls' principles of justice do, for the two conceptions of justice appear to rule out intolerable institutions in roughly the same range of conditions.

We can see, then, that the desire to avoid intolerable outcomes provides an insufficient argument in support of the maximin strategy, and that there is reason to suppose utilitarianism may satisfy this desire at least as well as Rawls' principles of justice do.

The Strains of Commitment: Psychological Stability

In the last three sections, we have seen Rawls' argument for claiming that the parties in the original position would be rational to employ the maximin strategy in selecting their principles of justice. The case appears far from conclusive. Inadequate support is offered for the inability of the parties to make probability estimates; and the putative existence of "satiation threshold" and "intolerable outcome" points does not show that maximin must be followed, since it may not achieve the former or avoid the latter, and other strategies might work as well. In addition we have seen evidence that utilitarianism might succeed as well as Rawls' principles in guaranteeing achievement of the satiation threshold and avoidance of intolerable institutions. However, Rawls adduces several other arguments to show that his principles, rather than utilitarianism, are the genuine maximin solution to the problem in the original position. We shall consider these in this section, the arguments from what Rawls calls the "strains of commitment," and "psychological stability."

The reasoning regarding the strains of commitment appears to go as follows. In selecting a principle of justice which will satisfy maximin, the parties assume their society will act in "strict compliance" with that principle. That is, they assume everyone will accept the principle, and know that the others accept the principle, and also assume that the basic social arrangements will satisfy and be known to satisfy the principle (8, 145, 454). But they are not to assume the impossible. If members of society would not be able to honor a given principle of justice under all circumstances, even the most onerous, then the principle is disqualified as one they may select (175–176). Rawls argues that his special conception of justice has an advantage over utilitarianism in this regard, because utilitarianism, unlike his principle, may require people to sacrifice their freedoms for the sake of greater good for others (176–177). We may grant that it would be psychologically possible for members of society to honor Rawls' special conception.[43] However, as we pointed out above, the empirical assumptions Rawls employs to argue for the priority of liberty under the special conception show that in circumstances where it would apply, utilitarianism would *also* refuse to trade the liberties of anyone for mere economic goods accruing to someone else. Thus honoring utilitarianism would be no more difficult, in these circumstances and for this reason, than honoring Rawls' special conception. We have also seen that Rawls' general conception of justice allows violations of liberties in some cases, and we have no conclusive argument that utilitarianism would do worse. We cannot conclude, then, at least on Rawls' own empirical assumptions, that it would be psychologically impossible to honor utilitarianism.

Rawls' reasoning concerning the psychological stability of a conception of justice has much the same flavor. The parties in the original position assume that they are choosing a conception of justice with which their society will strictly comply, in the sense explained above. However, society is an enduring entity, and strict compliance of the sort contemplated will only be achieved at the cost of social practices designed to maintain the relevant sense of justice in the members of society. The principles of justice must be promulgated and enforced; people must be trained to believe in those principles and to feel guilty when they violate them. The level and type of motivation necessary to maintain strict compliance may vary, depending on the content of the different principles of justice. In assessing a particular conception of justice, the parties in the original position must therefore take into account not only the effects of institutions which comply with that conception, but also the burden that maintaining compliance imposes on society. Rawls calls a conception of justice "stable" when public recognition of its realization by the social system tends to bring about the corresponding sense of justice, i.e., tendency to judge in accordance with the principles of that conception. Obviously, the more stable a conception is, the less burdensome the social cost of maintaining it (46, 177–183, § § 69, 76).

At some points in his discussion, Rawls suggests that different conceptions of justice must be compared with each other with respect to these burdens, and that a less burdensome conception is to be preferred, other things being equal (455, 498). At other points, he seems to suggest merely that an acceptable conception of justice must be *stable enough* (504). However, the structure of his argument implies that his position ought to be the following. The parties in the original position, according to him, must employ a maximin strategy, that is, select that principle of justice whose worst possible outcome is better than the worst possible outcome of any alternative principle. But the level of well-being of the worst-off individual in society depends not only, for example, on the economic arrangements mandated by the conception of justice but also on the social practices which are necessary to sustain compliance with that conception. Two different conceptions of justice might sanction precisely the same economic and political arrangements but differ from each other according to the ease with which allegiance to the conception is elicited, and therefore with respect to the amount of social resources which must be devoted to maintaining compliance. The naturally more attractive conception would then guarantee a *better* worst outcome. Therefore the parties must pay attention to the *relative* stability of the conceptions of justice they consider, for this affects what their expectations under these conceptions would be.

Let us look, then, at a simplified version of the complex argument to show that Rawls' conception of justice would be less burdensome, or more stable, than utilitarianism. Rawls points out that any conception of justice requires an individual to perform some acts which are not in accord with his self-interest, narrowly conceived. Therefore strict compliance can only be maintained if the pressure of self-interest is adequately offset, for example, by an opposing sense of justice, or a concern for the welfare of others (454, 497). He believes that such a sense of justice can be produced by two circumstances: (a) knowledge that the institutions satisfying that conception enhance one's own good—knowledge which enhances one's self-esteem, and creates the tendency to cherish and support those institutions and the governing conception of justice, and (b) thorough understanding both of the precepts of the governing conception of justice, and of the reasoning which supports it (177, 498–499).[44] He argues that his conception of justice would create both circumstances, and so produce a strong corresponding sense of justice. His principles prohibit forced sacrifice of one citizen's good for that of others, and they require that institutions be established from which everyone benefits (§ § 29, 76). Thus social arrangements satisfying these principles enhance the good of each member of society and would be known to do so. Moreover, he argues, his conception of justice is clear enough so that it is easy to understand and apply, largely because of its use of primary goods in measuring social expectations; in addition the reasons given for it are easily understood and accepted (§ 49, 501).

By contrast, Rawls argues, the institutions governed by utilitarianism may require us to make sacrifices, even of our liberties, in order to increase average welfare. Thus they need not enhance our good as individuals and so will not tend to produce the corresponding sense of justice throughout society. Compliance can then only be produced by inducing people to identify strongly with the interests of others, but this is not easy to bring about. Moreover, utilitarianism is difficult to understand and apply because of the problem presented by the necessity for making interpersonal comparisons of utility (§ § 15, 49, 76). Rawls concludes that the contract view offers greater stability (501).

It is difficult to assess an argument such as this which relies so heavily on empirical hypotheses which have received inadequate testing. I will confine myself to making three points. First, as we have already seen in "The First Extra-Contractarian Argument" above, there is room for disagreement with Rawls' claim that his principles "benefit everyone," whereas utilitarianism alone requires sacrifices of the interests of some for the good of others. According to Rawls, his principles benefit everyone primarily in the sense that each person (or representative group) would do better, if the principles govern society, than he or his group would have done if the primary goods had been divided equally (80).[45] We might grant that this is so. However, the question before us is whether or not persons living in a society governed by utilitarianism, or by Rawls' principles, would *feel* that anyone was being required to make sacrifices. As we noted before, someone who regards a given person as making sacrifices evaluates the position of that person relative to what minimal justice or morality requires of him. Thus to know if members of society would believe sacrifices were being made, we must know what *they* would believe justice requires of the members of society. One possibility of course is that they simply believe justice requires what the principle governing their society requires. If so, then obviously no one living under either utilitarianism or Rawls' principles would believe sacrifices were being made. The two conceptions of justice would be on an equal footing. Another possibility is that there is some independent, "natural," conception of justice which people tend to adhere to no matter what principles govern their society. If so, then it is possible that *either* utilitarianism *or* Rawls' principles, or both, require sacrifices relative to what that conception requires. If this "natural" conception calls for "equal shares for all," as perhaps Rawls assumes, then his principles would not call for sacrifices whereas utilitarianism might well. But there is no reason in advance to suppose the "natural" conception does call for equal shares. Certainly many in our society do not believe this and would believe that Rawlsian justice requires sacrifices by those who are better off for the sake of those who are worse off. Which conception of justice calls for greater sacrifices, and so is less stable, must be left an open question whose answer depends on resolution of the standard of "sacrifice" to be used and on empirical facts concerning human psychology.[46]

Second, it is far from clear that Rawls' principles have an advantage with respect to clarity and ease of application since as we saw before, the problem of indexing primary goods is in principle as difficult as the problem of making interpersonal comparisons of utility for utilitarianism. Moreover, the reasoning in favor of Rawls' principles is quite complex whereas some forms of reasoning in favor of utilitarianism have been quite simple (for example, Smart simply argues that utilitarianism is the principle that would be adopted by a perfectly benevolent person).[47]

Third, we have seen that it may be argued with some plausibility that utilitarianism would actually sanction much the same social arrangements as Rawls' principles. If so, it might be urged that utilitarianism would have the same effect on each person's good that the contract view would, hence would cause people to cherish just institutions to an equivalent degree, and hence develop an equally strong sense of justice. However, Rawls proposes a response to this line of thought. He points out that the affection elicited by a conception of justice depends not only on the consequences of the social arrangements which satisfy that conception, but also on the values which are expressed in the way the conception is stated. In particular he claims that the formulation of his conception of justice expresses respect for each member of society. According to him, expression by others of respect for oneself promotes one's own self-respect, and self-respect on the part of members of society increases the efficacy of social cooperation. Thus he claims that even if his principles mandate the same institutional arrangements as utilitarianism, public acceptance of his principles would increase the amount of self-respect in society, so make it more efficient, and so raise the expectations of every member of society relative to what they would be under utilitarianism. He concludes that the parties in the original position have reason to choose his conception of justice rather than utilitarianism (178–183).

According to Rawls, his conception of justice expresses respect for each member of society because it includes everyone's good in a scheme of mutual benefit, so that public affirmation of this scheme affirms the worth of each person's life plan (178–179). However, we have already seen it is far from clear that persons living under Rawlsian justice would view institutions satisfying his conception as benefiting everyone. They might well feel that those higher up on the social scale were being asked to sacrifice their life plans for those lower down. Thus we cannot be sure that his conception of justice would really promote universal self-respect in the manner described.

Rawls offers a variant on this argument. He suggests in another context that his conception of justice has an advantage over utilitarianism because members of a utilitarian society would constantly be aware that the guarantee of their civil liberties rests on certain assumptions concerning empirical facts, assumptions which may at any time be found erroneous, and facts which may change with the alteration of social conditions. Thus civil liberties are not assured once and for all, and the members of society may feel insecure in this knowledge. Under Rawlsian justice, it is claimed on the contrary that the priority of liberty is built right into the principles and cannot be taken away even if new facts come to light (159–161).

We may concede that members of a utilitarian society would necessarily be aware that their liberties rest on empirical assumptions about the importance of liberty, and so are not immune to change. Thus there is a built-in uncertainty which might have psychological cost. (One might ask whether this will necessarily be a *cost*, however. Why should the members of society be so concerned about the possible loss of something which would only be removed on the finding that they care rather little for it?) However, in all probability, as we have seen before, a situation in which utilitarianism does not support equal liberties for all is also a situation in which Rawls' special conception of justice, which grants liberties a special place, would no longer be appropriate. The special conception rests on empirical assumptions just as the derivation of civil liberties from utilitarianism rests on empirical assumptions. Members of a society governed by the special conception must recognize that these assumptions may prove false, or that the facts may change. What are they to imagine their options in such a situation would be? One possibility is that nothing could be done, i.e., that they are stuck with the special conception of justice and the priority of liberty, even if it turns out for example that they prefer wealth to liberty. It would appear that knowing one lived under a conception of justice which could not be overturned, even if the empirical assumptions on which it rests turn out to be false, would involve just as high a psychological burden as that envisioned for members of a utilitarian society. A second possibility Rawls could allow is that members of this society would know that if the facts which mandate application of the special conception fail to obtain, then their society would shift to the general conception of justice. Thus they need not fear being stuck with an unwanted priority of liberty. However, this scenario would mean that they could not feel, any more than members of a utilitarian society could, that their civil liberties are guaranteed. If this knowledge in itself is costly, members of Rawlsian society must bear it as well. Moreover they must bear an additional cost. Members of a utilitarian society will know that their principle of justice is sensitive to *any* change in personal values. Members in a Rawlsian society cannot rest assured of this, for their society has only two options, the general or the special conceptions of justice. Society must accept one or the other of these even though there are possible, indeed probable, preference structures on the part of society's members which would make neither one appropriate (for example, they might rank wealth lexicographically relative to liberty). The moral to be drawn here is that any conception of justice which is not directly committed (rather than committed only on the basis of possibly false empirical assumptions) to the fundamental values of members of society will necessarily entail some psychological cost for those who live under it. But Rawls has hardly shown conclusively that the cost to be borne in a utilitarian society would be greater than that borne in a Rawlsian society.

Harsanyi's Argument for Utilitarianism from an Original Position

We argued in "The First Feature" above that the desire to avoid utilitarianism was Rawls' main ground for denying that the parties in the original position have knowledge of the course of history or (more importantly) of the probability of their being a given individual in the society they enter. Those who do not find utilitarianism objectionable will not of course be moved by this consideration. By allowing the parties in the original position knowledge that they have an equal chance of becoming any member of society, Harsanyi and Vickrey have developed an argument to show that utilitarianism, rather than Rawls' conception of justice, would be chosen.[48] Let us look at this argument (the first detailed *positive* reasoning for utilitarianism we have seen so far), and Rawls' response to it.

Stated simply, the argument proceeds as follows. Suppose one were in the original position and knew that one was going to become a member of a given society about which one knew almost all the relevant details: the social structure of the society, the expectations of its members, their number, and their preference orderings. One does not know, however, which member of society one will turn out to be, although one knows that one has an equal chance of being any given member. Most theorists, including Rawls, agree that when probabilities can be taken into account, it is rational to choose the alternative which maximizes one's expected utility. Thus persons in this version of the original position would follow a strategy of maximizing their expected utility, and this dictates choosing a principle of justice whose public recognition would maximize average utility in the society they will enter. (If the levels of welfare of the members of that society are u_1, u_2, u_3, ..., u_n, then the total utility of the society would be the sum of these or Σu_i, and the average utility would be the total utility divided by the number of members of society or $\Sigma u_i/n$. Assuming that one has an equal chance of being any member of that society, the probability of being a particular member is 1/n. This allows us to arrive at one's expected prospect for being in that society by weighting the utility of being a particular member (e.g., u_1) by the probability of being that member (1/n) and summing the results $1/n(u_1) + 1/n(u_2) + 1/n(u_3) + \ldots + 1/n(u_n)$ to get $\Sigma u_i/n$. Since this figure just *is* the average utility of society, one's prospect is equal to that average (165)). This is true for *any* society one might enter, whatever the structure, prospects, number, or preferences of its members. Thus if one did not know anything about the society one was to enter, except that one had an equal chance of being any member of it, and one also knew that a given principle of justice would maximize average utility in every society, then one would select that principle of justice. It maximizes one's expectations, even when one does not know which society one will be a member of. It is then assumed that the principle of maximizing average utility, when strictly complied with, actually succeeds in maximizing utility in each society. Consequently it is the one, not Rawls' conception of justice, which the parties in the original position ought to select.

Most of Rawls' responses to Harsanyi's proposal have already been examined above under other topics. However, he suggests, and David

Gauthier elaborates on, an argument which is specific to the debate with Harsanyi. Rawls' and Gauthier's reasoning is as follows.[49] Let us take it for granted, as Harsanyi must, that it is possible to make interpersonal comparisons of utility. Imagine, now, an individual Jones whose society I may possibly enter. Jones derives a utility of ten from experiencing an hour's worth of pleasure. Of course, ten utiles for him is worth ten utiles for me. However, it does not follow that I also assign a utility of ten to being Jones and experiencing an hour's worth of that same pleasure. My tastes—that is, my utility function—may differ, and that hour may only be worth eight utiles to me. In light of this, let us ask what utility I should assign to the prospect of entering Jones's society as Jones and experiencing an hour's worth of this pleasure. One might suppose, and Harsanyi does suppose, that the utility for me of being Jones during this hour is ten utiles. But in fact (the argument continues) the utility *for me* of being Jones and experiencing his pleasure is only *eight* utiles—since I am concerned with the utility *for me now*, in the original position, not the utility for me after I have become Jones. It is claimed this fact invalidates Harsanyi's argument, for his argument depends on the identification of my utility for being various members of society with their own utility for being themselves. Since the identification is incorrect, Harsanyi's argument does not succeed. Rawls and Gauthier conclude we cannot assume, then, that a principle of justice which maximizes average utility in a society will necessarily maximize the expected utility of a person in the original position who will enter that society as one of its members.

It is dubious that this objection to Harsanyi succeeds. First, as stated, it assumes that the parties in the original position know their own utility functions. However, Harsanyi cannot allow this. If a party in the original position knows what his utility function is, then he will know that he cannot turn out to be any member of society whose utility function is different from his own. If this knowledge is allowed, the interests of all members of society will not be equally taken into account. Of course, even if a person in the original position is not allowed to know his own utility function, he may know that it differs from that of some members of the society, for he knows that his is identical with that of one member of society, and he may know that the members of society have different utility functions from each other. But he must think about the situation as follows. When he tries to assess the utility to him of being Jones, he knows that if he *is* Jones, then his present utility function is identical with that of

Jones. Thus his utility for being Jones is the same as Jones' utility for being Jones. And this is true for every other member of society as well, even though their utility functions may differ. Consequently, his expected utility for entering that society is equal to the average utility level in the society, just as Harsanyi's argument requires, even though the expected utility figure is computed on the basis of different utility functions. There seems to be nothing in principle faulty about such a procedure, despite Rawls' hesitation on this score (175).

Even if we had to assume for some reason that the person in the original position must view himself as being *transformed* into a member of society who may have a different utility function from his own (unknown) one, it is still not obvious that it is illegitimate for him to evaluate the life of a given member of society in terms of that member's own utility function. We might understand the case as parallel to the following one. Suppose you must choose whether to enroll in a graduate program in philosophy or one in business. If you do the former, you will be poor but famous. If you do the latter, you will be rich but unknown. Right now you prefer being famous to being rich. However, whichever course of action you choose, you will undergo a character transformation and come to prefer being rich to being famous. Which of these three utility functions should be taken into account in your decision whether to enroll in the philosophy or the business program? A simple egoism-of-the-moment would dictate that you take into account only your *present* preferences, and so go into philosophy. However, it seems wholly appropriate to take into account instead the preferences of the future philosopher or businessperson, since they, as future aspects of yourself, will be the ones to actually lead and endure the lives in question. We might now transfer this solution to Harsanyi's original position since the time interval itself seems to make no difference. Thus even if the person in the original position knows that his utility function may be different from that of the member of society he will become, it may be appropriate for him to evaluate the life of that member in accord with the preferences of the member himself since he is the one who will actually live the life. He should not be concerned about the fact that, as chooser in the original position, he might "now" have a different utility function. It is unclear whether or not this appropriateness is a matter of rational prudence or rather a matter of moral principle. If it is the latter, then the parties in the original position, who are not themselves moved by moral considerations, cannot themselves argue on moral grounds that they should use the utility functions of the members of society. However, it is open to Harsanyi to stipulate it as one of the conditions of the original position that they so judge the lives of the members of society, in order to ensure the fairness of the decision, just as he stipulates that they judge themselves to have an equal chance of becoming any member of society.

The argument from different utility functions therefore does not appear to succeed as stated. However, it should be noted that Harsanyi's whole enterprise depends on the posssibility of making appropriate interpersonal comparisons of utility. Harsanyi's own suggestion for how this may be done appears to be undercut by the possibility that two individuals may have different utility functions for the very same experiences.[50] Until some more satisfactory method has been arrived at for making such comparisons, Harsanyi's argument remains at best problematic. Thus we cannot say that the original-position argument in favor of utilitarianism has been made completely compelling.

SUMMARY AND CONCLUSIONS

Let us summarize, although briefly, what has been discovered in the course of our examination of Rawls' arguments against utilitarianism. These arguments were divided into two categories, those which are independent of the contractarian standpoint, and those which depend on it. Among the former, the most important is the argument that utilitarianism accords less well with our considered moral judgments than does Rawls' own conception of justice, and in particular that utilitarianism violates our conviction that the liberties of some may not be limited so that others may benefit economically. We saw that the actual extent to which utilitarianism violates common egalitarian precepts is unclear because the empirical facts necessary to determine this remain unknown. But we also saw that Rawls' own assumptions about people's utility functions for such goods as income do not leave him in a strong position to press this point. We saw in addition that if Rawls' assumption about our relative preference for liberty is correct, then utilitarianism and his special conception may treat the protection of civil liberties in very much the same way, since it would not in realistic situations promote utility to trade the liberties of one person for an increase in economic goods for others. The contrast between Rawls' general conception and utilitarianism with regard to liberty must also remain unsettled, because of our ignorance of relevant empirical matters; but Rawls himself offers no reason to suppose utilitarianism would violate common precepts in any worse fashion than his general conception. The other extra-contractarian arguments he offers were also questioned: the complaint that utilitarianism illegitimately merges persons, and the complaint that it improperly disregards the source of the desires whose satisfaction is to be maximized, seemed unwarranted in the main part. The objection that utilitarianism has a serious problem in making interpersonal comparisons of utility was granted as a debilitating difficulty. But it was also pointed out that Rawls' own reliance on primary social goods to measure social expectations is subject to difficulties which in principle are just as grave. Thus on the whole we must conclude that Rawls' extra-contractarian arguments fail to show that utilitarianism is unacceptable—at least in comparison to Rawls' own principles, and judged on the basis of the empirical assumptions Rawls makes in arguing for his own conception of justice.

The arguments from within the contractarian standpoint do not fare significantly better. The three features of the original position which Rawls adduces to show that the parties in it must employ a maximin strategy in choosing a principle of justice to govern their society, fail to show that maximin, rather than some related strategy, must be used. It seems dubious that all of these features would hold true in an empirically plausible original position, and one feature at least seems to be a restriction added solely to avoid the derivation of utilitarianism from the original position. Given Rawls' empirical assumptions, it cannot clearly be argued that his principles of justice, rather than utilitarianism, constitute the unique best choice for the parties, even if these three features are all present. Rawls argues in addition that the parties in the original position would know they would be unable as members of society to adhere to the requirements of utilitarian justice, but we saw that utilitarianism rules out slavery and other forms of servitude in the same circumstances that Rawls' own principles do, and hence that there is no more reason to suppose it could not be adhered to. The argument from stability has serious flaws as well: it was shown that Rawls' principles would probably be seen as calling for sacrifices, just as utilitarianism might be, and hence that both would have some trouble eliciting popular support. It was also argued that utilitarianism is not significantly more difficult to understand or argue for than Rawls' principles, and so not less likely to command allegiance on those grounds. In addition we questioned whether Rawls' principles would be psychologically more reassuring than utilitarianism for members of society. Finally, we inspected Rawls' and Gauthier's argument against Harsanyi's attempt to derive utilitarianism from an original position, and saw that it seemed answerable, even though Harsanyi's own project is handicapped by lack of an acceptable method for making interpersonal comparisons of utility.

Rawls' book has revolutionized contemporary discussions of political theory; it seems likely to be the most profound work in the field to be published in this century. His extended argument against utilitarianism has raised important new issues and forced us to examine the old ones from a new perspective. But contrary to what many critics have supposed, the argument does not appear to ring the death-knell for utilitarianism; defenders of that theory, and those of contractarianism, must feel that the battle is far from over.[51]

NOTES

1. See Rawls (22-23n.); "Utilitarianism" *The Encyclopedia of Philosophy* (1967), pp. 7 and 8, 206-212, Dan W. Brock, "Recent Work in Utilitarianism," *American Philosophical Review* 10, no. 4 (October 1973): 241-276; and Samuel Gorovitz, ed., *Mill: Utilitarianism* (Indianapolis: The Bobbs-Merrill Company, Inc., 1971).

   Some utilitarians believe that the welfare of *all* sentient creatures, not just human beings, should be taken into account, but I shall not pursue that line here.
2. William K. Frankena, *Ethics*, 2nd ed. (Englewood Cliffs, N.J.: Prentice-Hall, Inc., 1973), p. 52.

   It should be pointed out that some "ideal" utilitarians *do* face a similar problem, for they believe that disparate kinds of things must all be recognized as good in themselves and balanced against each other.
3. A.M. MacLeod, "Critical Notice of Rawls' Theory of Justice," *Dialogue*, March 1974, p. 158, as quoted in Jan Narveson, "Rawls and Utilitarianism," unpublished paper presented at the Conference on the Limits of Utilitarianism held at Virginia Polytechnic Institute and State University, May 18-21, 1978. See also Joel Feinberg, "Rawls and Intuitionism," in Norman Daniels, ed., *Reading Rawls* (New York: Basic Books, Inc.), p. 116.
4. See Rawls (302-303) for the final statements of these principles.
5. See Feinberg, "Rawls and Intuitionism," pp. 108-116 for an illuminating discussion of the relations between justice, overall rightness, and utilitarianism.
6. Strictly speaking, his argument for the average view makes use of the original position perspective, but I shall assume it has general application.

7. See Richard Brandt, *A Theory of the Good and the Right*, Chapters 13 and 16 for useful discussion of the problems with the desire-satisfaction theory, and for an innovative account of rational desire.
8. On Rawls' version of utilitarianism, the welfare to be taken into account is restricted to that experienced by members of the society in question, rather than all of humanity, although the latter would be more in the spirit of classical utilitarianism (22). This makes no difference to the points I shall discuss, but merits further investigation.
9. Rawls also invokes the "Kantian conception" as a justification for the contractarian approach, but the gap between this conception and utilitarianism is too large to attempt dealing with in this paper.
10. See Marshall Cohen, "Review of a Theory of Justice," *New York Times Book Review* (16 July 1972), pp. 1, 16, and Hugo Bedau, "Founding Righteousness on Reason," *The Nation* (11 September 1972), pp. 180–181, as quoted in David Lyons, "Nature and Soundness of the Contract and Coherence Arguments" in Daniels, *Reading Rawls*, p. 143.
11. Peter Singer, "Sidgwick and Reflective Equilibrium," *Monist* 58 (1974): 490-517.
12. Lyons, "Nature and Soundness," p. 148.
13. See Rawls (28). Allan Gibbard discusses this theory of ordinary moral judgments, as Sidgwick states it, in "If the Morality of Common Sense is Unconsciously Utilitarian, Does that Give Us Any Reason to be Utilitarians?" unpublished paper presented at the utilitarianism conference at Virginia Polytechnic Institute and State University, May 18–21, 1978.
14. For further discussion on the role of moral intuitions, see Brandt, *A Theory of the Good and the Right*, Chapter 1, and Ronald Dworkin, "The Original Position," in Daniels, *Reading Rawls*, pp. 27–37.
15. This was pointed out to me by Allan Gibbard.
16. John Rawls, "Justice as Fairness," in Wilfrid Sellars and John Hospers, eds., 2nd ed., *Readings in Ethical Theory* (New York: Appleton-Century-Crofts, 1970), p. 592.
17. See Lyons, "Nature and Soundness," p. 148.
18. Rawls actually admits that the special conception itself would admit slavery when it constitutes an improvement over a current unjust practice, for example if enslavement of prisoners of war were substituted for their automatic execution (248). Unfortunately it is unclear from his discussion whether he intends this as an application of the special conception in nonstrict compliance theory, and so not strictly relevant to its adequacy in a well-ordered society, or intends it to fall under the strict-compliance priority rule which stipulates that a less than equal liberty must be acceptable to those citizens with the lesser liberty (250). If he intends the latter, then the possibility is relevant to the assessment of the special conception in a well-ordered society. Presumably utilitarianism would allow slavery in these circumstances as well, so no contrast can be drawn.

19. Narveson, "Rawls and Utilitarianism," pp. 16-17; Kenneth J. Arrow, "Some Ordinalist-Utilitarian Notes on Rawls' Theory of Justice," *The Journal of Philosophy* LXX, no. 9 (May 10, 1973), 250; Brian Barry, *The Liberal Theory of Justice* (Oxford: The Clarendon Press, 1973), p. 106; Lyons, "Nature and Soundness," pp. 142-145.
20. See Arrow, "Ordinalist Notes," p. 250.
21. Rawls also argues that his conception of justice handles justice between generations more effectively than utilitarianism does (286). I will not attempt here to resolve this difficult issue.

    A number of authors have argued that Rawls' principles actually give rise to *less* intuitive results than utilitarianism does. See, for example, Arrow, "Ordinalist Notes," and Barry, *Liberal Theory of Justice*.
22. Brandt, *A Theory of the Good and the Right*, Chapter 12. The "impersonality" of Rawls' parties was pointed out to me by Gary M. Busch.
23. Arrow, "Ordinalist Notes," p. 257.
24. See Jane Bryant Quinn, "Perquisites: A Status Report," *Newsweek*, July 24, 1978, p. 13c.
25. For a discussion of this issue and the ways in which Rawls might try to avoid it, see Allan Gibbard, "Disparate Goods and Rawls' Difference Principle," forthcoming in *Theory and Decision*.
26. Some work has been done on the measurement of power, but it is unclear what the relation is between *power* and Rawls' notion of *powers*. On the measurement of power, see Alvin I. Goldman, "Toward a Theory of Social Power," *Philosophical Studies* 23 (1972): 221-268, and "On the Measurement of Power," *The Journal of Philosophy* LXXI, no. 8 (May 2, 1974): 231-252. The first of these contains references to literature in the social sciences.
27. See Arrow, "Ordinalist Notes," p. 254.
28. Frederick Schick, "A Calculus of Liberalism," unpublished paper presented at the conference on utilitarianism at Virginia Polytechnic Institute and State University, May 18-21, 1978, p. 2.
29. Arrow, "Ordinalist Notes," p. 254.
30. Rawls' citation of the three "features" follows William Fellner, *Probability and Profit* (Homewood, Ill.: R.D. Irwin, Inc., 1965), pp. 140-142 (154n.).
31. Barry, *Liberal Theory of Justice*, p. 91; R. Duncan Luce and Howard Raiffa, *Games and Decisions* (New York: John Wiley and Sons, Inc., 1957), Chapter 13.
32. See Narveson, "Rawls and Utilitarianism," p. 21, and Thomas Nagel, "Rawls on Justice," in Daniels, *Reading Rawls*, pp. 11-12.
33. John C. Harsanyi, "Can the Maximin Principle Serve as A Basis for Morality? A Critique of John Rawls' Theory," *The American Political Science Review* LXIX (June 1975), 598.
34. Narveson, "Rawls and Utilitarianism," pp. 21-22.
35. Although Nagel has noted, significantly, that the decision is "important" only within the range of social arrangements where disaster is a possibility;

with respect to more socially developed circumstances, the "importance" argument looks far less compelling (Nagel, "Rawls on Justice," p. 11).

36. R.M. Hare, "Rawls' Theory of Justice," in Daniels, *Reading Rawls*, p. 103.
37. Narveson, "Rawls and Utilitarianism," pp. 10-11; Barry, *Liberal Theory of Justice*, pp. 97-98; Nagel, "Rawls on Justice," p. 12.
38. Rawls himself does not state this explicitly.
39. Barry, *Liberal Theory of Justice*, p. 105.
40. Barry, *Liberal Theory of Justice*, p. 98.
41. Narveson, "Rawls and Utilitarianism," p. 23.
42. See Hare, "Rawls' Theory of Justice," pp. 104-105, and Nagel, "Rawls on Justice," p. 12.
43. There are interesting problems here, however, about the nature of "psychological possibility." Rawls' remarks suggest that it may be psychologically impossible for a member of society to accept a given principle of justice if he does rather poorly under it, *and* if he knows he personally would have done better under some other principle of justice (174-175). But of course people living under Rawlsian principles might know this.
44. Rawls also mentions as a third circumstance the recognition of those who follow the governing principle of justice as being admirable. However, this appears to play a less significant role in his argument that his conception of justice fares better than utilitarianism.
45. Rawls also identifies a second sense in which his principles benefit everyone, but it relies on empirical assumptions on which he wishes to rest no weight, which many commentators have found suspect, and which, if true, would render utilitarianism and the difference principle equivalent in their prescriptions (80, 82). I shall therefore ignore this second sense.
46. See Robert Nozick, *Anarchy, State, and Utopia* (New York: Basic Books, Inc., 1974), pp. 190-197, for an illuminating discussion of the problem of "sacrifice."
47. J.J.C. Smart, "An Outline of a System of Utilitarian Ethics," in J.J.C. Smart and Bernard Williams, *Utilitarianism: For and Against* (Cambridge: The University Press, 1973), p. 7.

    Rawls may have in mind here the sort of argument which it would be necessary to use when selecting a principle of justice in the original position, although it is not clear this restriction would be fair. In any event, the argument from the original position for utilitarianism is no more difficult than the argument for his own principles.
48. John C. Harsanyi, "Cardinal Utility in Welfare Economics and the Theory of Risk Taking," *Journal of Political Economy* 61 (1953), and "Cardinal Welfare, Individualistic Ethics, and Interpersonal Comparisons of Utility," *Journal of Political Economy* 63 (1955); and W.S. Vickrey, "Utility, Strategy, and Social Decision Rules," *Quarterly Journal of Economics* 74 (1960). See also Rawls' presentation of this argument in Section 27.
49. Rawls (173-175); David Gauthier, "On the Refutation of Utilitarianism," unpublished paper presented at the conference on utilitarianism at Virginia

Polytechnic Institute and State University, May 18–21, 1978, pp. 18–22.

50. Harsanyi appears to suggest that we can derive interpersonal comparisons of utility in the following manner. Suppose the problem is whether to provide Jones or Smith with an hour's pleasure of a certain sort. We arrange for Jones to understand exactly what being Smith and experiencing that pleasure would be like for Smith, and we also arrange for Smith to understand exactly what being Jones and experiencing that pleasure would be like for Jones. We then ask each to choose between the following alternatives: (a) taking a fifty-fifty chance of being Jones or Smith, and Jones' experiencing the pleasure, or (b) taking a fifty-fifty chance of being Jones or Smith, and Smith's experiencing the pleasure. It is assumed they would make the same choice, and that the choice of, say, alternative (a) shows that Jones experiencing the pleasure has greater value than Smith's. However, as Allan Gibbard points out, this procedure does not work if Jones places a different value on the sort of experience that Smith would have than Smith himself does. And it seems possible that Jones and Smith may indeed have different utility functions for the same subjective experiences.

51. I wish to thank John G. Bennett, Richard Brandt, Alvin Goldman, Jan Narveson, and particularly Allan Gibbard for their assistance with this paper.

Rawls and Marx

Joseph P. DeMarco
CLEVELAND STATE UNIVERSITY

INTRODUCTION

John Rawls' almost immediate success with *A Theory of Justice* suggests that he is able to articulate some beliefs about justice important in contemporary Western social and political thinking. He does this by taking a position within the social contract tradition which has had great importance as a foundation of political thoughts, in a way that seems to support current demands for equal opportunity and for greater economic equality. His work is meant as a challenge to basic patterns of institutional life, but the standards he sets are not out of line with some fundamental predispositions in Western societies. His position is basically individualistic; he is not a radical egalitarian—instead he is theoretically willing to tolerate even wide economic and social inequalities. His call for equal liberty is restricted to political liberties, and his demand for full equal opportunity is somehow seen by him as consistent with predictable disabilities in initial life prospects accruing from basic class differentiations.[1] Of course, these concessions are not to be viewed as a commitment to basic patterns of social and economic inequality; his clear intent is to force such inequalities into a position in which they carry the burden of proof. A defense of inequality must include everyone—it is only in mutual benefit through greater efficiency that inequalities become tolerable. Rawls taps dominant sentiments: productive efficiency and individual self-concern are essential ingredients of his theory.

It seems that Rawls' work stands as a kind of bellwether of contemporary Western democracies. He is able to capture some dominant historical trends, and, simultaneously, he offers a critical perspective that apparently promises reform of some serious social maladies. Rawls consciously intends to perform a critical function such as this, as his notion of considered judgments in reflective equilibrium suggests. This basically means that the main principles of his theory are to be judged by the extent to which they support *and* guide widely held, carefully considered, beliefs about justice. Such an undertaking deserves success; but it will attract its own form of critical commentray: a wide variety of objections can be made to any philosophical position, but with Rawls' theory a central question will be whether or not it does indeed reflect and guide "our" considered judgments on justice. Part of the philosopher's critical role is to attempt to answer this question.

The main weight of this essay, however, is an attempt to carry such a critique one step further. It may be true that Rawls is in step with current trends in Western democracies, but to stop there is not to carry to completion the analytic and critical function of the philosopher and of the social critic. The main problem is twofold: in a closely interrelated world in which concerns over justice seriously affect everyone, a theorist using the test of considered judgments must look beyond sentiments in Western societies. And, secondly, some of the dominant inclinations apparently supporting Rawls' theory may not be internally consistent or well enough formulated to withstand critical scrutiny. The purpose of Rawls' theory is to guide and support well-established judgments; the point raised here is that care must be taken when these considered beliefs about justice are selected and evaluated. In short, basic predispositions must be subjected to a careful, thorough critique.

This exploration, which relates the Marxian position to Rawls', can push the analysis further for a variety of reasons, regardless of our attitudes toward Marxism. First of all, what counts as a considered judgment, that is, a firm belief about justice, is partly determined by awareness of alternatives and by what is taken to be facts about social arrangements. Marxism provides alternatives for consideration and constitutes a theory of society. Secondly, if our considered judgments are to occupy the theoretical role Rawls gives to them as a point from which we can judge his theory, it is crucial that the "our" is pushed to include the greatest possible number and variety of people. We want to get as much agreement as possible over what sorts of views are held as considered judgments because justice is a social notion, prescribing the relationships that ought to exist between members of societies. An overwhelming number of people today live under Marxian governments, and many of the people in these countries advocate Marxism. Perhaps more importantly many people in other countries, e.g., India, Italy, Spain, Portugal, are convinced that a Marxian state is the only just state. Theoretically, an understanding of Marx is clearly relevant in testing the extent to which Rawlsian justice captures and guides such widely held views on justice.

Beyond that, we live in a world made dangerous partly by basic ideological differences; these differences, by blocking concerted action, tend to perpetuate injustices now clearly rampant in the world. Bridging such gaps, if possible, will bring a small world in which interaction is extensive closer to justice and thereby eliminate the misery of exploitation and injustice. So a comparison between Rawls and Marx should strengthen a critique of the Rawlsian model and may aid in the establishment of a fuller social dialogue.

These reasons are sufficient to justify the comparison; yet there is a further perspective on the comparison which, while more difficult to defend, is probably as important as the other. This perspective concerns a trend with an almost universal impact in intellectual climate, and this trend is clearly inspired by Marx. Marx was an economic "determinist." That is, Marx believed that social and political institutions are basically molded by economic conditions and that great historical movements result from the interplay of basic economic factors. To some degree or other, such a "determinism" infects much of the contemporary perspective. Occasionally non-Marxian scholars express their debt to Marxian thought. For example, Patrick Gardner writes, "By stressing the relevance to historical explanation of technical and economic factors in the particular way he did, Marx in effect redrew the map of history. In doing so he made it difficult for historians ever to look at this subject in quite the same fashion as they had done before; this is surely the mark of a considerable and original thinker."[2] While the central role of economic conditions in social life is well recognized in Marxian and non-Marxian circles, political philosophers in other traditions often fail to examine the influencing force of economic factors. The closed systematic structure of a philosophical position such as Rawls' makes it tempting to ignore a side of social life otherwise kept in the foreground. The examination of Rawls in relation to Marx should help to bring the determining economic conditions into the forefront so that a critique of Rawls can be approached with greater depth and thereby greater ability to assess its plausibility and consequences. This is not to say that a Marxian economic determinism is to be uncritically accepted—actually it seems to be clearly mistaken in its strongest statement. Rather it is looked to, as Marx's basic position, to find whether Rawls' theory shows weaknesses or strengths in relation to economic and other derivative social forces.

So the Marxian point of view stands as a challenge to Rawls in two ways: It centers on economic determinism and it offers an alternative set of basic predispositions. While I am neither a Rawlsian nor a Marxist, I think that viewing the two theories together shows flaws in both. In my view, there is much strength in a position which combines some of the key features of both. The concluding section of this chapter attempts to present such a view after the evaluation of the strengths or weaknesses of both in comparison. In short, I will attempt to develop a synthesis which captures some of the most important views of both.

Throughout, this essay focuses on some basic elements in Marx's thought: economic determinism, class struggle, surplus value, and the movement of history. These will be compared with the basic features of Rawls' thought: the original position, the difference principle, the priority of equal liberty and equal opportunity. It might not be surprising that on each of these, Marx and Rawls would have had fundamental disagreements. Precise determination of the grounds of the disagreement will be attempted. But the essay also includes such hypothetical quesions as, How would Marx have constructed the original position *if* he found such a model useful?

The second section covers the basic elements of Marx's thought. Although the description is quite brief it should give the fundamental flavor of his position. It not only attempts to explain his economic determinism, but also tries to show why he believed that all non-communistic societies are exploitative and inalterably gripped by basic class hostilities.

The following section explores Marx's explicit sentiments on what a theory of justice is all about. To him, as a determinist, theories such as Rawls' lack efficacy or are merely apologistic fudges covering the harsh realities of class conflict. This claim is explored in a critical fashion, especially in relationship to Rawls. The conclusion is that the claim is not specific enough to be fruitfully evaluated. So we turn instead to a detailed analysis of Rawls' theory in view of Marx's basic doctrines.

The fourth section considers the ways in which Marx might have reacted to Rawls' original position. His view would have been overwhelmingly negative—some of what he might have said seems to be unjustified, but much has significant merit. For example, Marx held a social view of human nature which conflicts with Rawls' "individualism." A Marxian original position occupied by social individuals yields results that are at odds with Rawls. This is instructive because it shows that a particular commitment necessary for accepting Rawls' original position falls far short of being universally appealing.

Rawls' principles are examined from the Marxian perspective in the fifth section, with easily predictable results. Marx would have rejected all of the main ingredients of Rawls' principles—from equal liberty to the difference principle. I develop the theory that a basic reason for such rejection is that Marx took a broad historical evolutionary view; he tended to judge current practices by their efficacy in leading to an ulterior historical goal. Rawls, on the other hand, is interested in judging current arrangements without taking a longer view.

Both perspectives are overly narrow, and so in the final section I offer a synthesis in which a view fairly close to Rawls' is adopted for judging current policies provided we take a view something like Marx's as an ideal to be approached in the long run future. Such a view has substantial merit on its own, but even if it is rejected in its details, it seems to me to point out a crucial need for the balancing of such a two-fold time perspective.

THE ESSENTIALS OF MARX'S THOUGHT

As some of the basic elements in Marx' thought are presented, the reader may be aware of a tone or style that is basically different from Rawls'. Rawls' work is highly abstracted from specific social contingencies; it is also prescriptive, with the underlying assumption of the efficacy of value judgments; and it is utopian, especially in the final chapters, in that it argues for a harmony of social interests under the guidance of the principles of justice. Marx, on the other hand, often argued from the perspective of a particular historical period; he did not believe in value judgments as a vehicle of social change; and he was pessimistic in that he saw social classes as necessarily living in social strife.

These differences suggest that the conflict between Rawls and Marx is going to be significant. Perhaps the most important point leading to conflict is Marx's notion of the efficacy and status of philosophical speculation. While Rawls believes that principles of justice can influence social and economic arrangements, Marx maintained that such principles are derived from economic arrangements and merely serve to rationalize and support already existing institutions. Marx's view is dependent on the fundamental feature of his thought, "economic determinism." The foundation of this position rests on the contention that economic conditions determine social institutions. He claimed,

> In the social production of their existence, men inevitably enter into definite relations, which are independent of their will, namely relations of production appropriate to a given stage in the development of their material forces of production. The totality of these relations of production constitutes the economic structure of society, the real foundation, on which arises a legal and political superstructure and to which correspond definite forms of social consciousness. The mode of production of material life conditions the general process of social, political and intellectual life. It is not the consciousness of men that determines their existence, but their social existence that determines their consciousness.[3]

Marx once proclaimed that people need to eat before they can think. The above statement shows this sentiment in a more sophisicated form. The central aspect of social life is the way in which goods are produced, distributed, and consumed; in this Marx included the physical process of production—machines, labor and the materials of production. And he also included the *roles* various people play in relation to physical production—the owner of capital, the wage laborer, slave and master, serf and lord, etc. (called the relations of production). It is not simply that this is the basic aspect of society—the one that absorbs the most time and energy—but it is also the aspect of society which strongly influences all other important patterns in social life. Marx, in the above statement, was claiming that institutions such as the state, the legal system, the family, and even the style in which people worship and think is determined, or made to be what they are, by economic conditions. And the way people think includes, of course, the kind of philosophy they write.

Scholars disagree (and even Marx and Engels said conflicting things) about Marx's intention in using the strong word "determines"; so it is not clear just how far Marx believed social institutions could be independent of economic conditions or how far social institutions could, in their turn, influence basic patterns in production. But there is nearly unanimous agreement that for Marx economic conditions form by far the main influencing factor in social life. And, to make the claim more plausible, we should keep in mind that Marx was talking about *basic* patterns of life in broadly defined historical periods. As an example, he held that the dominant religion of the middle ages was a product of feudal economic organization. He did not maintain that some given individual could not think different thoughts about religion, nor did he believe that the dominant religion could not go through minor alterations independent of economic changes. His position simply applies to basic patterns in social life and how these get to be the way they are.

From his nineteenth century vantage point, Marx could see the profound social effects of the movement away from feudalism in various European countries, with England leading the way. Concomitant with new materials and relations of production he could see basic changes in religion, laws, philosophy, the state, and even family structure. From his perspective it seems reasonable to believe that the way people's work routine changed did usher in a new historical age.

It is not enough for a theory to claim some sort of correlation—the question is why such a correlation exists. Marx's answer has to do with the power or the lack of power that attends one's place in the relations of production. In short, economic conditions involve social classes of unequal power; these classes are defined by their role in the economic process. The dominating class, in capitalism the "owners of the means of social production and the employers of wage-labor,"[4] have the preponderance of social power through which they can, as a class, manipulate social institutions. Their power, not as individuals but as a class, succeeds in the production (in ways not made clear by Marx) of a social superstructure (the major social institutions), most notably the state and the legal structure, functioning as the protector and the facilitator of the dominant class. The relations of production serve to facilitate the production process in a society, and the superstructure facilitates and maintains the smooth operation of the society from the point of view of the dominant class. The major features of a society function, in the Marxian theory, as the means used by the dominating class to put the life of a society in its service. For example, in capitalism the state serves as the protector of unequal property and the facilitator of trade, and religion keeps the people in line and instills a "work ethic."

A stable historical period comes about as the result of stable class relations where the balance of power rests with some particular class. The equilibrium, though it might be stable for hundreds of years, is not a happy state. Instead it conceals a network of class conflicts and tensions, occasionally coming into full view. So Marx and Engels confidently stated, "The history of all hitherto existing society is the history of class struggles."[5] If, in a society, people simply had different occupational duties, "class struggle" might not be found. But Marx's analyses went beyond functional differences, and involved exploitation—this exploitation explains the tension and struggle attendant on the presence of classes.

Exploitation has a fairly precise meaning in the Marxian system—it has to do with the expropriation of "surplus value." Surplus value is the total value of goods produced in a society beyond what is needed to keep itself functioning as a productive force. In any society a high proportion of the material produced is needed simply for survival at a minimal level. This level is determined by the needs of the productive system; in a society such as ours, a high level of educational support may be required to insure a properly skilled work force. Therefore much of the expense in education should be considered socially necessary. Of course, items such as food, clothing, basic transportation and housing are crucial to the viable economic survival of this society. Surplus value is *extra* value in the sense that it goes beyond the essential needs of the productive system. It is that part of production above and beyond what is really needed.

One could imagine a society in which everyone had to work very long hours in order to keep a society alive as an economic unit. This would be a society without surplus value. It is unattractive because life would be so difficult. But since, by and large, everyone has to work for survival, it would be, on Marx's view, a society without any single group engaging in the exploitation of another group. Exploitation here means, quite simply, taking goods away from a group. In such a state of scarcity taking goods from a group is not feasible, because the group that is exploited is living at the edge of subsistence and would be destroyed as a group by further deprivation.

But if a social surplus comes about, say by the development of some new technique of production, then one class could exploit another. The opportunity would be present for some people to, say, enslave the rest, making them produce and taking from them all that was not needed to keep that producing class functioning. That which the enslavers get is surplus value. This is, more or less, what Marx believed happens in a pure capitalistic system. He thought that wage labor is paid just enough to keep it functioning as a producing class—indeed in a fairly wretched state (an obvious condition in his day). In this way the capitalistic class appropriates surplus value and uses it in large part to amass wealth and power.

The notion of exploitation is the philosophical counterpart of the labor theory of value, used by Marx to show that all economic value comes by means of labor. The goods of society are produced by labor and exchanged at rates based on the amount of labor needed to produce the goods. While all value comes from labor, some gain goods without laboring. This is possible in capitalism, Marx believed, because labor is not paid its full value, and the unpaid part accrues to capitalists, landowners, etc. Consequently the capitalistic class increases in wealth. This is Marx's doctrine of "wage-slavery."

The capitalist can pay wage-laborers less than the value of their production because the laborers are forced to work at subsistence. They have no capital of their own. If they do not work, chances of survival are lessened. Many are unemployed so competition among workers can be relied on to keep wages at a social minimum. The capitalistic system with its private ownership of the means of production is, Marx thought, a thoroughly exploitative system.

It is easy to see why Marx believed that classes are antagonistic; for him the existence of classes means that some group(s) are exploiting, or taking from, other groups. This sort of thing is only feasible when there is unequal power, and with unequal power those in the exploiting class(es) erect (in a social way) the superstructure, the institutional life, of a society in order to preserve their benefits. And he also believed that their power is based on their role in the productive process. But the way things are produced changes—for example, large factories replace handicraft. With such changes the nature of those controlling the life of society changes. As the economic base shifts through the introduction of new materials of production and through rearrangements of the relations of production, the relative strength of economic classes also shift. That is, the exploiting class grows weaker as its style of production becomes unworkable, and some other class grows stronger. When the balance of power fatally tips, a new period of history, with its new superstructure, supercedes the old.

This he thought was going to happen within a short time to capitalism. He believed that the capitalistic system contained a variety of what he called "contradictions" or what we might call "basic conflicts." For example, in the system people buy goods for consumption in relatively small units—a single person buys a shirt to wear. Yet production is for profit in large units—the shirt is produced in a factory in order to make a profit. Production is social (viz., large scale) yet ownership is individual. Such forces contribute, among other things, to overproduction and consequently depressions, or "panics" as they used to be called. This is so because the gigantic productivity of the capitalistic system is uncoordinated so that the amount produced is determined by individual and thereby limited readings of the amount of goods that can be profitably produced. When supply outstrips effective demand, production is cut back and, when this occurs on a large enough scale, demand is further curtailed by layoffs. Finally a depression results.

These depressions tend to destroy the weaker capitalists and force them into the ranks of the working class. In turn larger and larger productive units are developed, and this exacerbates the contradiction between social production and individual ownership. In Marx's scenario this leads to a serious weakening of the power of the capitalist class (mainly the consolidation of business in bigger units and consequently the numerical weakening of the capitalist) and thereby strengthens the workers. With increased power the workers rebel against being exploited and usher in a new epoch. But the unusual feature of the new order would be the absence of any classes at all. The workers and the owners of the means of production are the main classes in the capitalist era. So when the capitalists are destroyed as capitalists, only one group is left, and hence class struggle would eventually disappear.

Marx's vision for the future includes a classless society in which production is for use and not for profit, in which people freely cooperate without the need of a superstructure containing a state and laws (which simply existed to protect the dominating class). People would receive what they need and would contribute what they could. Money would not be used; work would be limited because of extensive use of machinery; the arts and sciences would flourish in a society without the debilitating inequalities of class differentiation.

MARX AND JUSTICE

In moving on to more specific aspects of Marx's thought that explicitly relate to justice, his "deterministic" system should be kept in mind. A major part of that system is the analytic use of the relations between classes leading to institutional structures (state, law, religion, etc.) and to historical movement from one economic system to another. These class relationships are always exploitative. "Exploitation" is a value-laden word; it suggests something bad, something that needs to be overcome. And Marx knew that exploitation leads to genuine human misery. In a variety of places Marx graphically related the real horrors of the nineteenth century economic production in England. With this in view it is easy to read Marx's work as a consistent effort to overcome exploitation and thereby reach the just and non-exploitative state. Since exploitation is rather clearly defined as the expropriation of surplus value in the capitalist system, a theory of justice in Marx could be structured from which a comparison with Rawls could be drawn. While many have read Marx in this way,[6] other features of his writings make this judgment more complex. This complexity is, however, to our advantage because it should bring us to a deeper understanding of the gap between Rawls and Marx.

Characterizing Marx as a person with passion for justice is problematic. How could Marx suggest changes in the name of "justice" when he claimed that "justice" merely rationalizes an existing system? He apparently believed that "justice" language is either nonsense or else so system-bound as to be useless to his purposes.[7] As a matter of fact, Marx, in all of his copious writings, hardly ever used the term "justice," and when he did it was often in a pejorative sense. For example Marx cynically wrote:

> Do we really know anything more about the 'usurer' when we say that his actions conflict with 'eternal justice,' with 'eternal equity,' with 'eternal mutuality' and with other 'eternal verities'—then the Fathers of the Church knew when they said that the actions of the usurer conflicted with the 'eternal grace,' with the 'eternal faith,' with the 'everlasting will of god'?[8]

And he even claimed, in seeming contradiction to his supposed passion for justice, that exploitation of the wage-labor is "a piece of good luck for the buyer, but by no means an injury to the seller."[9]

Some sense of this odd feature of Marx can be made in ways which will aid in an eventual comparison with Rawls. First of all, the base-superstructure model relegates morality to the superstructure where it serves the interests of the dominant class. Any widely held account of justice is going to be "determined" by the kind of productive relationships in society. In short, there is no "eternal idea" of justice but merely conceptions functioning as lubricants of a society's productive machinery. That is what talk about justice is all about. Within a capitalistic system it makes little sense for the laborer to talk of unjust treatment because of exploitation; the capitalist system only works with such exploitation. The worker can validly claim that an injustice is committed if he or she does not receive the wages agreed on by contract—but that, after all, is part of the capitalist notion of justice. The exploitation of a wage-labor contract is simply part of the system. One might want to argue here that the notion of exploitation can be turned into a conception of justice in order to show that capitalism is, in Marx's view, a bad system. But this overlooks Marx's belief that capitalism was needed in the historical movement to communism; it was needed because it brought with it the enormous productive capacity that eventually would enable a genuine classless society to function. Without exploitation the advantages of capitalism would be lost. Marx was not unequivocably opposed to capitalism—but he thought that it had already served its purpose on countries like England, and therefore it was *fated* to be overturned, not by talk about justice, but by movement of economic events. To claim an injustice to workers is to fail to take the historical view that capitalism and exploitation are needed in the movement toward communism.

Marx's point, that "justice" is in the service of the superstructure, should put the student of Rawls on guard—Rawls is, after all, offering a theory of justice good for all times and places. Marx thought that we cannot have such a concept without suffering illusion, and the predicted illusion would be that Rawls maintains a notion suitable to his time and society (or rather to the dominant forces of his age) and extends it to all times. It is necessary, of course, to deal with the specific ways in which Marx might have claimed that Rawls' view functions within a capitalist environment, but for now it is enough to point out that the Marxian would be anxious to expose ideologically motivated capitalistic leanings in Rawls' conception.

The second, and perhaps even more important reason for Marx's rejection of "justice," is that he may have viewed it as a term that is used in the stabilization of harmful class conflicts.[10] For Marx "justice" is not a utopian term; it is a term used in an environment of conflict as the effort to bring that conflict to equilibrium. On the social level the significant conflicts are class conflicts. But the very existence of classes means exploitation in a less than optimum society. Marx's utopian element calls for the abolition of such differences of interest. Justice as a notion calls for the stabilization and the harmonization of such conflicts. Marx was a long run thinker; he thought in terms of great historical movements of economic systems. The stabilization of conflict within a particular system could not have been, for him, eternal or universal justice. If he took a short run view, he might have had more respect for harmonizing conflicts since, given the existence of classes with different interests, it is best to bring those interests into the most satisfying equilibrium. But Marx would have viewed such an equilibrium if genuinely stable, as in opposition to necessary historical movement. Hence, in the long run, justice is unnecessary and in the short run it is either useless (as a universal philosophical notion) or in the interest of the dominant class (as a legal notion). To add some credence to his view, we find Rawls agreeing that "justice" is used to stabilize social conflict:

> ...although a society is a cooperative venture for mutual advantage, it is typically marked by a conflict as well as by an identity of interest....A set of principles is required for choosing among the various social arrangements which determine this division of advantages and for underwriting an agreement on the proper distributive shares (4, all parenthetical citations are to John Rawls, *A Theory of Justice*, (Cambridge, Mass.: Harvard University Press, 1971)).

Rawls obviously intends his system as one leading to a stabilization of conflict and, as shall be seen, such a stabilization would be at the class level. Marx would have seen this as an attempt to grant a seal of objective permanent validity to a transient aspect of social life, viz., the conflict of class interests.

So the Marxist would offer a response to the Rawlsian which would be equally applicable to almost any attempt at a theory of justice: (1) A theory of justice (being part of the superstructure) is dominated by the relations of production in a particular society. Attempts to make it seem otherwise are illusory. (2) Theories of justice, such as Rawls', are riddled through with an invalid willingness to accept, for all times, basic class differences in society. Given those two objections, it is doubtful that the orthodox, hard-line Marxist would give any sort of sympathetic reading to Rawls' theory.

I think this is a serious mistake. The a priori rejection of Rawls goes too far. It is not by accident that many have noted Marx's passion for injustice. He did use terms like "exploitation," "equality," "freedom," "wage-slavery," and "alienation." And he did offer a utopian vision of future social life. The rejection of "justice" as ideological seems to argue for the overthrow of Marx's favorite terms and his vision. It seems then that Marx's use of "justice" was idiosyncratic. If "justice" is a term used to show how people ought to be related in society in terms of social benefits and burdens and without necessary tie to class membership, then Marx can be read as advocating a particular (albeit classless) conception of justice. He might not have held, as Rawls does, that justice is the first virtue of a society. But he would have held that the most rewarding, the freest and the most productive society is one without classes, without a state and without money. Although Marx would not have called this a theory of justice, it appears to many to be one.

The prima facie rejection of Rawls is premature; the dialogue between Rawls and Marx needs to deal with specifics; the Marxian ought to take Rawls seriously. In the following sections we shall attempt such a point by point examination of the main features of Rawls' theory.

MARX AND THE ORIGINAL POSITION

A central piece of Rawls' theory is the original position because it seems to establish the rationale for the acceptance of the two principles of justice. Although it seems to occupy such an important place, its foundational status has been thrown into doubt by Rawls himself. When his views were first presented in journal articles in the late fifties, Rawls seemed to think that the features of the original position formed the self-evident starting point, or an axiomatic base, for the development of rigorously proved principles of justice. He was criticized for this view in 1969, basically because the features of the original position are not self-evident;[11] they are peculiarly value-laden because they *assume* important aspects of the principles they are to defend. Rawls explicitly accepts this line of criticism in the preface to *A Theory of Justice* (xi). Apparently in answer to this charge, Rawls develops a rationale for the main features of the contract situation—considered judgments in reflective equilibrium.[12] That is, Rawls devises a technique which could be used to defend the main features of the original position instead of simply presenting those features as the self-evident starting point of his theory. The revision establishes a give and take between our considered beliefs and the original position, allowing both to be modified. So in the revised version Rawls devises the original position in such a way that it either leads to principles that support our most secure judgments about justice or else causes us to modify our judgments so that they are brought into line with the principles. If the original position is designed in a way that fails to produce such effective principles, it needs to be modified until it does so. In this process, our considered judgments may yield and shift with increasingly refined versions of the original position until an equilibrium point exists. At that equilibrium point, we can be confident that we have reached the most suitably structured original position which then spins forth the best principles of justice.

Now the whole contract situation is relativised in an important way: our considered views, even if modified, become the real base of the theory. And, of course, our views can be considered to be historically conditioned to some significant degree. This may indeed be the best way to proceed in the theory of justice, but Rawls goes on to hold that he has formulated the principles of justice for all times and places. Either Rawls is contradictory here, or else he believes that when our views are pressed to their most abstract rationality—when they are tested and refined—the conclusions are the same as would follow from any set of carefully considered and duly refined judgments. This is hard to believe, especially given that people throughout the ages have had such dramatically different beliefs about justice. For example, Aristotle believed that some people are natural slaves.

So we are faced with conflicting views of the original position. Starting with the view that the original position only functions well as relative to a given historically conditioned set of considered judgments, Marx would have claimed that such judgments are part of an economically dominated superstructure. Rawls, Marx would have insisted, is simply setting up a point to be regarded as rational, because refined and tested, when actually it cannot help but to serve dominant interests because these are the only views which are ever significantly held to be considered. These views are part of the superstructure. When we look at the sorts of views Rawls points to as considered—those, for example, that reject slavery and racial prejudice—we find that these are very much like the judgments Marx claimed served the capitalist mode of production in which a mobile and relatively capable force of *wage* labor is required. Marx believed that the "bourgeois" notion of freedom and slavery, both consistent with being subject to wage exploitation (or "wage-slavery"), always served the interest of the capitalist class. In this way, Marx would have argued that only judgments consistent with capitalism would be the ones admitted into Rawls' test.

Rawls might reply that some of the stringent requirements of the original position—full equality, the veil of ignorance—clearly go beyond any demonstrable connection with the economic base of current economic conditions. In fact, Rawls might point out that what could be called Marx's normative view on justice (his call for a classless society without wage exploitation) is a philosophical value judgment (whether Marx likes it or not) that seems to go beyond a bound ideology. Rawls might, quite sensibly, reject Marx's argument as overly a priori and unproven by careful argumentation. In other words, Marx's own theory suggests we can transcend narrow values. So the real argument between Marx and Rawls should be about whether the original position helps us to formulate a fruitful theory of justice.

While Rawls seems safe against the a priori charge that his theory is unavoidably bound up with capitalism, Marx would have an easier time arguing against the claim that the original position is the basis for a theory of justice for all times; Rawls never adequately defends this. Perhaps at this point I am interjecting my own point of view too much, but I find Rawls entirely unappealing here. We are, after all, children of our age--we live here and now and we need a theory for here and now. Even physicists, much further ahead than ethical philosophers in their brand of theory, would not claim that any particular theory is good for all times.

I think the real argument between Rawls and Marx is simply over the extent to which our considered judgments are independent, or can be made to be independent, of the economic base. The burden of proof here is on Marx; he has never adequately shown that thought is thoroughly conditioned. Marx seems to have held (as we have seen) that some views can be independent of the economic base, so in the argument against Rawls, the Marxian needs to show that Rawls' view and its main features, such as, fairness, equality, etc., are dependent.

The important question should be whether the original position is an aid to objective thinking. I tend to think that it is not, but I do not side with Marx's rejection of all philosophical speculation. Rather it seems to me that the original position is superfluous given Rawls' doctrine of considered judgments in reflective equilibrium, since it seems to serve only as a kind of "middle-man."

The Marxian might further argue that the principles derived from the deliberations in original position are to be put into effect within different periods of history. Each of these periods has its own mode and relations of production. The Marxist is thoroughly convinced that each historical period, until the communist stage, is burdened by its own special handicaps relating to its productive capacity, and the burdens cannot be wished away. They involve, inevitably, the existence of classes and exploitation. On the Marxian view, the members of the original position, knowing this, would then try to reconcile the conflicts that arise in any set of antagonistic relationships. In other words, they would try to make the best of the circumstances which they would encounter. A fair resolution of conflicts is given the honorific title of "justice," but Marx would have held that such a stabilization of conflict is not ideal. What is needed is a society without exploitation and conflict. So Rawls could be read as doing with the theory of justice precisely what Marx wished to avoid.

Rawls would be foolish, given his principles, not to acknowledge that we might indeed face a system of class stratification involving Marxian exploitation. In fact, Rawls does use the term "class," and admits that one class may justifiably have better life prospects than another class. He does this most explicitly. But Rawls does not use the term "exploitation,"—a term already connoting injustice. Instead he offers his theory as a way to test whether or not injustice exists in certain class relationships. The test he offers is whether or not rational, self-interested, free and equal individuals would assent to it. Of course, when inequities are unavoidable, such people, even when so "fairly" defined, are likely to accept all sorts of uncomfortable circumstances. It is rational to maximize your condition even when it is *horrible!* I do not want to exaggerate here; I want to make the theoretical point that under Rawlsian fairness the conflicting requirements of different classes may be taken into account, and the position of fairness operates as the vantage point from which the last bit of benefit is drained from such situations. So Rawls would answer that given a stable mode of production the only rational thing to do is to optimize one's position in it and thereby reach a maximally acceptable social equilibrium.

On this point Rawls seems to be on the losing end. He does seem to speculate in terms of given social circumstances—he attempts to rationalize a society with classes and does not consider Marxian questions about basic class exploitation. This will be a central issue in forthcoming sections. For now, I'll simply suggest, without a full defense, what is wrong with Rawls' position. The people in the original position are saddled with the difficult task of designing a set of principles that maximizes their position, and they decide to do so with a very general, abstract set of principles. The trouble is that the principles eventually need to be applied. But they must always be applied relative to some set of other constraints defined mainly by the workings of an economic system. The problem is that his theory contains no theory of economic constraints as Marx's does. Rawls claims that the position of the least well-off class must by made as rich in primary goods as possible. In this he assumes that there may be a least well-off class. The main reason for some classes having more goods than others would be that an economic system demands or needs inequalities to serve as incentives in order to promote productivity. Marx believed that capitalism needed such incentives and explained in his social theory that they worked through exploitation. He believed this need could be overcome when capitalism failed. Rawls does not give us a perspective from which we can judge whether a social inequality needed to increase productivity is unjust, a genuine need, a short run need or a relatively permanent feature of a system. On the other hand, Marx believed that these sort of constraints in capitalism were going to be short-lived. Given Marx's view of the future variability of those constraints, it seems nothing less than a sham to consider a society which has only reached a fair balance given the constraints upon it as "eternally" just. Without treating productivity promoting needs at greater length, Rawls seems unable to give an adequate account of the extent to which such needs are just.

This, however, is not the place to proceed fully on this issue. It will, I hope, be clearer when we examine Rawls' difference principle. I simply conclude that Marx would be right to say that as Rawls construes the original position, the members might be too willing to accept a stratified system based on current needs.

All of these issues are on such a broad level that it may be hard to see exactly what sorts of specifics would have bothered Marx about Rawls and what he might have accepted. Also, it is relatively hard to evaluate the comparative merit of such abstract positions, because it is difficult to argue over the extent that economic needs determines ethical judgments. So now we turn to a more specific debate about the original position. In this the pretence will be made that Marx is willing to play the original position game. Of course Marx's view of ethics would have caused him to reject any sort of original position, so we must keep in mind that we are making a counterfactual supposition.

Two options can be speculatively examined. (1) We will first assume that Marx accepts the original position more or less as it is defined by Rawls. The problem would then be to determine what sorts of results the Marxian would derive from the position. (2) Secondly, we will simply assume that Marx is willing to play the game, but we will allow him to make changes in the definition of the position.

The first view, that Marx more or less accepts the Rawlsian definition of original position, has been examined by Richard Miller.[13] Miller centers on the fact that the parties to the original position know the general facts about social life. Rawls actually makes the members extraordinarily intelligent; they know, for example, all the general principles of economic theory. The veil of ignorance only applies to those sorts of personal interest which tend to separate one person from another. If we know what group we are in, we might always want those things helping our particular group. So Rawls rules our knowledge of our own race, sex, I.Q., etc. but he does not rule out theoretical knowledge.

So Miller hypothesizes that since Rawls allows for knowledge of a general theory of social life, the occupants of the original position would know and accept all the theoretical points of the Marxian. This would not be a basic change in Rawls' position because he does not tell us what sorts of theoretical principles the members hold. So, naturally, if a Marxian played Rawls' game, the general principles assumed would be Marxian. This, according to Miller, means that the occupants would understand the nature and significance of class struggles. Since they know how strongly people in exploiting classes feel about their exceptional position in social life, those in the original position know that excessive wealth is monumentally important to people in richer classes. These people could not accept social life without such wealth. But Rawls' theory explicitly rejects this by claiming that rational people put little value on excessive wealth. When excessive wealth becomes vitally important, the people in the original position may be willing to gamble for the large rewards resulting from exploitation and would count as unrealistic attempts to dramatically limit such gains.

Rawls, of course, would disagree with Miller's point; for Rawls the original position is precisely designed to preclude making judgments based on personal biases which tend to skew rational deliberation. Those with wealth may indeed consider it crucial, but when examined from behind the veil of ignorance, it looks less so because the members would also know about the miserable subsistence life of labor. Rawls' (supposed) answer makes good sense; Miller does center too much on the needs of the best off. Rawls' strictures on the original position preclude these sorts of interests from being given so much consideration. Nevertheless, Rawls' answer does not completely address the general point.

Marx does give a theory of society in which capital accumulation depends on an attempt at building wealth. So, for Marx, having a lot of money does not mean much from the rich individual's perspective. Many capitalists in Marx's day were, as a matter of fact, quite frugal. The point of the system (which was, for Marx, nearly a necessary phase of human development) is the massive accumulation of capital so that productive capacity could be enormously increased. People *need* wealth in the system, not just to suit their egos, but to build for the coming days of plenty. The problem is to find out how well off the least well-off class would be if the wealth of capitalist class was significantly reduced, given the demands of the system of capital production. After all, investment provides one form of effective demand that keeps the system healthy and thereby supports the income of workers. So to answer, more knowledge is needed; for example, how effective would investment be without an excessively rich investing class, and how effective would entrepreneurship be when increased equality enters the picture? The trouble with this is that it does not seem to give "justice" much of a role. The system itself (and remember that Marx considers that system nearly unavoidable) has already distributed entrepreneurial skills and incentive needs used to keep productivity at a high level. Under these conditions the least well off may genuinely depend on unequal rewards bestowed on those better off. So Miller's point may be reinterpreted from the perspective of the least well-off by claiming that (in the Marxian view) capitalists will only perform when offered extravagant wealth. In such a case the least well-off are hurt unless such wealth is granted. The demands of the difference principle are thus met.

This brings the analysis back to the problem of evaluating as just or unjust needs of various classes in relation to the production of goods. Part of the problem centers on the duration of such needs. Rawls theorizes from a relatively short run view which includes only a few generations. The classical economists (including Marx) tended to be long run thinkers. They wanted to examine the changes that a society would undergo over long periods of time so they could easily think in terms of hundreds of years, during which many generations pass. Rawls' thought makes the best sense when the lifetime of only one generation is considered; after all, that would be the most feasible view of an entirely self-interested individual. This view is faulty because the life of a society goes on and a selfish generation can effectively cripple succeeding generations. So Rawls, realizing this, extends the point of view to cover two generations—still the short run from the point of view of shifting historical circumstances.

The point I want to make is that in the short run, class needs may be relatively stable even though they may be molded by "unjust" practices. The capitalist may actually need exorbitant privileges in order to perform the services of entrepreneurial innovation and the accumulation of wealth. Without such a class and its relative position of power, surplus value might not be used for more and better capital—it might instead be used for a present consumption. Without the control over production that the current system has, class equality might have results to the present and future detriment of everyone. It may be that the attitudes of the capitalists, no matter how formed, are essential considerations in the application of Rawls' principles.

Yet Rawls' theory labels satisfaction of those sorts of needs "just" provided it maximizes the position of the least well-off in the short run. Marx refused to consider such questions in relation to justice because the system he held to be needed (capitalism) was also exploitative. If the system contains certain "needs," Marx simply accepted that as a fact subject to change over the long haul. To call it "just" merely gives such needs a stamp of approval which might tend to forestall the eventual arrival of a new day through its potentially soothing effects. This, of course, goes back to the point already made that Marx refused to speculate about justice. The result of all of this is that Marx would not have played the original position game as Rawls defines it. Yet *if* Marx played the game he may very well have adopted the same principles as Rawls. But this is not terribly interesting—it merely says that Rawls knows how to derive a conclusion (principles) from the premise (the original position) of his system. The more interesting point is: How would Marx have altered the original position if he were willing to play and was allowed to change the rules? With success in answering this point, a position could be established from which Marx's basic evaluative stance could be justified; that is, an original position might be formulated which could support Marx's (utopian) views on justice.

Marx and Rawls have a basically different perspective on the nature of a human person and therefore on what is to be rational.

Rawls seems to consider a person to be an individual in the sense that a person has autonomous desires and ambitions, and views the successes or failures of the society in relation to his or her burdens and gains. So for Rawls social life is to be judged in terms of a tendency toward harmony of autonomous individual interests. Consequently, Rawls defines the members of the original position as mutually self-interested individuals.

Marx would have great difficulties accepting a model projecting atomic decision-making individuals. For him, a person *is* social. He wrote, "...when I am active *scientifically*, etc.,—when I am engaged in activity which I can seldom perform in direct community with others—then I am *social*, because I am active as a *man*. Not only is the material of my activity given to me as a social product (as is even the language in which the thinker is active): My *own* existence *is* social activity, and therefore that which I make of myself, I make of myself for society and with the consciousness of myself as a social being."[14] When humans are thought of as fundamentally social, they are thought of as adopting different standards than they would when thought of as autonomously individual. In Marx's model the members of the original position would not ask how the principles of justice affect each individual but rather what kind of society would the principles produce.

Those positions seem to be far apart, with Marx looking like the kind of utilitarian Rawls criticizes. Actually both positions are complex, with the complexities bridging some of the gap. For Rawls individuals in the original position are not what we ordinarily think of as individuals. Instead they are (aside from their veil of ignorance) *representative* individuals: this means that each individual in the position stands for (represents) the *standard* interests of similarly socially endowed people. For example, one position represented would be that of unskilled labor. Of course, the standard interests of a social class are not, strictly speaking, autonomously formed, nor are they necessarily equivalent to the actual interests of individual members. Regardless, the interests of the various representative individuals are fragmented—they do not necessarily support the "interests" of the whole society. But these interests must be read as social (albeit fragmented) even in Rawls' model. Marx, on the other hand, rebelled against fragmented interests and, in effect, believed that a society could only be decent when no fragmentation of class interests existed. This all makes it difficult to decide just what kind of people Marx would want populating his original position. It would appear that he would have wanted people with a desire for the elimination of fragmentation so that all social interests could merge into *one representative* position.

This has its dangers. By giving people a social sense in the original position Marx would open up a possibility that Rawls wanted to avoid, namely a willingness among those in the position to make genuine social sacrifices for the benefit of the group. If we keep in mind that Marx takes the viewpoint of the long evolution of society, eventuating in a final communistic, classless society, then we can begin to see what use he would make of this willingness to make sacrifices. Because each class makes a specific contribution to the final achievement (for example, capitalists invest for the expansion of productive capacities), each historical period may be judged differently by principles supporting its own contribution toward the ultimate goal. Such historically conditioned principles may require considerable sacrifice which Rawls would not allow. Note, though, that theoretically Rawls always would permit final inequalities that Marx found intolerable. That is, Marx's communistic society would not tolerate class inequalities; Rawls' view is designed to provide rational standards by which class inequalities may be validated.

With the Marxian revision of the nature of the occupants, the notion of gaining as much as one can for oneself in the original position becomes inoperable. This view serves a purpose for rational *individuals;* but for social beings interested in a movement toward the conflation of interests, maximizing one's own rewards is not important. The standard they would impose would be one that demands that each social position in each historical period maximally advance toward the classless society. Such a principle would demand that until a classless society is achieved that each group must occupy a social position, defined by the relations of production, that most effectively contributes, given the historical period, to the movement toward a classless system.

This amounts to drawing up a "principle" which articulates Marx's contention that society ought to be moving toward advanced communism. The members of Marx's original position all take a long run view, but they also make demands on the short run. The demands are consistent with a rational consciousness, in each period, formed by Marx's view on history. This notion seems strained, however, because Marx did not deem it realistic to attempt to prescribe formulae for a period dominated by exploiting interests.

Marx never claimed each period worked at maximal efficiency; he merely thought that each period did (in the long run) move through the dialectic to the hoped for goal.

We are back now at the point from which we started this section. Marx would, as a matter of fact, reject the whole original position game as ideologically dominated. But we did find out how Rawls and Marx differ on human individuality and, perhaps even more importantly, we found that one can get out of an original position most anything wanted, providing its main features are skillfully designed.

We might be better off examing Rawls' principles. These might be valid even without the derivation from the original position, and they might reflect the spirit of our times better than the artificial original position.

MARX, EQUAL LIBERTY, EQUAL OPPORTUNITY AND THE DIFFERENCE PRINCIPLE

Rawls' system divides the "goods" of a society into two types: one has to do with social and economic goods which clearly are distributable in that what one person has another lacks. The other has to do with "goods" such as "freedom" and "opportunity" which have no clear distributable features. In fact, with something like freedom of conscience or religious freedom, the freedom another has may increase my freedom. Opportunity may be more like freedom than like wealth;[15] equal opportunity is relatively costless, especially when one considers the increases in human capital resulting from equalized opportunity. On the other hand, equal opportunity does have clear costs (say, for better schools), but no group has a long-lasting individual claim on using the system of opportunities in the way they do on using their own wealth. This, it seems to me, is behind the easy acceptance in America of the relatively strong commitment to freedom and opportunity for all. Wealth and power are competitively considered, so there is little sentiment in this country for such social equality. But freedom and opportunity are true prerequisites for a "fair" competition.

Rawls, then, seems to be following such sentiments when he declares, in his principles, that equal liberty and equal opportunity take precendence over a fair distribution of social and economic goods. And when we get to the latter, inequalities are permitted.

Marx, as we might expect, would have reacted strongly against singling out freedom and equality of opporutnity as having priority on the grounds that such rights are illusory in a system of social and economic inequality.

Given Marx's basic beliefs, such a view is quite predictable. Rights of political participation, liberty of thought and religion all fall in the domain of the superstructure; as a result, their reality is diminished when they are not supported by freedom in the economic base. This is what Marx had in mind when he said "...a state can be a *free state* without men becoming *free men*."[16] Furthermore, the sorts of freedoms Rawls deals with are of the sort that benefit the capitalist mode of production, Marx would have claimed. Religious freedom, following the view that religion is the opium of the people, would be considered a means of domination. Political freedom is merely *a* way of reinforcing the notion that workers are autonomous and self-ruling even while they are economically compelled to sell their labor at rates entailing exploitation. Marx would have insisted that the value of freedoms are greatly curtailed under such a system of wealth and power. A freedom to vote, to assemble, and to petition are not very valuable to those who are not able to use wealth and influence to back their political views. Freedom of travel is not especially valuable to a person who cannot afford to travel. Marx would have held that to really maximize equal liberty, one must broaden the notion of freedom to include the worth of freedom. The worth of freedom concerns the ways in which we are able to use our freedoms. If we have the right to organize politically in favor of some cause, but our time is dominated by efforts to earn a living, the worth of our freedom is diminished. We are not able to cash freedom in by actually organizing. Rawls, on the other hand, wants to deal with liberty and not with the worth of liberty.

Opportunity, which Rawls intends to equalize mainly through compensatory education, is even more patently affected by unequal class status. Even while calling for equal opportunity, Rawls contends that permissible class inequality may lead to greater initial prospects in life for some than others (78). Thus, for Rawls, equal opportunity may have a different social value (or expected life value) for some than others. Even if two children from unequal social classes are educated in the same school, and even if those from the poorer class receive extra compensatory education, the experiences of growing up in different classes may tend to restrict or enhance these external opportunities. The style of life learned in a social class may be crucial to membership in that class. If this is so, in Marx's eyes Rawls' concern for such opportunity is also consistent with the high level of exploitation that goes on within the capitalist society.

It seems to me that while Marx's position may be an exaggeration of the extent to which liberty and opportunity lack effectiveness, he is right to claim that the network of social relations does bind together liberty and power. Rawls' separation of the two thus appears weak at the places he defends the priority on liberty and opportunity because he seems to contradict himself when, after demanding *equal* liberty and *equal* opportunity, he permits each to be unequal in his first and second priority rules. He writes in the fullest statement of his principles: "...liberty can be restricted only for the sake of liberty. Then are two cases: (a) a less extensive liberty must strengthen the total system of liberty shared by all; (b) a less than equal liberty must be acceptable to those with lesser liberty (302–303)." He does this, I think, because the demand for equal liberty is not consistent with the aim of the people occupying the original position. They want more freedom, and they are not jealous of the freedom of others. So when unequal freedom actually gives those with less more freedom than they would otherwise have, they would be foolish to opt for equality.

With the provision for unequal liberty and for unequal opportunity in the fullest statement of his principles in *A Theory of Justice* (as partially stated above), Rawls uncovers the central role of the "difference principle" which prescribes that goods are to be equally distributed unless inequality is to the maximal benefit of those with less. Here Rawls is dealing with all major social goods, so Marx cannot claim that Rawls is merely dealing with illusory items. With this principle, Rawls seems to be pushing equality to its rational limits; after all, if equality hurts those with less it appears to be counterproductive and unreasonable. So inequality is justified in terms that take maximal account of those with less. Marx, whose concern has always seemed to center on those with less, seems to bear the burden of the argument; he must show why this justification is not in the interest of those who face exploitation.

We already know that Marx would have rejected the difference principle on the basis of its (and any other moral principle's) lack of meaningful social efficacy because non-communistic societies are dominated by class interests, but I pointed out such a view was unproven. So a more concrete Marxian criticism of the difference principle is sought. It seems plausible to speculate that Marx would have begun by reminding us that Rawls is not presenting a full political perspective, but one applicable only within a given social structure, with already existing means of production and relations of production. The difference principle then seems to require us to ask, given such a system, what distributional pattern is in the maximal interests of the least well off. Consider how Rawls would apply his principles. He says,

> ...those starting out as members of the entrepreneurial class in property-owning democracy, say, have a better prospect than those who begin in the class unskilled laborers. It seems likely that this will be true even when the social unjustices which now exist are removed. What, then, can possibly justify this kind of initial inequality in life prospects? According to the difference principle, it is justifiable only if the difference in expectation is to the advantage of the representable man who is less well off, in this case the representation unskilled worker. The inequality in expectation is permissible only if lowering it would make the working class even more worse off (78).

Rawls here certainly seems to accept as his starting point a given system with a given class structure. Then, of course, he sets out with his difference principle to judge that structure. Rawls is not committed to maintaining any given structure, but simply asks how well the least well off do in it. If they could do better without it, or rather with a new structure, then it should be changed. But any attempt to make those changes in that structure might hurt the least well off—i.e., make them worse off. Systems, as we all know, tend to have a tenacious staying power. Tampering with an already functioning system could have serious affects, even on the least well off, especially if the least well off are actually dependent on those with more. And the system itself, functioning over long periods of time, may have ensured that dependency. As soon as the system is accepted as the starting point, the risk is that the system itself will have a veto power over the extent to which it may be modified (from the point of view of difference principle). This, of course, is a realistic feature in Rawls. To attempt to change a system because it looks unjust, with results that make the least well off even worse off, seems itself a certain kind of injustice, no matter how well intended the changes were. Rawls, looking at life from his short run perspective, allows such realistic considerations to function within the criteria of justice. The result is somewhat unfortunate because what we otherwise might want to call an unjust system may be allowed to establish its own validity.

Marx would cynically claim that this sort of principle would simply stabilize the dependency of the non-property holders on those who hold property, because attempts at equalization would disrupt the relations of production that as a matter of fact do lubricate the capitalistic scheme of production. Given a class of unskilled labor, it is not surprising to find that they are dependent on an entrepreneurial class.

Rawls might reply that it would be unreasonable for the least well off to demand equality when this means they will get even less. As a matter of fact, we are faced with a given class structure and a given mode of production. Remember Rawls is a short run thinker. What is needed is to rationally seek the greatest gains possible for all, based on a rational view of human needs, from a given system.

Marx would have countered this claim by recalling that the "eternal view" of justice based on current exploitation is not acceptable; something is not "just" because a person has no rational options. Remember Marx's "view" of justice demands the sort of equality that comes from the absence of social classes; Marx also insisted that people should get according to their needs and contribute according to their abilities. But these criteria must be read in terms of Marx's non-exploitative society. All needs in that sort of society are genuine human needs equally distributed across social groups such as blacks and whites. All work contributions are intended to be humanly fulfilling and are therefore not to be considered as human burdens. Both of these criteria are on a level different from that on which Rawls argues. Any decent social system takes account of needs and varying abilities—he does not, of course, rule these out. Rawls simply is not talking about them: he remains at a level on which there are basic class differences in society. And these he is willing to permit; Marx would not permit them in an advanced communistic state.

Rawls, Marx would have maintained, is using a device to stabilize a vicious scheme in the name of eternal justice. Furthermore, Marx would have insisted that by permitting basic class inequalities Rawls denies a society the ability to realize any of the demands that the difference principle stipulates. The difference principle allows the kind of class power that can, as a matter of fact, disallow, through its control of the state, opinion, etc., any basic benefits not in its interests. This, of course, is at the base of Marx's rejection of justice language; gains cannot be made unless current and repressive controlling forces approve those gains. And this, of course, is against their interests. So we find Marx appealing in what we call his theory of justice to the long run state brought by historical forces not in one's immediate control.

In all of this there is an odd juxtaposition. At the beginning of this essay I pointed to a basic difference between Marx and Rawls. One is an economic determinist and the other a reformer with some confidence in the efficacy of philosophical theory. Rawls, the reformer, scrutinizes a short run period and allows evaluations of the given political structure to be constrained by current circumstances precisely because current circumstances may effect the extent to which the least well off may be made better off. So a realistic view of the staying power of basic institutions would suggest that Rawls is best a modifier and not a radical. Consequently his presumed rejection of a deterministic economic base is not very far-reaching. Marx, the determinist, on the other hand, stood as a revolutionary, even a visionary, looking forward with approval to a day without classes and even without stultifying work conditions. Marx rejected any attempts to judge current practices as just, and hence to reform the current political structure, because he was so future oriented. Reform of the current political structure is inconsistent with his deterministic, utopian, long run view. Rawls, the non-determinist, only looks to the constrained short run which flaws his insistence on the efficacy of ethical theory.

This claim can be succinctly put: Marx accepted, in his pessimism, the short run as is, but was a long run radical. Rawls insists on subjecting the short run to modification but does not take the long run into his vision. These two positions are quite at odds—unfortunately (for these theorists) societies face both time dimensions; furthermore, some individuals may also face both.

There may be some theoretical strangeness here, but it does not answer any questions about which view is superior. Certainly the present structure always seems unyielding and needs to be dealt with on a day-to-day basis with that in mind. On the other hand, current "necessities" can be changed with our own visions of the future in mind. Both Marx and Rawls seem to ignore important aspects of social life. Marx seems to turn his back on those who attempt to make gains within a particular structure, and Rawls seems to offer less than a genuine theory of basic justice.

In one sense Rawls certainly appears theoretically weaker than Marx. Marx gave a theory of society into which a theory of justice can be placed. Rawls does not give a theory of society, so whether some given social arrangements are to be accepted is placed into doubt. One does not know how far he takes current arrangements to be intransigent. For this reason, Rawls' willingness to accept a class structure seems undefended by a theoretical base. As a result the value of applying the difference principle is heavily compromised.

The very fact that one theorist is a short run thinker and that the other takes a long view suggests that one can shore up the other's weakness. In the following section we attempt a synthesis of Rawls and Marx in which the difference principle occupies an important role. Basically the synthesis (as the reader might guess) will use Rawls' theory in short run situations in a way that allows for a movement to a long run Marxian ideal.

RAWLS AND MARX: A SYNTHESIS

The analysis of Marx's "critique" of Rawls began with the claim that this could broaden the base of the critical appraisal of Rawls. Now, at the conclusion, it should be apparent that we have exposed some flaws in the Rawlsian view, the most significant being his short run acceptance of an institutional base and his ad hoc espousal of the primacy of liberty and opportunity. His main strength seems to be his attempt to derive the greatest amount of rationality from given arrangements; this means that he challenges current structures with the intention of pushing equality to the limit. Marx's strength lies in his unwillingness to accept as just the mediation of any unequal class structure; he was concerned only with a long run movement to equality. His major weakness (in terms of the theory of justice) seems to be his utter unwillingness to evaluate the justness of any current class structure; he only offered a revolutionary model applicable under certain limited historical conditions now seen by many as difficult to achieve.

Both suffer from an unsupported "determinism." Marx refused to allow efficacy to philosophical theories not adequately supported in the economic base. His hopes for "just" social relations rested on "autonomous" developments in the relations of production. Nevertheless, he called for a revolution and was confident that a revolution would take place, at least partly as a result of his call. So his determinism seems tempered by his revolutionary hopes. Rawls seems to believe in the possible efficacy of theory, but theory seems incapable, in his view, of guiding long run instituional change. It is limited to maximum gains in the short run. So his optimism is tempered (much as Marx's pessimism) by the obdurancy of current basic structures. In brief, Rawls (like most liberals since Keynes) is a short run thinker; Marx, like other classical economists, was a long run thinker. Neither adequately defends the adoption of one perspective to the exclusion of the other.

The synthesis that suggests itself is some combination of the long and the short run view. This shall be attempted, but first I try to give a clearer meaning to the necessarily vague reference to the short and the long run. The definition follows the lead of microeconomic analysis, where the short run is the period of time during which some of a firm's productive inputs cannot be varied. Generally this is taken to mean that period during which a firm's basic plant and equipment do not vary.[17] The long run is consequently the period in which all of a firm's inputs may be varied. In relation to Rawls and Marx the short run may be defined as the period in which *basic* political and economic arrangements are relatively constant. The long run is the period in which basic institutional life may significantly vary. (These definitions are not precise because they leave open for further determination whether changes are significant; however, the definitions do have some rough serviceability.)

The synthesis begins with the contention that in the short run meaningful changes in distribution can be accomplished through political and social action based on conceptions of justice. Further, short run changes can lead to significant long run changes in basic institutional life. And these long run changes, fostered by short run ideals, may be guided by different standards than those used to judge the short run situation. This model gives efficacy to philosophical conceptions in both the short and the long run. It means that a theory of justice can have two sets of complimentary principles, one specifying a long run goal and the other serving to maximize the tendency of changes, in the short run, to be made in conformity with the long run goal. On this view, a policy may be considered just in the short run if it adheres to short run principles, and a basic institutional pattern is considered just only if it conforms to long run principles. It is important to note the distinction between policies and an institution; in the short run we judge what is done, given an institution; in the long run an institution is judged. So a certain public action may be judged just even though it might take place within unjust institutional arrangements.

In the short run one faces constraints on what may be done, in a way analogous to a firm which cannot quickly vary the size of its physical plant. But in looking to the long run one can allow that all social constraints are subject to thorough overall change (at least in all respects relevant to the theory of justic). What may be done is to establish a long run ideal of justice and then develop a set of short run principles which give guidance for policies given present constraints on the realization of the long run ideal. This guidance should do two things: (1) It should attempt to undermine the relevant constraints, and (2) it should prescribe the way to maximize for the present the values stressed in the long run ideal.

Before specifying the long and short run principles and more about how they would operate, the feasibility of this sort of two-fold structure should be examined. Since justice deals with real social issues, I offer as an instructive case a description of an actual process of social change related by Gunnar Myrdal, involving a process in which an action consistent with an economic base came to be antithetical to that base. Myrdal talks about the actions of colonial powers in the Nineteenth and early Twentieth Centuries:

> ...the imperial powers themselves had created an educated class to provide administrative and professional services in the colonies. This class, and particularly an upper stratum steeped in Western Ideology, was, in the main, not the product of economic development but of legal, administrative, and educational structures built up in order to rule and advance the colonies according to the interests and ideals of the metropolitan countries. Such an indigenous elite had been growing for a longer time and was quantitatively and qualitatively stronger in British Indian, Ceylon, and the Philippines than elsewhere, but was nowhere entirely absent. Particularly in the period between the two world wars, many of the colonial governments began to share their power by permitting members of the elite to qualify as administrators of relatively high rank and by setting up consultative assemblies with appointed and/or elected members. When welfare became a concern of the policy-makers, the indigenous elite were called on to assume more responsibility for their own people. As this elite grew, they came to press for more posts for their kind and for more responsibility at higher levels. The most important observation that can be made about this development in the context of the dissolution of colonialism is that it introduced a trend which was antithetical to colonial rule.[18]

The point that I want to make about this case is that "ideals" (note the talk about concern for welfare) were efficacious to some degree in the short run, but yet they functioned within an unjust system. Action according to ideals was part of the movement that led to the dissolution of some (but very few) of the coarser elements of the basically unjust situation, even though the actions were not intended in this way. In Marx's terminology, the superstructure contributed to the overthrow of the base with which it was initially consistent and even supported. This does not mean that the ideals themselves caused the change—just that they contributed to the change. So, in effect, we can look at this case in two ways: (1) First of all, the policy of giving more power to native administrators may have contributed to a higher level of welfare within a relatively stable system. This is a short run view; given that the system was not going to be replaced quickly, such a reform may be just. (2) But this action *also* contributed to a long run change—the fall of colonialism. The colonial system may be judged unjust in the long run since the system needs to be changed. Just short run reforms may or may not lead to such a change; but actions in the short run should be engaged in so as to produce long run changes. A long run perspective may help to guide some short run actions. Thus, in the example from Myrdal two principles may be seen as operative: (1) (Partly) judge a society by its economic and political independence. (This is a long run principle.) (2) Do those things which will promote (a) the greatest gains for indigenous people and (b) move the society gradually closer to full independence. In this case we might view the education and power given to the native elite as just, while viewing the basic structures unjust. But eventually just short run actions lead to a sort of long run justice.

Of course, I do not intend to set those principles up as the principles of justice, but they serve as an example of the kind of interaction between the short and long run I have in mind.

Another case, involving India after independence, may help to show the practicality of writing short and long run goals. In this example, we can see that a similar perspective was actually attempted by economic planners trying (even if in a very limited way) to come to grips with the tremerndous problems facing their country. In India's *First Five Year Plan (1951-1956)*, the planners claimed they wanted increased equality, but in the short run they claimed that it would be counter-productive. The following statement from the *Plan* contains in an inchoate form the sort of synthesis I have in mind.

> Precisely for the reason that the development of a country is a somewhat long-term process, the institutional and other factors which affect it can be changed to the desired extent and in the desired direction through conscious effort. Moreover, a programme of development even for the short period would fail to have direction and prospective unless it is in some way

> linked to certain long-term targets and objectives relating to the kind of economy and social framework which it is proposed to evolve. In other words, while it is important to preserve throughout a pragmatic and non-doctrinaire approach, and also to bear in mind the limitations involved in any long-term development possibilities, it is of the essence of planning that it must have a wider time-horizon than immediate requirements and calculations.[19]

Here the view is that both a long and short run perspective must be taken. One view to the exclusion of the other would be myopic. This is the issue in developing a synthesis between Rawls and Marx.

In the model I wish to present, Rawls' difference principle serves as a partial guide for short run policies, with the intention that they tend to promote a long run state such as Marx argued for. In the long run state, full group equality ought to reign, but in the short run inequalities are constantly hammered at by eliminating any class gain that does not further the interests of the least well off (given basic unyielding institutional arrangements). But furthermore, basic institutional arrangements ought to be altered, when feasible, in accord with the demand for equality.

This can be stated more formally as follows:

I. A society is just only if there is full *social* equality, that is, all social *groups* are socially equal as groups.

II. Whenever the attainment of equality is unfeasible without harm to those with less, just policy demands (a) the maximization of the position of the least well off and (b) the long run move toward the elimination of the conditions which constrain the movement toward full equality.

This model makes sense along several lines. It assumes that reforms are possible and thereby denies the unrealistic block to action supported by a full determinism, yet it is realistic enough to accept the relative permanency of basic institutions. It does not ask the least well off to sacrifice maximal gains in the name of equality; and it keeps in mind the goal of equality as this becomes increasingly feasible. Also by straining all the rationality out of current practices—that is, by getting all we can for the least well off—it places greater and greater value on equality. The least well off move toward greater equality because they can be expected to gain as the difference principle narrows inequalities and as long run efforts to eliminate constraints take effect. Further, as the difference principle is satisfied, the movement away from inequality, we may expect, opens further possibilities along the path toward equality. This would tend to be true because the need for inequalities is largely a function of incentives; as the society grows more equal, smaller and smaller differentials at the class level may serve the incentive function.

To be faithful to the Marxian model in the long run, the model would have to include production for need, diversity of function, the absence of money and of the state. These may be difficult features to accept, so I have presented the long run view as one which omits these features and centers on class equality.

The model here is offered as a synthesis of Rawls and Marx. This model seems to solve some of the problems in each—but that alone does not make it valid. If some form of Rawls' considered judgment test is accepted, one would have to carefully compare it with considered judgments before giving full approval. I believe that it would pass the test in a more satisfying way than would Rawls' theory. It would do this because considered judgments are flexible enough to operate on both a long and short run perspective.

Whether one accepts this model may hinge on the relatively unlikely coincidence of finding both Rawls and Marx plausible. But since it does provide a synthesis, it might be appealing to many people in countries facing developmental problems who have not yet decided their basic ideological commintment. Short of this, the model does show the need to consider both the long and the short run in a theory of justice.

NOTES

1. Rawls' call for equal opportunity and for full liberty are ambiguous. In his fullest statement of his principles he allows less than equal opportunity and less than equal liberty (306-7, all parenthetical citations are to John Rawls', *A Theory of Justice* (Cambridge, Mass.: Harvard University Press, 1971)). This may be why he is willing to permit differential intial prospects for the less well off (78).
2. Patrick Gardner, *Theories of History* (Glencoe, Ill.: The Free Press, 1959), p. 125. See also crane Brenton, *The anatomy of Revolution* (New York: Vintage Books, 1965), p. 28.
3. Karl Marx, *A Contribution to the Critique of Political Economy*, translated by S. Ryazanskaya and edited by M. Dobb (New York: International Publishers, 1970), pp. 20-21.

4. Marx and Engels, *The Communist Manifesto*, translated by S. Moore and edited by S.H. Beer (New York: Appleton-Century-Crofts, 1955), p. 9.
5. *Ibid.*
6. For example, Harold J. Laski, *Karl Marx* (New York: League for industrial Democracy, 1933), p. 46, and Sidney Hook, *From Hegel to Marx* (New York: The Humanities Press, 1950), p. 53.
7. Lately a good deal of attention has been given to this problem. For a fuller account see W.L. Bride, "The Concept of Justice in Marx, Engels, and Others," *Ethics*, 85, no. 3 (April 1975), 204-218; R. Tucker, *The Marxian Revolutionary Idea* (New York: W.W. Norten and Company, 1969), pp. 37-53; and A. Woods, "The Marxian Critique of Justice," *Philosophy and Public Affairs*, I, no. 3 (Spring 1972), 244-282.
8. Marx and Engels, *Selected Correspondence 1846-1895* (New York: International Publishers, 1942), p. 128.
9. Karl Marx, *Capital, Vol. I*, translated by S. Moore and E. Aveling and edited by F. Engels (New York: International Publishers, 1967), p. 194.
10. This point is based on R. Tucker's well argued claim that "Marx's philosophy expressed a search for unity—for a world beyond all antagonisms and therefore beyond justice as equilibrium of them." Tucker, *Marxian Revolutionary Idea*, p. 3.
11. Norman Care, "Contractualism and Moral Criticism," *The Review of Metaphysics*, 23 (1969), 85-101.
12. For another discussion of reflective equilibrium see "The Original Position and the Veil of Ignorance" by Louis Katzner in chapter one of this volume.
13. Miller devotes nearly all of his article, "Rawls and Marxism," in *Reading Rawls*, ed. N. Daniels (New York: Basic Books, Inc., 1976). pp. 206-230, to this issue.
14. Karl Marx, *Economic and Philosophic Manuscripts of 1844*, translated by M. Milligan and edited by D. Struik (New York: International Publishers, 1964), p. 137.
15. For this point I am indebted to my colleague, Samuel A. Richmond, Cleveland State University.
16. Karl Marx, "On the Jewish Question," in *Writings of the Young Marx on Philosophy and Society*, translated and edited by L.D. Easton and K.H. Guddat (New York: Doubleday & Company, Inc., 1967), p. 223.
17. For example, see E. Mansfield, *Microeconomics, Theory and Application*, 2nd edition (New York: W.W. Norton & Company, 1975), pp. 121-122.
18. Gunnar Myrdal, *Asian Drama: An Inquiry Into the Poverty of Nations*, Vol. I (New York: Pantheon, 1968), p. 135.
19. India, Government of, Planning Commission, *The First Five Year Plan* (New Delhi, 1952), pp. 17-18.

Responses to Rawls from the Political Right

Alan H. Goldman
UNIVERSITY OF MIAMI

INTRODUCTION

It should be abundantly clear by now that the most striking feature of Rawls' theory, and the one most responsible for its recent popularity, is its blend of the traditional libertarian ideal of individual freedom and the egalitarian ideal of a more equal distribution of wealth and power. On the one hand, Rawls supports the priority of the freedom of the individual; on the other hand, however, he emphasizes the limits which must be placed on the individual to insure a fair distribution of society's goods. The first reaffirms the foundations of Western liberal, capitalist democracies; the second accepts the validity of much of the socialist critique of capitalist freedoms. The central question confronting Rawls' work, therefore, is whether it is possible to have it both ways. Is it possible to satisfy the legitimate "leftist," "socialist" critics of Western capitalism within a broadly liberal, capitalist and democratic framework?

As might be expected, neither the political left nor the polictical right has been happy with Rawls' attempt to reconcile their traditionally opposed perspectives, and Rawls has found himself increasingly caught between attacks from the left and from the right. Those on the political left naturally feel Rawls has not gone far enough in his constraints on the traditional freedoms of the individual, while those on the right believe he has gone too far. The situation is not unlike political attitudes in the United States toward "welfare statism." When limits are placed on traditional freedoms in the name of social justice, criticism is immediately voiced from the left that this does not go far enough and from the right that it goes too far toward an equal distribution of national wealth.

It is necessary to specify what is meant by criticisms from the political right. The "political right" is notoriously difficult to define, and the term is used in everyday contexts to refer both to militarists who see little danger in the abridgment of civil liberties and rights in the name of "security," as well as to those who urge vigorous *protection* of liberties and personal rights against the intrusions of governmental regulations and bureaucracy. Indeed many American politicians and voters who think of themselves as comprising the political right endorse with questionable consistency *both* these ideologies on different issues. In political philosophy the term "right" is generally applied these days to those right-wing libertarians who uphold the value of personal rights.[1] Present day libertarians are perhaps ideologically closer on some issues to classical liberals, like Locke or Mill, than to classical conservatives, like Burke. Be that as it may, and despite the historical vagaries in the use of the term "right," I will center this discussion on objections to Rawls which reflect the libertarian view. Since Rawls' egalitarianism is the central issue of dispute, I will include objections centering on the egalitarian thrust of his theory put forth by utilitarians as also coming from the right.

The right's general objection to Rawls is that his principle for the distribution of economic goods places too great an emphasis upon the value of equality at the expense of other values and rights, especially the value of economic freedom and the right to property. Libertarians recognize a right to keep what one has earned and to contract freely to exchange it or give it away. Rawls' claim that an unequal distribution of economic goods is justified only if it is to the advantage of society's worst-off individuals conflicts with property rights and economic freedoms stressed by libertarians. The picture a libertarian draws of Rawlsian society is that of a society which constantly equalizes by taking from those who have earned what they have acquired through free contracts and exchanges, and gives this wealth to those who probably do not deserve it.

It is argued by those on the right that for a society to redistribute wealth and power, until those on the bottom of the social and economic ladder have the most they possibly could have, would involve extreme coercion of those in other social positions. The expropriation of wealth for such massive redistribution would amount to an extreme violation of natural property rights. When the goal of equality is emphasized to this degree, those who are most productive must be sacrificed to those who are least productive. Merit and productivity cannot earn their just rewards since productive people cannot expect to keep the wealth earned by their services or products, and initiative must be restricted or directed towards maximum benefit to those who lack it. In this essay I will try to support this general complaint with specific arguments.

The arguments to be presented are constructed from various suggestions of philosophers of somewhat different persuasions, though all have a right-wing thrust in the sense just indicated. While I have constructed or reconstructed the arguments to be presented, they should not be taken to reflect my views, although I will briefly indicate at the end what I take to approach an acceptable compromise position between Rawls and some of the more reasonable points of his critics to the right.

The criticisms fall into two categories. First, the central methodological question raised is: "Are just rules those which would be chosen in the original position under the veil of ignorance as Rawls defines it?" The second and more substantive question is whether The Difference Principle and The Principle of Equal Opportunity would be chosen from this position, whether The Principle of Equal Basic Liberty would be given priority, and whether these principles are intuitively acceptable. Let us begin with the second and more concrete question.

LIBERTARIAN OBJECTIONS TO RAWLS' PRINCIPLES OF JUSTICE

The Difference Principle

Most of the criticism of the right centers on the Difference Principle which states that inequalities are justified only to the extent that they benefit those in society who are worse off. This is equivalent to demanding that benefits be maximized for those on the bottom. The principle requires that the economic system be structured so that the advantages some individuals may have simply from their own natural endowments, such as intelligence or industriousness, must bring maximum benefit to those who lack these natural endowments. Rawls contrasts his principle with an even more extreme principle of redress which calls for the elimination of all effects of natural endowment and initial social position upon subsequent distributions (101, all parenthetical citations are to John Rawls, *A Theory of Justice* (Cambridge, Mass.: Harvard University Press, 1971); but it is clear that his principle as stated is still radically egalitarian in treating natural talents as purely common or social assets, to be used to the maximum benefit of those who do not possess, develop or utilize them.

One striking feature of the Difference Principle to which some on the right have objected is its neglect of the notion of desert (as a result of effort or productivity). The concept of desert is in fact absent throughout the ground level of Rawls' theory, although it may seem to some readers the central notion behind our intuitions regarding distributions.[2] Is it fair for one person to have more than another just because he was lucky enough to have been born with more intelligence and ambition? Rawls seems to say no. But, libertarians ask whether it is fair to take something away from a person who has worked hard for it and give it to someone who couldn't or wouldn't produce it himself? Obviously not, according to the libertarian. For Rawls the initially just distribution is always equality, departures from equality being justified only to benefit those who end up on the bottom. To hold, as does the Difference Principle, that equality is always to constitute the base from which departures must be justified, and that departures from it can be justified only when they are to the advantage of those who are relatively worse off, amounts to a refusal to allow *any* differences among individuals, including prior agreements, efforts or productivity to be grounds for differential distributions of benefits. It is true that Rawls' principles are meant to apply to the design of basic social institutions, and that when individuals within those institutions satisfy specific requirements, they then become differentially entitled to benefits. Once an economic structure is established in accord with the Difference Principle, individuals may then enter into agreements and become entitled to different portions of wealth and income. But it is also true that such differential entitlements are to be permitted in general only when they collectively benefit those who are least entitled. The central question then is whether society has the right to design its institutions to appropriate and freely use personal differences in talent, effort and productivity in the service of those least talented or productive.

I should make clear that those to the right of this extreme egalitarianism criticize the Difference Principle as it is stated initially, not as Rawls tends to apply it later in his book. How egalitarian it works out to be in practice depends upon how broadly we construe the concept of lowest relevant position for whom benefits are to be maximized. Rawls applies the Difference Principle not to maximize benefits to the worst off individual, but to the worst off representative social and economic positions (95–8). I take it, however, that this is a practical necessity rather than a theoretical desideratum from a Rawlsian point of view, and that the goal really is to maximize benefits to the worst off individuals (or if not, I cannot see why not, given Rawls' arguments regarding the strategy of the contractors in the original position).[3] Nevertheless Rawls is conservative in the application of the principle, allowing, for example, inequalities to be justified as incentives to attract the most competent people to various positions. Rawls argues that once suitable minimum standards of living are established by income transfers, pay by marginal contribution, as in a free market, is justified. It is justified according to him for reasons of efficiency (277) and to create necessary incentives for productive people to occupy those positions in which they are most needed (305–6, 311). This strikes me as false accoring to Rawls' own criterion, since highest paying jobs are often the most pleasant as well.[4] These jobs would continue to be sought under the more egalitarian pay scales which I think the Difference Principle would demand. In any case, those on the right take the principle to have strongly egalitarian practical implications and criticize it under that assumption. Even if that is incorrect, there is still a moral question about the way the principle conceives of individuals and their talents and efforts in relation to society.

The central problem, as Rawls himself recognizes, is how to justify the Difference Principle to those in society who have superior natural endowments or simply make greater socially productive efforts. The problem is not that well endowed egoists would not agree to the principle, knowing that they would do better if left free to make their own particular agreements, but that the principle must accord with *our* intuitions of what is just treatment of the better endowed; we must agree that the state has the right to treat their natural assets and willingness to work as so much common property to be divided or utilized to the maximum benefit of others. Further, after the veil of ignorance is lifted and the Difference Principle is applied, a stable society must result; the better off must not be driven to resistance out of a sense of injustice done them.

How could we explain to these individuals that as their talent, effort and productivity increase, they are to be forced to give greater percentages of what they earn to those who are less well endowed or simply choose to work less, and to do this up to the maximum benefit for these others? Rawls' main complaint against utilitarianism is that it may require us to treat some individuals as means to the welfare of others. He writes on the third page of his book:

> Justice does not allow that the sacrifices imposed on a few are outweighed by the larger sum of advantages enjoyed by many.

Justice cannot demand that some accept lower life prospects for the sake of others. The libertarian points out that Rawls is guilty of exactly the same kind of injustice in demanding that those with talent who work hard sacrifice up to the maximum benefit of others.[5] Rawls must simply presuppose that sacrifices toward the top are unobjectionable, while those toward the bottom are not.[6] But then his argument against utilitarianism is misleading at best.

His attempt to justify the Difference Principle to those who are better endowed consists of the argument that since their talents are of use only in a context of social cooperation, they must expect the benefits of such cooperation only on reasonable terms acceptable to those on the bottom. The Difference Principle is held to express such reasonable terms (102-103). This seems clearly a bad argument, perhaps the weakest in the book; and in fact there seems to be no egoist appeal of this type which could work. Rawls not only tries to show that advantages through natural endowments are unjust; he tries to get those who are more highly endowed to *agree* that it is in their interest not to use their talents solely for their own gain. This "egoist" argument from the self-interest of the most talented individuals seems doomed to failure. For one thing, even without any general agreement on state-enforced redistributive mechanisms of justice, there will be social cooperation through particular exchange contracts for purely egoist reasons, and those better endowed could enter into such contracts on their own terms. Clearly they will fare better under such free cooperative agreements than under the cooperative arrangements dictated by the terms of the Difference

Principle. Rawls misrepresents the choice open to these individuals as that between chaos and cooperation made universal on his terms. This is the view which pictures equality as the basically just distribution from which deviations must always be justified to all concerned. The libertarian, on the other hand, sees free and unhindered contractual agreements for cooperative endeavors as the basis for distributing the products of such endeavors. These free agreements will tend to give a more central place to relative productivity than to absolute equality as the basis for just distributions. If we imagine a cooperative scheme among the better endowed and a separate one among those with fewer talents and propensities for work, it seems obvious that it is the latter group who benefit most from any free agreement for mutual cooperation.[7] So we are left with the question of why those in the former group should accept the Difference Principle which looks not to their benefits at all in setting the terms of the agreement.

Rawls perhaps should have avoided justifications which appeal to egoist motives altogether and simply pressed the argument that natural endowments are morally undeserved and hence no ground for differential distributions. But while the latter claim is true, it can still be maintained that to force those who produce more to sacrifice up to maximum benefits for those who produce least and end up on the bottom of the social scale, is to press an egalitarian bias at the expenses of other values intuitively relevant to justice. There is foremost the problem of desert: we naturally feel that those who make greater efforts in a socially productive way deserve to receive a greater share of the social product to which they contribute. And this seems a basic, if not the basic distributive consideration. Rawls it seems has conflated the concept of distributive justice at the base level into that of equality alone. As one critic points out, Rawls' principle appears more egalitarian than even Marx's (as summarized in the slogan: "From each according to his ability; to each according to his need.") While Marx recognized differences arising from need, and required each to contribute to the social product up to the maximum of his ability, Rawls refuses to accord a central place in his theory to differential needs and is willing to maximize benefits to the worst off, likely to be the least productive, without demanding maximal effort or contribution relative to ability from them.[8]

There is in fact no more egalitarian principle which it could be prudent for those who contribute least to accept. It is no exaggeration to say that distributive justice *is* equality for Rawls, departures from this norm being justified on purely prudential grounds, because those on bottom would be stupid not to accept greater benefits. In fact we can imagine that even if the contractors in the original position were to adopt a maximin strategy and seek to protect themselves against unsatisfied desires as much as possible, they might still reject the Difference Principle with its base of absolute equality in distribution of actual goods. The reason is that those who in the least favorable positions are likely to be those who contribute least to the social product. Many of these may do so out of choice, because it is not worth the effort to them to work for a better position (especially if a satisfactory minimum providing for the satisfaction of basic needs is guaranteed). Thus once we guarantee a reasonable minimum level and provide for equal opportunities, to proceed to maximize benefits for those who contribute least will be to add to the benefits of those who might not care enough to work for them, at the expense of those who are already contributing to the maximum of their ability, and hence cannot remedy their unsatisfied wants.[10] To have unremediable unsatisfied wants appears worse than to have a lower absolute share of goods when one can acquire more by working harder. Thus the Difference Principle, which aims at the best absolute amount of primary goods for those who have least, might be rejected as too egalitarian even in the original position.[11]

Independently of the previous argument which accepts the Rawlsian framework for justifying principles of justice, it strikes us as unfair to take from those who contribute more through their efforts, to benefit those who contribute least, if the latter do so by choice. Before pressing this argument, however, we should clear up a possible ambiguity in interpreting the Difference Principle itself. Rawls sometimes writes as if the least advantaged individuals to whom the Difference Principle is to afford maximum benefits are those with least innate ability and those born into the lowest social classes (75). Indeed it may seem just for a social system to attempt to contribute most toward the future development of those individuals in order to compensate for undeserved unequal starts in life. But this is taken care of by the Principle of Equal Opportunity. In the initial statement of the principles of justice (60), and in most later references to the Difference Principle, it seems to be interpreted as providing maximum benefits for those who actually end up with least primary goods, including income and wealth, for whatever reason. That is how the principle is most often interpreted by critics and how I am interpreting it here. The equation of justice with equality implied in the Difference Principle so construed is inconsistent with our moral intuitions, since it treats those we consider unequal in desert as equals, a sin on a par, according to Aristotle, with treating equals differently. Our intuition is that the contributions of individuals are not to be treated as common social assets to benefit social noncooperatives. At a certain point at least, equality as a value must be balanced against liberty and merit. Rawls ignores merit in his quest to negate differences in natural endowments.

This last statement again must be qualified somewhat. He does introduce a concept of desert, but only secondarily as a concept of legitimate expectations in relation to existing social rules which are subordinate to the more fundamental Difference Principle. One deserves a specific good only when he fulfills the social regulation governing such entitlements. But the regulations themselves are to be formulated in terms of the Difference Principle. Thus desert is ultimately subordinate to that principle as well. Rawls argues convincingly against the distribution of goods on the basis on the basis of absolute and abstract moral virtue (310-13). Mainly from this argument, he concludes that desert must reduce to legitimate expectation in relation to existent social rules. Deserving is therefore not a *fundamental* parameter of justice but a dependent one. But our concept of desert is not, as Rawls supposes, based on piety or moral virtue. We rather have a notion of desert based upon effort and social contribution; this is neither reducible to altruistic or pious moral virtue, nor subordinate to particular social rules either—certainly not to Rawls' Difference Principle.[12] The latter violates this sense of desert by departing from strict equality only to produce incentives to benefit those most who contribute least. If there are differential claims to goods independent of specific social rules, and if these include factors like effort or contribution or free agreement, then Rawls' reduction of justice to equality, or to institutions which aim at equality or at only universally prudent departures from it, cannot be correct.

Rawls does briefly consider the criterion of social contribution as desert. In dismissing the primacy of this concept in the theory of distributive justice, he points out that contribution is relative to such nonmoral factors as supply and demand and native talents (311). But to thereby dismiss or slight the notion of contribution seems to assume that distributive criteria must be morally deserved, that their satisfaction ought to vary with moral virtue. But Rawls rejects this claim as well, as just indicated. A person's social contribution represents a combination of effort, social advantage, natural talent, and supply and demand, and in practice it may be impossible to completely separate them. It is possible to take different attitudes toward this combination of factors. We can, like Rawls, ignore them all in designing fundamental principles of justice, but this is extreme and unwarranted. That some of the factors which enter into social contribution are chance factors does not make social contribution itself irrelevant as a fundamental part in a theory of justice. When we distribute according to social contribution, we are not distributing solely on grounds of innate talent or chance contingencies. Why should we say that the former has no fundamental place in a theory of distributive justice just because it is affected by the latter? Rawls has not provided a full argument here, and the missing premise appears to be counterintuitive or false. For social contribution to entail desert on a basic level does not imply that *all* factors which causally lead to social contribution must be deserved.[13] To show this by analogy, we can imagine a person inspired by some chance personal event to work harder for the rest of his life. That he may not have deserved that inspirational moment certainly does not mean that he deserves no returns from his extra effort from then on. To speak of deserving the initial inspiration seems as out of place as to speak of deserving or not deserving one's natural assets, which Rawls seems to think makes sense. Yet the example shows that all causes of desert need not themselves be deserved. Thus we are not justified in ignoring social contribution in the fundamental principles of justice just because it is causally affected by factors which are undeserved.

This concept of desert negates the idea that a society's gross national product is somehow one undifferentiated social possession, to be distributed among individuals who have basically equal claims to it. Rawls' assumption that most of this product is the result of social cooperation does not establish the idea of equal claims. Would a group of individuals freely agreeing to cooperate in different ways in some joint venture, each of whom was to contribute to a different degree, all agree that the final claims to the to the products must be equal, simply because of the fact of cooperation? Let us take first a simple two-person case. Person A works hard and is smart, while person B is dumb and likes to sleep a lot. Should things be arranged so that B gets the maximum benefit from any joint project up to the point of equality, or the point at which A gives up working in disgust at seeing the difference between his work and its reward?[14] How does the fact that many people cooperate in society change our intuition here, when it is still possible to measure relative contribution to the social product? Such contribution still seems a relevant consideration at a fundamental level regarding deserved shares.[15] The product of society is the product of relatively small groups in society to which individuals contribute to differing degrees. Hence there are differential claims to portions of that product which are violated by the operation of the Difference Principle in the design of social institutions to govern distributions. The model for dividing up goods produced through varying efforts and free agreements cannot be the same as the model for dividing a pie to which no one has special claim.[16] Just as everyone does not have an equal claim to other individuals' natural endowments such as strength or intelligence, so not everyone has an equal claim to the products of other individuals' efforts. These are not one collective common asset, as Rawls tries to construe them.

Finally, even aside from considerations of effort, contribution or desert, it may strike us as unjust to judge the fairness of a distribution solely by the absolute position of those worst off under it. Aside from the question of differential claims, we might consider other factors, such as average utility or degree of spread between top and bottom, as relevant. Rawls recognizes that it is counterintuitive to call upon those who are better off to make very large sacrifices to generate small gains for those further down the social scale. But he argues that the situation in which they might be called upon to do so according to the Difference Principle as a matter of fact will not arise (157). One can counterargue first that there are situations in which the burdens are placed upon those in better positions and which call forth legitimate complaints. It has been a common complaint of recent years in this country that the middle class of some cities bears too large a burden for welfare and other transfers to those worse off. Public bonds which pay interest to the rich and finance welfare for the poor are sometimes said to place too large a tax burden on those in the middle, and are condemned on that ground. Second, whether this actually occurs or not, one can argue that ultimate criteria for evaluating the justice of situations should not depend upon what is or is not likely to occur emprically.[17] Rawls in fact attacks utilitarianism for excessive reliance upon such empirical probabilities. Here it seems that the utilitarian, like the libertarian, has a legitimate complaint against Rawls' defense of his Difference Principle and his treatment of the alternatives. It may be in fact that applications of the Difference Principle accord with intuitive judgments about just distributions only in those circumstances in which raising the position of those worse off does not damage the positions of others to a much greater degree. But in these circumstances, the results of applying the principle would more or less match the results of applying the principle of average of total utility.

The Principle of Liberty

The Principle of Equal Basic Liberty is the first of the principles of justice and states that each person is to have a right to the most extensive system of liberties compatible with a similar system for all, which Rawls sometimes takes to mean that liberty is to be restricted only for the sake of other and greater liberties. This may sound fine to the libertarians but is of little help in itself when liberties conflict, e.g. my liberty to move my fist versus your freedom from being punched in the nose, or my liberty to hold property versus your freedom to use what I have in my possession. Libertarians generally rely upon some version of Mill's harm principle which states that liberty is to be restricted only to prevent harm to others in such cases. Surprisingly this is not part of Rawls' Principle of Equal Basic Liberty. Rawls either has no method of adjudicating conflicting freedoms or, at best, has an unclear method. He does speak, for example, of a natural duty not to harm others (114). But natural duties apply to individuals rather than to the design of institutions, where the principles of justice operate. Natural duties and the principles of justice are not related to each other clearly in Rawls' account; it is difficult to know how to apply the principle of liberty in problem cases.[18]

To reduce the ambiguity of the general rule, Rawls introduces a list of basic liberties. The list includes political liberties, such as political participation, freedom of conscience and speech, and the right to hold personal property, but does not include protection for every action short of harm to others. The list appears too narrow to the libertarian. Other liberties Rawls classes as "permissions," which are actions we may perform which violate no obligations or natural duties (117). It seems that when we include permissions with natural duties, Rawls' view on liberty comes close to Mill's, and so might satisfy the libertarians. But in separating out certain liberties as those uniquely involved in social justice, and arguing that these are to be equalized and maximized in themselves, Rawls makes it difficult to see his overall position or to see how his principles are to be applied. My having a liberty subjects you to the disadvantages of my exercising it; and to balance these advantages and disadvantages, considerations beyond maximizing liberty are relevant, even in cases involving Rawls' basic liberties. We have laws against libel and slander, for example, to prevent harm from the exercise of freedom of speech, not to maximize the extent of that freedom, or even the extent of that freedom taken in conjunction with others.[19] Certainly many liberties may be restricted to prevent harm and not to simply maximize other liberties.

Despite these difficulties of interpretation, the main problem with the first principle from a libertarian viewpoint is that it is not taken seriously enough by Rawls himself, especially the clause which confers the right to control personal property once a certain level of material wealth is achieved. The first principle is said to have absolute priority over both parts of the second principle, the Difference Principle and Principle of Equal Opportunity. This means that in case of a conflict we must guarantee equal basic liberty first. And yet the right to control property seems blatantly contradicted by the Difference Principle.[20] According to the libertarian, the right to property is violated with every forced transfer of legitimately acquired goods to others, and violated to the ultimate degree when such transfers are to continue up to maximum benefits for those who acquire least. The liberty to hold personal property means nothing without the liberty to transfer it as one pleases, and this is severely limited by the forced redistribution required by the Difference Principle. Rawls' inclusion of the right to hold personal property in the list of basic liberties, his belief in the lexical priority of the Principle of Liberty over the Difference Principle, and his assumption that the Difference Principle is nevertheless to guide the distribution of wealth in society, appear inconsistent when considered together by the libertarian.

By thus ignoring his own stated priority of liberty over his principle for dividing wealth and other goods, his claim that that priority will *resolve* the conflict between increasing liberties and increasing wealth is surely misleading. The lexical priority of the first principle over the second, according to which we are not permitted to sacrifice liberties for wealth, is relevant only if we are generally faced with a choice of doing so.[21] But this is a moot point. Libertarians believe a basic liberty is the liberty to pursue wealth and other goods, and that these are generally maximized over society by allowing this liberty free reign. There is rarely a choice of giving up liberty for increased wealth, as Rawls seems to think, except, ironically, by the principle which does sacrifice the liberty of the more fortunate for the wealth of those with less. If these social facts were known to the contractors in the original position, it is doubtful that they would bother to arrange the Rawlsian principles in lexical order.

Finally, Rawls can be held to argue for his liberty principle on the wrong grounds. We cannot base the principle as he does on the claim that any rational man has a greater interest in liberty than in other goods. Some men may desire the security of an authoritarian regime without being the less rational. The point should be rather that such individuals have no right to bind others who value freedom more to such regimes. It is not that all people, or even all rational people, place such a great emphasis upon liberty in their scheme of values. It is rather that no one has a right to restrict certain liberties except to prevent harm to others.

From a utilitarian's point of view, it would make no sense to prohibit people from making small sacrifices in liberty for large material gains, were this possible.[22] Rawls argues that once a certain degree of material prosperity has been achieved by society, it cannot be worth it from the viewpoint of the original contractors to risk sacrifices in liberty for greater material prosperity. Restrictions upon liberty of conscience, for example, may prove to be beyond the limits of tolerability, and contractors selecting principles under the veil of ignorance will not risk selecting principles which could result in intolerable situations. An insistence on liberty is equally explained on utilitarian grounds without resorting to the lexical ordering of primary goods. If freedom is indeed worth so much more than wealth, then it will not be sacrificed according to the utilitarian principle either.

From the point of view of the libertarian it cannot matter whether most men in fact value money more than freedom—individuals simply do not have the right to compel others under authoritarian regimes, even if these were more efficient (which is also denied). The Rawlsian argument for the priority of liberty is that it is worse to be without liberty than without additional wealth. Whether or not this is true, it is insufficient for the libertarian as a ground of rights and freedom, which others simply have no right to abridge or infringe upon.

LIBERTARIAN OBJECTIONS TO RAWLS' METHODOLOGY

The Original Position

Libertarians charge that Rawls' conception of the original position as consisting of agents ignorant of their own individuating characteristics weights the procedure of choice in favor of egalitarian principles. Rawls represents his principles of justice as those which would be chosen from an initial position of equality, in which agents are unable to press for unfair advantages. His agents are defined as ignorant of their own values, social positions and natural endowments, as well as of the particular facts of their society. The idea is to eliminate factors which might bias the choice of principles. The fact that his principles would be chosen from this position of fairness is supposed to add to the intuitive plausibility of the principles.

Rawls' contract, it should be noticed, is very different from that in classical social contract theories. Since he never argues that actual men would all freely agree to his rules given the choice among alternatives, as does for example Hobbes, it is clear that he is not trying to justify his preferred social institutions on the basis of real interest or consent. The central notion in Rawls' original position is not in fact that of free choice, as it was in the early social contract tradition, but that of fairness or equality, as instantiated in the conditions of his veil of ignorance. If real agents would freely choose arrangements which would also be chosen by hypothetical agents ignorant of their social positions and natural endowments, there would be no reason to think about Rawls' original position at all. Although the "contracts" to which traditional social contract theory appealed were not real historical agreements, they were meant to be contracts to which real rational agents would agree, given the choice. Such agents were then seen to be bound, as by promises freely made. Rawls' contract, on the other hand, is one to which only his artificially defined contractors would agree. His contract and the rules chosen through it are meant to be acceptable to all when they emerge from behind the veil of ignorance, but only because their sense of justice convinces them that they ought to accept them. It must be antecedently shown, then, that such rules are just, and the basis of the argument cannot be actual free choice. But for the libertarian, arrangements arrived at on any basis other than free choice represent coercion of some real agents by others, and this in itself is not just.

While real contracts represent compromises or free exchanges, neither is present in Rawls' version, since his hypothetical agents are by definition all the same (each knows nothing of himself which could differentiate him from others), and there is nothing for them to compromise or exchange. He cannot argue from the agreements of such purely hypothetical agents alone that real people are bound to his rules of justice; he is only trying to dramatize by this method which rules for the distribution of social benefits are just and fair. The argument here is not that real rational agents *would* agree if given the choice, and thus should feel bound to his system as by a promise, but rather that they *should* agree to his rules of justice.[23] The central idea is to define a situation in which the choice of distributive rules must be fair and governed only by theorems of rational choice. This is to be accomplished by means of the veil of ignorance. The application of the theorems of rational choice, developed originally by economists to govern strategies in situations in which choices are made, makes some of Rawls' arguments sound pragmatic or prudential, though in relation to actual self-interested agents they are not. But for many libertarians, the only forceful arguments to guide conduct will be ones which are truly prudential, those which define the best available compromises for real agents.

The libertatian objects to the artificial constraints placed upon Rawls' contractors arranging for a just distribution of goods. He wonders why actual agents in the real world should feel bound by the choices of Rawls' hypothetical contractors under the peculiar circumstances in which they are placed. Why should not just arrangements be those which emerge from real contracts freely entered into by real agents in the real world, without artificial constraints of ignorance placed upon them? Normally, agreements reached out of ignorance are disqualified rather than justified. What right have we to restrict and rearrange real agreements of free agents in the name of some hypothetical and highly artificial Rawlsian model? How can we demand that those real persons who would not benefit from the outcome of the hypothetical contract, nevertheless acquiesce in it?

The first libertarian counterargument, then, develops directly from the fact that Rawls' original position is artificial and unreal, that agreements reached from it are not those that would be reached freely by real self-interested rational agents. If actual people act out of self-interest, then rules like Rawls', which are *not* agreed to freely by real agents, will have to be imposed on them without their prior consent, and they will have to be coerced into accepting them. This will not be coercion simply to prevent people from harming each other or breaking agreements, but coercion in order to further the interests of those at the lower end of the economic ladder at the expense of those who could have obtained much more by entering into genuinely free agreements. Such coercion is in itself a bad thing according to the libertarian. Of course Rawls holds that people act not only out of self-interest but out of an acquired sense of justice as well. In fact he claims the principles of justice will not be unacceptable to any one after the veil of ignorance is lifted, so that a society structured upon them will have inherent stability (498–500). But if no systematic coercion is required to stabilize such a society, we might ask why real agents cannot be left to their own real and free agreements.

The Rawlsian might reply that those who acquire a sense of justice will not need to be coerced, but that for others coercion for moral ends is not always a bad thing. But the burden of proof is now upon him to show that the conditions of ignorance in the original position do accord with our sense of what is just, and the right-wing critic has counterarguments to this claim as well. The veil of ignorance is meant to insure that no one can press personal interests or advantages not shared by all others. But to think it fair to bar all knowledge of differentiating traits presupposes that no one has legitimate differential claims to goods or any rights to advantages from his initial social or natural assets. But these assumptions, which are diametrically opposed to libertarian principles, clearly beg the question and must therefore be closely questioned. Is it true that we are all equally entitled to everything at the base level? Suppose that someone makes something himself? Is it nevertheless a common good, to be included among the social goods distributed according to rules chosen in the original position? But if it is the rightful property of whoever made it, why is he not also entitled to his share of contribution to cooperative efforts? But then there will be little in the way of material goods left to distribute according to Rawls' scheme. What this indicates is that while the concept of equality, which motivates the veil of ignorance, does enter into our concept of justice, it does not seem to exhaust that concept, even at the most fundamental level.

The central charge leveled against Rawls' conception of the original position is that it is arbitrarily rigged in favor of the liberal egalitarian rules which emerge from it. To have an independent justificatory force, the original position must be separately plausible through its connection with basic moral convictions, or better, with the very meaning of a moral or just point of view. But if one or more of its features lack such independent justification, then the description of the original position becomes viciously circular and loses all theoretical function.[25] It becomes circular by presupposing just what it wants to prove, that basic principles of justice are radically egalitarian. We have already hinted that the assumption that rules of justice are those which emerge from a hypothetical situation in which everyone is by definition the same presupposes that equality is the main or the only relevant consideration for justice. It presupposes that all differential rights to things are relative to particular rules chosen, and not ground-level considerations in a theory of justice. The specific features of the original position seem even more arbitrarily slanted toward the choice Rawls intends. In developing this objection, we may consider first features of the veil of ignorance and then the psychological make-up of the contracting parties.

The Veil of Ignorance

Can we expect the best choice of rules which govern our lives to be made in a condition of ignorance? As we will see, this forces the contractors not only to be fair, but paranoid as well. In total ignorance, one might pessimistically guard against the worst possibilities as Rawls argues. But why should such a psychology guide the choice of rules of justice? Even if we do conceive of rules of justice as those chosen according to an artificial model of fairness, Rawls' general model of the original position seems no more intuitively compelling than other possible models for impartiality and fairness. One alternative model is the impartial sympathetic observer theory. According to this model, which is often used to support a utilitarian conception of justice, there are not many contractors choosing under conditions of complete ignorance, but one ideal observer, sympathetic to the interests of all, but partial towards none, with complete knowledge of the society in question and its members, arranging for just distributions of goods within the society. Since such an observer can gauge distribution according to needs and other relevant factors, which Rawls' contractors cannot, we might imagine this a more suitable model of the original position.[26]

The central question to be raised here is whether it is necessary to hide so much knowledge behind the veil of ignorance in order to ensure fairness or whether some knowledge is hidden purely gratuitously. The occupants of the original position can not be completely ignorant, for then no choice of rules would emerge at all. Only knowledge which would tend to bias the choice is supposed to be denied to them. While they are to know nothing particular about themselves or their society, they make their choices on the basis of complete general knowledge from the social sciences. It is questionable whether it is so easy to separate general facts from particular preferences and value systems, and whether Rawls has succeeded in doing so.[27] The general facts which the original contractors are permitted to know seem to be those of contemporary welfare economics, some theories of rational choice, and some questionable psychology. But why not allow them the theories of surplus value or class structures of Marx, or the economic theories of Milton Friedman? Rawls appears very selective in what he regards as fact and what he considers value preference, although the division obviously will affect the choice of rules from the original position. Many apparent disagreements over value judgments and specifically over which distributions are just are grounded in disagreements over facts: the existence of God or the truth of the Bible, for example, or the basic equality of all people. Rawls allows psychological and social facts but not prior value preferences to guide choices of principles of justice, for the inclusion of the latter would make the method viciously circular, or, according to him, biased. We may wonder first whether he has succeeded in separating facts from values, and second whether some values are not necessary in the original position to generate any choice of rules. Perhaps value judgments are involved in the initial decision by Rawls as to what are permitted to count as facts.

Let us now move from general charges of circularity to more specific problems with the veil of ignorance. One prominent feature of the veil of ignorance is that those in the original position are to be ignorant not only their own places in society and in the division of natural talents, but also ignorant of the types of positions and persons in their own society and of the percentages of persons who fill each natural and social slot. Intuitively we recognize that when interests of actual agents clash, the number of individuals on opposing sides often constitutes a relevant moral consideration in deciding among them. If the interest of one individual is opposed to that of many, we generally consider this relevant to the question of which compromise to choose in resolving the dispute. If we were to judge impartially, or if, as in an original position, we knew that we were to end up on one side or the other, but did not know which, we would certainly tend to favor those in the majority. But since the contractors do not know percentages of people in various positions with opposing interests, they cannot gauge the choice of rules to take account of those percentages. The rules chosen from this situation therefore must be totally insensitive to numbers of individuals in different representative groups.

One cannot help feel, therefore, that preventing the contractors from having such information about their own society serves only to force them toward a principle like Rawls', which takes no account of such percentages. If it were known, for example, that the chance of ending up in the worst relevant representative position were extremely slight, it would seem irrational to opt for the maximin strategy which maximizes benefits for those in that position. Rather, given knowledge of the relevant probabilities, rational agents might maximize their expected utility from the original position by multiplying the expected return to each representative individual by the chance of ending up as that individual under each prospective rule. That such probabilities are not known in Rawls' original position seems designed simply to rule out the maximization of expected utility or average utility by barring any definite expectations. Without an independent moral reason for preventing such knowledge, the original position is revealed to be circular or slanted towards its liberal-egalitarian outcome. And we have seen that independent moral reason appears to be lacking.

The Rawlsian might offer several replies here. First, he might argue that basic rules of justice are not relative to particular structures of specific societies, and that in order to have them apply across societies, knowledge of such particulars must be prohibited in the original position from which they are chosen. The rules of justice themselves ought to operate, when necessary, to change the structure of particular societies rather than conservatively treating specific structures as given. There is time later (at the stage of choosing a constitution and framing legislation) for making adjustments in application to specific social circumstances (199–200). Rawls' own main argument for barring such knowledge in the original position is that justice must apply across generations as well as within them, and thus rules of justice cannot be framed to fit a particular society at a particular stage of social and economic development (137).

But these arguments do not seem wholly adequate to meet the objection. For one thing, there may be no rules of justice which apply to all social situations indifferently, and Rawls himself ultimately allows for different versions of his rules to apply to societies at different stages of economic development. For another thing, various versions of the utilitarian principle are as general in scope of application as are Rawls' priniciples, and yet ignorance of social structures and percentages of persons at various levels in society in the original position helps to decide against such principles. The problem of justice across generations could be handled by giving more information rather than less in the original position. For example, we might have representatives of present and later generations who must reach a compromise, and we might give them knowledge of the structure of present society and its likely courses of future development under different principles of arrangement.[29] The utilitarian principle does not in itself necessarily militate in favor of one specific generation; and there cannot be anything intuitively sacred about ruling out bias in the choice of rules by stipulating sweeping ignorance, especially when such ignorance prejudices the choice away from certain perfectly general and impartial rules.

In defending the prohibition of such knowledge, the Rawlsian might finally argue that it is precisely to avoid having to aggregate competing interests in adjudicating disputes once the veil of ignorance is lifted, that the veil extends across these particular facts in the original position. The basic rules of justice are to determine the specification of individual rights, and a central feature of rights is that they prohibit sacrificing certain interests of individuals to the opposing interests of the greater number. (For example, if I have a right to free speech, the number of people I might offend is not a sufficient reason for silencing me.) Thus a good reason for this feature of the original position is that if the probabilities of ending up in various positions were known, based on the number of people likely to be in each position, the contractors would be willing to sacrifice the interests of some to those of others, thereby choosing some version of the utilitarian principle over the conception of rights which Rawls endorses. But this simply shows the veil of ignorance begs the question against the adoption of less egalitarian principles than Rawls'. It simply brings out the circularity of the method for specifying the original position.

This objection is most likely to be expressed by the utilitarian since it is this feature which helps to propel the choice of rules away from a principle of utility and towards Rawls' more egalitarian principles. The libertarian would endorse the utilitarian's charge of circularity in Rawls' method, as well as his objection to the artificiality of the constraints of the veil of ignorance. But the libertarian is more likely to center his objections to the veil of ignorance upon its abstraction from existing social positions and the natural endowments of real individuals. Such abstraction guarantees that no differential features of individuals can figure prominently as basic considerations in deciding how goods are to be divided. Natural as well as social differences are not only ignored but nullified as grounds for unequal distributions.

Objections to the nullification of natural endowments like strength or intelligence are the easier ones to raise, and these could also be endorsed by those whose overall position lies somewhere between that of the libertarian and Rawls, so I will concentrate upon them. Disallowing knowledge of such personal characteristics in the original position amounts to treating personal assets as so much common property, to be used to the maximum benefit of society as a whole. By what right does society appropriate personal abilities? Rawls' principal argument is that natural abilities are arbitrary from a moral point of view, a matter of chance, and so not to be the basis in themselves for unequal distributions. Of course, society will still wish to encourage the development of natural abilities for the benefit of all. But since we need only a marginal amount of incentive to encourage the development of natural abilities, and since, according to Rawls, individuals derive their highest pleasure from the development of their abilities anyway (426), Rawlsian society would not need to stimulate the maximum flowering of such talents as would a free market situation. It is one thing to ignore natural differences in establishing a framework for distributing goods, so that rewards are based solely on productivity and not upon natural abilities alone. It is another thing to nullify all the effects of such abilities, except those that benefit everyone.[30]

If we recognize a fundamental right of each individual over his own person, it seems that this might include a right to exercise his natural abilities and a right to the fruits of their exercise under free agreements. As Robert Nozick points out, the logical outcome of the nullification of differential abilities by the veil of ignorance in the original position might be a call for a more equitable redistribution of natural assets themselves, i.e. the redistribution of arms, legs and brains (as soon as technology made this practicable and painless).[31] But this runs counter to our intuitive recognition of each person's right over his own body as perhaps the most fundamental right of all. And how much difference is there in fact between simply redistributing natural endowments, were this genetically or technologically feasible, and nullifying their effects upon distribution of social goods to gain maximum benefits for those who have fewer endowments? Can the former be prohibited and the latter required by our most basic intuitions concerning justice? The inviolability of the individual person, which is argued by Rawls to be the ground for preferring his principles of justice over the utilitarian principle, seems to be ignored here.

Finally, we may question here, as we began to in an earlier paragraph, Rawls' prohibiting the original contractors from knowing their own conception of what is good. Our own views about what is right and wrong, just and unjust, are influenced by our values, by what we consider good, valuable or worth having. According to Rawls, however, knowledge of values or conceptions of the good in the original position either would prevent a unanimous choice of rules of justice, or would bias the choice, as each contractor would attempt to foster his own values. Of course without any values, no preferences for distributive arrangements could emerge at all, as there would be no preferences for goods to distribute. Rawls' solution is to adopt a "thin theory of the good," which consists of a list of primary goods, which he thinks it rational for all agents to want, whatever else they want. These primary goods include wealth and power, which Rawls sees as universal means to other goods. But such goods are means to the fulfillment of certain life plans and not others, and they are more highly valued in themselves by certain individuals than by others.[32] Thus once again the original position and the veil of ignorance fail to be value free. More importantly, the play of individual preferences, which the libertarian seeks to protect, becomes lost in the Rawlsian methodology which considers all individuals as equal, i.e. the same.[33]

The Psychology of the Contractors

Even with the stipulated veil of ignorance, which involves choosing the alternative with the best worst outcome, ignoring other possible outcomes and the probability of their occuring, the choice of the maximin strategy is not the inevitable result from the original position. In the absence of information regarding the percentage of people occupying each relevant social position, the parties to the contract would still treat all relevant positions as equi-probable and opt for average utility as a maximizing scheme.[34] Rawls cannot complete the argument against this alternative without additional premises. What is required to complete the argument according to Rawl's opponents is that the contractors in the original position have a peculiar and abnormal psychology with a total aversion to risk and a strongly materialistic, yet strangely limited, desire for primary goods like wealth and power.[35]

First, it can be pointed out that in ordinary life we normally do not act in a maximim fashion even if we are uncertain about the probability of various situations occuring. If it is a nice day and the chances of rain seem slight, we do not walk around with raincoat and umbrella on the grounds that the worst possible outcome would be to get caught in the rain without them. Rather we play percentages to maximize expected utility. It could be replied that the seriousness of the choices in the original position renders this example irrelevant; but, to take another common case, how many of us risk catastrophe by flying when we travel rather than taking the bus or train?[36]

In order to avoid the charge that the choice of his rules depends upon some socially relative psychology, Rawls claims that the desire for primary goods is universal among rational persons, and yet that they care little for what they can acquire of these goods beyond the minimum guaranteed by the adoption of the maximin strategy and the resultant Difference Principle. These are not psychological assumptions as far as Rawls is concerned, but part of the definition of rationality for his agents. He also claims that what underlies the adoption of the maximin strategy is not an unusual aversion to risk, but rather the desire for stability in the system of justice which is to be instituted once the veil of ignorance is lifted. An abnormal psychological aversion to risk is not necessary, according to him, because the contractors know that they should not adopt rules which some of them will not be able to endorse or willingly obey in real social situations (172). Strategies other than the maximin will result in a choice of rules which may call upon some to make severe sacrifices for the sake of others, according to Rawls. Thus he concludes that the need for inherently stable social rules in itself dictates the maximin strategy which results in a selection of rules which guarantee a satisfactory minimum level of goods to everyone.

The problem with this argument is that while those on the bottom will do better with this kind of strategy than they would do with any other, those in other positions will be called upon to give up what they could acquire in a free market situation up to the maximum possible benefit for less productive people. Since those in socially better positions are generally also in better positions to change the system, we might think Rawls' system even more inherently unstable than others, given a realistic appraisal of motives. Rawls includes among motivations of persons in society a sense of justice, but he cannot appeal to this motive in justifying the choice of certain rules of justice themselves. Furthermore, he himself argues that this sense of justice develops only towards rules recognized to operate for the betterment of all (471, 473–4). Since those better endowed or more socially productive will recognize that rules which emerge from a maximin strategy will not be to their benefit as compared to conceivable alternatives (including real free association), they will not be motivated to uphold Rawls' system by a sense of allegiance. Hence it seems we cannot conclude that the social framework which results from maximin is more stable than others. Hence, further psychological premises are required to motivate the adoption of a maximin strategy in the original position.

At least we can say for Rawls that the psychological features of the contractors are not socially relative. There may never have been a society whose members matched the combination of materialism and extreme cautiousness Rawls insists upon, certainly not Western democracies in their recent histories. The whole development of capitalism as well as the settling of this country demanded people who took high risks in the face of uncertainty.[37] (It might even be necessary in real social situations to take high risks sometimes to raise the minimum level in a society, a seeming paradox for Rawls.[38]) For the libertarian, who values freedom above all else and generally takes an optimistic view of the prospects for those willing to take reasonable risks in the face of uncertainty, Rawls' contractors will appear obsessed with security and extremely pessimistic in acting as if their futures were to be determined by their enemies (152). Given full knowledge of the risks involved, one who is willing to take such risks for the chance of better life prospects cannot be condemned as irrational. Indeed we generally condemn those who fail to seize opportunities to better themselves for fear of the risks involved. And yet Rawls makes the adoption of a maximin strategy in the face of uncertainty of the original position part of the definition of rationality itself.

The willingness of those more fortunate to abide by the Difference Principle in an actual society might be viewed as morally praiseworthy, indeed, extremely altruistic and self-sacrificing. But Rawls does not demand altruism or the love of one's fellow men either of his contractors, or of his citizens once the veil of ignorance is lifted (281, 476). Indeed for altruists, notions of justice are unnecessary (281). Yet it is doubtful that any other attitude could generate the stability he seeks for his rules of justice in real society. And, while adherence to the Difference Principle by normally endowed real individuals might arouse moral admiration, adoption of the maximin strategy by Rawls' contractors out of self-interest appears only contemptible, abnormally cautious and lacking in spirit. To quote one critic on this point:

> Rawlsian man in the original position is finally a strikingly lugubrious creature: unwilling to enter a situation that promises success because it also promises failure, unwilling to risk winning because he feels doomed to losing, ready for the worst because he cannot imagine the best, content with security and the knowledge he will be no worse off than anyone else because he dares not risk freedom and the possibility that he will be better off—all under the guise of 'rationality.'[39]

Worse than the empirical oddness of Rawls' conception of the psychology of rational agents is its empirical inconsistency. Although he represents the desire for more primary goods as universally rational, in that these goods are seen as means to whatever else one values, it is clear that the ascription of such desires represents an empirical consensus from the majority of individuals who do desire these goods. Christian ascetics, for example, do not desire them, and rather than considering them universally valuable means, believe them to be detrimental to a worth-while earthly life. The ascription of these desires, therefore, represents an empirical average; and yet other features of the ascribed psychology—the attitude toward risk and the fact that the contractors care little for higher shares of the goods beyond a guaranteed minimum—are not at all average or usual. Those people who do desire such goods generally remain unsatisfied with minimal amounts of them, and they are willing to take considerable risks to acquire more. And, if Rawls' contractors care so little for higher shares of these goods, why do those with more talent need the incentives to prod them to work harder (Rawls' justification for inequality)?[40] Finally, while the contractors know nothing of their particular society, they seem to know that it is affluent enough to be able to guarantee a wholly satisfactory minimum level, which is not even true of the most affluent societies of recent years.[41]

The assumption that everyone desires material wealth and power, but that none care too much for amounts of these goods beyond the minimal guaranteed by the maximin strategy, amounts to an assumption of universal yet sharply diminishing marginal utility for the satisfaction of material desires. (Additional dollar is worth less to a millionaire, for example, than it is worth to someone with little money.) But under the assumption of diminishing marginal utility, Rawls' maximin strategy and the resultant Difference Principle would appear to conform to a utilitarian principle. Since marginal utility for additional units of these goods is assumed to decline as one acquires more of them, it can never maximize overall utility to benefit thsoe at the top more at the expense of those at the bottom. Thus to the extent that the psychological premise is correct, violation of the Difference Principle will not increase utility, and the utilitarian principle will not be eliminated as a rational choice for a principle of justice by the adoption of a maximin strategy in the original position.[42] And what else could account for the assumption that persons care little for additional primary goods beyond guaranteed minima besides the assumption of diminishing marginal utility for these goods? Yet Rawls is at pains to criticize utilitarians for reliance upon such empirical assumptions (159-160). It seems that this argument against utilitarianism collapses, for Rawls has only pushed the crucial empirical psychological premise further back in his theory to his definition of rationality for the contractors in the original position.[43] The premise of caring little for primary goods beyond the minima, like the premise regarding ignorance of probabilities discussed in the previous section, is necessary, according to Rawls himself, for the adoption of the maximin strategy to be rational in the orignal position (154-6). The circularity of the full methodology again appears: Rawls is able to derive from the original position the egalitarian principles he wants only by building into it questionable features (such as this peculiar notion of rationality) which lack independent intuitive appeal.

We could continue to question specific features of the underlying psychology of Rawls' contractors.[44] But it will be more profitable at this point to summarize and evaluate briefly the major criticisms of Rawls which have emerged.

CONCLUSION

I have concentrated upon those criticisms from the right which I take to be the relatively more plausible or compelling ones, although I do not agree with the full implications of all of them. Other broad lines of criticism, such as attacks upon the very notion of equal opportunity, or objections to the inherent mediocrity of egalitarian societies, I have ignored as more off the mark.[45] Thoroughgoing libertarians refuse to recognize any right to equal opportunity since they take any such purported right to violate the real right of individuals and corporations to control the disbursement of their assets, by hiring whom they please, for example. Since I have defended a principle of equal opportunity in other papers,[46] (albeit a more limited principle than Rawls'), I have not included attacks on the second part of Rawls' second principle in this discussion. Some choice of topics was necessary in any case, and little was lost by this omission since the force of these attacks is rearticulated in the criticisms of the Difference Principle.

The criticisms that were included centered on the claim that those above average in talents, effort or productivity are treated unjustly by the entire Rawlsian system. In light of the systematically brutal treatment of those on the bottom of the social scale in the history of this country, this complaint against Rawls may appear at first blush and in historical context relatively inconsequential. But given that he is interested primarily in developing a timeless theory of justice, a slightly closer reading perhaps does support the claim that he goes too far in the direction of complete egalitarianism. The utilitarian argues with some force that in exactly those contexts in which Rawls' principles diverge from the principle of utility, they become problematical in their treatment of those better off. Many of Rawls' arguments for the plausibility of his principles build in empirical assumptions as strong as those which he tends to criticize utilitarians for holding.

The libertarian attacks him not for shortchanging above average individuals in utility calculations, but for ignoring their rights—another ground upon which Rawls faults utilitarianism. It is interesting to note that both Rawls and the libertarian claim allegiance to the same deeper moral theory, a Kantian theory which opposes the collectivism of utilitarianism and takes rights seriously. Rawls interprets Kant's fundamental principle that moral rules be universalizable as the demand that rules be willed by all before particular positions or interests are known. His original position is a procedural interpretation of this demand, and its results are to accord with Kant's second formulation of the categorical imperative, (which forbids treating some individuals strictly as means to the welfare of others). The libertarian concentrates upon this second formulation, and argues that it is violated by any redistributive principle which treats above average individuals as collective assets to benefit those worse off. Whereas Rawls' Difference Principle constrains individuals within arrangements they would not agree to as actual agents in a free society, the libertarian substitutes for the artificial agreement of the original position actual free contracts of these real individuals. What results is a free market economy, with the state restricted to the prevention of harm and fraud, without redistributive functions. This is taken not only to maximize real freedom but to preserve the primacy of desert, since individuals will generally be paid in proportion to their marginal contribution to a socially demanded product. Just distributions are taken to be those which result from such free acquistions and transfers. Individuals can acquire what they desire enough to work for, within the limits of their capabilities.

The libertarian can be answered in turn that a system with totally free transfers will eventually cause some to start life at a considerable disadvantage to others. This has the effect of constraining the former within the bounds of poverty from which they can never escape to achieve that autonomy which Kant envisions. These individuals are then forced into agreements out of ignorance, fear or powerlessness, and there is certainly no guarantee that the distribution which thereby follows is fair. The individual's ability to formulate a rational life plan and pursue it within the bounds of morality, which is the ideal of the liberal Kantian tradition which envelops both Rawls and his libertarian critics, cannot be developed without the material means which render such plans practicable. A society in which some are constrained within the confines of poverty, and yet contribute as a class to the social product, can then plausibly be condemned as one which uses these individuals purely as means.[47] The Kantian injunction appears to be violated both by strict egalitarian and by strict libertarian distributive systems, but in relation to individuals at opposite ends of the social scale. One can rather easily interpret both as using some individuals as means to the welfare of others without their real consent.

There are clearly compromise positions between these two extremes which there is not space here to explore fully. For example, we can attempt to correct for unequal social starts in life without treating individual talents as common social assets. To provide equal opportunity by compensating for initially unequal social conditions does not appear to violate the rights of persons, as does the Difference Principle when applied to personal characteristics. Of course it is also difficult to separate natural endowments from what results from the early influence of parents in favorable social positions. While the egalitarian would argue that most apparent natural differences are really socially relative, the libertarian tends to turn this on its head by claiming that what appears the result of natural talent is more often the effect of hard work and training. Despite these complications, we can still discern a distinction which might guide educational and social policy toward the achievement of an equality of opportunity short of the Difference Principle. We also can insure a reasonable minimum level of welfare without attempting to maximize this minimum so as to benefit some who simply do not deserve it.[48]

The moral equality of all agents is central to a Kantian point of view, and it is clear that just rules cannot be slanted in favor of special interests. But there are different legitimate ways of concretely interpreting this equality and translating its demands into social institutions and policies.[49] Those to the right of Rawls aim, for example, at a social system which makes the same relative contribution to the welfare of each individual, or at one in which there is equal opportunity for rewards on the basis of contribution. The Difference Principle is a more extreme attempt to structure a just society, and those to the right of it are not amiss in arguing that the value of equality cannot completely override that of economic freedom and desert in a just and overall valuable social scheme.

NOTES

1. The leading spokesman for the right-wing libertarians has been Robert Nozick.
2. For discussions of desert in this context, see James Sterba, "Justice as Desert," *Social Theory and Practice*, 3, no. 1, (1974), 101-16; Michael Slote, "Desert, Consent, and Justice," *Philosophy & Public Affairs*, 2, no. 4, (1973), 323-47; and John Schaar, "Reflections on Rawls' Theory of Justice," *Social Theory and Practice*, 3, no. 1, (1974), 87.
3. Compare J.E.J. Altham, "Rawls' Difference Principle," *Philosophy*, 48, no. 183, (1973), 75-8; Robert Nozick, *Anarchy, State, and Utopia* (New

York: Basic Books, 1974), p. 190; David Braybrooke, "Utilitarianism with a Difference: Rawls' Position in Ethics," *Canadian Journal of Philosophy*, 3, no. 2, (1973), 323-4.

4. Especially according to Rawls' "Aristotelian Principle" which holds that people derive satisfaction by fully developing and utilizing their abilities.
5. This is implied throughout Norzick's discussion of Rawls in Nozick, *Anarchy*. See also, Kenneth Arrow, "Some Ordinalist-Utilitarian Notes on Rawls' Theory of Justice," *The Journal of Philosophy*, 70, no. 9, (1973), 257; and David Gauthier, "Justice and Natural Endowment: Toward a Critique of Rawls' Ideological Framework," *Social Theory and Practice*, 3, no. 1 (1974), 20.
6. Thomas Nagel, "Rawls on Justice," in *Reading Rawls.* edited by Norman Daniels (New York: Basic Books, 1975), p. 13.
7. Nozick, *Anarchy*, pp. 193-4.
8. Comparison with the Marxist slogan is found in Schaar, "Reflections," p. 89. Criticism of Rawls for ignoring differential needs can be found in Brian Barry, *The Liberal Theory of Justice* (London: Oxford, 1973), pp. 55-6; Benjamin Barber, "Justifying Justice: Problems of Psychology, Politics and Measurement in Rawls," in *Reading Rawls.* ed. Daniels, p. 311; Arrow, "Ordinalist-Utilitarian Notes," p. 254; and Braybrooke, "Utilitarianism," p. 318.
9. Compare David Lyons, "Nature and Soundness of the Contract and Coherence Arguments," in *Reading Rawls*, ed. Daniels, P. 152; Schaar, "Reflections," pp. 89-90; and Slote, "Desert," p. 343.
10. That the Difference Principle may benefit social noncooperatives is argued in Braybrooke, "Utilitarianism," p. 326-8.
11. The general argument of this paragraph was from Sterba, "Justice."
12. Compare Slote, "Desert," pp. 336-7; and David L. Norton, "Rawls' Theory of Justice: A 'Perfectionist' Rejoinder," *Ethics*, 85, no. 1, (1974), 54-55.
13. Nozick, *Anarchy*, p. 225.
14. For discussion of incentive blackmail, see Braybrooke, "Utilitarianism," p. 326.
15. This line of argument is drawn from Nozick, *Anarchy*, pp. 185-7.
16, Nozick, *Anarchy*, p. 198.
17. Barry, *Liberal Theory*, p. 112.
18. H.L.A. Hart, "Rawls on Liberty and its Priority," in *Reading Rawls*, ed. Daniels, pp. 240-42; and Norman Bowie, "Some Comments on Rawls' Theory of Justice," *Social Theory and Practice*, 3, no. 1, (1940), 71.
19. Hart, "Rawls on Liberty," p. 245.
20. Bowie, "Some Comments," pp. 71-2.
21. Barry, *Liberal Theory*, pp. 73-5.
22. Braybrooke, "Utilitarianism," pp. 311-13.
23. Compare Stanley Bates, "The Motivation to be Just," *Ethics*, 85, no. 1 (1974), 8, 12; and Dan Brock, "The Theory of Justice," *The University of Chicago Law Review*, 40, no. 3, (1973), 499.

24. Nozick, *Anarchy*, pp. 185-7; and Norton, "'Pefectionist' Rejoinder," p. 52.
25. See especially R.M. Hare, "Rawls' Theory of Justice," in *Reading Rawls*, ed. Daniels, pp. 81-107; Nagel, "Rawls on Justice,"; and Raymond Gastil, "Beyond a Theory of Justice," *Ethics*, 85, no. 3, (1975), 183-94.
26. Compare Hare, "Rawls' Theory," for a discussion of these different models and their implications, especially p. 89.
27. See Charles Frankel, "Justice, Utilitarianism, and Rights," *Social Theory and Practice*, 3, no. 1, (1974), 36; and Arrow, "Ordinalist-Utilitarian Notes," p. 255.
28. Compare Hare, "Rawls' Theory," pp. 90, 101-4.
29. Compare Hare, "Rawls' Theory," pp. 97-9.
30. Gauthier, "Justice and Natural Endowment," pp. 15-16.
31. Nozick, *Anarchy*, p. 206.
32. See Nagel, " Rawls on Justice," pp. 8-9; Lyons, "Nature and Soundness," p. 163; and Norton, "'Perfectionist' Rejoinder," p. 53.
33. Compare Frankel, "Rights," pp. 40, 42; Norton, "'Perfectionist' Rejoinder," p. 51; and Gastil, "Beyond a Theory," pp. 185-6.
34. For discussion of this Laplacian strategy as an alternative to maximin in the original position, see Arrow, "Ordinalist-Utilitarian Notes," p. 250.
35. That this is required is argued in Barry, *Liberal Theory*, p. 96; and Barber, Justifying Justice," p. 297.
36. These examples are from Barry, *Liberal Theory*, pp. 89, 107.
37. Barber, "Justifying Justice," p. 298.
38. *Ibid.*, pp. 306-7.
39. *Ibid.*, p. 299.
40. Barry, *Liberal Theory*, p. 97.
41. Nagel, "Rawls on Justice," p. 12.
42. Braybrooke, "Utilitarianism," p. 319; Lyons, "Nature and Soundness," pp. 166-7; Arrow, "Ordinalist-Utilitarian Notes," p. 252; Scott Gordon, "John Rawls' Difference Principle, Utilitarianism, and the Optimum Degree of Inequality," *The Journal of Philosophy*, 70, no. 9, (1973), 277-8; and Rolf Sartorius, *Individual Conduct and Social Norms* (Encino: Dickenson, 1975), p. 126.
43. Barry, *Liberal Theory*, p. 100.
44. *Ibid.*, pp. 45-9.
45. But for a forceful attack arguing the mediocrity of Rawlsian society, see Gastil, "Beyond a Theory."
46. In Alan Goldman, "Justice and Hiring by Competence," *American Philosophical Quarterly*, 14, no. 1, (1977), 17-28; and Alan Goldman, "The Principle of Equal Opportunity," *The Southern Journal of Philosophy*.
47. See Alan Goldman, "The Entitlement Theory of Distributive Justice," *The Journal of Philosophy*, 73, no. 21, (1976), 823-35.
48. For a discussion of a guaranteed minimum short of maximin, see Brock, "Theory of Justice," pp. 491-2; also Hare, "Rawls' Theory," pp. 104-5.
49. See Alan Goldman, "Rights, Utilities and Contracts," *Canadian Journal of Philosophy*, Supp. Vol., (Spring 1977).

Responses to Rawls from the Left

Leslie Pickering Francis
UNIVERSITY OF UTAH

A paper titled "Responses to Rawls from the Left" must begin with an explanation. "The left" is not a coherent entity, and it is not even easy to decide which criticisms of Rawls are "leftist."[1] Leftist critiques of Rawls are scattered and for the most part unsystematic. *A Theory of Justice* was widely reviewed in philosophy journals and liberal publications but barely mentioned in the leftist press or in journals such as *Radical Philosophy*. (All parenthetical citations are to John Rawls, *A Theory of Justice* (Cambridge, Mass.: Harvard University Press, 1971.)) Perhaps Rawls was correct to take utilitarianism as his major opponent, but this paper is written on the assumption that he was not: that the differences between Rawls and particularly Marxists are so deep and sustained that it is no wonder commentary on them is infrequent. This paper is a guide to those who would like to know what major issues have been discussed and where the discussion is to be found. It focuses on four areas: Rawls' methodology, his view of rationality, his account of private property and economic life, and his portrait of the good community. The principal charge is that Rawls fails to appreciate how private property may undermine individuals' abilities to lead satisfying lives in a community to which they are deeply attached because his justificatory methodology is ideological and his view of rationality too close to that of the bourgeois economists. For the most part, I will make little effort to arbitrate the issues between Rawls and his leftist critics; I am most inclined to break this rule in considering private property, economic life and the good community, which seem to me to have received far too cursory treatment in the Rawls literature to date.

In "Alienated Labour"[2] Marx starts from the presuppositions and laws of political economy (i.e., early capitalist economic theory) and attempts to argue that they have unacceptable and unforeseen consequences. One of his goals was to show that these consequences would be unacceptable to the capitalist "economists" themselves. This kind of criticism is an example of an "internal" criticism of Rawls. A number of internal criticisms of Rawls have appeared. Other criticisms of Rawls are "external," and proceed on the basis of values or assumptions which Rawls would not accept. Marx frequently chastised philosophical critics for their abstract unselfconsciousness about the material bases of their own premises.[3] Marx sometimes envisaged the unity of theory and practice as being achieved where theory motivates human purposive activity: "...theory itself becomes a material force when it has seized the masses. Theory is capable of seizing the masses when it demonstrates *ad hominem*, and it demonstrates *ad hominem* as soon as it becomes radical...Theory is only realized in a people so far as it fulfills the needs of the people."[4] Since recent discussions of Rawls have not even approached the question of whether his theory of justice is capable of fulfilling the needs of the people, this discussion of leftist objections to Rawls can be no more than a review of those external or internal criticisms of Rawls which seem most significant.

METHODOLOGY

Rawls' stated methodological ideal in *A Theory of Justice* was to argue that his principles of justice follow logically from "the original position," a set of uncontroversial assumptions about the conditions of societies in need of principles of justice, the nature of theories of right, and the character of human rationality and motivation. He admits he falls short of this goal; nonetheless, a central theme of the book is that Rawls' principles of justice can be justified by showing that they would be preferred in this original position to utilitarianism and several other alternatives. However, perhaps because Rawls himself is ambiguous, even his leftist critics do not agree about the kind of justification this original position argument is supposed to provide. On one view, in the original position Rawls is trying to find a value-neutral, "Archimedean" point from which to evaluate societies. On the other view, the original position need not be value neutral but only a plausible sketch of "the moral point of view;" what is important is that the original position and Rawls' principles of justice provide a consistent and mutally supporting account of a substantive theory of justice and the moral perspective lying behind it. An even further level of coherence is also crucial: that Rawls' principles fit more successfully than the alternatives with our most thoughtful judgments about particular moral situations—our "moral data," as it were. Passages from *A Theory of Justice* can be cited in support of either the Archimedean or the coherence view; Rawls emphasizes the coherence view in his abstract reflections on moral theory (cf. ss. 4, 9 and 87), the Archimedean in his descriptions of the details of his argument (cf. ss. 20, 41). The discussion which follows considers criticisms of Rawls by both leftist Archimedean and coherence interpreters; it does does not try to solve the somewhat futile question of which is the "correct" interpretation of Rawls' original position argument.[5]

Rawls' argument from the original position is basically that individuals subject to the conditions of the original position would choose his particular principles of justice over utilitarianism and several other alternatives. Individuals in the original position are, first, in the "circumstances of justice"—conditions of moderate scarcity where conflicts sometimes need to be settled but where "social cooperation makes possible a better life for all than any would have if each were to try to live solely by his own efforts" (126). Original position choosers are also subject to what Rawls calls "the constraints of the concept of right"—i.e., the principles they choose must have characteristics necessary for a principle to count as a moral principle about what it is right or wrong to do. These constraints are: finality (the principles must be chosen once and for all); universality (the principles must apply to all societies capable of principles of justice); generality (the principles must not contain proper names or descriptions which look general but are really designed to single out particular individuals); publicity; and the ability to order the conflicting claims of individuals in society. Further, individuals are behind the "veil of ignorance;" they must choose principles of justice without knowing anything about themselves that might enable them to tailor principles to their own advantage. It is as though both men and women, feminists and traditionalists, were asked to choose the proper marital institutions without knowing their sex or their particular persuasions—only on a much grander scale. Individuals, however, cannot choose if they are deprived of any motivational structures whatsoever; and so Rawls does assign "each" chooser knowledge of "primary goods"—things which it is rational for any man to want whatever else he may desire. Additionally, individuals are assumed to be rational in the sense that they want to get as much as possible for the least cost. Finally, they are not envious and have no interests—pro or con—in the fortunes of others.

How could individuals in the original position reason to principles of justice? Rawls argues that since they would want the best possible for themselves they would begin by selecting a principle of equality. But then they would notice that sometimes inequalities can make everyone better off, as when incentives encourage the production of things which are socially beneficial, so they would move to what he calls the general maximin conception: inequalities are impermissible unless they work to the advantage of the least well off individual. We might think of this theory as "rational egalitarianism."

Next, because of the role of liberties in ensuring the primary goods, liberties would be singled out for protection when that protection could be sure. A special first principle, guaranteeing each person "an equal right to the most extensive, or total system of basic liberties compatible with a similar system of liberty for all" (302) would take priority over a second principle requiring the arrangement of social and economic inequalities to work to the advantage of the least well off individual. These two principles make up what Rawls calls the "special" conception of justice. They win out over utilitarianism, Rawls claims, because no rational individual would want to be sacrificed (unless he had interests in the interests of others, which he is assumed not to have) to the benefit of others, or even to gamble on sacrifices for his own advantage if the possible gains are slight and the possible losses are catastrophic.

On the Archimedean interpretation of Rawls, the original position argument is supposed to support the principles of justice by showing they would be preferred to alternatives from a value neutral perspective. The most sweeping leftist critics challenge the possibility of value neutrality itself. Others urge that even if value neutrality is possible, it is so only at the cost of excessive abstraction and the loss of historical understanding. From this perspective, Archimedean critics argue that the original position conditions do not take sufficient account of historical change, and that the supposed deduction of Rawls' principles of justice depends upon highly problematic empirical assumptions. Rationality and the theory of primary goods pose particularly extensive problems which will be treated in the next section, but even leaving these problems aside it is clear that Rawls' Archimedean approach leaves much hostage to empirical fortune.

The standard leftist criticisms of Rawls' original position conditions are easily and frequently stated but extremely difficult to resolve. Some socialists who are perhaps utopian challenge Rawls' assumption that beyond a certain point of economic development, moderate scarcity is endemic; they urge that with appropriate socialization and technology, scarcity can be overcome. A more standard Marxist approach questions the mutually beneficial nature of social cooperation. Under some historical conditions, it is urged, social cooperation is not in the interest of the working class.[6] Of the constraints of the concept of right, universality and finality are challenged on the ground that it is irrational to choose moral principles for all societies, once and for all, since historical conditions change. Rawls agrees, to the extent that he distinguishes between the general maximin conception of justice which applies in conditions of scarcity and which requires that inequalities be distributed to benefit the least well off, and the special conception in which first principle liberties and fair equality of opportunity are given priority over the maximin conception when they can be ensured. After all, it is only under some historical conditions that liberties can be guaranteed. But then, the criticism continues, Rawls has laid himself open to the possibility that the value of liberty may vary much more widely with specific economic conditions than he realizes. Serious questions can be raised about when Rawls thinks the special conception of justice comes into play,[7] about whether the implications of Rawls' theory and utilitarianism are importantly different if Rawls admits that there are conditions under which liberties will not be given special priority[8] and about what the first principle guarantees are and whether Rawls has a clear method of arguing for them.[9] Daniels claims that if Rawls does have a method of arguing for the liberty guarantees, he is committed to greater egalitarianism than he realizes; liberties are to be given first principle priority because of their special importance; but isn't it then equally important that individuals not face inequalities of wealth which can impede the use of liberty in pursuit of their goals?[10]

The publicity condition is also thought to be somewhat removed from historical realities. Rawls himself stresses the condition because he thinks common knowledge of the moral principles actually in force in a society affirms the equal status of each member so critical to self-respect. That a utilitarian society might need secrecy about its basic principle in order to maximize utility (for knowledge of what was done in the general interest might make people worry) is seen by Rawls as a major flaw of utilitarianism. Marxists would, I think, agree that secrecy is not ultimately desirable. But they would want to consider the social circumstances; Leninists, for example, would charge that concealing the principles on which one acts is crucial in some revolutionary and immediately post-revolutionary situations. Insistence on a publicity condition under all social circumstances demonstrates naivete about power; so much can be said without defending Leninist dictatorships of the proletariat.

It is the veil of ignorance, however, which is the most troublesome of the original position conditions. The veil both takes away particular knowledge and perhaps more importantly guarantees available knowledge of general social science. Rawls describes it thusly:

> ...the only particular facts which the parties know is their society is subject to the circumstances of justice and whatever this implies. It is taken for granted, however, that they know the general facts about human society. They understand political affairs and the principles of economic theory; they know the basis of social organization and laws of human psychology. Indeed, the parties are presumed to know whatever general facts affect the choice of principles of justice. (137)

A generalized skepticism about the possibility of objective knowledge of "the laws" of social science would of course make this passage appear hopelessly confident. Short of such generalized skepticism, some charge that Rawls' distinction between general social science and particular social features cannot be sustained because social knowledge is knowledge of particular societies in specific historical circumstances, itself gotten in particular historical circumstances.[11] Others argue that while nonrelativized social knowledge is possible, Rawls is simply wrong in the assumptions he makes about societies. Barker, for example, argues that Rawls is at best jejune in assuming that tolerating the intolerant may persuade them to a belief in freedom, or that both socialist and private property economies are consistent with his principles.[12] Such challenges to Rawls' confidence about social science are serious, because judgments about the nature of societies enter into Rawls' argument that societies meeting his principles of justice would be chosen from the original position.

That Rawls requires troublesome empirical assumptions to provide an Archimedean defense for his principles emerges clearly with a consideration of whether his principles would be chosen in the original position. One central thrust of the leftist attack is that Rawls' principles would not be chosen because they guarantee too little to the worst off. The best way to get clear about the force of such criticisms of the Rawlsian derivation is to set up Rawls' argument as a problem in rational choice theory.[13] Suppose individuals with the above characteristics are faced with the following alternatives[14] :

(1) Remain in the state of nature.
(2) Adopt Rawls' two principles of justice.
(3) Adopt a first principle which requires guaranteeing to each the greatest amount of *effective* liberty compatible with a similar system of effective liberties for each, and a second principle which requires arranging the remaining economic inequalities to work to the advantage of the least fortunate representative individual.
(4) Adopt a principle which requires maximizing the minimum share of the benefits obtained from social cooperation, while leaving intact "naturally" based inequalities so far as these can be identified.
(5) Adopt the principle of utility.

Which alternative would it be rational to choose? In order to decide, the choosers must construct a "payoff matrix"—i.e., a chart listing the expected value of each alternative to each individual. Since original position choosers "all" have the same characteristics, the expected values will be the same for each. How, then, to assign the values? A standard suggestion for risky situations (situations in which one knows the probabilities of various outcomes and their value, but not which outcome will actually occur) is to sum a series of products: the value of each possible outcome times the probability of its occurring. In following this procedure, individuals would regard societies as lotteries; they would consider the kinds of societies generated by each alternative theory of justice, assess the probabilities of being in particular kinds of social positions in those societies, and multiply those probabilities times the value of the positions to the individuals occupying them. Rawls, however, rejects this method of assigning values to the alternatives: he thinks knowledge of the relevant probabilities is unobtainable under the veil of ignorance, and anyway the lottery procedure is a kind of irrational Russian roulette when losses might be severe and gains less important. Instead, as a guard against ill fortune in one's social position, he suggests evaluating each alternative theory of justice from the point of view of the least well off representative individual under that alternative; thus the payoff matrix is to be constructed by assigning to each alternative the value of that alternative to the least fortunate representative individual who lives under it, in any society to which it would be applied.

In the kinds of games usually discussed in game theory, assigning payoffs for each individual to each alternative is only the beginning; each individual must select a "strategy," because the outcome of the game will be the result of his and everyone else's choices. Such bargaining problems do not arise for Rawlsian choosers, since the values of alternatives to each individual are the same. They will unanimously agree on the alternative with the highest value—i.e., the alternative in which the worst off representative individual is best off. Rawls' own discussion concentrates on arguing for (2) as against (5); but a serious charge is that (3) is an alternative in which the worst off would be significantly better off. Daniels argues that if freedom of conscience is important enough to be assigned first principle equal protection, and if economic inequalities might threaten its exercise, then the worst off person under Rawls' principles will not have a guarantee which is admittedly important and which she/he would have if equal worth of liberty—that is, equality in what each individual can actually do with his liberties—were to be a first principle requirement.[15] For example, legal guarantees of freedom of thought and expression may have very different import for the lives of individuals with different economic resources. The "self-taught" coal miner was unusual enough to be worth remarking upon; money and, more importantly, time are needed even to develop one's thoughts on one's own. Isn't, then, the important guarantee equal effective exercise of freedom of conscience, rather than simply equal freedom of conscience? Rawls' reply is that (2) in comparison to (3) does not represent serious losses for the worst off individual because liberties are shored up as well as possible if inequalities must be to the benefit of the least well off; the extended discussion of economic life and community below is in large measure an evaluation of this defense.

Other critics charge that Rawls' principles of justice would not be chosen in the original position because identifiable groups in existing societies will feel that the original position choice is not to their advantage. As criticisms of Rawls' formal original position argument, these are not well taken, for Rawls does not claim that individuals in actual societies will find his principles to their advantage; if they would, the veil of ignorance device would be unnecessary. Nonetheless, these criticisms are worth noting because they point ahead to the problems Rawls will face in arguing that actual societies consistent with his two principles of justice will provide satisfying lives for their members. Gauthier, for example, argues that (4) would be the preferred alternative because individuals who knew they were naturally more favored would feel cheated by the knowledge that the values produced by their natural advantages were not assigned to them in an initial distribution. He thus thinks that the assumptions of Rawls' original position lead to less egalitarian conclusions than Rawls himself holds, for with values produced independently of social cooperation unavailable for redistribution, the worst off individual under (4) will be worse off than the worst off individual under Rawls' maximin principle. Gauthier portrays Rawlsian society as an instrument for the mutually advantageous furthering of natural advantages, rather than as a radically egalitarian understanding of others as ends.[16] His argument for the choice of (4) is that an individual who knows she/he would have been better off in the state of nature than under Rawls' principles—perhaps an individual of great natural talent and motivation whose gains are redistributed to others—would not find it reasonable to assume that the Rawlsian original position choice is the best choice for him/her. But Rawls does not claim that he should; he claims that (2) has a higher value than (4) in a payoff matrix constructed as described above. Rawls' appeal is to what original position choosers would select—not to what people in the real world would later find reasonable. Yet Gauthier's objection is not without point; individuals who evaluate societies in terms of what they are gaining may not feel much commitment to, or may even feel cheated by, a society which they do not believe advantageous to them. Restiveness among the talented may mean that Rawls' principles will not engender social stability.

Richard Miller's argument parallels Gauthier's, but it is the ruling class which Miller views as potentially unsatisfied.[17] Miller tries to show that if there are some societies fitting what he calls a weak Marxist description—societies in which no social arrangement acceptable to the best off class is acceptable to the worst off class, the best off class is a ruling class, and the need for wealth and power typical of the best off class is more acute than that typical of the rest of society—then no agreement on principles of justice would be forthcoming in the original position. In order to argue that the outcome of the original position would be stalemate, however, what Miller would need to show is not that some actual societies would suffer class conflict, but that disagreement over the situation of the worst off representative individual would make it impossible for original position choosers to decide when inequalities work to the benefit of the worst off. The problem raised here is whether Rawls' theory of primary goods enables original position choosers adequately to assess the situation of the worst off, and this is discussed in the next section. Miller does argue that in societies such as he describes, members of the ruling class would have self-interested reasons for not adhering to Rawlsian principles of justice. Thus, if societies with such ruling classes are compatible with Rawls' principles—and the social origins of desires for power is a topic Rawls leaves unexplored—Miller has isolated another potential source of dissatisfaction in Rawlsian society.[18]

The success of a Rawlsian Archimedean justification thus requires closer attention to life in societies governed by the two principles of justice. On the coherence interpretation, however, Rawls' principles can draw on an additional level of support: that they provide an illuminating systematization of "our considered judgments in reflective equilibrium." By our considered judgments Rawls means judgments about particular moral situations, made in Humean fashion: calmly, confidently and impartially. It will not do, then, to challenge these judgments as mere ideological abstractions; they are not generalizations.[19] But are they the kind of basic moral "data" on which we would agree without hesitation that Rawls seems to believe they are—data on the order of judgments about what "sounds right" by native speakers of a language?[20] If these judgments are ideological in nature, it is question-begging to test moral theories in comparison with them.[21] This is so even if one admits that moral systematization may require revisions of some considered judgments, for such revision amounts only in deciding which elements of an ideology are stronger or more central.

And there is reason to believe Rawlsian "considered judgments" are ideological. Rawls' description of them is revealing: "Considered judgments" are simply those rendered under conditions favorable to the exercise of the sense of justice, and therefore in circumstances where the more common excuses and explanations for making a mistake do not obtain" (47–48). Rawls thinks of these conditions as merely encouraging reasonable judgment, but the conditions favorable to the exercise of the sense of justice (roughly, the disposition to be just) are surely *moral.* If statements are "ideological" when they are influenced by a framework of values of which their maker is unaware, Rawls' own account of considered judgments is ideological. For Rawls believes that people who live in a society governed by his principles of justice will begin to desire those things which bring about justice. Of course, those with the sense of justice may well be aware that their judgments are influenced by the principles of justice under which they live, but this doesn't make it any less circular to test the principles in terms of the judgments they influence.

Suspicion about the justificatory force of Rawlsian considered judgments is fueled by some of Rawls' own examples. Favorite stalking horses of the left are the view that we should opt for tolerance of even the intolerant or religious fanatics, and the view that when liberties can be exercised it is irrational for anyone to trade them for material well-being. Such judgments, it is charged, are quintessentially liberal. Ironically, suspicion is also fueled by the dearth of considered judgments to be found in *A Theory of Justice.* There are very few judgments about particular cases; most of what passes for "considered judgments" (even the judgment about tolerance of the intolerant) appear to be generalizations of liberal theory.

To the social critic, coherence theory has far less appeal than Archimedean theory. At least the latter provides a perspective—however flawed—from which to view societies. Thus Rawls might have the best chance of convincing his leftist critics by ably defending the original position constraints and the derivation of his principles. Unfortunately, as will be shown below, the leftist verdict is that life in Rawlsian society simply would not bear out the empirical optimism of the original argument.

RATIONALITY AND PRIMARY GOODS

Rawls stipulates that original position choosers must be rational in the sense standard in rational choice theory: each attempts to advance his interests in the most efficient (i.e., least costly) manner possible. Some leftist critics reject efficiency as part of a theory of rationality because they think it implies a commitment to particular, usually egoist, goals. Strictly speaking, these critics are mistaken, because without additional assumptions rationality as efficiency is a purely formal notion. Advancing one's own interests does not imply selfishness if interests may include the interests of others. Nor does efficiency entail treating others as mere means to one's goals,[22] if these goals include broad, social goals. For example, one might strive to abolish alienated labor in the most economical manner.

Rather, what Rawls' critics should charge is that efficiency is not all there is to an account of rationality. In the rational choice literature, rationality as efficiency is associated with other seriously controversial views—such as the assumption that individuals do not have interests in the interests of others. Rawls links rationality as efficiency with similar controversial assumptions. For Rawls certainly cannot rely upon rationality as efficiency alone: since original position choosers are deprived of knowledge of their own interests, some substantive assumptions are required in order for them to be able to make choices at all. What the left charges is that Rawls' substantive additions characterize selfish, acquisitive—in a word, bourgeois—man.

To the formal notion of rationality, Rawls adds what he calls the assumptions of mutual disinterest and non-envy, the theory of primary goods, and the stipulation that each individual cares for at least one member of the next generation.[23] Envy is a desire for the lesser good fortune of another which could not benefit oneself; Rawls thinks that since envy is collectively disadvantageous, it may reasonably be excluded from the original position. To this point, the left cannot object; envy is not an appealing characteristic to attribute to moral choosers, and one would not want to claim it is such a constant of the human condition as to be built into the original position choice of moral principles. Of course, assuming that original position choosers are not envious entails nothing about whether there will be envy in particular societies.

Objections to the assumption of mutual disinterest are better taken. Rawls' description of the assumption sounds far removed from egoism: "Moreover, although the interests advanced by these plans are not assumed to be interests in the self, they are the interests of a self that regards its conception of the good as worthy of recognition and that advances claims on its behalf as deserving satisfaction. I shall emphasize this aspect of the circumstances of justice by assuming that the parties take no interest in one another's interests"

(127). Nonetheless, Rawls argues for assuming mutual disinterestness by saying that original position conditions must take as little as possible for granted, and so it would be a mistake to presuppose "extensive ties of natural sentiment" (129). Rawls is not assuming that individuals in actual societies *are* narrowly self-interested; but he *is* refusing to build affiliations into the point of view from which the moral principles are chosen. He thus loses what many would regard as an important opportunity to generate moral principles which might themselves influence the extent of altruism people possess.

The refusal to assume affiliative ties is especially striking in view of the assumptions Rawls makes about "primary goods." Primary goods are "things which it is supposed a rational man wants whatever else he wants" (92), and wants more of rather than less, because he needs these to get anything else. Rawls never makes clear whether these claims about the primary goods are supposed to be true by definition or as empirical generalizations. The primary goods are, in order of importance: self-respect, rights and liberties, opportunities and powers, and income and wealth. Rawlsian choosers need to be able to compare the desirability of different clusters of primary goods in order to decide which positions in society are worse off; but there are tremendous difficulties involved in defining the goods precisely and ranking them comparatively.[24] For example, education is an important opportunity and speech a central freedom; but social resources are consumed in policing either fair admissions policies or open forums, even in a relatively just society. If social resources are scarce, choices will need to be made among different possible mixtures of these primary goods. Very detailed evaluative judgments will be required in order to compare increments of educational opportunity with increments of free speech.

Leftist objections to the theory of primary goods, however, run far deeper than such problems of comparison. Rawls' theory published prior to his book was initially charged by the left with not being neutral, since the primary goods might prove more valuable to some kinds of lives than others.[25] Rawls anticipated this objection in *A Theory of Justice* and made a bad reply to it: it is rational for original position choosers to assume they prefer as much as possible of each primary good, he said, because in actual societies no one will suffer from an excess of any primary good. But this is surely false; while an ascetic can turn down extra wealth, he cannot turn down, and yet would suffer from, the general level of wealth or kinds of consumption patterns of his society. In an article published after *A Theory of Justice*, Rawls partially abandons the Archimedean perspective: the original position is not intended to be neutral, he says, but rather to incorporate the features of a society well-ordered by principles of justice, including giving different conceptions of the good equal opportunities to flourish.[26] Leftists should not attack him for this admission that the theory is not intended to be neutral; they themselves do not want to claim that all kinds of lives are of equal worth.[27]

Instead, the left should challenge Rawls' claim that societies ordered by his principles of justice do give different lives fair opportunities to flourish, and they should take a close look at the kinds of lives such societies might encourage.[28] Certainly, a society is not unfair merely because it makes some kinds of lives easy and actively discourages others—for example, lives predicated on injustice. But Rawls asserts that "If a conception of the good is unable to endure and gain adherents under institutions of equal freedom and mutual toleration, one must question whether it is a viable conception of the good, and whether its passing is to be regretted."[29] I have already touched on the important difference between liberty and what one can effectively do with it. If certain conceptions of the good are associated with being in a particular economic position, as a Marxist might claim they are for the working class, and if individuals in those positions are not effectively free to alter their economic positions, one might well ask whether these conceptions of the good actually have a fair opportunity to flourish. Similarly, one might ask whether conceptions of the good are treated fairly if they flourish with difficulty in societies in which most individuals pursue other conceptions. For example, would the lives of ascetics or individual craftsmen be treated fairly in a society in which there was extensive demand for cheaply produced material goods? I discuss below whether those whose conception of the good includes cooperative activity are treated unfairly in some Rawlsian societies.

If the flourishing of some kinds of lives within a society affects the fortunes of other kinds of lives, it is especially important which kinds of lives Rawlsian societies might encourage. Some have claimed that the theory of primary goods commits original position choosers to societies which encourage narrowly self-interested lives.[30] Rawls replies—correctly, I think—that the primary goods are not peculiarly valuable to acquisitive lives; if wealth is "(Legal) command over exchangeable means for satisfying human needs and interests,"[31] it will be valued by both a Marxist and Mill.[32] However, the left might well urge that Rawls' sins are those of omission; why are meaningful work, community and other sorts of altruistic activity not primary goods? Rawls' reply might be that if societies guarantee his list of primary goods, according to his principles of justice, these others will follow. But some of Rawls' primary goods might also follow from these other suggested candidates; for example, if people are guaranteed meaningful work and participation in community life, it is arguable they would possess appropriate amounts of the primary good of power. Furthermore, whether Rawls is correct in asserting the communitarian goods would follow depends on the more particular details of economic life and community in Rawlsian well-ordered societies.

PRIVATE PROPERTY AND ECONOMIC LIFE

Rawls' two principles of justice are highly abstract; they do not entail which social institutions are to be preferred for particular societies. On Rawls' view, the problem of institutional design for a particular society is to be solved from the original position in a series of four stages beginning with the choice of the principles of justice and subsequently limited by the principles. The first stage is the choice of the principles of justice. In the second stage, a constitution is chosen consistent with the principles of justice; Rawls believes the constitution must guarantee civil rights and set out fundamental political procedures. At the third, or legislative stage, individuals choose legislation consistent with the constitution and the principles of justice. And finally, in full knowledge of the facts, they make judgments applying the law to particular cases. In making these choices, individuals must know the "full range of general economic and social facts" (199) of their society.

Rawls places the choice of property rules at the legislative stage and thereby makes two highly controversial assumptions: that the choice of property rules is to be made in full knowledge of the features of one's society; and that property rules are only to be constrained by principles of justice and the constitution and bill of rights, but will themselves constrain only particular decisions about the application of laws. These initial commitments, it may be argued, reveal Rawls' underestimation of the impact of property relations on the ability of individuals to lead meaningful lives, and make possible his assertion that either private property or socialist institutions are permissible for advanced industrial societies.

At the legislative stage, Rawls provides his choosers with full knowledge except the particulars of their own situations, desires, and conceptions of the good. Those adopting rules governing property know the "full range of general economic and social facts" (199) of their society—whether it is well or poorly endowed with natural resources, what its level of economic development is, what kinds of things it produces and how production is arranged, and what kinds of material satisfactions its people enjoy. They will thus be able to tailor property institutions to specific features of their society but not to their individual preferences or advantages. So far, so good. But here the methodological questions about Rawlsian social science raised above reappear with immediate practical import. For permitting existing features of a society to shape the choice of its property institution raises the possibility that the chosen institutions will reflect biases already present in that society. For example, should it affect a society's choice of property institutions that its citizens generally prefer to work on things alone and take pride in individual rather than joint achievements, or vice versa? That members of the society enjoy competition or not? That, other things being equal, they would rather enjoy leisure time than work? That members of the society like material possessions and pleasures, that they love opera, or baseball? That the society already has market institutions in force and that people have expectations based upon them? Rawls understands that there is a problem about existing preferences; if individuals choosing property institutions know what members of their society desire, what is to prevent them from choosing economic institutions which merely pander to existing preferences, rather than having the perspective to recognize that economic institutions both shape and satisfy desires?

Perspective could be provided by giving the choosers a conception of the good in terms of which to criticize existing desires. However, Rawls is committed to the view that there are a number of different conceptions of the good consistent with his principles of justice, a view which is incompatible with perfectionist insistence upon one idea of the good. Rawls attempts to solve the problem by appealing to the primary goods and the previously chosen principles of justice (259). Desires to perform acts which are unjust themselves (e.g., the desire for material wealth of level w, where w is inconsistent with maximizing the situation of the least well off representative individual) are not to count in the deliberations of choosers. However, while this solution sounds quite forceful, it really is not; since the rules governing property institutions have not yet been chosen, we cannot say in advance which desires will be inconsistent with just property arrangements. Rawlsian theory will thus criticize desires only in the emphasis it gives to the primary goods and to discounting desires inconsistent with the general statement of the two principles of justice and the securing of first principle liberties. Prevailing attitudes and expectations towards work, competition, ownership and the market would presumably be known and taken into account by those choosing a system of property arrangements for their society.[33]

These difficulties in constructing the choice of economic institutions are not incidental. For *A Theory of Justice* was written under the assumption that "ideal" theory—the theory which is to govern "a well-ordered society under favorable circumstances" (245)—and "partial compliance" theory—"the principles for governing adjustments to natural and historical contingencies and the principles for meeting injustice" (246)—can be separated. What is more, Rawls devotes nearly all of the book to ideal theory. The standard criticisms of Rawls' concentration on ideal theory are that it represents a mistake in emphasis, that it splits theory and practice, and that as a result the view of ideal theory as representing "an ideal to guide the course of social reform" (245) is misconceived. But this discussion of the choice of property institutions suggests a different critique. As Rawls proceeds through the four-stage sequence to the point of choosing institutions for basic economic arrangements, the distinction between ideal and partial compliance theory becomes blurred. The choosers are allowed to know about features of their society which some thinkers would argue are themselves the product of injustices; and so it is not clear whether the economic arrangements they choose are ideal arrangements for their society or responses to existing injustices.

One way to try to argue that property arrangements are not merely responses to existing injustices would be to emphasize that their adoption is subject to constraints other than the ignorance assumption. By placing property at the legislative stage, Rawls assumes it is to be constrained by the two principles of justice, by whatever devices society has chosen to secure the greatest equal liberties for all and equal opportunity, and by the device chosen to make its collective decisions. If resources are needed to enforce liberties or run the political process, these needs take priority. Thus we may tax people to buy voting machines. The impact of the priority of the first principle, however, must not be overemphasized since Rawls distinguishes between liberty and the worth of liberty. The first principle guarantees to each individual a complete system of liberties of equal citizenship, but not the same "capacity to advance their ends within the framework the system defines" (204). It secures the right to publish what one wishes, but not the ability to buy a printing press. This is not to say that a society which meets the requirements of Rawlsian justice will do little to ensure the worth of their liberties to everyone; it is to say that Rawls does not regard the first principle as ensuring the equal worth of liberties, but rather thinks that it must fall to the second principle to secure liberty's worth to the extent that it can be secured. Resource allocations and property arrangements need not make us all equally capable of pursuing our ends; but any inequalities must work to the advantage of the least well off representative among us. If economic inequalities are arranged in this way, Rawls would say, liberty's worth is secured to the extent it can be. But is it really secured to a meaningful extent? This is an example of the sort of problem about the economic arrangements of advanced industrial societies which leads Marxists to argue that the constraints Rawls places on property are insufficient.

Rawls thinks that the legislative stage will not result in the choice of principles unique to any society; he thinks it will single out a set of permissible kinds of economic arrangements for various societies. In the case of an industrial society, Rawls says little about why some kinds of arrangements fall within the permissible range and others outside it. He discusses only why he thinks that private property and socialism fall within the range, and (briefly) why command economies—i.e., economies which are administratively planned—appear to fall outside it. As Rawls writes, the difference between a private property and a socialist economy is that the former uses the market for decisions about both the allocation of productive resources and consumption; the latter makes allocative decisions collectively but may use the market for decisions about consumption.[34] Either set of arrangements both can and would be subject to the constraints of first principle liberties, constitutional procedures and opportunity; either would need a "transfer branch" to guarantee the social minimum which works to the advantage of the least well off representative individual and a "distribution branch" which raises the money to support just institutions and which insures that concentrations of wealth threatening to first principle liberties or equalities of opportunity will not arise. Both can provide incentives to bring forth their members' best efforts, and both have the relative stability necessary to create and honor legitimate expectations. Both are compatible, Rawls says, with any number of different policies regarding conservation and the production of public goods.

However, from the discussion it is clear that Rawls thinks that private property institutions have some advantages over socialist ones. From the benefits of the market which he cites, we can tell a little more about why Rawls believes some kinds of economic institutions fall within the permissible range and others do not. Market institutions provide efficiency in the Pareto sense of full utilization of goods (i.e., there are no "valued" goods which could simply benefit some without a transfer of them disadvantaging others; any transfer of resources would have to "take away" from someone). They are relatively decentralized, so provide the flexibility needed for the production of a wide range of goods. This is important, since individuals in the society are assumed to have different conceptions of the good. They allow free choice in occupations, so individuals—given the background of equal opportunity—have maximum possible control of the kinds of lives they will lead. It is for this reason that Rawls rejects command economies as outside the permissible range and has doubts about the consequences for liberty of socialist allocative decisions. In short, economic arrangements which give wide scope for free choice of what individuals can have or do, are preferable.

But Rawls' treatment of the market overlooks a number of important problems—problems which, it might be urged, lend a hollow ring to the free choices the market is thought to be so good at protecting. I shall consider four: Rawls' understanding of equal opportunity; his notion of "free" choice of occupation; his view of wages as based upon reward according to "contribution"; and the short shrift he gives to the difficulties of producing what economists call public goods (i.e., goods such as national defense which cannot be provided to some citizens without being provided to others and which must be provided to a wide range of people).

Rawls' notion of equality of opportunity is not strictly speaking a problem of the market. But it exacerbates some other problems which are. According to Rawls, fair equality of opportunity exists when individuals similarly endowed and motivated in all sectors of society have similar chances in life (301). The family one has—which seems just as arbitrary from a moral point of view as the natural endowments one has—is highly likely to shape one's aspirations and motivations; Rawls is perfectly prepared to countenance such differences as consistent with fair equality of opportunity although it means that individuals will have different chances in life (201 ff.; 511 ff.). But he offers no argument for this willingness, beyond the claim that in a society which makes inequalities work to the advantage of the least fortunate such differences will not be a source of pain or resentment. In particular, although Rawls assumes that the family is a basic social institution, he says not a word in its defense. The plausibility of his argument for fair equality of opportunity thus hinges on whether differences in life chances attributable to family backgrounds would be sources of resentment; I suggest below that given some features of a market society they might well be.

Private property economies use the market to make decisions about both production and consumption. Decisions about what kinds of goods to manufacture are a function of consumer demand and the cost of supply. Thus consumer demands will crucially affect the availability of jobs in society—if individuals do not want a particular good or service, it will not be produced. (There are two exceptions to this: the provision of public services and of public goods. But their impact will be slight—more about this later.) This is the market background for "free choice of occupation" which Rawls thinks so important. Certainly, socially planned production will affect employment availability; but so do the various decisions of individual consumers.

Wages, too, will be determined by the market. This, Rawls says, is the appropriate way to understand the traditional canon of distributive justice, "to each according to his contribution":

> A firm's demand for workers is determined by the marginal productivity of labor, that is, by the net value of the contribution of a unit of labor measured by the sale price of the commodities that it produces. The worth of this contribution to the firm rests eventually on market conditions, on what households are willing to pay for various goods. Experience and training, natural ability and special know-how tend to earn a premium. Firms are willing to pay more to those with these characteristics because their productivity is greater. This fact explains and gives weight to the precept to each according to his contribution...(305–6)

In a market society, then, both what one can do and how much one can earn at it will be a function of consumer preference. Now, for Rawls the primary good of self-respect consists in having a plan for one's life and having the confidence that one is capable of carrying it out, and knowing that others have the same confidence in one's ability to carry out one's life-plan. When Rawls considers the problems of self-respect in market society, his concern is about individuals on the lower end of wage differentials. He claims that such individuals pose no problem because in a reasonably just society they will know that they are being made as well off as they can be by whatever inequalities exist. However, what the worst off are guaranteed is the best possible economic situation. No attention is paid to the plight of those who have difficulty doing what they want to do because of demographic shifts (e.g., unemployed teachers), technological advances (e.g., family farmers) or mere lack of demand (e.g., the perennial starving artist). Nor is attention devoted to the situation of those who can only find work which is dangerous or debilitating (e.g., miners). Socialist societies must also encounter difficulties such as these. But in making decisions about production collectively, such societies at least provide institutional recognition of the moral choices involved. In contrast, capitalist societies let the solution to such problems emerge from a series of expressions of individual preference, and may never raise the moral issues explicitly at all.

Constructing arrangements for the provision of public goods (i.e. goods which must be provided for a wide range of individuals, and which cannot be provided for some without also being provided for others) might be one way of incorporating collective normative judgments into market society. Rawls suggests that at the legislative stage individuals would establish an "exchange branch" for the provision of public goods; whenever there is a way of financing such goods by distributing the extra taxes among different kinds of taxpayers that will gain unanimous approval, then the exchange branch will make arrangements for their production (282). However, to impose this requirement of unanimous approval is to place a strong burden upon the production of public goods, especially rather expensive ones. For one thing, it too makes the provision of public goods ultimately a matter of existing individual preference—here, whether individuals would prefer being taxed for the good, to not having the good. What is more, the problems about choice of occupation and reward discussed above do not simply involve goods which are "public" in the economist's sense. Depending on what preferences exist, many non-public goods might go unprovided as well.

Thus one of the problems of private property institutions which Rawls does not consider is that handling allocation through the market lets the issue of providing meaningful work fall prey to private consumption decisions. There are of course many other problems raised by the left about Rawls' treatment of economic life. One is that Rawls fails to understand the possible political consequences of modes of production. For example, it is argued that private ownership of the means of production and exchange will undermine first principle liberties and fair equality of opportunity. Rawls' priorities are backwards; correct property relations ought to constrain the choice of a constitution and basic liberties, rather than vice versa. Rawls' reply is to argue that if the second principle is satisfied, serious threats to liberty and opportunity will not materialize. But as we have seen, Rawls' views about the worth of liberty and the nature of fair equality of opportunity are relatively weak, one may argue that what the maximin principle secures is a pale mockery of genuine liberty and opportunity. Robert Paul Wolff cites another political consequence of economic organization Rawls does not appear to understand: Rawls' discussion of redistribution cites no specific transfer institutions, and except in its in its mention of incentives is divorced from consideration of how the structure of production might influence possibilities for redistribution and the force of the maximin principle.[35] It is thus arguably a mistake to separate production and distribution as Rawls does, and attempt to offer a theoretical treatment of distribution on its own.[36]

Other problems raised by the left about Rawls' treatment of economic life center around his failure to analyze production itself. Rawls is faulted for not thinking that capitalist methods of production will yield class structure and class conflict.[37] In fact, except for his willingness to permit private ownership of the means of production and exchange, Rawls says almost nothing about the organization and control of the productive process. His argument for leaving the issues here open might be that how work is organized is not as crucial as whether the maximin principle is satisfied. The worst off will not lose self-respect if they know that society guarantees them the best package of primary goods. This reply can be criticized for offering a redistributive carrot to those in conditions of production which undermine self-respect; wages cannot compensate for shared control of the productive process. The charge here is that without an adequate treatment of production, Rawls cannot show that his societies provide adequate support for self-respect. In the discussion of community to follow, I consider whether Rawlsian societies have other methods for ensuring self-respect.

COMMUNITY

For Rawls, the good of community is achieved in a society which is governed by the principles of justice, and in which its members have self-respect and settled dispositions to uphold just institutions. Rawls' view of the good community can be criticized both in terms of Rawls' own goals and in terms of assumptions Rawls does not share. Some charge that there are social institutions—such as private property—which are compatible with Rawls' principles of justice but which will not generate the citizen willingness to accept those just institutions which Rawls believes are necessary for stability. Stability, for Rawls, requires both that individuals not ride free on the efforts of others and that they not cheat from fear that others will be free riders on goods produced by their efforts. Since Rawls thinks stability is a value, consistency with unstable societies would be a major flaw of his principles. Others charge that Rawls' notion of community is itself inadequate and so whatever stability his principles of justice have is hollow.

"The sense of justice" is Rawls' term for a person's collection of settled dispositions to uphold, institute and reform just institutions. Rawls holds that the sense of justice arises in three stages. The first stage is the morality of authority: through love and trust, children acquire dispositions to obey directives of parents or other significant caretakers. Next, individuals acquire dispositions to behave in accord with the morality of association. The content of the morality of association is given by the individual's role in various groups—the family, the workplace, even the nation. Just schemes of social cooperation are composed of a variety of associations, each with its own aims: the ideals and consequent virtues of particular roles within the association are defined by the association's aims. According to Rawls, in order to develop the morality of association, an individual must understand the aims of associations and their places in the scheme of social cooperation; must form attachments to others participating in associations, largely by extension from the more particular attachments of the morality of authority; and must believe that since the scheme of social cooperation is just its associations are beneficial to each member:

> "Since the arrangements of an association are recognized to be just..., thereby insuring that all of its members benefit and know that they benefit from its activities, the conduct of others in doing their part is taken to be to the advantage of each." (471)

Attachments to others dispose the members not to be free riders; the belief that everyone benefits instills confidence that others will not cheat.

Finally, individuals acquire the morality of principles. They understand the principles of justice and are able to apply them to new situations; and they are disposed to do so. On Rawls' view, knowledge of what the principles of justice require in a particular society is gotten by working within the morality of association. The appropriate motivation is supplied by the affiliations of the morality of association and by the realization that just institutions themselves benefit everyone.

The sense of justice is thus reinforced by both attitudes of affection and views about the connection between justice and the individual's good. For the development of morality at all three stages, human caring is crucial; Rawls goes so far as to say that lack of these moralities demonstrates the absence of important aspects of our humanity. On Rawls' view, the ties of affection must be reciprocal and known to be reciprocal, else they are likely to atrophy (494–5). But these natural attitudes are not sufficient to cement the bonds of justice; people must also believe that associations of just cooperative schemes benefit their members and that the principles of justice are themselves to the advantage of each individual. Otherwise, they will lack the confidence that others will comply and they themselves may be tempted to free ride—in spite of ties of affection. Reciprocal caring and beliefs in the good of justice interact to produce the sense of justice. If his principles of justice fail on either count, Rawls will need to find a different explanation for the development of the sense of justice.

And, it is charged, they do fail. I shall focus on objections to Rawls' view that in a society publicly ordered by his principles of justice, social arrangements will be thought to work to everyone's benefit. It is Rawls' view that strong affiliative ties will not flourish in an unjust society. In order to present and evaluate the charges, it is important to clear about how Rawls thinks the principles of justice do benefit each individual. His claim is not the usual answer to Thrasymachus: that the principles of justice maximize individuals' abilities to satisfy antecedently given ends, and so would be adopted by the rationally prudent individual (496–7). (Nor, I take it, would the left chastise Rawls for failing to refute the egoist.) Instead, Rawls' claim is that the sense of justice is "congruent" (501) with the good of each individual—that it is consistent with a rational plan of life for each individual. Actually, the bulk of Rawls' argument is directed to an even weaker claim: that the sense of justice is consistent with each individual's possession of enough of the primary goods to pursue a rational life plan. It is this that the left denies: Rawls' principles of justice, they charge, are consistent with social institutions which do not guarantee each individual self-respect, for Rawls the most important primary good of all.

Consider the situation of the worst-off representative individual. How will she/he feel about those who are better off; Rawls admits that she/he may feel regret that she/he is less well off; but if the society is admittedly just, he/she cannot feel resentful. His concern is whether she/he will feel too much general envy (i.e., hostility about the greater extent of goods (not particular items) of others even though those goods do not detract from his/her own advantage) to maintain self-respect. Rawls' precision here must be appreciated. While he thinks that the irrationality and contingency of envy suffices to explain why it must be ruled out of the moral point of view, he is explicit that eliminating envy from the moral point of view does not settle the question of whether individuals living under the principles of justice will in fact be envious. He does tend to discount the moral importance of sheer rancor, and to assume that little of it will exist in a reasonably just society. What concerns him is reasonable envy—envy which occurs when "a person's lesser position as measured by the index of objective primary goods may be so great as to wound his self-respect" (534). I think the left must follow Rawls to this extent, or risk assigning moral importance to Hobbesian characteristics.

The left's objections begin with Rawls' arguments to show that individuals in societies consistent with his principles of justice will not feel extensive amounts of reasonable envy. Rawls claims, first, that the priority of first principle liberties and fair equality of opportunity support self-esteem because they affirm the equal worth of everyone as citizens.[38] In society at large, individuals are most likely to encounter each other in the political forum, and so these priorities also help ensure that individuals are not frequently reminded of differential status. The left responds here by citing the weakness of first principle and opportunity guarantees, as discussed above. Another charge frequently made by leftist political scientists[39] is that first principle guarantees comprise too narrow a notion of the political process; equal rights do not guarantee equal participation in decision making. Others urge that in the face of the economic inequalities permitted by the difference principle, equal citizenship cannot suffice for self-respect.[40]

Rawls' next claim is that given that the maximin principle requires arranging inequalities for the benefit of the least well off representative, she/he will not lose self-respect. Self-respect consists in believing one's life-plan (roughly, one's set of long-range goals) is of value, that others believe one's plan is of value, that one is capable of carrying out one's life-plan, and that others believe one capable of carrying out one's life-plan. Rawls thinks that the maximin principle fosters self-respect, since arranging inequalities to the benefit of the least well off representative individual expresses concern for how she/he is faring, and structures social arrangements so as to give him/her the best opportunities for carrying out his/her life-plan. She/he thus has reason to believe others value his/her life-plan and think him/her capable of carrying it out. What is more, she/he knows that the principled basis for others' greater fortune is not moral worth or excellence, but the determination to arrange social institutions to his/her benefit. Nonetheless, it is objected, this is cold comfort to someone who has limited resources, who performs low prestige or uninteresting occupations, and who knows that particular individuals end up in particular places in part because of their natural talents and motivation and the families within which they were raised.[41]

According to Rawls, associations are "social unions" when individuals in them share ultimate ends, value the ends for their own sakes and engage in cooperative activities in pursuit of those ends. Rawls claims that within just societies, families, workplaces, and even political jurisdictions will be social unions. In support, he cites most frequently the shared final aim of justice itself. But here he begs the question, for whether individuals will share the final aim of justice itself depends upon whether they have self-respect in the just society. More interestingly, Rawls also appeals to what he calls the "Aristotelian principle" which stipulates that individuals prefer activities which develop their talents more fully and which enable them to exercise more complicated skills. But each individual can only develop some of his/her interests and talents; when she/he is exercising chosen skills, Rawls suggests, the achievements of others represent roads not taken for him/herself. (cf. 523) Even though others do better, the worst off individual knows that what she/he does is a contribution to a scheme of excellence. But in order to regard others' achievements as vicarious self-development, an individual must do more than observe that they benefit him/her. She/he must regard the aims and successes of others as his/her own. But Rawls provides no support for the claim that she/he will do so, or even for the claim that she/he will appreciate the value of others' aims in a society in which consumer preference shapes production. Instead, he is suspicious of principles of justice which depend too heavily on altruism, and he certainly does not want to treat the desires of each as part of one great individual system of desires. Thus he does not explain why in the just society individuals regard others' good fortune as extensions of their own, rather than as cause for jealousy.

Rawls' final attempt is to claim that members of social unions will share more particular aims and will develop bonds that will keep them from encountering the better fortune of others to a disturbing extent. But he provides no argument for thinking the closeness of social unions would not found resentment. Indeed, if as a Marxist would claim, Rawls' principles of justice are compatible with a class society, social unions might be the basis of class consciousness rather than mutual appreciation. Rawls once again may be mistaken about what societies governed by his principles will actually be like.

Other leftist critics argue that if Rawls believes societies ordered by his principles are genuine communities, he is mistaken about what genuine community means. Andrew Levine, for example, argues that even in a society made up of social unions, individuals are treated as means to the satisfaction of others' desires, since different social unions find their place in the social scheme depending upon how the activities practiced within them contribute to satisfying the desires of other individuals or groups in society. Had Rawls really been a Kantian, and divorced reason from satisfaction of desire as well as from the contingencies of particular circumstances, Levine asserts, he would have recognized the inadequacy of the bonds of social unions.[42] Now, to require that genuine communities not organize task differentiation on the basis of satisfaction of desires may seem excessively Kantian. But it is not excessively Kantian to be concerned about the extent to which uncriticized preferences may influence the structure of social union—as I argued above they could in market society.

Furthermore, Rawls fails to consider other desires which one might argue are critical to what it means for a society to be a community. Lawrence Crocker points to a family of what he calls "solidarity dispositions"; these include desires for situations of cooperation and mutual identification, desires to be part of a common team, and desires to shun distinctions and comparisons or competition.[43] Crocker suggests that desires such as these may only flourish in societies more egalitarian than the maximin principle requires. Rawls admits that gaps in income may foster differences in lifestyle which make friendships across social unions difficult. If such solidarity dispositions are critical to genuine community, Rawlsian societies are to the extent that they lack them, less than communities.

Rawls would, I think, be disturbed by these criticisms of the social nature of a just society. Self-respect is a crucial value. He wants society to provide mutual support for its members. It is not, as MacBride suggests, that he is an Hegelian valuing harmony and seeing it where it is lacking.[44] Rather, Rawls thinks liberal society can generate community. This provides the basis for perhaps the most devastating internal critique of Rawls' work: he claims to have captured a theory of justice which is the liberal theory; but his ultimate aims for society are not liberal at all. He does not find reason the rose in the cross of the present. Instead, he understands the flower that society might be, but produces principles of justice which are compatible with only a paper imitation.

NOTES

1. For example, is the charge that Rawls presupposes the family "leftist"? (For a discussion of Rawls on the family, see Jane English, "Justice Between Generations," *Philosophical Studies*, 31, (1977), 91-104.)
2. Karl Marx, "Alienated Labour," reprinted in *The Marx-Engels Reader*, ed. Robert C. Tucker (New York: Norton, 1972), pp. 56-67.
3. David Gauthier, "The Social Contract as Ideology," *Philosophy and Public Affairs*, 6, (1977), 130-164. This essay is a speculative effort to understand the material bases of the assumptions of contract theory, rare among critics of Rawls.

4. Tucker, *Marx-Engels Reader*, pp. 18-19.
5. For useful discussion of these two interpretations of Rawls, see David Lyons, "Nature and Soundness of the Contract and Coherence Arguments," reprinted in Norman Daniels, ed., *Reading Rawls* (New York: Basic Books, 1974), pp. 141-167; and C.F. Delaney, "Rawls on Method," *Canadian Journal of Philosophy*, Supplementary Volume III, (1977), 153-161. Some reviews of Rawls do not make the distinction clearly; an example is Thomas Nagel, "Rawls on Justice," reprinted in Daniels, *Reading Rawls*, pp. 1-16.
6. Cf. Richard Miller, "Rawls and Marxism," reprinted in Daniels, *Reading Rawls*, pp. 206-229.
7. Cf. Brian Barry, "John Rawls and the Priority of Liberty," *Philosophy and Public Affairs* 2 (1973), 274-290.
8. Lyons, "Nature and Soundness," pp. 143 ff.
9. H.L.A. Hart, "Rawls on Liberty and its Priority," reprinted in Daniels, *Reading Rawls*, pp. 230-252.
10. Norman Daniels, "Equal Liberty and Unequal Worth of Liberty," in Daniels, *Reading Rawls*, pp. 253-282.
11. This point is made by Milton Fisk, "History and Reason in Rawls' Moral Theory," in Daniels, *Reading Rawls*, pp. 53-80; and Robert Paul Wolff, *Understanding Rawls* (Princeton: Princeton University Press, 1977), pp. 119 ff.; among others.
12. Benjamin Barber, "Justifying Justice: Problems of Psychology, Politics and Measurement in Rawls," reprinted in Daniels, *Reading Rawls*, pp. 292-318.
13. I borrow here from Wolff, *Understanding Rawls*, pp. 71 ff.
14. Principle (3) is drawn from Daniels "Equal Liberty"; principle (4) from David Gauthier, "Justice and Natural Endowment: Toward a Critique of Rawls' Ideological Framework," *Social Theory and Practice*, 3, (1974), 3-26.
15. Daniels, "Equal Liberty," p. 264.
16. Gauthier, "Justice and Natural Endowment," pp. 24-26. Also Gauthier, "Rational Cooperation," *Nous*, 8, (1974), 53-65.
17. Miller, "Rawls and Marxism," *passim.*
18. There is another way of reading Miller's argument which does not commit him to the assumption that some societies fitting the weak Marxist description must be consistent with Rawls' principles. Miller interprets Rawls as holding that all of the most fundamental questions of justice, including problems of "partial compliance" theory, are to be solved from the original position; he is surely correct in thinking Rawls does believe that the original position should be used to select principles governing situations of injustice. However, Miller also appears to attribute to Rawls the view that ideal theory is *strategically* relevant to partial compliance theory—i.e., that individuals in unjust societies ought to work to further directly the proper principles of justice. On the basis of this interpretation, Miller may be claiming that the problem in ruling class societies is the unwillingness of major groups within them to work directly towards the realization of

Rawls' principles, rather than sheer instability. But there are hints that Rawls is unsure about whether ideal theory is relevant to more than just the criticism of unjust societies, because it is by comparing a society to the just society that we can understand its shortcomings. (cf. ss. 38 and 39). Unfortunately, it may be viewed as another illustration of his ahistoricity that Rawls says little about partial compliance theory, including about whether ideal theory sets strategic recommendations.

19. This point is made by Richard A. O'Neil, "On Rawls' Justification Procedure," *Philosophy Research Archives*, 2, no. 1099 (1976).
20. Nagel challenges this analogy in "*Rawls on Justice*," p. 1. But note that Rawls thinks that both the judgments of oridinary speakers and the judgments of moral practioners are revisable.
21. Cf. Lyons, "Nature and Soundness," p. 146.
22. *Contra* Gauthier, "Justice and Natural Endowment" and "Rational Cooperation."
23. This last is an *ad hoc* requirement designed to help Rawls in dealing with the problem of future generations; I ignore it.
24. Barber, "Justifying Justice," pp. 302-303.
25. See Nagel, "Rawls on Justice"; Adina Schwartz, "Moral Neutrality and Primary Goods," *Ethics*, 83, (1973); and Michael Teitelman, "The Limits of Individualism," *Journal of Philosophy*, 69, (1972).
26. John Rawls, "Fairness to Goodness," *Philosophical Review*, 84, (1975), 549 ff.
27. Cf. Wolff's refusal to attack the theory of primary goods by citing the life of the ascetic, *Understanding Rawls*, p. 134. What is more, many on the left would want to attack the idea of value neutrality in itself.
28. Mary Gibson, "Rationality," *Philosophy and Public Affairs*, 6, (1977), 193-225, is an extremely valuable discussion of the weakness of Rawls' notion of rationality, although the discussion is flawed by the assumption that Rawls intends his notion of rationality to be completely neutral as between conceptions of the good.
29. Rawls, "Fairness to Goodness," p. 549.
30. Nagel, "Rawls on Justice," p. 9.
31. Rawls, "Fairness to Goodness," p. 540.
32. Rawls, "Fairness to Goodness," p. 546.
33. This is what Nozick's "manna from heaven" critique misses (see *Anarchy, State and Utopia*, (New York: Basic Books, 1974), Ch. 7). While it is true that in the original position Rawlsian choosers do not presuppose anything about the ownership of things and so opting for a society in which all goods are treated as manna from heaven is an open option, it is also true that they are given assumptions about human motivation which appear to ensure that a manna from heaven society would be beyond the pale.
34. Nozick's assertion that a Marxist must forbid capitalist acts between consenting adults is a caricature. Cf. Robert Nozick, *Anarchy, State and Utopia*, Ch. 7.

35. Wolff, *Understanding Rawls*, p. 202.
36. Cf. Wolff, pp. 207-8. Also see Karl Marx, "Introduction" to the *Grundrisse*, tr. Martin Nicolaus (Middlesex, England: Penguin Books, 1973), pp. 81-114.
37. C.B. MacPherson, "Rawls' Models of Man and Society," *Phil. Soc. Sci.*, 3, (1973), 341-347.
38. For a generally clear discussion of Rawls' argument, see Henry Shue, "Liberty and Self Respect," *Ethics*, 85, (1974-75), 195-203. Shue attributes to Rawls the assumption that equal basic liberties and wealth are the two main competitors as bases of self-respect, and does not criticize the assumption. However, while an "equal shares" socialist might agree, a Marxist would argue that meaningful work is another important possibility.
39. See John Schaar, "Reflections on Rawls' Theory of Justice," *Social Theory and Practice*, 3, (1974), 75-100.
40. See Charles Frankel, "Justice, Utilitarianism, and Rights," *Social Theory and Practice*, 3, (1974), 33.
41. See Nagel, "Rawls on Justice," p. 12.
42. Andrew Levine, "Rawls' Kantianism," *Social Theory and Practice*, 3, (1974), 55 ff.
43. Lawrence Crocker, "Equality, Solidarity, and Rawls' Maximin," *Philosophy and Public Affairs*, 6, (1977), 262-66.
44. William L. McBride, "Social Theory *Sub Specie Aeternitatis:* A New Perspective," *Yale Law Journal*, 81, (1972), 1002-3.

Bibliography

Ake, Christopher. "Justice as Equality." *Philosophy and Public Affairs*, 5, (1975), 69-89.

Alexander, S.S. "Social Evolution Through Notional Choice." *The Quarterly Journal of Economics*, 88, (1974), 597-624.

Altham, J.E.J. "Rawls Difference Principle." *Philosophy*, 48, (1973), 75-8.

Andelson, Robert V. "*Vive La Difference?* Rawls' 'Difference Principle' and the Fatal Premise Upon Which It Rests." *The Personalist*, 56, (1975), 207-13.

Arrow, Kenneth J. "Gifts and Exchanges." *Altruism, Morality, and Economic Theory*. Ed. E.S. Phelps. New York: Russell Sage Foundation, 1975, 13-28.

———. *Social Choice and Individual Values*. 2nd. ed. New York: John Wiley & Sons, 1963.

———. "Some Ordinalist-Utilitarian Notes on Rawls' Theory of Justice." *The Journal of Philosophy*, 70, no. 9, (1973), 245-63.

———. " The Utilitarian Approach to the Concept of Equality in Public Expenditures." *The Quarterly Journal of Economics*, 85, (1971), 409-15.

Arthur, John and William Shaw, eds. *Justice and Economic Distribution*. Englewood Cliffs, N.J.: Prentice Hall, 1978.

Atkinson, A.B. "How Progressive Should Income Tax Be?" *Essays on Modern Economics*. Ed. M. Parkin. New York: Longmans, Green and Co. Inc., 1973.

Baier, Kurt. "Individual Moral Development and Social Moral Advance." A symposium with Richard G. Henson and Lawrence Kohlberg. *The Journal of Philosophy*, 70, (1973), 646-8.

———. "Moral Development." *The Monist*, 58, (1974), 601-15.

———. *The Moral Point of View: A Rational Basis for Ethics*. Ithaca: Cornell University Press, 1958.

———. "Rationality and Morality." *Erkenntnis*, 11, (1977), 197-223.

Barber, Benjamin. "Justifying Justice: Problems of Psychology, Politics, and Measurement in Rawls." *The American Political Science Review*, 69, (1975), 663-74.

Barker, Ernest, ed. *Social Contract*. Oxford: Oxford University Press, 1947.

Barnet, Richard J. and Ronald E. Müller. *Global Reach.* New York: Simon and Schuster, 1975.

Barry, Brian. "John Rawls and the Priority of Liberty." *Philosophy and Public Affairs*, 2, (1973), 274-90.

———. *The Liberal Theory of Justice.* Oxford: Clarendon Press, 1973, 59-82.

———. "Liberalism and Want-Satisfaction: A Critique of John Rawls." *Political Theory*, 1, (1973), 134-53.

———. *Political Argument.* London: Routledge and Kegan Paul, 1965.

———. "Rawls on Average and Total Utility: A Comment." *Philosophical Studies*, 31, (1977), 317-25.

———. "On Social Justice." *Justice and Equality.* Ed. H.A. Bedau. Englewood Cliffs, N.J.: Prentice-Hall, Inc., 1971, 103-15.

Bates, Stanley. "The Motivation to be Just." *Ethics*, 85. no. 1, (1974), 1-17.

Baumol, W.J. *Economic Theory and Operations Analysis.* 2nd. ed. Englewood Cliffs, N.J., 1965, ch. 24.

Baumrin, Bernard H. "Autonomy in Rawls and Kant." *Midwest Studies in Philosophy.* Studies in the History of Philosophy, Vol. 1, (1975), 55-7.

———. "Autonomy, Interest, and the Kantian Interpretation." *Midwest Studies in Philosophy*, 2, (1977), 280-82.

Beardsley, Monroe. "Equality and Obedience to Law." *Law and Philosophy.* Ed. Sidney Hook. New York: New York University Press, 1964, 35-42.

Beccaria, Cesare. *On Crimes and Punishment* (1764). Tr. Henry Paolucci. Indianapolis: The Bobbs-Merrill Company, 1963.

Becker, Edward F. "Justice, Utility, and Interpersonal Comparisons." *Theory and Decision*, 6, (1975), 471-84.

Bedau, Hugo Adam. "Founding Righteousness on Reason." *Nation*, Sept. 11, 1972, 180-1.

———. *Justice and Equality.* Englewood Cliffs, N.J.: Prentice Hall, 1971.

———. "Review of Brian Barry's *The Liberal Theory of Justice.*" *The Philosophical Review*, 84, (1975), 598-603.

Bell, Daniel. "On Meritocracy and Equality." *The Public Interest*, no. 29, (Fall, 1972), 26-69.

Benn, Stanley I. "Rights." *Encyclopedia of Philosophy*, 7, 197-99.

Benn, Stanley I. and Richard S. Peters. *Principles of Political Thought.* New York: Free Press, 1965. First published under the title *Social Principles and the Democratic State.* London: George Allen and Unwin, Ltd., 1959.

Bentham, Jeremy. *An Introduction to the Principles of Morals and of Legislation* (1789). New York: Hafner Publishing Co., 1948.

Bentley, D.J. "John Rawls: *A Theory of Justice.*" *The University of Pennsylvania Law Review*, 121, (1972-73), 1070-78.

Berlin, Isaiah. "Equality as an Ideal." *Justice and Social Policy: A Collection of Essays.* Ed Fredrich A. Olafson. Englewood Cliffs, New Jersey: Prentice-Hall, 1961, 128-50.

Bierman, A.K. "Chessing Around." *Philosophical Studies*, 23, (1972), 141-2.

Birnbaum, Pierre, Jack Lively and Geraint Parry, eds. *Democracy, Consensus and Social Contract.* Sage Modern Politics Series, Vol. 2. London and Beverly Hills: Sage Publications, 1978.

Bloom, Allan. "Justice: John Rawls vs. the Tradition of Political Philosophy." *The American Political Science Review*, 69, (1975), 648-62.

Bodenheimer, Suzanne. "Dependency and Imperialism: The Roots of Latin American Undevelopment." *Politics and Society*, 3, (1971), 327-57.

Bosanquet, Bernard. *The Philosophical Theory of the State.* London: The Macmillan Company, Ltd., 1923.

Bowie, Norman. "Some Comments on Rawls' Theory of Justice." *Social Theory and Practice*, 3, no. 1, (1974), 65-74.

———. *Towards a New Theory of Distributive Justice.* Amherst, Mass.: The University of Massachusetts Press, 1971.

Bowie, Norman E. and Robert L. Simon. *The Individual and the Political Order.* Englewood Cliffs, N.J.: Prentice-Hall, 1977.

Brandt, Richard B. *A Theory of the Good and the Right.* Oxford University Press, forthcoming.

———. "Utility and the Obligation to Obey the Law." *Law and Philosophy.* Ed. Sidney Hook. New York: New York University Press, 1964, 43-55.

Braybrooke, David. "Utilitarianism with a Difference: Rawls' Position in Ethics." *Canadian Journal of Philosophy*, 3, no. 2, (1973), 303-31.

Brenton, Crane. *The Anatomy of a Revolution.* New York: Vintage Books, 1965.

Bride, W.L. "The Concept of Justice in Marx, Engels, and Others." *Ethics*, 85, no. 3, (1975), 204-18.

Brierly, J.L. *The Law of Nations.* 6th ed. New York: Oxford University Press, Inc. 1963.

Brock, Dan W. "Contractualism, Utilitarianism, and Social Inequalities." *Social Theory and Practice*, 1, (1971), 33-44.

———. "John Rawls' Theory of Justice." A symposium with Ronald Dworkin and H.L.A. Hart. *The University of Chicago Law Review*, 40, (1973), 486-99.

———. "Recent Work in Utilitarianism." *The American Philosophical Quarterly*, 10, (1973), 241-76.

Brown, D.G. "John Rawls: John Mill." *Dialogue* (Canada), 12, (1973), 477-9.

Browne, D.E. "The Contract Theory of Justice." *Philosophical Papers* (South Africa), 5, (1976), 1-10.

Brownlie, Ian, ed. *Basic Documents in International Law.* 2nd. ed. Oxford: Clarendon Press, 1972.

———. "Categorical Imperatives and Moral Principles." *Philosophical Studies*, 31, (April, 1977), 249-60.

———. "Distributive Justice and Legitimate Expectations." *Philosophical Studies*, 28, (1975), 419-25.

———. "Revisability and Rational Choice." *Canadian Journal of Philosophy*, 5, (1975), 295-408.

Buchanan, Allen and W.C. Buch. "Political Constraints on Contractual Redistribution." *The American Economic Review*, 64, (1974), 153-7.

Buchanan, J.M. and G. Tullock. *The Calculus of Consent: Logical Foundations of Constitutional Democracy.* Ann Arbor, Michigan: The University of Michigan Press, 1962.

Buchanan, J.M. *The Limits of Liberty: Between Anarchy and Leviathan.* Chicago: The University of Chicago Press, 1975.

Buonarroti, Filippo Michele. *Babeuf's Conspiracy for Equality.* New York: A.M. Kelley, 1965.

Burkholder, L. "Rule-Utilitarianism and 'Two Concepts of Rules'." *The Personalist*, 56, (1975), 195-98.

Calabresi, Guido and Philip Bobbitt, *Tragic Choices*, New York: Norton, 1978.

Campbell, Richmond. "Review of Rawls' *A Theory of Justice.*" *Dalhousie Law Journal*, 1, (1973), 210-23.

Campbell, T.D. "Humanity Before Justice." *The British Journal of Political Science*, 4, (1974), 1-16.

Card, Claudia. "Retributive Penal Liability." *Studies in Ethics: The American Philosophical Quarterly Monograph*, 7, (1973), 17-35.

Care, Norman S. "Contractualism and Moral Criticism." *The Review of Metaphysics*, 23, (1969), 85-101.

———. "Review of Brian Barry's *The Liberal Theory of Justice.*" *Mind*, 85, (1976), 126-8.

———. "Runciman on Social Inequality." *The Philosophical Quarterly*, 18, (1968), 151-4.

Carr, Spencer. "Rawls, Contractarianism, and our Moral Intuitions." *The Personalist*, 56, (1975), 83-95.

Caws, Peter. "Changing Our Habits." *The New Republic*, May 13, 1972, 24-7.

Chapman, John W. "Justice as Fairness." *Nomos VI: Justice.* Ed. C.J. Friedrich and John W. Chapman. New York: The Atherton Press, 1963, 147-69.

———. "Natural Rights and Justice in Liberalism." *Political Theory and the Rights of Man.* Ed. D.D. Raphael. Bloomington, Indiana: Indiana University Press, 1967, 27-42.

———. "Rawls' Theory of Justice." *The American Political Science Review*, 69, (1975) 588-93.

Charvet, John. "The Idea of Equality as a Substantive Principle of Society." *Political Studies*, 17, (1969) 1-13.

Chevigny, P.G. "A Theory of Justice." *Civil Liberties*, 298, (1973), 4-5.

Choptiany, Leonard. "A Critique of John Rawls' Principles of Justice." *Ethics*, 83, (1973), 146-50.

Cobb, William J. "Review of *A Theory of Justice.*" *Journal of Public Law*, 22, (1973), 151-68.

Coburn, Robert. "Relativism and the Basis of Morality." *Philosophical Review*, 85, (1976), 87-93.

Cohen, Marshall. "The Social Contract Explained and Defended." *New York Times Book Review*, July 16, 1972.

Coleman, James S. "Beyond Pareto Optimality." *Philosophy, Science, and Method: Essays in Honor of Ernest Nagel.* Ed. Sidney Morgenbesser, Patrick Suppes, and Morton White. New York: St. Martins' Press, 1969, 415-39.

Coleman, S. "Inequality, Sociology and Moral Philosophy." *American Journal of Sociology*, 80, (1974), 739-64.

Collins, James. "Review of *A Theory of Justice.*" *Modern Schoolman*, 50, (1973), 396-7.

Cooper, Richard N. "Economic Interdependence and Foreign Policy in the Seventies." *World Politics*, 24, no. 2, (1972), 159-81.

Cooper, Wesley E. "The Perfectly Just Society." *Philosophy and Phenomenological Research*, 38, (1977), 46-58.

Copp, David. "Justice and the Difference Principle." *The Canadian Journal of Philosophy*, 4, (1974) 229-40.

Craig, Leon H. "Contra Contract: A Brief Against John Rawls' Theory of Justice." *The Canadian Journal of Political Science*, 8, (1975), 63-81.

Cranor, Carl. "Justice, Respect, and Self-Respect." *Philosophy Research Archives*, 3, no. 1120, (1976).

Crick, Bernard. "On Justice." *New Statesman*, May 5, 1972, 601-2.

Crocker, Lawrence. "Equality, Solidarity, and Rawls Maximin." *Philosophy and Public Affairs*, 6, (1977), 262-66.

Crompton, Louis, ed. *The Road to Equality: Ten Unpublished Lectures and Essays by Bernard Shaw.* Boston: Beacon Press, 1971.

Cunningham, R.L. "Justice: Efficiency or Fairness?" *The Personalist*, 52, (1971), 253-81.

Dalgarno, M.T. "Review of Rawls' *A Theory of Justice.*" *Philosophical Books*, 14, (1973), 26-8.

D'Amato, A. "International Law and Rawls Theory of Justice." *Denver Journal of International Law and Policy*, 5, (1975), 525-37.

Daniels, Norman. "Equal Liberty and Unequal Worth of Liberty." *Reading Rawls.* Ed. Norman Daniels. New York: Basic Books, 1975, 253-81.

———. "On Liberty and Inequality in Rawls." *Social Theory and Practice*, 3, (1974), 149-59.

———. *Reading Rawls: Critical Studies of a Theory of Justice.* New York: Basic Books, Inc., 1975.

Danielson, Peter. "Theories, Institutions and the Problem of World-Wide Distributive Justice." *Philosophy of the Social Sciences*, 3, (1973), 331-8.
osophy of the Social Sciences, 3, (1973), 331-8.

Darwall, Stephen. "A Defense of the Kantian Interpretation." *Ethics*, 86, no. 2, (1976), 164-70.

———. "The Inference to the Best Means," *The Canadian Journal of Philosophy*, 6, (1976), 49-58.

———. "Two Kinds of Respect." *Ethics*, 88, (1977), 36-49.

Dasgupta, Partha. "On Some Problems Arising from Professor John Rawls' Conception of Distributive Justice." *Theory and Decision*, 11, (1974), 325-44.

Delaney, C.F. "Rawls on Justice." *The Review of Politics*, 37, (1975), 104-11.

———. "Rawls on Method." *Canadian Journal of Philosophy*, Supp. Vol. III, (1977), 153-61.

DeMarco, Joseph P. "Equality—An American Dilemma." *Worldview*, 19, no. 4, (1976).

———. "A Note on the Priority of Liberty." *Ethics*, 87, no. 3, (1977), 272-75.

———. "Some Problems in Rawls' Theory of Justice," *Philosophy in Context*, 2, (1973), 41-48.

DeMarco, Joseph P. and S.A. Richmond. "Barry's Critique of Rawls' Liberalism." *Man and World*, 8, no. 4, (1975), 454-60.

DeNicola, Daniel R. "Genetics, Justice, and Respect for Human Life." *Zygon*, 11, (1976), 115-37.

Dias, R.W.M. "Review of Rawls' *A Theory of Justice.*" *Cambridge Law Review*, 30, (1972), 353-5.

Dryer, D.P. "Review of Rawls' *A Theory of Justice.*" *The University of Toronto Law Journal*, 5, (1972), 249-51.

Dworkin, Gerald, "Non-Neutral Principles." *The Journal of Philosophy*, 71, (1974), 491-506.

Dworkin, Ronald. "The Original Position." *The University of Chicago Law Review*, 40, (1973), 500-33.

———. *Taking Rights Seriously*. London: Gerald Duckworth and Co., Ltd., 1977.

Emmet, Dorothy and Alisdair Morrison. "Justice." *The Aristotelian Society Supplementary Volume*, 43, (1969), 109-40.

English, Jane. "Justice Between Generations." *Philosophical Studies*, 31, (1977), 91-104.

Eshete, Andreas. "Contractarianism and the Scope of Justice." *Ethics*, 85, (1974), 38-49.

Evans, Peter B. "National Autonomy and Economic Development." *Transnational Relations and World Politics.* Ed. Robert O. Keohane and Joseph S. Nye. Cambridge, Mass.: Harvard University Press, 1972.

Ewing, A.C. *The Morality of Punishment.* London: Kegan Paul, Ltd., 1929.

Falk, W.D. "Hume on Is and Ought." *Canadian Journal of Philosophy*, 6, (1976), 359-78.

———. "Hume on Practical Reason." *Philosophical Studies*, 27, (1975), 1-18.

Farrell, Daniel M. "Illegal Actions, Universal Maxims, and the Duty to Obey the Law: the Case for Civil Authority in the *Crito*" *Political Theory*, 6 (1978).

———. "Paying the Penalty: Justifiable Civil Disobedience and the Problem of Punishment." *Philosophy and Public Affairs*, 6, (1977), 166-84.

Feinberg, Joel. *Doing and Deserving.* Princeton: Princeton University Press, 1972.

———. "Duty and Obligation in the Non-Ideal World." *The Journal of Philosophy*, 70, (1973), 263-75.

———. "Justice, Fairness, and Rationality." *Yale Law Journal*, 81, (1972), 1004-31.

———. "The Nature and Value of Rights." *Journal of Value Inquiry*, 4, (1970), 243-57.

———. "Rawls and Intuitionism." *Reading Rawls.* Ed. Norman Daniels. New York: Basic Books, 1975, 108-23.

———. *Social Philosophy.* Englewood Cliffs, N.J.: Prentice-Hall, Inc., 1973.

Feldman, J. "Some Features of Justice and a Theory of Justice." *California Law Review*, 61, (1973), 1463-78.

Fellner, William. *Probability and Profit.* Homewood, Ill.: R.D. Irwin, Inc., 1965.

Ferguson, C.E. and J.P. Gould. *Microeconomic Theory.* 4th ed. Illinois: Richard D. Irwin, 1975.

Findlay, J.N. *Values and Intentions.* London: George Allen & Unwin, 1961.

Fingarette, Herbert. "Punishment and Suffering." *Proceedings and Addresses of the American Philosophical Association*, 50, no. 6, (1977), 499-525.

Fishkin, James. "Justice and Rationality: Some Objections to the Central Argument in Rawls' Theory." *The American Political Science Review*, 69, (1975), 615-29.

Fisk, Milton. "History and Reason in Rawls' Moral Theory." *Reading Rawls.* Ed. Norman Daniels. New York: Basic Books, 1975, 53-80.

Flathman, Richard E. *Political Obligation.* London: Croom Helm Ltd., 1973.

Flew, Antony. "Rawls' Theory of Justice," in Lewis, H.D. (ed.), *Contemporary British Philosophy.* London: George Allen and Unwin, 1976.

———. "Social Virtue and Blind Justice: On Rawls' Theory of Justice." *Encounter*, 41, (1973), 73-6.

———. "Three Questions About Justice in Hume's *Treatise.*" *The Philosophical Quarterly*, 26, (1976), 1-13.

Foot, Phillippa. "Morality as a System of Hypothetical Imperatives." *Philosophical Review*, 81, (1972), 305-16.

Frank, Andre Gunder. "The Development of Underdevelopment." *Dependence and Underdevelopment.* James D. Cockroft, et al. Garden City, N.Y.: Anchor Books, 1972, 3-18.

Frankel, Charles. "Justice and Rationality." *Philosophy, Science and Method: Essays in Honor of Ernest Nagel.* Ed. Sidney Morgenbesser, Patrick Suppes, and Morton White. New York: St. Martin's Press, 1969, 400-14.

———. "Justice, Utilitarianism, and Rights." *Social Theory and Practice*, 3, no. 1, (1974), 27-46.

———. "The New Egalitarianism and the Old." *Commentary*, Sept. 1973, 54-61.

———. "Review of *A Theory of Justice.*" *Columbia Human Rights Law Review*, 5, (1973), 547-64.

Frankena, William. *Ethics.* Englewood Cliffs, N.J.: Prentice-Hall, 1963.

———. "Some Beliefs about Justice." The Lindley Lecture, the University of Kansas, 1966, 16ff.

Fried, Charles. "Natural Law and the Concept of Justice." *Ethics*, 74, (1964), 237-54.

———. "Review of Rawls' *A Theory of Justice.*" *Harvard Law Review*, 85, (1971-72), 169-7.

Friedman, Wolfgang. "A Theory of Justice: A Lawyer's Critique." *The Columbia Journal of Transnational Law*, 11, (1972), 369-79.

Fuchs, Alan E. "The Concept of Morality in Rawls' Theory." *The Journal of Philosophy*, 72, (1975), 628-9.

Fullinwider, Robert K. "Hare on Rawls: A Worry About Possible Persons." *Philosophical Studies*, 29, (1976), 199-205.

Gardner, Michael. "Rawls on the Maximin Rule and Distributive Justice." *Philosophical studies*, 27, (1975), 255-70.

Gardner, Patrick. *Theories of History*. Glencoe, Illinois: The Free Press, 1959.

Gastil, Raymond. "Beyond a Theory of Justice." *Ethics*, 85, no. 3, 183-94.

Gauthier, David. "Reason and Maximization." *Canadian Journal of Philosophy*, 13 (1975).

———. "Justice and Natural Endowment: Toward a Critique of Rawls' Ideological Framework." *Social Theory and Practice*, 3, no. 1, (1974), 3-26.

———. "Economic Rationality and Moral Constraints." *Midwest Studies in Philosophy*, 3 (1978).

———. "Rational Cooperation." *Nous*, 8, (1974), 53-65.

———. "The Social Contract as Ideology." *Philosophy and Public Affairs*, 6, (1977), 130-64.

———. "On the Refutation of Utilitarianism." Unpublished paper presented at the Conference on the Limits of Utilitarianism held at Virginia Polytechnic Institute and State University, May 18-21, 1978.

George, Lawrence C. "Review of *A Theory of Justice.*" *The University of California Los Angeles Law Review*, 20, (1972-73), 856-63.

Gibbard, Allan. "Disparate Goods and Rawls' Difference Principle." *Theory and Decision*, forthcoming.

———. "If the Morality of Common Sense is Unconsciously Utilitarian, Does that Give Us Any Reason to be Utilitarians?" Unpublished paper presented at the Conference on the Limits of Utilitarianism held at Virginia Polytechnic Institute and State University, May 18-21, 1978.

Gibson, Mary. "Rationality." *Philosophy and Public Affairs*, 6, (1977), 193-225.

Gilbert, Joseph. "Interests Role Reversal, Universalizability, and the Principle of Mutual Acknowledgment." *Ethics and Social Justice*. Ed. Howard E. Kiefer and Milton K. Munitz. Albany, N.Y.: State University of New York Press, 1968, 164-70.

Glossop, Ronald J. "Is Hume A Classical Utilitarian?" *Hume Studies*, 2, (1976), 1-12.

Goff, Edwin L. "Affirmative Action, John Rawls, and a Partial Compliance Theory of Justice." *Cultural Hermeneatics*, 4 (1976), 43-60.

Goldman, Alan H. "The Entitlement Theory of Distributive Justice." *The Journal of Philosophy*, 73, no. 21, (1976), 823-35.

———. "Justice and Hiring by Competence." *American Philosophical Quarterly*, 14, (1977), 17-28.

———. "The Principle of Equal Opportunity." *The Southern Journal of Philosophy*, 15, no. 4, (1977), 473-85.

———. "Rawls' Original Position and the Difference Principle." *The Journal of Philosophy*, 73, (1976), 845-49.

———. "Rights, Utilities, and Contracts." *The Canadian Journal of Philosophy*, Supp. Vol., (Spring 1977).

Goldman, Alvin I. "On the Measurement of Power." *The Journal of Philosophy*, 73, (1974), 231-52.

———. "Toward a Theory of Social Power." *Philosophical Studies*, 23, (1972), 221-68.

Goodin, Robert E. *The Politics of Rational Man.* London: John Wiley and Sons, 1976.

Goodrun, Craig R. "Rawls and Equalitarianism." *Philosophy and Phenomenological Research*, 37, (1977), 386-93.

Gordon, Scott. "John Rawls' Difference Principle, Utilitarianism, and the Optimum Degree of Inequality." *The Journal of Philosophy*, 70, no. 9, (1973), 275-80.

Gourevitch, Victor. "Rawls on Justice." *The Review of Metaphysics*, 28, (1975), 485-519.

Gow, H.B. "Defining the Just Society." *The University Bookman*, (1973), 41-4.

Green, Ronald M. "Health Care and Justice in Contract Theory Perspective." *Ethics and Health Policy*. Ed. Robert Veatch and Roy Branson. Cambridge, Mass.: Ballinger Publishing Co., 1976.

Grey, Thomas C. "The First Virtue." *Stanford Law Review*, 25, (1973), 286-327.

Grice, Russell. *The Grounds of Moral Judgment.* London: Cambridge University Press, 1967.

Grisez, Germain. "Review of *A Theory of Justice*." *Review of Metaphysics*, 26, (1973), 764-5.

Grover, R.A. "The Ranking Assumption." *Theory and Decision*, 4, (1974), 277-99.

Haksar, Vinit. "Autonomy, Justice, and Contractarianism." *The British Journal of Political Science*, 3, (1973), 487-509.

———. "Coercive Proposals (Rawls and Gandhi)." *Political Theory*, 4, (1976), 65-79.

———. "Rawls and Gandhi on Civil Disobedience." *Inquiry*, 19, (1976), 151-92.

———. "Rawls' Theory of Justice." *Analysis*, 32, (1972), 149-53.

Hall, Everett. "Justice as Fairness: A Modernized Version of the Social Contract." *The Journal of Philosophy*, 54, (1957), 662-70.

Hampshire, Stuart. "A New Philosophy of the Just Society." *The New York Review of Books*, 3, no. 3, Feb. 24, 1972, 34-9.

Hancock, Roger N. *Twentieth Century Ethics.* New York: Columbia University

Press, 1974.

Hanfling, Oswald. "Promises, Games and Institutions." *Proceedings of the Aristotelian Society*, 75, (1974-75), 13-31.

Hare, R.M. *Freedom and Reason.* New York: Oxford University Press, 1969.

———. "Rawls' Theory of Justice." *Reading Rawls.* Ed. Norman Daniels. New York: Basic Books, 1975, 81-101.

Harris, C.E., Jr. "Rawls on Justification in Ethics." *The Southwestern Journal of Philosophy*, 5, (1974), 135-43.

Harsanyi, John C. "Can the Maximin Principle Serve as a Basis for Morality? A Critique of John Rawls' Theory." *The American Political Science Review*, 69, (1975), 594-606.

———. "Cardinal Utility in Welfare Economics and the Theory of Risk Taking." *Journal of Political Economy*, 61, (1953), 434-35.

———. "Cardinal Welfare, Individualistic Ethics, and Interpersonal Comparisons of Utility." *Journal of Political Economy*, 63, (1955), 309-21.

———. *Essays on Ethics, Social Behavior, and Scientific Explanation.* Dordrecht, Holland: D. Reidel, 1976, 37-63.

———. "Nonlinear Social Welfare Functions." *Theory and Decision*, 6, (1975), 311-32.

Hart, D.K. "Social Equity, Justice and the Equitable Administrator." *Public Administration Review*, 34, (1974), 3-11.

Hart, H.L.A. *The Concept of Law.* Oxford: Clarendon Press, 1961.

———. *Punishment and Responsibility.* Oxford: Oxford University Press, 1968.

———. "Rawls on Liberty and its Priority." *Reading Rawls.* Ed. Norman Daniels. New York: Basic Books, 1974, 230-52.

———. "Are There Any Natural Rights?" *Philosophical Review*, 64, (1955), 175-91.

Hay, William Henry. "Under the Blue Dome of the Heavens." *Proceedings of the American Philosophical Association*, 48, (1974-75), 54-67.

Hayek, F.A. *The Mirage of Social Justice*, Vol. 2 of *Law, Legislation and Liberty.* London: Routledge and Kegan Paul, 1976.

Hegel, G.W.F. *Philosophy of Right.* (1821). Tr. T.M. Knox. Oxford: Oxford University Press, 1942.

Held, Virginia. "On Rawls and Self-Interest." *Midwest Studies in Philosophy*, Vol. I: Studies in the History of Philosophy, (1976), 57-60.

Henson, Richard G. "Correlativity and Reversability." *The Journal of Philosophy*, 70, (1973), 648-9.

Hicks, Joe H. "Philosophers' Contracts and the Law." *Ethics*, 85, (1974), 18-37.

Hinton, William. *Fanshen: A Documentary of Revolution in a Chinese Village.* New York: Random House, 1966.

Hobbes, Thomas. *Leviathan.* Ed. Michael Oakeshott. Oxford: Basil Blackwell, 1960.

Hoekema, David A. *Coercion, Rights, and Punishment.* Ph.D. Diss. Princeton University.

Hoerster, Norbert. "Review of *A Theory of Justice.*" *Archi fur Rechts und Sozial Philosophie*, 61, (1975), 458-60.
Press, 1923.

Holborow, Les. "Desert, Equality, and Injustice." *Philosophy*, 50, (1975), 157-68.

Honderich, Ted. *Political Violence.* Ithaca: Cornell University Press, 1976.

———. *Punishment: The Supposed Justifications.* Salem, N.H.: Hutchenson, 1969.

———. "The Use of the Basic Proposition of a Theory of Justice." *Mind*, 84, (1975), 63-78.

Hook, Sidney. *From Hegel to Marx.* New York: The Humanities Press, 1950.

———. "Law, Justice, and Obedience." *Law and Philosophy.* Ed. Sidney Hook. New York: New York University Press, 1964, 56-60.

Hook, Sidney, ed. *Law and Philosophy.* New York: New York University Press, 1964.

Hospers, John. "A Review of Rawls' *A Theory of Justice.*" *The Personalist*, 55, (1974), 71-7.

Hubin, Clayton D. "Justice and Future Generations." *Philosophy and Public Affairs*, 6, (1976), 70-83.

Hymer, Stephen. "The Multinational Corporation and the Law of Uneven Development." *Economics and World Order.* Ed. J.N. Bhagwati. New York: Macmillan, 1972.

Jencks, Christopher et al. *Inequality: A Reassessment of the Effect of Family and Schooling in America.* New York: Basic Books, 1972.

Johnson, Conrad D. "Actual- vs (Rawlsian) Hypothetical - Consent. *Philosophical Studies*, 28, (1975), 41-8.

Johnson, Oliver A. "Autonomy in Kant and Rawls: A Reply to Stephen Darwall's 'A Defense of the Kantian Interpretation'." *Ethics*, 87, (1977), 251-54.

———. "Heteronomy and Autonomy: Rawls and Kant." *Midwest Studies in Philosophy*, 2, (1977), 277-79.

———. "The Kantian Interpretation." *Ethics*, 85, (1974), 58-66.

Johnson, Ronald. "Review of *A Theory of Justice.*" *Philosophy and Rhetoric*, 8, (1975), 133-5.

Jones, Hardy. "Fairness, Meritocracy, and Reverse Discrimination." *Social Theory and Practice*, 4, no. 2, (1977), 211-26.

———. "On the Justifiability of Reverse Discrimination." *Reverse Discrimination.* Ed. Barry R. Gross. Buffalo, N.Y.: Prometheus Books, 1977, 348-57.

Kalin, Jesse. "Grice's Contract Ground and Moral Obligation: The Inadequacy of Contractualism." *Philosophical Studies*, 29, (1976), 115-28.

Kant, Immanuel. "On the Common Saying: This May Be True in Theory but It Does Not Apply in Practice." *Kant's Political Writings*, Trans. H.B. Nisbett, Ed. Hans Reiss, Cambridge: University Press, 1970, 61-92.

———. *The Critique of Practical Reason.* Trans. L.W. Beck. Indianapolis: Bobbs-Merrill Co., Inc., 1956.

———. *Foundations of the Metaphysics of Morals.* Trans. L.W. Beck, Indianapolis: Bobbs-Merrill Co., Inc., 1959.

———. *The Metaphysical Elements of Justice.* Trans. John Ladd. Indianapolis: Bobbs-Merrill Co., Inc., 1965.

Kaplan, Morton A. *Justice, Human Nature and Political Obligation.* New York: The Free Press, 1976.

Katzner, Louis I. "Is the Favoring of Women and Blacks in Employment and Educational Opportunities Justified?" *Philosophy of Law.* Ed. Joel Feinberg and Hyman Gross. Encino, CA: Dickenson Publishing Co., 1975.

———. "Presumptions of Reason and Presumptions of Justice." *The Journal of Philosophy*, 70, no. 4, (1973), 89-100.

Kaufmann, Walter. *Hegel.* Garden City, N.Y.: Doubleday & Co., 1965.

———. *Without Guilt and Justice.* New York: Delta Books, 1973.

Kavka, Gregory. "Rawls on Average and Total Utility." *Philosophical Studies*, 27, (1975), 237-53.

Keat, Russell and David Miller. "Understanding Justice." *Political Theory*, 2, (1974), 3-31.

Keenan, Francis W. "Justice and Sport." *Journal of the Philosophy of Sport*, 11, (1975), 111-23.

Keyt, David. "The Social Contract as an Analytic, Justificatory and Polemic Device." *The Canadian Journal of Philosophy*, 4, (1974), 241-52.

Khatchadourian, H. "Institutions, Practices, and Moral Rules." *Mind*, 86, (1977), 479-96.

Kiefer, Howard E. and Milton K. Munitz. *Ethics and Social Justice.* Albany, New York: State University of New York Press, 1968.

Kleinberger, Aaron F. "The Social Contract Strategy for the Justification of Moral Principles." *Journal of Moral Education*, 5, (1976), 107-26.

Klevorick, Alvin K. "Discussion of Rawls' Maximin Criterion." *The American Economic Review*, 64, (1974), 158-61.

Kohlberg, Lawrence. "The Claim to Moral Adequacy of the Highest Stage of Moral Judgment." *The Journal of Philosophy*, 70, (1973), 630-46.
The Journal of Philosophy, 70, (1973), 630-46.

Konvitz, Milton. "Civil Disobedience and the Duty of Fair Play." *Law and Philosophy.* Ed. Sidney Hook. New York: New York University Press, 1964, 19-28.

Krislou, Samuel. "Justice as Formal Theory." *Polity*, 6, (1974), 574-8.

Ladd, John. "Law and Morality: Internalism versus Externalism." *Law and Philosophy.* Ed. Sidney Hook. New York: New York University Press, 1964, 61-71.

Ladenson, Robert F. "Rawls' Principle of Equal Liberty." *Philosophical Studies*, 28, (1975), 49-54.

Laski, Harold J. *Karl Marx.* New York: League for Industrial Democracy, 1933.

Lessnoff, Michael. "Barry on Rawls' Priority of Liberty." *Political Studies*, 4, (1974), 100-14.

———. "John Rawls' Theory of Justice." *Political Studies*, 19, (1971), 63-80.

Levin, J. "Review of Rawls' *A Theory of Justice.*" *Modern Law Review*, 36, (1973), 667-70.

Levine, Andrew. "Beyond Justice: Rousseau Against Rawls." *Journal of Chinese Philosophy*, 4, (1977), 123-42.

———. "Rawls' Kantianism." *Social Theory and Practice*, 3, (1974), 47-63.

Lewis, C.S. "The Humanitarian Theory of Punishment." *God in the Dock: Essays on Theology and Ethics.* Ed. Walter Hooper. Grand Rapids, Mich.: William B. Eerdmans, 1970, 287-95.

Lewis, David K. *Convention: A Philosophical Study*. Cambridge, Mass.: Harvard University Press, 1969.

Lindsay, A.D. *Karl Marx's Capital.* London, Geoffrey Cumberlige, 1947.

Loenen, J.H.M.M. "The Concept of Freedom in Berlin and Others: An Attempt At Clarification." *The Journal of Value Inquiry*, 10, (1976), 279-85.

Luce, Duncan R. and Howard Raiffa. *Games and Decisions.* New York: John Wiley and Sons, Inc., 1957.

Luegenbehl, Dale. "Some Remarks on the Difference Principle." *The Personalist*, 57, (1976), 292-98.

Lukes, Steven. *Individualism.* London: Basil Blackwell, Ltd., 1973.

———. "Relativism: Cognitive and Moral." *The Aristotelian Society*, 48, (1974), 165-89.

Lyons, David. "On Formal Justice." *Cornell Law Review*, 58, (1973), 833-61.

———. *Forms and Limits of Utilitarianism.* London: Oxford University Press, 1965.

———. "The Nature of the Contract Argument." *The Cornell Law Review*, 59, (1973-74), 1064-76.

———. "Nature and Soundness of the Contract and Coherence Arguments." *Reading Rawls.* Ed. Norman Daniels. New York: Basic Books, 1975, 141-67.

———. "Rawls versus Utilitarianism." *The Journal of Philosophy*, 69, (1972), 535-45.

Mabbott, J.D. *The State and the Citizen.* London: Arrow, Ltd., 1958.

Mabe, Alan R. "Review of *A Theory of Justice.*" *The Journal of Politics*, 35, (1973), 1018-20.

MacCormick, Neil. "Justice According to Rawls." *The Law Quarterly Review*, 89, (1973), 393-417.

Machan, Tibor R. "A Note on Independence." *Philosophical Studies*, 30, (1976), 419-22.

MacIntyre, Alasdair. "Justice: A New Theory and Some Old Questions." *Boston University Law Review*, 52, (1972), 330-4.

Mack, Eric. "Distributionism versus Justice." *Ethics*, 86, no. 2, (1976), 145-53.

Mackenzie, Nollaig. "An Alternative Definition of the Difference Principle." *Dialogue: Canadian Philosophical Review*, 13, (1974), 787-93.

———. "A Note on Rawls' Decision-Theoretic Argument for the Difference Principle." *Theory and Decision*, 8, (1977), 381-5.

Macleod, A.M. "Critical Notice: Rawls' Theory of Justice." *Dialogue: Canadian Philosophical Review*, 13, (1974), 139-59.

MacPherson, C.B. *Democratic Theory: Essays in Retrieval.* London: Oxford University Press, 1973.

———. *The Political Theory of Possessive Individualism.* Oxford: Clarendon Press, 1962.

———. "Rawls' Models of Man and Society." *Philosophy of the Social Sciences*, 3, (1973), 341-47.

Mandelbaum, Maurice. "Review of *A Theory of Justice.*" *History and Theory*, 12, (1973), 240-50.

Mansfield, E. *Microeconomics: Theory and Application.* 2nd ed. New York: W.W. Norton, 1975.

Margolis, Joseph. "Justice as Fairness." *The Humanist*, 33, (1973), 36-7.

Marshall, John. "The Failure of Contract as Justification." *Social Theory and Practice*, 3, (1975), 441-59.

Marshall, T.H. *Citizenship and Social Class.* Cambridge, England: University Press, 1950.

Marx, Karl. *Capital.* New York, International Publishers, 1970.

———. *Communist Manifesto.* New York: Appleton-Century-Crofts, 1955.

———. *Early Writings: Economic and Philosophical.* New York: McGraw-Hill, 1964.

———. *Grundrisse.* Tr. Martin Nicolaus. Middlesex, England: Penguin Books, 1973.

Marx, Karl and Frederick Engels. *Selected Correspondence 1846–1895.* New York: International Publishers, 1942.

Mason, H.E. "On the Kantian Interpretation of Rawls' Theory," *Midwest Studies in Philosophy*, Vol. I: *Studies in the History of Philosophy*, (1976), 47–55.

Masterson, M.P. "On Being Unfair to Rawls, Rousseau and Williams, or John Charvat and the Incoherence of Inequality." *The British Journal of Political Science*, 1 (1971), 209-22.

McBride, William L. "The Concept of Justice in Marx, Engels and Others." *Ethics*, 85, (1975), 204-18.

———. "Social Theory *Sub Specie Aeternitatis:* A New Perspective." *Yale Law Journal*, 81, (1972), 980-1003.

McClennen, Edward. "Comment." *Altruism, Morality, and Economic Theory.* Ed. E.S. Phelps. New York: Russell Sage Foundation, 1975, 133-9.

———. "Review of Brian Barry's *The Liberal Theory of Justice.*" *Social Theory and Practice*, 3, (1974), 117-22.

McCloskey, H.J. "Utilitarian and Retributive Punishment." *Journal of Philosophy*, 64, no. 3, (1967), 91-111.

Mead, Dale C. "Profit Maximization Strategies in Russian Roulette: *Rawls and Utilitarianism.*" *Dialogue* (Phi Sigma Tau), 19, (1977), 52-7.

Melden, A.I., ed. *Human Rights.* Belmont, California: Wadsworth Publishing Co., Inc., 1970.

———. *Rights and Persons.* Oxford: Blackwell, 1977.

Menninger, Karl. *The Crime of Punishment.* New York: Viking Press, 1968.

Merritt, Gilbert. "Justice as Fairness: A Commentary on Rawls' New Theory of Justice." *Vanderbilt Law Review*, 26, (1973), 665–86.

Meyer, Michel. "The Perelman-Rawls Debate on Justice." *Revue Internationale de Philosophie*, 29, no. 113, (1975), 316-31.

Michelman, Frank I. "In Pursuit of Constitutional Welfare Rights: One View of Rawls' Theory of Justice." *The University of Pennsylvania Law Review*, 121, (1972-73), 962–1019.

Miller, David. *Social Justice.* Oxford: Clarendon Press, 1976.

Miller, Richard. "Rawls and Marxism." *Philosophy and Public Affairs*, 3, (1974), 167-91.

———. "Rawls, Risk, and Utilitarianism." *Philosophical Studies*, 28, (1975), 55-61.

Moore, Ronald. "What Hath Rawls Got?" *Journal of Chinese Philosophy*, 4, (1977), 143-60.

Morgenbesser, Sidney, Patrick Suppes, and Morton White, eds. *Philosophy, Science, and Method: Essays in Honor of Ernest Nagel.* New York: St. Martin's Press, 1969.

Morris, Bertram, "Rawls' Egalitarianism." *Philosophical Research and Analysis*, 5, (1975), 2-3.

Morris, Herbert. "Persons and Punishment." *The Monist*, 52, no. 4, (1968), 475-501.

Morse, Edward L. "Transnational Economic Processes." *Transnational Relations and World Politics.* Ed. Robert O. Keohane and Joseph S. Nye. Cambridge, Mass.: Harvard University Press, 1972.

Mortimore, G.W. "An Ideal of Equality." *Mind*, 77, (1968), 222–42.

Mow, Joseph. "Rawls on Mercy: Pardon and Amnesty." *The Journal of West Virginia Philosophical Society*, Spring, (1975), 2–5.

Mueller, Dennis C. "Achieving the Just Polity." *The American Economic Review*, 64, (1974), 147-52.

———. "Intergenerational Justice and the Social Discount Rate." *Theory and Decision*, 5, (1974), 263–73.

Mueller, Dennis C., D. Tollison and T.D. Willit. "The Utilitarian Contract: A Generalization of Rawls' Theory of Justice." *Theory and Decision*, 4, (1974), 345-67.

Murphy, Cornelius. "Distributive Justice, Its Modern Significance." *The American Journal of Jurisprudence*, 17, (1972), 153-65.

Murphy, Jeffrey. *Punishment and Rehabilitation.* Belmont, Calif.: Wadsworth Publishing Co., Inc., 1973.

Murray, John Courtney, Jr. "The Problem of Mr. Rawls' Problem." *Law and Philosophy.* Ed. Sidney Hook. New York: New York University Press, 1964, 29–34.

Musgrave, R.A. "Maximin, Uncertainty, and the Leisure Trade-off." *The Quarterly Journal of Economics*, 88, (1974), 625–32.

Nagel, Ernest. "Fair Play and Civil Disobedience." *Law and Philosophy.* Ed.

Sidney Hook. New York: New York University Press, 1964, 72-6.

Nagel, Thomas. "Comment." *Altruism, Morality, and Economic Theory*. Ed. E.S. Phelps. New York: Russell Sage Foundation, 1975, 63-7.

———. *The Possibility of Altruism*. Princeton: Princeton University Press, 1978.

———. "Rawls on Justice." *The Philosophical Review*, 82, (1973), 220-34.

Narveson, Jan. *Morality and Utility*. Baltimore: Johns Hopkins Press, 1967.

———. "A Puzzle about Economic Justice in Rawls' Theory." *Social Theory and Practice*, 4, (1976), 1-28.

———. "Rawls and Utilitarianism." Unpublished paper presented at the Conference on the Limits of Utilitarianism held at Virginia Polytechnic Institute and State University, May 18-21, 1978.

Nathan, N.M.L. *The Concept of Justice*. London: The Macmillan Co., 1971.

———. "Some Prerequisites for a Political Causistry of Justice." *Inquiry*, 13, (1970), 376-93.

Neal, Patrick. "On the Contradictions in John Rawls' *A Theory of Justice*." *Journal of the West Virginia Philosophical Society*, 12, (1977), 7-9.

Nell, Onora. *Acting on Principle*. New York: Columbia University Press, 1975.

Nelson, William. "Special Rights, General Rights, and Social Justice." *Philosophy and Public Affairs*, 3, (1974), 411-30.

Nielsen, Kai. "The Choice Between Perfectionism and Rawlsian Contractarianism." *Interpretation*, 6, (1977), 132-39.

———. "A Note on Rationality." *The Journal of Critical Analysis*, 4, (1972), 16-19.

———. "On Philosophic Method." *International Philosophical Quarterly*, 16, (1976), 349-68.

———. "Our Considered Judgments." *Ratio*, 19, (1977), 39-46.

———. "Rawls and Classist Amoralism." *Mind*, 86, (1977), 19-30.

Nielsen, Kai and Roger Shiner, eds. *New Essays in Contract Theory. Canadian Journal of Philosophy, Supplementary Volume III*, 1977.

Nisbet, Robert. "The Pursuit of Equality." *The Public Interest*, Fall, (1973), 103-20.

Norton, David L. *Personal Destinies: A Philosophy of Ethical Individualism*. Princeton: Princeton University Press, 1976.

———. "Rawls' Theory of Justice: A 'Perfectionist' Rejoinder." *Ethics*, 85, no. 1, (1974), 50-7.

Nowell-Smith, P.H. "A Theory of Justice?" *Philosophy of the Social Sciences*, 3, (1973), 315-39.

Nozick, Robert. *Anarchy, State, and Utopia*. New York: Basic Books, Inc., 1974.

———. "Distributive Justice." *Philosophy and Public Affairs*, 3, (1973), 45-126.

———. "Moral Complications and Moral Structures." *Natural Law Forum*, 13, (1969), 1-50.

Oberdieck, Hans. "A Theory of Justice." *New York University Law Review*, 47,

(1972), 1012-28.
O'Connor, J. "Wolff, Rawls, and the Principles of Justice." *Philosophical Studies*, 19, (1968), 93-5.
O'Driscoll, L.H. "Abortion, Property Rights, and the Right to Life." *The Personalist*, 58, no. 2, (1977), 99-114.
O'Neil, Richard A. "On Rawls' Justification Procedure." *Philosophy Research Archives*, 2, no. 1099, (1976).
Orr, D. and W. Ramm. "Rawls' Justice and Classical Liberalism: Ethics and Welfare Economics." *Economic Inquiry*, 85, (1974), 50-7.
Parekh, B. "Reflections on Rawls' Theory of Justice." *Political Studies*, 20, (1972), 479-83.
Pastin, Mark. "The Reconstruction of Value." *Canadian Journal of Philosophy*, 5, (1975), 375-93.
Pattanaik, P.K. "Risk, Impersonality, and the Social Welfare Function." *The Journal of Political Economy*, 76, (1968), 1152-69.
Pennock, J. Roland. "The Obligation to Obey the Law and the Ends of the State." *Law and Philosophy*. Ed. Sidney Hook. New York: New York University Press, 1964, 77-85.
Perelman, Chaim. *Justice*. New York: Random House, Inc., 1967.
Pettit, Philip. "Another View of Rawls." *Proceedings of the XVth Worth Congress of Philosophy*, 6, (1973), Varna, Bulgaria, 279-84.
———. "A Theory of Justice?" *Theory and Decision*, 4, (1974), 311-24.
Phelps, E.S., ed. *Economic Justice*. Baltimore: Penguin Books, Inc., 1973.
———. "Taxation of Wage Income for Economic Justice." *The Quarterly Journal of Economics*, 87, (1973), 331-54.
Plott, Charles. "Rawls' Theory of Justice." *Caltech Social Science Working Paper No. 49*, Pasadena, California, Aug. 1974.
Pollock, Lansing. "A Dilemma for Rawls?" *Philosophical Studies*, 22 (1971), 37-43.
Pritchard, Michael S. "Human Dignity and Justice." *Ethics*, 82, (1972), 299-313.
———. "On Taking Emotions Seriously." *Journal for the Theory of Social Behavior*, 6, (1976), 211-32.
———. "Rawls' Moral Psychology." *Southwestern Journal of Philosophy*, 8, (1977), 59-72.
Proudfoot, Wayne. "Rawls on the Individual and the Social." *The Journal of Religious Ethics*, 2, no. 2, (1974), 107-28.
Quinn, Jane Bryant. "Perquisites: A Status Report." *Newsweek*, July 24, 1978.
Quinn, Michael Sean. "Practice Defining Rules." *Ethics*, 86, (1975), 630-47.
Rachels, James. "What People Deserve." *Justice and Economic Distribution*. Ed. John Arthur and William H. Shaw. Englewood Cliffs, N.J.: Prentice Hall, 1978.
Rae, Douglas. "The Limits of Consensual Decision." *The American Political*

Science Review, 69, (1975), 1270–94.

———. "Maximin Justice and an Alternative Principle of General Advantage." *The American Political Science Review*, 69, (1975), 630–47.

Rand, Ayn. "An Untitled Letter." *The Ayn Rand Newsletter*, II, no. 10, 11.

Ransdell, Joseph. "Constitutive Rules and Speech Act Analysis." *The Journal of Philosophy*, 68, (1971), 385–400.

Raphael, D.D. "Conservative and Prosthetic Justice." *Political Studies*, 12, (1964), 149–62.

———. "Critical Notice: Rawls' Theory of Justice." *Mind*, 83, (1974), 118–27.

———. "The Standard of Morals." *Proceedings of the Aristotelian Society*, 75, (1974–75), 1-12.

Rasmussen, Douglas B. "A Critique of Rawls' Theory of Justice." *The Personalist*, 55, (1974), 303-18.

Rawls, John. "The Basic Structure as Subject." *American Philosophical Quarterly*, 14, (1977), 159.

———. "Constitutional Liberty and the Concept of Justice." *Nomos VI: Justice*. Ed. C.J. Friedrich and John W. Chapman. New York: The Atherton Press, 1963, 98–125.

———. "Distributive Justice." *Philosophy, Politics and Society*. 3rd series. Ed. Peter Laslett and W.G. Runciman. London: Basil Blackwell Ltd., 1967, 58–82.

———. "Distributive Justice," in E.S. Phelps, ed., *Economic Justice*. Baltimore: Penguin Books, Inc., 1973.

———. "Distributive Justice: Some Addenda." *Natural Law Forum*, 13, (1968), 51-71.

———. "Fairness to Goodness." *The Philosophical Review*, 84, (1975), 536–54.

———. "The Independence of Moral Theory." Presidential Address to the American Philosophical Association, Eastern Division, 1974. *Proceedings and Addresses of the American Philosophical Association*, 48, (1975), 5-22.

———. "Justice as Fairness." *The Journal of Philosophy*, 54, (1957), 653-62.

———. "Justice as Fairness," *The Philosophical Review*, 67, (1958), 164-94.

———. "Justice as Reciprocity." *Utilitarianism*. Ed. Samuel Gorovitz. New York: Bobbs-Merrill Co. Inc., 1971, 242–68.

———. "The Justification of Civil Disobedience." *Revolution and the Rule of Law*. Ed. Edward Kent. Englewood Cliffs, N.J.: Prentice-Hall Inc., 1971, 30–45.

———. "A Kantian Conception of Equality." *Cambridge Review*, Feb. (1975), 94–99.

———. "Legal Obligation and the Duty of Fair Play." *Law and Philosophy*. Ed. Sidney Hook. New York: New York University Press, 1964, 1-18.

———. "Outline of a Decision Procedure for Ethics." *The Philosophical Review*, 60, (1951), 177-97.

———. "Reply to Alexander and Musgrave." *The Quarterly Journal of Economics*, 88, (1974), 633–55.

———. "Reply to Lyons and Teitelman." *The Journal of Philosophy*, 69, (1972), 556-7.

———. "The Sense of Justice." *The Philosophical Review*, 72, (1963), 281-305.

———. "Some Reasons for the Maximin Criterion." *American Economic Review*, 64, (1974), 141-46.

———. *A Theory of Justice*. Cambridge, Mass.: Harvard University Press, 1971.

———. "Two Concepts of Rules." *The Philosophical Review*, 64, (1955), 3-32.

———. "Utilitarianism." *The Encyclopedia of Philosophy*, 7 and 8. Ed. Paul Edwards. New York: Macmillan, 1967, 206-16.

Regan, Richard J. "Review of *A Theory of Justice*." *Thought*, 47, (1972), 634-5.

Reiman, Jeffrey. "A Reply to Choptiany on Rawls on Justice." *Ethics*, 84, (1974), 262-5.

Reiss, Hans, ed. *Kant's Political Writings*. Chicago: Chicago University Press, 1970.

Rempel, H.D. "Justice as Efficiency." *Ethics*, 79, (1969), 150-5.

Rescher, Nicholas. *Distributive Justice*. New York: Bobbs-Merrill Co., Inc., 1966.

Richards, David A.J. *The Moral Criticism of Law*. Encino, Dickenson: 1977.

———. *A Theory of Reasons for Actions*. London: Oxford University Press, 1971.

Rivello, J. Roberto. "Prison as a Surd Community: A Solution." *Aitia*, 4, (1976), 21-30.

Robins, Michael H. "Promissory Obligations and Rawls' Contractarianism." *Analysis*, 36, (1976), 190-98.

Rosen, Bernard. "Rules and Justified Moral Judgments." *Philosophy and Phenomenological Research*, 30, (1970), 436-43.

Ross, Geoffrey. "Utilities for Distributive Justice." *Theory and Decision*, 4, (1974), 239-58.

Runciman, W.G. *Relative Deprivation and Social Justice*. Berkeley, Calif.: The University of California Press, 1966.

———. "'Social' Equality." *The Philosophical Quarterly*, 17, (1967), 221-30.

Runciman, W.G. and A.K. Sen. "Games, Justice, and the General Will." *Mind*, 74, (1965), 554-62.

Sagel, Paul T. "What Rawls Says, and How Rawls Talks." *The Personalist*, 57, (1976), 93-95.

Samuels, P.L. "An Examination of Rawls' Theory of Justice." Unpublished Ph.D. Dissertation. University of Rochester, 1972.

Sartorius, Rolf. *Individual Conduct and Social Norms: A Utilitarian Account of Social Union and the Rule of the Law*. Encino and Belmont, California: Dickenson, 1975.

Scanlon, T.M. "Freedom of the Will in Political Theory." Unpublished ms.

———. "Nozick on Rights, Liberty, and Property." *Philosophy and Public Affairs*, 6, (1976), 3-25.

———. "Rawls' Theory of Justice." *The University of Pennsylvania Law Review*, 121, (1972-73), 1020-69.

Schaar, John H. "Equality of Opportunity and Beyond." *Nomos IX. Equality.* Ed. J. Roland Pennock and John W. Chapman. New York: Atherton, 1967, 228-49.

———. "Reflections on Rawls' Theory of Justice." *Social Theory and Practice*, 3, no. 1, (1974), 75-100.

———. "Some Ways of Thinking about Equality." *Journal of Politics*, 26, (Nov. 1964), 867-95.

Schaefer, David Lewis. "A Critique of Rawls' Contract Doctrine." *The Review of Metaphysics*, 28, (1974), 89-115.

———. "The 'Sense' and Non-sense of Justice: An Examination of John Rawls' *A Theory of Justice.*" *The Political Science Reviewer*, 3, (1973), 1-41.

Scheltens, D.R. "The Social Contract and the Principle of Law." *International Philosophical Quarterly*, 17, (1977), 317-38.

Schick, Frederick. "A Calculus of Liberalism." Unpublished paper presented at the Conference on the Limits of Utilitarianism held at Virginia Polytechic Institute and State University, May 18-21, 1978.

Schiffer, Walter. *The Legal Community of Mankind.* New York: Columbia University Press, 1954.

Schrag, Francis. "Justice and the Family." *Inquiry*, 19, (1976), 193-208.

Schuler, G.F. "Rawls on Promising." *Proceedings of the New Mexico-West Texas Philosophical Society*, (1974), 10-14.

Schwartz, Adina. "Moral Neutrality and Primary Goods." *Ethics*, 83, (1973), 294-307.

Schwyzer, Hubert. "Rules and Practices." *The Philosophical Review*, 78, (1969), 451-67.

Sen, A.K. *Collective Choice and Social Welfare.* San Francisco: Holden-Day, Inc., 1970.

———. *On Economic Inequality.* Oxford: At the Clarendon Press, 1973.

———. "Rawls versus Bentham: An Axiomatic Examination of the Pure Distribution Problem." *Theory and Decision*, 4, (1974), 301-9.

———. "Welfare Inequalities and Rawlsian Axiomatics." *Theory and Decision*, 7, (1976), 243-62.

Sennett, R. and J. Cobb. *The Hidden Injuries of Class.* New York: Vintage Press, 1973.

Sharp, Gene. *The Politics of Non-violent Action.* Boston: Porter Sargent, 1973.

Sher, George. "An Unsolved Problem About Punishment." *Social Theory and Practice*, 4, (1977), 149-65.

Shue, Henry. "The Current Fashions: Trickle Downs by Arrow and Close-Knits by Rawls." *The Journal of Philosophy*, 71, (1974), 319-27.

———. "Justice, Rationality, and Desire: On the Logical Structure of Justice as Fairness." *The Southern Journal of Philosophy*, 13, (1975), 89-97.

———. "Liberty and Self Respect." *Ethics*, 85, (1974-75), 195-203.

Sidgwick, Henry. *The Elements of Politics.* London, 1891.

Simson, G.J. "Another view of Rawls' Theory of Justice." *Emory Law Journal*, 23, (1974), 473-96.

Singer, Marcus G. "On Rawls on Mill on Liberty and So On." *Journal of Value Inquiry*, 11, (1977), 141-8.

Singer, Peter. *Democracy and Disobedience.* London: Oxford University Press, 1974.

———. "Famine, Affluence and Morality." *Philosophy and Public Affairs*, I, no. 3, (1972), 229-43.

———. "Sidgwick and Reflective Equilibrium." *The Monist*, 58, (1974), 490-517.

Skinner, B.F. *Science and Human Behavior.* New York: Macmillan Publishing Co., 1953.

Slote, Michael. "Desert, Consent, and Justice." *Philosophy and Public Affairs*, 2, no. 4, (1973), 323-47.

Smart, J.J.C. "An Outline of a System of Utilitarian Ethics." *Utilitarianism: For and Against.* Smart and Bernard Williams. Cambridge: Cambridge University Press, 1973.

Smith, James W. "Justice and Democracy." *The Monist*, 55, (1971), 121-33.

Smyth, J.L. "The Prisoner's Dilemma II." *Mind*, 81, (1972), 427-31.

Snare, Frank. "John Rawls and the Methods of Ethics." *Philosophy and Phenomenological Research*, 36, (1975), 100-12.

Sneed, Joseph D. "John Rawls and the Liberal Theory of Society." *Erkenntnis*, 10, (1976), 1-19.

Soble, Alan. "Rawls on Self-Respect." *The Journal of Philosophy*, 72, (1975), 629.

Speigelberg, Herbert. "Good Fortune Obligates: Albert Schweitzer's Second Ethical Principle." *Ethics*, 85, (1975), 227-34.

Sterba, James. "Justice as Desert." *Social Theory and Practice*, 3, no. 1, (1974), 101-16.

———. "Prescriptivism and Fairness." *Philosophical Studies*, 29, (1976), 1411-8.

———. "Retributive Justice." *Political Theory*, 5, (1977), 349-62.

Strassnick, Stephen. "Social Choice and the Derivation of Rawls' Difference Principle." *The Journal of Philosophy*, 73, (1976), 85-99.

Sullivan, Daniel. "Rules, Fairness, and Formal Justice." *Ethics*, 85, (1975), 322-31.

Tapp, June L. and Felice Levine. "Legal Socialization Strategies for an Ethical Legality." *Stanford Law Review*, 27, (1974), 1-72.

Tattershall, Gerald. "A Rawls Bibliography." *Social Theory and Practice*, 3, (1974), 123-7.

Taylor, Paul W. "Justice and Utility." *Canadian Journal of Philosophy*, 1, (1972), 327-50.

———. "Universalizability and Justice." *Ethics and Social Justice.* Ed. Howard E. Kiefer and Milton K. Munitz. Albany, New York: State University of New York Press, 1968, 142-63.

Taylor, Richard. "Justice and the Common Good." *Law and Philosophy.* Ed. Sidney Hook. New York: New York University Press, 1964, 86-97.

Taylor, Telford. "The Concept of Justice and the Laws of War." *The Columbia Journal of Transnational Law*, 13, (1974), 189-207.

Teitelman, Michael. "The Limits of Individualism." *The Journal of Philosophy*, 69, (1972), 545-56.

Thibaut, John, Laurens Walker, Stephen LaTour, and Pauline Holden. "Procedural Justice as Fairness." *Stanford Law Review*, 26, (1974), 1271-89.

Thomas, G.B. "On Choosing a Morality." *Canadian Journal of Philosophy*, 5, (1975), 357-74.

Thomas, Larry. "To *A Theory of Justice:* An Epilogue." *Philosophy Forum*, 14-15, (1974-75), 244-53.

Toulmin, Stephen. *The Place of Reason in Ethics.* Cambridge: Cambridge University Press, 1950.

Tucker, R. *The Marxian Revolutionary Idea.* New York: W.W. Norton & Co., 1969.

Tullock, Gordon. "Comment on Rae's 'The Limits of Consensual Decision'." *The American Political Science Review*, 69, no. 4, (1975), 1295-7.

United Nations General Assembly Resolution 3201 (S-VI). "Declaration on the Establishment of a New International Economic Order." *Official Records: Sixth Special Session*, Supp. No. 1 (A/9559), New York: United Nations General Assembly, May, 1974.

United Nations General Assembly Resolution 1803 (XVII). *Official Records: Seventeenth Session*, Supp. No. 17 (A/5217), New York: United Nations General Assembly, 1963.

"Universal Declaration of Human Rights (1948)." *Human Rights.* Abraham Irving Melden. Belmont, Calif.: Wadsworth Pub. Co., 1970, 143-49.

Urmson, J.O. "A Defense of Intuitionism." *Proceedings of the Aristotelian Society*, 75, (1974-75), 111-19.

Van Dyke, Vernon. "Justice as Fairness: For Groups?" *The American Political Science Review*, 69, (1975), 607-14.

Vickrey, W.S. "Utility, Strategy, and Social Decision Rules." *Quarterly Journal of Economics*, 74, (1960).

Vlastos, Gregory. "Justice and Equality." *Social Justice.* Ed. R.B. Brandt. Englewood Cliffs, N.J.: Prentice-Hall, Inc., 1962.

Waltz, Kenneth. "The Myth of National Interdependence." *The International Corporation.* Ed. Charles P. Kindleberger. Cambridge, Mass.: M.I.T. Press, 1970, 205-26.

Walzer, Michael. *Obligations: Essays on Civil Disobedience, War, and Citizenship.* Cambridge, Mass.: Harvard University Press, 1970.

Wasserstrom, Richard. "Rights, Human Rights, and Racial Discrimination." *Journal of Philosophy*, 61, (1964).

Wellbank, J.H. "Utopia and the Constraints of Justice." *Utopia/ Dystropia.* Ed. P.E. Richter. Cambridge, Mass.: Schenkman Publishing Co., 1975, 31-41.

Wicclair, Mark R. "Human Rights and Intervention." *Human Rights and United States Foreign Policy: Principles and Applications.* Eds. Peter G. Brown and Douglas MacLean. Lexington, Mass.: Lexington Books, 1979.

Wittman, Donald. "Punishment as Retribution." *Theory and Decision*, 4, (1974), 209-38.

Wolff, Robert Paul. *In Defense of Anarchism*. New York: Harper Torchbooks, 1970.

———. "On Strasnick's 'Derivation' of Rawls' Difference Principle." *The Journal of Philosophy*, 73, (1976), 849-58.

———. "A Refutation of Rawls' Theorum on Justice." *The Journal of Philosophy*, 63, (1966), 179-90.

———. *Understanding Rawls*. Princeton, N.J.: Princeton University Press, 1977.

Wood, A. "The Marxian Critique of Justice." *Philosophy and Public Affairs*, 1, no. 3, (1972), 244-82.

Young, Michael D. *The Rise of the Meritocracy, 1870-2033: the New Elite of Our Social Revolution*. London: Thames and Hudson, 1958.

Zaitchik, Alan. "Hobbes and Hypothetical Consent." *Political Studies*, 23, (1975), 475-85.

———. "Just Enough." *Philosophical Quarterly*, 25, (1975), 340-45.

Index